AN ENCYCLOPEDIA OF FAIRIES

KATHARINE BRIGGS

An Encyclopedia of Fairies

74027
HOBGOBLINS, BROWNIES, BOGIES, AND OTHER SUPERNATURAL CREATURES

PANTHEON BOOKS, NEW YORK

FIRST AMERICAN EDITION

Copyright © 1976 by Katharine Briggs

All rights reserved under International and Pan-American Copyright Conventions. Published in the United States by Pantheon Books, a division of Random House, Inc., New York. Originally published in England as *A Dictionary of Fairies* by Allen Lane, Penguin Books Ltd., London.

Library of Congress Cataloging in Publication Data

Briggs, Katharine Mary.
An Encyclopedia of Fairies.

First ed. published under title: A Dictionary of Fairies.
1. Fairies—Dictionaries.   I. Title.
GR549.B74   1977   398.2'1'03   76-12939
ISBN 0-394-40918-3

Manufactured in the United States of America

TO JOSEPHINE THOMPSON

who worked valiantly on this book
from start to finish,
with a zest and pleasure which would
be an encouragement to any author

Acknowledgements

In this dictionary I have quoted largely from earlier works, but I have obtained help and inspiration from many of my contemporaries. I have specially to thank the Editor of *Folklore* for permission to quote from many of the earlier numbers. I am most grateful for advice on the spelling and pronunciation of the Celtic fairies' names, to Alan Bruford, Robin Gwyndaf, Seán Ó Súilleabháin and Walter Clarke.

I am also indebted to several folklorists for oral information. Chief among these are Marie Campbell, the famous collector of the traditions of the Appalachian Mountains, Miss Joan Eltenton, who recorded for me the fairy beliefs which had migrated to Australia, and Susan M. Stevens, an anthropologist married to a chief of the Passamaquoddy Indians, who provided unique information about the two kinds of Little People who bear a remarkable resemblance to the Little People of Europe. Ruth L. Tongue has made her published works available to me and has from time to time given me her unpublished material as well. I am much obliged to her.

Contents

List of Plates

List of Text Figures

Preface

The word 'fairy' is used in various ways. There are a number of slang and cant usages of the word, varying from time to time, which are beside the point for this book. In fairy-lore, with which we are dealing here, there are two main general usages. The first is the narrow, exact use of the word to express one species of those supernatural creatures 'of a middle nature between man and angels' – as they were described in the seventeenth century – varying in size, in powers, in span of life and in moral attributes, but sharply differing from other species such as hob-goblins, monsters, hags, merpeople and so on. The second is the more general extension of the word to cover that whole area of the supernatural which is not claimed by angels, devils or ghosts. It is in this second, later and more generalized sense that I have often used the word in this book.

Exception might be taken to this use. The word 'fairy' itself is a late one, not used before medieval times and sometimes then with the meaning of mortal women who had acquired magical powers, as Malory used it for Morgan le Fay. The French *fai*, of which 'fairy' is an extension, came originally from the Italian *fatae*, the fairy ladies who visited the household at births and pronounced on the future of the baby, as the Three Fates used to do. 'Fairy' originally meant 'fai-erie', a state of enchantment, and was transferred from the object to the agent. The fairies themselves are said to object to the word, and people often think it better to speak of them euphemistically as 'the Good Neighbours', 'the Good Folk', 'the Seelie Court', 'Them Ones', or, more distantly, as 'the Strangers'. Throughout these islands many names are used for the fairies, the 'Daoine Sidh' in Ireland, the 'Sith' in the Highlands, the 'pisgies' in Cornwall. In the Lowlands of Scotland the Anglo-Saxon 'elves' was long used for the fairies, and Fairyland was called 'Elfame', but these names had limited and local usage, whereas the name 'fairies', however dis-trusted by the believers and debased by nineteenth-century prettification, was recognized everywhere.

At the inception of the book the idea had been to treat the whole area of fairy beliefs, as Thomas Keightley did in his *Fairy Mythology*; but to treat the fairies of the whole of Europe alone, even cursorily, would have been to produce a book ten times the size of this and founded on years of further research. I have occasionally mentioned a foreign fairy, for com-parison or elucidation, but only in passing. A complete work on the subject remains to be written, though the mammoth *Encyclopädie des Märchens*, now in preparation under the general editorship of Professor Kurt Ranke, will probably cover the subject adequately in its universal sweep. However, even within the range of our small islands and of some ten short centuries, enough matter will be found to enthral and horrify us.

This book is meant for browsing rather than for formal reference. As you read you will find words marked in small capitals. This indicates that there is a separate article on the subject, so that you can turn from one article to another as you pursue your explorations of the terrain.

The folklorist who specializes in fairy-lore is often asked if he believes in fairies – that is, in fairies as a subjective reality. Strictly speaking this is an irrelevant question. The business of the folklorist is to trace the growth and diffusion of tradition, possibly to advance theories of its origin or to examine those already put forward. When he speaks of 'true' fairy beliefs, he ordinarily means those actually believed by people as opposed to the fancies of literary storytellers, who are sometimes imbued with folk tradition and sometimes spin their material out of their own heads or follow the current literary fashion. Nevertheless it is of interest to know whether folklorists believe in the subjective truth of the traditions they record, for this affects their whole treatment of the subject. For myself, I am an agnostic. Some of the fairy anecdotes have a curiously convincing air of truth, but at the same time we must make allowance for the constructive power of the imagination in recalling old memories, and for the likelihood that people see what they expect to see.

Various suggestions have been made in the past for the classification of folk-tales and folk beliefs, among them a practical and suggestive outline by Professor Gomme in his *Handbook of Folk-Lore* (1890), but this was not taken up, and the pressure of newly collected tales became immense. The need was finally met by Antti Aarne's *Types of the Folktale* (1910), which, revised and supplemented by Professor Stith Thompson in 1928 and 1961, became the standard method of cataloguing folk-tales in all the archives of the world. So when a type number is given at the end of an article, it is to this work that I am referring. A *type* refers to a complete story, a cluster of motifs, while the *motif*, later classified by Professor Stith Thompson in his *Folk Motif-Index*, is the individual strand which makes up the tale. Cinderella, for instance, is Type 510 and is composed of motifs s31: Cruel stepmother; L55: Stepdaughter heroine; F311.1: Fairy godmother; D1050.1: Clothes produced by magic; F861.4.3: Carriage from pumpkin; N711.6: Prince sees heroine at ball and is enamoured; C761.3: Taboo: staying too long at ball. Must leave before certain hour; and H36.1: Slipper test. At the end of this book there is a list of the types and motifs to be found in the various anecdotes and beliefs mentioned in it.

True oral tradition is a great stimulus to creative imagination, and from time to time I have touched briefly on the creative writers who have been stimulated by fairy-lore and have in their turn influenced it. The rise of tradition into literature and the descent of literature into tradition is a fascinating study. The visual arts have also had their place here, and the small collection of fairy pictures in this book is an interesting comment on the fluctuations of traditional fairy beliefs through the centuries.

A Note on the Pronunciation of Celtic Names

The exact pronunciation of many of the Celtic names is hard to convey by English literation. A further difficulty is that the actual pronunciation varies in regional dialects, particularly in the Highlands and Islands of Scotland. Welsh is well standardized, but impossible for anyone of non-Cymric breeding to pronounce. We have consulted leading authorities on the Gaelic both of Ireland and Scotland, on Welsh and Manx, and they have kindly given us an approximation to the native pronunciations. These apply only to the titles of articles, but with the help of the specimens given the diligent reader may hope to pronounce the other names occurring in the text with some degree of accuracy. It seemed best to avoid peppering the articles with brackets.

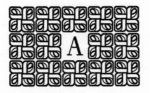

Abbey lubber. From the 15th century onwards, the luxury and wantonness of many of the abbeys began to be proverbial, and many folk satires were spread abroad about them. Among these were anecdotes of the abbey lubbers, minor devils who were detailed to tempt the monks to drunkenness, gluttony and lasciviousness. The best-known of these tales is that of FRIAR RUSH, who was sent to work the final damnation of a wealthy abbey. He had very nearly succeeded in doing so when he was unmasked, conjured into the form of a horse by the Prior, and finally banished. He took other service, and behaved more like an ordinary ROBIN GOOD-FELLOW until the Prior again caught up with him and banished him to a distant castle. After their experience with Rush, the friars repented and took to virtuous living, so that their last state was better than their first. Rush worked mainly in the kitchen, but abbey lubbers as a rule haunted the wine cellar. The Abbey Lubber has a lay colleague in the BUTTERY SPIRIT, which haunted dishonestly-run inns, or households where the servants were wasteful and riotous or where hospitality was grudged to the poor. There was a belief described by J. G. CAMPBELL in his *Superstitions of the Scottish Highlands* that FAIRIES and evil spirits only had power over goods that were unthankfully or grudgingly received or dishonestly gained. The Abbey Lubber and the Buttery Spirit must have owed their existence to this belief.

Aedh (*ay*). The son of Eochail Lethderg, Prince of Leinster, who was playing HURLING with his young companions when he was carried into a BRUGH, or palace, of Fairyland by two SIDH-women who were in love with him, and held captive there for three years. At the end of this time Aedh escaped and made his way to St Patrick, and begged him to free him from the fairy dominion. Patrick took him in disguise to Leinster to his father's court, and there restored him to humanity and freed him from the timeless life of the fairies (see TIME IN FAIRYLAND). This account from *Silva Gadelica* (pp. 204–20) is one of the earliest stories of CAPTIVES IN FAIRYLAND.
[Motif: F379.1]

Afanc (*avanc*). There was some doubt about the form taken by the monster which inhabited a pool called Llyn yr Afanc on the River Conwy in North Wales. It was generally thought to be an enormous beaver because the word *afanc* is sometimes used for beaver in local dialects. Llyn yr Afanc is a kind of whirlpool: anything thrown into it will whirl round about before it is sucked down. It used to be thought that it was the Afanc which dragged down animals or people who fell into the Llyn. It was thought to be either a monstrous beaver or a kind of crocodile. According to a 17th-century tradition told in Rhys's *Celtic Folklore* (p. 130), the Afanc, like the Unicorn, was allured by a maiden who persuaded it to lay its head in her lap and fall asleep. While it slept it was chained and the chains were attached to two oxen. When they began to draw it, it awoke and made for the pool, tearing away the maiden's breast which it was holding in its claw. Several men hauled on the chain, but it was the oxen's strength that was effectual, as the Afanc itself confessed. The men were disputing as to which of them had pulled the hardest when the captive suddenly spoke and said:

> 'Had it not been for the oxen pulling,
> The Afanc had never left the pool.'

[Motif: F420.1.4]

Aiken Drum. The name 'Aiken Drum' is best known in the Scottish nursery rhyme:

> There cam' a man to oor toun,
> To oor toun, to oor toun,
> There cam' a man to oor toun
> An' his name was Aiken Drum.

This is quoted in full by Iona and Peter Opie in *The Oxford Dictionary of Nursery Rhymes* as, 'There was a man lived in the Moon'. It is, however, the name given by William Nicholson to the Brownie of Blednoch in Galloway. William Nicholson wrote several ballads on folklore themes; 'Aiken Drum' is to be found in the third edition of his *Poetical Works* (1878). Aiken Drum in the nursery rhyme wears entirely edible clothes, a hat of cream cheese, a coat of roast beef, buttons of penny loaves, and so on, but the Brownie of Blednoch was naked except for a kilt of green rushes, and like all BROWNIES he was laid by a gift of clothing:

> For a new-made wife, fu' o' rippish freaks,
> Fond o' a' things feat for the first five weeks,
> Laid a mouldy pair o' her ain man's breeks
> By the brose o' Aiken-drum.

> Let the learned decide when they convene,
> What spell was him and the breeks between;
> For frae that day forth he was nae mair seen,
> And sair missed was Aiken-drum!

[Motif: F381.3]

Aillen Mac Midhna. A fairy musician of the TUATHA DE DANANN who came every year at Samhain Eve (All-Hallow Eve) out of Sidhe Finnachaid to Tara, the Royal Palace of the High King, playing so marvellously on his *timpan* (a kind of belled tambourine) that all who heard him were lulled asleep, and while they slept he blew three blasts of fire out of his nostrils and burnt up the Hall of Tara. This happened every Samhain Eve for twenty-three years, until FINN of the FIANNA Finn conquered Aillen and killed him (*Silva Gadelica*, vol. II, pp. 142–4). He conquered him by himself inhaling the fumes of his magic spear, whose point was so venomous that no one who smelled it could sleep, however lulling the music.

[Motifs: F262.3.4; F369.1]

Aine (*aw-ne*). The fairy goddess to whom, with her sister Fenne (or Finnen), Knock Aine and Knock Fennine on the shores of Lough Gur are dedicated. They were the daughters of Egogabal, a king of the TUATHA DE DANANN. Of Aine there is a version of the SWAN MAIDEN story, very similar to those of the GWRAGEDD ANNWN of Wales. One day, as Aine was sitting on the shore of Lough Gur combing her hair, Gerold, the Earl of Desmond, saw her and fell in love with her. He gained control over her by seizing her cloak, and made her his bride. Their child was Earl Fitzgerald, and the TABOO imposed upon his father was that he must never express any surprise at anything his son might do. One night, however, showing off his skill to some maidens, he jumped into a bottle and out again, and his father could not restrain a cry of surprise. Fitzgerald at once left the castle and was seen swimming across the lough in the form of a wild goose towards Garrod Island, under which his enchanted castle was said to lie. At the same time, Aine disappeared into Knock Aine. This story was collected from informants by Evans Wentz and included in *The Fairy Faith in Celtic Countries* (p. 79). A somewhat similar story is the more widely known LEGEND OF MULLAGHMAST.

[Motifs: C30; C31; F302.2]

Ainsel. This is a variant of the 'Noman' story and is told in Richardson's *Table-Book* about the FARIES of Northumberland. A widow and her little boy lived in a cottage near Rothley. One night the child was very lively and would not go to bed when his mother did. She warned him that the faries would come and fetch him if he sat up too late, but he only laughed and went on playing. She had not long blown out the candle when a lovely little creature jumped down the chimney and began to frisk about in front of the boy. 'What do they ca' thou?' he said fascinated. 'Ainsel,' she answered. 'And what do they ca' *thou*?' '*My* ainsel,' he answered, cannily, and they began to play together like two children of one race. Presently the fire got low and the little boy stirred it up so vigorously that a cinder blew out and burnt little Ainsel on the foot. She set up a yell quite disproportionate to her size, 'Wow! I'm brent!' 'Wha's done it? Wha's done it?' said a dreadful voice from the chimney, and the boy made one leap into bed as the old fary mother shot down on to the floor. 'My ainsel! My ainsel!' said the little fary. 'Why then,' said her mother, 'what's all this noise for: there's nyon to blame!' And she kicked Ainsel up the chimney.

[Type 1137. Motif: K602.1]

Allies's list of the fairies. Jabez Allies (1787-1856) in *Antiquities of Worcestershire* (second edition, 1852) included in the book an enlargement of an earlier pamphlet on 'The Ignis Fatuus or Will o' the Wisp and the Fairies', in which he linked many of the place-names of Worcestershire with the names of the FAIRIES in the anonymous 17th-century pamphlet the LIFE OF ROBIN GOODFELLOW and in Drayton's *Nimphidia*. One was a piece of popular journalism and the other a conspicuous example of the fashionable interest in the DIMINUTIVE FAIRIES among the Jacobean poets, but both works are founded on a common folk tradition which endured until well on into the 19th century.

From *The Life of Robin Goodfellow* Allies quotes:

> Pinch and Patch, Gull and Grim,
>   Goe you together;
> For you can change your shapes,
>   Like to the weather.
> Sib and Tib, Licke and Lull,
>   You have trickes too;
> Little Tom Thumb that pipes
>   Shall goe betwixt you.

And from Drayton's *Nimphidia* he quotes the list of Queen MAB's Maids of Honour:

> Hop, and Mop, and Dryp so clear,
> Pip, and Trip, and Skip that were
> To Mab, their sovereign, ever dear,
>   Her special maids of honour;

> Fib, and Tib, and Pinch, and Pin,
> Tick, and Quick, and Jil, and Jin,
> Tit, and Nit, and Wap, and Win,
>   The train that wait upon her.

To match these, Allies has collected, in Worcestershire alone, Drip's Hill, Grimsend, Lulsley, Patcham, Pinshill, Sibhay, Tibhay, Winstile and many others, to say nothing of those he has found scattered all over the country and collected from Anglo-Saxon place-names. 'It seems probable,' he says, 'that such places, or most of them, were so called after the corresponding names of some of the above-mentioned fairies.' It is arguable that these places may have taken their names from the fairies, and if so, the Anglo-Saxon names would argue a considerable antiquity for these particular fairies; but most of the names of the minor fairies who appear in *Nimphidia* and *The Life of Robin Goodfellow* seem to have been rather arbitrarily imposed by the authors. PINCH, GULL, LICKE and LULL might well be named after their activities, but it is possible that the names came first and the explanation afterwards; it is certainly so with GRIM, who was of a most respectable antiquity. The names of Drayton's maids of honour suggest the same origin. 'Hop, Mop, Dryp, Pip, Trip, Skip, Fib, Tib, Pinch, Pin, Tick, Quick, Jil, Jin, Tit, Nit, Wap and Win' might well be named *ex tempore* as one watched them. 'Wap and Win' are perhaps illuminated by a cant phrase quoted in Dekker's *O Per Se O*, 'If she will not wap for a win, let her trine for a make', translated by Dekker, 'If she will not O per Se O for a penny, let her hang for a halfpenny.' This suggests that hint of scurrility which lurks behind some of HERRICK's fairy poetry.

Allies gives lengthier notes on PUCK, JACKY LANTERN, ROBIN GOODFELLOW, DOBBY, HOB, ROBIN HOOD, the SEVEN WHISTLERS and WILL O' THE WISP.

Allison Gross. 'Allison Gross', No. 35 in F. J. Child's famous collection of ballads, was taken from the Jamieson-Brown collection and first printed in the *Jamieson Popular Ballads*. Mrs Brown was an old lady, the widow of a minister, who had a remarkable repertoire of popular ballads, particularly of ballads on supernatural themes, many of which we owe to her alone. This is a tale of witchcraft and of the FAIRY RADE. Allison Gross, 'the ugliest witch i the north country', allured the hero into her bower and made violent love to him, offering him various rich gifts if he would be her true love. He repulsed her advances uncompromisingly:

> 'Awa, awa, ye ugly witch,
>   Haud far awa, an lat me be;
> I never will be your lemman sae true,
>   An I wish I were out o your company.'

At the third refusal she blew on a grass-green horn, struck him with a silver wand and spun round three times muttering ill words, so that his strength failed and he fell senseless on the ground:

'She's turnd me into an ugly worm,
　　And gard me toddle about the tree.'

His only solace was from his sister Maisry, who came every Saturday night to wash and comb his locks. One night the Fairy Rade of the SEELIE COURT passed by and disenchanted him:

But as it fell out on last Hallow-even,
　　When the seely court was ridin by,
The queen lighted down on a gowany bank,
　　Nae far frae the tree where I wont to lye.

She took me up in her milk-white han,
　　An she's stroakd me three times oer her knee;
She chang'd me again to my ain proper shape,
　　An I nae mair maun toddle about the tree.

　　Child's ballad No. 36, 'The Laily Worm and the Machrel of the Sea', is very similar to this, but has two transformations by a wicked step-mother, the knight into a 'laily worm' and Maisry into a 'machrel of the sea'. It was taken down from recitation in the north of Scotland about 1802, and bears some resemblance also to 'The Laidley Worm of Spindleston Heughs', which was added as an appendix to ballad No. 34, 'Kemp Owyne'. It is a literary version of a Northumberland tradition. Further reference will be found to it in DRAGONS.
　　[Motifs: D683.2; D700; G269.4; G275.8.2]

Alp-Luachra (*alp-loochra*). The Irish version of the JOINT-EATER.

American fairy immigrants. There are at least two kinds of fairy immigrants from the Old World to the New. There is the straightforward story after the type of the old film, *The Ghost Goes West*, of the individual fairy who moves with his humans; and there are the fairy beliefs which have been carried over by the human immigrants. It may also be con-jectured that the LITTLE PEOPLE OF THE PASSAMAQUODDY INDIANS have been created from the traditions of the 17th-century Jesuit mis-sionaries, and for this reason they have been included in this book.
　　In the English tales of FAIRIES moving, the area is generally restricted. In the best-known of the stories, 'Aye George, we're flitting', the BOGGART who had made himself such a nuisance that the family decided to move to get away from him, merely packed himself up in the churn to be carried in the cart with the rest. In the Shropshire tale of 'The Saut Box', the GOBLINS followed the family on their own feet, carrying a

forgotten salt box with them. The humans got the better of the goblins in this tale, but by a very barbarous and unscrupulous method. In a ghost story version in oral transmission, the family heard sounds of ghostly packing in the attics and cellars the night before they left the house in the Midlands for one in the North of England, and the haunting moved with them. It is the Celtic spirits, however, who show real enterprise; they do not appear to be afraid of crossing the sea. In 1967 Ruth Tongue collected a story from a member of Combe Florey Women's Institute about a Westmorland tradition of her family, of TOM COCKLE, a domestic spirit who travelled with his family, or rather just before it, from Ireland to the Lake District. But it seems to be chiefly the Highland fairies that brace themselves to cross the Atlantic with their protégés. A very good example of this enterprising spirit is to be found in J. F. CAMPBELL's *Popular Tales of the West Highlands* (vol. II, p. 103). The hero of it is a BAUCHAN, which belongs to the same kind of class as the Lowland BROWNIE.

Sometimes the fairy beliefs were imported, and sometimes the stories. In the 1930s, Dr Marie Campbell made a remarkable collection of fairy legends of both kinds in the Appalachian Mountains. She is currently preparing these for publication, and they will appear shortly. Those to which I refer here have been collected from two narrators: Tom Fields, a postman and a miller, and Granny Caudill, a bedridden old lady with a very lively mind. The tales of both narrators are clearly derived from a Highland strain. The first relates to the belief in ELF-SHOT. The fairy bolt in this story was not a prehistoric arrowhead, but a tiny flint bird-point of the kind used by Indians for shooting birds and small game. Riding home in the dusk, Tom Fields had seen a small red-headed fairy no bigger than a tiny child, and a number of them dancing and whirling at a distance. She had run away to join them, something had whizzed past him and his horse had gone lame. He led it home and next day he came back to the place and searched until he found the arrowhead, and ever since he had been free of fairy enchantment, though he sometimes heard them singing. This was his story and it exactly corresponds to the Scottish beliefs about elf-shot and the efficacy of a fairy arrow against it.

The next story was also Tom Fields's. The CHANGELING tale has a wide distribution both in time and place, but the particular form which it took here is commonest in Scotland. In these stories the travelling tailor is the hero, which leads us to suspect that he was also the storyteller, for in common tradition a tailor is not a heroic character. This version of the story is not told as from far off, but is supposed to have been a local happening and was overheard by Tom Fields as a small boy. Here the tailor has become a sewing woman because in America it was the sewing woman who went from house to house, not the tailor, and the transition was therefore natural. There are two close parallels to this story, both Scottish. One is from Campbell (ibid., p. 68), though it is actually a Galloway tale; and the other, 'The Tailor of Kintalen', is from Bett's *English Myths and Traditions*. 'The Tailor and the Fairy' begins in just the same way as Tom Fields's version, with the stolen baby being accidentally handed to a mortal, and 'The Tailor of Kintalen' ends just like it, with the changeling being thrown into a deep pool and turning into an old man. Altogether, the resemblances are striking.

Granny Caudill recognized that her stories had travelled. Her first is a recollection of the legend about the famous Scottish pipers, the Mac-Crimmons, who were supposed to owe their special skill to a fairy gift. It is a kind of Cinderella story in which the despised youngest son, left at home to do the chores, is visited by a fairy man who gives him a magic chanter and teaches him how to use it. The name of MacCrimmon has gone, but the essentials of the story remain. This tale is still extant in Scotland and was recorded by Hamish Henderson from one of the travelling people. There are several written versions of it.

Another tale told by Granny Caudill is one of the stories of CAPTIVES IN FAIRYLAND. It is about the girl who was called into a fairy hill by the music and danced there all night. In the morning she wanted to leave, but was told she could not go till she had baked up the meal in the bin. There seemed very little there, but she could not come to the end of it until an old woman who had been a captive in the hill for many years told her the secret of bringing the supply to an end.

The help from a human captive is a common motif of many visits to Fairyland, English and Scottish. The being bound to an unending task of baking occurs in several Scottish MIDWIFE TO THE FAIRIES stories. In these it is often the patient, a captive bride, who tells her nurse how to end the task.

It is astonishing how this light freight, carried over the seas some hundred years ago or more, has retained its quality and flavour.

[Motifs: D2066; F262.2; F321; F321.1.1.2; F321.1.4.1]

Angus Mac Og. The god of youth and beauty, who was one of the TUATHA DE DANANN supposed to have been the gods of the Ancient Irish who later became the Irish HEROIC FAIRIES, the DAOINE SIDHE. In the Irish traditional history, the Tuatha de Danann were defeated and driven underground by the invading Milesians. They retreated to an underground realm, and their High King, DAGDA, apportioned his realms and palaces. He took two BRUGHS or palaces for himself and gave one to LUG, son of Ethne, and one to OGME, but his son Angus was away and was forgotten. When he returned and complained, Dagda ceded to him his own Brug na Boinne for a day and a night, but Angus was dissatisfied at the decision and claimed the Brug na Boinne for himself for ever.

Anu. Eleanor Hull, in *Folklore of the British Isles*, suggests tentatively that Anu is the same person as AINE, the mother of Earl Fitzgerald, to whom fires were lit at Midsummer, and who was the guardian of cattle and a health-giver. Anu is known to be one of the *Deae Matronae* of Ireland and was a goddess of fertility. Two neighbouring hills in Kerry are called the Paps of Anu. Eleanor Hull regards her as a local goddess, and rejects the suggestion that she has any connection with BLACK ANNIS of the Dane Hills in Leicestershire, though she thinks it possible that DANA and Anu are the same.

Aodh (*ay*). See AEDH.

Apple-Tree Man. In Somerset the oldest apple-tree in the orchard is called 'The Apple-Tree Man' and it seems that the fertility of the orchard is supposed to reside there. Ruth Tongue came across mentions of the Apple-Tree Man from time to time, and in 1920 heard a complete story about him from an old man at Pitminster. It is noteworthy that the Apple-Tree Man was willing to speak to the elder brother who had restored fertility to the orchard and wassailed the apple-trees. Ruth Tongue recorded the story in 1963 for publication in her *Folktales of England* (p. 44):

> There were a hard-working chap as was eldest of a long family, see, zo when his Dad die there wasn't nothing left for he. Youngest gets it all, and he do give bits and pieces to all his kith; but he don't like eldest, see, spoilt young hosebird he were, so all he do let he have is his Dad's old dunk, and a ox that was gone to a natomy (I s'pose it had the quarter-ail), and a tumbledown cottage with the two-dree ancient old apple-trees where his Dad had lived to with his granfer. The chap don't grumble, but he go cutting grass along lane, and old dunk begun to fatten, and he do rub the ox with herbs and say the words, and old ox he perk up hisself and walk smart, and then he do turn they beastses into orchet, and they old apple-trees flourish a marvel.
>
> But it don't leave him no time to find the rent! Oh yes, youngest was bound to have his rent. Dap on the dot too!
>
> Then one day he come into orchet and say, ''Twill be Christmas Eve come tomorrow, when beasts do talk. There's a treasure hereabouts we've all heard tell, and I'm set to ask your dunk. He mustn't refuse to tell me. Yew wake me just afore midnight and I'll take a whole sixpence off the rent.'
>
> Come Christmas Eve the chap 'e give old dunk and ox a bit extra and he do fix a bit of holly in the shippen, and he gets his last mug of cider, and mull it by ashen faggot, and outs to the orchet to give'n to the apple trees. . . Then the Apple-Tree Man he calls to the chap and 'e say, 'Yew take and look under this gurt diddicky root of ours.' And

there was a chest full of finest gold. ''Tis yours, and no one else,' say
the Apple-Tree Man. 'Put'n away zafe and bide quiet about'n.' So he
done that. 'Now yew can go call your dear brother,' say Apple-Tree
Man, ''tis midnight.'

Well, youngest brother he do run out in a terrible hurry-push and
sure enough the dunk's a-talking to the ox. 'Yew do know thic gurt
greedy fule that's a-listening to we, so unmannerly, he do want we
should tell where treasure is.'

'And that's where he never won't get it,' say the ox. 'Cause someone
have a-tooked he already.'

[Motifs: B251.1.2; N471; N541.1]

Arawn (*arrawn*). In the more recent Welsh legends, GWYNN AP NUDD
is always assumed to be the King of Annwn, the underworld kingdom of
the dead, but in the MABINOGION, Arawn, the friend of Pwyll Prince of
Dyfed, was King of Annwn, and it was he who gave to Dyfed the present
of pigs which were to play such an important part in Welsh legend. It was
perhaps the otherworld origin of pigs which made them so potent and
also so ominous in the Celtic world.

[Motif: A300]

Arkan Sonney (*erkin sonna*), or 'Lucky Piggy'. The name given to the
Fairy Pig of Man. Walter Gill in *A Manx Scrapbook* (p. 444) mentions a
fairy pig seen near Niarbyl by a child who told him about it some fifty
years later as an old woman. It was a beautiful little white pig, and as the
fairy pigs are supposed to bring luck, she called to her uncle to come and
help her to catch it. But he called back to her to leave it alone, and it soon
disappeared. Dora Broome has a tale of a little fairy pig in her *Fairy Tales
from the Isle of Man*. Her little pig is white, with red ears and eyes like
most Celtic FAIRY ANIMALS. It can alter its size, but apparently not its
shape.

Arthur of Britain. See GEOFFREY OF MONMOUTH; MATTER OF
BRITAIN; SLEEPING WARRIORS.

Ash. A substitute for ROWAN as a PROTECTION AGAINST FAIRIES.
Odd and even ash keys (seed-pods) were often used in divination.

Asrai, or water-fairies. Ruth Tongue recollects a tale, probably from
Shropshire, in *Forgotten Folk-Tales of the English Counties* (pp. 24–6).
The name is mentioned in Robert Buchanan's verses.

There are two tales almost identical from Cheshire and Shropshire.
In both a fisherman dredges up an asrai and puts it in the bottom of his
boat. It seems to plead to be set free, but its language is incomprehensible.

In the Cheshire tale he bound it, and the touch of its cold, wet hands burned him so that he was marked for life. In both stories he covered the asrai with wet weeds. It lay moaning in the bottom of the boat, but its moans grew fainter, and by the time he reached the shore it had melted away and left only a little water in the bottom of the boat.

Ruth Tongue heard other references to asrai from the Welsh Border, always in the same strain.

[Motif: F420.1.2*]

Assipattle. A good example of a Cinderlad, who is a particularly common hero in the Scottish fairy tales. The Opies point out in *The Classic Fairy Tales* that the heroine of the Cinderella stories was not usually a peasant or a beggar-girl raised by fairy help to a position to which her birth did not entitle her, but a princess or one of the nobility cast down by malice from her proper station into a condition of squalor. This is generally true of the Cinderellas, but it is not true of the Cinderlads, who are often the sons of poor widows and who have led a life of complete sloth, doing nothing to help towards the household expenses, idle, dirty, greedy, until suddenly they are roused into activity, and show great qualities of courage, resourcefulness and wit. Sometimes, as in the story of Tom Hickathrift, the tardiness is to allow time for abnormal growth in power and strength, just as the offspring of FAIRY ANIMALS in a human herd need to be fed for seven years with the milk of seven cattle. As a rule, however, the hero has no superhuman powers, but a reserve of energy from years of idleness. Most of these ne'er-do-well heroes are called 'Jack' or 'Jock', but the hero of the Orcadian story of 'Assipattle and the Mester Stoorworm' has a true Cinderella name, the same as that of 'Ashenputtle', the Highland Cinderella.

Assipattle is unlike the Jacks in being the son of a respectable Udaler who farms his own estate and is a member of the *Thing* (the Scandinavian parliament). His only daughter is lady-in-waiting to the Princess Gemdelovely. Assipattle is the seventh son of his father. He contrives to spend most of his time in idleness, though his brothers force him to perform the more menial duties of the farm, and his nights are spent lying among the ashes in the fireplace, stirring them about with his hands and feet. He is despised by everyone except his sister, who listens patiently to his stories of the great feats he is going to perform one day. Actually he is destined to be a dragon-slayer and to rescue the Princess from the MESTER STOORWORM, the greatest and most terrible DRAGON in the world. This tale, which is published in Douglas's *Scottish Fairy and Folk-Tales* (pp. 58–72), may owe something to the inventive fancy of its author, but it contains many interesting items of Orcadian social history.

[Type: 300. Motifs: A2468.3; B11.2.12; B11.10; B11.11; B184.1.1; D429.2.2; F420.1.4; H335.3.1; L101; L131.1; R227; T68.1]

Athach (*a-huch*). This, which means 'monster' or 'giant', is a general term for those most unpleasant creatures which haunted lonely lochans or gorges in the Highlands, such as LUIDEAG, the Rag, a female demon who haunted Lochan Nan Dubh Bhreac in Skye and slew what men she could catch; or the BOCAN, which can assume a variety of monstrous shapes; or the DIREACH of Glen Etive, with one hand out of his chest, one leg out of his haunch and one eye out of the front of his forehead, almost identical with the FACHAN. These monsters are described by D. A. Mackenzie, J. G. CAMPBELL and J. F. CAMPBELL.

Aubrey, John (1626–97). One of the most lovable of antiquarians. Many old customs and fairy anecdotes would have been lost to the world if he had not chronicled them. He tells us in his *Natural History of Surrey* of the Fairy Kettle of Frensham which was regularly lent to anyone who asked for it outside the Fairy Mound of Frensham, a good example of FAIRY LOANS; it is he who first gives us 'Horse and Hattock' as the master word in FAIRY LEVITATION, and gives us an early account of MEG MULLACH, the female BROWNIE, whose tradition in the Highlands of Scotland has lasted till this day. One passage, however, indubitably by Aubrey was quoted by HALLIWELL-PHILLIPPS in *Illustrations of the Fairy Mythology of Shakespeare* and has now disappeared. It was probably in the lost volume of *Hypomnemata Antiquaria* and a detailed note on this will be found in K. M. Briggs, *The Anatomy of Puck* (p. 34) in which the extract is printed:

In the year 1633–4, soone after I had entered into my grammar at the Latin Schoole at Yatton Keynel, (near Chippenham, Wilts), our curate Mr Hart, was annoy'd one night by these elves or fayries. Comming over the downes, it being neere darke, and approaching one of the faiery dances, as the common people call them in these parts, viz. the greene circles made by those sprites on the grasse, he all at once sawe an innumerable quantitie of pigmies or very small people, dancing rounde and rounde, and singing, and making all maner of small odd noyses. He, being very greatly amaz'd, and yet not being able, as he sayes, to run away from them, being, as he supposes, kept there in a kind of enchantment, they no sooner perceave him but they surround him on all sides, and what betwixt feare and amazement, he fell down scarcely knowing what he did; and thereupon these little creatures pinch'd him all over, and made a sorte of quick humming noyse all the time; but at length they left him, and when the sun rose, he found himself exactly in the midst of one of these faiery dances. This relation I had from him myselfe, a few days after he was so tormented; but when I and my bedfellow Stump wente soon afterwards, at night time to the dances on the downes, we saw none of the elves or fairies. But indeede it is saide they seldom appeare to any persons who go to seeke for them.

This passage is very characteristic of Aubrey's style and contains much that is characteristic of the FAIRIES of that period, their love of DANCING, their habit of pinching those that displeased them and their curious, indistinct manner of speech. Aubrey's *Miscellanies*, his *Remaines of Gentilisme* and his two County Histories, of Surrey and Wiltshire, contain many similar gems.

Aughisky (*agh-iski*), **the water-horse.** This is the same as the Highland EACH UISGE. YEATS, in *Irish Fairy and Folk Tales* (p. 94), tells us that the aughiska were once common and used to come out of the water – particularly, it seems, in November – and gallop along the sands or over the fields, and if people could get them away from the fields and saddle and bridle them, they would make the finest horses. But they must be ridden inland, for if they got so much as a glimpse of salt water they would gallop headlong away, carrying their riders with them, bear them deep into the sea and there devour them. It was said also that the untamed aughiska used to devour mortal cattle.

[Motifs: B184.1.3; F234.1.8; G303.3.3.1.3]

Aurora Borealis. See FIR CHLIS; PERRY DANCERS.

Australian fairy immigrants. British FAIRIES, and particularly those from the Highlands of Scotland, found their way into Australian folklore in the same way as the AMERICAN FAIRY IMMIGRANTS. The following record of an Australian fairy tradition is made available by the kindness of Miss Joan Eltenton of Oxford:

John Harley was born in Australia in the early '90s, of Highland parents who had emigrated some years earlier. He told me that his father kept and used an (illegal) whisky distiller, and when the whisky was 'ready' they always put out the first draw in a saucer 'for the fairies', who would protect this illegal hobby. One day, Mr Harley senior had to go up country, just at the critical time. He reminded his family not to forget the fairies, – they did forget to put the first whisky out for the fairies, and that day the excisemen caught up with them!

John assured me that as a child he had heard the fairies singing and whistling in the hills.

The family continued to speak Gaelic in Australia, and John did not learn English until he joined the army during the Great War, with the result that when I knew him, in his middle age, he still relapsed into Gaelic and the English of the British 'tommy'.

[Motif: V12.9]

Awd Goggie. A cautionary demon or NURSERY BOGIE from the East Riding of Yorkshire. Mrs Gutch quotes a mention of him in *County Folk-Lore* (vol. VI):

> There is another wicked sprite, who comes in most usefully as a protector of fruit. His name is *Awd Goggie*, and he specially haunts woods and orchards. It is evident, therefore, that it is wise on the children's part to keep away from the orchard at improper times, because otherwise 'Awd Goggie might get them.'

[Motif: F234.1.16]

Badb, or Badhbh (*bibe*). The Celtic goddess of war, who, according to Evans Wentz in *The Fairy-Faith in Celtic Countries* (pp. 302-5), incorporated the three goddesses NEMAN, MACHA and MORRIGU in a single form, that of a Royston or hoodie crow. The mythology has declined into folklore, and a crow perching on a house is often the form taken by the BANSHEE or 'fairy woman'. The narrative of the battle of Moytura in *The Book of Leinster* gives one of the most vivid descriptions of the activities of Badb and her attendant spirits.

[Motifs: A132.6.2; A485.1]

Banshee. An Irish death spirit, more correctly written BEAN SI, who wails only for members of the old families. When several keen together, it foretells the death of someone very great or holy. The Banshee has long streaming hair and a grey cloak over a green dress. Her eyes are fiery red with continual weeping. In the Scottish Highlands the Banshee is called the BEAN-NIGHE or LITTLE-WASHER-BY-THE-FORD, and she washes the grave-clothes of those about to die.

In the *Memoirs of Lady Fanshawe*, who lived from 1625–76, there is a first-hand account of a banshee that appeared to her when she was staying with Lady Honor O'Brien:

> There we stayed three nights. The first of which I was surprised by being laid in a chamber, when, about one o'clock I heard a voice that wakened me. I drew the curtain, and in the casement of the window, I saw, by the light of the moon, a woman leaning into the window, through the casement, in white, with red hair and pale and ghastly complexion: she spoke loud, and in a tone I had never heard, thrice,

'A horse'; and then, with a sigh more like the wind than breath she vanished, and to me her body looked more like a thick cloud than substance. I was so much frightened, that my hair stood on end, and my night clothes fell off. I pulled and pinched your father, who never woke during the disorder I was in; but at last was much surprised to see me in this fright, and more so when I related the story and showed him the window opened. Neither of us slept any more that night, but he entertained me with telling me how much more these apparitions were usual in this country than in England; and we concluded the cause to be the great superstition of the Irish, and the want of that knowing faith, which should defend them from the power of the Devil, which he exercises among them very much. About five o'clock the lady of the house came to see us, saying she had not been in bed all night, because a cousin O'Brien of her's, whose ancestors had owned that house, had desired her to stay with him in his chamber, and that he died at two o'clock, and she said, 'I wish you to have had no disturbance, for 'tis the custom of the place, that, when any of the family are dying, the shape of a woman appears in the window every night till they be dead. This woman was many ages ago got with child by the owner of this place, who murdered her in his garden and flung her into the river under the window, but truly I thought not of it when I lodged you here, it being the best room in the house.' We made little reply to her speech, but disposed ourselves to be gone suddenly.

Some two hundred years later Lady WILDE wrote a chapter in her *Ancient Legends of Ireland* (vol. I, pp. 259–63) on the beliefs about the Banshee. According to her, the Irish Banshee is more beautiful and poetic than the deformed Banshee of the Scottish Highlands. In the course of her description she says:

> Sometimes the Banshee assumes the form of some sweet singing virgin of the family who died young, and has been given the mission by the invisible powers to become the harbinger of coming doom to her mortal kindred. Or she may be seen at night as a shrouded woman, crouched beneath the trees, lamenting with veiled face; or flying past in the moonlight, crying bitterly: and the cry of this spirit is mournful beyond all other sounds on earth, and betokens certain death to some member of the family whenever it is heard in the silence of the night.

The Bean-Nighe is also sometimes thought of as a ghost, but the ghost of a woman who died in childbirth. J. G. CAMPBELL in *Superstitions of the Scottish Highlands* (p. 43) says: 'Women dying in childbed were looked upon as dying prematurely, and it was believed that, unless all the clothes left by them were washed, they should have to wash them themselves till the natural period of their death.' Yet the Bean-Nighe's washing was supposed to foreshadow the violent death of some member of the clan, whose grave-clothes she was washing. The Highland Banshee, like the other FAIRIES, has some physical DEFECTS. She has only one nostril, a large protruding front tooth and long hanging breasts. A mortal who is bold enough to creep up to her as she is washing and lamenting and suck her long breast can claim to be her foster-child and gain a wish from her. Since the word 'banshee' means 'fairy woman', the beliefs about her are various, and occasionally the GLAISTIG is spoken of as a banshee, though she has nothing to do with the Bean-Nighe.

[Motif: F254.1]

Baobhan Sith (*baavan shee*). This Highland word is the same as BAN-SHEE, and means 'fairy woman', but it is generally employed to mean a kind of succubus, very dangerous and evil. D. A. Mackenzie in *Scottish Folk Lore and Folk Life* (p. 236) retells a story from C. M. Robertson's *Folk-Lore from the West of Ross-shire*.

Four young men were on a hunting trip and spent the night in an empty shieling, a hut built to give shelter for the sheep in the grazing season. They began to dance, one supplying mouth-music. One of the dancers wished that they had partners. Almost at once four women came in. Three danced, the fourth stood by the music-maker. But as he hummed he saw drops of blood falling from the dancers and he fled out of the shieling, pursued by his demon partner. He took refuge among the horses and she could not get to him, probably because of the IRON with which they were shod. But she circled round him all night, and only disappeared when the sun rose. He went back into the shieling and found the bloodless bodies of the dancers lying there. Their partners had sucked them dry.

[Motifs: E251.3.3; F471.2.1]

Barguest. A kind of BOGY OR BOGEY-BEAST. It has horns, teeth and claws and fiery eyes. Henderson describes the Barguest as closely allied to PADFOOT and the HEDLEY KOW. Like them it can take various forms, but usually appears as a shaggy BLACK DOG with huge fiery eyes. It is generally regarded as a death portent. William Henderson in *Folk-Lore of the Northern Counties* (pp. 274–5) said that it used to haunt a piece of wasteland between Wreghorn and Headingley Hill near Leeds. At the death of any notable person in the district it would appear, followed by all the dogs in the district, howling and baying. Henderson reports that he met an old man who claimed to have seen the procession as a child. Hone's *Everyday Book* (vol. III, p. 655) gives a lively report of an encounter with a barguest:

> You see, sir, as how I'd been a clock dressing at Gurston (Grassington), and I'd staid rather lat, and maybe getten a lile sup o' spirit; but I war far from being drunk, and knowed everything that passed. It war about eleven o' clock when I left, and it war at back end o' t' year, and

a most admirable neet it war. The moon war verra breet, and I nivver seed Kylstone Fell plainer in a' my life. Now, you see, sir, I war passing down t' Mill loine, and I heerd summat come past me – brush, brush, brush, wi' chains rattlin' a' the while, but I seed nothing; and I thought to myself, now this is a most mortal queer thing. And I then stuid still and luiked about me; but I seed nothing at aw, nobbut the two stane wa's on each side o' t'mill loine. Then I heard again this brush, brush, brush, wi' the chains; for you see, sir, when I stood still it stopped, and then, thowt I, this mun be a Barguest, that sae much is said about; and I hurried on toward t' wood brig; for they say as how this Barguest cannot cross a watter; but, Lord, sir, when I gat o'er t' brig, I heerd this same again: so it mun either have crossed t' watter or have gone round by the spring heed! And then I became a valiant man, for I were a bit freekend afore; and, thinks I, I'll turn and hev a peep at this thing; so I went up Greet Bank towards Linton, and heerd this brush, brush, brush, wi' the chains aw the way, but I seed nothing; then it ceased all of a sudden. So I turned back to go hame; but I'd hardly reached the door when I heerd again this brush, brush, brush, and the chains going down towards t' Holin House; and I followed it, and the moon there shone verra breet, and I seed its tail! Then thowt I, thou owd thing, I can say I'se seen thee now; so I'll away hame.

When I gat to the door there was a grit thing like a sheep, but it war larger, ligging across the threshold o' t' door, and it war woolly like; and I says, 'Git up!' and it wouldn't git up. Then says I, 'Stir thysel!' and it wouldn't stir itself. And I grew valiant, and I raised t' stick to baste it wi'; and then it luiked at me, and sich oies, they did glower, and war as big as saucers and like a cruelled ball. First there war a red ring, then a blue one, then a white one; and these rings grew less and less till they cam to a dot! Now I war none feared on it, tho it grin'd at me fearfully, and I kept on saying, 'Git up', and 'Stir thysel', and the wife heerd as how I war at t' door, and she came to oppen it; and then this thing gat up and walked off, for it war mare freeten'd o' t'owd wife than it war o' me; and I told the wife, and she said as how it war Barguest; but I never seed it since – and that's a true story.

[Motifs: F234.0.2; F234.1.9; G302.3.2; G303.4.1.2.4; G303.4.6]

Barrenness. See HARD DELIVERY OR BARRENNESS.

Bathing fairies. The medicinal baths and spas so fashionable in 18th-century England seem also to have been patronized by the FAIRIES. A lively account of them bathing one early morning at Ilkley Wells in Yorkshire is to be found in the *Folk-Lore Record* for 1878 (pp. 229–31). It is recorded by Charles Smith from the report of John Dobson:

William Butterfield . . . always opened the door the first thing in the morning, and he did this without ever noticing anything out of the common until one beautiful quiet mid summer morning. As he ascended the brow of the hill he noticed rather particularly how the birds sang so sweetly, and cheerily, and vociferously, making the valley echo with the music of their voices. And in thinking it over afterwards he remembered noticing them, and considered this sign attributable to the after incident. As he drew near the Wells he took out of his pocket the massive iron key, and placed it in the lock; but there was something 'canny' about it, and instead of the key lifting the lever it only turned round and round in the lock. He drew the key back to see that it was all right, and declared 'it was the same that he had on the previous night hung up behind his own door down at home.' Then he endeavoured to push the door open, and no sooner did he push it slightly ajar than it was as quickly pushed back again. At last, with one supreme effort, he forced it perfectly open, and back it flew with a great bang! Then whirr, whirr, whirr, such a noise and sight! all over the water and dipping into it was a lot of little creatures, all dressed in green from head to foot, none of them more than eighteen inches high, and making a chatter and jabber thoroughly unintelligible. They seemed to be taking a bath, only they bathed with all their clothes on. Soon, however, one or two of them began to make off, bounding over the walls like squirrels. Finding they were all making ready for decamping, and wanting to have a word with them, he shouted at the top of his voice – indeed, he declared afterwards he couldn't find anything else to say or do – 'Hallo there!' Then away the whole tribe went, helter skelter, toppling and tumbling, heads over heels, heels over heads, and all the while making a noise not unlike a disturbed nest of young partridges. The sight was so unusual that he declared he either couldn't or daren't attempt to rush after them. He stood as still and confounded, he said, as old Jeremiah Lister down there at Wheatley did, half a century previous, when a witch from Ilkley put an ash riddle upon the side of the river Wharfe, and sailed across in it to where he was standing. When the well had got quite clear of these strange beings he ran to the door and looked to see where they had fled, but nothing was to be seen. He ran back into the bath to see if they had left anything behind; but there was nothing; the water lay still and clear as he had left it on the previous night. He thought they might perhaps have left some of their clothing behind in their haste, but he could find none, and so he gave up looking, and commenced his usual routine of preparing the baths; not, however, without trotting to the door once or twice to see if they might be coming back; but he saw them no more.

These small green-clad fairies may well have been ELVES. Their chirping, bird-like voices and DRESS AND APPEARANCE are true to a tradition that goes as far back as the 16th century, and it is noticeable that they had no wings, but scampered and leapt like squirrels. This is one of those strangely vivid accounts which can be found from time to time and which strike one with a shock of authenticity.

[Motif: F265.1]

Bauchan (*buckawn*) **or Bogan.** A HOBGOBLIN spirit, often tricksy, sometimes dangerous, and sometimes helpful. J. F. CAMPBELL in *Popular Tales of the West Highlands* (vol. II, p. 103) gives a story of one who followed his master when he emigrated to America.

Callum Mor MacIntosh had a little farm in Lochaber. A bauchan haunted the place, and there was a kind of love–hate relationship between the two. They often fought, but the bauchan helped Callum at need. One day, for instance, as Callum came back from the market the bauchan waylaid him and they had a fight. When they had parted and Callum got home he found he had lost his best handkerchief which he prized because it had been blessed by a priest. He was sure the bauchan had it and he went back to look for it. Sure enough he found the bauchan rubbing the handkerchief on a rough stone. 'It's well you've come, Callum,' said the bauchan. 'I'd have been your death if I'd rubbed a hole in this. As it is you'll have to fight me for it.' So they fought and Callum won back his handkerchief. A little later, however, when they had run out of firewood and the snow prevented Callum from fetching a birch he had felled, he heard a great thud at his house door, and there was the tree, lugged through the snow by the bauchan. When he had to move house the bauchan brought a great cart that he had left behind, and saved him a ten-mile tramp across difficult country.

Some years later came the deportations, and Callum was one of the first to land in New York. He had to stay some time in quarantine, and when he got to his new plot of land the first person to meet him was the bauchan in the form of a goat. 'Ha, ha! Callum,' he said. 'I am before you.' The bauchan was very helpful in clearing Callum's new land. He thus became an example of the AMERICAN FAIRY IMMIGRANTS.

[Motifs: F482.3.1; F482.5.5]

Bean-nighe (*ben-neeyeh*), **or 'the Washing Woman'.** She occurs both in Highland and Irish tradition as one of the variants of the BANSHEE. A good account of her is given in L. Spence's book *The Fairy Tradition in Britain* (pp. 54–5). The name and characteristics vary in different localities. She is to be seen by desolate streams washing the blood-stained clothing of those about to die. She is small and generally dressed in green, and has red webbed feet. She portends evil, but if anyone who sees her before she sees him gets between her and the water she will grant him three wishes. She will answer three questions, but she asks three questions again, which must be answered truly. Anyone bold enough to seize one of her hanging breasts and suck it may claim that he is her foster-child and she will be favourable to him. But the CAOINTEACH of Islay, which is the same as the Bean-Nighe, is fiercer and more formidable. If anyone interrupts her she strikes at his legs with her wet linen and often he loses the use of his limbs. It is said that the bean-nighe are the ghosts of women who have died in childbirth and must perform their task until the natural destined time of their death comes

The bean-nighe, sometimes called the LITTLE-WASHER-BY-THE-FORD, chiefly haunt the Highlands and Islands of Scotland, but Peter Buchan collected a washer story in Banffshire.

[Motifs: F232.2; M301.6.1]

Bean Si (*banshee*). Bean Si is the Gaelic for 'fairy woman', and is commonly written BANSHEE, as it is pronounced, because it is one of the best-known of the Celtic FAIRIES. In the Highlands of Scotland she is also called BEAN-NIGHE, or the LITTLE-WASHER-BY-THE-FORD, because she is seen by the side of a burn or river washing the blood-stained clothes of those about to die.

[Motif: M301.6.1]

Beithir (*behir*). This is a rather rare Highland name for one of the large class of FUATHS. It haunted caves and corries. The word was also used for 'lightning' and 'the serpent'. It is given by D. A. Mackenzie in *Scottish Folk Lore and Folk Life* (p. 247), but I have been unable to find it in J. F. CAMPBELL, Kennedy, Carmichael or other Gaelic authorities.

[Motif: F460]

Bells. These had a dual use. In the first place they were used by mortals as a PROTECTION AGAINST FAIRIES and other evil spirits. The church bells, the gargoyles and the weathercock – the symbol of sunrise and day – were popularly supposed to be the three defences against the Devil. The FAIRIES were also repelled by the sound of church bells. Jabez ALLIES's anecdote of the fairy who was heard lamenting

> 'Neither sleep, neither lie,
> For Inkbro's ting-tang hangs so high'

is the first of quite a number that record the fairies' dislike of church bells. Another protective use of bells was that of the Morris Men, whose leg-bells are generally supposed to drive anti-fertility spirits from the neighbourhood.

In the second place, the fairies themselves used bells. No account of the FAIRY RADE is complete without a mention of the jingling bells ringing from the horses' harness. We hear of it, for instance, in YOUNG TAMLANE and in the Galloway account of the Fairy Rade. It is never explained why the fairy bells rang, unless it be from their great love of music, but it is generally supposed that these fairies, in spite of their general habit of kidnapping human beings and purloining human food, belonged to the SEELIE COURT, and it might be conjectured that these bells rang to scare away the evil creatures who made up the UNSEELIE COURT.

Bendith Y Mamau (*bendith er mamigh*), **or 'The Mother's Blessing'.** The Glamorganshire name for the FAIRIES. They steal children, elf-ride horses and visit houses. Bowls of milk were put out for them.

In *Celtic Folklore* (vol. I, pp. 262–9) Rhys gives a circumstantial account of the kidnapping of a child, the substitution of a CHANGELING and the three stages of disenchantment by which the mother gained her child again. The Bendith y Mamau are described as stunted and ugly. The story related by Rhys happened at a time when many children were taken by these fairies, and a young widowed mother guarded her beautiful only child with great care, for the neighbours were sure that he would be coveted by the fairies. One day, when the child was about three years old, the mother heard a strange lowing among the cattle and went to see what was the matter, and when she came back the cradle was empty. She searched desperately for her child and found a little wizened boy who greeted her as Mother. She was sure that it was a CRIMBIL, for it never grew, and after a year she went to a cunning man, who advised her first to test the child. This she was to do by a variant of the brewery of egg-shells. She was to take the top off a raw egg and stir up the contents. When the crimbil asked her what she was doing she replied that she was mixing a pasty for the reapers. He exclaimed, 'I heard from my father – he heard it from his father and that one from his father – that an acorn was before the oak; but I have neither heard nor seen anybody mixing the pasty for the reapers in an eggshell.' This saying established his identity as a changeling, but the mother had yet to discover if her child was with the Bendith y Mamau. For this purpose, she had to go to the place where four roads meet above Rhyd y Gloch when the full moon was four days old and watch there till midnight. The procession of the Bendith y Mamau would pass by, but she must remain silent and still or all would be lost. She waited a long time till she heard the FAIRY RADE approach-ing, and as it passed by she saw her own dear child. With a great effort she stayed still, and went next day to the cunning man. He told her what she must do to get her son. She must procure a black hen without a white or coloured feather on it, wring its neck and roast it without plucking it on a fire of wood. When every feather dropped off, and not before, she might look at the changeling. With great difficulty she got the coal-black hen and obeyed the cunning man exactly. When she turned to look at the crimbil he had disappeared, and outside the door she heard the voice of her own son. He was thin and worn and remembered nothing that had happened to him except that he had been listening to pleasant music. It is unusual to find all these motifs combined in one story.

[Motifs: F321; F321.1; F321.1.1.1; F321.1.3]

Ben-Varrey (*bedn varra*). The Manx name for the MERMAID, of which many tales are told round the coasts of Man. She bears the same general character as mermaids do everywhere, enchanting and alluring men to their death, but occasionally showing softer traits. In Man the Mermaid shows, on the whole, the softer side of her nature. In Dora Broome's *Fairy Tales from the Isle of Man* the Mermaid of Purt-le-Murrey sets her love on a man and nearly succeeds in alluring him into the sea, but his boat-mates save him by a counter-charm. Here she is a siren, but apparently actuated by true love. In the same book a fisherman who carries a stranded mermaid back into the sea is rewarded by the information of how to find a treasure. He finds it, but it is of antique gold and he does not know how to dispose of it. In the end the strange coins are thrown into the sea by a roaming simpleton; but that is hardly the fault of the Ben-Varrey. There is also a story of a baby mermaid who coveted a little human girl's doll and stole it, but was rebuked by her mother and sent to give the girl her necklace of pearls to atone for the theft. A pleasant story in Sophia Morrison's *Manx Fairy Tales*, 'The Mermaid of Gob-Ny-Ooyl', tells of the friendly relations of the Sayle family with the local mermaid. They were a large fishing family, with a well-tended croft to eke out their living, and everything prospered with them. It was noticed that old Sayle had a great liking for apples, and always took a pile of them in the boat when they were ripe. But the time came for him to retire, and then things began to go less well. There was soon not enough to keep them all, and one by one the boys went to be sailors, till there was only the youngest, Evan, left to look after his parents and the farm. One day when Evan had set the lobster creels and was climbing among the rocks to search for sea-birds' eggs, he heard a sweet voice calling him and when he came down he found the Ben-Varrey sitting on a shoal of rock. He was half afraid, but she spoke pleasantly and asked after his father, and he told her all their troubles. When he got home his father was well pleased to hear what had happened, and told him to take some apples with him next day. The mermaid was delighted to get her 'sweet land eggs' again, and everything began to flourish once more. But Evan loved the mermaid's company so much that he spent all his time in his boat, and people began to fault him for idleness. Evan was so bothered by this that he decided to go for a sailor, but before he went he planted a little apple tree on the cliff above the Ben-Varrey's Bay, and told her that when the tree was old enough the sweet land-eggs would ripen and drop down into the sea. So, though he went, she still brought good luck on the place; but the apple-tree was slow in growing and the mermaid grew weary of waiting, and went off to look for Evan Sayle. The apples ripened in the end, but Evan and the Ben-Varrey never came back to gather them.

Walter Gill in *A Manx Scrapbook* (p. 241) recalls a tradition of a friendly warning by a mermaid near Patrick when the Peel boats were fishing at the Wart off Spanish Head. A mermaid rose suddenly among the boats and called out, '*shiaull er thalloo*', that is 'sail to land'. Some of the boats ran for shelter at once, those that remained lost their tackle and some lives. From these tales it will be seen that though some of the Ben-Varrey are regarded as dangerous sirens, the picture of them is on the whole more favourable than that of most mermaids.

[Motifs: B53.0.1; B81.7; B81.13.4; F420.3.1]

Biasd Bheulach (*beeast veealuch*). The monster of Odail Pass on the Isle of Skye, and one of the Highland demon spirits. It is described by J. G. CAMPBELL in *Witchcraft and Second Sight in the Scottish Highlands* (pp. 207-8). It seems to have been a nasty creature to meet.

> Sometimes it bore the form of a man, sometimes of a man with only one leg; at other times it appeared like a greyhound or beast prowling about; and sometimes it was heard uttering frightful shrieks and outcries which made the workmen leave their bothies in horror. It was only during the night it was seen or heard.

> It was not only horrible to see and hear, it seemed to be hunting for blood to appease it.

> It ceased when a man was found dead at the roadside, pierced with two wounds, one on his side and one on his leg, with a hand pressed on each wound. It was considered impossible that these wounds could have been inflicted by human agency.

The distinction between demon spirits and demonic ghosts is hard to draw, and people might well have accounted for Biasd Bheulach as the ravening ghost of a murdered man, hungry for revenge.

Big Ears. The name given in the Highlands to a demon cat said to appear at the end of the ferocious magical ceremony of TAGHAIRM. In an account of the last performance of this rite which appeared in the *London Literary Gazette* of 1824, Big Ears, when he finally appeared, perched upon a stone which was still pointed out in the writer's day. The marks of his claws were still visible.

[Motifs: B871.1.6; G302.3.2]

Billy Blind. A household spirit of the HOBGOBLIN kind, who only seems to appear in the ballads. His speciality was giving good advice, but in 'Young Bekie' (No. 53 of the Child collection of ballads), which is a variant of the story of à Becket's father, Burd Isabel, the French princess who has helped young Bekie to escape and plighted her troth with him, is warned by the billy blind that young Bekie is on the point of marrying someone else, and assists in a magical journey to England in time to prevent the celebration of the nuptials, hailing a magic ship which the billy blind himself steered across the sea.

Another ballad in which he appears is No. 6 in the Child collection, 'Willie's Lady', in which Willie's mother, a rank witch, is preventing the birth of his child by various cantrips. The billy blind advises them to announce the birth of a child and summon the mother-in-law to the christening of a dummy. The mother-in-law expresses her surprise in a soliloquy which gives away the methods by which she has been preventing the birth and enables them to counteract them, as, for instance, by killing the master kid beneath her bed. It is rather strange that this spirit only occurs in the ballads. 'Billy' means a companion or a warrior.

[Motif: F482.5.4]

Billy Winker. The Lancashire version of WEE WILLIE WINKIE of Scotland, Old Luk Oie of Hans Andersen and, even less credible as a folk figure, The Dustman. These are all nursery spirits, and it is doubtful if they ever enjoyed full grown-up credence. Unlike the NURSERY BOGIES, these are all gentle spirits, worthy to be invoked by weary nurses and mothers of obstinately wakeful children.

Black Annis. A cannibal hag with a blue face and iron claws supposed to live in a cave in the Dane Hills in Leicestershire. There was a great oak at the mouth of the cave in which she was said to hide to leap out, catch and devour stray children and lambs. The cave, which was called 'Black Annis' Bower Close', was supposed to have been dug out of the rock by her own nails. On Easter Monday it was the custom from early times to hold a drag hunt from Annis' Bower to the Mayor of Leicester's house. The bait dragged was a dead cat drenched in aniseed. Black Annis was associated with a monstrous cat. This custom died out at the end of the 18th century. Black Annis and GENTLE ANNIE are supposed to derive from ANU, or DANA, a Celtic mother goddess. Donald A. Mackenzie suggests a connection with the Irish AINE, the mother of Earl Fitzgerald. The *Leicester Chronicle* of 1842 mentions a tomb in Swithland Church to Agnes Scott, an anchoress, and suggests that she was the original of Black Annis. Ruth Tongue in her *Forgotten Folk-Tales of the English Counties* reproduces a tale about Black Annis the hag. It was told by an evacuee from Leicester in December 1941. Her description seems to show that the tradition of Black Annis was still alive just over thirty years ago:

Black Annis lived in the Danehills.

She was ever so tall and had a blue face and had long white teeth and she ate people. She only went out when it was dark.

My mum says, when she ground her teeth people could hear her in time to bolt their doors and keep well away from the window. That's why we don't have a lot of big windows in Leicestershire cottages, she can't only get an arm inside.

My mum says that's why we have the fire and chimney in a corner.

The fire used to be on the earth floor once and people slept all round it until Black Annis grabbed the babies out of the window. There wasn't any glass in that time.

When Black Annis howled you could hear her five miles away and then even the poor folk in the huts fastened skins across the window and put witch-herbs above it to keep her away safe.

A full account of the various traditions about Black Annis is given by C. J. Billson in *County Folk-Lore* (vol. I). It has been suggested that she is MILTON's 'blew meager hag'.

[Motifs: A125.1; G211.1.7; G214.1; G261; G262.0.1]

Black dogs. Stories of black dogs are to be found all over the country. They are generally dangerous, but sometimes helpful. As a rule, the black dogs are large and shaggy, about the size of a calf, with fiery eyes. If anyone speaks to them or strikes at them they have power to blast, like the MAUTHE DOOG, the Black Dog of Peel Castle in the Isle of Man. In England they are often the form taken by a human ghost. Such a one was said to be laid at Finstock in Oxfordshire with the help of prayers, a mother with a new-born child and a pair of clappers which were parted and put into the two separate ponds in the village. When the two clappers come together it is said that the Black Dog of Finstock will reappear. In 'The Collingbourne Kingston Black Dog' in Ruth Tongue, *Forgotten Folk-Tales of the English Counties* (pp. 48–9), the animal is an instrument of justice. Another type of black dog is the CHURCH GRIM. An account is given in HARTLAND's *English Fairy and Folk Tales* (pp. 234–44), but the fullest treatment is by T. Brown in *Folklore* (vol. 69, p. 175).

[Motifs: E423.1.1; E423.1.1.1; F234.1.9; G302.3.2]

Blights and illnesses attributed to the fairies. The word 'STROKE' for a sudden paralytic seizure comes directly from fairy belief. It is an abbreviation of 'fairy stroke' or 'elf stroke', and was supposed to come from an ELF-SHOT or an elf-blow, which struck down the victim, animal or human, who was then carried off invisibly, while a STOCK remained to take its place. Sometimes this was a transformed fairy, sometimes a lump of wood, transformed by GLAMOUR and meant to be taken for the corpse of the victim. The legend about KIRK, the author of *The Secret Commonwealth*, illustrates this. Kirk was accustomed to wander round the fairy hills by night, and one morning he was found unconscious on the Fairy Knowe of the Sith Bruach at Aberfoyle. He was carried to bed, and died without fully regaining consciousness. His wife was pregnant, and the night before his child was born a kinsman, Grahame of Duchray, dreamt that Kirk appeared to him and told him that he was not dead but had been carried away into the fairy KNOWE. If his child was christened in the manse, however, he would have power to appear, and if on his appearance Grahame struck his dirk into Kirk's arm-chair he would be freed. It was believed that Kirk appeared as he had promised, but Grahame faltered back at the sight of him and failed to draw his dirk, so Kirk is still a prisoner in Fairyland. In 1944 it was still said that if a child was christened in the manse, Kirk could be disenchanted if a dagger was stuck into his chair, which had never been moved from the manse. Presumably he would have crumbled into dust, but his soul would still have been freed.

Many other ailments were supposed to be inflicted by the FAIRIES. Rheumatism, slipped discs, anything that twisted or deformed the body could be supposed to be due to fairy blows and wounds dealt invisibly but painfully. Paralysis was attributed in BOVET's *Pandaemonium* to the invisible presence of a FAIRY MARKET. A night traveller had seen this market on Blackdown in Somerset and had ridden up to see it closer. When he got near to it, it disappeared, but he felt a pressure all round him as if he was being thronged, and when he got out of the press a deadness struck him, all on one side, and he was paralysed for the rest of his life.

For more temporary offences, people were often afflicted with cramps or with bruising supposed to be the marks of pinching fingers. W. B. YEATS claimed to know an old man who was tormented with the fairies. 'They had um out of bed and thumped um,' he said. Wasting diseases, phthisis and tuberculosis were often blamed on the fairies, although they might also be ascribed to witchcraft. CONSUMPTION was chiefly ascribed to compulsive nightly visits to the fairy mounds, so that every morning the victim returned exhausted and unrefreshed. A typical example of this infliction is to be found in the Orcadian story of KATE CRACKERNUTS, which is rich in both fairy and witchcraft beliefs. Sometimes the wasting is ascribed to a single amatory experience which leaves unsatisfied yearnings behind it, as an encounter with the GANCONER would do, or the vampire-like embraces of a LAMIA; sometimes, as in Christina Rossetti's GOBLIN MARKET, it could be due to eating FAIRY FOOD. Fairies also, who were in the main fertility spirits, could be blamed for HARD DELIVERY OR BARRENNESS though, again, this was more commonly attributed to witchcraft. IMPETIGO and many other skin diseases were a fairy infliction, and they could also be responsible for a plague of lice.

Many animal diseases were thought to be inflicted by the fairies. Cattle taken suddenly ill were supposed to have been previously slaughtered and eaten by the fairies. An example of this is the story of 'The Three Cows' in Jacobs's *English Fairy Tales* (p. 82). Brucellosis, swine fever and fowl pest were all attributed to the fairies. In fact, what witches could do fairies could do.

INFANTILE PARALYSIS was not recognized as a disease by country

people, but believed to show that a CHANGELING had been substituted
for the true child. Incredibly harsh treatment was generally recommended
as a cure. Indeed, if officious neighbours took a hand, it sometimes ended
in the death of a child.

[Motif: F362]

Blue Burches. A harmless HOBGOBLIN who played BOGGART pranks
in a shoemaker's house on the Blackdown Hills in Somerset. The cobbler's little boy was friendly with him, and had seen him once in his true
shape, an old man in baggy blue burches, or breeches. The cobbler and
his family took all his pranks in good part. When heavy steps were heard
descending the stairs and a wisp of blue smoke drifted across the room,
the cobbler only said, 'Never mind old Blue Burches; he never do no
harm.' And he went on proudly to boast of how Blue Burches ran across
the room like a little black pig and jumped into the duck-pond without a
splash, and how, when they were coming back late from market, he would
set the house all a-glow to make them think it was on fire. He told his tale
to the wrong audience, one of the church-wardens, who took old Blue
Burches for the Devil himself and got a couple of parsons along to exorcize him. They came up and found an old white horse grazing by the
duck-pond. 'Who's that?' said the parson to the little boy. 'That be old
Blue Burches, sir,' said the boy. 'Can you put a bridle on him?' said the
parson. The boy was proud to show how friendly old Blue Burches was,
and he slipped the bridle over his head. At once both the parsons cried out
together: 'Depart from me, you wicked!' Old Blue Burches plunged into
the pond, and never came out again; at least, not in so friendly a form.
This anecdote of Blue Burches was told to Ruth Tongue by her school-
fellows in 1909 and by some harvesters at Trull in 1907–8. The story
probably dates from the end of the 19th century.

[Motifs: D610; F382; F401.3.1; F473.2.4; F475]

Blue-cap. An industrious mine spirit, who worked as hard as any
BROWNIE, but, unlike a brownie, expected to be paid a working man's
wages. An account of him appeared in the *Colliery Guardian* in May
1863:

> The supernatural person in question was no other than a ghostly
> putter, and his name was Blue-cap. Sometimes the miners would
> perceive a light-blue flame flicker through the air and settle on a full
> coal-tub, which immediately moved towards the rolly-way as though
> impelled by the sturdiest sinews in the working. Industrious Blue-cap
> required, and rightly, to be paid for his services, which he moderately
> rated as those of an ordinary average putter, therefore once a fortnight
> Blue-cap's wages were left for him in a solitary corner of the mine. If
> they were a farthing below his due, the indignant Blue-cap would not

pocket a stiver; if they were a farthing above his due, indignant Blue-cap left the surplus revenue where he found it.

At the time when this was written, the belief in Blue-cap – or Blue-bonnet, as he was called in some of the mines – was already on the wane.
[Motifs: F456; F456.1; F456.2; F456.2.1]

Blue Men of the Minch. The Blue Men used particularly to haunt the strait between Long Island and the Shiant Islands. They swam out to wreck passing ships, and could be baulked by captains who were ready at rhyming and could keep the last word. They were supposed to be fallen angels.

The sudden storms that arose around the Shiant Islands were said to be caused by the Blue Men, who lived in under-water caves and were ruled by a chieftain.

J. G. CAMPBELL in his *Superstitions of the Scottish Highlands* (p. 200) summarizes a tale of a Blue Man who had been captured sleeping on the surface of the sea.

> He was taken on board and, being thought of mortal race, string twine was coiled round and round him from his feet to his shoulders, till it seemed impossible for him to struggle, or move foot or arm. The ship had not gone far when two men (Blue Men) were observed coming after it on the waters. One of them was heard to say, 'Duncan will be one man,' to which the other replied 'Farquhar will be two.' On hearing this, the man who had been so securely tied sprang to his feet, broke his bonds like spider threads, jumped overboard and made off with the two friends who had been coming to his rescue.

In this story the creatures had human names. D. A. Mackenzie in *Scottish Folk-Lore and Folk Life* devotes a chapter to 'The Blue Men of the Minch'. They are believed in only in the area of the Straits of Shiant, and he brings forward the theory that the belief originated in the Moorish captives called 'Blue Men' who were marooned in Ireland in the 9th century by Norwegian pirates. The account is well documented, the chief source being *The Annals of Ireland* by Duald Mac Firbis, and it seems likely that the theory has a solid foundation. If so, this is one more example of the fairy tradition being founded on memories of an extinct race.
[Motif: F420.5.2.7.3]

Bocan (*buckawn*), **or Bogan.** This is another form of the Highland BAUCHAN, one of which had a love–hate relationship to Callum Mor MacIntosh, and finally went with him to America, an excellent example of the AMERICAN FAIRY IMMIGRANTS. The Bocan was also to be found in Ireland.

Bodach (*budagh*). The Celtic form of BUGBEAR, or BUG-A-BOO. He comes down the chimney like a NURSERY BOGIE to fetch naughty children. The Bodach Glas is a death token, and William Henderson, in *Folk-Lore of the Northern Counties* (p. 344), cites it among Highland beliefs in his account of death tokens:

> Such a prophet of death was the Bodach Glas, or Dark Grey Man, of which Sir Walter Scott makes such effective use in *Waverley* towards the end of Fergus MacIvor's history. Its appearance foretold death in the clan of —, and I have been informed on the most credible testimony of its appearance in our own day. The Earl of E—, a nobleman alike beloved and respected in Scotland, and whose death was truly felt as a national loss, was playing on the day of his decease on the links of St Andrews the national game of golf. Suddenly he stopped in the middle of a game, saying 'I can play no longer, there is the Bodach Glas. I have seen it for the third time; something fearful is going to befall me.' He died that night at M.M—, as he was handing a candlestick to a lady who was retiring to her room. The clergyman from whom I received the story endorses it as authentic, and names the gentleman to whom Lord E— spoke.

[Motif: E723.2]

Bodachan Sabhaill (*botuchan so-will*), **the Little Old Man of the Barn**. A barn BROWNIE who took pity on old men, and threshed for them. D. A. Mackenzie gives us a verse about him in his *Scottish Folk Lore and Folk Life* (p. 230):

> When the peat will turn grey and shadows fall deep
> And weary old Callum is snoring asleep . . .
>   The Little Old Man of the Barn
>   Will thresh with no light in the mouth of the night,
>   The Little Old Man of the Barn.

[Type: ML6035. Motifs: F346; F482.5.4]

Bogan (*buckawn*). See BAUCHAN; BOCAN; BUGGANE.

Boggart. A mischievous BROWNIE, almost exactly like a poltergeist in his habits. The best-known story about him, told by William Henderson, KEIGHTLEY and several others, is that about his accompanying the family when they move to get rid of him.

There was once a Yorkshire farmer called George Gilbertson whose house was much tormented by a boggart. He played his tricks on everyone about the house, and especially on the children. He would snatch away their bread and butter and upset their porringers and shove them into corners and cupboards; and yet not a glimpse of him was ever seen.

There was an elf-bore in one of the cupboards, a hole where a knot of wood had been, and one day the youngest boy stuck an old shoehorn into it. It was pushed back so hard that it popped out of the hole and hit him on the forehead. After this the children loved to play with the boggart by thrusting sticks into the hole and seeing them shot back. But the boggart's tricks got worse and worse, and poor Mrs Gilbertson became so anxious for the children that at last they decided to move. So on the day of the flitting their nearest neighbour, John Marshall, saw them following their last creaking carts out of the empty yard.

'And so you're flitting at last, Georgie?' he said.

'Aye, Johnny lad, I'm forced tull it; for that domned boggart torments us soa we can neaither rest neet nor day for't. It seems to have sech a malice against t' poor bairns that it omost kills my poor dame at thowt on't. And soa ye see we're forced to flit like.'

A sudden unexpected echo to his words came in a deep voice out of the old upright churn in the last cart.

'Aye, Johnny lad, we're flitting, ye see.'

'It's the domned boggart!' said George. 'If I'd a knowed thou'd been there I hadn't a stirred a leg. Turn back, Mally,' he said to his wife. 'We mun as well be tormented in t'owd house as in another that's not to our liking.'

So back they went; and the boggart played about their farm till he was tired of the sport.

[Types: ML7010; ML7020. Motifs: F399.4; F482.3.1.1; F482.5.5]

Bogey-beast. See BOGY, OR BOGEY-BEAST.

Boggle-boos. See BUGS, *et al.*

Bogies. 'Bogies', 'BOGLES', 'BUGS' or 'bug-a-boos' are names given to a whole class of mischievous, frightening and even dangerous spirits whose delight it is to torment mankind. Sometimes they go about in troops, like the HOBYAHS, but as a rule they may be described as individual and SOLITARY FAIRY members of the UNSEELIE COURT. A nickname of the Devil in Somerset is 'Bogie', presumably to play him down a little, for bogies generally rank rather low in the retinue of hell. They are often adepts at SHAPE-SHIFTING, like the BULLBEGGAR, the HEDLEY KOW and the PICKTREE BRAG. These are generally no more than mischievous. The well-known BOGGART is the most harmless of all, generally a BROWNIE who has been soured by mistreatment; among the most dangerous are the fiendish NUCKELAVEE and the DUERGAR, and other examples appear under BOGY OR BOGEY-BEAST.

Some bogies, like minor devils, are simple and gullible. Sternberg's story, 'The Bogie's Field', in his *Dialect and Folk-Lore of Northampton-*

shire (p. 140), is a common type of trickster tale. Several versions of it are told about the Devil and one about a boggart:

Once there was a bogie that laid claim to a farmer's field. The farmer did not think it fair; but after a long argument they decided that, though the farmer should do the work, they should divide the produce between them. So the first year in spring the farmer said: 'Which will you have, tops or bottoms?'

'Bottoms,' said the bogie.

So the farmer planted wheat; all the bogie got was stubble and roots. Next year he said he would have tops, and the farmer planted turnips; so he was no better off than before. He began to think he was getting the worst of it; so the next year he said: 'You'll plant wheat, and we'll have a mowing match, and him who wins shall have it for keeps.' 'Agreed,' said the farmer, and they divided the field up into two equal halves. A little before the corn ripened, however, the farmer went to the smith and ordered some hundreds of thin iron rods, which he stuck all over the bogie's half of the field. The farmer got on like a house on fire, but the poor bogie kept muttering to himself, 'Darnation hard docks, 'nation hard docks!' and his scythe grew so blunt that it would hardly cut butter. After about an hour he called to the farmer, 'When do we wiffle-waffle, mate?' for in a match all the reapers whet their scythes together.

'Waffle?' said the farmer. 'Oh, about noon, maybe.'

'Noon!' said the bogie. 'Then I've lost,' and off he went, and troubled the farmer no more.

[Types: 1030; 1090. Motifs: K42.2; K171.1]

Bogles. On the whole, these are evil GOBLINS, but according to William Henderson in *Folk-Lore of the Northern Counties*, who quotes from HOGG's 'Woolgatherer', the bogles on the Scottish Borders, though

formidable, are virtuous creatures: 'Then the Bogles, they are a better kind o' spirits; they meddle wi' nane but the guilty; the murderer, an' the mansworn, an' the cheaters o' the widow an' fatherless, they do for them.' Henderson tells a corroborative story of a poor widow at the village of Hurst, near Reeth, who had had some candles stolen by a neighbour. The neighbour saw one night a dark figure in his garden and took out his gun and fired at it. The next night while he was working in an outhouse the figure appeared in the doorway and said, 'I'm neither bone nor flesh nor blood, thou canst not harm me. Give back the candles, but I must take something from thee.' With that he came up to the man and plucked out an eyelash, and vanished. But the man's eye 'twinkled' ever after.

On the other hand, Henderson has another story of a bogle which was banished by an open bible.

Mrs Balfour uses 'bogles' in her Lincolnshire tales in *Folk-Lore* (vol. II) as completely evil creatures. It is a little doubtful if the word is true Lincolnshire or was imported by her.

Bogy, or Bogey-beast. A malicious GOBLIN, one name for the Devil, which was once in common use for frightening children. E. M. Wright in *Rustic Speech and Folk-Lore* gives as an example: 'If tha doesna leave off shrikin', I'll fetch a black bogy to thee', and cites a ghostly bogy which haunted its murderer as a skeleton, wailing: 'Oi waant my booans! I waant my booans!' It was universal over England, but the use of cautionary demons and NURSERY BOGIES has gone out of fashion in modern education. Now 'bogy' serves as a generic name for BOGIES in general, including a number of frightening and mischievous characters: BARGUEST, BOGGART, BRAG, BUGGAN, BUGGANE, HEDLEY KOW, MUMPOKER, PADFOOT, TANTERABOGUS, TRASH, and so on. The respectable and mediocre Colonel Bogey, whose golf score is always dead average, seems to have no right to his name.

Boneless. One in the famous lists of spirits given by Reginald SCOT as those that used to fright his grandmother's maids. There is no further information about him by Scot, but one presumes that he was one of those formless things whose chief function it was to terrify travellers, or children in their beds, not unlike the Shetland IT. Lately, however, Ruth Tongue has disinterred a story told to her in 1916 about a pedlar going to the Oxford market by night; and later still, she picked up an account of a policeman whose beat was along the Minehead–Bridgwater road, and who had to be moved to another district after a terrifying encounter with Boneless as he bicycled along on his round one night. The report was confirmed to her by Mr H. Kille and by Colonel Luttrell.

The apparition was later described to Ruth Tongue by the policeman's sister-in-law:

> He told her it was darksome over above Putsham Rise and the tide was in far below – he could hear it plain down two hill fields, and then his lamp lit up a white Summat across the road. It weren't fog. It were alive – kind of woolly like a cloud or a wet sheep – and it slid up and all all over him on his bike, and was gone rolling and bowling and stretching out and in up the Perry Farm Road. It was so sudden he didn't fall off – but he says it was like a wet heavy blanket and so terrible cold and smelled stale.

The thing in the Oxford story is expressly called Boneless, and is described as:

A shapeless Summat as slides behind and alongside in the dark night. Many's have died of fright through his following on. They can't never tell about him except he's a big shadow and shapeless.

This is one of those creatures called 'Frittenings'.
[Motif: F402.1.12]

Boobrie. A gigantic water-bird, which inhabits the lochs of Argyllshire. It has a loud harsh voice and webbed feet and gobbles up sheep and cattle. J. F. CAMPBELL thinks the Boobrie is one form taken by the WATER-HORSE, but he gives no reason for thinking so. He gives an eye-witness account in *Popular Tales of the West Highlands* (vol. IV, p. 308) from a man who claimed to have seen it. He waded up to his shoulders in the waters of a loch in February to get a shot at it, but had only come within eighty-five yards when the creature dived. It looked like a gigantic Northern Diver, but was black all over. Its neck was two feet eleven inches long, its bill about seventeen inches long and hooked like an eagle's. Its legs were very short, the feet webbed and armed with tremendous claws, its footprints were found in the mud to the north of the loch, its voice was like the roar of an angry bull, and it lived on calves, sheep, lambs and others.
[Motif: B872]

Booman. In Orkney and Shetland, 'Booman' is a BROWNIE-like HOBGOBLIN. Its name is preserved elsewhere in singing games, 'Shoot, Booman, shoot', and 'Booman is dead and gone'. These are to be found in Alice Gomme's *Dictionary of British Folk-Lore*, Part I: *Traditional Games* (vol. I, p. 43).

Bottrell, William (1816–81). He was born at Raftra near Land's End and educated at Penzance Grammar School. His first writings were in the *Cornish Telegraph* of 1869, on 'The Penzance of our Grandfathers'. He wrote regularly for the *Cornish Telegraph*, as well as in the periodicals *One and All* and *The Reliquary*. Most of these articles were reproduced in the first volume of *Traditions and Hearthside Stories of West Cornwall* in 1870, the second volume of which came out in 1873, and the last, called *Stories and Folk-Lore of West Cornwall*, in 1880. Before this came out he was stricken by paralysis, and he died in August the following year.

In 1865, HUNT published *Popular Romances of the West of England*, very largely based on Bottrell's work, both his articles and stories told by him (more than fifty).

Bovet, Richard. Towards the end of the 17th century, before the rationalism of the 18th century overwhelmed it, a number of books appeared with a strong bias towards the supernatural, and a more

credulous attitude towards FAIRIES than had been found in the Elizabethan period, whose writers were apt to treat belief in the fairies as a
rustic superstition. We have AUBREY's *Remaines of Gentilisme* in 1686,
Baxter's *The Certainty of the Worlds of Spirits* in 1681, Joseph Glanvil's
Saducismus Triumphatus in 1681, KIRK's *The Secret Commonwealth* in
1691, William Lilly's *History of His Own Times* in 1681, and Cotton
Mather's *The Wonders of the Invisible World* in 1693. Among the most
interesting of them is Richard Bovet's *Pandaemonium, or The Devil's
Cloyster*, published in 1684. Richard Bovet lived out of the intellectual
ferment of London society. He belonged to a puritanical family in
Taunton, and there is even some rumour of his having suffered under
Judge Jeffreys after the Monmouth Rebellion. That he was not entirely

out of touch with the thought of his time is shown by his dedication of his book to Dr Henry More, the author of *Philosophical Poems* (1647). He tells us more about fairy-lore than Glanvil or Baxter. His two most important contributions to our knowledge are his account of the FAIRY MARKET on Blackdown between Pitminster and Chard, and a report from a Scottish correspondent of the Fairy Boy of Leith. His style is lucid and plain. The frontispiece of the book is worth studying, for it covers the whole ground of Bovet's supernatural beliefs. In the background is an enchanted castle with a DRAGON rising out of it and a horned porter at the door. A witch is riding a rather smaller dragon in the sky. In front of the castle is a fairy ring. To the right of the foreground a friar protected by a magic circle and a rosary is controlling a rather bewildered group of IMPS, one of whom is scratching his head while the one behind the friar is clawing at his gown in the hope of pulling him out of the circle and snatching him down to Hell. Behind him is a witch's cottage; to the left of the picture a witch, also protected by a circle, is raising what she fondly imagines is a dead woman, demurely dressed in a shroud with a top-knot above it, though the cloven hoof just showing beneath her skirt shows that it is not a corpse that the witch is raising, but a devil. This is in accordance with the orthodox Puritan belief of the time, according to which apparent ghosts were really disguised devils.

The general tone and style of the book gives an impression of a pleasant personality. It is to be hoped that he did not fall into Judge Jeffreys's hands.

Brag. One of the mischievous SHAPE-SHIFTING kinds of GOBLINS. Like the Irish PHOOKA, he often takes the form of a horse. He belongs to the Northern Counties, which are rich in HOBGOBLINS.

In *Folk-Lore of the Northern Counties*, William Henderson quotes some tales of the PICKTREE BRAG told by Sir Cuthbert Sharpe in *The Bishoprick Garland*. It kept changing its form. Sometimes it was like a calf, with a white handkerchief round its neck, sometimes like a dick-ass; it appeared once as four men holding a white sheet, once as a naked man without a head. One old lady had a tale about her uncle. He had a suit of white clothes which always brought him bad luck. The first time he put it on he met the brag, and once, as he was returning from a christening in that very suit, he met the brag again. He was a brave man, so he leapt on its back.

> But when he came to the four lonin ends, the Brag joggled him so sore that he could hardly keep his seat; and at last it threw him into the middle o' the pond, and ran away, setting up a great nicker and laugh, for all the world like a Christian.

The DUNNIE and HEDLEY KOW behave in the same kind of way. [Motif: F234.0.2]

Bran (*bran*) **and Sceolan** (*shkeolawn*). Bran and Sceolan were the two
favourite hounds of FINN Mac Cumhal. They were so wise and knowing
that they seemed human in knowledge, and so indeed they were. According to the Irish story, this was how they were born. One time Finn's
mother Muirne came to stay with him in Almhuin (Allen) which was the
headquarters where he lived with the FIANNA, and she brought her sister
Tuiren with her. And Iollan Eachtach, an Ulster man and one of the
chiefs of the Fianna there, was with him at the time, and he asked
Tuiren's hand in marriage from Finn, and Finn granted it, but he said
that if Tuiren had any reason to be displeased with her bargain, Iollan
should allow her to return freely, and he made Iollan grant sureties for it
and Iollan gave sureties to Caoilte and Goll and Lugaidh Lamha before
he took Tuiren away. Now, whether Finn had any inkling of it or not it is
certain that Iollan had already a sweetheart among the SIDHE and she
was Uchtdealb of the Fair Breast, and when she heard that Iollan was
married she was bitterly jealous. She took on the appearance of Finn's
woman messenger and, going to Ulster to Tuiren's house, she said: 'Finn
sends all good wishes and long life to you, queen, and bids you prepare a
great feast, and if you will come aside with me I will tell you how it must
be.' Tuiren went aside with her, and when they got out of sight Uchtdealb took out a rod and smote her with it, and at once she turned into a
most beautiful little bitch, and she led her away to the house of Fergus
Fionnliath, the king of the harbour of Gallimh. She chose Fergus because
he hated dogs more than anything in the world, and, still in the shape of
Finn's messenger, she led the little bitch in to Fergus and said to him:
'Finn wishes you to foster and take charge of this little bitch and she is
with young, and do not let her join the chase when her time is near';
and she left the hound with him. Fergus thought it a strange thing that
this charge should have been put on him, for everyone knew what a
hatred he had of dogs, but he had a great regard for Finn, so he did his
best, and the little hound was so swift and so clever that soon he changed
his notions altogether and began to like hounds as much as he had hated
them.

In the meantime it became known that Tuiren had disappeared, and
Finn called Iollan to account for it, and Iollan had to say that she was
gone and that he could not find her. At that his sureties pressed him so
hard that he begged for time to search for her. When he could not find
her he went to Uchtdealb and told her in what danger he stood, and she
consented to free Tuiren if he would be her sweetheart for ever. She went
to Fergus's house and freed Tuiren from her shape, and afterwards Finn
married her to Lugaidh Lamha. But the two whelps were already born,
and Finn kept them and they were always with him.

The Highland version is different. In this Bran and Sceolan are
monstrous dogs, won by Finn from a kind of Celtic version of the
monster Grendel in *Beowulf*, who had been stealing babies from a young

champion's house. There is something monstrous about them – a strange mixture of colours and great savagery in some versions. In one form, collected and translated by J. Macdougall in *Waifs and Strays of Celtic Tradition* (vol. III), Sceolan is called 'The Grey Dog' and is most dangerous, only to be controlled by Bran's gold chain. Any trace of relationship between Finn and the hounds is lost here.

[Motifs: D141.1; F241.6; F302.5.2]

Bran Mac Febail (*bran mock feval*). See BRAN SON OF FEBAL.

Bran (*bran*) son of Febal. The hero of a legend somewhat similar to that of OISIN and even closer to the story of KING HERLA. Bran was summoned by MANANNAN SON OF LIR to visit one of his islands far over the sea, Emhain, the Isle of Women. And this was the way in which he was summoned. He was walking one day near his own dun when he heard a sound of music so sweet that it lulled him to sleep, and when he woke he had a silver branch in his hand covered with silver-white apple blossom. He carried the branch back with him into his dun. And when all his people were gathered round him, suddenly there was a woman in strange clothing standing in front of him, and she began to sing him a song about Emhain, the Isle of Women, where there was no winter or want or grieving, where the golden horses of Manannan pranced on the strand and the games and sports went on untiringly. She summoned Bran to seek out that island, and when her song was over she turned away, and the apple branch jumped from Bran's hand into hers, and he could not retain it. On the next morning he set out with a fleet of curraghs. They rowed far across the sea until they met a warrior driving a chariot as if it might be over the land, and he greeted them and told them that he was Manannan son of Lir, and he sang about the island of Emhain, inviting Bran to visit it. On the way they passed the Island of Delight and tried to hail the inhabitants, but got nothing but shouts of laughter and pointing hands. So Bran put one of his men on shore to talk to them, but he at once burst out laughing and behaved just as the inhabitants had done. So in the end Bran went on, and they soon got to the Isle of Women, where the Chief Woman was waiting for them and drew them ashore. They enjoyed every delight on the many-coloured island, but after what seemed a year Bran's companions began to pine for Ireland, and Nechtan son of Collbrain was urgent to return. The woman who was Bran's lover warned them that sorrow would come of it, but Bran said he would just visit the land and return to it. At that she warned him, as Niam had warned Oisin, that he could look at Ireland and talk to his friends, but that no one of his party could touch it. So they sailed away and approached the shores of Ireland at a place called Srub Bruin. People on the shore hailed them, and when Bran told them his name they said that no such man was now alive, though in their oldest stories there were mentions of how Bran son of Febal had sailed away to look for the Island of Women. When Nechtan heard this he leapt out of his curragh and waded through the surf; but as he touched the strand of Ireland his mortal years came on him and he crumbled into a handful of dust. Bran stayed awhile to tell his countrymen of all that had befallen him; then he turned his fleet of curraghs away from the shore, and he and his companions were never seen in Ireland again.

This story is told in Lady Gregory's *Gods and Fighting Men* (Chapter 10), and a comparative study of the legend is to be found in Alfred Nutt's *The Voyage of Bran*, with beautiful translations of the Irish by Kuno Meyer.

[Type: 766 (variant). Motifs: FI11; FI12; F302.3.1; F373; F377]

Bran (*brarn*) **the Blessed.** There are three Brans mentioned in Celtic mythological and legendary matter: BRAN, the famous hound of FINN; BRAN SON OF FEBAL, the Irish hero who was allured away to the Isle of Women, the Western Paradise of MANANNAN SON OF LIR; and Bran the Blessed, the brother of Manawyddan and the son of LLYR, whose story is told in the MABINOGION. It is clear that the Irish and the Welsh mythologies are closely connected in these two groups, but Bran the Blessed represents a much earlier and more mythological strain of belief, obviously a primitive god. It has been surmised by Professor Rhys that he was a Goidelic or even pre-Goidelic divinity who was grafted on to later Celtic tradition.

Bran was of monstrous size, so large that no house could contain him, but he was one of the beneficent GIANTS and had magical treasures which enriched Britain, and chief among them was the Cauldron of Healing which came from Ireland and was destined to return to it. Manawyddan and his brother Bran had a sister Branwen, and Manawyddan had two half-brothers on his mother's side, Nissyen and Evnissyen. One was gentle and delighted in making peace between those who were at enmity, but the other was malicious, and if people were at peace he set strife between them. And it was through Evnissyen that two great peoples were destroyed.

One day Matholwch King of Ireland came to Britain to ask Bran the Blessed to give him the hand of Branwen in marriage, so that there might be a league for ever between Britain and Ireland. This seemed good to Bran, and he called his Council and everything was agreed between them, and they moved to Aberffraw where the wedding celebrations were held. When they were all assembled, Evnissyen, who had been away, arrived at Aberffraw and saw all the magnificent horses of Matholwch ranged between the encampment and the sea. He asked whose they were, and when he heard that they belonged to King Matholwch who had just been married to his sister he was furious at this being done without his leave. He rushed like a madman on the horses and mutilated them all most cruelly. When Matholwch heard what had been done to his horses, he was bitterly wounded and retired towards his ships. Bran sent embassies after and offered one atonement after another, and at length, after liberal payment of money and of horses, he offered the Cauldron of Healing. Then Matholwch was pacified and consented to come back, and in the end he departed with Branwen and the full toll of horses and gold, and all seemed at peace. But after he had got home, Matholwch's people and his foster-brothers grew more and more angry at the thought of the insult that had been put on him and after Branwen's little son had been born, Matholwch banished her from his bed and put on her every insult he could devise, and if any Briton came to Ireland, he was not allowed to go home for fear Bran should hear how savagely she was treated. But Branwen, confined to tne chopping-block in the yard, tamed a starling that she hid there, taught it to talk and instructed it how to go to Bran and to give him the letter that she fastened under its wing. And after three years of painful teaching the starling carried the message across the sea to Bran. Then Bran was more angry than he had ever been, and he summoned a mighty fleet and a mighty armament, and they set out, Bran wading the sea because no ship would hold him. A few days later King Matholwch's swineherds, sitting by the sea-shore, saw a strange spectacle approaching them across the sea: a moving forest with a great headland towering behind it, at the summit of which was a great ridge of rock dividing two lakes. They hurried to tell the king, who at once uneasily connected it with Bran. The only person who could explain the phenomenon was his wife, so he sent messengers to Branwen and described the vision to her. 'What is the meaning of the moving forest?' they asked her. 'My brothers are bringing a great fleet against you. That is the forest,' she answered. 'And the great headland moving towards us out of the sea?' 'That is my brother Bran wading the channel; no boat can hold him,' she answered. 'But the sharp cliff dividing two great lakes?' 'My brother is angry as he looks towards Ireland. The cliff is his nose, the two lakes are his eyes, large and suffused with anger.'

The whole of Ireland was in a panic at her words, but they had a way of retreat. If they crossed the river Linon and broke down the great bridge across it, it would be impassable, for there was a loadstone that lay in the bed of the river that drew all boats down to it. So they crossed the river and broke down the bridge: but when Bran reached it he stretched his great length over it, and all the mighty armies crossed the river in safety.

As Bran raised himself from the ground, ambassadors from Matholwch approached him. They told him that Matholwch had given the kingdom to Branwen's son Gwern and had put himself at Bran's disposal to atone for the wrongs he had done to Branwen. At first Bran would not be appeased, but Matholwch proposed other terms, that he would build a great house, large enough to hold Bran for whom no house had yet been built, and here the Irish and the British would meet and make a lasting peace. And to this Bran agreed.

The great meeting-house was built with a door at each end, and all went well while it was building. But the Irish had not made the agreement in good faith. On each of the hundred pillars of the house were two brackets, and on the night of the Peace Meeting there was a leather bag hanging on each bracket with an armed man inside it. Evnissyen came in early to look at the hall, and he looked sharply at the leather bags. 'What is in this bag?' he said. 'Meal, good soul,' said the Irishman who was showing him round. Evnissyen put up his hand and felt till he found the rounded shape of a skull. Then he pinched it so sharply that his fingers met through the splintered bone. He went on to the next. 'And what is in this?' he asked. And he went on his round till he came to the end of the two hundred. Then the Irish came in at one door and the British at the other, and they greeted each other with great cordiality and the peace was concluded. When all was decided, Gwern, the new little king, was brought out and went merrily from one of his kinsmen to another, and they all loved him. When he had gone round them all, Evnissyen called him and he went to him gladly. Then, before anyone could stop him, Evnissyen took the child by the ankles and thrust him head-first into the blazing fire. That was the end of peace. Every man snatched his arms and the battle went on all night. In the morning Evnissyen saw the dead bodies of the Irish being put into the cauldron and rising up as well as before, except that they were dumb, but no Welshmen were put in. And remorse came on Evnissyen, and he flung himself down among the Irish, and when he was thrown into the cauldron he gave a great stretch and burst the cauldron, but his own heart burst at the same time. After that some small measure of victory came to the Britons, but it was little enough. Bran was wounded with a poisoned dart on the foot and when he knew that he was dying he told them to cut off his head and carry it back to Britain, and bury it under the White Tower in London to guard the land as long as it was there. And the head would be good company to them wherever they went. And good company it was. But only eight of all that great host got back to Britain, and one of them was Branwen, and when she got home her heart burst with grief to think of the great destruction which had come through her. As for Ireland, all that were left alive in it were five pregnant women hiding in a cave. And Ireland was re-peopled through them, and they founded the Five Kingdoms.

[Motifs: A523; A525; F531; F1041.16]

Bread. The prototype of food, and therefore a symbol of life, bread was one of the commonest PROTECTIONS AGAINST FAIRIES. Before going out into a fairy-haunted place, it was customary to put a piece of dry bread into one's pocket.

Brewing of eggshells. See CHANGELINGS.

Brigit, or Brid (*breed*). The Irish goddess Brigit seems to have been so much beloved that the Early Church could not bring itself to cut her off from the people and she became St Bridget of Ireland.

Lady Gregory, in *Gods and Fighting Men*, says of her (p. 2):

> Brigit . . . was a woman of poetry, and poets worshipped her, for her sway was very great and very noble. And she was a woman of healing along with that, and a woman of smith's work, and it was she first made the whistle for calling one to another through the night. And the one side of her face was ugly, but the other side was very comely. And the meaning of her name was Breo-saighit, a fiery arrow.

Various sources of the fairy beliefs have been suggested among the THEORIES OF FAIRY ORIGINS, and with good reason. They have been called the dead, or traditions of primitive men or nature spirits, but there seems little doubt that in Ireland at least some of them were descendants of this early Pantheon.

Brochs. A broch is a type of round, stone-walled farmhouse covered with turf to make a smooth hill which is to be found in the ancient Pictish areas of Scotland. The entrance to a broch is by a single door, and they have no shaft connecting them with the outer air such as are found in the howes. Inside are winding low passages leading to several chambers. They are defensive rather than offensive in design. R. W. Feachem, who contributes Chapter 3 to *The Problem of the Picts*, considers that they were constructed not by the Picts but by the Proto-Picts, the heterogeneous tribes which were finally blended together to produce the Picts of history, that mysterious people who contribute their part to the THEORIES OF FAIRY ORIGINS. These brochs, like other knolls and howes, were often called Fairy KNOWES and play their part in sustaining the theories of David MAC RITCHIE.

Broken Ped, the. Versions of these legends give an example of GRATE-FUL FAIRIES. The FAIRY PED theme is always the same: a FAIRY or PIXY is heard by a kindly ploughman lamenting a broken stool, shovel or kirn-staff. He mends it and is given a delicious little cake as a reward. The TABOO against eating FAIRY FOOD is not operative in this case, for, often against the warning of a companion, he eats it, and is prosperous ever after. The latest example of this anecdote is collected by Ruth Tongue from Somerset. Other examples can be found in K. M. Briggs, *A Dictionary of British Folk-Tales*:

> A farm labourer whose way took him across Wick Moor heard the sound of someone crying. It was someone small, and within a few steps

he came across a child's ped (spade or shovel) broken in half. Being a kindly father himself, he stopped and took a few moments to mend it neatly and strongly, never noticing that he was standing close to the barrow called 'Pixy Mound'.

Putting down the mended ped, he called out, 'There 'tis then – never cry no more,' and went on his way.

On his return from work the ped was gone, and a fine new-baked cake lay in its place.

Despite the warnings of his comrade, the man ate it and found it 'proper good'. Saying so loudly, he called out, 'Good night to 'ee,' and prospered ever after.

[Type: ML5080. Motifs: F271.10; F330; F338; F343.19]

Brollachan. The Gaelic for a shapeless thing. J. F. CAMPBELL, in *Popular Tales of the West Highlands* (vol. II, p. 203), tells a Brollachan story which seems to be a variant of 'Maggie Moulach and the Brownie of Fincastle Mill' (see under BROWNIE), which is one form of the 'Nemo' story. In this version, however, the point is missed of the human naming himself 'Me Myself'. It is a widespread tale, best known in England as AINSEL.

There was once a cripple called Ally Murray who lived in the Mill of the Glens on the charity of the miller and his neighbours, who put a handful into his bowl for every bag of grain ground there. The lamiter usually slept in the mill, and one cold night when he was lying by the fire a brollachan came in, the child of a FUATH, or 'vough', who lived in the millstream. This brollachan had eyes and a mouth, but it could say only two words, 'Mi-phrein' and 'Tu-phrein', that is, 'Myself' and 'Thyself'. Beyond his eyes and his mouth he had no shape that you could describe. This brollachan stretched itself in front of the fire, which began to burn low. Murray threw a fresh peat on it, and the hot embers flew about and burnt the brollachan, who yelled and shrieked fearsomely. The 'vough' rushed in very fierce, crying, 'Och my Brollachan, who then burnt you?' But all it could say was 'Me and thou!' 'Were it any other,' she said, 'wouldn't I be revenged!' Murray slipped the peck measure over himself, and lay there among the machinery all night, praying with all his might to be saved. And so he was, for the brollachan and the vough left the mill. But the vough grew suspicious, for she chased a poor woman who was out alone that night, who put on a great turn of speed and got safe to her own house, safe except for her heel, and that the vough clawed off. The poor woman walked lame all the rest of her life.

[Type: 1137]

Broonie. The Lowland type of BROWNIE, as in:

> 'Ha! ha! ha!
> Broonie has't a'!'

[Type: ML7015. Motif: F405.11]

Brother Mike. We know this as a fairy name from the pathetic cry of a little frairy (see FRAIRIES) captured near Bury St Edmunds and reproduced from 'Suffolk Notes and Queries' in the *Ipswich Journal* of 1877. It is to be found in *County Folk-Lore* (vol. II, pp. 34–5) and forms a particularly sad example of a CAPTURED FAIRY:

There wus a farmer, right a long time ago, that wus, an he had a lot o' wate, a good tidy lot o' wate he had. An he huld all his wate in a barn, of a hape he did! but that hape that got lesser and lesser, an he kount sar how that kum no how. But at last he thout he'd go and see if he kount see suffun. So off of his bed he got, one moanlight night, an he hid hiself hind the oud lanetew, where he could see that's barn's doors; an when the clock struck twelve, if he dint see right a lot of little tiddy frairies. O lork! how they did run – they was little bits o' things, as big as mice, an they had little blue caoots and yaller breeches an little red caps on thar hids with long tassels hangin down behind. An they run right up to that barn's door. An if that door dint open right wide of that self. An lopperty lop! over the throssold they all hulled themselves. Well, when the farmer see they wus all in, he kum nigher an nigher, an he looked inter the barn he did. An he see all they little frairies; they danced round an round, an then they all ketched up an air o' wate, an kopt it over their little shouders, they did. But at the last there come right a dear little frairie that wus soo small that could hardly lift that air o' wate, and that kep saying as that walked –

> 'Oh, how I du twait,
> A carrying o' this air o' wate.'

An when that kum to the throssold, that kount git over no how, an that farmer he retched out his hand an he caught a houd o' that poooare thing, an that shruck out, 'Brother Mike! Brother Mike!' as loud as that could. But the farmer he kopt that inter his hat, an he took that home for his children; he tied that to the kitchen winder. But that poooare little thing, that wont ate nothin, an that poyned away and died.

[Type: ML6010. Motifs: F239.4.3; F387]

Brown Man of the Muirs. A guardian spirit of wild beasts that inhabits the Border Country. Henderson quotes a story of an encounter with him sent by Mr Surtees, author of *The History of Durham*, to Sir Walter

SCOTT. Two young men were out hunting on the moors near Elsdon in 1744, and stopped to eat and rest near a mountain burn. The youngest went down to the burn to drink, and as he was stooping down he saw the Brown Man of the Muirs on the opposite bank, a square, stout dwarf dressed in clothes the colour of withered bracken with a head of frizzled red hair and great glowing eyes like a bull. He fiercely rebuked the lad for trespassing on his land and killing the creatures that were in his care. For himself he ate only whortleberries, nuts and apples. 'Come home with me and see,' he said. The lad was just going to jump the burn when his friend called him and the Brown Man vanished. It was believed that if he had crossed the running stream he would have been torn to pieces. On the way home he defiantly shot some more game and it was thought that this had cost him his life, for soon after he was taken ill, and within a year he died.

[Motifs: C614.1.0.2; F383.2; F419.3.1*; F451.5.2; N101.2]

Browney. The Cornish guardian of the bees. When the bees swarm, the housewife beats a can and calls 'Browney! Browney!' and the browney is supposed to come invisibly to round up the swarm. It is possible, how-ever, that 'Browney' is the name of the bees themselves, like 'Burnie, Burnie Bee' in the Scots folk rhyme.

Brownie. One of the fairy types most easily described and most recog-nizable. His territory extends over the Lowlands of Scotland and up into the Highlands and Islands, all over the north and east of England and into the Midlands. With a natural linguistic variation he becomes the BWCA of Wales, the Highland BODACH and the Manx FENODOREE. In the West Country, PIXIES or PISGIES occasionally perform the offices of a brownie and show some of the same characteristics, though they are essentially different. In various parts of the country, friendly LOBS AND HOBS behave much like brownies.

The Border brownies are the most characteristic. They are generally described as small men, about three feet in height, very raggedly dressed in brown clothes, with brown faces and shaggy heads, who come out at night and do the work that has been left undone by the servants. They make themselves responsible for the farm or house in which they live; reap, mow, thresh, herd the sheep, prevent the hens from laying away, run errands and give good counsel at need. A brownie will often become personally attached to one member of the family. In return he has a right to a bowl of cream or best milk and to a specially good bannock or cake. William Henderson in *Folk-Lore of the Northern Counties* (p. 248) describes a brownie's portion:

He is allowed his little treats, however, and the chief of these are knuckled cakes made of meal warm from the mill, toasted over the embers and spread with honey. The housewife will prepare these, and lay them carefully where he may find them by chance. When a titbit is given to a child, parents will still say to him, 'There's a piece wad please a Brownie.'

A point to notice in this little extract is that the housewife was careful not to offer the titbit to the brownie, only to leave it in its reach. Any offer of reward for its services drove the brownie away; it seemed to be an absolute TABOO. This was accounted for in various ways. In Berwickshire it was said that the brownie was the appointed servant of mankind to ease the weight of Adam's curse and was bound to serve without payment; another suggestion was that he was of too free a spirit to accept the bondage of human clothes or wages; sometimes again that he was bound to serve until he was considered worthy of payment; or again, it might be the quality of the goods offered that offended him, as in the story of the Lincolnshire brownie, who, most unusually, was annually given a linen shirt, until a miserly farmer, succeeding to the farm, left him out one of coarse sacking, on which he sang:

> 'Harden, harden, harden hamp!
> I will neither grind nor stamp.
> Had you given me linen gear,
> I had served you many a year,
> Thrift may go, bad luck may stay,
> I shall travel far away.'

With which he left the farm never to return. The traditional brownie's song:

> 'What have we here, Hempen, Hampen!
> Here will I never more tread nor stampen,'

which was quoted by Reginald SCOT in the 16th century, suggests that other brownies may have had the same grievance. Whatever the reason, it is not to be doubted that the gift of clothes to brownies or any hobgoblins doing brownie work will infallibly drive them away.

It was indeed very easy to offend a brownie, and either drive him away or turn him from a brownie to a BOGGART, in which case the mischievous side of the HOBGOBLIN nature was shown. The Brownie of Cranshaws is a typical example of a brownie offended. An industrious brownie once lived in Cranshaws in Berwickshire, where he saved the corn and thrashed it until people began to take his services for granted and someone remarked that the corn this year was not well mowed or piled up. The brownie heard him, of course, and that night he was heard tramping in and out of the barn muttering:

> 'It's no weel mowed! It's no weel mowed!
> Then it's ne'er be mowed by me again:
> I'll scatter it ower the Raven stane,
> And they'll hae some wark e'er it's mowed again.'

Sure enough, the whole harvest was thrown over Raven Crag, about two miles away, and the Brownie of Cranshaws never worked there again.

Where he was well treated, however, and his whims respected, a brownie would be wholly committed to the interests of his master. He would sometimes, indeed, make himself rather unpopular with the servants by exposing their misdeeds, or punishing them; as when two maids who had a stingy mistress had stolen a junket and sat down to eat it between them when the brownie squeezed himself into the middle of the bench and invisibly consumed most of the dish.

There are several stories of a brownie fetching the midwife to his mistress when she was suddenly taken in labour, of which the best-known is the story of the Brownie of Dalswinton. There was a brownie who once haunted the old pool on the Nith, and worked for Maxwell, the Laird of Dalswinton. Of all human creatures he loved best the laird's daughter, and she had a great friendship for him and told him all her secrets. When she fell in love it was the brownie who helped her and presided over the details of her wedding. He was the better pleased with it because the bridegroom came to live in his bride's home. When the pains of motherhood first came to her, it was he who fetched the cannie wife. The stableboy had been ordered to ride at once, but the Nith was in spate and the straightest path went through the Auld Pool, so he delayed. The brownie flung on his mistress's fur cloak, mounted the best horse, and rode across the roaring water. As they rode back, the cannie wife hesitated at the road they came.

'Dinna ride by the Auld Pool,' she said, 'we mecht meet the brownie.'

'Hae nae fear, gudwife,' said he, 'ye've met a' the brownies ye're like to meet.'

With that he plunged into the water and carried her safely over to the other side. Then he turned the horse into the stable, found the boy still pulling on his second boot and gave him a sound drubbing.

The story ended sadly, for Maxwell of Dalswinton told the minister, and he persuaded him that so helpful a servant deserved to be baptized. So he hid in the stable with a stoup of holy water, and when the brownie crept in to begin his labours, he poured it over him and began the office of baptism. He never finished, for as the first drop touched him the brownie gave a yell and vanished. He never came back to Nithsdale again.

From these stories we can make out a general picture of the Brownie. It was a common thing for a brownie to be attached to a stream or pool, and outside his own home he was often feared. However benevolent he might be, he was afraid of Christian symbols. He fits in well with MAC RITCHIE's suggested THEORY OF FAIRY ORIGINS as a shaggy aboriginal hanging round the farm, attached to its service by food and kindness but distrustful of anything that could bind him. Some touches are added in local descriptions to the appearances of brownies. It is sometimes said that they have no noses, only holes for nostrils, unlike KILLMOULIS, who had an enormous nose but no mouth. In Aberdeenshire it was sometimes believed that they had no separate fingers, a thumb and the other four fingers joined in one. They would commonly be described as SOLITARY FAIRIES and all male, but in the Highlands they occasionally seem to gather together in small bands. They are sometimes larger than the Lowland brownies, and there is an occasional female among them. AUBREY mentions one in his *Miscellanies* (pp. 191–2), MEG MOULACH, that is, Hairy Meg, attached to the Grants of Tullochgorm. She mourned the deaths in the family like a BANSHEE, performed brownie labours and helped the chief in games of CHESS. She was acute, but her son BROWNIE-CLODD was stupid, a DOBIE, and the servants played tricks on him. In the present century, the mill at Fincastle in Perthshire was haunted by brownies: a small band of them according to one story; a single brownie, with his mother, Maggy Moloch, close at hand, according to another. This story, told by Andrew Stewart and preserved in the archives of the School of Scottish Studies, is interesting as showing the ambivalent character of the brownies. It is one of the AINSEL stories, and a similar tale is told about a BROLLACHAN. Fincastle Mill was never worked at night, for it had the name of being haunted. One night a girl was making a cake for her wedding and she found she had run out of meal, so she asked her father to go up to the mill and grind some for her, but he didn't care to go, so she had to go up herself. She asked the miller to grind it up for her, but he wouldn't, so she just had to go herself. She lit a big fire in the mill and put a pot on to boil and began to grind the meal. At twelve o'clock the door opened and a wee hairy man came in. It was the Brownie of the Mill. 'Who are you?' said the girl, 'and what are you doing here?' 'What are you doing yourself? And what's your name?' said the brownie. 'Oh, I'm Mise mi fein' (me myself), said the girl. She kept sitting by the fire, and the brownie kept edging up to her grinning and grinning till she got frightened, and poured a dipperful of water from the pot over him. He went for her then, and she drenched him with the boiling water. He ran screaming out of the door, and in the wood beyond she heard old Maggy Moloch crying, 'Who's done this to you?' 'Me myself! Me myself!' he cried, dying. 'If it had been any mortal man,' said Maggy Moloch, 'I would have been revenged, but if it was you yourself I can do nothing.'

So the girl finished grinding her meal and made her cake and was married, and moved to Strathspey, and the mill was left empty, for Maggy Moloch moved off too. But the girl did not escape for ever, for one night at a ceilidh the young bride was asked for a story and she told how she had tricked the brownie at Fincastle Mill. But Maggy Moloch was near, for a voice from outside called: 'Aye, was it you killed my man? Ye'll no kill another!' and a three-legged stool shot in at the door and killed the girl on the spot. Then Maggy Moloch moved again and found a home near a farm, where the servants hired her well with bread and cream and she did good service about the farm so long as they all stayed. When the farmer decided to dismiss them and rely on her help, she went on strike and became a boggart instead of a brownie, nor would she stop tormenting him until he re-engaged the whole of his former staff. It was better not to take liberties with old Maggy Moloch, and the same holds good with even the gentlest brownies.

[Types: ML6035; ML7010; ML7015. Motifs: F332.0.1; F346; F381.3; F382; F403; F403.2; F475; F482; F482.5.4; F482.5.4.1; F482.5.5]

Brownie-Clod. The companion of MEG MOULACH, the most famous of the Highland BROWNIES. It was perhaps he who was scalded to death in the Mill of Fincastle in a story told in the preceding entry. The fullest account of him is given by Grant Stewart in *Popular Superstitions of the Highlanders of Scotland* (pp. 142–3):

The last two brownies known in this quarter of the Highlands were long the appendages of the ancient family of Tullochgorm in Strath-spey. They were male and female, and, for aught we know, they might likewise have been man and wife. The male was of an exceedingly jocose and humorous disposition, often indulging in little sports at the expense of his fellow-servants. He had, in particular, a great trick of flinging clods at the passengers, and from thence he got the name of 'Brownie-Clod'. He had, however, with all his humour, a great deal of simplicity about him, and became, in his turn, the dupe of those on whom he affected to play. An eminent instance of this appears from a contract into which he foolishly entered with the servants of Tulloch-gorm, whereby he bound and obliged himself to thrash as much corn and straw as two men could do for the space of a whole winter, on con-dition he was to be gratified with an old coat and a Kilmarnock cowl, pieces of apparel for which, it seems, he had a great liking. While the servants were reclining themselves at their ease upon the straw, poor Brownie-Clod thrashed on unremittingly, and performed such Herculean tasks as no human constitution could bear for a week together. Some time before the expiry of the contract, the lads, out of pure gratitude and pity, left the coat and cowl for him on a mow of corn in the barn, on receipt of which he instantly struck work, and, with the greatest triumph at the idea of taking in his acquaintances, he sneeringly told them, that, since they were so foolish as to give him the coat and cowl before he had wrought for them, he would now decline to thrash another sheaf.

> 'Brownie has got a cowl and coat,
> And never more will work a jot.'

[Motif: F488]

Brugh, or Bru (*broo*). According to J. G. CAMPBELL in his *Super-stitions of the Scottish Highlands*, the word 'brugh' means the interior of a fairy mound or KNOWE and is the same word as 'borough'. It generally means a place where quite a number of fairies live together, and not just the home for a family. The outside of the brugh is the SITHIEN.

Bruising. The appearance of small round bruises clustered together was supposed to show the marks of fairy fingers pinching. People who spied on the FAIRIES, and so were responsible for an INFRINGEMENT OF FAIRY PRIVACY, or who betrayed their secrets, were particularly liable to be pinched, and it was also a penalty for careless, dirty ways since the fairies applauded NEATNESS. In Ben Jonson's *Entertainment at Althorpe* we have:

> Shee, that pinches countrey wenches
> If they rub not cleane their benches,
> And with sharper nayles remembers,
> When they rake not up their embers.

And in Marston's *Mountebanks Masque* we have:

> If lustie Doll, maide of the Dairie,
> Chance to be blew-nipt by the fairie.

In fact, in the early 17th century, pinching was one of the fairy charac-teristics most commonly remembered. See BLIGHTS AND ILLNESSES ATTRIBUTED TO THE FAIRIES.

Bucca, or Bucca-boo. Margaret Courtney, in *Cornish Feasts and Folk-Lore* (p. 129), says:

> Bucca is the name of a spirit that in Cornwall it was once thought necessary to propitiate. Fishermen left a fish on the sands for bucca, and in the harvest a piece of bread at lunch-time was thrown over the left shoulder, and a few drops of beer spilt on the ground for him, to ensure good luck.

He seems to have declined from a godling to a HOBGOBLIN, for she further says:

> Bucca, or bucca-boo, was until very lately (and I expect in some places it still is) the terror of children, who were often, when crying, told that 'if they did not stop he would come and carry them off'.

She also says that there were two buccas: Bucca Dhu and Bucca Gwidder. One version of a 'Mock Ghost/Real Ghost' story is given by BOTTRELL in *Traditions and Hearthside Stories* (vol. I, p. 142), as 'The White Bucca and the Black'.

[Motif: V12.9]

Buckie. One of a long list given in the DENHAM TRACTS (vol. II, p. 78) of supernatural creatures feared by our ancestors. There is a rhyme quoted by G. F. Northall in *English Folk-Rhymes* which he relates to Buckie (some relation probably of bug-a-boo, see BUGS, etc.). The lines were recited by Devonshire children when they had to go through passages in the dark.

> Bucky, Bucky, biddy Bene,
> Is the way now fair and clean?
> Is the goose ygone to nest?
> And the fox ygone to rest?
> Shall I come away?

'Bene' was the Old English for a prayer, and 'bidding' for asking, as in the 'Bidding Prayer' for the Benefactors of Oxford. 'Bucky' suggests the goatish form assumed by the Devil and IMPS.

Bugan. Bugan is a form of the now obsolete BUG and a variant of BOCAN and bug-a-boo. It is mentioned in Mrs Wright's *Rustic Speech and Folk-Lore* (p. 198) as known in the Isle of Man, Cheshire and Shropshire.

Buggane (*bug airn*). The Manx Buggane is a particularly noxious type of GOBLIN, adept at SHAPE-SHIFTING like the PICKTREE BRAG and the HEDLEY KOW, but more dangerous and vicious. Walter Gill in *A Manx Scrapbook* (p. 487) seems to identify the Buggane with the CABBYL-USHTEY, the WATER-HORSE of Man. One haunted Spooty Wooar, the Big Waterfall in the Patrick District. Gill says:

> The Buggane who lives here has been seen by many people in time past, and not very long past; he was usually shaped like a big black calf, which sometimes crossed the road and jumped down into the pool with a sound as of chains being shaken. In a more human form he came to a house at the Glen May end of Glen Rushen, picked up a girl who was working near it, slung her over his back, and carried her down to his place under the dub into which the spooty falls. But just as they were coming to it, she, having a sharp knife in her hand with which she had been slicing up turnips, managed to cut the string of her apron and get free.

Walter Gill thought it likely that even in his human form the Buggane had the ears or hoofs of a horse.

In Dora Broome's excellent little book, *Fairy Tales from the Isle of Man*, there are three Buggane stories, in all of which he is a shape-shifter, capable of growing into monstrous size and extremely mischievous, but not so dangerous as the Buggane of Glen May, unless we except the Buggane who made a habit of tearing the roof off the little Church of St Trinian at the foot of Mount Greeba. This is a version of the Highland story of the Haunted Church of Bewley, except that in the Highland version the tailor finishes his shirt and in the Manx one he is one button short. The point of each story is the gradual emergence of the BOGIE from the tomb: head, hands, arms – and when the first leg is out it is time to be gone. The Buggane of the Smelt is a magnificent tale of shape-shifting.

Bugs, bug-a-boos, boggle-boos, bugbears, etc. These are all generally treated as NURSERY BOGIES, set up to scare children into good behaviour. They are discussed in some detail by Gillian Edwards in *Hobgoblin and Sweet Puck* (pp. 83–9) as an extension from the early Celtic '*bwg*'. Most of these words are applied to imaginary fears along the lines of 'How easy is a bush supposed a bear'. This use of a bugbear is illustrated in a translation of an Italian play published *c*. 1565 called *The Buggbear*. It is about mock conjurors.

Bullbeggar. A word from the long list of supernatural terrorizers given by Reginald SCOT. Its meaning is unspecified, but it did not perish with the 16th century, for there is still a Bullbeggar Lane in Surrey, which once contained a barn haunted by a bullbeggar, and traditions of a bull-beggar who haunted Creech Hill near Bruton in Somerset were recollected by Ruth Tongue from oral tradition in 1906 and published by her in *County Folk-Lore* (vol. VIII, pp. 121–2). In the 1880s two crossed bodies were dug up in quarrying operations, and crumbled to dust when they were exposed to the air. For some unexplained reason they were supposed to have been a Saxon and a Norman, and after this finding, Creech Hill had a bad name and was supposed to be haunted by following footsteps and a black uncanny shape. A farmer coming home late one night saw a figure lying on the road and went to its help. It suddenly shot up to an uncanny height and chased him to his own threshold. His family ran to his rescue and saw it bounding away with wild laughter. Another night traveller was attacked on Creech Hill and held his own from midnight to cockcrow with the help of an ashen staff. This bullbeggar was considered a BOGY OR BOGEY-BEAST rather than a ghost because two bodies were found.

Burton's account of the fairies. Robert Burton (1577–1640), in his *Anatomy of Melancholy*, Part I, section 2, in a sub-section called 'Digression of Spirits', gives a fairly full account of the various kinds of FAIRIES believed in at that time. Like many of the 17th-century Puritans, and of the Scottish Highlanders whose beliefs were recorded by J. G. CAMPBELL and Evans Wentz, Burton thought of the fairies as a lesser order of devils. I give his own account, for it is a pity to deprive the reader of Burton's rich, closely packed style.

Water-devils are those *Naiades* or water Nymphs which have been
heretofore conversant about waters and rivers. The water (as *Paracelsus*
thinks) is their Chaos, wherein they live; some call them *Fairies*, and
say that *Habundia* is their Queen; these cause Inundations, many
times shipwracks, and deceive men divers wayes, as *Succuba*, or otherwise, appearing most part (saith *Tritemius*) in womens shapes. *Paracelsus* hath several stories of them that have lived and been married to
mortal men, and so continued for certain years with them, and after
upon some dislike, have forsaken them. Such a one as *Aegeria*, with
whom *Numa* was so familiar, *Diana*, *Ceres*, etc. *Olaus Magnus* hath a
long narration of one *Hotherus* a King of *Sweden*, that having lost his
company, as he was hunting one day, met with these water Nymphs or
Fairies, and was feasted by them; and *Hector Boethius*, or *Mackbeth*,
and *Banco*, two Scottish Lords, that as they were wandring in the
Woods, had their Fortunes told them by three strange women. To
these heretofore they did use to Sacrifice, by that *hudromanteia*, or
divination by waters.

Terrestrial devils, are those *Lares*, *Genii*, *Faunes*, *Satyrs*, Wood-
nymphs, Foliots, Fairies, *Robin Goodfellowes*, *Trulli*, etc. which as they
are most conversant with men, so they do them most harme. Some
think it was they alone that kept the Heathen people in awe of old, and
had so many Idols and Temples erected to them. Of this range was
Dagon amongst the Philistines, *Bell* amongst the Babylonians, *Astartes*
amongst the Sydonians, *Baal* amongst the Samaritans, *Isis* and *Osyris*
amongst the Aegyptians, etc. some put our Fairies into this rank,
which have been in former times adored with much superstition, with
sweeping their houses, and setting of a pail of cleane water, good
victuals, and the like, and then they should not be pinched, but finde
money in their shooes, and be fortunate in their enterprizes. These are
they that dance on Heathes and Greens, as *Lavater* thinks with
Tritemius, and as *Olaus Magnus* addes, leave that green circle, which
we commonly finde in plain fields, which others hold to proceed from
a Meteor falling, or some accidental rankness of the ground, so Nature
sports her self; they are sometimes seen by old women and children.
Hicrom. Pauli. in his description to the City of *Bercino* in *Spain*,
relates how they have been familiarly seen near that town, about
fountaines and hils; *Nonnunquam* (saith *Tritemius*) *in sua latibula
montium simpliciores homines ducant, stupenda mirantibus ostentes
miracula, nolarum sonitus, spectacula*, etc. *Giraldus Cambrensis* gives
instance in a Monk of *Wales* that was so deluded. *Paracelsus* reckons
up many places in *Germany*, where they do usually walk in little coates
some two foot long. A bigger kinde there is of them, called with us
Hobgoblins, & *Robin Goodfellows*, that would in those superstitious
times, grinde corne for a mess of milk, cut wood, or do any maner of
drudgery work. They would mend old Irons in those *Aeolian* Iles of

Lypara, in former ages, and have been often seen and heard. *Tholosanus* cals them *Trullos* and *Getulos*, and saith, that in his dayes they were common in many places of *France*. *Dithmarus Bleskenius* in his description of *Island*, reports for a certainty, that almost in every family they have yet some such familiar spirits; & *Foelix Malleolus* in his book *de crudel. daemon.* affirmes as much, that these *Trolli*, or *Telchines*, are very common in *Norwey*, *and seen to do drudgery work*; to draw water, saith *Wierus lib*. I. *cap*. 22. dress meat, or any such thing. Another sort of these there are, which frequent forlorn houses, which the Italians call *Foliots*, most part innoxious, *Cardan* holds; *They will make strange noyses in the night, howle sometimes pittifully, and then laugh again, cause great flame and sudden lights, fling stones, rattle chaines, shave men, open doores, and shut them, fling down platters, stooles, chests, sometime appear in the likness of Hares, Crowes, black Dogs, etc.*

He goes on from this to various ghost stories, from classical times onward and from them to the Ambulones

that walk about midnight on great Heaths and desart places, which saith *Lavater draw men out of the way, and lead them all night a by-way, or quite bar them out of their way*; these have several names in several places; we commonly call them *Pucks*. In the Desarts of *Lop* in *Asia*, such illusions of walking spirits are often perceived, as you may read in *M. Paulus* the *Venetian* his travels; If one lose his company by chance, these devils will call him by his name, and countefeit voyces of his companions to seduce him.

After speaking of deceiving spirits of the BOGY OR BOGEY-BEAST type he goes on to the Subterranean Devils 'as common as the rest', and cites the often-quoted Georgius Agricola. Of these, he says, there are two kinds, the 'Getuli' and the 'Cobali'. He ascribes earthquakes and mine disasters to their agency.

Burton here covers a large number of fairy types and a wide range of time and place; but his attitude towards the fairies is ungenial.

Buttery spirits. These spirits are the lay form of the ABBEY LUBBERS who used to be supposed to haunt rich abbeys, where the monks had grown self-indulgent and idle. As a rule it was thought that FAIRIES could feed on any human food that had not been marked by a cross. The story of the TACKSMAN OF AUCHRIACHAN is an example of this. But, by an extension of this belief, it was sometimes thought that the fairies could take any food that was ungratefully received or belittled or anything that was dishonestly come by, any abuse of gifts, in fact. It was under these circumstances that the abbey lubbers and buttery spirits worked. A very vivid account of a buttery spirit is to be found in Heywood's *Hierarchie of the Blessed Angels* (Book 9).

A pious and holy priest went one day to visit his nephew who was a cook, or rather, it seemed, a tavern keeper. He was hospitably received, and as soon as they sat to meat the priest asked his nephew how he was getting on in the world, for he knew he was an ambitious man, anxious for worldly success. 'Oh Uncle,' said the taverner, 'my state is wretched; I grow poorer and poorer, though I'm sure I neglect nothing that can be to my profit. I buy cattle that have died of the murrain, even some that have been found dead in ditches; I make pies of dogs' carcasses, with a fine pastry and well spiced; I water my ale, and if anyone complains of the fare I outface them, and swear I use nothing but the best. I use every trick I can contrive, and in spite of that I grow poorer and poorer.'

'You'll never thrive using these wicked means,' said his Uncle. 'Let me see your Buttery.' 'Nothing easier,' said the Cook. 'If I open this casement you can look straight into it.' The priest crossed himself, and said, 'Come and look with me.' They looked through, and saw a great, fat, bloated fellow, gouty with over-eating, guzzling the food set around. Pies, loaves, joints, all disappeared like smoke. He tapped a cask and emptied it almost to the dregs in a twinkling. 'How does this scoundrel come here?' said the taverner. 'By what right does he devour my goods?' 'This is the Buttery Spirit,' said his Uncle, 'who has power over all ill-got gains and all dishonestly prepared food. If you wish to prosper you must leave these wicked ways. Seek God, deal honestly, serve your guests with good will. Your gains will be small but certain, and you will be happy.' With that he left his nephew, and did not return for several years. When he came back he saw a different scene. The tavern was clean and prosperous, the food was good, the taverner was in high repute in the town and on his way to becoming a burgess. The priest told him to open the window again and there they saw the wretched Buttery Spirit, lean, hollow-bellied, tottering on a stick, stretching out in vain for the good things which were set on the shelves, with no strength to lift even an empty glass, let alone a bottle, in the last extremity and fast withering away. The taverner had found that honesty is the best policy. George MACDONALD mentions another spirit, the Cellar Demon, but he seems to be of a different kind, for his function is to protect the cellar from depredations, while the Buttery Spirit has no moral intentions and inadvertently brings it about that ill-gotten gains do not prosper.

[Motif: F473.6.3]

Bwbachod (*boobachod*). The Welsh equivalent of the BROWNIES, whom they very closely resemble both in their domestic helpfulness and their capacity for obstreperous and even dangerous behaviour when they are annoyed. According to Sikes in *British Goblins* (pp. 30–31), they have one outstanding characteristic, which is their dislike of teetotallers and of dissenting ministers. Sikes tells a story of a Cardiganshire bwbach who took a special spite against a Baptist preacher, jerking away the stool from under his elbows when he was kneeling, interrupting his prayers by clattering the fire-irons or grinning in at the window. Finally he frightened the preacher away by appearing as his double, which was considered to be ominous of death. This was a BOGY OR BOGEY-BEAST prank beyond the range of most BROWNIES, otherwise the Bwbach differed only linguistically. See also BWCA.

[Type: ML7010. Motif: F482.5.5]

Bwca (*booka*). The Welsh BROWNIE (but see also BWBACHOD). A story collected by John Rhys (*Celtic Folk-Lore*, pp. 593–6) shows how close the connection can be between the Brownie and BOGGART, or the Bwca and BUGAN. Long ago a Monmouthshire farm was haunted by a spirit of whom everyone was afraid until a young maid came, merry and strong and reputed to be of the stock of the BENDITH Y MAMAU, and she struck up a great friendship with the creature, who turned out to be a bwca, who washed, ironed and spun for her and did all manner of household work in return for a nightly bowl of sweet milk and wheat bread or flummery. This was left at the bottom of the stairs every night and was gone in the morning; but she never saw him, for all his work was done at night. One evening for sheer wantonness she put some of the stale urine used for a mordant in his bowl instead of milk. She had reason to regret it, for when she got up next morning the bwca attacked her and kicked her all over the house, yelling:

> 'The idea that the thick-buttocked lass
> Should give barley-bread and piss
> To the bogle!'

After that she never saw him again, but after two years they heard of him at a farm near Hafod ys Ynys, where he soon made great friends with the servant girl, who fed him most delicately with constant snacks of bread and milk and played no unseemly pranks on him. She had one fault, however, and that was curiosity. She kept on asking to be allowed to see him and to be told his name – without success. One night, however, she made him believe that she was going out after the men, and shut the door, but stayed inside herself. Bwca was spinning industriously at the wheel, and as he span he sang:

> 'How she would laugh, did she know
> That GWARWYN-A-THROT is my name.'

'Aha!' cried the maid, at the bottom of the stairs, 'now I have your name, Gwarwyn-a-Throt!' At which he left the wheel standing, and she never saw him again.

He went next to a neighbouring farm, where the farm-hand, Moses, became his great friend. All would have gone well with poor Gwarwyn-a-Throt but that his friend Moses was sent off to fight Richard Crookback and was killed at Bosworth Field. After the loss of this friend the poor bwca went completely to the bad and spent all his time in senseless pranks, drawing the ploughing oxen out of the straight and throwing everything in the house about at night-time. At length he became so destructive that the farmer called in a *dyn cynnil* (wise man) to lay him. He succeeded in getting the bwca to stick his long nose out of the hole where he was hiding, and at once transfixed it with an awl. Then he read an incantation sentencing the bwca to be transported to the Red Sea for fourteen generations. He raised a great whirlwind, and, as it began to blow, plucked out the awl so that the poor bwca was swept away and never was seen again. It seemed that the bwca had changed his shape with his nature, for brownies were generally noseless, and he was nicknamed in this farm 'Bwca'r Trwyn', 'the Bwca with the Nose'.

[Type: ML7010. Motif: F482.5.5]

Cabyll-Ushtey. The Manx WATER-HORSE, pale-greyish in colour, as dangerous and greedy as the Highland EACH UISGE, though there are not so many tales told about it. Walter Gill in *A Manx Scrapbook* (p. 226) has a story of a cabyll-ushtey who for a short time visited Kerroo Clough on the Dark River. A farmer's wife found one of her calves missing with no trace except some tufts of hair; the next day the farmer saw a monstrous thing rise out of the river, seize one of the calves and tear it to pieces. They drove the cattle far from the river after that, but they had a worse loss to endure, for a few days later their daughter and only child diasppeared and was never heard of again. The Cabyll-Ushtey never troubled them after that.

[Motif: B17.2.1]

Caillagh ny Groamagh, or the 'Old Woman of Gloominess'. This is the Manx version of the Highland CAILLEACH BHEUR and the Irish CAILLEACH BERA (CALLY BERRY in Ulster). The Manx Caillagh, as Gill tells us in *A Manx Scrapbook* (pp. 347–9), seems to be particularly unlucky, for she fell into the crevice called after her in trying to step from the top of Barrule to the top of Cronk yn Irree Lhaa. The mark of her heel is still to be seen. The Manx Caillagh, like all the rest, is a weather spirit. In Scotland winter and bad weather belong to her, but in Man she seems to operate all through the year. If St Bride's Day (1 February) is fine, she comes out to gather sticks to warm her through the summer; if it is wet, she stays in, and has to make the rest of the year fine in her own interests. A fine St Bride's Day is therefore a bad omen for the rest of the year. She is said to have been seen on St Bride's Day in the form of a gigantic bird, carrying sticks in her beak. Cronk yn Irree Lhaa is supposed to be the usual home of the 'Old Woman of Gloominess'.

[Motif: A1135]

Cailleach bera (*kill-ogh vayra*), **or beara.** This, in Ireland, is almost identical with the CAILLEACH BHEUR of the Highlands except that she is not so closely connected with winter nor with the wild beasts. She is a great mountain builder, and, like many other gigantic HAGS, she carried loads of stone in her apron and dropped them when the string broke. Eleanor Hull gives interesting information about both the Irish and the Highland Cailleachs in *Folklore of the British Isles* (pp. 50–53). Mackenzie in *Scottish Folk-Lore and Folk Life* (pp. 136–55) decides that the Highland tradition of the Cailleach is older and more deeply rooted than the Irish.

[Motif: A1135]

Cailleach Bheur (*cal'yach vare*). The Cailleach Bheur of the Highlands, the blue-faced lean HAG who personifies winter, seems one of the clearest cases of the supernatural creature who was once a primitive goddess, possibly among the ancient Britons before the Celts. There are traces of a very wide cult: BLACK ANNIS of the Dane Hills in Leicestershire with her blue face, GENTLE ANNIE of Cromarty Firth, the loathly hag in Chaucer's WIFE OF BATH'S TALE, MILTON's 'blew, meager hag', the GYRE-CARLINE in the Lowlands of Scotland, CALLY BERRY in Ulster, the CAILLAGH NY GROAMAGH in the Isle of Man, and many other scattered references. We learn most about her, however, in the Highlands of Scotland. The variety of aspects in which she is presented is indicative of an ancient origin and a widespread cult. There are many mentions of her and folk-tales about her in the works of J. F. CAMPBELL and J. G. CAMPBELL, Mrs W. J. Watson, and her father Alexander Carmichael, Mrs K. W. Grant and J. G. Mackay, but the most comprehensive survey of the subject is to be found in Donald Mackenzie's *Scottish Folk-Lore and Folk Life*, in which he devotes a chapter, 'A Scottish Artemis', to an examination of the activities of the Cailleach Bheur and the various facets of her character, in which he finds a striking resemblance to the primitive form of the Greek goddess Artemis. At first sight she seems the personification of winter. She is called 'the daughter of Grianan', the winter sun. There were two suns in the old Celtic calendar, 'the big sun' which shines from Beltane (May Day) to Hallowe'en, and 'the little sun' which shines from All Hallows to Beltane Eve. The Cailleach was reborn each

All Hallows and went about smiting the earth to blight growth and calling down the snow. On May Eve she threw her staff under a holly tree or a gorse bush – both were her plants – and turned into a grey stone. One can guess that many lonely standing stones were once sacred to her.

This is the first aspect of the Cailleach Bheur, but there are others. According to some traditions, she did not turn to stone at the end of winter, but changed into a beautiful maid. J. F. Campbell in his *Popular Tales of the West Highlands* (vol. III) tells a tale of a loathsome hag who appeared at the house where the FEENS lay and begged for a place to warm herself at the fire. FIONN and OISIN refused her, but Diarmaid pleaded that she might be allowed to warm herself at the fire, and when she crept into his bed did not repulse her, only put a fold of the blanket between them. After a while he gave 'a start of surprise', for she had changed into the most beautiful woman that men ever saw. There is a striking similarity between this tale and 'The Marriage of Sir Gawain', or 'The Wife of Bath's Tale'.

If this were taken as part of the primitive legend it would seem that the Cailleach Bheur represented a goddess of both winter and summer, but that must be a matter of speculation. In another version of the legend, she kept a beautiful maiden prisoner, with whom her son fell in love. The two escaped, and the Cailleach launched bitter winds against them to keep them apart. This is a version of the NICHT NOUGHT NOTHING story with the sexes inverted. Presumably the escaping maiden was the summer. However that may be, it is undoubted that the Cailleach is the guardian spirit of a number of animals. The deer have the first claim on her. They are her cattle; she herds and milks them and often gives them protection against the hunter. Swine, wild goats, wild cattle and wolves were also her creatures. In another aspect she was a fishing goddess. The Cailleach Bheur was also the guardian of wells and streams, though sometimes a negligent one, as a tale told by Mrs Grant in *Myth, Tradition and Story from Western Argyll* will show.

There are many tales of wells that were allowed to overflow from the negligence of a human guardian, but it is here more appropriately attached to a supernatural creature. The Cailleach was in charge of a well on the summit of Ben Cruachan. Every evening she had to staunch its flow with a slab at sunset and release it at sunrise.

But one evening, being aweary after driving her goats across Connel, she fell asleep by the side of the well. The fountain overflowed, its waters rushed down the mountain side, the roar of the flood as it broke open an outlet through the Pass of Brander awoke the Cailleach, but her efforts to stem the torrent were fruitless; it flowed into the plain, where man and beast were drowned in the flood. Thus was formed Loch Awe. . . The Cailleach was filled with such horror over the result of her neglect of duty that she turned into stone.

This is one among many legends of the Cailleach Bheur. Indeed, a whole book rather than a chapter might be written about the Cailleach Bheur and the crowd of variants that surround her.

[Motifs: AI135; F436]

Cait Sith (*cait shee*). The Highland fairy cat. J. G. CAMPBELL, in his *Superstitions of the Scottish Highlands* (p. 32), describes it as being as large as a dog, black, with a white spot on its breast, with an arched back and erect bristles. This, probably, would be when it was angry. He says that many Highlanders believed that these cats were transformed witches, not FAIRIES. An even larger and more ferocious cat, the demonic god of the cats, appeared in answer to the wicked and ferocious ceremony of the TAGHAIRM, which consisted in roasting successive cats alive on spits for four days and nights until BIG EARS appeared and granted the wishes of the torturers. The last ceremony of Taghairm was said to have been performed in Mull and was described in detail in the *London Literary Gazette* (March 1824). The account is quoted by D. A. Mackenzie in *Scottish Folk-Lore and Folk Life* (p. 245). But Big Ears was a monstrous demon cat who had only a slight connection with the Cait Sith.

Cally Berry. The Ulster version of the Highland CAILLEACH BHEUR. The Cally Berry is not, as in the Highlands, a nature spirit, the personification of winter and the guardian of the wild deer, but a malignant supernatural HAG.

Campbell of Islay, John Francis (1822–85). J. F. Campbell was the author of perhaps the most famous collection of Scottish Folktales, *Popular Tales of the West Highlands, Orally Collected*. He was a cousin of the Duke of Argyll, a grandson of the Earl of Wemyss, was educated at Eton and Edinburgh University, and became a barrister. He had much practical work to do in the world; as Secretary to the Lighthouse Commission and Coal Commission he had detailed and voluminous reports to prepare, but as a child he had been brought up in Islay with a Gaelic-speaking nurse and had made many close friends among the island people. In a time when Gaelic was despised and suppressed by the village dominies, and often by the ministers as well, Campbell of Islay upheld it, and searched out the surviving storytellers and the traditions of history, legend and belief that were still lingering in the Highlands and Islands. His method of collection was an exemplar to all later collectors, for he trained a team of Gaelic speakers and threw a great network over the whole area. Sometimes he travelled with his collectors and trained them assiduously to accurate and lively oral transmission. He published only the four volumes of his *Popular Tales*, but left behind him a vast manuscript collection, much of which has been translated and printed bilingually, according to the standard which he established. A full and lively account of his life and the impact he made on his contemporaries can be found in R. M. Dorson's classic work, *The British Folklorists*.

Campbell of Tiree, John Gregorson (1836–91). Among the 19th-century collectors of Highland tales and traditions, two of the name of Campbell are of outstanding importance: J. F. CAMPBELL and J. G. Campbell. They were members of a band of collectors, among them J. McDougall and D. McInnes, encouraged and directed by Lord Archibald Campbell. They pursued the same method of oral collection of Gaelic sources with translations into English. Campbell of Islay's *Popular Tales of the West Highlands* is well known, but Campbell of Tiree's contribution to folk knowledge is nearly as important.

John Gregorson Campbell was born in Kingairloch, Argyllshire, the son of a sea-captain. His first schooling was in Appin, from which he went to high school at Glasgow, and later to the university, where he already began to collect oral traditions and cultivate the acquaintance of good storytellers. He was called to the ministry, and in 1860 the Duke of Argyll appointed him to the ministry of Tiree and Coll, where he worked for the rest of his life in a very happy relationship with his parishioners.

In the course of his work he provided material for two volumes of the series *Waifs and Strays of Celtic Tradition*, wrote *Superstitions of the Highlands and Islands of Scotland*, and contributed stories to various Celtic journals. He corresponded with his fellow collectors, and particularly with John Campbell of Islay. It was a time of keen intellectual activity in the Highlands, not rivalled until the School of Scottish Studies began its researches.

Caoineag (*konyack*), or 'Weeper'. One of the names given to the Highland BANSHEE (CAOINTEACH is another). She belonged to the class of FUATHS. Unlike the BEAN-NIGHE, she is not seen and cannot be approached to grant wishes. She is heard wailing in the darkness at a waterfall before any catastrophe overtakes a clan. Carmichael in *Carmina Gadelica* (vol. II, p. 227) says that before the Massacre of Glencoe the Caoineag of the Macdonalds was heard to wail night after night.

[Motif: M301.6.1]

Caointeach (*kondyuch*). A localized form of the CAOINEAG, the Highland BANSHEE, which belongs to Argyllshire, Skye and some of the neighbouring islands, and was attached to the Macmillans, Mathisons, Kellys, Mackays, Macfarlanes, Shaws and Curries. The name means 'wailer', and she has a peculiarly loud and lamentable cry, rising at times to a kind of scream. Sometimes she beats clothes on a stone like the BEAN-NIGHE. She has been described as a child or a very little woman in a short green gown and petticoat with a high-crowned white cap. It is not certain whether she is like a banshee in having no nose and one monstrous tooth, but her habits seem to be the same. Lewis Spence gives an account of her in *The Fairy Tradition in Britain* (pp. 47–8), and there is a story about her in Macdougall and Calder's *Folk Tales and Fairy Lore* (p. 215). In this tale she wore a green shawl for mourning and served the Mackays. One wet cold night she was keening softly outside the door, and a compassionate member of the family put out a plaid for her. She was thus laid like any BROWNIE, and has never come back to mourn for the Mackays.

[Motif: M301.11]

Capelthwaite. The name given to a Westmorland local BOGIE of the BLACK DOG type. He could apparently assume any form at will, but preferred that of the calf-sized black dog. There used to be a barn near Milnthorpe called Capelthwaite Barn which was the home of one of these creatures. He was well disposed towards the farm people, and used to round up their sheep and cattle for them. The story was told about him which is more commonly told of various HOBGOBLINS of how he once rounded up a hare among the sheep, and complained of having had more trouble with the little lamb than with any of the rest. Towards strangers, however, he was very spiteful and mischievous, so that in the end the Vicar of Beetham laid him with due ceremony in the river Bela. Since then he has not been seen, except that one man came back from the fair capless, coatless and much dishevelled and told his wife that Capelthwaite had chased him and thrown him into the hedge. William Henderson, who tells this story in *Folk-Lore of the Northern Counties* (pp. 275–6), seems to regard this adventure with some scepticism.

Captives in Fairyland. From very early times there have been traditions of mortals carried away into Fairyland, or detained there if they ventured into a fairy hill and were inveigled into tasting FAIRY FOOD or drink, and so partaking of the fairy nature. An early example is the story of MALEKIN given in the MEDIEVAL CHRONICLE of Ralph of Coggeshall. Here we have an example of the most common form of captive, a mortal CHANGELING, stolen from his mother's side while she was working in the fields, and apparently believing that he had a chance of regaining his freedom every seven years. These little captives, fed from infancy on fairy food and cosseted by fairy mothers, would presumably be accepted in the end as full FAIRIES. There was, however, a more sinister reason given for their capture; it was said in both Ireland and Scotland that, once in seven years, the fairies had to pay a tribute to Hell, and that they preferred to sacrifice mortals rather than their own kind. It will be remembered that in the ballad of THOMAS THE RHYMER, the Queen of Elfland had some fears that Thomas might be chosen for the TEIND.

Older children were sometimes thought to be in danger too, particularly if they strayed on to fairy territory. In J. F. CAMPBELL's

Popular Tales of the West Highlands (vol. II, pp. 57–60) the smith's only son, a lad of fourteen, was taken and a 'sibhreach' or changeling left in his place. By the old ruse of the brewery of eggshells, the smith drove out the changeling; but his son did not automatically return, so the smith set out to recover him from the fairy KNOWE, armed with a dirk, a bible and a cock. He saw his son working at a forge with other human captives in a far corner of the hill, and rescued him. The boy afterwards became noted for his skill in smithy work. It was perhaps curious that the fairies, who in this very story were kept at bay by IRON, should deal in wrought-iron work. There seems to be some confusion with the GNOMES here. Lady WILDE confirms the use of mortals as bond-slaves in her *Ancient Legends of Ireland* (vol. II, p. 213): 'The young men,' she says, 'that they beguile into their fairy palaces become their bond-slaves, and are set to hard tasks.' They are also valued for the help of a mortal arm in faction fights between the fairies, or in HURLING matches, but these are generally temporary loans and are well rewarded.

According to Lady Wilde, too, young men are often lured away if they are gifted with powers of song and music, as Thomas the Rhymer was, or especially handsome ones are desired as lovers by fairy princesses.

Women, however, are in much more danger of capture by the fairies than men. Nursing mothers are in great demand to suckle fairy babies (for the quality of fairy milk seems to be poor), and the time between child-birth and churching is one of great danger. There are many stories of precautions successfully taken, or of the attempted rescue of wives from the power of the fairies. Sometimes the fairies were intercepted as they were carrying off their victim and never got into Fairyland with her. 'The LAIRD OF BALMACHIE'S WIFE' is an example of this and an exposure of the fairy method of capture. Sometimes the victim was successfully rescued, as in SCOTT's story of MARY NELSON. But there were tragic stories of failure in the attempt. One among many is the tale of 'The Lothian Farmer's Wife' which Douglas tells in *Scottish Fairy and Folk Tales* (p. 129), when the husband made an attempt to rescue his wife from the FAIRY RADE (an attempt which had succeeded with YOUNG TAMLANE):

> The wife of a farmer in Lothian had been carried off by the fairies, and, during the year of probation, repeatedly appeared on Sunday, in the midst of her children, combing their hair. On one of these occasions she was accosted by her husband; when she related to him the unfortunate event which had separated them, instructed him by what means he might *win* her, and exhorted him to exert all his courage, since her temporal and eternal happiness depended on the success of his attempt. The farmer, who ardently loved his wife, set out on Hallowe'en, and, in the midst of a plot of furze, waited impatiently for the procession of the fairies. At the ringing of the fairy bridles, and the wild, unearthly

sound which accompanied the cavalcade, his heart failed him, and he suffered the ghostly train to pass by without interruption. When the last had rode past, the whole troop vanished, with loud shouts of laughter and exultation; among which he plainly discovered the voice of his wife, lamenting that he had lost her for ever.

In another tale, 'Katherine Fordyce of Unst', there are several interesting features. The child named after Katherine Fordyce is given fairy blessings, though there is no mention of Katherine's own child, and the TABOO against eating food in Fairyland is mentioned, though apparently the name of God would have availed even against that. The tale comes from Edmonston and Saxby's *The Home of a Naturalist*, and is reproduced in *County Folk-Lore* (vol. III, pp. 23-5):

There was a woman called Katherine Fordyce and she died at the birth of her first child – at least folks thought she died. A neighbour's wife dreamt shortly after Katherine's death that she came to her and said 'I have taken the milk of your cow that you could not get, but it shall be made up to you; you shall have more than that if you will give me what you will know about soon.' The good wife would not promise, having no idea what Katherine meant, but shortly afterwards she understood it was a child of her own to which Katherine referred. The child came and the mother named it Katherine Fordyce; and after it was christened this Trowbound Katherine appeared to the mother again and told her all should prosper in her family while that child remained in it. She told her also that she was quite comfortable among the Trows but could not get out unless somebody chanced to see her and had presence of mind enough to call on God's name at the moment. She said her friends had failed to sain her (guard by spells) at the time of her child's birth, and that was how she fell into the power of the Trows.

Prosperity came like a high tide upon the good wife's household until the child Katherine married. On the girl's wedding night a fearful storm came on; 'the like had no' been minded in the time o' anybody alive.' The Broch was overflowed by great seas that rolled over the Skerries as if they had been beach stones. The bride's father lost a number of his best sheep, for they were lifted by the waves and carried away and 'some folk did say that old men with long white beards were seen stretching their pale hands out of the surf and taking hold of the creatures'. From that day the good wife's fortunes changed for the worse. A man named John Nisbet saw that same Katherine Fordyce once. He was walking up a daal near her old home, when it seemed as if a hole opened in the side of this daal. He looked in and saw Katherine sitting in a 'queer-shaped armchair and she was nursing a baby.' There was a bar of iron stretched in front to keep her a prisoner. She was dressed in a brown poplin gown – which folk knew by John's description to be her wedding-dress. He thought she said, 'O Johnnie! what's sent de *here*?' And he answered, 'And what keeps you *here*?' And she said, 'Well; I am well and happy but I can't get out, for I have eaten their food!' John Nisbet unfortunately did not know or forgot to say 'Güde be aboot wis,' and Katherine was unable to give him a hint and in a moment the whole scene disappeared.

The capture of beautiful young women to be brides to fairy kings or princes was almost as common as that of nursing mothers, and these seem often to have been the patients for whom fairy midwives were called out. A very clear example of this is J. Rhys's story of EILIAN OF GARTH DORWEN. Here the fairy's bride went willingly and had always had something uncanny about her. Her GOLDEN HAIR made her particularly attractive to the fairies. There was no need to rescue her. This is the most complete MIDWIFE TO THE FAIRIES story that we possess.

Lady Wilde's ETHNA THE BRIDE is a representative of a FAIRY THEFT of a young bride and of her rescue out of Fairyland. The classic Irish story of MIDHIR AND ETAIN is the epic version of the tale, and the medieval KING ORFEO, in which Hades becomes Fairyland, follows something on the same lines.

The Cornish 'FAIRY DWELLING ON SELENA MOOR' tells of the failure to rescue a human captive, but here the girl seems kept as a nursemaid rather than a bride. Again the eating of fairy food was her undoing.

One aspect of the fairy captives is of especial interest and that is the friendly warning they often give to humans who have inadvertently strayed into Fairyland. In 'The TACKSMAN OF AUCHRIACHAN' it is a neighbour supposed to have been recently dead who warns him of his danger, hides him and helps him to escape. Often the midwife is advised by her patient what to do for her safety. As a rule this patient is a captive bride, and one can presume that it is so in Lady Wilde's story of 'The DOCTOR AND THE FAIRY PRINCESS'. In the Irish tales there are many examples of a 'red-haired man' who intervenes to rescue people enticed into Fairyland, and who is supposed to be a mortal captive there. One example is perhaps enough, drawn from Lady Wilde's *Ancient Legends of Ireland* (vol. I, pp. 54–6). It is about a girl who was enticed into a fairy dance, and, after dancing with the prince, she was led down to a gorgeous banquet:

> She took the golden cup the prince handed to her, and raised it to her lips to drink. Just then a man passed close to her, and whispered –
> 'Eat no food, and drink no wine, or you will never reach your home again.'
> So she laid down the cup, and refused to drink. On this they were angry, and a great noise arose, and a fierce, dark man stood up, and said –

'Whoever comes to us must drink with us.'

And he seized her arm, and held the wine to her lips, so that she almost died of fright. But at that moment a red-haired man came up, and he took her by the hand and led her out.

'You are safe for this time,' he said. 'Take this herb, and hold it in your hand till you reach home, and no one can harm you.'

And he gave her a branch of the plant called *Athair-Luss* (the ground ivy).

This she took, and fled away along the sward in the dark night: but all the time she heard footsteps behind her in pursuit. At last she reached home and barred the door, and went to bed, when a great clamour arose outside, and voices were heard crying to her –

'The power we have over you is gone through the magic of the herb; but wait – when you dance again to the music on the hill, you will stay with us for evermore, and none shall hinder.'

However, she kept the magic branch safely, and the fairies never troubled her more; but it was long and long before the sound of the fairy music left her ears which she had danced to that November night on the hillside with her fairy lover.

Thomas the Rhymer is the one mortal-born inhabitant of Fairyland who appears again and again as the leader and counsellor of the fairies, and seems to have no backward looks towards Middle Earth and no remorse for human mortals. Thomas of Ercildoune actually lived in Scotland in the late Middle Ages, and the very tree where he met the Fairy Queen is still pointed out. Robert KIRK, the 17th-century author of *The Secret Commonwealth*, was another who was believed to have been carried into a fairy hill, the Fairy Knowe at Aberfoyle. He was an unwilling prisoner and was thought to be held because of his betrayal of fairy secrets.

It will be seen that various motives were ascribed for captures of mortals: the acquisition of bond-slaves, amorousness, the enrichment brought by musical talent, human milk for fairy babies, but perhaps the chief motive was to inject the dwindling stock with fresh blood and human vigour.

[Type: ML4077*. Motifs: F300; F301.3; F321.1.1.1; F321.1.4.3; F372; F375; F379.1]

Captured fairies. The marriage of a human man with a fairy wife seems generally to have been a marriage by capture, except for the GWRACHS of Wales, who generally yielded to wooing. Like the captured brides, however, they imposed a TABOO, which was in the end always violated. WILD EDRIC is an early example of a captured FAIRY BRIDE, complete with the taboo and the wife's final return to Fairyland. Many other wives are SELKIES or SEAL MAIDENS, captured by the theft of their

seal skins. When, after years of married life, they regain their skins, they
hurry down to the sea at once.

Ralph of Coggeshall's early tale of the GREEN CHILDREN is an
unusual one of FAIRIES captured, for of the pair, the boy pined and died
and the girl never went back to her subterranean land, but married and
lived on like a mortal, keeping still some of the fairy wantonness.

There are scattered tales all over the country of the capture of small
helpless fairies, most of whom escape in the long run. The most famous
of these are the LEPRACAUNS. The man who is bold enough to seize one
hopes to threaten him into surrendering his pot of gold, for the Lepracaun
is a hoarder, but there has been no recorded case of success. The rule first
laid down by KIRK that a fairy can only be seen between two blinks of an
eye holds good with him. However fast your grip, you must keep your
eye on him through rough and smooth, or he will slip between your
fingers like water. Perhaps the same rule held good for the pixy (see PIXIES)
at the Ockerry, of whom William Crossing wrote in his *Tales of Dartmoor
Pixies*. An old woman who lived on the Moors was going home with an
empty basket from the market after selling her goods. When she got near
the bridge which spans Blackabrook at the Ockerry a small figure leapt
on to the road and began capering in front of her. He was about eighteen
inches high, and she recognized him as a pixy. She paused for a moment,
wondering if she should turn back for fear of being PIXY-LED; but she
remembered that her family would be waiting for her, and pressed
steadily on. When she got to the bridge the pixy turned and hopped
towards her, and she suddenly stooped down, picked him up, popped
him into her empty basket and latched down the lid, for she thought to
herself that instead of the pixy leading her she would lead the pixy. The
little fellow was too tall to leap about in the basket, but he began to talk
and scold in an unknown gibberish, while she hurried proudly home,
longing to show her catch to the family. After a time the stream of
gabbling stopped, and she thought he might be sullen or asleep. She
thought she would take a peep at him, and lifted a corner of the lid very
cautiously, but there was no sight or feel of him, he was gone like a piece
of dried foam. No harm seems to have come to her, and, in spite of losing
him, she felt proud of her exploit.

Two Lancashire poachers, putting their sacks at the mouth of two
rabbit-holes and sending a ferret down the third, were rewarded with
struggling creatures inside the sacks. They secured their ferret, and each
picked up his sack. As they climbed Hoghton Brow they heard to their
horror a little voice from one sack calling, 'Dick, where art thou?' and
from the other sack a voice piped up:

> 'In a sack
> On a back,
> Riding up Hoghton Brow.'

As one man they flung down their sacks in a panic and ran for home. Next morning when they ventured timidly up the hill they found the two sacks neatly folded, but no sign of the fairies. They had had such a fright that they gave up their poaching ways and became industrious weavers, like the rest of the village. This tale is to be found in James Bowker's *Goblin Tales of Lancashire*, and one like it about the theft of a pig is given by C. Latham in 'West Sussex Superstitions', *Folk-Lore Record* (vol. I). SKILLYWIDDEN and COLEMAN GRAY tell of little fairies who were carried into human houses but got back to their own family in the end. In the sadder tale of BROTHER MIKE the little captive never escaped, but pined away and died. Ruth Tongue has a story of a rather rare water-spirit, an ASRAI, who pined and melted away under the heat of the sun like a stranded jelly-fish when a fisherman caught it and tried to bring it home to sell.

Most of these fairies, great or small, seem powerless to avenge the wrong offered to them, though other fairies avenge much more trifling injuries with BLIGHTS AND ILLNESSES, or even death.

[Type: ML6010. Motif: F387]

Cauld Lad of Hilton, the. One of the domestic spirits which is half BROWNIE, half ghost. It was supposed to be the spirit of a Northumbrian stable boy killed by one of the past Lords of Hilton in a fit of passion.

He was heard working about the kitchen at nights, but he was a perverse spirit, for like PUDDLEFOOT or the SILKY of Haddon Hall, he would toss about and disarrange whatever had been left tidy, but clean and tidy whatever had been left dirty or in disorder. He used to be heard singing sadly at night:

        'Wae's me, wae's me;
        The acorn's not yet
        Fallen from the tree,
        That's to grow the wood,
        That's to make the cradle
        That's to rock the bairn,
        That's to grow to a man,
        That's to lay me.'

He was unnecessarily pessimistic, however, for the servants put their heads together and laid out a green cloak and hood for him. At midnight he put them on, and frisked about till cock-crow, singing,

        'Here's a cloak and here's a hood,
        The Cauld Lad of Hilton will do nae mair good!'

And with the dawn he vanished for ever.
  [Motifs: F346; F381.3; F405.11]

Cearb (*kerrap*), **or 'the killing one'.** Recorded by D. A. Mackenzie in *Scottish Folk-Lore and Folk Life* (p. 244) as widely but vaguely referred to in the Highlands: a killer of men and cattle.
  [Motif: F402.1.11]

Ceasg (*keeask*). The Highland MERMAID, also known as *maighdean na tuinne* or 'maiden of the wave'. The body is that of a beautiful woman and the tail that of a grilse (a young salmon), though presumably larger. If caught, she may be prevailed upon to grant three wishes, and the SEAL MAIDEN stories of marriage with humans are sometimes told about the Ceasg. Notable pilots are said to descend from these unions. The darker side of her nature is shown by a tale told of her in George Henderson's book *The Celtic Dragon Myth* in which the hero is swallowed by a sea maiden, but the sweet playing of his betrothed draws the mermaid to the shore, and he escapes. She is still dangerous, however, and is only overcome by the destruction of her SEPARABLE SOUL. Mackenzie, in *Scottish Folk Lore and and Folk Life* (p. 252), suggests that the maiden of the wave may once have been a sea spirit to whom human sacrifices were offered.
  [Motif: B81]

Cellar demon. See BUTTERY SPIRITS.

Changelings. The eagerness of FAIRIES to possess themselves of human children is one of the oldest parts of the fairy beliefs and is a specific form of FAIRY THEFT. Mentions of the thefts of babies are to be found in the MEDIEVAL CHRONICLES of Ralph of Coggeshall and

GERVASE OF TILBURY among others, through the Elizabethan and Jacobean times, and right down to the beginning of the present century. The fairies' normal method was to steal an unchristened child, who had not been given proper PROTECTION, out of the cradle and to leave a substitute in its place. This 'changeling' was of various kinds. Sometimes it was a STOCK of wood roughly shaped into the likeness of a child and endowed by GLAMOUR with a temporary appearance of life, which soon faded, when the baby would appear to die and the stock would be duly buried. More often a fairy child who did not thrive would be left behind, while the coveted, beautiful human baby was taken. More often still the changeling would be an ancient, withered fairy, of no more use to the fairy tribe and willing to lead an easy life being cherished, fed and carried about by its anxious foster-mother, wawling and crying for food and attention in an apparent state of paralysis.

The 'stock' method was most usually employed when the fairies had designs against the mother as well as the child. A good example of a frustrated attempt at such a theft is the Shetland tale 'Mind [Remember] da Crooked Finger'. The wife of a Shetland crofter had just given birth to her first child, and as her husband was folding his lambs he heard three loud knocks coming from underground. He closed the folds and walked up through the cornyard. As he came through the stacks he heard a loud voice say three times, 'Mind da crooked finger.' His wife had a crooked finger and he had a shrewd notion that the GREY NEIGH-BOURS were planning an attack on his wife and his little bairn. But the goodman knew what to do. He went quickly to the house, lighted a candle, took down a clasp-knife and a bible and opened them. As he did so a great clamour and wailing broke out in the byre, which was built against the house. He stuck the knife in his mouth with the blade pointing forward, held the lighted candle in one hand and the opened bible in the other, and made for the byre, followed by most of the neighbours who were visiting his wife. He opened the byre door and threw the bible inside, and as he did so the wailing redoubled, and with a great rush the fairies sped past him. They left behind them a wooden stock, carved feature by feature and joint by joint in the form of his wife. He lifted it up and carried it into the house. 'I've won this from the grey neighbours,' he said, 'and I'll make it serve my turn.' And for years afterwards he used the image as a chopping-block, and the wife was never molested by the fairies again.

A touching story of the weakling fairy child is told by Lady WILDE in *The Ancient Legends of Ireland*. This was of a very daring raid against a newly-born child. The mother and father were lying asleep when the door burst open and a tall, dark man came into the house, followed by an old HAG with a wizened, hairy child in her arms. The mother roused her husband, who put up a vigorous resistance. His candle was twice blown out, but he seized the tongs, and forced the old hag out of the house.

They re-lit the candle, and then they saw that their own baby was gone, and the hairy changeling was in its place. They burst into lamentations, but the door opened and a young girl wearing a red handkerchief came in. She asked them why they were crying, and when they showed her the changeling she laughed with joy and said, 'This is my own child that was stolen from me tonight because my people wanted to take your beautiful baby, but I'd rather have ours; if you let me take him I will tell you how to get your child back.' They gave the changeling to her with joy, and she told them to take three sheaves to the fairy hill, and to burn them one by one, threatening to burn everything that grew on the hill if the fairies did not return their baby safe and sound. They did so, and got their own child back again. The threat to burn the thorns on the fairy hill is sometimes employed to win back full-grown humans.

When the changeling is supposed, like this one, to be a fairy child it is often tormented or exposed to induce the fairy parents to change it back again. This method has been responsible for a dreadful amount of child suffering, particularly in Ireland. Even at the beginning of this century a child was burned to death by officious neighbours who put it on a red-hot shovel in the expectation that it would fly up the chimney. Waldron in his *Isle of Man* gives a tragic account of a dumb child who was supposed to be a changeling. Infantile paralysis or any other unfamiliar disease among the various BLIGHTS AND ILLNESSES that came on suddenly would be accounted for by supposing that the child had been changed, and as a rule the parents would be advised to beat it, expose it on a fairy hill or throw it on to the fire. Only occasionally were they advised to treat the child kindly so that their own children might be kindly treated in return.

Where the changeling was an old fairy it was thought possible to trick it into betraying its age. The method used was so common that it is surprising that the fairies were not forewarned of it. It was to take some two dozen empty eggshells, set them carefully up on the hearth and go through the motions of brewing. Then the constant sobbing and whining would gradually cease, the supine form would raise itself, and in a shrill voice the thing would cry 'I have seen the first acorn before the oak, but I have never seen brewing done in eggshells before!' Then it only remained to stoke up the fire and throw the changeling on to it, when he would fly up the chimney, laughing and shrieking, and the true baby would come to the door. Sometimes the child would not be returned and the parents would have to go and rescue it from the fairy hill.

Children were supposed to be stolen into Fairyland either to pay a TEIND to the Devil, to reinforce the fairy stock or for love of their beauty. Where older people were stolen it was for specific qualities and they were replaced by some form of the 'stock' and generally seemed to be suffering from a 'stroke', which is indeed 'the fairy stroke', generally given by ELF-SHOT. The true changelings are those fairy creatures that replace the stolen human babies. See also CAPTIVES IN FAIRYLAND.

[Type: ML5085. Motifs: F321; F321.1; F321.1.1.2; F321.2; F321.1.4; F321.1.4.3]

Cheerfulness. A cheerful wayfarer, a cheerful giver and a cheerful worker are all likely to gain the patronage of the FAIRIES, who dislike nothing so much as grumbling and moaning. See also VIRTUES ESTEEMED BY THE FAIRIES.

Cheney's Hounds. In the Parish of St Teath in Cornwall an old squire called Cheney used to hunt his own pack of hounds. Little is known of him, but he must have been unpopular, for after his death he was supposed to lead a spectral pack as DANDO did. HUNT thinks that Cheney's dogs were WISH HOUNDS.

'Cherry of Zennor'. A version of the story of the FAIRY WIDOWER, which appears in HUNT's *Popular Romances of the West of England* (pp. 120–26). It is very closely allied to JENNY PERMUEN, also to be found in Hunt. 'Cherry of Zennor' is a curious story, and throws a number of side-lights on fairy beliefs. Sometimes one is tempted to believe that the story had a naturalistic foundation, and that it is an unsophisticated girl's interpretation of a human experience. On the other hand, it gives one quite a picture of the real traditions of underground Fairyland, such as that which was entered by TRUE THOMAS.

Cherry was one of a large family living in Zennor, a small village in Cornwall, and when she got to the age of fourteen it was time for her to go out into the world. She set out to be hired at the local fair, but her courage failed her, and on the Lady Downs she sat down and cried. Whilst she was still weeping a handsome, well-dressed gentleman stood beside her, and asked what was troubling her. After some conversation he said that he was going out to hire a neat, tidy girl to look after his little son, because he had recently been left a widower. He praised Cherry's neatly-mended clothes and tidy looks, and hired her to go along with him. They went an immense way, down and down twisting lanes with high hedges closing above them. The gentleman lifted Cherry over several streams and at length they came to a gate into a garden where flowers of all seasons grew and flowered together. Birds were singing all round them, and Cherry thought she had never seen so lovely a place. A little sharp-eyed boy ran out to greet them, followed by an old, cross-looking woman. 'That's my wife's mother,' said the gentleman, 'but she will only stay a few days to put you in the ways of the place, and then she shall go.' The old woman looked crossly at Cherry and took her in, muttering that she knew Robin would choose a fool. It was a strange place, with long passages and a big room locked up, into which the old woman led Cherry. It was full of what Cherry thought of as dead people –

presumably statues – and there was a coffin-like box in the middle of the room which Cherry was set to polish. When she rubbed it hard it made a strange, groaning sound, and Cherry fell down in a faint. Her master ran in, picked her up and took her out, kissed and comforted her, and sent the old woman away.

Cherry's duties were very light and pleasant; she had to play with the little boy, milk a cow who appeared mysteriously when she was called, and anoint the little boy's eyes every morning with green ointment. The pleasantest of her duties was to help her master work in the garden. At the end of every row he gave Cherry a kiss, and she would have been very happy there if it had not been that her master disappeared for many hours together, and when he came back went into the locked room from which strange sounds proceeded. Her little charge would answer none of her questions, but only said 'I'll tell Grannie' if she asked him anything; but she fancied that he saw much more than she did, and his eyes were very bright; so one morning she sent him off to pick some flowers and slyly put a crumb of the ointment in her own eye. This produced a transformation: the garden was swarming with little creatures. Her eyes smarted and she ran to the well to wash out the ointment. At the bottom of the well she saw numbers of tiny people dancing, and to her fury she saw her master among them, as tiny as they were, and on very familiar terms with the little fairy ladies. Soon she saw her master coming back as his normal size. He went up to the locked room and went inside. Cherry followed him and peeped through the keyhole. He lifted the lid of the coffin and a lady came out, sat down, and began to play upon the coffin, and all the statues began to dance. Cherry ran away weeping, and when her master called her to weed the garden with him, she was very sulky. At the end of the first row he tried to kiss her, but she pushed him away saying: 'Go and kiss your little midgets at the bottom of the well.' Her master looked very sad. 'Cherry, you have been using the ointment that you were told not to use. I am sorry, but you must go home, and old Grace must come back again.' Cherry cried and besought, but he made her pack her clothes, and led her back by the long uphill way on to the Lady Downs. She never saw him again, and like many people who have visited Fairyland, she did no good in the mortal world, but hung about the Lady Downs hoping Robin her master would come back and see her. This is one occasion on which the seeing eye was not blinded. Cherry's master had shown great restraint.

An interesting feature of this story is that old Grace kept the village school. She was evidently a mortal, and therefore Robin's first wife must have been mortal too. The FAIRY OINTMENT would have been necessary to give the little half-fairy fairy sight. It is as yet uncertain if this needed to be used by whole fairies.

[Type: ML4075. Motifs: F235.4.1; F370; F372; F376]

Chess. The ancient oriental game of chess came into Celtic Britain at a very early date, and was much esteemed as the Game of Kings, who learned tactics and strategy from it, and the art of hiding their thoughts when they were in conflicts. It was a game at which the aristocratic fairies, the DAOINE SIDHE of Ireland and the SIDH of Scotland, had great skill, and it was the habit of wandering members of the sidhe to win great contests against mortals by challenging them to three games, at each of which the winner was to choose his stake. Invariably the mortal won the first two games and chose rich prizes, but the supernatural stranger won the third, and imposed some almost fatal task or asked for some next-to-impossible gift. It was by such a game that MIDHIR won ETAIN from EOCHAID. This motif is also common in Highland folk-tales, as, for instance, in one of McKay's *More West Highland Tales*, 'How the Great Tuairisgeal was Put to Death', in which the Young Tuairisgeal, winning the third game of chess, puts the Young King of Erin under binding spells to find out how the Great Tuairisgeal was put to death and to bring back with him the Sword of Light by which he was slain. The young king succeeds in the quest by the help of the woman and the horse which he won in the first two games. This is a standard pattern in both Highland and Irish tales.

Chess as a sport of kings is illustrated in the tale of FINN, in the episode when Young Finn, serving his stepfather, the King of Carraighe, incognito, displayed both his ingenuousness and his royal blood by winning seven games in succession against the king, who guessed his paternity and sent him quickly away.

[Motif: H509.3]

Chessmen of Lewis. In 1831 a high tide on the coast near Uig in the Isle of Lewis washed away a sand-bank and exposed a cave in which there was a small beehive-shaped building rather like the little domestic grinding querns to be found in the Highlands. A labourer working near found it, and, thinking it might contain some treasure, broke into it. He found a cache of eighty-four carved chessmen ranged together. They had an uncanny look, and he flung down his spade and ran, convinced that he had come on a sleeping company of fairies. His wife was of sterner stuff and made him go back and fetch them. The greater part of them are now in the British Museum. Replicas have been made of them, but the originals, all mustered together, are much more impressive. A tradition has arisen about them. It is said that the guards who take the guard-dogs round at night cannot get them to pass the Celtic chessmen. They bristle and drag back on their haunches. So perhaps the Highlander's super-stition can be excused.

Church Grim. There is a widespread tradition that the churchyards were guarded from the Devil and witches by a spirit that usually took the form of a BLACK DOG. Those who saw it generally took it as a death warning. Mrs Gutch mentions it in *County Folk-Lore* (vol. II, pp. 127–8), and William Henderson discusses it in *Folk-Lore of the Northern Counties* (p. 274). He attributes it to a foundation sacrifice and points out that the Kyrkogrim of Sweden appears in the form of a lamb because, in the early days of Christianity in Sweden, a lamb was buried under the altar, while in Denmark the Kirkegrim took the form of a 'grave-sow'. Thomas WRIGHT in his *Essays* (p. 194) says that the Yorkshire church grim can be seen about the church in dark stormy weather by day and night. It sometimes tolls the bell at midnight before a death, and at a funeral the clergyman would see it looking out from the tower, and could tell by its aspect whether the soul of the corpse was destined for Heaven or Hell.

In her *County Folk-Lore* collection (vol. VIII, p. 108), Ruth Tongue says that when a new churchyard was opened it was believed that the first man buried there had to guard it against the Devil. To save a human soul from such a duty a pure black dog was buried in the north part of the churchyard as a substitute. In the Highlands, according to J. G. CAMP-BELL in his *Superstitions of the Highlands and Islands of Scotland* (p. 242), a similar belief was held. It was the duty of the last-buried corpse to guard the graveyard till the next funeral.

[Motif: F401.3.3]

Churchyard mould. Mould which came from an ancient churchyard, where all the soil consisted of mouldering bodies, was valuable in spells, but was also considered protective as a counter-charm against FAIRIES or spirits. See also PROTECTION AGAINST FAIRIES.

Churnmilk Peg. The unripe nut thickets in West Yorkshire are guarded by Churnmilk Peg. According to Mrs Wright, who mentions her among the cautionary GOBLINS in *Rustic Speech and Folk-Lore*, she beguiles her leisure by smoking a pipe. In the North Country generally, MELSH DICK performs the same function.

Cinderlad. See ASSIPATTLE.

Cipenapers. According to Gerard Manley Hopkins in his *Journal* (p. 263), this is an attempt to reproduce the English word 'kidnappers' in Welsh; 'kidnappers' is given as a name for the FAIRIES in the long list of fairy names to be found in the DENHAM TRACTS (vol. II, p. 78).

Ciuthach (*kew-uch*). This Highland character, latterly a cave-haunting monster, was a noble cave-dwelling giant in earlier romances. W. J. Watson in the *Celtic Review* (vol. IX, pp. 193–209) says:

In view of the fact that traces of Ciuthach are found, one may say, from Clyde to the Butt of Lewis, it is clear that at one time he played a great role in the traditions of the West. Among all the confusion of the traditions as they have come down to us, there may be, and probably is, an ultimate historical basis . . . Throughout the references to him there runs the feeling that Ciuthach was a hero, or the hero of a race different from the Gael.

Watson suggested that he might be a Pict; Professor MAC RITCHIE, in the next number of the *Celtic Review*, put forward the theory that he was a Finn. Gill, in his *Second Manx Scrapbook* (p. 252), points out that it was Ciuthach whose cave was visited by Diarmuid and Grania on their flight.

Clap-Cans. This Lancashire BOGIE is one of the least offensive of the frightening spirits. It is mentioned by Mrs Wright in *Rustic Speech and Folk-Lore* (p. 194). It is invisible and impalpable and is only feared for the frightening noise it makes.

Clean hearth. The first recipe in old days for encouraging fairy visits and gaining fairy favours was to leave the hearth swept and the fire clear. This seems some indication of the contention that domestic fairies were of the type of the *Lares*, the ancestral spirits who were the ghosts of those who had been buried under the hearth according to the primitive custom in pre-classical times. See also VIRTUES ESTEEMED BY THE FAIRIES.

Clear water. A bowl of clear, fair water had to be left in any place where the fairy ladies were supposed to resort with their babies to wash them by the fire. Dirty water or empty pails were commonly punished by pinching or lameness. See also FAULTS CONDEMNED BY THE FAIRIES; VIRTUES ESTEEMED BY THE FAIRIES.

Clodd, Edward (1840–1930). A prominent figure in the early years of the Folklore Society, Clodd was by profession a banker, and much respected in his profession, but he was also widely read in anthropology and folklore, and in 1895 was made President of the Folklore Society. He was a rationalist, and did not hesitate to examine Christianity as a source of pagan survivals. He wrote many books. Our chief interest in the fairy-lore context is his work on TOM TIT TOT, the English Rumpelstiltskin, on which he wrote a monograph, *Tom Tit Tot, an Essay on Savage Philosophy in Folk-Tales* (1898). After his retirement in 1915, he entertained many folklorists and writers in his cottage at Aldeburgh: the Gommes, Andrew Lang, John Rhys, HARTLAND and Frazer, as well as Leslie Stephen, Thomas Hardy, H. G. Wells, J. M. Barrie and many others. Further particulars of his life may be found in Joseph McCabe, *Edward Clodd, a Memoir* (London, 1932).

Clover. See FOUR-LEAFED CLOVER.

Cluricaune (*kloor-a-cawn*), or **Cluracan.** One of the SOLITARY
FAIRIES of Ireland. Thomas Crofton CROKER has several stories of him
as a kind of BUTTERY SPIRIT, feasting himself in the cellars of drunkards,
or scaring dishonest servants who steal the wine. Sometimes he makes

himself so objectionable that the owner decides to move, but the Cluricaune pops into a cask to move with him, as the BOGGART did in Lancashire. The Cluricaune described by Crofton Croker wore a red nightcap, a
leather apron, pale-blue long stockings and silver-buckled, high-heeled
shoes. Presumably his coat was red, for solitary fairies were generally
supposed to be distinguished from TROOPING FAIRIES by wearing red
instead of green coats.

Coblynau (*koblernigh*). The Welsh MINE GOBLINS, not unlike the
KNOCKERS of Cornwall. Wirt Sikes devotes some room to them in
British Goblins (p. 24). He says they are about eighteen inches in height,
dressed something after the manner of the miners and grotesquely ugly.
They are good-humoured and propitious to see and hear. By their
knocking they indicate where rich lodes of ore are to be found. If they
are mocked they throw stones, but these do no harm. They appear to be
very busy, but they actually perform nothing. In this they are like the
'Goblins who labour in the mines', so often cited from Georgius Agricola
by the 17th-century writers.
  [Motif: F456]

Colann Gan Ceann (*kulan gone kyown*). See COLUINN GUN CHEANN.

Coleman Gray. A Cornish example of the CAPTURED FAIRIES, this
is the name of a little PISKY boy who was adopted by a human. It is
given by HUNT in *Popular Romances of the West of England* (p. 95), from
T. Quiller Couch in *Notes and Queries*.

There is a farmhouse of some antiquity with which my family have a close connection; and it is this circumstance, more than any other, that has rendered this tradition concerning it more interesting to us, and better remembered than many other equally romantic and authentic. Close to this house, one day, a little miserable-looking bantling was discovered alone, unknown, and incapable of making its wants understood. It was instantly remembered by the finder, that this was the way in which the piskies were accustomed to deal with those infants of their race for whom they sought human protection; and it would have been an awful circumstance if such a one were not received by the individual so visited. The anger of the piskies would be certain, and some direful calamity must be the result; whereas, a kind welcome would probably be attended with great good fortune. The miserable plight of this stranger therefore attracted attention and sympathy. The little unconscious one was admitted as one of the family. Its health was speedily restored, and its renewed strength, activity, intelligence and good-humour caused it to become a general favourite. It is true the stranger was often found to indulge in odd freaks; but this was accounted for by a recollection of its pedigree, which was not doubted to be of the piskie order. So the family prospered, and had banished the thought that the foundling would ever leave them. There was to the front door of this house a hatch, meaning a half-door that is kept closed when the whole door behind it is open, and which then serves as a guard against the intrusion of dogs, hogs, and ducks, while air and light are freely admitted. This little being was one day leaning over the top of this hatch, looking wistfully outward, when a clear voice was heard to proceed from a neighbouring part of the townplace, calling, 'Coleman Gray, Coleman Gray!' The piskie immediately started up, and with a sudden laugh, clapped its hands, exclaiming, 'Aha! my daddy is come!' It was gone in a moment, never to be seen again.

[Type: ML6010. Motifs: F329.4.1; F387]

Colepexy. KEIGHTLEY, quoting from Brand's *Popular Antiquities* (vol. II, p. 513), says:

In Dorset the Pixy-lore still lingers. The being is called *Pexy* and *Colepexy*. The fossil belemnites are named Colepexies-fingers; and the fossil echini, Colepexies-heads. The children, when naughty, are also threatened with the Pexy, who is supposed to haunt woods and coppices.

Colour of fairy clothes. See DRESS AND APPEARANCE OF THE FAIRIES.

Colt-pixy. This is the Hampshire name for a spirit like the Northern BRAG or DUNNIE. KEIGHTLEY in *Fairy Mythology* (p. 305) quotes a

Captain Grose as saying: 'In Hampshire they give the name of Colt-
Pixy to a supposed spirit or fairy, which in the shape of a horse *wickers*,
i.e. neighs, and misleads horses into bogs, etc.' In Somerset, however,
the colt-pixy, again in the form of a colt, is an orchard-guardian who
chases apple-thieves. Ruth Tongue, in *County Folk-Lore* (vol. VIII), suggests that he is a form taken by LAZY LAWRENCE (p. 119). The Dorset
COLEPEXY sounds as if it might be a variant of the same name.

Coluinn gun Cheann (*collun g'n chyown*), or 'the Headless Trunk'.
J. F. CAMPBELL in *Popular Tales of the West Highlands* describes a
BAUCHAN who was a kind of tutelary spirit of the Macdonalds of Morar,
but who was extremely hostile to anyone else in the neighbourhood. He
hovered about Morar House, which is on the mainland just opposite the
point of Sleat on Skye, but at night he commonly haunted 'the Smooth
Mile', a path which ran from the river of Morar to Morar House, and
made it a very perilous track for any solitary man to tread at night-time.
The mutilated body of any man who ventured there was likely to be
found in the morning. The Bauchan never did any harm to women or
children and never appeared to any going in company, so that it was
useless to send out a party against him. This went on for a long time,
until at length Coluinn gun Cheann killed a friend and distant cousin of
the Macleods of Raasay, a very dear friend of 'Big John, the son of
Macleod of Raasay', a man of remarkable strength and prowess. He told
his stepmother of his friend's death and sought her counsel, as he always
did, and she advised him to attempt the destruction of the monster. He
met the Coluinn just after sunset and they fought all night long. Before
dawning Big John got the victory, and he was anxious to see the thing he
had been fighting, so he tucked it under his arm to carry it to the light.
The Coluinn had never been heard to speak, but it spoke now, and said,
'Let me go.' 'I will not let you go,' said Big John. It was getting towards
daybreak, and like all ghosts and BOGLES the Coluinn could not abide
the break of day. It said again, 'Let me go, and I shall never be seen here
any more.' Big John had pity on him and said, 'If thou swear that on the
book, on the candle and on the black stocking, you may be gone.' And he
made the Bauchan swear it on his knees, then he released it and it flew
away lamenting:

> 'Far from me is the hill of Ben Hederin,
> Far from me is the pass of murmuring.'

He sang it over and over until his voice faded into the distance, and
women and children at Morar still sing the lament. Campbell identifies
this Bauchan with that which served Callum Mor Mackintosh in the
story of the Bauchan, but he does not give the reasons for this identification.

[Motifs: E422.1.1; E461]

Consumption. The popular name for tuberculosis. It was sometimes blamed upon witches, who were supposed to turn their victims into horses and ride them by night to the sabbats so that they became 'hag-ridden'; but it was more commonly supposed to be a fairy affliction. Young girls or young lads were summoned night after night to dance in the fairy revels and wasted away because they had no rest by night or day. It is noticeable that this belief was commonest where there was a close connection between the FAIRIES and the dead. FINVARRA, an Irish king of the fairies, was also the king of the dead. Lady WILDE in her *Ancient Legends of Ireland* gives a number of legends of Innis-Sark in which the fairies and the dead appear to be interchangeable. See also BLIGHTS AND ILLNESSES ATTRIBUTED TO THE FAIRIES.

Co-Walker. KIRK, in his *Secret Commonwealth*, names a double, such as the Germans call a *Doppelgänger*, a 'Co-walker'. In the North it is called a WAFF and is said to be a death token. Kirk, however, considers it to be one of the FAIRIES, and says (1933 edition, p. 69):

> They are clearly seen by these Men of the Second Sight to eat at Funeralls (and) Banquets; hence many of the Scottish–Irish will not teast Meat at these Meittings, lest they have Communion with, or be poysoned by, them. So are they seen to carrie the Beer or Coffin with the Corps among the midle-earth Men to the Grave. Some men of that exalted Sight (whither by Art or Nature) have told me they have seen at these Meittings a Doubleman, or the Shape of some Man in two places; that is, a superterranean and a subterranean Inhabitant, per-fectly resembling one another in all Points, whom he notwithstanding could easily distinguish one from another, by some secret Tockens and Operations, and so go speak to the Man his Neighbour and Familiar, passing by the Apparition or Resemblance of him.

And on the next page he continues:

> They call this Reflex-man a Co-walker, every way like the Man, as a Twin-brother and Companion, haunting him as his shadow, as is oft seen and known among Men (resembling the Originall), both before and after the Originall is dead; and wes also often seen of old to enter a Hous, by which the People knew that the Person of that Liknes wes to Visite them within a few days. This Copy, Echo, or living Picture, goes att last to his own Herd.

Cowlug sprites. Strictly local spirits, haunting the Border villages of Bowden and Gateside. Henderson in *Folk-Lore of the Northern Counties* (p. 262) quotes from the Wilkie manuscript, but the report is very vague.

> The villages of Bowden and Gateside had a strange belief that on a certain night in the year (thence called 'Cowlug E'en') a number of

spirits were abroad with ears resembling those of cows; but he could not discover the origin of the belief, nor which night was thus distinguished.

Cramps. These were often the penalty for annoying the FAIRIES. Scolding and ill-temper were specially punished in this way. See also BLIGHTS AND ILLNESSES ATTRIBUTED TO THE FAIRIES.

Crimbil. The Welsh for a CHANGELING; quoted in BENDITH Y MAMAU.

Crodh Mara. The Highland fairy cattle or sea cattle are less dangerous than the EACH UISGE, just as the TARROO USHTEY of Man is less dangerous than the CABYLL USHTEY. They are 'hummel', or hornless, and generally dun in colour, though those in Skye are said to be red and speckled, and are often described as black. The bulls of the water-cattle sometimes mate with the mortal cattle to the great improvement of the stock. In one way they are a danger to the farmer, according to J. G. CAMPBELL in *Superstitions of the Highlands and Islands* (p. 29). Sometimes one of the fairy cattle joins a mortal herd who follow her everywhere, and she leads them towards a fairy KNOWE which at once opens for her. If the cowherd does not turn his own cows back, they follow the fairy cow into the mound and are never seen again. The opposed characters of the WATER-HORSE AND THE WATER-BULL are well shown in a story about Islay told by J. F. CAMPBELL in *Popular Tales of the West Highlands* (vol. IV, pp. 304–6). There was a farmer on the north of the island who had a large herd of cattle and one day a calf was born to one of the cows with round ears. An old woman who lived on the farm and whose advice was always taken recognized it as the calf of a water-bull and told them to keep it separate from the other calves for seven years and feed it each day with the milk of three cows. As she said, so they did. Some time after this a servant lass went out to watch the cattle, who were grazing near the loch. A young man drew near and, after some talk, sat down beside her and asked her to clean his head. It was an attention often paid by lasses to their lads. He laid his head on her lap and she began to part and straighten his locks. As she did so she saw with horror that there was green seaweed growing amongst his hair, and knew that he must be the dreaded Each Uisge himself. She did not scream or start, but went on rhythmically with her task until she had lulled the creature to sleep. Then she slowly untied her apron, worked her way from under the head and ran for home. When she was nearly there she heard a dreadful thunder of hoofs behind her and saw the water-horse hard on her heels. He would have seized her and carried her into the loch to be torn to pieces, but the old woman loosed the bull. The bull charged at the horse and the two went fighting into the loch. Next morning the mangled body of the bull drifted to the shore, but the water-horse was never seen again.

See also FAIRY ANIMALS; GWARTHEG Y LLYN.

[Motifs: B184.2.2.2; F241.2]

Croker, Thomas Crofton (1798–1854). The first field-collector of folk-tales in Ireland, and indeed the first in the British Isles if we except Walter SCOTT. The first volume of *Fairy Legends and Traditions of the South of Ireland* appeared in 1823 when Crofton Croker was working in London as clerk to the Admiralty. It was an immediate and immense success; Jacob Grimm translated it into German and Scott wrote a lengthy and eulogistic letter which Croker printed in the second volume of 1828. The success of the first volume had been so great that its publisher, John Murray, sent Croker at once to Ireland to collect material for the second, which did not, however, come out until the third of the series was also ready. The third volume contained a translation of an essay by Grimm on the ELVES, and was devoted to the fairy-lore of England, Wales and Scotland. The first two volumes, however, deal entirely with the fairy spirits of Ireland, the CLURICAUNE, in whom the LEPRACAUN is merged, the SHEFRO, the FIR DARIG, the PHOOKA, the MERROW, and others, mostly of the HOBGOBLIN kind, except for a couple of stories on the BANSHEE and a few headed 'Thierna Na Oge' (see TIR NAN OG). The stories are often amusing, even jocular, in manner, but nevertheless they represent genuine folk traditions, and a few of them are described as written down verbatim. Most attempt to convey the background and setting in which the stories were told. Before he had completed the three volumes of *The Fairy Legends*, Crofton Croker brought out a kind of guide book of his travels in Cork, Waterford and Limerick, *Researches in the South of Ireland, illustrative of the scenery, architectural remains, and the manners and superstitions of the peasantry*. This provides additional comment on the fairy-lore which he gathered on his travels.

Croker met Sir Walter Scott, corresponded with Grimm, and indeed with most of the leading folklorists of his time, and maintained a high reputation as an authority on fairy-lore which has long outlasted his life.

Cross. From the earliest days of Christianity the cross was believed to be a most potent protective symbol against FAIRIES and all evil spirits. It is even possible that cross-roads had a pre-Christian significance, as sacred to the god of limits and a place of sacrifice. The cross in all its forms was protective – the 'saining' or crossing of one's own body or that of another, a cross scratched on the ground or formed by four roads meeting, a cross of wood, stone or metal set up by the roadside, a cross worn as a trinket round the neck, all these were believed to give substantial protection against devils, ghosts or FAIRIES. Sometimes this protection was reinforced by carrying a cross of a particular material – of ROWAN wood, for instance, for this wood was a protection of itself – or for trinkets crosses of coral or amber, both of some potency.

An example of the efficacy of 'saining' as a means of rescuing a CAPTIVE IN FAIRYLAND is to be found in Walter SCOTT's 'Alice Brand', a ballad from *The Lady of the Lake*:

> 'But wist I of a woman bold,
> Who thrice my brows durst sign,
> I might regain my mortal mould,
> As fair a form as thine.'

Literary though this is, it is the work of a man who knew almost all there was to be known about the fairy-lore of the Scottish Border.

For the wayside cross, it will be remembered that when Burd Janet went into Carterhaugh Woods to rescue YOUNG TAMLANE, she took her stand by Miles Cross, where both she and he could expect some protection. For the metal cross, mothers, to protect their babies from the fairies, would hang open scissors over the cradle to make a cross of cold IRON, and stick pins into their clothing in the form of a cross.

[Motifs: D788; F382.1]

Cu Chulainn (*koo chul-inn*). See CUCHULLIN.

Cu Sith (*coo-shee*). This, the FAIRY DOG of the Highlands, was different from other Celtic fairy hounds in being dark green in colour. It is described by J. G. CAMPBELL in *Superstitions of the Scottish Highlands* (pp. 30–32). It was the size of a two-year-old stirk (yearling bullock). It was shaggy, with a long tail coiled up on its back, or plaited in a flat plait. Its feet were enormous and as broad as a man's; its great footmarks were often seen in mud or snow, but it glided along silently, moving in a straight line. It did not bark continuously when hunting, but gave three tremendous bays which could be heard by ships far out at sea. As a rule the fairy dogs were kept tied up inside the BRUGH to be loosed on intruders, but sometimes they went with women looking for human cattle to milk or to drive into the SITHEIN, and sometimes a cu sith would be allowed to roam about alone, taking shelter in the clefts of the rocks. This cu sith would be terribly formidable to mortal men or dogs, but those loosed in the Brugh in J. F. CAMPBELL's tale of the 'ISLE OF SANNTRAGH' were driven back by the mortal dogs when they approached human habitations. BRAN, FINN's elfin dog, was different in appearance. Other fairy dogs are generally white with red ears, and the commonest supernatural dogs in England are BLACK DOGS.

[Motif: F241.6]

Cuachag (*cooachack*). According to Mackenzie in *Scottish Folk Lore and Folk Life*, and also to Professor W. J. Watson in *History of Celtic Place-Names in Scotland*, the Cuachag was a FUATH. It was a river sprite, which haunted Glen Cuaich in Inverness-shire, which is connected to it by name. Like all the Fuathan, it is a dangerous spirit.

Cuchullin, or Cuchulain (*koo chul-inn*). This is the hero of the *Ulster Cycle*, one of the earliest of the Irish collections of heroic legends. He was a mortal, born for death, set apart by curious, abnormal characteristics and destined from the beginning to a strange fate. Though human, he was, like a Greek hero, the son of a god, LUGH of the Long Arm. The unusual features of his appearance were that he had seven pupils in each eye, seven fingers on each hand and seven toes on each foot. His cheeks were streaked yellow, green, blue and red. His hair was dark at the roots, red as it grew out and fair at the tips. He was bedizened with ornaments, a hundred strings of jewels on his head and a hundred golden brooches on his chest. Such was his appearance in times of peace, and it was apparently admired. When he was seized by war frenzy he was completely changed. He turned round inside his own skin, so that his feet and knees were to the rear and his calves and buttocks were to the front. His long hair stood on end and each hair burned with a spark of fire, a jet of flame came out of his mouth and a great arch of black blood spouted from the top of his head. One eye shot out on to his cheek and the other retreated back into his skull; on his forehead shone 'the hero's moon'. His frenzy was so great that he had to be plunged into three vats of icy water to bring him down to normal temperature. These strange transformations seem to have been characteristic of heroes, for something similar is reported of Lancelot of the Lake in *Lanzelet*, the German translation of a 12th-century romance.

Even as a child, Cuchullin's strength was enormous, for at seven years old he killed the ferocious dog of Culain the Smith, which guarded the King of Ulster's Court. To atone for this he offered to take the dog's place and guard Ulster. His name was changed from Sétanta to Cuchullin – 'Culain's Hound', and he guarded Ulster until his death. Like other heroes he was skilled in poetry, music and magic as well as in the arts of war, but tragedy hung over him and he made many enemies in following his vocation. The bitterest was Queen Medhb, or MAEVE, who encountered him in the Cattle Raid of Cuailagne and systematically reared MAGICIANS to fight against him. In the end she entangled him in contradictory GEASAS and brought about his downfall. He died heroically, having bound himself to a pillar so that he could stand against his enemies to the end.

Eleanor Hull's book *The Cuchullin Saga* gives a scholarly account of the whole legend.

[Motifs: A511.1.3.1; A526.1; A526.5; A526.6; A526.8; A536.1]

Cughtagh (*cootah*). A cave-dwelling spirit, but, according to Gill in *A Second Manx Scrapbook* (p. 252), the Cughtagh is seldom mentioned now, though the creature is merged into the class of cave-haunting BUGGANES. Gill thinks that the Highland CIUTHACH, now a disagreeable cave spirit, but earlier a more noble character, a chivalrous GIANT, is closely related to it.

Cutty Soams. Mentioned by HUNT as one of the spirits of the Cornish mines, he actually belonged, as one might imagine by his name, to the North Country, and Hunt lifted his story from the *Monthly Chronicle* of 1887, quoted in the DENHAM TRACTS:

> Cutty Soams was a coal-pit Bogle, a sort of Brownie, whose disposition was purely mischievous, but he condescended sometimes to do good in an indirect way. He would occasionally bounce upon and thrash soundly some unpopular over-man or deputy viewer; but his special business and delight was to cut the traces or 'soams' by which the poor little assistant putters (sometimes girls) used then to be yoked to the wooden trams underground. It was no uncommon thing in the morning, when the men went down to work, for them to find that Cutty Soams had been busy during the night, and that every pair of rope-traces in the colliery had been cut to pieces. By many he was supposed to be the ghost of one of the poor fellows who had been killed in the pit at one time or other, and who came to warn his old marrows of some misfortune that was going to happen. At Callington Pit, which was more particularly haunted, suspicion fell upon one of the deputies named Nelson, and soon after two men, the under-viewer and the over-man, were precipitated to the bottom of the pit, owing to this man Nelson cutting the rope by which they descended, all but one strand. As a climax to this horrible catastrophe, the pit fired a few days afterwards, and tradition has it that Nelson was killed by the damp. Cutty Soams Colliery, as it had come to be nicknamed, never worked another day.

[Motifs: F456; F456.1; F456.3; F456.3.1]

Cwn Annwn (*koon anoon*). The Welsh hell hounds, something of the same kind as the GABRIEL RATCHETS, the WISH HOUNDS and the SEVEN WHISTLERS. Like these they are death portents, but they do not, like the DEVIL'S DANDY DOGS, do actual destruction. Sikes in *British Goblins* (p. 233) describes their howl, which grows softer as they draw closer. Near at hand they sound like a cry of small beagles, but in the distance their voice is full of wild lamentation. Sometimes a voice sounds among the pack like the cry of an enormous bloodhound, deep and hollow. To hear them is taken as a certain prognostication of death.

[Motif: E501.13.4]

Cyhyraeth (*kerherrighth*). The Welsh form of the Highland CAOINEAG (the 'Weeper'). Unlike the GWRACH Y RHIBYN, it is seldom seen, but is heard groaning before a death, particularly multiple deaths caused by an epidemic or disaster. Sikes in *British Goblins* (pp. 219–22) gives several oral accounts of the Cyhyraeth. Prophet Jones described the noise it made as 'a doleful, dreadful noise in the night, before a burying'. Joseph Coslet of Carmarthenshire was more explicit. He said that the sound was common in the neighbourhood of the river Towy, 'a doleful, disagreeable sound heard before the deaths of many, and most apt to be heard before foul weather. The voice resembles the groaning of sick persons who are to die; heard at first at a distance, then comes nearer, and the last near at hand; so that it is a threefold warning of death. It begins strong, and louder than a sick man can make; the second cry is lower, but not less doleful, but rather more so; the third yet lower, and soft, like the groaning of a sick man almost spent and dying.' This reminds one of the three approaching cries of the CWN ANNWN. Like the Irish BANSHEE, the Cyhyraeth wailed for the death of natives who died away from home. On the Glamorganshire coast, Cyhyraeth passes along the sea before a wreck, and here it is accompanied by a kind of corpse-light. Like corpse candles (see under WILL O' THE WISP), this foretells the path a corpse is to take on the way to the churchyard. In a story about St Mellon's churchyard a ghost is reported as having been seen, but, as a rule, Cyhyraeth is an invisible and bodiless voice.

[Motif: M301.6.1]

Dagda (*dagda*). The High King of the TUATHA DE DANANN, the immortal fairy people of Ireland, who were conquered by the Milesians, the human invaders who forced the Danaans to take refuge under the hollow hills. Though in hiding, they were still powerful over the growth of the land, and they destroyed all the wheat and milk of the Milesians, for whom neither grass nor grain grew until they had concluded a treaty with Dagda. Dagda had four great palaces in the depths of the earth and under the hollow hills, and he made a distribution of them to his sons. To LUG son of Ethne he gave one and to OGME another, and he kept two for himself, and the chief of these was Brugh na Boinne, which was very great and full of wonders, but ANGUS MAC OG got this from him by the help of MANANNAN SON OF LIR. For Angus had been away when Dagda distributed his palaces, and he was angry to find himself left out. But

Manannan advised him to ask for Brugh na Boinne for a day and a night, and he would work a magic so that Dagda could not refuse it. Dagda gave him the BRUGH for a day and a night, but when the time was over Angus said that it had been given him for ever, for all time consisted of a day and a night following each other for ever. Dagda rendered it up to him, for though he was High King of the great race of Danu, he could be conquered by cunning.

Dagda had another and greater sorrow to bear, for he had another son AEDH, who had the same mother as Angus; and this son went with his father to his other palace near Tara. It happened that a great man of Connacht, Corrgenn, came to visit him and brought his wife with him. It seemed to Corrgenn that there was more between Aedh and his wife than there should have been, and he struck Aedh down and killed him before his father's eyes. Everyone expected that Dagda would kill Corrgenn for this, but Dagda said that if Corrgenn was not mistaken he had reason for what he did, so he would not kill him; but he put a GEASA on him that was worse than death. He had to carry the body of Aedh with him until he found a stone the exact size to cover him, and then he must dig a grave on the nearest hill and bury Aedh and put the stone over him. It was many a long mile that Corrgenn walked until he found a stone on the shore of Loch Feabhail. On the hill nearby he dug the grave, and laid Dagda's son there and carried the stone to cover him. The great labour was too much for him and his heart burst and he died. Dagda had a wall built round the tomb and the hill has been called the Hill of Aileac, that is, the Hill of Sighs, ever since. It is not certain whether Corrgenn was a mortal man, but it is certain that Aedh was an immortal and the son of immortals, but he could be killed in battle, and this is true of all the Tuatha de Danann unless they have some special magic that revives them.

Daisies. It is sometimes said that the habit of dressing children in daisy-chains and coronals comes from a desire to protect them against being carried off by the fairies. Daisies are a sun symbol and therefore protective magic. See also PROTECTION AGAINST FAIRIES.

Dana, or Danu (*thana*). One of the Mother Goddesses of early Ireland, the ancestress of the TUATHA DE DANANN, who later dwindled to the DAOINE SIDHE, the FAIRIES of Ireland. Lady Gregory begins her book *Gods and Fighting Men* with an account of how the Tuatha de Danann came to Ireland, led by Nuada, and fought with the FIRBOLGS under their king EOCHAID. Among the goddesses who fought under Nuada she mentions BADB and MACHA and the MORRIGU, Eire and Fodla and Banba, the daughters of DAGDA, and Eadon and BRIGIT, the two goddesses of the poets, and she adds, 'And among the other women there

were many shadow-forms and great queens; but Dana, that was called
the Mother of the Gods, was beyond them all.'

Dancing. The festive exercise most widely attributed to the FAIRIES,
large or small. Beautiful or hideous fairies are alike adept in it. In literature, from the 16th century onwards, we find constant references to the
fairies as dancers. In the anonymous *The Maides Metamorphosis* (see
DIMINUTIVE FAIRIES), produced about the same date as a MID-
SUMMER NIGHT'S DREAM, we have a pleasing set of fairy revels, with
their accompanying song:

> By the moone we sport and play,
> With the night begins our day;
> As we daunce, the deaw doth fall;
> Trip it little urchins all,
> Lightly as the little Bee,
> Two by two and three by three:
> And about go wee, and about go wee.

And later in the century we have the jovial Bishop Corbet in 'Farewell
Rewards and Fairies':

> At morning and at evening both
> You merry were and glad,
> So little care of sleepe and sloth
>   These prettie ladies had;
>
> When Tom came home from labour,
> Or Ciss to milking rose,
> Then merrily merrily went their tabor,
>   And nimbly went their toes.

In the 19th century, when fairy stories had begun to be freed from the
18th-century compulsion towards moralizing and allegory, we find the
grotesque DWARFS in 'Amelia and the Dwarfs' by J. H. EWING as fond
of dancing as the most delicate and elegant fairy of them all. All these
literary embroideries are true to the old tradition of the fairies' love of
dancing and music. In one of the earliest of the EARLY FAIRY ANEC-
DOTES, the hero of WILD EDRIC sees his future fairy wife dancing in a
house of the Forest of Clun. In the many Welsh variants of 'Rhys at the
Fairy Dance' we have the tale of a young man who steps into a fairy ring
or an old mill and is lost to the sight of his companion, who can only hear
the music and sees nothing. In many of the versions, the companion is
accused of the murder of his friend, but fortunately only after a year has
almost elapsed. He manages to persuade his judges to accompany him to
the place where his friend disappeared. They all hear the music, and while

someone holds his coat-tails he puts one foot over the ring and pulls his friend out, wretchedly emaciated and still with the cask over his shoulder which he carried into the ring. He imagines that single dance is not yet finished.

The TROWS of Shetland have two kinds of dances; the HENKIES perform a grotesque kind of 'goose-dance', squatting on the ground with their hands clasped round their thighs, bounding up and down and kicking out alternate legs; the other trows dance exquisitely with intricate steps.

John AUBREY, in a passage already quoted, describes a true fairy-ring dance, seen by his school-teacher, with the pinching by which they punished an intruder. The miniature, amorous fairies with whom Anne JEFFERIES claimed intercourse, danced and revelled in the palatial place to which they conveyed her. It is impossible ever to list all the occasions on which fairies have been watched dancing, but it is perhaps well to mention that many dance tunes are supposed to have been memorized by a skilful fiddler or piper. Perhaps the best-known of these are the 'Fairy Dance' of Scotland and the 'Londonderry Air'.

'Dando and his Dogs'. The story of a priest, Dando, who lived in the village of St Germans in Cornwall, is an example of the way in which the Devil's hunt becomes attached to a wicked human being. Dando was a priest who cared for nothing but sensual pleasures and hunting. Week-days and Sundays were alike to him, and he thought nothing of leading the hunt out, however sacred the day. One fine Sunday Dando and his rout were hunting over the estate of Earth, as it was called, and had had a fine and prosperous hunt, with many kills. When they paused to bait their horses, Dando found that no drink was left in the flasks of any of his attendants. He clamoured for it, and said, 'If none can be found on Earth, go to Hell for it!' At that a stranger who had joined the hunt unperceived, rode up and offered him a drink, saying that it was the choicest brew of the place he had just mentioned. Dando drank it eagerly, and emptied the whole flask. 'If they have drink like this in Hell, I will willingly spend Eternity there.' In the meantime the stranger was quietly collecting all the game. Dando demanded it back again with furious curses. The stranger said, 'What I have, I hold.' Dando leapt off his horse and rushed at the stranger, who lifted him by the scruff of the neck as Dando shouted out, 'I'll follow you to Hell for it!' and the stranger said, 'You shall go with me.' With that he spurred his horse with a great leap into the middle of the stream, with Dando sitting before him. A burst of flame came up from the stream; the stranger, the horse and Dando disappeared. But not for ever: for since that day Dando and his hounds are from time to time heard in wild chase over the countryside. This is one of the stories that HUNT tells in *Popular Romances of the West of England* (pp. 220-23).

The same kind of origin is given in Scandinavian tradition to Jon, who succeeds OD IN as the ghastly huntsman.

[Motifs: G303.17.2.4; M219.2.4]

Danes. There is a certain amount of confusion in Somerset between the Danes, whose incursions are still remembered, and the FAIRIES. The name 'Danes' may be connected, in this Celtic pocket of England, with the DAOINE SIDHE, the children of DANA. The Leicestershire Dane Hills may have the same origin. Ruth Tongue in *County Folk-Lore* (vol. VIII, p. 111) quotes an informant at Ashridge in 1907 who was convinced that the traditional buried treasure on Dolbury Camp was put there by the Fairies, not by the Danes.

There be a bit of verse as do go

> If Dolbury digged were
> Of gold should be the share,

but nobody hasn't found the treasure yet. And for why? Well, to start up with it don't belong to they, and so they won't never meet up with it. 'Twill go on sinking down below never mind how deep they do dig. I tell 'ee 'tis the gold of they Redshanks as used to be seed on Dolbury top. To be sure there's clever, book-read gentlemen as tell as they was Danes, and another say 'twere all on account of their bare legs being red with the wind, but don't mind they.

My granny she did tell they was fairies, ah, and all dressed in red, and if so the treasure med be theirs. If they was Danes how do 'ee explain all they little clay pipes as 'ee can find on Dolbury Camp. They did call 'em 'fairy pipes', old miners did. An' if there be fairy pipes then there was fairies, and nobody need doubt they was the Redshanks.

Daoine Sidhe (*theena shee*). These are the fairy people of Ireland, generally supposed to be the dwindled gods of the early inhabitants of Ireland, the TUATHA DA DANANN, who became first the Fenian heroes and then the FAIRIES. Other names are however given them for safety's sake, 'the GENTRY', the 'GOOD PEOPLE', the 'Wee Folks', 'the People of That Town', or other EUPHEMISTIC NAMES. A good account of these Irish fairies is given by YEATS in the first few pages of his *Irish Fairy and Folk Tales*. They are the typical HEROIC FAIRIES, enjoying the pleasures and occupations of the medieval chivalry. Even in modern times their small size is not invariable; they are occasionally of human or more than human stature. Their habitations are generally underground or underwater, in the green raths or under the loughs or in the sea. These underwater fairies are well described by Lady WILDE in *Ancient Legends of Ireland* (vol. I, p. 68). They are supposed to be those of the Fallen

Angels, too good for Hell: 'Some fell to earth, and dwelt there, long before man was created, as the first gods of the earth. Others fell into the sea.'

D'Aulnoy, Madame la Comtesse (*c.* 1650–1705). The wife of François de la Motte, Comte d'Aulnoy, Madame d'Aulnoy followed closely on the heels of the fashion for fairy stories initiated by Charles PERRAULT, but while Perrault's stories were true folk-tales only adorned by the admirable style in which they were told, her fairy stories were the undisciplined product of her own lively imagination. She indeed knew something of folk traditions, but used them in an arbitrary way. For instance, the theme of the bartered bed and the magic nuts is used in 'The Blue Bird', but the fairies are entirely unconvincing, a piece of arbitrary machinery. The stories have the quality of engaging attention, but the style is purely literary. They are the forerunners of the *Cabinet des Fées*, that monstrous collection in which the voice of tradition grows fainter almost with each successive tale, and the style increasingly flatulent.

'Dead Moon, The'. An unusual story to find in English folk tradition, for it is a mythological story, though in no way an origin myth. It was collected in the Lincolnshire Fens by Mrs Balfour, and published in 'Legends of the Cars' (*Folk-Lore*, vol. II). The personified Moon is the heroine of the story. She heard of black doings on the Fens, with the witches and BOGLES and the dead folk and creeping horrors and WILL O' THE WYKES leading travellers out of the way, and one moonlight night she wrapped herself in a black cloak and went to see. As she passed lightly over the Fens a stone turned under her feet and a willow snag twisted round her wrists and drew her down into the bog. All the evil spirits of the Fens came round her and buried her under a great stone, setting a Will o' the Wykes to guard her, and for more than a month no moon shone and the creeping horrors gained in strength until the Fenmen began to fear that they would invade their own hearths. At length, by the advice of a wise woman, the Fenmen set out to look for the buried Moon in dead silence, and in silence said the charms that freed her. They lifted the great stone and she rose up into the heavens and drove the black spirits away. This is one of a group of stories so unusual that some folklorists have doubted their genuineness. Mrs Balfour, however, published the notes which she took at the time, which established the general accuracy of the tales, though an occasional Scottish word may have strayed in, and there is no doubt from subsequent collection that the Fen area was a unique confine of legends and traditions.

[Motifs: A106.2.1.1; A753; A754.1.1; A758]

Dee, John (1527–1608). One of the greatest mathematicians of his age, Dr Dee was a man of great and wide learning with that extraordinary capacity for concentrated study which seemed to characterize the men of the Renaissance. He was astronomer and astrologer to Queen Elizabeth I, with a subtle and profound intellect, fascinated by mysticism and entangled in it, and yet so innocent and guileless that he was an easy dupe to an impostor. He would have no place in this book if he had not been so, for it was Edward Kelly who introduced him to the dubious company of spirits who beguiled him for so long. He had already been attracted towards intercourse with angels by means of a mirror or crystal and through the intervention of 'a scryer' or medium, but in 1582 Kelly presented himself at Mortlake, and a partnership was established which lasted for over six years, all the initiative being in Kelly's hands, since he alone could obtain any response from the crystal. Dee was already much hated by the common people as a WIZARD, though he was still supported by the Queen. In 1583, Dee, Kelly and their wives left Mortlake and travelled to Holland, and the house was no sooner empty than a mob attacked it and sacked Dee's magnificent library of over 4,000 volumes. For six years they travelled over Europe, one patron after another wearying of Kelly's impostures, but Dee remaining blindly loyal. The first converse on the crystal had been through angels, but these deteriorated to spirits who seemed nearer to FAIRIES than anything else, though they were intolerable prattlers. Sometimes the angels returned, and on one occasion they went too far, for they advised that the two philosophers should hold everything in common, including their wives. Jane Dee was much better-looking than Mrs Kelly. Dee regretfully agreed, but the wives objected, quarrels broke out and the two associates parted, though a correspondence was maintained between them. Dee's journal of the intercourse with the spirits was published by Méric Casaubon under the title of *A true and faithful relation of what passed for many years between Dr J. Dee and some spirits*. It did no good to Dee's reputation, which has, however, been largely vindicated by the writings of Dr Frances A. Yates.

Defects of the fairies. Among the many beliefs held about the FAIRIES, there is one strand which describes them as beautiful in appearance, but with a deformity which they cannot always hide. The Scandinavian ellewomen, for instance, have beautiful faces, but if looked at from behind are seen to be hollow. The evil but beautiful GLAISTIGS of the Highlands wear trailing green dresses to conceal their goat's hoofs. The Shetland HENKIES were given that name because they limped in their dancing. J. G. CAMPBELL, in his *Superstitions of the Highlands and Islands of Scotland*, says: 'Generally some personal defect is ascribed to them by which they become known to be of no mortal race. In Mull and the neighbourhood they are said to have only one nostril, the other being imperforate.' The physical defects of the BEAN SIDHE as described by him are such that she could never under any circumstance be called beautiful: 'The Bean Sith was detected by her extraordinary voracity (a cow at a meal), a frightful front tooth, the entire want of a nostril, a web foot, preternaturally long breasts, etc.'

According to George MACDONALD, the Aberdeenshire BROWNIES had a thumb with the rest of the fingers joined together.

It seems likely that these characteristics were given to the fairies by people who believed them to be fallen angels, or yet more closely related to the Devil. The Devil's cloven hoof is perhaps one of the most common articles of folk belief. As Alexander Roberts put it in his *Treatise of Witchcraft*, 'Yet he cannot so perfectly represent the fashion of a man's body but that there is some sensible deformity by which he bewrayeth himself.'

[Motif: F254.1]

Denham Tracts, The. The author of these, Michael Aislabie Denham, died in 1859, nearly thirty years before the Folk-Lore Society was founded. Nevertheless, he worked at the study of folklore for a great part of his life, and contributed to Hone's *Everyday Book* and Richardson's *Table Book*. *A Collection of Proverbs and Popular Sayings* was published for him by the Percy Society, and he printed quite a number of pamphlets and short books during the last years of his life. A great deal of this, however, was scattered and dispersed when he died, and when the Folk-Lore Society was first founded in 1878, W. J. Thoms suggested that Denham's papers should be collected and published. The result of this suggestion was the publication by the Folk-Lore Society of *The Denham Tracts* in two volumes (1892 and 1895). The first volume chiefly consists of local sayings and proverbs, but spirit and fairy traditions are to be found scattered about in the second, which contains much that is quotable. Of particular interest is the voluminous list (vol. II, pp. 77–80) of the FAIRIES and other night fears which troubled our ancestors. One section of it is borrowed straight from the list given by Reginald SCOT in his *Discovery of Witchcraft*, but a great deal of local lore has been added to this, and many of the spirits mentioned have received separate treatment in the present dictionary, though it requires rather a long stretch to include some among spirits:

> Grose observes, too, that those born on Christmas Day cannot see spirits; which is another incontrovertible fact. What a happiness this must have been seventy or eighty years ago and upwards, to those chosen few who had the good luck to be born on the eve of this festival, of all festivals; when the whole earth was so overrun with ghosts, boggles, bloody-bones, spirits, demons, ignis fatui, brownies, bugbears, black dogs, spectres, shellycoats, scarecrows, witches, wizards, barguests, Robin-Goodfellows, hags, night-bats, scrags, breaknecks, fantasms, hobgoblins, hobhoulards, boggy-boes, dobbies, hobthrusts, fetches, kelpies, warlocks, mock-beggars, mum-pokers,

Jemmy-burties, urchins, satyrs, pans, fauns, sirens, tritons, centaurs, calcars, nymphs, imps, incubusses, spoorns, men-in-the-oak, hell-wains, fire-drakes, kit-a-can-sticks, Tom-tumblers, melch-dicks, larrs, kitty-witches, hobby-lanthorns, Dick-a-Tuesdays, Elf-fires, Gyl-burnt-tails, knockers, elves, raw-heads, Meg-with-the-wads, old-shocks, ouphs, pad-fooits, pixies, pictrees, giants, dwarfs, Tom-pokers, tutgots, snapdragons, sprets, spunks, conjurers, thurses, spurns, tantarrabobs, swaithes, tints, tod-lowries, Jack-in-the-Wads, mormos, changelings, redcaps, yeth-hounds, colt-pixies, Tom-thumbs, black-bugs, boggarts, scar-bugs, shag-foals, hodge-pochers, hob-thrushes, bugs, bull-beggars, bygorns, bolls, caddies, bomen, brags, wraithes, waffs, flay-boggarts, fiends, gallytrots, imps, gytrashes, patches, hob-and-lanthorns, gringes, boguests, bonelesses, Peg-powlers, pucks, fays, kidnappers, gally-beggars, hudskins, nickers, madcaps, trolls, robinets, friars' lanthorns, silkies, cauld-lads, death-hearses, goblins, hob-headlesses, buggaboes, kows, or cowes, nickies, nacks (necks), waiths, miffies, buckies, gholes, sylphs, guests, swarths, freiths, freits, gy-carlins (Gyre-carling), pigmies, chittifaces, nixies, Jinny-burnt-tails, dudmen, hell-hounds, dopple-gangers, boggleboes, bogies, redmen, portunes, grants, hobbits, hobgoblins, brown-men, cowies, dunnies, wirrikows, alholdes, mannikins, follets, korreds, lubberkins, cluricauns, kobolds, leprechauns, kors, mares, korreds, puckles, korigans, sylvans, succubuses, black-men, shadows, banshees, lian-hanshees, clabbernappers, Gabriel-hounds, mawkins, doubles, corpse lights or candles, scrats, mahounds, trows, gnomes, sprites, fates, fiends, sybils, nick-nevins, whitewomen, fairies, thrummy-caps, cutties, and nisses, and apparitions of every shape, make, form, fashion, kind and description, that there was not a village in England that had not its own peculiar ghost. Nay, every lone tenement, castle, or mansion-house, which could boast of any antiquity had its bogle, its spectre, or its knocker. The churches, churchyards, and cross-roads, were all haunted. Every green lane had its boulder-stone on which an apparition kept watch at night. Every common had its circle of fairies belonging to it. And there was scarcely a shepherd to be met with who had not seen a spirit!

Departure of the fairies. From the time of Chaucer onwards, the FAIRIES have been said to have departed or to be in decline, but still they linger. Some 200 years later, Bishop Richard Corbet pursues the same theme:

> Farewell rewards and fairies,
>   Good housewives now may say;
> For now foul sluts in dairies
>   Do fare as well as they.

> And though they sweep their hearths no less
> Than maids were wont to do,
> Yet who of late for cleanliness
> Finds sixpence in her shoe?

A little later AUBREY has a story of a fairy driven away when BELLS were hung in Inkberrow Church. He was heard lamenting:

> 'Neither sleep, neither lie,
> Inkberrow's ting-tang hangs so high.'

Some two centuries later, Ruth Tongue picked up a similar story in Somerset, to be found in *County Folk-Lore* (vol. VIII, p. 117). It was about the farmer of Knighton Farm on Exmoor, who was on very friendly terms with the PIXIES. They used to thresh his corn for him and do all manner of odd jobs, until his wife, full of good-will, left suits of clothes for them, and of course, like BROWNIES, they had to leave. But they did not lose their kindly feeling for the farmer, and one day, after the Withypool bells were hung, the pixy father met him.

> 'Wilt gie us the lend of thy plough and tackle?' he said.
> The farmer was cautious – he'd heard how the pixies used horses.
> 'What vor do 'ee want'n?' he asked.
> 'I d'want to take my good wife and littlings out of the noise of they ding-dongs.' The farmer trusted the pixies, and they moved, lock, stock and barrel over to Winsford Hill, and when the old pack horses trotted home they looked like beautiful two-year-olds.

Those were only partial moves, not total evacuations, but they illustrate one of the factors that were said to drive the fairies out of the country. KIPLING's 'Dymchurch Flit' in *Puck of Pook's Hill* is probably founded on an actual Sussex folk tradition.

Somewhere at the beginning of the 19th century, Hugh Miller recorded what was supposed to be the final departure of the fairies from Scotland at Burn of Eathie. It is to be found in *The Old Red Sandstone* as a footnote in Chapter 11.

> On a Sabbath morning ... the inmates of this little hamlet had all gone to church, all except a herd-boy, and a little girl, his sister, who were lounging beside one of the cottages; when, just as the shadow of the garden-dial had fallen on the line of noon, they saw a long cavalcade ascending out of the ravine through the wooded hollow. It winded among the knolls and bushes; and, turning round the northern gable of the cottage beside which the sole spectators of the scene were stationed, began to ascend the eminence toward the south. The horses were shaggy, diminutive things, speckled dun and grey; the riders, stunted, misgrown, ugly creatures, attired in antique jerkins of plaid, long grey cloaks, and little red caps, from under which their wild uncombed

locks shot out over their cheeks and foreheads. The boy and his sister stood gazing in utter dismay and astonishment, as rider after rider, each one more uncouth and dwarfish than the one that had preceded it, passed the cottage, and disappeared among the brushwood which at that period covered the hill, until at length the entire rout, except the last rider, who lingered a few yards behind the others, had gone by. 'What are ye, little mannie? and where are ye going?' inquired the boy, his curiosity getting the better of his fears and his prudence. 'Not of the race of Adam,' said the creature, turning for a moment in his saddle: 'the People of Peace shall never more be seen in Scotland.'

Aberdeenshire is in the Northern Lowlands; the Highlanders would not so easily bid the fairies farewell. Indeed, in all the Celtic parts of Britain living traditions still linger. Even in the Midlands, in Oxfordshire, A. J. Evans, writing about the Rollright Stones in the *Folk-Lore Journal* of 1895, gives the last recorded tradition of the fairies. An old man, Will Hughes, recently dead when Evans wrote, claimed to have seen them dancing round the King Stone. They came out of a hole in the ground near it. Betsy Hughes, his widow, knew the hole: she and her playmates used to put a stone over it, to keep the fairies from coming out when they were playing there.

Yet, however often they may be reported as gone, the fairies still linger. In Ireland the fairy beliefs are still part of the normal texture of life; in the Highlands and Islands the traditions continue. Not only in the Celtic areas, but all over England scattered fairy anecdotes are always turning up. Like the chorus of policemen in *The Pirates of Penzance*, they say, 'We go, we go,' but they don't go.

[Motif: F388]

Dependence of fairies upon mortals. The FAIRIES appear to have an independent existence of their own, to lead their lives in subterranean or subaqueous countries, or on enchanted islands across the sea. They ride, revel, dance and hold their FAIRY MARKETS, they pursue their own crafts, spin, weave, make shoes and labour in the mines; and yet from time to time we come across extraordinary examples of their dependence upon humanity. The commonest stories about them are of their thefts of human babies and their periodic need of a human MIDWIFE TO THE FAIRIES. It is possible that these last may be for the human brides stolen, but here again we see the fairy dependence. Mortal blood seems needed to replenish the fairy stock. Sometimes it is needed literally: in the Isle of Man it was believed that if water was not left out for the fairies to drink, they would suck the blood of the sleepers in the house. This was reported by Evans Wentz in *The Fairy-Faith in Celtic Countries* (p. 44). The other most obvious example of dependence was on human food. Again and again we are told of FAIRY THEFTS of grain, milk or butter, or of them carrying away the FOYSON or goodness of food or cattle and leaving only a simulacrum behind. In some of the stories, such as the medieval tale of MALEKIN, the explanation might be that it was a human CHANGELING who wished to return to the world again and so refrained from FAIRY FOOD, but the instances are too frequent to allow of that as the sole explanation. In the friendly intercourse of FAIRY BORROWING, they sometimes beg for a suck of milk from a human breast for a fairy baby, or a loan of human skill to mend a broken tool such as a BROKEN PED. In Ireland in particular human strength is needed to give power to the fairy arms in faction fights or in HURLING matches. Evans Wentz gives a report of this (p. 44). KIRK suggests that many of the spectacles seen among the fairies are imitations or foreshadowings of human happenings, as some of the FAIRY FUNERALS are supposed to be. Indeed, however much the fairies may seem to resent human prying and INFRINGEMENTS OF FAIRY PRIVACY, it would appear that the affairs of humanity are of more importance to them than they would wish us to suppose.

[Motifs: D2066; F267; F391]

Derricks. The derricks of Devon are described by E. M. Wright in *Rustic Speech and Folk-Lore* (p. 207) as 'dwarfish fairies, of somewhat evil nature', but they may have a better reputation in Hampshire. In 1962 a visitor from Hampshire suggested to Ruth Tongue that a little green-dressed, good-humoured fairy who directed a stranger lost on the Berkshire downs might be a derrick. The Devonshire derricks would be more likely to lead travellers astray.

Devil's Dandy Dogs. This is a Cornish version of the WILD HUNT, closely attached to DANDO AND HIS DOGS, to the GABRIEL RATCHETS

and the WISH HOUNDS, the Welsh CWN ANNWN and, more loosely, to
HERLA'S RADE. This last is the legend that has the closest fairy connection; most of the other spirits are more nearly allied to beliefs about
the Devil than about FAIRIES. The Devil and his dandy dogs are the
most dangerous of all the diabolical packs. HUNT, in *Popular Romances
of the West of England* (pp. 223–4), quotes a story of T. Quiller Couch's
in which a herdsman is only saved from being torn to pieces by the
dandy dogs by kneeling and praying:

> A poor herdsman was journeying homeward across the moors one
> windy night, when he heard at a distance among the Tors the baying of
> hounds, which he soon recognized as the dismal chorus of the dandy-
> dogs. It was three or four miles to his house; and very much alarmed,
> he hurried onward as fast as the treacherous nature of the soil and the
> uncertainty of the path would allow; but, alas! the melancholy yelping
> of the hounds, and the dismal holloa of the hunter came nearer and
> nearer. After a considerable run, they had so gained upon him, that on
> looking back, – oh horror! he could distinctly see hunter and dogs. The
> former was terrible to look at, and had the usual complement of
> *saucer-eyes*, horns, and tail, accorded by common consent to the
> legendary devil. He was black, of course, and carried in his hand a long
> hunting-pole. The dogs, a numerous pack, blackened the small patch
> of moor that was visible; each snorting fire, and uttering a yelp of
> indescribably frightful tone. No cottage, rock, or tree was near to give
> the herdsman shelter, and nothing apparently remained to him but to
> abandon himself to their fury, when a happy thought suddenly flashed
> upon him and suggested a resource. Just as they were about to rush
> upon him, he fell on his knees in prayer. There was strange power in
> the holy words he uttered; for immediately, as if resistance had been
> offered, the hell-hounds stood at bay, howling more dismally than
> ever, and the hunter shouted, 'Bo Shrove,' which (says my informant)
> means in the old language, '*The boy prays,*' at which they all drew off
> on some other pursuit and disappeared.

The Cornish devil hunts human souls. The prey of many devils are
witches; but in the Scandinavian legend it is ODIN, lately become like
DANDO a demi-devil, who leads the hunt, and it is the elf-women whom
he pursues. One can see in all these varying hunts how close the connection between devils, fairies and the dead can be.

[Motifs: G303.7.1.3; G303.16.2]

Diminutive fairies. The first very small traditional FAIRIES that we
know are the PORTUNES recorded by GERVASE OF TILBURY. They were
probably carried on in the stream of tradition by the fairies' connection
with the dead, for the soul is often thought of as a tiny creature which
comes out of a sleeping man and wanders about. Its adventures are the

sleeper's dreams. By this means or others the tradition continued, and came up into literature in the 16th century. The first poet to introduce these small fairies into drama was John Lyly in *Endimion*. They are brought in for a short time, to do justice on the villain by the pinching traditional to the fairies. They punish not only the wrong done to Endimion, but the INFRINGEMENT OF FAIRY PRIVACY. Corsites has been trying to move the sleeping Endimion when the fairies enter, and pinch him so that he falls asleep. They dance, sing and kiss Endimion:

> 'Pinch him, pinch him, blacke and blue,
> Sawcie mortalls must not view
> What the Queene of Stars is doing,
> Nor pry into our Fairy woing.'

The Maides Metamorphosis, published the same year as A MIDSUMMER NIGHT'S DREAM, has a scene reminiscent of Bottom's introduction to TITANIA's elves, and their song makes their tiny size apparent:

> 1 FAY: 'I do come about the coppes
>   Leaping upon flowers toppes;
>   Then I get upon a Flie,
>   Shee carries me abouve the skie,
>   And trip and goe.'

> 2 FAY: 'When a deaw drop falleth downe
>   And doth light upon my crowne,
>   Then I shake my head and skip
>   And about I trip.'

Drayton's *Nimphidia* is quite a long narrative poem, a parody of a courtly intrigue in miniature. The fairies in it are among the tiniest in the poetry of the period, but not strictly to scale. The Queen, Pigwiggen and all her ladies of honour take refuge in a cowslip bell, but the ladies ride a cricket, about ten times the size of their room, and the Queen's coach is a snail's shell. Neither the King nor the Queen has the powers that belong to Shakespeare's OBERON and Titania, not even the power of swift motion; the witch-fairy Nimphidia is the only potent one among them, and she relies on herbs and charms which might be used by mortal witches. The chief charm of the poem is in the littleness of the actors, the stampede of tiny ladies-in-waiting, the preparation of Pigwiggen for the tourney:

> 'When like an uprore in a Towne,
> Before them every thing went downe,
> Some tore a Ruffe, and some a Gowne,
>   Gainst one another justling:

> They flewe about like Chaff i' th' winde,
> For hast some left their Maskes behinde;
> Some could not stay their Gloves to finde,
>   There never was such bustling . . .
>
> And quickly Armes him for the Field,
> A little Cockle-shell his Shield,
> Which he could very bravely wield:
>   Yet could it not be pierced:
> His Speare a Bent both stiffe and strong,
> And well-neere of two Inches long;
> The Pyle was of a Horse-flyes tongue,
>   Whose sharpnesse naught reversed.'

With PUCK we get back on to the plain road of folklore, HOBGOBLIN
with his SHAPE-SHIFTING tricks:

> 'This *Puck* seemes but a dreaming dolt,
> Still walking like a ragged Colt,
> And oft out of a Bush doth bolt,
>   Of purpose to deceive us.
> And leading us makes us to stray,
> Long Winters nights out of the way,
> And when we stick in mire and clay,
>   *Hob* doth with laughter leave us.'

William Browne of Tavistock belonged to the same set as Drayton and
was one of the group who called themselves the 'Sons of Ben Jonson'. He
and Drayton were both lovers of antiquities and both wrote long poems
on the beauties of England, Drayton *Polyolbion* and Browne the delightful,
unfinished *Britannia's Pastorals*, which incorporates a rambling narrative
in his topography. The fairies play an important part in it. They are a
little larger than Drayton's fairies, riding mice instead of insects, and a
little more of folk fairies, having their fairy palace underground and to
be seen through a SELF-BORED STONE as the Selkirkshire lassie saw
HABETROT and her spinners. Like Habetrot, they too were great spinners
and weavers, but do not seem to have been deformed by it:

> And with that he led
> (With such a pace as lovers use to tread
> By sleeping parents) by the hand the swain
> Unto a pretty seat, near which these twain
> By a round little hole had soon descried
> A trim feat room, about a fathom wide,
> As much in height, and twice as much in length,
> Out of the main rock cut by artful strength.

> The two-leav'd door was of the mother pearl,
> Hinged and nail'd with gold. Full many a girl
> Of the sweet fairy ligne, wrought in the loom
> That fitted those rich hangings clad the room.

The two types of Robert HERRICK's fairy writings may be sampled in an extract from *Oberon's Feast* and in *The Fairies*. The first is full of fanciful turns:

> His kitling eyes begin to runne
> Quite through the table, where he spies
> The hornes of paperie Butterflies,
> Of which he eates, and tastes a little
> Of that we call the Cuckoes spittle.
> A little Fuz-ball-pudding stands
> By, yet not blessed by his hands,
> That was too coorse; but then forthwith
> He ventures bodly on the pith
> Of sugred Rush, and eates the sagge
> And well bestrutted Bees sweet bagge:
> Gladding his pallat with some store
> Of Emits eggs; what wo'd he more?

The second little poem is straightforward folklore:

> If ye will with *Mab* find grace,
> Set each Platter in his place:
> Rake the Fier up, and get
> Water in, ere Sun be set.
> Wash your Pailes, and clense your Dairies;
> Sluts are loathsome to the Fairies:
> Sweep your house: Who doth not so,
> _ *Mab* will pinch her by the toe.

Simon Steward was another of the fellowship, but only one poem of his was published, and that in a small pamphlet called *A Description of the King and Queene of Fayries* (1635). There are one or two pleasant touches in this piece, which commemorates a New Year's custom used in the human court as well as among the fairies, for it is called 'Oberon's Apparell: A Description of the King of Fairies Clothes, brought to him on New Yeares Day in the morning, 1626, by his Queens chambermaids'. It is one of the most attractive of these little fairy poems:

> His belt was made of Mirtle leaves
> Pleyted in small Curious theaves
> Besett with Amber Cowslipp studdes
> And fring'd a bout with daysie budds

> In which his Bugle horne was hunge
> Made of the Babling Echos tungue
> Which sett unto his moone-burnt lippes
> Hee windes, and then his fayries skipps.
> Att that the lazie Duoane gan sounde
> And each did trip a fayrie Rounde.

The eccentric but engaging Duchess of Newcastle pursued the theme of the littleness of fairies with her usual enthusiasm. Her theory was that the fairies were natural phenomena, much less spiritual than witches or ghosts. By the time she has finished with them they have no more spiritual qualities than microbes:

> Who knowes, but in the *Braine* may dwel
> Little small *Fairies*; who can tell?
> And by their severall actions they may make
> Those *formes* and *figures*, we for *fancy* take.
> And when we sleep, those *Visions*, *dreames* we call,
> By *their* industry may be raised all;
> And all the *objects*, which through *senses* get,
> Within the *Braine* they may in order set.
> And some pack up, as *Merchants* do each thing,
> Which out sometimes may to the *Memory* bring.
> Thus, besides our owne *imaginations*,
> *Fairies* in our *braine* beget *inventions*.
> If so, the *eye's* the *sea* they traffick in,
> And on *salt watry teares* their ship doth swim.
> But if a *teare* doth breake, as it doth fall,
> Or wip'd away, they may a *shipwrach* call.

The diminishers have done their worst; no numinosity is left to these fairies any more.

Dinny-Mara, or Dooinney Marrey (*dunya mara*). The MERMAN of Man seems to have been a less fierce character than the English Merman, and nearly as amiable as the Irish MERROW. The MERMAID of Cury in the Cornish legend of LUTEY AND THE MERMAID, herself harmless enough, was afraid that her husband would eat their children if she did not get home in time to feed him, but the Dinny-Mara in Dora Broome's story, 'The Baby Mermaid', seems to have been an affectionate father, who romped with his baby and gave her presents. Otherwise less is heard of the Dinny-Mara than of the BEN-VARREY.

Direach, or Dithreach (*jeeryuch*). In J. F. CAMPBELL's *Popular Tales of the West Highlands* (vol. IV, p. 298) there is a description of a FACHAN, Direach Ghlinn Eitidh, that is, 'the desert creature of Glen Eiti', who was a peculiarly ugly specimen of his ugly class. 'Ugly was the make of the Fachin; there was one hand out of the ridge of his chest, and one tuft out of the top of his head, it were easier to take a mountain from the root than to bend that tuft.' It was also mentioned that he had one leg out of his haunch and one eye in the middle of his forehead. He was a GIANT.

Dobbs, or Master Dobbs. The Sussex BROWNIE, supposed to be specially kind to old men, like the Highland BODACHAN SABHAILL. The belief has now gone, but it has left its trace in the proverbial saying quoted by Mrs Wright, 'Master Dobbs has been helping you,' when someone has got through more work than was expected. In Yorkshire the same character was called DOBBY.

Dobby. A friendly name for a HOBGOBLIN in Yorkshire and Lancashire. He is very like a BROWNIE, but perhaps more likely to play mischievous pranks. In fact he is much like ROBIN GOODFELLOW. Mrs Wright mentions Dobby in *Rustic Speech and Folk-Lore* (p. 202).

Dobie. One type of BROWNIE, but, according to William Henderson in *Folk-Lore of the Northern Counties* (p. 247), he is not nearly so acute as a brownie, and people are often heard saying, 'She's but a Dobie,' or, 'Ye stupid Dobie!' It used to be the custom in unsettled times on the Border to bury one's valuables and commit them to the charge of a brownie. If no brownie was to be had, people used to fall back on a dobie, which was always willing, but very gullible. There was, however, another use of the name as a tutelary family ghost. It will be remembered that the CAULD LAD OF HILTON, who behaved like a brownie and was laid in the traditional way by a gift of clothes, was supposed to be the ghost of a stableboy killed by one of the Lords of Hilton. In the same way the SILKIE is often described as a ghost, and Lady WILDE describes the Irish BANSHEE as the spirit of some beautiful girl of the family, dead long ago but still concerned with its fortunes. In something the same way, the Dobie of Morthan Tower, Rokeby, is said to be the ghost of a long-past wife of the Lord of Rokeby, who was murdered by her jealous husband in the glen below. It is said that the blood which dripped from his dagger left indelible stains on the stairs. This dobie was more of a ghost than a HOBGOBLIN, for it seemed to haunt the house in a ghostly way, and neither keened nor undertook domestic duties. In the end it was laid, not by a gift of clothes but by exorcism.

'Doctor and the Fairy Princess, The'. Lady WILDE, in her *Ancient Legends of Ireland* (vol. II, p. 191), has an unusual version of the MIDWIFE TO THE FAIRIES story, in which a famous doctor, not a midwife, delivers the fairy lady. The FAIRY OINTMENT does not occur in this story, and the doctor is saved from being held CAPTIVE IN FAIRYLAND by following the advice of his patient, evidently a fellow captive:

Late one night, so the story goes, a great doctor, who lived near Lough Neagh, was awoke by the sound of a carriage driving up to his door, followed by a loud ring. Hastily throwing on his clothes, the doctor ran down, when he saw a little sprite of a page standing at the carriage door, and a grand gentleman inside.

'Oh, doctor, make haste and come with me,' exclaimed the gentleman. 'Lose no time, for a great lady has been taken ill, and she will have no one to attend her but you. So come along with me at once in the carriage.'

On this the doctor ran up again to finish his dressing, and to put up all that might be wanted, and was down again in a moment.

'Now quick,' said the gentleman, 'you are an excellent good fellow. Sit down here beside me, and do not be alarmed at anything you may see.'

So on they drove like mad – and when they came to the ferry, the doctor thought they would wake up the ferryman and take the boat; but no, in they plunged, carriage and horses, and all, and were at the other side in no time without a drop of water touching them.

Now the doctor began to suspect the company he was in; but he held his peace, and they went on up Shane's Hill, till they stopped at a long, low, black house, which they entered, and passed along a narrow dark passage, groping their way, till, all at once, a bright light lit up the walls, and some attendants having opened a door, the doctor found himself in a gorgeous chamber all hung with silk and gold; and on a silken couch lay a beautiful lady, who exclaimed with the most friendly greeting –

'Oh, doctor, I am so glad to see you. How good of you to come.'

'Many thanks, my lady,' said the doctor, 'I am at your ladyship's service.'

And he stayed with her till a male child was born; but when he looked round there was no nurse, so he wrapped it in swaddling clothes and laid it by the mother.

'Now,' said the lady, 'mind what I tell you. They will try to put a spell on you to keep you here; but take my advice, eat no food and drink no wine, and you will be safe; and mind, also, that you express no surprise at anything you see; and take no more than five golden guineas, though you may be offered fifty or a hundred, as your fee.'

'Thank you, madam,' said the doctor, 'I shall obey you in all things.'

With this the gentleman came into the room, grand and noble as a prince, and then he took up the child, looked at it and laid it again on the bed.

Now there was a large fire in the room, and the gentleman took the fire shovel and drew all the burning coal to the front, leaving a great space at the back of the grate; then he took up the child again and laid it in the hollow at the back of the fire and drew all the coal over it till it was covered; but, mindful of the lady's advice, the doctor said never a word. Then the room suddenly changed to another still more beautiful, where a grand feast was laid out, of all sorts of meats and fair fruits and bright red wine in cups of sparkling crystal.

'Now, doctor,' said the gentleman, 'sit down with us and take what best pleases you.'

'Sir,' said the doctor, 'I have made a vow neither to eat nor drink till I reach my home again. So please let me return without further delay.'

'Certainly,' said the gentleman, 'but first let me pay you for your trouble,' and he laid down a bag of gold on the table and poured out a quantity of bright pieces.

'I shall only take what is my right and no more,' said the doctor, and he drew over five golden guineas, and placed them in his purse. 'And now, may I have the carriage to convey me back, for it is growing late?'

On this the gentleman laughed. 'You have been learning secrets from my lady,' he said. 'However, you have behaved right well, and you shall be brought back safely.'

So the carriage came, and the doctor took his cane, and was carried back as the first time through the water – horses, carriage, and all – and so on till he reached his home all right just before daybreak. But when he opened his purse to take out the golden guineas, there he saw a splendid diamond ring along with them in the purse worth a king's ransom, and when he examined it he found the two letters of his own name carved inside. So he knew it was meant for him, a present from the fairy prince himself.

All this happened a hundred years ago, but the ring still remains in the doctor's family, handed down from father to son, and it is remarked, that whoever wears it as the owner for the time has good luck and honour and wealth all the days of his life.

'And by the light that shines, this story is true,' added the narrator of the tale, using the strong form of asseveration by which the Irish-speaking peasants emphasize the truth of their words.

Don. The Welsh goddess Don was the equivalent of the Irish goddess DANA, and it seems likely that she was an immigrant from Ireland, for the Children of Don correspond closely in character and functions to the Children of Dana. Govannan the smith was the British equivalent of the Irish Gobniu, Ludd or Nudd of Nuada, for both had silver hands and GWYDION was a many-skilled god like LUG. The Children of Don were in frequent conflict with the Children of LLYR, who were the British equivalents of the Irish Children of Lir.

Dooinney-Oie (*dunya-oi*), **or the 'Night-Man'.** A kindly spirit who gave warnings of storm, sometimes by a voice shouting, sometimes by a misty appearance of a man who spoke and gave warning, and sometimes by the blowing of a horn, which must have sounded rather like a Swiss alpen-horn. Gill mentions the Dooinney-Oie in *A Second Manx Scrapbook* (p. 246), and gives a longer account of various warnings received in *A Manx Scrapbook* (pp. 241–4) without mentioning the Dooinney-Oie by name. An amusing story of a Dooinney-Oie who got too fond of playing his horn is told in Dora Broome's *Fairy Tales from the Isle of Man*. HOWLAA seems almost indistinguishable from Dooinney-Oie, except that he never speaks, but only howls before storms.

Dooinney Marrey. See DINNY-MARA.

Doonie. A Scottish variant of the Northumberland DUNNIE. Like the Dunnie, the Doonie appeared in the form of a pony, but often as an old man or woman. It was far more benevolent than the Dunnie; the stories about it are of guidance or rescue. Hannah Aitken quotes one published in the *Gallovidian Annual* (vol. v, 1903) in which a school-boy, climbing the steep rock that overhangs Crichope Linn in Dumfriesshire to take young rock-doves, slipped, and fell right down the precipice. He caught hold of a hazel bush, but it only gave him a few moments' grace. He looked down to see if he would be drowned in the Linn or dashed to pieces on the rocks – there seemed no other choice – when he saw a strange old woman standing on a ledge some way beneath him, who held out her apron and told him to jump into it. He jumped, for he had no choice. The apron gave way and he fell into the Linn, but as he rose to the surface the old woman pulled him out by the scruff of his neck, and led him to safety by a hidden path which he never found again. Then she told him to get home and never to harry the doves again, 'Or maybe,' she said, 'the Doonie'll no be here tae kep ye.' With that she was gone.

Double, or Doppelgänger. See CO-WALKER.

Dragons. The dragon slain by St George was an heraldic dragon, with bat's wings, a sting in its tail and fiery breath. We find it in some of the English fairy-tales, and it is to be seen in church carvings and in many of the Italian pictures of St George, such as the Carpaccio painting, where the dragon is pathetically small. Most of the British dragons, however, are WORMS after the Scandinavian pattern, wingless, generally very long, with a poisonous rather than a fiery breath and self-joining. Nearly all the Celtic dragons are worms. Worms and dragons have some traits in common. Both are scaly, both haunt wells or pools, both are avid for maidens and particularly princesses, both are treasure-hoarders and are extremely hard to kill. It seems as if the model on which both are founded is the fossilized remains of prehistoric monsters.

In England there are legends of a few winged, fiery dragons, the

Dragon of Kingston, for instance, who 'cooked his meat to a turn' according to the tradition picked up by Ruth Tongue in 1911 from Cothelstone harvesters and recorded in *County Folk-Lore* (vol. VIII, pp. 129–30). He was choked by a great boulder rolled down the ridge into his mouth as he opened it to belch out flames. The Dragon of Wantley was a true dragon, typical in his attributes, behaviour and the method of killing him, though this was also used against worms. A condensed version of the rhymed account given by Harland and Wilkinson in *Legends and Traditions of Lancashire* (pp. 265–70) is representative. One item worth noting is the anointing of the champion by a black-haired maiden, for maidens played a large part in the dragon legends:

> This dragon was the terror of all the countryside. He had forty-four iron teeth, and a long sting in his tail, besides his strong rough hide and fearful wings.
>
> He ate trees and cattle, and once he ate three young children at one meal. Fire breathed from his nostrils, and for long no man dared come near him.
>
> Near to the dragon's den lived a strange knight named More of More Hall, of whom it was said that so great was his strength that he had once seized a horse by its mane and tail, and swung it round and round till it was dead, because it had angered him.

Then, said the tale, he had eaten the horse, all except its head. At last the people of the place came to More Hall in a body, and with tears implored the knight to free them from the fearful monster, which was devouring all their food, and making them go in terror of their lives. They offered him all their remaining goods if he would do them this service. But the knight said he wanted nothing except one black-haired maid of sixteen, to anoint him for the battle at night, and array him in his armour in the morning. When this was promised, he went to Sheffield, and found a smith who made him a suit of armour set all over with iron spikes, each five or six inches in length.

Then he hid in a well, where the dragon used to drink, and as it stooped to the water, the knight put up his head with a shout and struck it a great blow full in the face. But the dragon was upon him, hardly checked by the blow, and for two days and a night they fought without either inflicting a wound upon the other. At last, as the dragon flung himself at More with the intention of tossing him high into the air, More succeeded in planting a kick in the middle of its back. This was the vital spot: the iron spike drove into the monster's flesh so far, that it spun round and round in agony groaning and roaring fearfully, but in a few minutes all was over, it collapsed into a helpless heap, and died.

The Serpent of Handale in Yorkshire seems to have been half-way between a serpent and a dragon, for it had fiery breath and a venomous sting. It was a devourer of maidens, and a young man called Scaw killed it to rescue an earl's daughter.

The dragon who haunted Winlatter Rock in Derbyshire was said to be the Devil himself, taking that form, and was driven off by a monk who planted himself on the rock with his arms outstretched in the shape of a CROSS. So great was his concentration that his feet sank deep into the rock and left the impression of two holes there. In the second part of the tale, a concerted effort of the neighbouring villagers drove off the dragon. He sought refuge down Blue John Mine and the Derbyshire springs have tasted sulphurous and warm ever since.

Drayton, Michael (1563–1631). See DIMINUTIVE FAIRIES.

Dress and appearance of the fairies. The FAIRIES of Britain vary as much in dress as they do in appearance and SIZE. Most people, asked off-hand about the colour of the fairies' clothes, would answer 'green' without hesitation, and they would not be far astray. Green is generally acknowledged to be the fairy colour, particularly in Celtic countries, and for this reason is so unlucky that many Scotswomen refuse to wear green at all. Red runs green very close, and in Ireland the small TROOPING FAIRIES, the DAOINE SIDH and the SHEFRO, wear green coats and red caps while the SOLITARY FAIRIES, such as the LEPRACAUNS, the CLURICAUN and the FEAR DEARG, generally wear red. William Allingham describes

> Wee folk, good folk, trooping all together,
> Green jacket, red cap and white owl's feather.

This seems to be a typical costume of the small trooping fairies. The LIL' FELLAS of Man, about three feet in height, are described by Sophia Morrison as wearing green coats and red caps, or occasionally leather ones on hunting expeditions. Their hunting dogs were of all fancy colours, green, blue, red. Red caps were very common for all kinds of the homelier fairies. Even the MERROW in Crofton CROKER's story wore a red cap to enable him to go through the sea to a dry land under it, and gave a similar one to his human friend, which had to be thrown back when he returned to land. Red, blue and white caps were used in various stories of FAIRY LEVITATION. GRIGS, little South Country fairies, wore red caps. A CLURICAUNE of the ABBEY LUBBER type is described by Crofton Croker as wearing a red nightcap, a leather apron, long light-blue stockings and high-heeled, buckled shoes. Even the mourners at the FAIRY FUNERAL in Bowker's *Goblin Tales of Lancashire*, though they were sombrely clad otherwise, wore bright red caps. The green-clad fairy ladies enjoyed a touch of red as much as the fairy men, but they introduced it in their slippers, like the little lady in 'The Fairies of Merlin's Crag' from Gibbings's *Folk-Lore and Legends, Scotland* who was eighteen inches high, with long GOLDEN HAIR hanging to her waist, a long green dress and red slippers. The tiny fairy gentleman who wooed Anne JEFFERIES was too much of a dandy to wear a red cap, but he brightened his green clothing by a red feather in his hat. In Somerset the fairies are said to wear red, and the rougher PIXIES green. This is the opposite way round to the Irish colour scheme. ELVES wear green. Many of the Green Ladies of Scotland were connected with the dead, and so naturally wore green, for green is the Celtic colour of death. The SILKIES of the North of England generally wore glistening white silk, the WHITE LADIES of Man wore white satin, and the TYLWYTH TEG of Wales wore white. Isobel Gowdie, the self-confessed witch who gave a vivid account of her TRAFFIC WITH THE FAIRIES, described the Fairy Queen rather prosaically: 'The Qwein of Fearrie is brawlie clothed in whyt linens, and in whyt and browne cloathes.' A Fairy Queen whose visit to a Galloway cottage is described in J. F. CAMPBELL's *Popular Tales of the West Highlands* (vol. II, pp. 67–8) was more glamorous:

> She was very magnificently attired; her dress was of the richest green, embroidered round with spangles of gold, and on her head was a small coronet of pearls. . . One of the children put out her hand to get hold of the grand lady's spangles, but told her mother afterwards that she felt nothing.

This magnificent vision came on a prosaic errand; she wanted to borrow a bowl of oatmeal. In the Celtic legend of ST COLLEN AND THE FAIRY KING, blue is introduced with red; the king's pages wear liveries of scarlet and blue, impolitely denounced by the saint as, 'Blue for the eternal cold and red for the flames of hell.' Manx fairies sometimes wore blue. In Gill's *Second Manx Scrapbook* (p. 248) we are told of a little gnomish man seen between Ramsey and Milntown, about two feet high,

> wearing a red cap and a long blue coat with bright buttons, white hair and bushy whiskers. Face very wrinkled. Very bright, very kind eyes, carrying a small but very bright lantern.

In Jenkinson's *Guide to the Isle of Man, 1876* (p. 75) he reports being told by a farmer's wife that her mother always maintained that she had actually seen the fairies, and described them as young girls with 'scaly, fish-like hands and blue dresses'. The little mouse-sized fairies in the Suffolk story of BROTHER MIKE wore blue coats, yellow breeches and little red caps. The fairies described by a friend to Walter Gill as seen in Glen Aldyn were greyish all over, something the colour of a fungus, a foot to eighteen inches high. The earth-bound TROW in Shetland was also grey. A sombre note is struck too in Hugh Miller's account in *The Old Red Sandstone* of the DEPARTURE OF THE FAIRIES: the horses 'shaggy diminutive things, speckled dun and grey, the riders stunted, misgrown, ugly creatures, attired in antique jerkins of plaid, long grey cloaks, and little red caps, from which their wild, uncombed locks shot out over their cheeks and foreheads'. This confirms KIRK's much earlier statement that the fairies wore the costume of their country, as tartan in the Highlands.

John Beaumont's fairies, whose visits to him he describes in *A Treatise of Spirits* (1705), were dressed in a most unusual fashion:

> They had both black, loose Network Gowns, tied with a black sash about their Middles, and within the Network appear'd a Gown of a Golden Colour, with somewhat of a Light striking through it; their Heads were not dressed with Topknots, but they had white Linnen Caps on, with lace about three Fingers breadth, and over it they had a Black loose Network Hood.

A rather engaging dress on little people of three feet high, but not at all the kind of costume one would expect to see on a fairy.

There were other eccentric costumes. The GUNNA, a Highland fairy boy who had been banished from the court, wore fox skins; the kind, solitary GHILLIE DHU dressed in leaves and green moss; the sinister Northumbrian DUERGAR wore a coat made of lambskin, trousers and shoes of moleskins and a hat of green moss decorated with a pheasant's feather. The BROWN MAN OF THE MUIRS wore clothes of withered bracken. In the more literary descriptions of fairies from the 16th century onwards, they are said to wear clothes made of flowers, of gossamer spangled with dew and of silvery gauze, but these clothes are not so often found in the traditional accounts, though we can quote the foxglove caps of the Shefro. Beyond these there are a number of fairies of all kinds who were naked. The ASRAI, the water-spirits, were beautiful, slender and naked, only covered by their long hair. Many of the nymph-like fairies danced naked in their rounds, as the witches were said to do, a fashion imitated by the modern witches. Many of the HOBGOBLINS were naked. BROWNIES generally wore ragged clothes, but other hobgoblins were often hairy and naked. The FENODEREE is one of these hairy monsters. There is LOB-LIE-BY-THE-FIRE, HOB, OR HOBTHRUST, the BOGAN, and the URISG who was like a satyr in shape. The Shetland BROONIE 'King of the Trows' was presumably naked, since he was laid by a gift of clothing. One naked little hobgoblin, however, was not shaggy, if we may trust his own pathetic description of himself:

> 'Little pixie, fair and slim,
> Not a rag to cover him.'

It is no wonder that that lament called forth the gift of clothing that laid him, but he did not go weeping away like the GROGACH of Man, but ran away merrily, as Mrs Bray tells us, chanting:

> 'Pixy fine, Pixy gay!
> Pixy now will run away.'

Some fairies wore clothes indistinguishable from those of mortals, fine and fashionable like those of Cherry's Master in the tale CHERRY OF ZENNOR, or homely and old-fashioned; or sometimes archaic, like the costume of the market people seen at the FAIRY MARKET at Blackdown:

> Those that had occasion to travel that way, have frequently seen them there, appearing like Men and Women of a stature generally near the smaller size of Men; their habits used to be of red, blew or green, according to the old way of Country Garb, with high crown'd hats.

The descriptions I have given of fairy clothing and appearance have not dealt with those skilled in SHAPE-SHIFTING, who can change their size and appearance at will, nor do they make allowance for the power of GLAMOUR possessed by most of the fairies, which can only be penetrated by the use of the FAIRY OINTMENT, or a FOUR-LEAFED CLOVER.

Droll, or droll-teller. See WANDERING DROLL-TELLER.

Duergar. These are rather vaguely described in *Northumberland Words* as 'the worst and most malicious order of fairies'. In other words, the UNSEELIE COURT, or rather, some obscure members of it, for in the

Highlands the SLUAGH or Host makes up the most numerous part of the Unseelie Court. Duergars are the Black DWARFS of the North of England, always full of malice and the enemies of mankind. They are mostly SOLITARY FAIRIES. A representative story about a duergar is told in F. Grice's *Folk-Tales of the North Country*. It is set in the Simonside Hills of Northumberland. A stranger, making his way to Rothbury, lost himself on the hills and was overtaken by darkness. He knew no landmarks to guide him and the ground was very treacherous, so he decided that the only thing to do was to shelter for the night under a rock and wait till morning. But as he came up to the rock he saw a faint light at a little distance, and when he had fumbled his way towards it he found that the light came from a small smouldering fire inside a rough stone hut, such as the shepherds build for shelter. There were two grey stones on each side of the fire, to the right of which was a pile of kindling and to the left two great logs. There was no one there. The traveller went in with a thankful heart, for he might well have died of exposure on the hillside, revived the fire with some of the kindling and sat down on the right-hand stone. He was hardly seated when the door burst open and a strange figure came into the room. He was a dwarf, no higher than the traveller's knee, but broad and strong. His coat was made of lambskin, his trousers and shoes of moleskins, his hat of green moss, decorated with a pheasant's feather. He scowled at the traveller, but said not a word, stumped past him and perched himself on the other stone. The traveller did not dare to speak first, for he guessed that this was a duergar, and bitterly hostile to men. So they sat staring at each other across the fire, which began to die down. It grew bitterly cold, and at last the traveller could bear it no longer, and put some more kindling on the fire. The dwarf looked at him with anger and disdain, leaned back and picked up one of the two great logs. It was twice as long as he was and thicker than his body, but he broke it across his knee as if it had been matchwood and wagged his head at the traveller as much as to say, 'Why can't you do the like?' The fire blazed up for a time, but soon it began to die down. The kindling was all spent. And the dwarf looked at the traveller as if to challenge him to put on the last log. The traveller thought there was some catch in it, and did nothing. The fire faded out and they sat on in cold darkness. Then in the far distance a cock crew and a faint light showed in the sky. At the sound the dwarf vanished, and the hut and fire with him. The traveller was still sitting on his stone, but it was the topmost peak of a steep crag. If he had moved to the left to pick up the log in answer to the duergar's silent challenge, he would have fallen into the deep ravine and there would have been nothing left of him but broken bones.

[Motif: F451.5.2]

Dun cow of Kirkham. Harland and Wilkinson, in their *Legends and Traditions of Lancashire* (p. 16), give the story of 'The Dun Cow and the Old Rib', a slightly humorous version of a legend which is to be found both in Wales and Ireland. The Lancashire legend is of a great dun cow which wandered over the Lancashire moors and freely allowed herself to be milked by all who came. However many there were their pails were always filled, until one day a malicious Lancashire witch set up a sieve and milked the cow into it. She milked all day and the sieve, which had an open mesh, was never filled. At evening the cow died, exhausted by her efforts. The size of the cow can be judged by an enormous rib, which once belonged to a whale, set up over the doorway of an old fortified farmhouse, called 'The Old Rib', in the parish of Kirkham. Though a jocular turn is given to this version of the tale, it is part of an ancient tradition of a heavenly cow which appeared in a time of famine and fed all who needed it until it was destroyed by man's greed or malice. John Rhys gives the Welsh version of the legend.

Lastly, let me add a reference to the *Iolo Manuscripts*, pp. 85, 475, where a short story is given concerning a certain Milkwhite Sweet-milk Cow (*y Fuwch Laethwen Lefrith*) whose milk was so abundant and possessed of such virtues as almost to rival the Holy Grail. Like the Holy Grail also this cow wandered everywhere spreading plenty, until she chanced to come to the Vale of Towy, where the foolish inhabitants wished to kill and eat her: the result was that she vanished in their hands and has never since been heard of.

An even closer parallel is the legend of GLASGAVLEN, the supernatural cow of Ireland, which presented herself before every door to be milked, until an avaricious woman, to obtain more than her pailful, milked her into a sieve, when she left Ireland for ever.
[Motif: B184.2.2.2]

'Dun Cow of Mac Brandy's Thicket, The'. There was a man called Mackenzie who was one of the tenants of Oonich in Lochaber, and after a time it happened that every night his cattle-fold was broken down and the cattle grazed through his cornfield. He was sure that it was neither the neighbours nor the cattle who were responsible, and concluded that it must be the FAIRIES, so he fetched his brother, the one-eyed ferryman – who had the second sight – to watch with him. Late in the night they heard a sound as of stakes being pulled up, and the one-eyed ferryman, moving quietly towards the far side of the fold, saw a dun, polled cow throwing the stakes aside and butting the cattle to their feet. She then drove them through the broken fence into the cornfield. The One-Eyed Ferryman followed her silently, and saw her go up to the Fairy Knoll of Derry Mac Brandy. The knoll opened before her and she went in. The ferryman hastened after her in time to stick his dirk into the turf at the door, so that it would not shut. The light streamed out of the knoll and he saw everything. In the centre of the knoll sat a circle of big old grey men round a fire on which a cauldron was burning. By this time the farmer had come up, but could see nothing until he put his foot on his brother's foot and then the whole scene was clear to him, and he was very much alarmed, and wanted to go away. But the Ferryman called out in a loud voice: 'If your dun cow ever troubles Oonich fold again, I will take everything out of the knoll, and throw it out on Rudha na h-Oitire.' With that he pulled out the dirk and the door shut itself. They went down home, and the dun polled cow never troubled them again.

This tale is to be found in MacDougall and Calder's *Folk Tales and Fairy Lore* (pp. 280–83). It is an unusual example of a mischievous fairy cow. Fairy bulls, like those of the CRODH MARA, may occasionally be formidable, but the cows are generally gentle and fortunate to a herd.

Dunnie. Good accounts of the Northumbrian Dunnie can be found both in the DENHAM TRACTS (vol. II, pp. 157–9), and in Henderson's *Folk-Lore of the Northern Counties* (p. 263). According to Denham, the Dunnie is an individual spirit, from Hazelrigg on Belford Moor. It is surmised that he was originally the ghost of a Border reiver, who was caught and killed robbing a granary. He had a considerable amount of plunder hidden in one of the caves in a crag called Bowden Doors, and he died without disclosing it, which is one of the prime reasons for haunting. The rhyme which he was in the habit of reciting, and which is given by Henderson, certainly bears out this assumption:

> 'Cocken heugh there's gear enough,
>   Collier heugh there's mair,
> For I've lost the key o' the Bounders,
>   An' I'm ruined for evermair.'

But if he is a ghost he has all the SHAPE-SHIFTING powers and the practical-joking tastes of the regular GOBLIN, the PICKTREE BRAG, the HEDLEY KOW and others of their tribe. A favourite form he took was that of a horse, though Mrs Balfour in *County Folk-Lore* (vol. IV, p. 14) seems to have come across him more often as a donkey. He would assume the form of the farmer's own horse, and one of his favourite times to play pranks was when the farmer rode to fetch a midwife. He would carry the farmer to fetch the midwife prosperously enough, but on the way back after the birth he would slip from under them with a loud whicker, dropping them in the stream. Or he would pretend to be the ploughman's steady old plough-horse, allow himself to be harnessed, led out and hitched to the plough, and then suddenly disappear, leaving his harness fallen to the ground, and be seen galloping and plunging away into the distance. He seemed sometimes to be seen in semi-human form, for a crag above one of the quarries was shown as a favourite spot for him to sit through the night dangling his legs over the cliff. Even in 1870, however, he was spoken of in the past rather than in the present.

1. Arthur Rackham: 'Butter is made from the roots of old trees'

2. Arthur Rackham: 'A band of workmen, who were sawing down a toadstool, rushed away, leaving their tools behind them'

3. Henry Fuseli: Cobweb

4. Henry Fuseli: 'Oberon Squeezes a Flower on Titania's Eyelids'

5. Richard Dadd: 'Come unto these yellow sands'

6. John Anster Fitzgerald: The Chase of the White Mice

7. Richard Dadd: Bacchanalian Scene

8. John Anster Fitzgerald: Fairy Gifts

9. Richard Doyle: A Fairy Celebration

10. Richard Doyle: The Fairy Tree

11. J. Simmons: A Fairy

12. J. Simmons: A Midsummer Night's Dream

Dunters. These Border spirits, also called POWRIES, like the more sinister REDCAPS inhabit old peel-towers and Border keeps. They make a constant noise, like beating flax or grinding barley in a hollow stone quern. William Henderson mentions them in *Folk-Lore of the Northern Counties* (pp. 255–6) and says that if the sound gets louder it is an omen of death or misfortune. He mentions that the foundation of these towers, supposed to have been built by the Picts, were according to tradition sprinkled with blood as a foundation sacrifice. The suggestion is that dunters and redcaps were the spirits of the original foundation sacrifices, whether human or animal.

Dwarfs. Germany is the great home of dwarfs, and the Isle of Rügen has dwarfs both black and white. The Swiss mountains are also the homes of dwarfs, but though there are many stunted and grotesque figures in English fairy-lore, it is doubtful if they were ever explicitly called 'dwarfs'. The best candidates for the name would be the pygmy king and his followers who accosted KING HERLA in Walter Mapes's story in his *De Nugis Curialium*; but he is described as more like a satyr; the SPRIGGANS of Cornwall are small and grotesque and travel in troops like some of the German dwarfs, but they are never so called. There are more SOLITARY FAIRIES of the dwarfish kind, such as the 'wee, wee man' of one of the Child ballads (No. 38), who is stunted and grotesque and of great strength. His description is anticipated in a 14th-century poem quoted in the Appendix to No. 38. The nearest approach to a black dwarf is the North Country DUERGAR, and the BROWN MAN OF THE MUIRS is like him. Dwarfs are often mentioned as attendants on ladies in Arthurian legends, but these ladies hover so much between a fairy and a mortal estate that their attendants are equally nebulous. On the whole it is best, as KIRK would say, to 'leave it to conjecture as we found it'.

[Motif: F451]

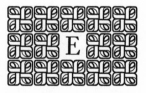

Each Uisce (*agh-iski*). See AUGHISKY.

Each Uisge (*ech-ooshkya*). This, the Highland WATER-HORSE, is perhaps the fiercest and most dangerous of all the water-horses, although the CABYLL USHTEY runs it close. It differs from the KELPIE in haunting the sea and lochs, while the Kelpie belongs to running water. It seems also to transform itself more readily. Its most usual form is that of a sleek and handsome horse, which almost offers itself to be ridden, but if anyone is so rash as to mount it, he is carried at headlong speed into the lake and devoured. Only his liver is rejected, and floats to shore. It is said that its skin is adhesive, and the rider cannot tear himself off it. It also appears sometimes as a gigantic bird and sometimes as a handsome young man. (For a story about this transformation, see CRODH MARA.) J. F. CAMPBELL has a long passage devoted to the Each Uisge in *Popular Tales of the West Highlands* (vol. IV, pp. 304–7). When we come to Each Uisge in his horse form, it is hard to select among the stories about him. A wide-spread tale which is possibly cautionary in origin is of several little girls being carried away by him. A good version is told of a small lochan near Aberfeldy. Seven little girls and a little boy were going for a walk on a Sunday afternoon when they saw a pretty little pony grazing beside the loch. One of the little girls mounted him, and then another and another until all seven were seated on his back. The little boy was more canny, and he noticed that the pony grew longer to accommodate each new rider. So he took refuge among the high rough rocks at the end of the loch. Suddenly the pony turned its head and noticed him. 'Come on little scabby-head,' it cried, 'get on my back!' The boy stayed in shelter and the pony rushed towards him, the little girls screaming, but unable to pull their hands from its back. To and fro they dodged among the rocks, but the pony could not reach the boy, and at length it tired of trying, and plunged into the loch with its sevenfold prey on its back. Next morning the livers of the seven children were washed up on the shore.

The tale of the killing of a water-horse is told in McKay's *More West Highland Tales* (vol. II). There was a smith in Raasay. He had a herd of cattle and his own family herded it. One night his daughter did not return, and in the morning they found her heart and lungs on the loch side known to be haunted by the Each Uisge. The smith was heartbroken, and determined to destroy the monster. He set up a forge by the loch and he and his boy forged great iron hooks and made them red-hot in the fire. They roasted a sheep on the fire and the scent of it went out over the water. A steaming mist arose, and the water-horse, like an ugly, shaggy yearling, rose out of the loch. It seized the sheep and they grappled it with the hooks and killed it there. But in the morning there were no bones nor hide, only a heap of what looked like star-shine. (Star-shine is a jelly-like substance found on the shore, probably the remnants of stranded jellyfish, but supposed by the Highlanders to be all that is left of a fallen star.) And that was the end of the Water-Horse of Raasay. A similar story is told by Walter Gill of the Cabyll Ushtey.

[Motifs: B184.1.3; F401.3.1; F420.1.3.3; G302.3.2; G303.3.3.1.3]

Eairkyn Sonney. See ARKAN SONNEY.

Early fairy anecdotes. For an account of early fairy anecdotes, see under MEDIEVAL CHRONICLES. See also articles on GEOFFREY OF MONMOUTH, GERVASE OF TILBURY and GIRALDUS CAMBRENSIS; and ELIDOR AND THE GOLDEN BALL, the GREEN CHILDREN, KING HERLA and WILD EDRIC.

Eilian of Garth Dorwen. Eilian was the name of the golden-haired maidservant who used to spin with the TYLWYTH TEG on moonlight nights and at last went to live with them. The tale – from *Celtic Folklore* by John Rhys – is told in full in MIDWIFE TO THE FAIRIES. It is a tale of particular interest, for not only does it widen the scope of the fairy midwife tale by showing that the patient to be attended was a human CAPTIVE IN FAIRYLAND and that the child to be anointed was half-human, but is also a variation of the story of the FAIRIES as spinners and shows the importance they assigned to GOLDEN HAIR. It is of interest also that the field where Eilian was last seen was long called 'Eilian's Field', or 'The Maid's Meadow'.

[Motifs: F300; F301.3]

Elaby Gathen. Name of a fairy contained in magicians' spells in the 17th century. See SPELLS TO OBTAIN POWER OVER FAIRIES.

Elder tree. See OLD LADY OF THE ELDER TREE.

Elf-bull, the. Jamieson's *Northern Antiquities* gives the story of the most famous of the CRODH MARA, the cow bred by the visit of a water-bull and of the farmer too mean for gratitude:

The elf-bull is small, compared with earthly bulls, of a mouse-colour; *mosted* [crop-eared], with short *corky* horns; short in the legs; long, round, and *slamp* [supple] in the body, like a wild animal; with short, sleek, and glittering hair, like an otter; and supernaturally active and strong. They most frequently appear near the banks of rivers; eat much green corn in the night-time; and are only to be got rid of by, etc., etc. (*certain spells which I have forgot*).

A certain farmer who lived by the banks of a river, had a cow that was never known to admit an earthly bull; but every year, in a certain day in the month of May, she regularly quitted her pasture, walked slowly along the banks of the river, till she came opposite to a small holm covered with bushes; then entered the river, and waded or swam to the holm, where she continued for a certain time, after which she again returned to her pasture. This went on for several years, and every year, after the usual time of gestation, she had a calf. They were all alike, mouse-coloured, mosted, with corky horns, round and long-bodied, grew to a good size, and were remarkably docile, strong, and useful, and all ridgels. At last, one forenoon, about Martinmas, when

the corn was all 'under thack and raip', as the farmer sat with his
family by the *ingleside*, they began to talk about killing their *Yule-Mart*.
'Hawkie,' said the gudeman, 'is fat and sleek; she has had an easy life,
and a good goe of it all her days, and has been a good cow to us; for she
has filled the plough and all the stalls in the *byre* with the finest steers
in this country side; and now I think we may afford to pick her old
bones, and so she shall be the *Mart*.'

The words were scarcely uttered, when Hawkie, who was in the byre
beyond the *hallan*, with her whole bairn-time, tyed by their *thrammels* to
their stalls, walked out through the side of the byre with as much ease
as if it had been made of brown paper; turned round on the midding-
head; lowed once upon each of her calves; then set out, they following
her in order, each according to his age, along the banks of the river;
entered it; reached the holm; disappeared among the bushes; and
neither she nor they were ever after seen or heard of. The farmer and
his sons, who had with wonder and terror viewed this phenomenon
from a distance, returned with heavy hearts to their house, and had
little thought of Marts or merriment for that year.

[Type: ML6060]

Elf-shot. Illness or disability attributed to a STROKE from one of the
flint arrow-heads to be found in downland country. Isobel Gowdie, the
Scottish witch who claimed collusion with the FAIRIES, in her strange
voluntary confession said that she visited the elf-hills and saw the boss-
backed elf-boys shaping and dighting the arrows under the direction of
the Devil. The witches were given them to take on their devil-accom-
panied rides through the air, to flip at any passing people or cattle. They
generally appeared to be remarkably bad shots. See BLIGHTS AND
ILLNESSES ATTRIBUTED TO THE FAIRIES.

[Motif: D2066]

Elidor and the golden ball. GIRALDUS CAMBRENSIS in *Itinerarium
Cambriae*, the account of his journey through Wales in 1188, gives a
remarkable narrative of a boy's visit to Fairyland, the translation of
which by R. C. Hoare is included by KEIGHTLEY in his *Fairy Mythology*
(pp. 404–6). It contains so much information in so short a space that it
deserves to be included in full. It is one of the best of the EARLY FAIRY
ANECDOTES:

A short time before our days, a circumstance worthy of note occurred
in these parts, which Elidurus, a priest, most strenuously affirmed had
befallen himself. When he was a youth of twelve years, – since, as
Solomon says, 'The root of learning is bitter, although the fruit is
sweet,' – and was following his literary pursuits, in order to avoid the

discipline and frequent stripes inflicted on him by his preceptor, he ran away, and concealed himself under the hollow bank of a river; and, after fasting in that situation for two days, two little men of pygmy stature appeared to him, saying, 'If you will come with us, we will lead you into a country full of delights and sports.' Assenting, and rising up, he followed his guides through a path, at first subterraneous and dark, into a most beautiful country, adorned with rivers and meadows, woods and plains, but obscure, and not illuminated with the full light of the sun. All the days were cloudy, and the nights extremely dark, on account of the absence of the moon and stars. The boy was brought before the king, and introduced to him in the presence of the court; when, having examined him for a long time, he delivered him to his son, who was then a boy. These men were of the smallest stature, but very well proportioned for their size. They were all fair-haired, with luxuriant hair falling over their shoulders, like that of women. They had horses proportioned to themselves, of the size of greyhounds. They neither ate flesh nor fish, but lived on milk diet, made up into messes with saffron. They never took an oath, for they detested nothing so much as lies. As often as they returned from our upper hemisphere, they reprobated our ambition, infidelities, and inconstancies. They had no religious worship, being only, as it seems, strict lovers and reverers of truth.

The boy frequently returned to our hemisphere, sometimes by the way he had first gone, sometimes by another; at first in company with others, and afterwards alone, and confided his secret only to his mother, declaring to her the manners, nature, and state of that people. Being desired by her to bring a present of gold, with which that region abounded, he stole, while at play with the king's son, the golden ball with which he used to divert himself, and brought it to his mother in great haste; and when he reached the door of his father's house, but not unpursued, and was entering it in a great hurry, his foot stumbled on the threshold, and, falling down into the room where his mother was sitting, the two Pygmies seized the ball, which had dropped from his hand, and departed, spitting at and deriding the boy. On recovering from his fall, confounded with shame, and execrating the evil counsel of his mother, he returned by the usual track to the subterraneous road, but found no appearance of any passage, though he searched for it on the banks of the river for nearly the space of a year. Having been brought back by his friends and mother, and restored to his right way of thinking and his literary pursuits, he attained in process of time the rank of priesthood. Whenever David the Second, bishop of St David's, talked to him in his advanced state of life concerning this event, he could never relate the particulars without shedding tears.

He had also a knowledge of the language of that nation, and used to recite words of it he had readily acquired in his younger days. These words, which the bishop often repeated to me, were very conformable to the Greek idiom. When they asked for water, they said, *Udor udorum*, which signifies 'Bring water;' for Udor, in their language, as well as in the Greek, signifies water. When they want salt, they say, *Halgein udorum*, 'Bring salt.' Salt is called a'λς in Greek, and Halen in British; for that language, from the length of time which the Britons (then called Trojans, and afterwards Britons from Brito, their leader) remained in Greece after the destruction of Troy, became, in many instances, similar to the Greek.

[Motif: F370]

Elidurus. See ELIDOR.

Elizabethan fairies. The FAIRIES OF THE MEDIEVAL ROMANCES grew out of the Celtic tradition of the HEROIC FAIRIES, the knights and ladies of the MABINOGION, the DAOINE SIDH who encountered the Milesians in love or battle; but the poets and dramatists of the Elizabethan age brought a different strand of fairy tradition into prominence. This was partly because the rise of the yeoman class, as the 16th century went on, had brought a spread of literacy and produced a new class of writers, drawn from the country up to town as Shakespeare was drawn, and bringing with them their own country traditions. The fairy ladies of the romances had become more humanized and sophisticated as time went on, and though SPENSER clung to them still, they were perhaps slightly out of date. Classical mythology was a perennial source of allusions familiar to every lettered man, even if he only came from a small-town grammar school. Still, there had been a good deal said and sung about Mars and Venus and naiads and dryads and nymphs; a new source of reference would be a welcome change, and it was at hand in the English countryside. There are two main types of FAIRIES which were novelties in literature: the HOBGOBLINS, with which we may rate the BROWNIE and the PUCK, and the small, flower-loving fairies such as we find pre-eminently in MIDSUMMER NIGHT'S DREAM and which became all the fashion for the JACOBEAN FAIRIES. These fairy writings came in towards the end of the century, in the hey-day of the drama.

Among the prose writers, Nashe in his *Terrors of the Night* gives us a characteristic picture of the hobgoblin type:

> The Robbin-good-fellowes, Elfes, Fairies, Hobgoblins of our latter age, which idolatrous former daies and the fantasticall world of Greece ycleaped *Fawnes, Satyres, Dryades,* & Hamadryades, did most of their merry prankes in the Night. Then ground they malt, and had hempen shirts for their labours, daunst in rounds in greene meadowes, pincht maids in their sleep that swept not their houses cleane, and led poore Travellers out of their way notoriously.

Here Nashe, with a journalist's eye, lights on most of the things which became most noteworthy in his period, the brownie labours and the gift of a shirt that brought them to an end, the DANCING in fairy rings, the love of order and NEATNESS and the punishment for untidy ways and the misleading of night wanderers.

Shakespeare puts in all of these, except the pinching, which is being forever mentioned in the masques and poems, but he adds the fairy smallness and their love of flowers, which were to become so characteristic of the Jacobean fairies. The Elizabethans struck a new note in literature there, though it was not new in tradition. It is to be found in GERVASE OF TILBURY and GIRALDUS CAMBRENSIS.

[Motifs: F239.4.3; F261.1.1; F482]

Ellylldan (*ethlerthldan*). The Welsh form of WILL·O' THE WISP, or JACKY LANTERN, or SPUNKIE, with a variety of names all over the country but only one activity: that of misleading night travellers into fens and bogs. They have not a monopoly of this sport, for PUCK, PWCA, and the Somerset PIXIES play exactly the same trick, though they are much more complex characters.

[Motifs: F200-399; F491; F491.1]

Ellyllon (*ethlerthlon*). This is the name given to the Welsh ELVES. According to Wirt Sikes in *British Goblins* (pp. 13-17) these are tiny, diaphanous fairies whose food is toadstools and 'fairy butter', a fungoid substance found in the roots of old trees and in limestone crevices. Their queen is MAB, and they are smaller than the TYLWYTH TEG. In a story which Sikes collected orally at Peterstone, near Cardiff, they appear less ethereal and more like the Somerset PIXIES. This is the tale of an unfortunate farmer named Rowli Pugh who seemed to be the butt of misfortune. If blight came anywhere, it fell on his crops; when all other cattle were flourishing, his were ailing. His wife was an invalid with no strength to do anything about the house or farm, and he was thinking sadly one day that he must sell up the farm and leave, when he was accosted by an ellyl who told him not to be troubled any longer, to tell his wife to leave a lighted candle and sweep the fire clean, and the Ellyllon would do the rest. The ellyl was as good as his word. Every night Rowli and Catti went early to bed leaving the coast clear, every night they heard laughter, merriment and bustle below them, and every morning farm stock and farmhouse were in apple-pie order. Rowli and Catti grew strong and sleek and crops and stock prospered. This went on for three years till Catti grew avid for a glimpse of the little people. One night she left her husband sound asleep, tiptoed downstairs and peeped through a crack of the door. There was the merry throng laughing, gambolling, working at top speed. Their merriment was so infectious that Catti burst out laughing too. At once the candle was blown out, there was a cry and a scamper, and all was quiet. The Ellyllon never came back to work at Pugh's Farm, but he had got into the way of prosperity and his ill-fortune did not return. A very similar story is told about the Somerset pixies. It is one of many stories about the INFRINGEMENT OF FAIRY PRIVACY.

Elves. Already in Scandinavian mythology the fairy people were elves and were divided into two classes, the light elves and the dark elves, like the Scottish SEELIE COURT and UNSEELIE COURT. The name came over into Britain, and in the Anglo-Saxon Leechdoms we find remedies against ELF-SHOT and other sinister elvish activities. The mythological light elves were not unlike the small TROOPING FAIRIES of England as we find them in Shakespeare's MIDSUMMER NIGHT'S DREAM and many common traditions. In Christian times the Scandinavians continued to believe in the elves, or huldre folk, who showed many of the same characteristics as the Scottish FAIRIES, both Highland and Lowland. They stole humans away, destroyed their cattle and avenged any injuries done to them. The huldre girls were beautiful and alluring, wearing grey dresses and white veils, but the DEFECT OF THE FAIRIES by which they could be recognized was their long cows' tails. A man who was dancing with a huldre girl saw her tail and realized what she was. He did not betray her, but only said, 'Pretty maid, you are losing your garter.' His tact was rewarded by perpetual prosperity. The defect of the Danish elves or ellewomen is that though they appeared beautiful and engaging from the front, they were hollow behind. The Danish elves were great thieves of dough and other human foods. In Lowland Scotland and in England the usage differed. In Scotland the fairy people of human size were often called elves and Fairyland was Elfame; in England it was the smaller trooping fairies who were called elves, and the name was particularly applied to small fairy boys. TITANIA's 'To make my small elves coats' is a typical example of the later use. 'Elf', however, was as unpopular with the fairies themselves as the tactless name of 'fairy', if we may judge from the rhyme given by Chambers in his *Popular Rhymes of Scotland* (p. 324):

> Gin ye ca' me imp or elf,
> I rede ye look weel to yourself;
> Gin ye ca' me fairy,
> I'll work ye muckle tarrie;
> Gin guid neibour ye ca' me,
> Then guid neibour I will be;
> But gin ye ca' me seelie wicht,
> I'll be your freend baith day and nicht.

[Motif: F200–399]

Endimion (Lyly). See DIMINUTIVE FAIRIES.

Eochaid (*ughy*). King of the FIRBOLGS when the TUATHA DE DANANN invaded Ireland. Firbolgs were a rougher, less magical people than the Tuatha de Danaan, but the two races spoke the same language and were able to agree on the same conventions of warfare. The Firbolgs were as the Titans to the Olympians, and, like the Titans, they were overthrown.

Etain (*aideen*). Etain of the TUATHA DE DANANN was the heroine of the great fairy love story, MIDHIR and Etain. It has inspired much poetry and drama, and is perhaps best known to English people through Fiona Macleod's fairy play, *The Immortal Hour*. The original story is well told by Lady Gregory in *Gods and Fighting Men*. Etain was the second wife of Midhir, the king of the Fairy Hill of Bri Leith. His first wife Fuamach was bitterly jealous, and with the help of the Druid Bresal Etarlaim, she finally contrived to turn Etain into a small fly and blew her away with a bitter blast into the mortal land of Ireland, where she was blown about in great misery for seven long years. But as for Fuamach, when her evil doings were known, ANGUS MAC OG, son of DAGDA, smote her head from her body.

After seven years of wretchedness, Etain was blown into the hall where Etar, of Inver Cechmaine, was feasting, and she fell down from the roof into the golden cup of Etar's wife, who swallowed her with the wine, and after nine months she was born as Etar's daughter, and was again named Etain, and she grew into the most beautiful woman in the length and breadth of Ireland. When she was grown Eochaid saw her and courted her, and took her back with him to Teamhair (Tara). But all this time Midhir knew where she was, and had once appeared to her though she did not remember him. At the wedding feast Eochaid's younger brother Ailell was suddenly smitten with a desperate love and longing for Etain. He suppressed it, but he pined and a deadly sickness fell on him. The king's doctor said it was love-longing, but he denied it. Eochaid became very anxious about him. The time came when Eochaid had to ride on his circuit over the whole of Ireland receiving homage from the tributory kings, and he committed Ailell to the care of Etain while he was away. Etain did all she could for Ailell, and she tried all she could to persuade him to tell her what it was that was bringing him down to the gates of death. At last she made out that it was unsatisfied love for her that ailed him. Then she was very sad, but she continued to do all that she could for him, but he only grew worse, until in the end it seemed to her that the only way was for her to yield to his longing, and she appointed to meet him very early next morning at a dun outside the town. Ailell was filled with rapture, and all night he lay sleepless, but at dawn a deep sleep fell on him and he did not go. But Etain rose early and went out to the dun. And at the time when she had appointed to meet Ailell she saw a man that looked like him walking up to her with pain and weakness, but when he came close she saw that it was not Ailell. They looked at each other in silence, and the man went away. Etain waited a little and then went back and found Ailell newly awakened and full of anger at himself. He told her how it had been, and she appointed to meet him next morning, but the same thing happened. And on the third morning she spoke to the strange man. 'You are not the man I have appointed to meet,' she said. 'And I have not come out for wantonness but to heal a man who is laid under sickness for my sake.'

'You would be better to come with me, for I was your first husband in the days that were long ago.' 'And what is your name?' she said. 'It is easy to tell that. I am Midhir of Bri Leith.' 'And how was it that I was taken from you?' 'Fuamach, my first wife, put a spell upon you and blew you out of the Land of TIR NAN OG. Will you come back with me, Etain?' But she said, 'I will not leave Eochaid, the High King, and go away with a stranger.' He said: 'It was I put the yearning upon Ailell, and it was I that put a spell on him that he could not come to you and your honour was saved.' She went back to Ailell and found that the yearning had left him and that he was healed. She told him all that had happened, and they were both rejoiced that they were saved from doing a treachery to Eochaid. Soon after Eochaid came back, and they told him all that had happened, and he gave great praise to Etain for her kindness to Ailell.

Midhir appeared once again to Etain in the likeness of the stranger she had seen when she was a girl. No one saw him or heard the song he sang praising the beauties of Tir Nan Og and begging her to come with him. She refused to leave Eochaid. 'If he renders you to me, will you come?' he said. 'If he does that I will come,' she answered, and he left her. Soon after this a stranger appeared to Eochaid and challenged him to three games of CHESS. They played for stakes, but, according to custom, the stakes were named by the winner after the game was won. Twice Eochaid won, and he set high stakes, the first a great tribute of horses and the second three tasks which it took all Midhir's fairy hosts to accomplish. The third time Midhir won and he asked for Eochaid's wife. Eochaid refused, and Midhir modified the demand for the right to put his arms round her and kiss her. Eochaid granted that and set the time of granting at the end of a month. At the end of that time Midhir appeared. Eochaid had drawn all his forces round him and secured the doors as soon as Midhir entered so that he should not carry her away. Midhir drew his sword with his left hand, put his right arm round her and kissed her. Then they rose together through the roof and the warriors rushing out saw two white swans flying over the Palace of Tara linked with a golden chain.

That was not the end of the story, for Eochaid could not rest without Etain, and after years of searching he tracked her to Bri Leith, and made war on the whole realm of fairy, and made great havoc there until at length Etain was restored to him. But the wrath of the Tuatha de Danaan rested on Eochaid and all his descendants because of the great harm they had wreaked upon the land of Tir Nan Og.

I have gone into this tale at some length as an example of the subtle and poetic treatment of the HEROIC FAIRY themes in the Irish legends. The challenge to games of chess occurs in many Celtic legends and fairy tales. The theme of metempsychosis or reincarnation occurs often in the early legends.

[Motifs: F68; F392 (variant)]

Ethna the Bride. Finvarra, or FIN BHEARA, the Irish fairy king who was also king of the dead, though he had a beautiful queen of his own, was amorous of mortal women, and any woman who was renowned for her beauty stood in special danger from him. Lady WILDE in her *Ancient Legends of Ireland* tells of one Ethna the Bride who was said to be the most beautiful woman then in Ireland and who was stolen by Finvarra. Ethna was newly married, and the young lord her husband was so proud of her beauty that he held festivities day after day. His castle was near the fairy hill which covered Finvarra's palace, but they had been long friends, and from time to time he set out offerings of wine to the fairy king, so he had no fear of him. Nevertheless one evening, as Ethna was floating through the dance, shining like moonlight in her silver dress, her hand slipped from her partner's and she fell to the ground in a swoon. Nothing would revive her, and they carried her to bed where she lay motionless. In the morning she seemed to revive, but would speak of nothing but a beautiful country which she had visited, and to which she longed to return. At night she sank deep again into sleep. Her old nurse was set to guard her, but in the silence of the night she too fell asleep, and when she woke at sunrise Ethna had gone. The whole castle was roused, and they searched high and low, but no sight, sound nor trace of her was to be found. It was clear that the FAIRIES had some part in her disappearance, and the young lord rode off at top speed to Knock-Ma under which his friend Finvarra lived, to seek his counsel as to how to find her. When he reached the Rath he dismounted, and had begun to climb its slope when he heard voices above him in the air. 'Finvarra is happy now,' said one, 'when he has carried Ethna the Bride into his palace. Her husband will never see her again.' 'Yet he could win her back,' said another, 'if he could dig a deep hole down into the heart of the Rath and let the light of day into it; but he will never win his way down, for Finvarra is more powerful than any mortal man.' 'Yet I will conquer him,' thought the young lord; and he sent for workmen far and wide and they dug down into the hill, a deep, wide trench, so that when darkness fell they thought that their task was more than half done, and that they would reach Finvarra's palace by the next day. So they went to rest in high hopes. But next morning the trench was gone, and the grass grew over the hill as if it had never been disturbed. Then most men despaired, but the young lord had a brave heart, and he added more diggers to the many who were working, and that day they got even deeper than the day before, but the next morning all trace of their labour had disappeared. And the third morning it was the same again. Then the young lord was ready to die for grief, when he heard a voice in the air above him saying 'Sprinkle the earth with salt and your work will be safe.' Hope sprang up again in his heart, and he sent round and gathered salt from all his people, and that night they covered all the piles of earth with salt before they left them. Next morning their work had been untouched, and they set to work with a good heart, and before the day was over they were so near to Fairyland that when they put their ears to the clay they could hear fairy music, and voices speaking. And one voice said: 'Finvarra is sad now, for he knows that if one human spade cuts into his palace wall it will crumble into dust.' Another answered: 'But if the king sends Ethna back to her lord, we shall all be saved.' Then the voice of Finvarra rang out: 'Lay down your spades, men of earth, and at sunset Ethna shall return to her lord.' At that the lord told his men to stop digging, and at sunset he rode up to the mouth of the Glen, and Ethna came walking up the deep cleft, shining like silver, and he snatched her up to his horse's back and rode with her to his castle; but Finvarra had played him false, for when he carried her in she lay in his arms without speech or movement, and when they laid her on the bed she lay there like a waxen image and nothing would rouse her, so that they began to fear that she had eaten FAIRY FOOD and that her soul had remained in Fairyland. One night as the lord was riding sadly home he heard the friendly voices in the air. And one said: 'It is a year and a day since Ethna came home to her lord, and still she lies motionless, for Finvarra has her soul with him still in his palace under Knock-Ma.' And the other answered: 'Yet her husband could win her back to mortal life if he undid the girdle round her waist and took out the fairy pin with which it is fastened. If he burned the girdle and sprinkled the ashes outside her door, and buried the pin in the earth, then her human soul would come back to her.' The young lord turned his horse, and rode back like lightning. With great difficulty he untangled the girdle and disengaged the fairy pin. He burnt the girdle and scattered the ashes outside the door. Still she never moved. Then he took the pin and buried it under a fairy thorn where no one would disturb it. When he came back, Ethna sat up in bed and stretched out her arms to him. She knew and remembered everything, except that the year she had spent in Fairyland was like the dream of a single night. Finvarra never troubled them again, and they lived out their mortal lives in great happiness. They have long gone, but the deep cleft is still left in Knock-Ma, and is still called the Fairy Glen.

Though Finvarra behaved with such treachery it is clear that there were more scrupulous spirits among his people.

Since Finvarra rules over the dead his story is very near to KING ORFEO, the medieval version of *Orpheus and Eurydice* in which Pluto is called the King of the Fairies.

[Motifs: F322; F322.2; F375]

Euphemistic names for the fairies. Just as the Furies were called 'The Eumenides', the 'Kindly Ones', so were the FAIRIES called laudatory names by the country people. As KIRK says, 'These *Siths*, or Fairies, they call *Sleagh Maith*, or the Good People, it would seem, to prevent the Dint of their ill Attempts, (for the Irish use to bless all they fear Harme of;).' E. B. Simpson in *Folk Lore in Lowland Scotland* (p. 93) gives a list of some of these euphemisms.

> The invisible and alert fairies for the same reason were always mentioned with a honeyed tongue. The wily, knowing not where they might be lurking, were careful to call them 'the GOOD NEIGHBOURS', 'the honest folk', 'the little folk', 'the GENTRY', 'the hill folk', and 'the forgetful people', the 'men of peace'.

The folk-rhyme given by Chambers, quoted under ELVES, contains the fairies' own caution on the subject.

[Motif: C433]

Ewing, Juliana Horatia (1841–85). One of the writers who, in the second half of the 19th century, wrote sensible and well-informed fairy stories and other books for children. Almost from her nursery days, Mrs Ewing had been the family story-teller, and the magazine edited by her mother, Mrs Gatty, was called *Aunt Judy's Magazine*, after the nickname given her by the family because of this talent. Most of her stories first came out in it. The ones that deal with FAIRIES are 'The Brownies', 'Lob-Lie-by-the-Fire', 'Amelia and the Dwarfs' and a book of short stories, *Old-Fashioned Fairy Tales*. The first three all give a naturalistic explanation of the happenings in the tales, but are soundly founded on folk tradition, generally that of her native Yorkshire. In 'The Brownies' two little boys, the children of a poor widowed tailor living in an old farmhouse which has long belonged to the family, try to persuade the BROWNIE which deserted the place many generations ago to return to them, and having been convinced that they are the only brownies available, play the part. The brownie story, as told by the old grandmother after much coaxing, is in the central stream of the brownie tradition:

> 'He lived in this house long enough,' said the old lady. 'But it's not lucky to name him.'

'O Granny, we are so hungry and miserable, what can it matter?'

'Well, that's true enough,' she sighed. 'Trout's luck is gone; it went with the Brownie, I believe.'

'Was that *he*, Granny?'

'Yes, my dear, he lived with the Trouts for several generations.'

'What was he like, Granny?'

'Like a little man, they say, my dear.'

'What did he do?'

'He came in before the family were up, and swept up the hearth, and lighted the fire, and set out the breakfast, and tidied the room, and did all sorts of house-work. But he never would be seen, and was off before they could catch him. But they could hear him laughing and playing about the house sometimes.'

'What a darling! Did they give him any wages, Granny?'

'No! my dear. He did it for love. They set a pancheon of clear water for him over night, and now and then a bowl of bread and milk, or cream. He liked that, for he was very dainty. Sometimes he left a bit of money in the water. Sometimes he weeded the garden, or threshed the corn. He saved endless trouble, both to men and maids.'

'O Granny! why did he go?'

'The maids caught sight of him one night, my dear, and his coat was so ragged, that they got a new suit, and a linen shirt for him, and laid them by the bread and milk bowl. But when Brownie saw the things, he put them on, and dancing round the kitchen, sang,

"What have we here? Hemten hamten!
Here will I never more tread nor stampen,"

and so danced through the door, and never came back again.'

The story about LOB-LIE-BY-THE-FIRE is rather like 'The Brownies' in plot. A deserted gipsy baby is adopted by two old ladies, runs away when he becomes old enough to work under the farm bailiff, and after his penitent return works secretly in the house at night, and is taken for the family LOB. 'Amelia and the Dwarfs' is a tale of fairy kidnapping. In this case the fairies, or DWARFS, carry off Amelia with a benevolent motive, to reform her many faults, but as they succeed they become fond of her, and she only escapes from them by means of a FOUR-LEAFED CLOVER. The description of the underground Fairyland, illumined by a half-light but unlit by sun or moon, reminds one of St Martin's Land from which the GREEN CHILDREN came. The *Old-Fashioned Fairy Tales* are some of them in the French tradition, some of them parables, but some so like the traditional fairy anecdotes that it is difficult to distinguish them from folk-tales.

External soul. See SEPARABLE SOUL.

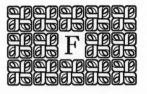

Fachan. J. F. CAMPBELL in *Popular Tales of the West Highlands* (vol. IV, p. 298) gives a description of a fachan (Glen Eitli the Son of Colin): 'With one hand out of his chest, one leg out of his haunch, and one eye

out of the front of his face . . .' Further on he slightly amplifies the description:

Ugly was the make of the Fachin; there was one hand out of the ridge of his chest, and one tuft out of the top of his head, it were easier to take a mountain from the root than to bend that tuft.

Douglas HYDE came across a fachan, though unnamed, in an Irish manuscript and gives a vivid description of the creature in the Preface to *Beside the Fire* (p. xxi):

And he [Iollann] was not long at this, until he saw the devilish mis-formed element, and the fierce and horrible spectre, and the gloomy disgusting enemy, and the morose unlovely churl; and this is how he was: he held a very thick iron flail-club in his skinny hand, and twenty chains out of it, and fifty apples on each chain of them, and a venomous spell on each great apple of them, and a girdle of the skins of deer and roebuck around the thing that was his body, and one eye in the forehead of his black-faced countenance, and one bare, hard, very hairy hand coming out of his chest, and one veiny, thick-soled leg supporting him and a close, firm, dark blue mantle of twisted hard-thick feathers, protecting his body, and surely he was more like unto devil than to man.

Faerie Queene, The. The 16th-century poet Edmund Spenser used Fairyland, as many lesser writers were afterwards to do, for the material of moral allegory. His fairyland adjoined Arthurian Britain, and the elfin and Arthurian knights moved to and fro across the borders. By a double symbolism, Fairyland was also contemporary Britain. Poor Spenser, in his unhappy exile in Ireland, might well feel that England was a fairyland. The moral pattern of the allegory is firmly and clearly traced. Its object is to illustrate the Twelve Virtues of Man, as laid down by Aristotle. There were to have been twelve books, each consisting of twelve cantos. Only six of these were completed, of which the first three were separately published in 1590. Even so, it is a monumental work. Each book has a hero, with his lady, engaged on a quest in the course of which he will perfect one virtue. The hero of the whole is Prince Arthur, who brings help to the heroes in each episode. He is destined to be himself the hero of the last tale and illustrates the crowning quality of magnanimity, in which all other virtues are contained. In the end he will gain the hand of Gloriana, the Faerie Queene.

The first book is about Holiness; its hero is St George, the Red Cross Knight, his companion and lady is Una, or Truth, and his quest is to slay the Dragon Error and save Una's land from devastation. The hero of the second book is Guyon, who stands for Temperance, Alma is his lady. Guyon's quest is to defeat Acrasie, or Lust, and destroy her. The third book is about Chastity, and the warrior princess Britomart represents that virtue, with her irresistible spear. The subject of the fourth book is Friendship, represented by the two young knights, Campbell and Triamond, with their two ladies, Canacee and Cambina, sisters to the two knights respectively and both skilled in magic. It is by a magic draught given by Cambina that the two knights are knit in friendship. The fifth book is about Justice, with Artegall as its hero and an iron man, Talus or Punishment, as his page. His lady is Britomart. He has been sent to free Irene from Grantorto. The virtue of the sixth book is Courtesy, with Sir Calidore as its hero, whose quest is to defeat the Blatant Beast (False Report) and whose lady is Pastorella.

The political application of the allegory is less clear. Queen Elizabeth is both Gloriana and Belphoebe, possibly also Britomart. Prince Arthur is probably Leicester, Artegall Lord Grey, under whom Spenser served in Ireland, Timias Sir Walter Raleigh and Calidore Sir Philip Sidney.

The good characters in the allegory are perpetually deceived, waylaid and persecuted by a wicked MAGICIAN, Archimago, a false witch, Duessa, and a variety of GIANTS, HAGS, DRAGONS and malevolent ladies. Both good and bad characters have a variety of magical instruments at their disposal: a magic mirror, an irresistible spear, a shield of adamant, a magic draught, a ring which saves the wearer from loss of blood, the Water of Life and the Tree of Life. We hear of fairy CHANGELINGS, of SHAPE-SHIFTING and GLAMOUR of all sorts, and at least one English fairy tale, the story of Mr Fox (which may be found in Jacobs's *English Fairy Tales*, p. 148), is referred to. There is a profuse mixture of fairy types, for we have a number of references to Arthurian legend, particularly to Merlin, but there are even more classical references, and much of the machinery is drawn from Ovid and Homer. It is something of a feat to read the book straight through, though there is a compulsiveness about it which leads one on, and it is full of passages of particular beauty.

Fair dealing. Although the FAIRIES have personally no scruples about appropriating anything that they fancy through FAIRY THEFTS or FAIRY BORROWINGS, they take a rigorous view of mortal dishonesty, and it is very unwise to try to cheat them in a bargain, though this can be accomplished with certain simple-minded BOGLES. See FAIRY MORALITY and VIRTUES ESTEEMED BY THE FAIRIES.

Fair Family, the. See TYLWYTH TEG.

Fairies. The word 'fairies' is late in origin; the earlier noun is FAYS, which now has an archaic and rather affected sound. This is thought to be a broken-down form of *Fatae*. The classical three Fates were later multiplied into supernatural ladies who directed the destiny of men and attended childbirths. 'Fay-erie' was first a state of enchantment or GLAMOUR, and was only later used for the fays who wielded those powers of illusion. The term 'fairy' now covers a large area, the Anglo-Saxon and Scandinavian ELVES, the DAOINE SIDHE of the Highlands, the TUATHA DE DANANN of Ireland, the TYLWYTH TEG of Wales, the SEELIE COURT and the UNSEELIE COURT, the WEE FOLK and GOOD NEIGHBOURS and many others. The TROOPING FAIRIES and the SOLITARY FAIRIES are included in it, the fairies of human or more than human size, the three-foot fairies and the tiny fairies; the domestic fairies and those that are wild and alien to man; the subterranean fairies and the water fairies that haunt lochs, streams or the sea. The supernatural HAGS, MONSTERS and BOGIES might be considered to belong to a different category, and there are, of course, FAIRY ANIMALS to be considered.

Fairies of medieval romances. The earliest of the medieval romances clearly mark their characters as fairy people. SIR LAUNFAL is a FAIRY BRIDE story, with the TABOO enforced by Tryamour, though to a less fatal issue than usual; KING ORFEO makes the connection between the FAIRIES and the dead as explicit as it is in many later accounts of the ORIGIN OF THE FAIRIES. The German *Lanzelet* is equally explicit about the fairy nature of the LADY OF THE LAKE and the TIR NAN OG fairyland which she inhabits. As the French sophisticated writers with their chivalric subtleties took over the primitive matter of Celtic legends, the fairy ladies became more of enchantresses and the magically-endowed knights lost their god-like powers. One true fairy-tale, SIR GAWAIN AND THE GREEN KNIGHT, appears, late in time and treated with great subtlety but with full supernatural quality. Here we have the Celtic story of the beheading match, with the SUPERNATURAL WIZARD appearing as challenger. Here we have MORGAN LE FAY as a full evil fairy, able even to assume a dual form as the old hag and the tempting lady simultaneously. This story too shows a primitive form in giving a full heroic stature to Sir Gawain. But if the shape of the story is primitive, the style of the poetry is most accomplished. The north-west had a poet of quality in the anonymous author of *Sir Gawain* and *The Pearl*.

[Motif: F300]

'Fairies on the Eastern Green'. This tale of an encounter between FAIRIES and a band of smugglers is about Zennor in Cornwall, and is supposed to be told by an innkeeper there. It comes from William BOTTRELL's *Stories and Folk-Lore of West Cornwall*, Series III (pp. 92-4):

> During the evening, after much coaxing, our host told the story which his wife had spoken of as a true one; telling how a company of smugglers, of his acquaintance, had been driven away from Market-jew Green by small-folks (fairies).
>
> There is some hope that all the fairy-folk have not yet entirely forsaken this neighbourhood, as there are persons now living who have seen them dancing and holding their revels on the Eastern Green within the last fifty years. At that time, however, there were many acres of grass-grown sandy banks there; and a broad belt of soft greensward, which skirted the carriage road, afforded a pleasant walk from Chyannour to Market-jew bridge. Great part of this green has now been swept away by the waves, and much of what the sea spared has been enclosed by the grasping owners of adjacent land, though their right to this ancient common is very questionable.
>
> The following fairy adventure was told to me a short time since by a grave elderly man who heard it related by the principal person concerned in it.

Tom Warren of Paul, was noted as one of the boldest smugglers round. On a summer's night, about forty years ago, he and five other men landed a boat-load of smuggled goods at a short distance from Long Rock. The brandy, salt, etc., having been taken above high-water mark, two of the men departed for Market-jew, where their best customers lived, and one went over to Newtown to procure horses that the goods might be secured before daybreak.

Tom and the other two, being very tired, lay down by a heap of goods, hoping to get a doze whilst their comrades were away. They were soon disturbed, however, by the shrill 'tweeting' of 'feapers' (slit quills or reeds, which give a shrill note when blown in.) Besides there was a constant tinkling, just like old women make by rattling pewter plates or brass pans to frighten their swarming bees home, or to make them settle.

The men thought this noise might be from a company of young folks keeping up a dance on the Green till a very late hour. Tom went to see who they were and to send them home, for it wasn't desirable for everybody to pry into the fair traders' business. Having passed the beach, he mounted a high sand-bank to have a look round, as the music seemed very near.

At a little distance, in hollows, between sand-banks, he saw glimmering lights, and persons like gaily dressed dolls skipping about and whirling round. Going nearer, he beheld, perched on a pretty high bank in their midst, a score or so of little old-looking chaps; many of them blew mouth-organs (Pan's pipes); some beat cymbals or tambourines; whilst others played on jew's-harps, or tweeted on May whistles and feapers.

Tom noticed that the little men were rigged all in green, except for their scarlet caps (small people are so fond of that coloured head-gear that they used to be nicknamed 'red-caps'). But what struck him and tickled his fancy most was to see the little, old, grave-looking pipers with their long beards wagging.

In moving their mouths over the reeds, stuck in their breasts, they looked more like buck-goats than anything human, so Tom said; and that for the life of him he couldn't forbear shouting – 'Will e be shaved – will e be shaved old red-caps?' He hailed them twice, and was about to do so again when all the dancers, with scores and hundreds more than he noticed at first sprang up, ranged themselves in rank and file; armed themselves in an instant with bows and arrows, spears and slings; then faced about, looking like vengeance. The band being disposed alongside, played a quick march, and the troops of 'spriggans' stamped on towards Tom, who saw them getting taller as they approached him. Their threatening looks were so frightful that he turned tail and ran down to his comrades, roused them, saying, 'Put to sea for your lives. There's thousands of small people and bucca-boos 'most on our backs! They'll soon surround us!' Tom made off to the boat, and his comrades followed close at his heels; but on the way a shower of pebbles fell on them, and 'burned like coals o' fire wherever they hit them'.

The men pulled many fathoms from shore before they ventured to look up, though they knew themselves safe when on the sea, because none of the fairy tribe dare touch salt water.

At length, casting a glance landward, they saw, ranged along the shore, a company of as ugly-looking creatures as they ever beheld, making threatening gestures and vain endeavours to sling stones at them.

When a furlong or so from land, the men rested on their oars, and kept watching their assailants till near daybreak; then horses being heard galloping along the road from Market-jew, the small people retreated to the sand-banks and the smugglers rowed to land.

The smugglers collected their gear successfully and were not again molested by SPRIGGANS or BUCCA-boos, but bad luck was said to have followed Tom after the encounter.

This is a neat example of the fairies' resentment of the INFRINGE-MENT OF FAIRY PRIVACY.

[Motifs: F236.1.6; F236.3.2; F361.3]

Fairy animals. The very numerous fairy animals, of which there are many traditions in the British Isles, may be divided into two main classes. There are wild ones, that exist for their own purposes and in their own right, and the domesticated ones bred and used by the FAIRIES. It is sometimes difficult to distinguish between these two types, because the fairies occasionally allow their creatures to roam freely, as, for instance, the CU SITH of the Highlands, which is generally kept as a watch dog in the BRUGHS, but is at times free to roam at its pleasure, and the CRODH MARA, which sometimes visit human herds. But the distinction is generally clear.

The two kinds of fairy creatures occur very early in our traditions and are mentioned in the MEDIEVAL CHRONICLES. Examples are the GRANT, a medieval BOGEY-BEAST mentioned by GERVASE OF TIL-BURY, and the small dogs and horses to be found in GIRALDUS CAM-BRENSIS' story of ELIDOR.

Examples of the free FAIRY HORSES are the dangerous EACH UISGE of the Highlands, the hardly less dangerous KELPIES, the CABYLL USHTEY of the Isle of Man, and such BOGIES as the BRAG, the TRASH and the SHOCK. All these have some power of SHAPE-SHIFTING. The horses used by the fairies occur everywhere in the HEROIC FAIRY legends, wherever there is the FAIRY RADE in which they are to be found. They have been taken over by the Devil where he haunts with the

YETH HOUNDS or the DEVIL'S DANDY DOGS, and even with the CWN ANNWN, which once explicitly belonged to GWYN AP NUDD. The fairy horses of the TUATHA DE DANANN are the most explicitly remembered.

The BLACK DOGS are the most common of the wild dogs in England, but there are many bogey-beast dogs, the BARGUEST, the GALLY-TROT, the MAUTHE DOOG of Man, and the Shock. The domestic FAIRY DOGS most vividly remembered are BRAN AND SCEOLAN, the hunting dogs of FINN, and in the Cu Sith; but traditions of the HOUNDS OF THE HILLS still linger in Somerset.

The fairy cattle were less fierce than the wild fairy horses. Occasionally these were independent, like the DUN COW OF KIRKHAM, and they were beneficent, not dangerous. The ELF-BULL was a lucky visitor to any herd, and so were the GWARTHEG Y LLYN of Wales. There were, however, ferocious ghost bulls like the GREAT BULL OF BAGBURY.

Of miscellaneous creatures, the most famous were the seal people, the SELKIES and ROANE. Cats were almost fairies in themselves, but there was a fairy cat in the Highlands, the CAIT SITH, and a demon-god cat, BIG EARS, which appeared after horrible invocations.

AFANC was a river monster of Wales, something like a giant beaver, and the BOOBRIE was a monstrous water-bird.

Goats and deer may be said to have been fairies in their own proper shape, and many birds, particularly the eagle, the raven, the owl and the wren, had strong fairy associations. Certain trout and salmon were fairy creatures, and even insects had their part: the GOOSEBERRY WIFE appeared as a gigantic hairy caterpillar. In fact the whole of these islands is rich in fairy zoology.

Fairy borrowing. One proof of the DEPENDENCE UPON MORTALS of the FAIRIES is their eagerness to borrow from their human neighbours. This is particularly frequent in Scotland. They borrow grain and occasionally implements. They borrow the use of mills and of human fires. The story of the ISLE OF SANNTRAIGH is one which was used by MAC RITCHIE to enforce his contribution to the THEORIES OF FAIRY ORIGINS. Indeed, all these examples of fairy borrowing fit in well with the suggestion that the first fairies were the remnants of a conquered people gone into hiding and yet creeping nervously around their conquerors for what pickings they could find, and the subject overlaps with FAIRY THEFTS.

[Motif: F391]

Fairy brides. From early classical times, the legends of the visits of goddesses and nymphs to human mortals and their loving intercourse with them have touched humanity with tragedy and splendour; for the ends of all these intercourses between immortality and mortality have been tragic. The fairy traditions carry on the tale, particularly in Celtic countries. There have been many stories of weddings between creatures of more than human beauty and stature and human men, often ones with outstanding qualities of leadership. WILD EDRIC, the champion of resistance against the Normans on the Welsh Borders, is one that immediately comes to mind. Walter Map, in his 12th-century collection of strange happenings, *De Nugis Curialium*, as well as 'Wild Edric' gives us 'The Fairy Wife of Brecknock Mere', whose beginning is very like GWRAGEDD ANNWN, 'The Fairy of Fan y Fach'. It is to be found in *De Nugis Curialium* (p. 91):

> Welshmen tell us of another thing, not a miracle but a marvel. They say that Gwestin of Gwestiniog waited and watched near Brecknock Mere (Llangorse Lake), which is some two miles around, and saw, on three brilliant moonlight nights, bands of dancing women in his fields of oats, and that he followed these until they sank in the water of the pond; and that, on the fourth night, he detained one of the maidens. The ravisher's version of the incident was that on each of the nights after they had sunk, he had heard them murmuring under the water and saying, 'Had he done thus and so, he would have caught one of us'; and he said that he had thus been taught by their lips how to capture this maiden, who yielded and married him. Her first words to her husband were: 'I shall willingly serve thee with full obedience and devotion until that day when in your eagerness to hasten to the shouting (*clamores*) beyond Llyfni you will strike me with your bridle-rein.' Now Llyfni is a river near the pond. And this thing came to pass. After the birth of many children, she was struck by him with his bridle-rein and, on his return from his ride, he found her fleeing with all her offspring. Pursuing, he snatched away with great difficulty one of his sons, Triunein Nagelauc (Trinio Faglog) by name.

Here we see at least a token capture, though, as in the story of 'The Fairy of Fan y Fach', there is some murmured instruction as to the method of wooing to be followed. There is also the TABOO imposed, forbidding an accidental blow with a bridle, as in a later version of the story. Possibly the element of cold IRON is involved here.

A more goddess-like fairy is Tryamour in the metrical romance of SIR LAUNFAL, which is nearer to the legend of OSSIAN, for here the hero is fetched away into Fairyland, though in this tale the departure into Fairyland makes the happy ending after the violation of taboo has been punished and forgiven. It is possible that this may be a literary element in the tale. The SEAL MAIDENS play a large part in the fairy bride tales. They are always unwillingly captured by the theft of their sealskins, and escape as soon as they can get them back. The SWAN MAIDENS are also captured by impounding their feathers, but they part with them more willingly, and seem generally to be swans by enchantment rather than by birth.

A more sinister supernatural wife, though not truly native to Britain, is MELUSINE, the beautiful water-spirit who becomes a serpent at the touch of water. Walter Map gives a version of the Melusine story, set in Normandy, the tale of Henno Cum Dentibus who married a beautiful and modest-seeming girl who turned into a DRAGON when sprinkled with HOLY WATER. But these Melusines were thought of as devils rather than fairies.

[Motifs: C31; C31.1.2; C31.2; C31.5; C31.8; C984; F300; F302.2; F302.4.2.1]

Fairy crafts. The FAIRIES have a great reputation for various skills. They are seen and heard working on their own account, they teach skills to mortals and they do work for them. A vivid account of their activities is given by J. G. CAMPBELL in *Superstitions of the Highlands and Islands of Scotland* (p. 15):

> The Fairies, as has been already said, are counterparts of mankind. There are children and old people among them; they practise all kinds of trades and handicrafts; they possess cattle, dogs, arms; they require food, clothing, sleep; they are liable to disease, and can be killed. So entire is the resemblance that they have even been betrayed into intoxication. People entering their brughs, have found the inmates engaged in similar occupations to mankind, the women spinning, weaving, grinding meal, baking, cooking, churning, etc., and the men sleeping, dancing, and making merry, or sitting round a fire in the middle of the floor (as a Perthshire informant described it) 'like tinkers'. Sometimes the inmates were absent on foraging expeditions or pleasure excursions. The women sing at their work, a common practice in former times with Highland women, and use distaff, spindle, handmills, and such like primitive implements.

Their skill in spinning and weaving is famous, as is shown in such tales as HABETROT and TOM TIT TOT, but there is some qualification to this. In the Isle of Man the looms and spinning-wheels are guarded from the LIL' FELLAS at night because they are likely to spoil the webs. This opinion is illustrated in a passage from Sophia Morrison's *Manx Fairy Tales* about a fairy visit to a Manx house, a memorat taken down from James Moore:

> I'm not much of a believer in most of the stories some ones is telling, but after all a body can't help believing a thing they happen to see for themselves.
> I remember one winter's night – we were living in a house at the

time that was pulled down for the building of the Big Wheel. It was a thatched house with two rooms, and a wall about six foot high dividing them, and from that it was open to the scrabs, or turfs, that were laid across the rafters. My Mother was sitting at the fire busy spinning, and my Father was sitting in the big chair at the end of the table taking a chapter for us out of the Manx Bible. My brother was busy winding a spool and I was working with a bunch of ling, trying to make two or three pegs.

'There's a terrible glisther on to-night,' my Mother said, looking at the fire. 'An' the rain comin' peltin' down the chimley.'

'Yes,' said my Father, shutting the Bible; 'an' we better get to bed middlin' soon and let the Lil' Ones in to a bit of shelter.'

So we all got ready and went to bed.

Some time in the night my brother wakened me with a: 'Shish! Listen boy, and look at the big light tha's in the kitchen!' Then he rubbed his eyes a bit and whispered: 'What's Mother doin' now at all?'

'Listen!' I said, 'An' you'll hear Mother in bed; it's not her at all; it must be the Little Ones that's agate of the wheel!'

And both of us got frightened, and down with our heads under the clothes and fell asleep. In the morning when we got up we told them what we had seen, first thing.

'Aw, like enough, like enough,' my Father said, looking at the wheel. 'It seems your mother forgot to take the band off last night, a thing people should be careful about, for it's givin' Themselves power over the wheel, an' though their meanin's well enough, the spinnin' they're doin' is nothin' to brag about. The weaver is always shoutin' about their work, an' the bad joinin' they're makin' in the rolls.'

I remember it as well as yesterday – the big light that was at them, and the whirring that was going on. And let anybody say what they like, that's a thing I've seen and heard for myself.

A story given by W. W. Gill in *A Manx Scrapbook* (p. 291) is of spinning ostensibly done by spiders, but he thinks almost certainly by the fairies:

A story, of which the following is the gist, has a limited currency in the district; it reached me from an elderly sheep-farmer of the neighbouring hills. The Rabyhouse was inhabited by an old woman named K— and her servant-girl. One morning when there was a great deal of spinning on hand the girl ran off and left her, and she was at her wits' end to get it done. Finally, in despair she went down to the river and asked it, or asked the spiders – accounts differ on this point – to help her; and it, or they, promised to do so. Not only did they spin her wool for her, but after the work was finished they wove her, all out of their own silk thread, a shawl of miraculous delicacy and beauty. It was preserved in the family for several generations, but has now disappeared, like the two Fairy Cups, the Mylecharaine Cross, and other Insular treasures.

Gill confirms this story by one from the Isle of Mull in which the fairies came at a spoken wish and performed the acts of spinning and weaving by a simple invocation. They then clustered round the table expecting to be fed, but as the woman had nothing to give them, she had at last to clear the house by the simple stratagem of raising an alarm of fire in their fairy hill.

This story raises the question of whether the fairy spinning was an actual performance or a piece of GLAMOUR which deceived human senses. It will be remembered that in the Cornish version of TOM TIT TOT, 'Duffy and the Devil', all TERRYTOP's spinning disappeared when he was routed, and the Squire had to walk home naked. This perhaps is not a fair parallel, for Terrytop is explicitly described as a devil, not a fairy.

Of the other crafts in which fairies are distinguished, the most curious and contradictory is smithy work, when we consider the fairies' fear of cold IRON. GNOMES were, from of old, reputed metal-workers, and many famous swords and breastplates were wrought by them, but in the tale of 'The ISLE OF SANNTRAIGH' the fairies, who were governed by the dirk stuck into the hillside, taught their captives unusual skill in metal-work, from which the rescued boy afterwards profited. As is common in folk-lore, there is no explanation of this anomaly. A notable literary use of this theme is made by Rudyard KIPLING in 'Cold Iron', one of the stories in *Puck of Pook's Hill*.

LEPRACAUNS were reputed to be highly skilled at their trade, but since there is no record that they made shoes for other than fairy feet, there is no means of testing this.

GOBLINS labouring in the mines were proverbial in the 17th century for producing no results by their deedy labours. Boat-building, on the other hand, was a work on which they nightly laboured and which they could transfer to human protégés. Evans Wentz, in *The Fairy-Faith in Celtic Countries* (pp. 106–7), collected a story from a Barra piper about how an apprentice boat-builder, who had picked up a fairy's girdle, was given the gift of a master's skill when he returned it to her. The gift remained even after he had told how he acquired it.

One undoubted gift of the fairies was that of skill in music, and there are many stories of how the MacCrimmons, the most famous family of Scottish pipers, were given their skill by the gift of a black chanter to a despised younger son of the family. The gift was accompanied by tuition. Many songs and airs have come out of fairy hills and have survived the change into the human world. It is clear that whatever fairy skills are the work of glamour, their music survives in its own right.

[Motifs: F262; F262.1; F271.0.1; F271.4.2; F271.4.3; F271.7; F271.10]

Fairy cup, the. The story of the fairy cup, told by William of New-bridge, the 12th-century chronicler, is an early example of THEFTS FROM THE FAIRIES. Thomas KEIGHTLEY quotes it from *Guilielmi Neubrigensis Historia, sive Chronica Rerum Anglicarum* (Book 1, Chapter 28):

> In the province of the Deiri (Yorkshire), not far from my birth-place, a wonderful thing occurred, which I have known from my boyhood. There is a town a few miles distant from the Eastern Sea, near which are those celebrated waters commonly called Gipse... A peasant of this town went once to see a friend who lived in the next town, and it was late at night when he was coming back, not very sober; when lo! from the adjoining barrow, which I have often seen, and which is not much over a quarter of a mile from the town, he heard the voices of people singing, and, as it were, joyfully feasting. He wondered who they could be that were breaking in that place, by their merriment, the silence of the dead night, and he wished to examine into the matter more closely. Seeing a door open in the side of the barrow, he went up to it, and looked in; and there he beheld a large and luminous house, full of people, women as well as men, who were reclining as at a solemn banquet. One of the attendants, seeing him standing at the door, offered him a cup. He took it, but would not drink; and pouring out the contents, kept the vessel. A great tumult arose at the banquet on account of his taking away the cup, and all the guests pursued him; but he escaped by the fleetness of the beast he rode, and got into the town with his booty. Finally, this vessel of unknown material, of un-usual colour, and of extraordinary form, was presented to Henry the Elder, king of the English, as a valuable gift, and was then given to the queen's brother David, king of the Scots, and was kept for several years in the treasury of Scotland; and a few years ago (as I have heard from good authority), it was given by William, king of the Scots, to Henry the Second, who wished to see it.

[Type: ML6045. Motifs: F352; F352.1]

Fairy dogs. There are a number of varieties of fairy dogs. There are those domesticated to the FAIRIES, either as watch-dogs or as hunting dogs. (For these, see CU SITH, CWN ANNWN, which also fulfil the func-tion of the spectral pack (see below), the HOUNDS OF THE HILL, with individuals such as BRAN AND SCEOLAN and FARVANN.) There are solitary dogs of the BOGEY-BEAST type, BLACK DOGS, with the GUAR-DIAN BLACK DOG and the CHURCH GRIM as a contrast, GALLY-TROT, the GRANT and the MAUTHE DOOG as menacing individuals, and there are the spectral packs, usually accompanied by demonic huntsmen: CHENEY'S HOUNDS, DANDO AND HIS DOGS, the DEVIL'S DANDY

DOGS, GABRIEL HOUNDS, GABRIEL RATCHETS, and YETH HOUNDS.
All these are types of the fairy dog, and some particulars will be found of
them under their appropriate entries.
[Motifs: F241; F241.6]

'Fairy Dwelling on Selena Moor, the'. A most interesting legend of
a VISIT TO FAIRYLAND is given in BOTTRELL's *Traditions and Hearthside Stories of West Cornwall* (vol. II, pp. 95–102), which illustrates very
well the beliefs on the ORIGINS OF THE FAIRIES and social history still
held in Cornwall at the middle of the last century. It is a homelier fairyland than that imagined in Bottrell's other story of Richard Vegoe's
experiences, but it gives a complete illustration of the origin belief of the
FAIRIES as the pagan dead, of the dangers of tasting FAIRY FOOD and of
the dwindling size and powers of the fairies. A condensed version of this
long and interesting story will be sufficient to give its flavour. These
fairies with their dwindling powers and reality give an impression that
reminds one somehow of Swift's Struldbrugs:

> The tale is about a Mr Noy, a well-liked farmer, who lived near
> Selena Moor and who went out to the neighbouring inn one night to
> order drink for the Harvest Home next day. He left the inn, but never
> arrived home. They searched for him for three days, and at last, passing
> within half a mile of his home, they heard dogs howling, and a horse
> neighing. They went over the treacherous bogland of the moor, and
> found a great thicket, where Mr Noy's horse was tethered, with the
> dogs beside it. The horse had fed well on the rich grass, but the dogs
> were very thin. The horse led them to a ruined bowjey (or barn) and
> there they found Mr Noy fast asleep. He was surprised to see that it
> was morning already, and was very dazed and bewildered, but at last
> they got his story from him. He had made a short-cut through the
> moor, but had lost his way and had wandered, he thought, many miles
> over country unknown to him, until he saw lights in the distance and
> heard music. He hurried towards it, thinking that he had come at last
> to a farmhouse, where they were perhaps holding a Harvest Home
> supper. His horse and dogs shrank back and would not come with him,
> so he tied his horse to a thorn, and went on through a most beautiful
> orchard towards a house, outside which he saw hundreds of people
> either dancing or sitting drinking at tables. They were all richly dressed,
> but they looked to him very small, and their benches and tables and
> cups were small too. Quite close to him stood a girl in white, taller than
> the rest, and playing a kind of tambourine. The tunes were lively, and
> the dancers were the nimblest he had ever seen. Soon the girl gave the
> tambourine to an old fellow near, and went into the house to fetch out
> a black-jack of ale for the company. Mr Noy, who loved dancing and

would have been glad of a drink, drew near to the corner of the house, but the girl met his eyes, and signed to him to keep back. She spoke a few words to the old fellow with the tambourine, and then came towards him.

'Follow me into the orchard,' she said.

She went before him to a sheltered place, and there in the quiet starlight, away from the dazzle of the candles, he recognized her as Grace Hutchens, who had been his sweetheart for a long time, but had died, or was thought to have died, three or four years before.

'Thank the stars, dear William,' she said, 'that I was on the look-out to stop ye, or ye would this minute be changed into the small people's state, like I am, woe is me!'

He would have kissed her, but she warned him anxiously against touching her, and against eating a fruit or plucking a flower if he wished ever to reach his home again.

'For eating a tempting plum in this enchanted orchard was my undoing,' she said. 'You may think it strange, but it was all through my love for you that I am come to this. People believed, and so it seemed, that I was found on the moor dead; what was buried for me, however, was only a changeling or a sham body, never mine, I should think, for it seems to me that I feel much the same still as when I lived to be your sweetheart.'

As she said this several little voices squeaked, 'Grace, Grace, bring us more beer and cider, be quick, be quick!'

'Follow me into the garden, and remain there behind the house; be sure you keep out of sight, and don't for your life touch fruit or flower.'

Mr Noy begged her to bring him a drink of cider too, but she said she would not on his life; and she soon returned, and led him into a bowery walk, where all kinds of flowers were blooming, and told him how she came there. One evening about dusk she was out on Selena Moor looking for a stray sheep, when she heard Mr Noy hallooing to his dogs, so she took a short-cut towards him, and got lost in a place where the ferns were above her head, and so wandered on for hours until she came to an orchard where music was sounding, but though the music was sometimes quite near she could not get out of the orchard, but wandered round as if she was pixy-led. At length, worn out with hunger and thirst, she plucked a beautiful golden plum from one of the trees, and began to eat it. It dissolved into bitter water in her mouth, and she fell to the ground in a faint. When she revived she found herself surrounded by a crowd of little people, who laughed and rejoiced at getting a neat girl to bake and brew for them and to look after their mortal babies, who were not so strong, they said, as they used to be in the old days.

She said their lives seemed unnatural and a sham. 'They have little sense or feeling; what serves them in a way as such, is merely the remembrance of whatever pleased them when they lived as mortals – maybe thousands of years ago. What appear like ruddy apples and other delicious fruit are only sloes, hoggins (haws) and blackberries.'

Mr Noy asked her if any fairy babies were born, and she answered that just occasionally a fairy child was born, and then there was great rejoicing – every little fairy man, however old and wizened, was proud to be thought its father. 'For you must remember that they are not of our religion,' she said in answer to his surprised look, 'but star-worshippers. They don't always live together like Christians and turtle-doves; considering their long existence, such constancy would be tiresome for them; anyhow, the small tribe seem to think so.'

She told him also that she was now more content with her condition, since she was able to take the form of a small bird and fly about near him.

When she was called away again Mr Noy thought he might find a way to rescue them both; so he took his hedging gloves out of his pocket, turned them inside out and threw them among the fairies. Immediately all vanished, Grace and all, and he found himself standing alone in the ruined bowjey. Something seemed to hit him on the head, and he fell to the ground.

Like many other visitors to Fairyland, Mr Noy pined and lost all interest in life after this adventure.

[Type: ML4075. Motifs: C211.1; F370; F372; F375]

Fairy food. There are various accounts of fairy food. The small, homely FAIRIES, such as that in the Worcestershire story of the BROKEN PED and its variants, bake small, delicious cakes which they give to their benefactors. Those fairies about whom tales of FAIRY BORROWING are told often beg for loans of grain, and return it honestly. According to J. G. CAMPBELL in his *Superstitions of the Highlands and Islands of Scotland* (p. 22), they often borrow oatmeal and return double measure, but always of barley meal, for barley seems to be their natural grain. The fairies also steal the essential good out of human food, and leave an un-nourishing substance behind them. KIRK speaks of their stealing away the 'FOYSON' of human food, and Campbell uses the Gaelic '*toradh*'. The tale of the TACKSMAN OF AUCHRIACHAN illustrates this trait. Otherwise their food, though it appears by GLAMOUR to be rich and elegant, consists of weeds. St Collen, in the tale of ST COLLEN AND THE FAIRY KING, scornfully dismisses the fairy banquet as 'the leaves of a tree'. According to Campbell (p. 21) it consists of brisgein (that is, the roots of silverweed), stalks of heather, milk of red deer and goats, and barley meal. HERRICK's minute fairy king has a banquet fitted to his small size, but not very appetizing to the ordinary mortal:

A little mushroome table spred,
After short prayers, they set on bread;
A Moon-parcht grain of purest wheat,
With some small glit'ring gritt, to eate
His choyce bitts with; then in a trice
They make a feast lesse great then nice.

And now, we must imagine first,
The Elves present to quench his thirst
A pure seed-Pearle of Infant dew,
Brought and besweetned in a blew
And pregnant violet; which done,
His kitling eyes begin to runne
Quite through the table, where he spies
The hornes of paperie Butterflies,
Of which he eates, and tastes a little
Of that we call the Cuckoes spittle.
A little Fuz-ball-pudding stands
By, yet not blessed by his hands,
That was too coorse; but then forthwith
He ventures boldly on the pith
Of sugred Rush, and eates the sagge
And well bestrutted Bees sweet bagge:
Gladding his pallat with some store
Of Emits eggs; what wo'd he more?
But Beards of Mice, a Newt's stew'd thigh,
A bloated Earewig, and a Flie;
With the Red-capt worme, that's shut
Within the concave of a Nut,
Browne as his Tooth. A little Moth,
Late fatned in a piece of cloth:
With withered cherries; Mandrakes eares;
Moles eyes; to these, the slain-Stags teares:
The unctuous dewlaps of a Snaile;
The broke-heart of a Nightingale
Ore-come in musicke; with a wine,
Ne're ravisht from the flattering Vine,
But gently prest from the soft side
Of the most sweet and dainty Bride,
Brought in a dainty daizie, which
He fully quaffs up to bewitch
His blood to height; this done, commended
Grace by his Priest; *The feast is ended*.

It is doubtful if this diet has any folk foundation. It may well be the
product of Herrick's own fancy. In one of Lady WILDE's more grue-

some tales, the rich banquet served up to the fairy court had appeared to
a mortal visitor in the kitchen to be the body of an old HAG. It is certain
that all the food served in Fairyland was spiced and transformed by
glamour.

[Motifs: F243; F243.1]

Fairy funerals. Allan Cunningham in his *Lives of Eminent British
Painters* (pp. 228–9) records that William Blake claimed to have seen a
fairy funeral. 'Did you ever see a fairy's funeral, madam?' said Blake to
a lady who happened to sit next to him. 'Never, Sir!' said the lady. 'I
have,' said Blake, 'but not before last night.' And he went on to tell how,
in his garden, he had seen 'a procession of creatures of the size and colour
of green and grey grasshoppers, bearing a body laid out on a rose-leaf,
which they buried with songs, and then disappeared'.

Most people would deny the possibility of a fairy funeral, believing the
FAIRIES to have lives co-terminous with this earthly world, or else that they
dwindle and disappear in the course of ages, like the SMALL PEOPLE of
Cornwall. Yet, here and there, people claim, like Blake, to have seen fairy
funerals. One of these is preserved in the archives of the School of
Scottish Studies among the fairy experiences of Walter Johnstone, one of
the travelling people of Perthshire. He found a ruined house near Tom
na Toul with a well near it. He was just going to dip his can into the well
when he saw a light coming out of the bushes. Two wee men came out,
about six inches tall, carrying a coffin between them. They were wearing
bowler hats, not the 'lum hats' usually worn at Scottish funerals. Dr
T. F. G. Paterson of Armagh Museum collected a similar account from
one of the old people:

> A man once followed a fairy funeral. He was up late at night an'
> heard the convoy comin'. He slipped out an' followed them an' they
> disappeared into Lisletrim Fort (a triple-ringed fort near Cullyhanna).
> He heard the noise of them walking plain, but he saw none of them.

KIRK in his incomparable work puts a period to fairy lives and also
mentions funerals.

> There Men travell much abroad, either presaging or aping the dis-
> mall and tragicall Actions of some amongst us; and have also many
> disastorous Doings of their own, as Convocations, Fighting, Gashes,
> Wounds, and Burialls, both in the Earth and Air. They live much
> longer than wee; yet die at last, or at least vanish from that State.

A little later he says: 'They are not subject to sore Sicknesses, but
dwindle and decay at a certain Period, all about ane Age.'

Some people are not certain that their funerals are not part of this
'presaging or aping the dismall and tragicall Actions' of men; at least it is
so in Bowker's 'Fairy Funeral', in his *Goblin Tales of Lancashire*. Two

men were once walking home towards Langton village on a clear moon-light night. One was the old cow-doctor, Adam, and the other was a lively young fellow called Robin. As they came up to the church the first stroke of twelve sounded and they passed it as the chimes pealed out. A moment later they stopped, for the peal of the passing-bell began to ring. They counted the strokes, and after twenty-six they stopped – Robin was twenty-six years old. They wondered who it could be among his companions, but decided that they would know in the morning, and hurried on towards home. But as they reached the drive and lodge of the ancient abbey, the gate swung open and a little dark figure came out with a red cap on his head. He was waving his arms and singing a sweet but mournful dirge, and he was followed by a procession dressed like him which bore in the midst of it a tiny coffin with the lid pushed back so that the face was visible. The two men drew back into the hedge, but as the coffin passed old Adam leant forward, and in the moonlight saw the face of the corpse. 'Robin, mi lad,' he said, 'it's the picter o' thee as they hev i' the coffin!' Robin started forward, and saw that it was indeed the miniature of his own face. The bell still tolled and the funeral cortège passed on towards the church. Robin took it for a death warning and determined to know the appointed time. Adam tried to restrain him, but he hurried after the FEEORIN, and, touching the leader, he asked, trembling, 'Winnot yo' tell mi heaw lung I've to live?' At once, with a flash of lightning and a spatter of rain, the whole procession vanished, and the two men made their way homeward as best they could through wind and rain.

From that time Robin was a changed man. There was no more riot and merriment for him. His only comfort was to sit with old Adam at night and talk over what they had seen and heard. In a month's time he fell from a stack and was fatally injured.

This is the fullest account of a warning funeral, but there are reports of them in Galloway and Wales. The Welsh corpse-candles are among the WILL O' THE WISP phenomena discussed by AUBREY and Sikes, but these are ascribed to the spirits of the dead rather than to the fairies.

The funeral of a genuine fairy, indeed the Fairy Queen, is described by HUNT in *Popular Romances of the West of England* (p. 102). This is a shortened version of his tale.

One night an old man called Richard was returning home late with a load of fish from St Ives when he heard the bell of Lelant Church tolling out, with a heavy, muffled sound, and saw a light from the windows. He drew near and peered in. The church was brightly lighted, and a crowd of little people were moving along the central aisle, with a bier carried between six of them. The body was uncovered; it was as small as the tiniest doll, and of waxen beauty. The mourners were carrying flowering myrtle in their hands, and wearing wreaths of small roses. A little grave had been dug near the altar. The body was lowered into it, and the

fairies threw their flowers after, crying aloud: 'Our queen is dead!'
When one of the little grave-diggers threw in a shovelful of earth so
dismal a cry arose that Richard echoed it. At once the lights went out,
and the fairies rushed past him like a swarm of bees, piercing him with
sharp points. Richard fled in terror, and thought himself lucky to have
escaped with his life.

It is notable that these fairies, though they showed the normal dislike of prying intruders, and hence of an INFRINGEMENT OF FAIRY
PRIVACY, were undeterred by crucifix (see CROSS) or consecration. They
must indeed have belonged to the SEELIE COURT.

[Motifs: D1825.7.1; F268.1; F361.3]

Fairy godmothers. The fairy godmothers of the sophisticated fairy
tales of PERRAULT, Madame D'AULNOY and the later authors of the
Cabinet des Fées are something of an anomaly. The wild FAIRIES would
be by their nature entirely out of place at a Christian service, but there
is a deep-rooted foundation for their appearance at a heathen name-
giving. It was on such occasions, indeed, that the norns, the parcae and
the fortunae – the ancestresses of our FAYS – made their appearance.

The Perrault fairy-stories were retold folktales, which presupposed,
however, a courtly audience who knew the custom of courts and the
emphasis placed on courtly sponsors for royal and noble children. 'The
Sleeping Beauty' is the typical example of a courtly christening, with the
influential fairies invited to the christening and the haggish and ugly
fairy neglected and taking umbrage in consequence. A parallel example
is to be found in the 13th-century interlude, the *Jeu de Folie du Trouvère
Adam de la Halle*, in which three fairy ladies, Arcile, Morgue and
Maglore, are summoned to attend a banquet laid for them in a summer
hall in the churchyard, and Maglore is angered at the inadequacy of the
cutlery set out for her, and lays a curse of baldness on her host. This is
no christening, however, but a pagan rite set out by ancient custom in the
churchyard, already a sacred place in heathen times.

There are plenty of supernatural patrons in the folktales of all nations.
Sometimes these are animals, often the spirit of the murdered mother,
sometimes old men or old women who have been obliged by the pro-
tagonist, sometimes spirits of wells, rivers or mountains. In most stories
the plot is much the same, but the trappings are different. The idea of the
fairies at the christening has indeed captured the literary fairy-stories,
and one finds it used as the blueprint for a fairy-tale by George MAC-
DONALD, E. M. Nesbit, Andrew Lang, Mrs Baldwin and many others.

[Motifs: F311.1; F316]

Fairy horses of the Tuatha de Danann, the. All the HEROIC FAIRIES
spent a great part of their time in solemn rides, and their horses, large or
small according to the riders, were often described. The FAIRIES

described by ELIDOR were small, but noble, and they had horses and hounds proportioned to their size, the Welsh GWRAGEDD ANNWYN rode on milk-white horses and the FAIRY RADE described in the Scottish ballads was on horses of varying colours richly caparisoned with tinkling bells. The TUATHA DE DANANN, who were conquered and driven underground by the Milesians and who afterwards dwindled down into the DAOINE SIDHE, were the very cream of the heroic fairies, and their horses were eloquently described by Lady WILDE in her *Ancient Legends of Ireland* (vol. I, pp. 178–9 and 182–3):

> And the breed of horses they reared could not be surpassed in the world – fleet as the wind, with the arched neck and the broad chest and the quivering nostril, and the large eye that showed they were made of fire and flame, and not of dull, heavy earth. And the Tuatha made stables for them in the great caves of the hills, and they were shod with silver and had golden bridles, and never a slave was allowed to ride them. A splendid sight was the cavalcade of the Tuatha-de-Danann knights. Seven-score steeds, each with a jewel on his forehead like a star, and seven-score horsemen, all the sons of kings, in their green mantles fringed with gold, and golden helmets on their head, and golden greaves on their limbs, and each knight having in his hand a golden spear.
>
> And so they lived for a hundred years and more, for by their enchantments they could resist the power of death.

A few pages later she tells of the last of these royal steeds:

> Of the great breed of splendid horses, some remained for several centuries, and were at once known by their noble shape and qualities. The last of them belonged to a great lord in Connaught, and when he died, all his effects being sold by auction, the royal steed came to the hammer, and was bought up by an emissary of the English Government, who wanted to get possession of a specimen of the magnificent ancient Irish breed, in order to have it transported to England.
>
> But when the groom attempted to mount the high-spirited animal, it reared, and threw the base-born churl violently to the ground, killing him on the spot.
>
> Then, fleet as the wind, the horse galloped away, and finally plunged into the lake and was seen no more. So ended the great race of the mighty Tuatha-de-Danann horses in Ireland, the like of which has never been seen since in all the world for majesty and beauty.

[Motifs: F241.1; F241.1.1.1]

Fairy levitation. It is very rare in traditional fairy tales for FAIRIES to travel by means of wings. They generally fly through the air on transformed ragwort stems, twigs or bundles of grasses, using them as witches use broomsticks, and most commonly levitated by a magic password. AUBREY in his *Miscellanies* gives us one of the earliest examples of these passwords, 'Horse and Hattock'. This apparently had power to levitate objects as well as people, for Aubrey tells us that a schoolboy, seeing a cloud of dust whirl by and hearing shrill cries of 'Horse and Hattock' coming out of it, called out, 'Horse and Hattock my top', and at once his top rose into the air and joined the party. 'Hupp, Horse and Handocks' is another cry. A longer one given in the *Shetland Folk Book* (vol. III) is slightly more elaborate:

> Up hors, up hedik
> Up will ridn bolwind
> And I kin I's reyd among yu.

In the short tale of 'The Black Laird of Dunblane' included by Simpkins in *County Folk-Lore* (vol. VII) the instructions are short and explicit: 'Brechin to the Bridal' and 'Cruinan to the Dance!', but the Black Laird never learned their final destination, for he broke a TABOO by calling out, 'Well dune, Watson's auld ploughbeam!' – for that was his mount – and found himself alone, and back in the furrow from which he had started.

The commonest fairy levitation stories are those in which the guest on the flight goes with his hosts, fairies, PISKIES, TROWS or witches, to carouse in a distant cellar, drinks too much and finds himself alone in the cellar in the morning with a gold cup in his hand and no convincing way of accounting for his presence.

When the revellers are witches, the means of levitation are often red caps, but there is one fairy legend, given in E. M. Leather's *The Folk-Lore of Herefordshire*, in which white caps are used. The plot and the final rescue of the boy is much closer to the witch stories:

> Once there was a boy who wandered away from the right path on a journey to his home, and lost himself in a big wood; night came on, and he lay down tired out, and fell asleep. When he woke, two or three hours after, he could see that a bear was lying beside him, with its head on his little bundle of clothes. It got up, and the boy was very much frightened at first, but, finding the bear was quite tame and gentle, he allowed the animal to lead him out of the wood, to a spot where he could see a light. Walking towards it, he found it came from a little turf hut. In answer to his knock, a little woman opened the door, kindly inviting him to enter. There he saw another little woman sitting by the fire. After a good supper, he was told he must share with them the only bed, and lying down, he fell fast asleep, to be wakened when the clock struck twelve by his bedfellows, who sprang up, putting on little white caps, which hung at the bed's head. One said, 'Here's off,'

and the other, 'Here's after,' and they suddenly disappeared, as though flying. Afraid to stay in the hut alone, and seeing another white cap hanging at the bed's head, the boy seized it, saying, 'Here's after.' He was immediately transported to the fairy ring outside the door of the hut where the little women were dancing merrily. Then one said, 'Here's off to a gentleman's house,' and the other, 'Here's after,' so the boy did likewise, and found himself on the top of a tall chimney. The first fairy said, 'Down the chimney,' and the others repeating the usual formula, down they went, first to the kitchen, and then to the cellar. Here they began collecting bottles of wine to take away; they opened one, and gave it to the boy, who drank so greedily that he fell asleep; on waking, he found himself alone, and in fear and trembling, went up to the kitchen, where he met the servants, and was taken before the master of the mansion.

He could give no satisfactory account of himself, and was condemned to be hanged.

On the scaffold he saw, pushing eagerly through the crowd, a little woman carrying a white cap, and wearing a similar one. She asked the judge if the prisoner might be hanged in the cap, and he gave his consent. So she walked up to the scaffold, and placed it on the lad's head, saying, 'Here's off!' He quickly said, 'Here's after!' and away they went like lightning to the turf hut. Here the fairy explained that she had been displeased by his taking the magic cap, and that if befriended by fairies he must in future never take liberties with their property. This he promised, and after a good meal was allowed to depart to his home.

Fairies were also in the habit of levitating buildings, castles and churches if their situation did not suit them. Sometimes they removed the building material to the preferred location. In many of the stories it is a monstrous animal, a cat or a pig who is the agent; sometimes it is the Devil, but occasionally it is a crowd of fairies, as in the anecdote given by George Henderson in *The Popular Rhymes, Sayings and Proverbs of the County of Berwickshire*, 'The Fairies and Langton House'. Their levitation rhyme was:

> Lift one, lift a',
> Baith at back and fore wa' –
> Up and away wi' Langton House,
> And set it down in Dogden Moss.

Fortunately their intention was frustrated by a hastily-uttered prayer.
[Type: ML5006*. Motifs: F241.1.0.1; F282; F282.2]

Fairy loans. If FAIRIES often made FAIRY BORROWINGS borrowed from humans, they were also ready to lend in their turn, either utensils or food. The most famous utensil lent was the Frensham Caldron, mentioned by AUBREY in *The Natural History of Surrey* (vol. III). There was a fairy hill near Frensham, to which everyone who needed an unusually large cooking pot resorted, asked for the loan of the pot, mentioned the need he had of it and the date at which he would return it, on which the pot was handed out to him. Aubrey unfortunately does not mention whether the fairy was invisible or seen. The arrangement worked smoothly until one unpunctual borrower forgot to return the caldron on the specified day. When at length he brought it back it was not accepted, so it was brought back and hung in the vestry of Frensham Church, where it was to be seen in Aubrey's day, though it has since disappeared.

J. G. CAMPBELL has a passage in his *Superstitions of the Highlands and Islands of Scotland* on fairy loans and borrowing. He says:

> When a loan is returned to them, they accept only the fair equivalent of what they have lent, neither less nor more. If more is offered they take offence, and never give an opportunity for the same insult again.

They themselves, however, return loans of grain with a generous interest, though they always give back barley for oats. In spite of this handsome testimonial, however, Campbell gives the fairies a bad character, and says that no one is the better for their gifts, and that all TRAFFIC WITH THE FAIRIES is to be avoided.

Fairy market, or fair. The most famous of the fairy markets was held in Somerset at Blackdown near Pitminster. It is first mentioned in detail by BOVET in his *Pandaemonium, or The Devil's Cloyster* (p. 207). It is quoted by KEIGHTLEY:

> At some times they would seem to dance, at other times to keep a great fair or market. I made it my business to enquire among the neighbours what credit might be given to that which was reported of them, and by many of the neighbouring inhabitants I had this account confirmed.
>
> The place near which they most ordinarily showed themselves was on the side of a hill, named Black-down, between the parishes of Pittminster and Chestonford, not many miles from Taunton. Those that have had occasion to travel that way have frequently seen them, appearing like men and women, of a stature generally near the smaller size of men. Their habits used to be of red, blue or green, according to the old way of country garb, with high crowned hats. One time about fifty years since, a person living at Comb St Nicholas, a parish lying on one side of that hill, near Chard, was riding towards his home that way, and saw, just before him, on that side of the hill, a great company of people, that seemed to him like country folks assembled at a fair. There were all sorts of commodities, to his appearance, as at our

ordinary fairs; pewterers, shoemakers, pedlars, with all kind of trinkets, fruit and drinking booths. He could not remember anything which he had usually seen at fairs but what he saw there. It was once in his thoughts that it might be some fair for Chestonford, there being a considerable one at some time of the year; but then again he considered that it was not the season for it. He was under very great surprise, and admired what the meaning of what he saw should be. At length it came to his mind what he had heard concerning the Fairies on the side of that hill, and it being near the road he was to take, he resolved to ride in amongst them, and see what they were. Accordingly he put on his horse that way, and, though he saw them perfectly all along as he came, yet when he was upon the place where all this had appeared to him, he could discern nothing at all, only seemed to be crowded and thrust, as when one passes through a throng of people. All the rest became invisible to him until he came to a little distance, and then it appeared to him again as at first. He found himself in pain, and so hastened home; where, being arrived, lameness seized him all on one side, which continued on him as long as he lived, which was many years; for he was living in Comb, and gave an account to any that enquired of this accident for more than twenty years afterwards; and this relation I had from a person of known honour, who had it from the man himself.

There were some whose names I have now forgot, but they then lived at a gentleman's house, named Comb Farm, near the place before specified; both the man, his wife, and divers of the neighbours, assured me they had, at many times, seen this *fair-keeping* in the summer-time, as they came from Taunton-market, but they durst not adventure in amongst them; for that everyone that had done so had received great damage by it.

These FAIRIES evidently felt the common fairy dislike of human prying and INFRINGEMENTS OF FAIRY PRIVACY, and an even more sinister fair, merry and beautiful as it appeared at first sight, is to be found in Lady WILDE's *Ancient Legends of Ireland*, 'November Eve' (vol. I, p. 145), in which the fairies are described as fairies and yet are identified with the dead.

The fairies of Blackdown, however, seem to have had their gentler moods. Ruth Tongue in *County Folklore* (vol. VIII, p. 112) says that the PIXIES have now taken over Somerset from the fairies and hold their fair in the same place. She tells of a covetous old fellow who saw the pixy fair and took a fancy to a gold mug there. He urged his pony into the middle of the fair, seized the mug and made off. In the morning, when he went to look at his prize, it had turned into a great toadstool, and the pony was scamble-footed, or lame, for the rest of his days.

In a rather earlier story, pieced together in Miss Tongue's youth, pixies are called 'vairies' and receive an old friend courteously, rewarding his GOOD MANNERS by turning an apparent payment of withered leaves into gold, reversing the more usual procedure.

There were a Varmer over-right our place did zee the vairies to their Market, and comed whoame zafe tew. Mind, he did'n never vorget to leave hearth clean 'n a pail of well water vor'n at night, 'n a girt dish of scalt cream tew. My granny did zay her'd get'n ready vor'n many's the time. Zo when her rode up tew stall, zee, all among the Vair, 'n axed mannerly vor a zider mug a-hanging up, the vairies answers 'n zo purty as if they were to Taunton Market. With that Varmer lugs out his money-bag 'n pays, 'n what do 'ee believe! They gived 'n a heap of dead leaves vor his change, quite serious like, Varmer he took 'n serious tew, then her wishes 'n 'Good-night, arl,' 'n her ride whoame. He d' put zider mug on table, 'n spread they dead leaves round 'n careful, then he d' zay, 'Come morn, they won't none o' they be yur, but 'twere worth it to zee the liddle dears' Market.'

Come morn, when Varmer went to get his dew-bit avore ploughing what do 'ee zee on table but a vine silver mug 'n lumps of gold all round 'n.

Here we have the fairies at their most benign; Christina Rossetti's GOBLIN MARKET shows them at their most sinister. It is true enough to some fairy traditions, but it is possible that she evolved it out of her own imagination. It was not, at any rate, the fairies' own market, but a travelling show designed to beguile and entrap mortals.

[Motif: F258.1]

Fairy midwife. See MIDWIFE TO THE FAIRIES.

Fairy morality. Wherever there were fairy beliefs there has always been a distinction drawn between the good and the bad fairies, the SEELIE COURT and the UNSEELIE COURT, as they put it in Scotland, as between the HOSTS and the fairies in the Highlands. An old Barra piper interviewed by Evans Wentz in *The Fairy-Faith in Celtic Countries* (p. 106) made a distinction between the two.

'Generally,' he said, 'the hosts were evil and the fairies good, though I have heard that the fairies used to *take* cattle and leave their old men rolled up in the hides. . . I saw the men who used to be lifted by the hosts. They would be carried from South Uist as far south as Barra Head, and as far north as Harris. Sometimes when these men were ordered by the hosts to kill men on the road they would kill instead either a horse or a cow; for in that way, so long as an animal was killed, the injunction of the hosts was fulfilled.'

This habit, so frequently described, is part of the DEPENDENCE OF

FAIRIES UPON MORTALS. It will be noticed that even the 'good fairies' were not scrupulous about stealing cattle from mortals.

In England, the picture was the same, though more naïvely expressed. In Leather's *The Folk-Lore of Herefordshire*, for instance, the house-keeper at Pontrilas Court told of the beliefs of old Mary Phillips when she was young.

> She told us how to be very careful not to offend the wicked old fairies, or they would do us dreadful injury. These always accompanied the pretty bright fairies, who were always draped in white, with wands in their hands and flowers in their hair.

In general it may be said of the good fairies that they hold to the saying, 'All that's yours is mine, all that's mine is my own', at least as far as humans are concerned (see FAIRY THEFTS). They are more scrupulous about dealings among themselves. In Jessie Saxby's *Shetland Traditional Lore* (Chapter 10), there is the story of a TROW boy who was guilty of theft from a Trow:

> There was said to be a boy sometimes seen wandering about the mires o' Vaalafiel, the Sma' Waters, and the burn which meanders from Helyawater to the Loch of Watley.
> Whenever the boy was seen he was clad in grey and weeping sadly. His history, which I got from a woman belonging to Uyeasound, who called it 'Gude's truth', is here given as nearly as I can remember.
> 'The Trows are not honest. They will klikk (steal) anything they can find. But they never, never tak aught frae one o' themselves. No! that wad be the worst faut o' any! They are aubar (very greedy and eager) to get silver, and a boy o' their ain stole a silver spoon frae a Kongl-Trow. He was banished frae Trowland on the moment and condemned to wander *for ever* among the lonesome places o' the Isle. But once a year – on Yule Day – he was allowed to veesit Trowland for a peerie start; but a' he got was egg-shells to crack atween his teeth, followed by a lunder upon his lugs, and a wallop ower his back. So he wanders wanless, poor object! But so it *Maun* be for dat's their law!'

Here we see a stern morality at work, which reminds us of ELIDOR's fairies, and an even higher tone is shown by the PLANT RHYS DWFEN, those fairies who inhabited an invisible island off Cardiganshire. An account of these people by John Rhys will be found in his *Celtic Folklore* (pp. 158–60). They were great traders, and riches from all the world were on their small island. Once they were very friendly with a certain Gruffyd ab Einon, and took him with them to their home, where they showed him their treasures and loaded him with presents before taking him back to the mainland. Before he parted with his guide he asked him how they secured their land, even beyond the virtue of the magic herbs that grew on it. 'For surely,' he said, 'there might grow up a traitor amongst you who

could lead an enemy to your land.' 'Traitors cannot grow upon our soil,'
said his guide. And the narrative – quoted from the *Brython* (vol. I) –
continues:

> 'Rhys, the father of our race, bade us, even to the most distant
> descendant, honour our parents and ancestors; love our own wives
> without looking at those of our neighbours; and do our best for our
> children and grandchildren. And he said that if we did so, no one of us
> would ever prove unfaithful to another, or become what you call a
> traitor. The latter is a wholly imaginary character among us; strange
> pictures are drawn of him with his feet like those of an ass, with a nest
> of snakes in his bosom, with a head like the devil's, with hands some-
> what like a man's, while one of them holds a large knife, and the
> family lies dead around the figure. Good-bye!' When Gruffyd looked
> about him he lost sight of the country of *Plant Rhys*, and found himself
> near his home.

The Welsh fairies seem to have been rather unusually high-souled.
As a rule the most people expected of the good fairies was a general
readiness to be helpful, and fairness in their dealings; that is, the return
of FAIRY BORROWINGS, gratitude for kindness done to them, patronage
of true love, delight in music and DANCING and a general interest in
fertility, in NEATNESS, order and beauty.

Even bad fairies did not lie; they only equivocated.

The goodwill of a fairy, however, might at times prove rather embarrassing, like the goodwill of a savage with a code of morality different
from one's own. They might, for instance, avenge one's wrongs with a
disproportionate severity or enrich one at the expense of a neighbour.
This might be illustrated by the tale of 'The Fairy Threshers', to be
found in J. R. W. Coxhead, *Devon Traditions and Fairy-Tales*. It is a tale
of a Devon farmer in whose barn a troop of fairies one day started to
thresh the corn unloaded there. He was a man well versed in fairy
etiquette, and he strictly forbade his men to go near the barn while the
sounds of threshing continued. In the evening they found that the
threshed corn was all piled on one side of the barn and the straw neatly
piled on the other. The farmer left a generous meal of bread and cheese in
the barn and closed the door. Every day the same thing happened and
every day the farmer left his bread and cheese. The strange thing was that
even after all the corn on the farm was carried in the grain continued to
appear, drawn, they concluded, from some neighbouring farm, and as the
year went on more and more far-fetched grain enriched the farmer who
had shown how well he understood how to receive fairy favours. The
farmer might well have felt himself to be in a dilemma: on the one hand
he was guilty of enriching himself by another's loss, on the other, he
could not risk offending a benevolent but touchy set of patrons; but there
is no evidence in the story that the farmer felt any uneasiness at all. Here

is perhaps an explanation of the ambivalent strain in the morals of the good fairies. The tales were conceived when the morals of the community were on the same pattern as that of a savage. The narrators felt no uneasiness about partial charity or disproportionate punishment because considerations of abstract morality had never been presented to them.

[Motifs: D2066; F172.1; F365]

Fairy ointment. The salve, sometimes an oil and sometimes an ointment, by which human eyesight penetrates the GLAMOUR which FAIRIES can cast over it, and sees things as they really are. It also penetrates the spells which cause invisibility. We are told most about it in stories of the MIDWIFE TO THE FAIRIES. The first version of the tale is told in the 13th-century writings of GERVASE OF TILBURY in the account of the Dracae of Brittany. Early as it is, it is the complete story: the fetching of a human midwife at night to an unknown house, the ointment given her to anoint the eyes of the newborn child and the strange enlightenment that follows her casual use of it on one of her own eyes; and it is followed, as in all the later stories, by the innocent betrayal of her forbidden vision and the blinding of the seeing eye. There are dozens of such stories with slight modifications, but Professor John Rhys in *Celtic Folklore* (vol. I, pp. 211–13) gives what may well be the complete story, the tale of EILEAN. The fairy ointment occurs in another, slightly different story, CHERRY OF ZENNOR. In this story in HUNT's collection a country girl seeking service is engaged by a FAIRY WIDOWER as nursemaid to his little boy, and one of her duties is to anoint the eyes of her charge every morning. Her master is amorous and friendly and she is very happy with him, until curiosity about the strange things that happen in her new home leads her to use the ointment on her own eyes, when she sees all sorts of things going on around her, her master as amorous with the midget fairies at the bottom of the spring as he ever was with her. Jealousy leads her to betray herself, and her master regretfully dismisses her though he does not injure her sight. It is clear from the story that the fairy master's first wife was a mortal, which suggests that the ointment was needed only for hybrid fairies, for whole fairies by their own nature could see through the glamour.

[Motifs: F235.4.1; F361.3]

Fairy origins. See ORIGIN OF THE FAIRIES; THEORIES OF FAIRY ORIGINS.

Fairy ped, the. One of the tales of the small, homely FAIRIES who are glad of human help is told by Ruth Tongue in *County Folklore* (vol. VIII, pp. 116–17) in a story of a BROKEN PED:

A farm labourer whose way took him across Wick Moor, heard the sound of someone crying. It was someone small, and within a few steps he came across a child's ped (spade or shovel) broken in half. Being a kindly father himself he stopped and took a few moments to mend it neatly and strongly, never noticing that he was standing close to the barrow called 'Pixy Mound'.

Putting down the mended ped he called out, 'There 'tis then – never cry no more,' and went on his way.

On his return from work the ped was gone, and a fine new-baked cake lay in its place.

Despite the warnings of his comrade the man ate it and found it 'proper good'. Saying so loudly, he called out, 'Goodnight to 'ee,' and prospered ever after.

It is noticeable in the stories of this type that no ill-consequences come of eating FAIRY FOOD outside Fairyland. This man was well versed in fairy etiquette. He expressed appreciation of the food, but he did not give thanks for it. These small fairies seem powerless enough, but they are believed to have control over good and bad luck.

Fairy rade, the. One of the commonest occupations of the HEROIC FAIRIES, and indeed of all branches of the TROOPING FAIRIES, is to go on solemn rides and processions. We come upon it in the early tale of WILD EDRIC, in HERLA'S RADE and in KING ORFEO. In the small number of traditional ballads that relate to the FAIRIES the Fairy Rade takes a prominent part in YOUNG TAMLANE and ALLISON GROSS. In Ireland we have FINVARRA'S Rade, though a large part of the Irish fairies travelled by FAIRY LEVITATION. The riding and the horses of the DAOINE SIDHE were famous. In Scottish literature we find a vivid if grotesque description of the Fairy Rade. In the beginning of the 19th century, Cromek, in his *Remains of Galloway and Nithsdale Song* (pp. 298–9), gives an old woman's account of the Rade of the small but beautiful fairies of that period. Cromek is always very favourable to the fairies:

I' the night afore Roodsmass I had trysted wi' a neeber lass, a Scots mile frae hame, to talk anent buying braws i' the fair:–we had nae sutten lang aneath the hawbuss, till we heard the loud laugh o' fowk riding, wi' the jingling o' bridles, and the clanking o' hoofs. We banged up, thinking they wad ryde owre us; – we kent nae but it was drunken fowk riding to the fair, i' the fore night. We glowred roun' and roun', and sune saw it was the *Fairie fowks' Rade*. We cowered down till they passed by. A leam o' light was dancing owre them, mair bonnie than moon-shine: they were a wee, wee fowk, wi' green scarfs on, but ane that rade formost, and that ane was a good deal langer than the lave, wi' bonnie lang hair bun' about wi' a strap, whilk glented lyke stars.

They rade on braw wee whyte naigs, wi' unco lang swooping tails, an'
manes hung wi' whustles that the win' played on. This, an' their
tongues whan they sang, was like the soun' of a far awa Psalm. Marion
an' me was in a brade lea fiel', whare they cam by us, a high hedge o'
hawtrees keepit them frae gaun through Johnnie Corrie's corn; – but
they lap a' owre't like sparrows, an' gallop't into a green knowe beyont
it. We gade i' the morning to look at the tredded corn, but the fient a
hoof mark was there nor a blade broken.

[Motif: F241.1.0.1]

Fairy thefts. Even setting aside their thefts of human beings, mortal
babies, beautiful maidens, nursing mothers and so on, there is no doubt
that the FAIRIES, like all wild creatures, felt themselves to have a right to
any human possessions, particularly food (see FAIRY MORALITY).
According to KIRK and J. G. CAMPBELL, the Highland fairies do not
steal actual food – except for grain and occasionally meal – but leave the
appearance of the thing and take the substance out of it, the 'FOYSON',
as Kirk calls it, or the '*toradh*' according to the Gaelic word used by
Campbell. They can take the goodness out of cheese, so that it floats in
water like a cork, out of butter, bread or bannocks. Sometimes they
allure cattle away into the fairy KNOWES, but more often they leave the
appearance of a beast behind, as the ox is left in the tale of the TACKSMAN
OF AUCHRIACHAN. Similar stories are told of the Shetland TROWS.
Campbell denies that the fairies ever take milk, and this may be true in
the Highlands, but it is not so everywhere. HUNT has a story of a cow
who was a great favourite with the fairies and who always held back some
of her milk for them. They were invisible to human sight as they milked
her, until one night the dairymaid, who was milking the cows in the
meadow, plucked a FOUR-LEAFED CLOVER in the pad of grass with which
she softened the pail on her head, and saw the tiny people swarming about
with their little pipkins, caressing the cow and milking her. In stories
about the FAIRY OINTMENT, the owners of the seeing eye generally
detect the fairies pilfering in the market place, scraping over the pats of
butter and so on. Tales of FAIRY BORROWING exhibit them in a very
different character, for they are generally scrupulous about returning what
they have borrowed, and often give something in addition to those who
obliged them. Campbell says that the fairies can only take what people do
not deserve to have, what they have grumbled at or refused to share,
which gives them some resemblance to the ABBEY LUBBER and his kind.
There may be some foundation for this, but it does not seem to be borne
out by all the anecdotes he tells. However, many of the stories seem to
illustrate the old saying that ill-gotten gains never prosper.

[Motif: F365]

Fairy trees. Nearly all trees have some sacred association from very early times, but some are more sacred than others. There is the magical trilogy of Oak and ASH and Thorn. There are the fruit-bearing trees, especially Apple and Hazel; there are ROWAN, Holly and Willow, Elder and Alder. Some trees seem to be regarded as having a personality of their own, and some are more specifically a haunt of FAIRIES or spirits. Most people would probably think first of an oak as a sacred tree, worshipped by the Druids, and it is strong enough certainly to stand in its own right, though everyone knows the couplet,

> Fairy folks
> Are in old oaks,

and many oak coppices are said to be haunted by the sinister OAKMEN. Hawthorn has certain qualities of its own, but it is primarily thought of as a tree sacred to or haunted by the fairies. This is especially so of solitary thorns growing near fairy hills, or of a ring of three or more hawthorns. White may in blossom was supposed to bring death into the house, and although it was brought round on May Morning it was hung up outside.

Ruth Tongue collected a folk-song in Somerset whose chorus illustrates the popular belief about three very different trees:

> Ellum do grieve,
> Oak he do hate,
> Willow do walk
> If you travels late.

Possibly because of the vulnerability of elms to disease, it was thought that if one elm was cut down a neighbouring elm would pine and die in sympathy. Oaks, however, as fitted their ancient, god-like status, bitterly resented being cut, and an oak coppice which sprang from the roots of a felled oakwood was malevolent and dangerous to travel through by night, more especially if it was a blue-bell wood. Willows were even more sinister, for they had a habit of uprooting themselves on a dark night and following a solitary traveller, muttering. TOLKIEN is faithful to folk tradition in the ogre-ish behaviour of Old Man Willow. Wood-Martin, in his *Traces of the Elder Faiths of Ireland*, devotes some attention to tree beliefs. For instance, speaking of the sacred ash, he mentions one in the parish of Clenor in County Cork, whose branches were never cut, though firewood was scarce all round, and another in Borrisokane, the old Bell Tree, sacred to May Day rites, of which it was believed that if any man burnt even a chip of it on his hearth his whole house would be burned down. A similar fate was brought down on himself by a cottager who tried to cut a branch from a sacred elder overhanging a saint's well. He tried three times; twice he stopped because his house seemed to be on fire, but found it a false alarm. The third time he determined not to be put off by appearances and carried the branch home, only to find his cottage burnt to the ground. He had had his warning. There are two views of the elder. It has been a sacred tree, as we may see from Hans Andersen's 'Elder-Flower Mother'. In Lincolnshire, too, it used to be thought necessary to ask the tree's permission before cutting a branch. The formula was 'Owd Gal, give me of thy wood, an Oi will give some of moine, when I graws inter a tree' (*County Folk-Lore*, vol. v, p. 21). The flowers and fruit were much esteemed for wine, the tree was a shelter against flies, and it was said also that the good fairies found protection under it from witches and evil spirits. On the other hand, in Oxfordshire and the Midlands, many elders were strongly suspected of being transformed witches, and they were supposed to bleed if they were cut. The witch of the Rollright Stones took the form of an elder tree according to the popular legend. D. A. Mac Manus in *The Middle Kingdom*, an explanation of comparatively modern fairy beliefs in Ireland, devotes a chapter to fairy trees, and gives many examples of the judgements falling on people who have destroyed sacred thorn trees. He believes some trees to be haunted by fairies and others by demons, and gives one example of a close group of three trees, two thorns and an elder, which was haunted by three evil spirits. He says that when an oak and ash and thorn grew close together, a twig taken from each, bound with red thread, was thought to be a protection against spirits of the night.

In England, ash was a protection against mischievous spirits, but in Scotland the mountain ash, rowan, was even more potent, probably because of its red berries:

> Rowan, lammer (amber) and red threid
> Pits witches to their speed,

as the old saying went. Red was always a vital and conquering colour. A berried holly was potent for good. On the other hand, a barren one – that is, one that bore only male flowers – was thought to be malevolent and dangerous. Two fruit-bearing trees, apple and hazel, had specially magical qualities. Hazel-nuts were the source of wisdom and also of fertility, and apples of power and youth. There was some danger attached to each of them. An 'ymp-tree' – that is, a grafted apple – was under fairy influence, and a man who slept under it was liable, as Sir Lancelot found, to be carried away by fairy ladies. A somewhat similar fate befell Queen Meroudys in the medieval poem of KING ORFEO. The fertility powers of nut-trees could be overdone, and the Devil was said to be abroad in the woods at the time of nut-gathering; 'so many cratches, so many cradles', goes the Somerset saying quoted by Ruth Tongue in *County Folklore* (vol. VIII). On the other hand, the hazel-nuts eaten by trout or salmon gave their flesh a power of imparting wisdom at the first taste of it. It was to this that FINN owed his tooth of wisdom.

Mac Manus mentions other fairy trees, Scots fir, birch, blackthorn and broom, though this last is a shrub rather than a tree. A beech is a holy tree, with no connection with fairies. It is said that the prayers spoken under it go straight to Heaven. Otherwise it is difficult to think of a tree which has not some fairy connection.

[Motifs: A2766.1; D950.2; D950.6; D950.10; D950.13; D1385.2.5]

'Fairy Widower, The'. This story, which comes in HUNT's *Popular Romances of the West of England* (pp. 114–18) is another story on the same general theme as 'CHERRY OF ZENNOR', but rather more romantically conceived and with no mention of a TABOO or of the FAIRY OINTMENT. It may be described as one of the VISITS TO FAIRYLAND, for Jenny was returned home punctually after her year and a day.

Not many years since a very pretty girl called Jenny Permuen lived in Towednack. She was of poor parents, and lived in service. There was a good deal of romance, or what the old people called nonsense, in Jenny. She was always smartly dressed, and she would arrange wild-flowers very gracefully in her hair. As a consequence, Jenny attracted much of the attention of the young men, and again, as a consequence, a great deal of envy from the young women. Jenny was, no doubt, vain; and her vanity, which most vain persons will say is not usual, was accompanied by a considerable amount of weakness on any point connected with her person. Jenny loved flattery, and being a poor, uneducated girl, she had not the genius necessary to disguise her frailty. When any man told her she was lovely, she quite admitted the truth of the assertion by her pleased looks. When any woman told her not to be such a fool as to believe such nonsense, her lips, and eyes too, seemed to say you are only jealous of me, and if there was a pool of water near, nature's mirror was speedily consulted to prove to herself that she was really the best-looking girl in the parish. Well, one day Jenny, who had been for some time out of a situation, was sent by her mother down to the lower parishes to 'look for a place'. Jenny went on merrily enough until she came to the four cross roads on the Lady Downs, when she discovered that she knew not which road to take. She looked first one way and then another, and she felt fairly puzzled, so she sat down on a boulder of granite, and began, in pure want of thought, to break off the beautiful fronds of ferns which grew abundantly around the spot she had chosen. It is hard to say what her intentions were, whether to go on, to return, or to remain where she was, so utterly indifferent did Jenny appear. Some say she was entirely lost in wild dreams of self-glorification. However, she had not sat long on this granite stone, when hearing a voice near her, she turned round and saw a young man.

'Well, young woman,' says he, 'and what are you after?'

'I am after a place, sir,' says she.

'And what kind of a place do you want, my pretty young woman?' says he, with the most winning smile in the world.

'I am not particular, sir,' says Jenny; 'I can make myself generally useful.'

'Indeed,' says the stranger; 'do you think you could look after a widower with one little boy?'

'I am very fond of children,' says Jenny.

'Well, then,' says the widower, 'I wish to hire for a year and a day a young woman of your age, to take charge of my little boy.'

'And where do you live?' inquired Jenny.

'Not far from here,' said the man; 'will you go with me and see?'

'An it please you to show me,' said Jenny.

'But first, Jenny Permuen,' – Jenny stared when she found the stranger knew her name. He was evidently an entire stranger in the parish, and how could he have learnt her name, she thought. So she looked at him somewhat astonished. 'Oh! I see, you suppose I didn't know you; but do you think a young widower could pass through Towednack and not be struck with such a pretty girl? Beside,' he said, 'I watched you one day dressing your hair in one of my ponds, and stealing some of my sweet-scented violets to put in those lovely tresses. Now, Jenny Permuen, will you take the place?'

'For a year and a day?' asked Jenny.

'Yes, and if we are pleased with each other then, we can renew the engagement.'

'Wages,' said Jenny.

The widower rattled the gold in his breeches-pocket.

'Wages! well, whatever you like to ask,' said the man.

Jenny was charmed; all sorts of visions rose before her eyes, and without hesitation she said –

'Well, I'll take the place, sir; when must I come?'

'I require you now – my little boy is very unhappy, and I think you can make him happy again. You'll come at once?'

'But mother' –

'Never mind mother, I'll send word to her.'

'But my clothes' –

'The clothes you have will be all you require, and I'll put you in a much gayer livery soon.'

'Well, then,' says Jane, ''tis a bargain' –

'Not yet,' says the man; 'I've got a way of my own, and you must swear my oath.'

Jenny looked frightened.

'You need not be alarmed,' said the man, very kindly; 'I only wish you to kiss that fern-leaf which you have in your hand, and say, "For a year and a day I promise to stay."'

'Is that all?' said Jenny; so she kissed the fern-leaf and said –

'For a year and a day
I promise to stay.'

Without another word he walked forward on the road leading east-ward. Jenny followed him – she thought it strange that her new master never opened his lips to her all the way, and she grew very tired with walking. Still onward and onward he went, and Jenny was sadly weary and her feet dreadfully sore. At last poor Jenny began to cry. He heard her sob and looked round.

'Tired are you, poor girl? Sit down – sit down,' says the man, and he took her by the hand and led her to a mossy bank. His kindness completely overcame her, and she burst into a flood of tears. He allowed her to cry for a few minutes, then taking a bunch of leaves from the bottom of the bank, he said, 'Now I must dry your eyes, Jenny.'

He passed the bunch of leaves rapidly first over one and then over the other eye.

The tears were gone. Her weariness had departed. She felt herself moving, yet she did not know that she had moved from the bank. The ground appeared to open, and they were passing very rapidly under the earth. At last there was a pause.

'Here we are, Jenny,' said he, 'there is yet a tear of sorrow on your eyelids, and no human tears can enter our homes, let me wipe them away.' Again Jenny's eyes were brushed with the small leaves as before, and, lo! before her was such a country as she had never seen previously. Hill and valley were covered with flowers, strangely varied in colour, but combining into a most harmonious whole; so that the region appeared sown with gems which glittered in a light as brilliant as that of the summer sun, yet as mild as the moonlight. There were rivers clearer than any water she had ever seen on the granite hills, and water-falls and fountains; while everywhere ladies and gentlemen dressed in green and gold were walking, or sporting, or reposing on banks of flowers, singing songs or telling stories. Oh! it was a beautiful world.

'Here we are at home,' said Jenny's master; and strangely enough he too was changed; he was the most beautiful little man she had ever seen, and he wore a green silken coat covered with ornaments of gold. 'Now,' said he again, 'I must introduce you to your little charge.' He led Jenny into a noble mansion in which all the furniture was of pearl and ivory, inlaid with gold and silver, and studded with emeralds. After passing through many rooms, they came at length to one which was hung all over with lace, as fine as the finest cobweb, most beautifully worked with flowers; and, in the middle of this room was a little cot made out of some beautiful sea-shell, which reflected so many colours that Jenny could scarcely bear to look at it. She was led to the side of this, and she saw, as she said, 'One of God's sweetest angels sleeping there.' The little boy was so beautiful that she was ravished with delight.

'This is your charge,' said the father; 'I am the king in this land, and I have my own reasons for wishing my boy to know something of human nature. Now you have nothing to do but to wash and dress the boy when he wakes, to take him to walk in the garden, and to put him to bed when he is weary.'

Jenny entered on her duties, and gave, and continued to give, satisfaction. She loved the darling little boy, and he appeared to love her, and the time passed away with astonishing rapidity.

Somehow or other she had never thought of her mother. She had never thought of her home at all. She was happy and in luxury, and never reckoned the passing of time.

Howsoever happiness may blind us to the fact, the hours and days move onward. The period for which Jenny had bound herself was gone, and one morning she awoke and all was changed. She was sleeping in her own bed in her mother's cottage. Everything was strange to her, and she appeared strange to everybody. Numerous old gossips were called in to see Jenny, and to all Jenny told her strange tale alike. One day, old Mary Calineck of Zennor came, and she heard, as all the others had done, the story of the widower, and the baby, and the beautiful country. Some of the old crones who were there at the time said the girl was 'gone clean daft.' Mary looked very wise – 'Crook your arm, Jenny,' said she.

Jenny sat up in the bed and bent her arm, resting her hand on her hip.

'Now say, I hope my arm may never come uncrooked if I have told ye a word of a lie.'

'I hope my arm may never come uncrooked if I have told ye a word of a lie,' repeated Jenny.

'Uncrook your arm,' said Mary.

Jenny stretched out her arm.

'It is truth the girl is telling,' said Mary; 'and she has been carried by the Small People to some of their countries under the hills.'

'Will the girl ever come right in her mind?' asked her mother.

'All in good time,' said Mary; 'and if she will but be honest, I have no doubt but her master will take care that she never wants.'

Howbeit, Jenny did not get on very well in the world. She married and was discontented and far from happy. Some said she always pined after the fairy widower. Others said they were sure she had misbehaved herself, or she would have brought back lots of gold. If Jenny had not dreamt all this, while she was sitting picking ferns on the granite boulder, she had certainly had a very strange adventure.

A story even more similar to 'Cherry of Zennor' is told by BOTTRELL in *Traditions and Hearthside Stories* (II, pp. 175–95). It is called 'The

Fairy Master', the heroine is Grace Treva and the Fairy Master is Bob o' the Carn. The fairy ointment and the return to her home occur in this tale, but Grace is given her wages, and after some little time of pining she married a farmer and settled down to a happy human life. In this tale the old mother-in-law, Aunt Prudence, kept a village school. It is therefore probable that Bob o' the Carn's first wife was human, and that the child needed the ointment to give him fairy sight.

[Type: ML4075. Motifs: D965; D971.3; F211.3; F370; F372; F376]

Fairyland. See CAPTIVES IN FAIRYLAND; TIME IN FAIRYLAND.

Fane. Jamieson in his *Scottish Dictionary* mentions Fane as the Ayrshire name for a fairy, and it is also listed by Lewis Spence in *The British Fairy Tradition*. In Grant's *Scottish National Dictionary*, however, it is traced to J. Train's *Poetical Reveries* (1806), and it is suggested that it was possibly coined by Train as a Scottish version of the English FAY. The lines quoted are:

> The story ran to ilka ane
> How Kate was haunted wi' a fane.

In default of further evidence, the name should possibly be listed as literary. MAC RITCHIE, however, in his *Testimony of Tradition* suggests a connection with the FEENS, or Fians, which he thinks almost identical with the PECHS.

Farisees, or Pharisees. KEIGHTLEY in *The Fairy Mythology* (p. 305) quotes Brand in confirmation of 'farisees' as the Suffolk name for fairies. The Suffolk children used to be confused between the farisees and the biblical mentions of the Pharisees. Brand in *Popular Antiquities* (vol. II, p. 503) says:

> Not many years ago a butcher near Woodbridge went to a farmer's wife to buy a calf, and finding, as he expressed it, that 'the cratur was all o' a muck' he desired the farmer to hang a flint by a string in the crib, so as to be just clear of the calf's head. 'Becaze,' said he, 'the calf is rid every night by the *farisees*, and the stone will brush them off.'

AUBREY recommends a SELF-BORED STONE hung above the mangers in the same way to prevent horses from being elf-ridden.

Farvann (*farbhann*). The name of the FAIRY DOG loosed on Hugh Macleod of Raasay when he stole the FAIRY CUP from a fairy BRUGH. See also THEFTS FROM THE FAIRIES.

[Motif: F241.6]

Fary. The dialect name for fairy in Northumberland is 'fary', written in this way, but pronounced as if with a double r. KEIGHTLEY gives several stories of the faries from Richardson's *Table-Book*, three about FAIRY OINTMENT, one of which is the standard tale of the MIDWIFE TO THE FAIRIES. In one a doctor takes the place of the midwife, and in the third a fary is brought to be fostered by a mortal woman, and it is the husband not the foster-mother who steals the ointment and whose curiosity is punished in the usual way. A fourth story is that of AINSEL, a version of the 'Noman' story of which there are several different variants in these islands.

Fashions in fairy-lore. Even the most flaccid and degenerate of the literary FAIRIES have some point in common with the fairies in folk tradition, but, as a rule, the poets and story-tellers pick out one aspect from the varied and intricate world of fairy tradition, and the aspect chosen differs not only from poet to poet but from one period to another. The FAIRIES OF MEDIEVAL ROMANCES are among the HEROIC FAIRIES in type, of human size and often amorous of mortals, expert in enchantment and GLAMOUR, generally beautiful but occasionally hideous HAGS. Many of them are half-forgotten gods and goddesses, euhemerized into mortals with magical powers. The goddesses are more frequent than the gods. It was literary fashion which chose out this type because the romances derived from Celtic hero tales founded on the Celtic Pantheon; scattered references in the MEDIEVAL CHRONICLES show that very different types of fairies were available to the medieval poets if they had chosen to use them.

A different type of spirit, though no less true to tradition, appears among the ELIZABETHAN and JACOBEAN FAIRIES. It is true that Spenser uses the fairies, enchanters and witches of the Arthurian legends in the machinery of his FAERIE QUEENE, but on the whole the spotlight is turned upon the DIMINUTIVE FAIRIES. They appear in John Lyly's *Endimion*, in the anonymous *Maides Metamorphosis* and the WISDOME OF DR DODYPOL, and above all in a MIDSUMMER NIGHT'S DREAM. Queen MAB in *Romeo and Juliet* is even more minute than the ELVES who waited on TITANIA. The Jacobean poets followed hard on the fashion. The diminutive fairies in Drayton, HERRICK, *et al.*, made an extravaganza of Shakespeare's little fairies until, with the Duchess of Newcastle, they became miracles of littleness. Even MILTON in *Paradise Lost* used the elves to illustrate diminution and small size. The exception to these dainty and miniature fairies is the rougher, homely HOBGOBLIN, by whatever name he is called – ROBIN GOODFELLOW, PUCK or the LUBBARD FIEND. Since that period, the tiny fairies have constantly haunted literature.

The 18th century was the first period in which books were written expressly for the edification of children. Educational text books had been written before – one of the first books printed was Caxton's *Babees Book* to train pages in etiquette, and there were Latin and French conversation books, but works of fiction were first written expressly for children in the 18th century. At the end of the 17th century the sophisticated French fairy-stories of PERRAULT and Madame D'AULNOY were translated into English. They began as real traditional tales, polished to meet the taste of the French court, and they were equally popular in England. Half the court seem to have tried their hands at them, and as time went on they moved farther away from their original. The FAIRY GOD-MOTHERS, already at one remove from folk fairies, became relentless moralists, driving their protégés along the path to virtue. The trend persisted into the 19th century, and it was not until a quarter of it had passed that the researches of the folklorists began to have some effect on children's literature. The Romantic Revival, however, had begun before this to affect the writings of the poets. Collins, SCOTT, HOGG and Keats wrote in the folk-fairy tradition, and as the century went on writers of children's stories followed them; Jean INGELOW and J. H. EWING are among the best. At the beginning of the 20th century, an extreme tenderness and sensibility about children almost overwhelmed the folk fairies and turned them into airy, tenuous, pretty creatures without meat or muscles, made up of froth and whimsy. Rudyard KIPLING fought against this tendency in *Puck of Pook's Hill*, and now, in TOLKIEN, his predecessors and successors, we enjoy a world in which imagination has superseded fancy; but whimsy is still with us in the works of the weaker writers.

Faults condemned by the fairies. The FAIRIES have a code of morality of their own and are strict in enforcing it (see FAIRY MORALITY). We can deduce something of their nature from the degree of severity with which they punish infringements of their code. In the first place, they are a secret people and punish any attempts at spying or INFRINGE-MENTS OF FAIRY PRIVACY, often to the utmost of their power. In the various FAIRY OINTMENT stories, there are varying degrees of culpability. Sometimes the MIDWIFE TO THE FAIRIES touches her own eye inadvertently with a finger still smeared with the ointment, and often she is allowed the benefit of the doubt and only the fairy sight is taken from her. In the tale of 'CHERRY OF ZENNOR', Cherry had wilfully offended to spy on her master from jealousy and she was left the sight of her human eye and only banished from Fairyland. In the parallel story of JENNY PERMUEN, Jenny made no mention of the fairy ointment and reported herself as sent back from Fairyland when the year and a day for which she had been hired was over. No penalty except that of inability to return was imposed on them for reporting their adventures. The most severe punishment was rightly inflicted on Joan, Squire Lovell's housekeeper, in HUNT's story in *Popular Romances of the West of England*

(p. 111) of 'How Joan Lost the Sight of her Eye'. This was inflicted for sheer meddling. Joan was on no legitimate business, but was merely paying a friendly call on Betty Trenance, reputed to be a witch but actually a fairy. Peeping through the latch-hole before she knocked, she saw Betty anointing her children's eyes with a green ointment, which she hid carefully away before answering the door. Joan, however, contrived to get hold of the ointment, and touched her eye with it with the usual result. When she betrayed her fairy sight to Betty's husband, he not only blinded her right eye but tricked her into a ride on a devilish horse who nearly carried her into Toldava fowling pool in the company of the Devil and all his rout.

People who spied on the fairy revels or boasted of fairy favours were generally punished, sometimes with BLIGHTS AND ILLNESSES, and those who stole fairy treasures did so in danger of their lives. Spies were often punished only by pinching, like Richard of Lelant, the old fisherman who saw Lelant Church lit up and climbed up to peep in at a window. Inside the church he saw the funeral procession of a fairy queen, and foolishly betrayed himself by an exclamation of surprise. At once the fairies flew past him, pricking him with sharp weapons. He only saved his life by flight (Hunt, *Popular Romances*, p. 102). The old MISER ON THE FAIRY GUMP in Hunt's story (p. 98), who tried to capture the royal dais and table at the revels on the Gump, deserved a severer punishment. Just as he raised his hat to cover the high table, a whistle rang out, a thousand cobwebs were thrown over him and he was bound to the earth, pinched, pricked and tormented till cockcrow. In the morning he hobbled down to the town, no richer than he had been, and permanently tormented by RHEUMATISM. It must be acknowledged that he deserved it.

Lack of GENEROSITY, rudeness and selfishness are all unpopular with fairies, as many traditional fairy-tales show. Gloomy fellows are disliked, and a merry heart is popular.

One of the most notable traits of the fairies is their strong interest in NEATNESS and orderly ways. They expect to find the hearths that they visit swept clean, with fresh water set out for their use. A breach of this habit is often punished, as in the tale of the milkmaid who forgot to leave out clean water for the fairy babies and refused to get up when reminded of it. Her companion dragged herself out of bed to set the water and was rewarded with a silver sixpence, but the milkmaid was punished by seven years' painful lameness. Scolds and wife-beating husbands are both likely to be punished. Ruth Tongue gives a story in *County Folklore* (vol. VIII) of an old bully of a farmer, the scourge of his family, who met his death in a bog because of the ill-will of the fairies. In short, the faults chiefly condemned by them are undue curiosity, meanness, sluttishness, ill-temper and bad manners.

[Motifs: F235.4.1; F361.3; F361.14]

Fays. 'Fay' was the earliest form in which the word 'fairy' appears. It is generally supposed to be a broken-down form of 'Fatae', the Fates, which in Romance tradition became less formidable and multiplied in number. The word 'fairy' was originally 'fayerie', the enchantment of the fays, and only later became applied to the people working the enchantment rather than to the state of illusion.

Fear Dearig. See FIR DARIG.

Feens, or Fians. FINN and his FIANNA Fin were in the Scottish Gaelic tradition translated into Finn and the Feinne, and the Fenian BROCHS were said to be built by them. According to David MAC RITCHIE, in his *Testimony of Tradition* and other writings, the Feens were a dwarfish Ugrian people who were spread over Finland, Lapland, Norway, Sweden, Denmark, northern Germany, England, Scotland, Ireland and Wales, and who were conquered and driven underground by the Milesians or Scots. This follows the old Irish traditional history (see TUATHA DE DANANN) and is plausibly presented by Mac Ritchie with a wealth of evidence, though with more attention to that which confirms his theory than to that which tends to disprove it. He also makes the SILKIES and ROANE a part of the same pattern, Finmen and Finwomen in their sealskin kayaks. If we subscribe to his theory, we have to abandon the great figure of OSSIAN, towering on his white horse above the puny modern men, for a stunted, cunning MAGICIAN with almost superhuman strength of muscle, but we may leave them their music, tale-telling and wealth of golden treasure.

Feeorin. James Bowker in his *Goblin Tales of Lancashire* uses 'Feeorin' as a collective noun for fairies. The word has a Celtic sound, reminiscent of the Manx FERRISHYN. It is the small fairy that is indicated, green-coated, generally red-capped, and with the usual fairy traits of love of DANCING and music. In Bowker's account of a FAIRY FUNERAL (p. 83), the Feeorin are seen conducting a miniature funeral with all the sounds of grief and chanting, carrying with them a tiny coffin, the corpse lying in it with its face uncovered. The two spectators of the ceremony see with horror that the face is that of one of them – Robin, the younger of the pair, who was indeed killed a month later. However gruesome the spectacle, the Feeorin may be thought to be acting a friendly part, for their warning gave Robin, who had been wild and thoughtless, an opportunity for repentance and amendment. These phantom funerals are common in folk tradition, but the actors in them are not usually fairies. In HUNT's 'Fairy Funeral' the little corpse was the Fairy Queen herself.
[Motif: D1825.7.1]

Fennel, or Finnen. See AINE.

Fenoderee, or Phynnodderee (*fin-ord-er-ree*). There are about five ways of spelling the name of this, which is generally described as the Manx BROWNIE. Indeed, he fulfils all the functions of a brownie, though he is more like LOB-LIE-BY-THE-FIRE, whom MILTON calls 'the LUB-BARD FIEND'. He is large, hairy and ugly, but of enormous strength. There is a story, told by Sophia Morrison in *Manx Fairy Tales*, that when the Fenoderee was working in Gordon he happened to meet the blacksmith one night and offered to shake hands with him. The blacksmith prudently held out the sock of a plough which he was carrying, and Fenoderee twisted it almost out of shape, and said with satisfaction: 'There's some strong Manxmen in the world yet.' Similar tales are told about OSSIAN in his old age and about the last of the PECHS. Curiously enough, this uncouth creature is said to have been once one of the FERRISHYN, banished from Fairyland. He had fallen in love with a mortal girl who lived in Glen Aldyn, and had absented himself from the Autumn Festival to dance with her in the Glen of Rushen. For this he had been transformed into a hairy shape and banished until Doomsday. He still kept a kindly feeling for humanity, however, and willingly performed all sorts of tasks when his help was needed. Every collection of Manx fairy tales contains some anecdotes about the Fenoderee. It seems he was an individual, not a class, but he was sometimes confused with the GLASHAN, a Manx HOBGOBLIN whose memory has faded and who is now blended with the GLASTYN, a very different kind of creature. He seems to be multiple because he went from place to place, either having been offended or banished by the offer of clothes. KEIGHTLEY quotes several anecdotes, told by Train in his *Account of Man* (vol. II, p. 148). It is he that tells of Fenoderee's banishment. He also tells of how the Fenoderee was offended because a farmer criticized his grass cutting, saying that it was not close enough. After this he gave up helping the farmer, but followed him, grubbing up the roots so fiercely that the farmer's legs were endangered. Train also gives one account of the gift of clothes. A gentleman was building a large house at Sholt-e-Will at the foot of Snafield Mountain. All the stones were lying ready quarried on the beach, among them a large and beautiful block of white marble which was too heavy for all the masons together to lift. However, Fenoderee carried it and all the rest up from the shore to the site in one single night. The gentleman, wishing to reward him, ordered a fine suit of clothes to be made for him. Fenoderee picked them up one by one, saying:

> 'Cap for the head, alas, poor head!
> Coat for the back, alas, poor back!
> Breeches for the breech, alas, poor breech!
> If these be all thine, thine cannot be the merry glen of Rushen.'

And with that he went wailing away.

Sophia Morrison tells a rather different version of the story in which

Fenoderee was working for the Radcliffes of Gordon. During his time there he was dissatisfied with Big Gordon, the farmer, because he blew hot and cold with the same breath, blowing on his fingers to warm them and his porridge to cool it. But he left Gordon in the end because of a gift of clothes, and with a very similar rhyme. In his next place he put himself to great trouble to round up a hare with the sheep, as so many HOBS have done. In Sophia Morrison's tale he seems rather more of a BOGIE, for he once terrified the miller's wife in Glen Garragh Mill, and was set by her to draw water with a sieve so that she could bake him a cake. According to Miss Morrison, too, the Fenoderee has a wife with whom he quarrels like an ordinary stone-throwing GIANT. There seems to be some confusion here.

Walter Gill, in *A Second Manx Scrapbook* (p. 326), translates 'Yn Folder Gastey', 'The Nimble Mower', a delightful song about the Fenoderee:

> Finoderee stole at dawn to the Round-field,
>   And skimmed the dew like cream from a bowl;
> The maiden's herb and the herb of the cattle,
>   He was treading them under his naked sole.
>
> He was swinging wide on the floor of the meadow,
>   Letting the thick swath leftward fall;
> We thought his mowing was wonderful last year,
>   But the bree of him this year passes all!
>
> He was lopping the blooms of the level meadow,
>   He was laying the long grass ready to rake;
> The bog-bean out on the rushy curragh,
>   As he stroked and mowed it was fair ashake!
>
> The scythe that was at him went whizzing through all things,
>   Shaving the Round-field bare to the sod,
> And whenever he spotted a blade left standing
>   He stamped it down with his heel unshod!

Later he says:

Finoderee's handling of his *yiarn mooar* was ... masterly, as might have been expected from one of his superb physique. Moreover, in that age of gold, before he suffered his rebuff from the thankless farmer near St Trinian's, he was more willing and more energetic than ever since. He was more numerous, or more ubiquitous, too, and most of the larger farms were lucky enough to possess one of him. As we may gather from the song, he was then not too shy to start work at daybreak and let himself be seen and admired in the grey light by the respectful villagers, while they peeped over each other's shoulders through the sallies and alders that screened the little verdant meadows of the Curragh Glass. In the days ere he lost confidence in Manxmen he not only mowed for them, he raked and carried for them, reaped, made bands, tied sheaves and built the stack for them, threshed it and stacked the straw again, herded sheep and cattle, and whisked horse-loads of wrack and stone about the land like the little giant he was. He attacked his jobs like a convulsion of nature, making the hard ground soft and the soft ground water – hence the Curraghs. When he mowed he flung the grass to the morning star or the paling moon without heed to the cock's kindly word of warning from the near-by farmyard. He could clear a daymath in an hour and want nothing better than a crockful of bithag afterwards. The concentrated fury of his threshing resembled a whirlwind, an earthquake, Doomsday; his soost was a blur and the air went dark with the flying husks. In the zeal and zest of his shepherding he sometimes drove an odd animal over the cliffs, allowing, but he made up for that by folding in wild goats, purrs and hares along with the sheep. For he was a doer, not a thinker, mightier in thew than in brain, and when he should have been cultivating his intelligence at the village school between his nights of labour he was curled up asleep in some hiding-place he had at the top of the glen.

It will be seen in this passage that Gill thinks it possible that the Finoderee was plural, not singular, but this would discount the story of his banishment.

Dora Broome, in *Fairy Tales from the Isle of Man*, has a rather different story, in which Fenoderee is invoked by a foolish man to cure his little red cow. Fenoderee appears and cures the cow but carries it off in the end. It is interesting to see how many of the widely-spread anecdotes, some of them international tale types, have attached themselves to the Fenoderee.

[Motifs: F252.4; F381.3; F405.11]

Feriers, or Ferishers. A Suffolk name for the FAIRIES. They are also called FARISEES or FRAIRIES. Camilla Gurdon in *County Folk-Lore* (vol. I, p. 36) quotes an extract from Hollingworth's *History of Suffolk* about these little Feriers.

Stowmarket Fairies. Fairies (Feriers) frequented several houses in Tavern Street about 80 to 100 years since. They never appeared as long as any one was about. People used to lie hid to see them, and some have seen them. Once in particular by a wood-stack up near the brick-yard there was a large company of them dancing, singing, and playing music together. They were very small people, quite little creatures and very merry. But as soon as they saw anybody they all vanished away. In the houses after they had fled, on going upstairs sparks of fire as bright as stars used to appear under the feet of the persons who disturbed them.

From the same source there is an account of a child just saved from being carried off by the Feriers, and another of a woman who found a CHANGELING in her baby's place, but contrary to the ordinary practice, she was so kind to it that the Feriers were grateful and left a small piece of silver in her pocket every morning.

Ferishers. See FERIERS.

Ferries. The most usual name for the Shetland and Orcadian FAIRIES is TROWS, and all the usual elfish and fairy legends are told about them. Occasionally, however, they are called 'Ferries', but there seems to be no difference of meaning in the two words except that ferry is more often used as an adjective as in 'ferry tuns', tunes learnt from the Trows or overheard from the fairy KNOWES. Passages quoted in *County Folk-Lore* (vol. III, pp. 20–30) contain some mention of the Ferries.

Ferrishyn (*ferrishin*). A Manx name for the fairie tribe; the singular is 'Ferrish'. Gill supposes it to be derived from the English 'Fairies'. He gives a list of names of places and plants in which 'ferrish' occurs in *A Second Manx Scrapbook* (pp. 217–18). The Ferrishyn were the TROOP-ING FAIRIES of Man, though there does not seem to be any distinction between them and the SLEIH BEGGEY. They were less aristocratic than the fairies of Ireland and Wales, and they have no named fairy king or queen. They were small, generally described as three feet in height, though sometimes as one foot. They stole human babies and left CHANGE-LINGS, like other FAIRIES, and they loved to frequent human houses and workshops when the inhabitants had gone to bed. Their favourite sport was hunting, and they had horses and hounds of their own. The hounds were sometimes described as white with red ears, like FAIRY DOGS else-where, but sometimes as all colours of the rainbow, red, blue, green, yellow. The huntsmen wore green coats and red caps, so the hunt must have been a gay sight as they passed. They could hear whatever was said out of doors. Every wind stirring carried the sound to their ears, and this made people very careful to speak of them in favourable terms.

Fetch. A name common all over England for a double or CO-WALKER, very similar to the North Country WAFF. When seen at night, it is said to be a death portent, and is at all times ominous. AUBREY in his *Mis-cellanies* (pp. 89–90) records that:

> The beautiful Lady Diana Rich, daughter to the Earl of Holland, as she was walking in her father's garden at Kensington, to take the fresh air before dinner, about eleven o'clock, being then very well, met with her own apparition, habit, and every thing, as in a looking-glass. About a month after, she died of the small-pox. And it is said that her sister, the Lady Isabella Thynne, saw the like of herself also, before she died. This account I had from a person of honour.

[Motif: E723.2]

Fianna (*feen-a*), **the.** The great fighting force of Ireland, serving under the Ard Righ, or High King, and it was at its greatest when FINN Mac Cumhal was its last and greatest leader. The account of the Fianna and of the career of Finn Mac Cumhal, drawn from the Ancient Manuscripts of Ireland, is to be found in Lady Gregory's *Gods and Fighting Men* and also in O'Grady's *Silva Gadelica*. An account of the manuscript sources of these tales is given in Professor O'Curry's *Lectures on the MS. Materials of Ancient Irish History*. James Stephens's *Irish Fairy Tales*, illustrated by Arthur Rackham, gives a delightfully humorous turn to some of the stories.

The Fianna were an order of chivalry whose qualifications were even more rigid than those of King Arthur's Round Table. They are given in detail in *Gods and Fighting Men* (pp. 169–70):

And the number of the Fianna of Ireland at that time was seven score and ten chief men, every one of them having three times nine fighting men under him. And every man of them was bound to three things, to take no cattle by oppression, not to refuse any man, as to cattle or riches; no one of them to fall back before nine fighting men. And there was no man taken into the Fianna until his tribe and his kindred would give securities for him, that even if they themselves were all killed he would not look for satisfaction for their death. But if he himself would harm others, that harm was not to be avenged on his people. And there was no man taken into the Fianna till he knew the twelve books of poetry. And before any man was taken, he would be put into a deep hole in the ground up to his middle, and he having his shield and a hazel rod in his hand. And nine men would go the length of ten furrows from him and would cast their spears at him at the one time. And if he got a wound from one of them, he was not thought fit to join with the Fianna. And after that again, his hair would be fastened up, and he put to run through the woods of Ireland, and the Fianna following after him to try could they wound him, and only the length of a branch between themselves and himself when they started. And if they came up with him and wounded him, he was not let join them; or if his spears had trembled in his hand, or if a branch of a tree had undone the plaiting of his hair, or if he had cracked a dry stick under his foot, and he running. And they would not take him among them till he had made a leap over a stick the height of himself, and till he had stooped under one the height of his knee, and till he had taken a thorn out from his foot with his nail, and he running his fastest. But if he had done all these things, he was of Finn's people.

It was good wages Finn and the Fianna got at that time; in every district a townland, in every house the fostering of a pup or a whelp from Samhain to Beltaine, and a great many things along with that. But good as the pay was, the hardships and the dangers they went through for it were greater. For they had to hinder the strangers and robbers from beyond the seas, and every bad thing, from coming into Ireland. And they had hard work enough in doing that.

This royal band were served by a great retinue of Druids, physicians, minstrels and musicians, messengers, door-keepers, cup-bearers and huntsmen, besides fifty of the best serving-women in Ireland, who worked all the year round making clothes for the Fianna in a rath on Magh Femen.

There was constant intercourse with the TUATHA DE DANANN; many of the men had fairy mistresses and FAIRY BRIDES; Finn's chief musician was the fairy Cnu Deireoil, the 'Little Nut', a little man with GOLDEN HAIR, about four feet high, said to be a son of LUG of the Long Hand; a fairy helper would suddenly join them, and they would be constantly assailed by hideous supernatural HAGS, GIANTS and WIZARDS. It was an active life, full of delights and dangers, and it went on until old age overtook Finn, and his Fianna went down under dissensions, jealousies and deaths.

[Motif: H900]

Fians. See FEENS.

Fideal, the. One of the evil water-demons of the Highlands. Mackenzie, in *Scottish Folk-Lore and Folk Life* (p. 233), suggests that the Fideal was a personification of the entangling bog grasses and water weeds. She haunted Loch na Fideil in Gairloch and was supposed to allure men and drag them under the water. A champion named Ewen attacked and conquered her at the expense of his life. 'Ewen killed the Fideal and the Fideal killed Ewen.'

[Motif: F420.5.2]

Fin Bheara (*fin-vara*). The Fairy King of Ulster. Lady WILDE seems to regard him as the king of the dead. In 'November Eve', a story in her *Ancient Legends of Ireland* (vol. I), she tells how a fisherman, Hugh King, negligently returning late from the fishing on November Eve, once got caught up in a Fairy Fair and found that all the dancers were dead men whom he had known. Finvarra and his wife drove up to the fair in a coach with four white horses: 'Out of it stepped a grand, grave gentleman all in black and a beautiful lady with a silver veil over her face.' In another tale, ETHNA THE BRIDE, we see Finvarra as the thief of beautiful human women, a theme reminiscent of the medieval KING ORFEO. In vol. II there is another story of Finvarra as a horseman on a black horse who lent one of the Kirwans of Galway a jockey by means of whom his horse won a great race, and afterwards took him to dinner in a grand mansion – actually, probably Knockma, Finvarra's fairy mound – where he gradually recognized the splendid company as the dead whom he had known. Though he ate the banquet and drank the fairy wine, he came to less harm than most mortals who violate the TABOO against partaking of FAIRY FOOD. He was escorted safely home; the only harm he received was a burnt ring round his wrist left by a girl whom he had loved in old days and who had died before their marriage.

The brief mentions of Finvarra in Wentz's *The Fairy-Faith in Celtic Countries* lay less stress on his role as king of the dead and more on his territorial holding.

[Motifs: F109; F160.0.2; F167.12; F184; F252.1]

Finn, or Fionn (*f-yoon*). The last and greatest leader of the FIANNA. He was the son of Cumhal ('Coo-al') Mac Baiscne, who had been head of the Fianna of Ireland and had been killed by the sons of Morna who were contending against him for the headship. Finn's mother was Muirne, granddaughter of Nuada of the TUATHA DE DANANN, and of Ethlinn, the mother of LUG of the Long Hand, so he was of godlike and fairy race. After Cumhal was killed, Finn's mother sent him away to the care of a female Druid, for the sons of Morna were looking for him to kill him too. There he was trained, strenuously and in secret, and sent from place to place for safety and further education. He was trained in poetry, and he acquired two magical skills; whilst he was in training to the poet Finegas he accidentally tasted the salmon of knowledge and gained his magic tooth, and he drank a mouthful of water of the well of the moon which gave him the power of prophecy. At last his training was complete, and he went up at the time of Samhain ('Sow-in') to the High King's palace at Teamhair ('Tara'). The High King recognized him by his likeness to his father, and putting the smooth horn into his hand, which gave him immunity from attack, he asked him who he was. Finn told him his whole story and asked to be admitted to the Fianna; and the king granted it to him, for he was the son of a man whom he had trusted. Now every year at Samhain for the past nine years the Hall of Teamhair had been burned down by a fairy musician called AILLEN MAC MIDHNA, who played so sweet an air that no one who heard it could help falling asleep, and while they slept he loosed a burst of flame against the place so that it was consumed. That night the king asked the Fianna if any man among them would attempt the watch, and Finn offered to do so. While he was going the round an old follower of his father offered him a magic spear of bitterness, which smelt so sharply that it would keep any man awake. By the use of this spear, Finn killed Aillen and rescued the Hall for ever. He was made leader of the Fianna, and Goll Mac Morna, his chief and most bitter enemy, made willing submission to him, and was ever after his true follower and friend, though he still picked quarrels with all his kinsmen. Many stories of his adventures were told, of his hounds and cousins, BRAN AND SCEOLAN, of the birth of his son OISIN, the poet and warrior, of his old age, and the last sad moment when he let the saving water trickle through his fingers, leaving Diarmuid to die in revenge for his unwilling abduction of Grania, Finn's young queen.

[Motifs: A511.2.3; A511.3; A524.1.1; A527.2]

Fionn. See FINN.

Fir Bholg (*fir vulag*). See FIRBOLGS.

Fir Chlis, the, or the 'Nimble Men' or 'Merry Dancers'. The Highland name for the Aurora Borealis. Mackenzie, in *Scottish Folk-Lore and Folk Life* (p. 222), gives a good account of the tradition about the Fir Chlis, distinguishing their 'everlasting battle' from the more hurtful activities of the SLUAGH. He himself was told of the 'Nimble Men' engaging in fights between the clans of two chiefs, rivals for the possession of a fairy lady. The bright red sky sometimes seen beneath the moving lights of the aurora is sometimes called 'the pool of blood'. J. G. CAMPBELL, in his *Superstitions of the Highlands* (p. 200), says that the blood of the wounded, falling to the earth and becoming congealed, forms the coloured stones called 'blood stones', known in the Hebrides also by the name of *fuil siochaire* ('fairy blood'). In Ireland, according to William Allingham's poem 'The Fairies', the spirits composing the aurora are more truly 'Merry Dancers', for the old fairy king is described as:

> Going up with music on cold starry nights
> To feast with the Queen of the gay Northern Lights.

According to Lewis Spence in *The Fairy Tradition* (p. 58), the Fir Chlis were supposed to be those fallen angels whose fall was arrested before they reached the earth. This Christian theory of the ORIGIN OF FAIRIES was particularly prevalent in the Highlands, for almost every Highlander was a theologian. The Suffolk name for the Northern Lights is PERRY DANCERS.

Fir Darrig, or Fir Dhearga (*fir yaraga*). Of the Fir Darrig, YEATS says in *Irish Fairy and Folk Tales* (p. 80):

> The *Far Darrig* (fear dearg), which means the Red Man, for he wears a red cap and coat, busies himself with practical joking, especially with gruesome joking. This he does, and nothing else.

The example he gives is 'The Far Darrig in Donegal' (pp. 90–93), which is a version of 'The Story-Teller at a Loss', in which a man who fails to produce a story on request suffers a succession of macabre experiences which prove to be illusions designed to provide him with material for a story. The Far Darrig in this story is described as the big man, 'a gigantic fellow, the tallest of the four'. The Fear Dearg of Munster was, according to Crofton CROKER, a little old man, about two and a half feet in height, wearing a scarlet sugar-loaf hat and a long scarlet coat, with long grey hair and a wrinkled face. He would come in and ask to warm himself by the fire. It was very unlucky to refuse him. The CLURICAUNE in his account was only six inches high. There is, however, another Fir Darrig, a red-headed man, who occurs in stories of humans trapped in Fairyland. He is generally taken to be a human captive in Fairyland, and it is his advice and help which enables the human visitor to escape. Examples are to be found in Lady WILDE's *Ancient Legends of Ireland* (vol. I), 'Fairy Music' and 'Fairy Justice', and the same character occurs in many of the Scottish stories.

[Motifs: F233.3; F369.4; F375]

Firbolgs (*fir vulag*). The first inhabitants of Ireland, according to ancient traditions, were the Firbolgs, who were conquered and driven into the Western Islands by the TUATHA DE DANANN. The Firbolgs became the first FAIRIES of Ireland, GIANT-like, grotesque creatures. They and the Tuatha De Danann may be compared with the Titans and the Olympic gods of Greece.

[Motif: A1657.2]

Foawr, the (*fooar*). The Manx equivalent of the Highland FOMOR-IANS. Like them, the Foawr are stone-throwing GIANTS. They are great ravishers of cattle, but do not seem to be OGRES. Dora Broome in *Fairy Tales from the Isle of Man* has a story, 'Chalse and the Foawr', of a light-hearted young fiddler caught and carried home by a Foawr. One would expect it to end like the Polyphemus incident, but Chalse escapes by climbing up the giant's chimney. Nothing much is told of the giant who rode JIMMY SQUAREFOOT, except that he threw stones at his wife, but in one of Sophia Morrison's *Manx Fairy Tales* we have a complete TOM TIT TOT story in which the spinning is done by a giant whose name is Mollyndroat. The prize of the guessing contest in this tale is the possession of the woollen thread spun. Mollyndroat was the least grasping of all the GOBLIN spinners.

Foidin Seachrain (*fodeen shaughrawin*). See STRAY SOD.

Fomorians, the. A race of demons, hideous and evil, against whom most of the successive invaders of Ireland had to fight. There is no record of their arrival, so presumably they had been there from the beginning, surviving the various hazards that exterminated the successive waves of colonizers. According to the *Book of Conquests*, the first unnamed in-habitants had perished in the Great Flood. Then came the children of

Partholon, who waged war against the Fomorians and were finally destroyed by a great pestilence. After them came the people of Nemed, who fared even worse against the Fomorians than their predecessors, for they were enslaved by them and had to pay every November a yearly tribute of two thirds of their children and two thirds of their cattle. At length in a great battle they conquered the Fomorians and killed Conann, their king; but they themselves were so cruelly diminished in numbers that they left the country. Then came the FIR BOLGS, who had no trouble with the Fomorians, but were defeated by another wave of invaders, the TUATHA DE DANANN. The Tuatha conquered the Fir Bolgs, but allowed them to retain the province of Connacht. They also came into conflict with the Fomorians, but compromised with them to a certain extent, even to intermarriage. However, the war broke out again in the end, and the Fomorians were finally conquered at the second battle of Moytura. It has been suggested among the THEORIES OF FAIRY ORIGINS that these successive waves of invasion describe the conflicts of religious cults and practices. If this is so, the Fomorians would represent a primitive religion that entailed barbaric human and animal sacrifices.

The Highland Fomorians were a race of giants, less evil than the Irish demons.

[Motifs: A1659.1; A1659.1.1; G100.1; S262]

Foul-Weather. This Cornish version of TOM TIT TOT or 'Rumpel-stiltskin' is a church-building tale. It is given in *Old Cornwall* (vol. II).

There was once a king of a far country who had set his heart on building the most beautiful cathedral in his kingdom; he had it all planned, but by the time the foundations were laid all the money in his coffers was exhausted and he could think of no way of finishing it without laying heavy taxes on his people. One day he went out alone on the mountains pondering what he could do, and there he met a strange old man. 'Why art thou so gone into thought?' the old man asked him.

'Why should I not be gone into thought,' answered the king, 'since I have begun a great cathedral and have not money to finish it.'

'Never make lamentation on that account,' said the little man. 'I myself will build thee a right fair church, better than any in the realm, without asking thee for a dime of money.'

'What wilt thou take from me then?' said the king.

'If you can tell me my name by the time the church is built,' said the dwarf, 'I shall do it for nothing; but if you cannot I will take your heart for forfeit.'

The king knew then that the little old man was a GNOME of the Mountain, but he thought to himself that he might well be dead before the work was finished, and if his life was gone he would care little what happened to his heart, so he consented.

The cathedral rose as if by magic. No work was done on it by day, but

at night swarms of gnomish creatures toiled on it. The king suggested one
addition after another, but he had only to suggest it for it to be done next
day, until he despaired of delaying it any further. One evening he went
out alone up to the mountains, trying to make up something more he
could ask for. He wandered about until he came to the mouth of a cave.
A prodigious roaring was coming out of it, a gnomish baby yelling and
being soothed. As his mother dandled it she sang

> 'Weep not, weep not my darling boy;
> Hush altogether
> And then Foul-Weather,
> Thy dad, will come
> Tomorrow home,
> Bringing a king's heart for thy joy
> To play withal, a pretty toy.'

Loudly and harshly she sang, but her song was music to the king, for it
told him the name of his adversary. He crept past the cave and ran down
the whole way into his city. It was dark by that time and the gnome was
up on the topmost spire fixing the gilded weathercock that would complete the building. The king stood and called at the top of his voice: 'Set
it straight, FOUL-WEATHER.' At that the gnome fell with a crash straight
down from the tower, and was broken into smithereens, as if he had been
made of glass. And the weathercock on that great cathedral has been
crooked from that day to this.

[Type: 500. Motifs: C432.1; F381.1; H512; H521; N475]

Four-leafed clover. A four-leafed clover is regarded as a PROTECTION
AGAINST FAIRIES. It is chiefly used to dissolve GLAMOUR in spells cast
either by FAIRIES or MAGICIANS. The FAIRY OINTMENT which
enabled mortals to see through the glamorous appearance of the fairies
was said to be compounded from four-leafed clover. There are various
stories of enchantments pierced by someone who is carrying a sprig of
the herb unknowingly in a pack of hay or a handful of grasses. An example is one told by HUNT in *Popular Romances of the West of England*
(pp. 107-9).

There was a most beautiful cow called Daisy in a farm at West Buriens,
who was in milk for long seasons with a splendid quality of milk, but she
never let down more than two gallons, then she would prick her ears
forward, give a soft low and hold back her milk. One evening a milkmaid
was milking the cows in the meadows when this happened. She put a pad
of grass on her head to soften the weight of the pail, picked up the pail
and started for home. As she crossed the stile she glanced back at Daisy
and saw that she was surrounded by fairies, who swarmed over her with
little pipkins in their hands. They patted and stroked her, and Daisy was
clearly delighted with their company. One rather bigger than the rest,

whom she recognized as a PIXY by his impudent grin, was lying on his back with his feet in the air, and the others took turns in standing on them to milk the cow. The girl hurried home to tell her mistress, who would not believe her until she had pulled the wad of grass to pieces by the light of the stable lantern and found a four-leafed clover in the heart of it. Then she was convinced, but unfortunately she did not leave well alone. She consulted her mother, who was a witch, about the best way of driving off the fairies. They concocted a brew of brine and stock-fish and painted Daisy's udder with it. That drove off the fairies effectually, but the farm was none the better of it, for Daisy pined for the loss of her friends, dwindled to skin and bone, and gave no milk at all. A similar tale, but without the sad sequel, is told in the DENHAM TRACTS about a milkmaid at Nether Witton.

A secondary use of a four-leafed clover is to grant wishes. This is the use made of it in J. H. EWING's story 'Amelia and the Dwarfs'. Here Amelia, held prisoner among the fairies, is able to escape when she finds a four-leafed clover during the fairy dance.

[Motif: F235.4.6]

Foyson. The term used by KIRK for the essential goodness that is taken out of food by the FAIRIES. See also FAIRY THEFTS.

Frairies. In Norfolk and Suffolk, a local version of the word 'fairies' is 'frairies'. KEIGHTLEY (p. 306) describes an interview with a Norfolk girl about the frairies. He says:

> We once questioned a girl from Norfolk on the subject of Fairy-lore. She said she had often heard of and even seen the *Frairies*. They were dressed in white, and lived under the ground, where they constructed houses, bridges, and other edifices. It is not safe, she added, to go near them when they appear above ground.

[Motifs: F211.3; F236.1.3]

Friar Rush. The chapbook story of 'Friar Rush' is the 16th-century adaptation of a Danish legend which satirizes the sloth and gluttony of the monastic friars, a popular subject in England, as elsewhere, from the 14th century onwards which led to the ABBEY LUBBER stories among others. The English treatment is unsystematic, and Friar Rush becomes more and more of a HOBGOBLIN and less and less of a devil as the wandering tale trickles on. It starts with a commission from Hell of the kind treated in Ben Jonson's *The Divell is an Ass*, by which Rush is sent on temptation duty to an abbey of friars, whom he faithfully leads into gluttony, lechery and sloth until he is unmasked, changing into the form of a horse, and banished to haunt an uninhabited castle. Even in this part he displays a kind of innocent good-fellowship, for he delights in visiting village taverns and seems to find real pleasure in the company of the rustics. When he leaves his castle and enters into other service, he becomes very much of a ROBIN GOODFELLOW, doing prodigious labours for his new master and playing tricks upon the lascivious friar who is making love to his mistress. In his next service, he changes sides so much as to tell his new master that his young mistress is possessed by a devil and to recommend him to send her to the now-reformed abbot for exorcism. There is nothing in the end of the story to suggest that he eventually becomes a WILL O' THE WISP, though it might well be that he was banished from Hell for his treachery, and, not being eligible for Heaven, assumed the form of the IGNIS FATUUS, as in other legends whose heroes were ineligible for either place. At least it makes it quite plausible to suggest that MILTON's 'Friar's lanthorn' was a reference to Friar Rush, though Kittredge in his monograph *The Friar's Lantern* is inclined to think that there is no ground for the identification.

[Motifs: F470.0.1; G303.3.3.1.3; G303.9.3.1; G303.9.4; K1987]

Frid. A supernatural creature which lives under or inside rocks in the Highlands and which devours all milk or crumbs of bread spilt on the ground. Mackenzie, in *Scottish Folk Lore and Folk Life* (p. 244), thinks it likely that the Fridean were the original beings to which the libations of milk were poured upon the hills of Gairloch, Ross and Cromarty. He suggests that the fairly widespread tale of a piper who, followed by his dog, explored the windings of an underground cavern and never returned from it, though the sound of his music was followed above ground for several miles, is related to the Fridean. The dog returned hairless, as dogs do from encounters with FAIRIES, and died when it came out into the open.

[Motif: V12.9]

Frittenings. See BONELESS.

Fuath (*foo-a*). 'The Fuathan' was the generic term for a number of spirits, generally malicious and dangerous, who had a close connection with water, lochs, rivers and sometimes the sea. J. F. CAMPBELL counts them as water spirits, though J. G. CAMPBELL denies that they are invariably so, but Mackenzie in *Scottish Folk Lore and Folk Life* agrees with J. F. Campbell. The PEALLAIDH was a fuath, so were the FIDEAL, SHELLYCOAT, many at least of the URISKS, and presumably NUCKELAVEE, if he was not too Lowland a character. The word is sometimes written 'vough' by those who had not seen it written and relied on the sound. It was a VOUGH who was the mother of the BROLLACHAN in Campbell's version of the NEMO story.

[Motifs: F420.5.2; F470.]

Gabriel Hounds. The cries and wing-beats of migrating birds, particularly geese, are sometimes taken to be the baying of superterrestrial spirits, a pack of spectral hounds, sometimes called 'sky yelpers', sometimes the GABRIEL RATCHETS. They were known as the 'Gabriel Hounds' in Lancashire, and were said to be monstrous dogs with human heads who travelled high up in the air. Brockie, quoted in *County Folk-Lore* (vol. IV), says that sometimes they seem to hover over a house, and this foretells death or misfortune to the inmates. Lewis Spence, in *The Fairy Tradition in Britain*, calls them the Lancashire version of the YETH HOUNDS and of the CWN ANNWN.
    [Motif: G303.7.1.3]

Gabriel Ratchets. A variant of GABRIEL HOUNDS. 'Ratchet' is an archaic term for a hound that hunts by scent. By the 17th century they were called 'Lyme Hounds' as opposed to 'Gaze Hounds'. The archaic name is a proof of the antiquity of the belief.
    [Motif: G303.7.1.3]

Galley-beggar. The Galley-beggar seems to be closely allied to the BULLBEGGAR, which comes from the North Country and Suffolk as well as from Somerset. The first part of its name, from 'gally', means to frighten, scare, and is also used for a ghostly apparition. Ruth Tongue in *County Folklore* (vol. VIII, pp. 122–3) reports a headless galley-beggar who used to toboggan on a hurdle down the hill between Over and Nether Stowey, his head tucked firmly under his skeleton arm and shrieking with laughter. It was only on dark nights that he rode, but a strange light surrounded him, and he would slide, yelling with laughter, right down into Castle Street.

Gally-trot. An apparition known in the North Country and in Suffolk. It takes the form of a white shaggy dog, about the size of a bullock and indeterminate in outline, which pursues anyone who runs from it. 'Gally' means to frighten. See also GALLEY-BEGGAR.

Ganconer, or Gean-cannah, the Love-Talker. A kind of fairy who appears in lonesome valleys, smoking a *dudeen* (that is, a short clay pipe), who makes love to country maidens, then fades away, leaving them to pine to death. Ethna Carbery's poem 'The Love-Talker' gives the whole picture:

> I met the Love-Talker one eve in the glen,
> He was handsomer than any of our handsome young men,
> His eyes were blacker than the sloe, his voice sweeter far
> Than the crooning of old Kevin's pipes beyond in Coolnagar.
>
> I was bound for the milking with a heart fair and free –
> My grief! my grief! that bitter hour drained the life from me;
> I thought him human lover, though his lips on mine were cold,
> And the breath of death blew keen on me within his hold.
>
> I know not what way he came, no shadow fell behind,
> But all the sighing rushes swayed beneath a faery wind,
> The thrush ceased its singing, a mist crept about,
> We two clung together – with the world shut out.
>
> Beyond the ghostly mist I could hear my cattle low,
> The little cow from Ballina, clean as driven snow,
> The dun cow from Kerry, the roan from Inisheer,
> Oh, pitiful their calling – and his whispers in my ear!
>
> His eyes were a fire; his words were a snare;
> I cried my mother's name, but no help was there;
> I made the blessed Sign; then he gave a dreary moan,
> A wisp of cloud went floating by, and I stood alone.
>
> Running ever through my head, is an old-time rune –
> 'Who meets the Love-Talker must weave her shroud soon.'
> My mother's face is furrowed with the salt tears that fall,
> But the kind eyes of my father are the saddest sight of all.
>
> I have spun the fleecy lint, and now my wheel is still,
> The linen length is woven for my shroud fine and chill,
> I shall stretch me on the bed where a happy maid I lay –
> Pray for the soul of Mairè Og at dawning of the day!

In a story, however, which YEATS quotes from the *Dublin and London Magazine* in his *Irish Fairy and Folk Tales* (pp. 206–11), the Ganconers appear in a troop playing at HURLING like ordinary DAOINE-SIDHE, and carry a poor widow's cow to an underwater fairyland at the bottom of Loughleagh.

[Motif: F301.2]

Gean-cannah. See GANCONER.

Geasa. A kind of TABOO.

Generosity. Any mortal who wishes to be esteemed in any way by the FAIRIES must show generosity in his dealings. A man who will not give freely will receive nothing. See also VIRTUES ESTEEMED BY THE FAIRIES.

Gentle Annis, or Annie. The weather spirit responsible for the south-westerly gales on the Firth of Cromarty. The firth is well protected from the north and east, but a gap in the hills allows the entry of spasmodic squally gales. These give Gentle Annis a bad reputation for treachery. A day will start fine and lure the fisher out, then, in a moment, the storm sweeps round and his boat is imperilled. D. A. Mackenzie suggests that Gentle Annis is one aspect of the CAILLEACH BHEUR. 'Annis' may come from the Celtic goddess ANU, which has been suggested as the origins of BLACK ANNIS of the Dane Hills. It may be, however, that these half-jocular personifications have no connection with mythology.

[Motif: F430]

Gentry, the. One of the many EUPHEMISTIC NAMES FOR THE FAIRIES, used in Ireland. As KIRK says, 'the Irish use to bless all they fear Harme of'.

[Motif: C433]

Geoffrey of Monmouth (1100?–1154). The suppositious author (though the supposition is well supported) of the *Vita Merlini*, who must be recorded as the first inspiration of the Arthurian Romances. His *Historia Britonum* gives the history of Arthur from the intrigues which led to his birth, from his discovery and through his career to the time of his death. Arthur, who had been almost certainly a patriot and cavalry leader who led the defence of the Britons against the Saxons in post-Roman days, was already a legendary figure entwined with mythology and fairy-lore in Wales and in Brittany, but it was the works of Geoffrey of Monmouth which introduced him to literature both in France and England. Geoffrey was a man versed in all the learning of his time and of considerable charm of manner, a member of the pleasant circle of 12th-century scholars. Some people denounced *Historia* as 'a lying book', and told jocular stories about how favourably it was received by possessing devils, but it had a considerable influence, and played a valuable part in welding the Saxons, Britons and Normans together into a nationality, as well as pro-viding the MATTER OF BRITAIN with a source upon which poets and romancers could draw from that time till the present day.

Georoidh Iarla. See 'LEGEND OF MULLAGHMAST'.

Gervase of Tilbury (1150?–1235?). An Englishman, born at Tilbury in the second half of the 12th century and brought up in Rome, who became a teacher of law in Bologna. While still a young man he was clerk in the household of the Archbishop of Rheims, but after a time he returned to England and became a close friend of young King Henry, the son of Henry II, who died before his father in 1183. After his death, he returned to the Continent and was appointed Marshal of the Kingdom of Arles by Otto IV, to whom he dedicated his great work, *Otia Imperialia*. The last years of his life were spent in England. One of his chief friends there was Ralph of Coggeshall, another writer of the MEDIEVAL CHRONICLES, to whom he communicated a good deal of information. The *Otia Imperialia* (finished in 1211) is in three parts, of which the third is of especial interest for our knowledge of the folklore of the period, for it is a record of marvels, though Part One contains matter of some importance. From these too we obtain the story of the PORTUNES, the earliest record of DIMINUTIVE FAIRIES, and the Dracae of Brittany, about whom a FAIRY OINTMENT story is told; also a version of the well-known story, 'The Hour has come but not the Man'. In the first part of the books he mentions the werewolves of England, and the FAIRIES, with the legend of the fairy horn, an example of THEFTS FROM THE FAIRIES.

Ghillie Dhu, or Gille Dubh. Osgood Mackenzie in his *Hundred Years in the Highlands* describes the Ghillie Dhu as the best-known Gairloch 'fairie' of modern times. He lurked among the birch woods and thickets at the southern end of Loch a Druing. He was called 'Gille Dubh' because of his black hair, not from a dark tartan, for his clothing was made of leaves of trees and green moss. He was generally regarded as a benevolent fairy, though only one person had heard him speak. She was little Jessie Macrae, who was lost one night in the woods. The Ghillie Dhu looked after her all night with great kindness and took her safely home in the morning. For all that, some years later Sir Hector Mackenzie of Gairloch invited four other Mackenzie lairds to join him in a shoot to destroy the Ghillie Dhu. He gave them great entertainment, and they rested on heather couches in John Mackenzie's barn by Loch a Druing, before they went out to range the woods around for Ghillie Dhu. By that time Jessie Macrae had grown up and married John Mackenzie. One may imagine that she was much relieved that the five lairds could find no trace of the Ghillie Dhu, though they hunted all night. This incident took place at the end of the 18th century.

[Motif: R131.12]

Giants. Almost the only trait that giants have in common is their enormous size and strength. Some of them, such as BRAN THE BLESSED, have obviously once been gods. Bran was so large that no house could contain him, so large indeed that he looked like an approaching mountain as he waded the channel between Wales and Ireland. His strength was tremendous, but he was essentially benevolent and his decapitated head

brought a blessing wherever it was carried, and protected Britain from
invaders so long as it was safely lodged in London. The two great hill
figures that still remain in England, the Cerne Abbas Giant and the
Long Man of Wilmington, represent god-like figures of the same kind.
The Cerne Abbas giant is plainly a fertility god as well as a protective
figure. Some kind and protective giants continue down to comparatively
modern times. An example is the Giant of Grabbist, whose character and
exploits are described by Ruth Tongue in *County Folklore* (vol. VIII).
He was one of the stone-throwing giants, of which many are reported,
good and bad, and spent a good deal of his time in contests with the
Devil. He was full, too, of active benevolence, and once lifted a fishing-
boat that was in difficulties and set it down safely in harbour. There is a
touch of comedy, even farce, in the tales about the Giant of Grabbist,
and it is noticeable that as time went on the giants became gradually
more foolish. The kind old Cornish giant of Carn Galva, whose sad story
is told by BOTTRELL in *Traditions and Hearthside Stories of West
Cornwall* (vol. I, pp. 47–8), is an example:

> The giant of Carn Galva was more playful than warlike. Though the
> old works of the giant now stand desolate, we may still see, or get up
> and rock ourselves upon, the logan-stone which this dear old giant
> placed on the most westerly carn of the range, that he might log himself

to sleep when he saw the sun dip into the waves and the sea-birds fly to their homes in the cleaves. Near, the giant's rocking-seat, one may still see a pile of cubical rocks, which are almost as regular and shapely now as when the giant used to amuse himself in building them up, and kicking them down again, for exercise or play, when alone and when he had nothing else to do. The people of the northern hills have always had a loving regard for the memory of this giant, because he appears to have passed all his life at the carn in single blessedness, merely to protect his beloved people of Morvah and Zennor from the depredations of the less honest Titans who then dwelt on Lelant hills. Carn Galva giant never killed but one of the Morvah people in his life, and that happened all through loving play.

The giant was very fond of a fine young fellow, of Choon, who used to take a turn over to the carn, every now and then, just to see how the old giant was getting on, to cheer him up a bit, play a game of bob, or anything else to help him pass his lonely time away. One afternoon the giant was so well pleased with the good play they had together that, when the young fellow of Choon threw down his quoit to go away home, the giant, in a good-natured way, tapped his playfellow on the head with the tips of his fingers. At the same time he said, 'Be sure to come again tomorrow, my son, and we will have a capital game of bob.' Before the word 'bob' was well out of the giant's mouth, the young man dropped at his feet; – the giant's fingers had gone right through his playmate's skull. When, at last, the giant became sensible of the damage he had done to the brain-pan of the young man, he did his best to put the inside workings of his mate's head to rights and plugged up his finger-holes, but all to no purpose; for the young man was stone dead, long before the giant ceased doctoring his head.

When the poor giant found it was all over with his playmate, he took the body in his arms, and sitting down on the large square rock at the foot of the carn, he rocked himself to and fro; pressing the lifeless body to his bosom, he wailed and moaned over him, bellowing and crying louder than the booming billows breaking on the rocks in Permoina.

'Oh, my son, my son, why didn't they make the shell of thy noddle stronger? A es as plum (soft) as a pie-crust, doughbaked, and made too thin by the half! How shall I ever pass the time without thee to play bob and mop-and-heede (hide and seek)?'

The giant of Carn Galva never rejoiced any more, but, in seven years or so, he pined away and died of a broken heart.

It seems as if these giants were half-playfully invented to account for scattered boulders or other natural features, or for prehistoric monuments.

In contrast to these gentle, foolish giants, we have the cruel, blood-thirsty giants or OGRES, such as those which Jack the Giant-Killer

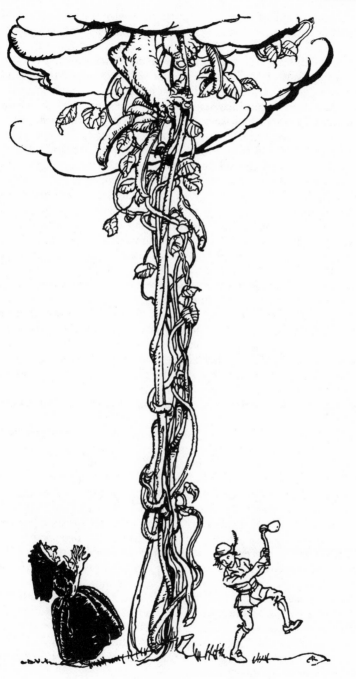

conquered. Some of these were MONSTERS with several heads, most of them not overburdened with sense, all man-eaters. The Highland giants were much more astute, some of them MAGICIANS, like that in 'The Battle of the Birds', the Highland version of NICHT NOUGHT NOTHING. The grim giant of 'A King of Albainn' in *Waifs and Strays of Celtic Tradition* (vol. II), collected by D. MacInnes, may be a magician as well as a giant, for a magical hare enticed his victims into the cave where the giant and his twelve sons were waiting for them and the giant gave them the choice of deadly games: 'the venomous apple' or 'the hot gridiron'. In the end they had to play both. There is another giant in the story, who has carried off the old king's daughter, an activity to which giants are very prone. Both giants are conquered by a supernatural helper called 'The Big Lad'. This may either be an incomplete version of a 'grateful dead' type of story, or more probably the ghost of the young king's father, for whom he has been mourning inordinately. Another dangerous and evil giant, 'The Bare-Stripping Hangman', also occurs in *Waifs and Strays of Celtic Tradition* (vol. III). This giant is a magician, for he has a SEPARABLE SOUL which has to be destroyed before he can be killed. There is a series of giants to be destroyed, one-headed, two-headed and three-headed. In the same volume is a story of a guileless giant who does not know how formidable his strength is, a human giant after the type of Tom Hickathrift, whose story Joseph Jacobs tells in *More English Fairy Stories* (pp. 42–9). He was suckled by his mother for twenty years and so gained supernatural strength. His frightened master sets him a succession of tests in order to destroy him, but he succeeds in them all, and in the end settles down happily with his old mother in the house he has won for himself. It will be seen that there is a great variety of giants in British tradition.

[Type: ML5020. Motifs: A523; A963.5; A977.1; F531; F628.2.3; N812]

Giraldus Cambrensis (1146?–1220?). Giraldus de Barri, called Cambrensis, belonged to one of the ancient families of Wales and was remarkable from childhood for his love of learning. It is therefore not surprising that he became one of the compilers of the MEDIEVAL CHRONICLES. Because of his high connections in Wales he was handicapped in his career in the Welsh Church by the Norman policy of appointing only Normans to the episcopacy, but he was made Chaplain to Henry II and sent to accompany Henry's son on his expedition to Ireland. He wrote *Typographica Hibernica* on returning from this tour. He picked up some interesting pieces of folk tradition in Ireland, notably a sympathetic account of a pair of werewolves and a tradition of a disappearing island which was made visible by firing a fairy arrow at it, but the most interesting piece of fairy-lore is to be found in the *Itinerary through Wales*, the story of ELIDOR AND THE GOLDEN BALL, perhaps our earliest account of the social life of the FAIRIES.

Glaistig. A composite character, included by J. F. CAMPBELL among the FUATHAN. She sometimes has the attributes and habits of the CAILLEACH BHEUR, sometimes assumes animal form, often that of a goat, but more often she is described as half-woman, half-goat. She is a water-spirit, and when she is regarded as a FUATH she is murderous and dangerous. As the Green Glaistig, however, she is more like a BANSHEE, mourning the death or illness of her favourites, and even undertaking domestic duties. (For this aspect of her nature, see under GRUAGACHS.) D. A. Mackenzie gives a full chapter to her in *Scottish Folk Lore and Folk Life*, and she has also been given detailed treatment by Lewis Spence in *The Fairy Tradition in Britain*. She was often said to have been a human woman, taken and given fairy nature by the FAIRIES. Many traditions are given about her by J. G. CAMPBELL and J. F. Campbell, by Carmichael of *Carmina Gadelica* and by his daughter, Mrs Watson. In her benign form, she was fond of children and often took old people under her protection. She frequently herded the cattle of the farm she haunted, and expected libations of milk. URISKS, in their satyr-like form, often associated with the glaistigs.

Glamour. Originally a Scottish word, a variation of 'gramarye' or 'glaumerie'. We find it in undoubted use first in the 18th century, in Ramsay's publication of *The Gipsy Counties*:

> As soon as they saw her weel faur'd face
> They cast their glamourie o'er her O!

It generally signified a mesmerism or enchantment cast over the senses, so that things were perceived or not perceived as the enchanter wished. Gipsies, witches and, above all, the FAIRIES had this power, so that a MIDWIFE TO THE FAIRIES, called to a patient's home, would see it as a neat cottage or a stately home with a beautiful lady lying in a four-poster bed until she happened to touch her eyes while she anointed the baby, when she found herself in a poor cave, surrounded by a crowd of skinny IMPS, with her patient on a withered heap of rushes. The FAIRY OINTMENT had virtue to break the power of glamour, as a FOUR-LEAFED CLOVER could do. Indeed it was said that the ointment itself was made of sprigs of four-leafed clover.

[Motifs: D2031; D2031.2]

Glasgavlen. One of the FAIRY ANIMALS, a fairy cow which appeared out of various lakes and whose legend is briefly told in Wood-Martin's *Elder Faiths of Ireland*. See the DUN COW OF KIRKHAM.

[Motif: B184.2.2.2]

Glastyn, the, or Glashtin. One of the Manx forms of the EACH UISGE, though the almost extinct GLASHAN is confused with him and he

is sometimes described as a kind of FENODEREE. Gill points this out in
A Second Manx Scrapbook (p. 253). The Glastyn is, in his human form,
much handsomer than the great shambling Fenoderee, a dark, splendid
young man, with flashing eyes and curling hair, but to be distinguished
by his ears, which though fine and delicate, are pointed like a horse's. A
typical story of the Glastyn is to be found in Dora Broome's *Fairy Tales
from the Isle of Man* (pp. 48–53). It is of a girl, Kirree Quayle, who was
left in her lonely cottage when her father went to Doolish market to sell
his fish. He told her to bolt the door and not to open it till he knocked
three times. She was not nervous, but when a great storm got up and
her father did not return she began to be anxious. At last, very late at
night, there came three knocks on the door. She ran to open it and a
stranger came in, drenched and dripping. He spoke in a foreign tongue,
but he seemed to ask to be allowed to warm himself at the fire. He would
eat nothing she offered him, but he lay down by the fire and fell asleep.
The candle and lamp had gone out, but she cautiously blew up the fire,
and she saw that there were fine, pointed ears half-hidden by his dark
curls. She knew at once that he was the dreaded Glastyn, who might at
any moment take his horse's shape and drag her out into the sea to devour
her in the waves. If only dawn would come and the little red cock would
crow she would be saved. She sat as still as a stone, and that was not an
easy thing to do, but the night seemed to grow dark. Too soon a peat
broke and blazed and the stranger woke. He sat up and drew out a long
string of pearls which he dangled before her eyes, inviting her to come
with him. She pushed them aside and he caught her dress. She screamed
aloud, and the little red cock sitting on the rafter woke and crowed. The
thing dashed out, and she heard the trampling of horses' hoofs outside
among the stones. The light brightened and the thing was gone, the
storm had ceased and down by the shore she saw her father coming home.

A variant of the tale is mentioned by J. F. CAMPBELL in his *Popular
Tales of the West Highlands*. There is a strong resemblance here to the
WATER-HORSE of the Highlands. The Glastyn is not as closely tied to its
horse form as the CABYLL-USHTEY. It performs other cantrips, and
might sometimes be confused with the BUGGANE. There are some
rumours of him as a kind of BROWNIE, discussed by J. Rhys in *Celtic
Folklore* (p. 258), but he is inclined to think this is mere confusion. It
would certainly seem he would not be very safe to have about the house.

[Motif: B184.1.3]

Gnomes. These cannot properly be classed as FAIRIES, GOBLINS,
BOGIES, or even as IMPS. They belong rather to dead science than to
folk tradition. They are members of a very small class consisting of four:
the four elementals, Gnomes, Sylphs, Salamanders and Nereids, who
belong to the four elements, Earth, Air, Fire and Water. Man and all
mortal creatures were made up of these four elements, variously com-

pounded, but the elementals were pure, each native to and compounded of its own element. This was the hermetic and neo-Platonic doctrine, and all medieval science and medicine was founded on it. As the Renaissance matured and empirical science gained ground, the belief in the Four Elements gradually faded. The first description of gnomes as the elementals of Earth is to be found in Paracelsus (1493–1531) in his *De Nymphis . . .* (1658). It is doubtful if he invented the word; the *Oxford English Dictionary* suggests that it is an elision of *genomus*, earth-dweller. At any rate, the gnomes were supposed to live underground, moving through earth as freely as if it were air, and their function was supposed to be to guard the treasures of the earth. In popular tradition, they were called DWARFS or Goblins. Other mine spirits were the KNOCKERS of Cornwall, but there was no suggestion that they were elementals.

[Motif: F456]

Goblin Market. The Goblin Market in Christina Rossetti's poem is entirely unlike the traditional FAIRY MARKET or PIXIES' fair. These fairy markets are held between the FAIRIES themselves. If humans come to harm in them it is from their INFRINGEMENT OF FAIRY PRIVACY or as a punishment for human greed. People approaching them courteously have even been able to trade with them to advantage. The Goblin Market of the poem, on the other hand, was a murderous show got up to entice mortals to taste the glistening fruits of death, the work of the UNSEELIE COURT. It is true to the more sombre tradition of the fairies of FINVARRA's court, the sinister fairies of Innis-Sark. The goblins' attempts to force Lizzie with pinchings and buffetings reminds one of the sinister dancers in Lady WILDE's story of 'November Eve'. In the same book is the story of a ring of flowers by which a girl was allured into the Fairyland of the dead to meet her love, and the whole tale is similar in mood to the motif of Laura's pining after the lost fairy fruits. Christina Rossetti's GOBLINS are much like BOGIES, various in appearance, masters of GLAMOUR. They are not unlike George MACDONALD's goblins, though they were more uniform in shape and it was their beasts which were diverse.

The plot of the poem is a variant of three main fairy themes: the danger of peeping at the fairies, the TABOO against eating FAIRY FOOD, and the rescue from Fairyland.

The metre of the poem and the scurrying pace of the lines is evocative of many of the traditional fairy rhymes:

> Laughed every goblin
> When they spied her peeping:
> Came towards her hobbling,
> Flying, running, leaping,

> Puffing and blowing,
> Chuckling, clapping, crowing,
> Clucking and gobbling,
> Mopping and mowing.

The helter-skelter doggerel is exactly suited to carry the mood of the story.

Goblins. A general name for evil and malicious spirits, usually small and grotesque in appearance. The sting is taken from the name by prefixing it with 'HOB', for the HOBGOBLINS were generally thought of as helpful and well-disposed to men, if sometimes rather mischievous. The Puritans, however, would not allow this, and so we have Bunyan in his hymn coupling 'hobgoblin' and 'foul fiend' together. The highland FUATH cover the same kind of ground as the English goblin and the French *gobelin*.

[Motif: F470]

Golden hair. Some of the FAIRIES were golden-haired, as presumably were the TYLWYTH TEG, or Fair Family, many of the FAIRIES OF MEDIEVAL ROMANCES and the Irish fairies of the TIR NAN OG, but

many of them were black-haired and brown-skinned. Fair or dark, however, they all set great store by golden hair in mortals. A golden-haired
child was in far more danger of being stolen than a dark one. It was often
a golden-haired girl who was allured away to be a FAIRY BRIDE, as
EILIAN OF GARTH DORWEN was; sometimes, too, the fairies adopted
girls of especial beauty, and above all golden-haired, as their special
charges; and when they could not protect them they avenged their
wrongs. The story of 'the Golden-Haired Girl of Unst' told by Jessie
Saxby in *Shetland Traditional Lore* (Chapter 10) is a good example of this
patronage of beauty. Here it is the TROWS who loved and cared for the
child:

> There was a girl whose mother had been bewitched by the Trows at
> the girl's birth, who grew up to be a lovely creature with golden hair
> of wonderful beauty. It fell in sunny waves about her, and such an
> unusual mode of wearing it created much wonder. No child or maiden
> ever permitted her hair to fall as it pleased, except this girl, and folk
> did say that whenever she tried to bind it to her head the bright locks
> refused to obey her fingers, but slowly untwined themselves until they
> became natural ringlets again.
>
> The girl was a sweet singer – and singing is a fairy gift – and she
> would wander about lilting softly to herself, while neighbours won-
> dered and young men lost their hearts. It was believed that she was
> under the special care of Trows, for everything seemed to go smooth
> for her, and her golden hair was called 'the good gift of them that
> liked her well'. But it happened that a witch began to covet the Trow
> gift; and one day, when the girl lay down among some hay and went
> to sleep, the witch cut off her beautiful hair.
>
> The poor young thing returned to her home shorn of her glory, and
> after that she pined away. The song died from her lips, the light from
> her eyes.
>
> When she lay dead in her teens, folk said that the golden hair began
> to grow again, and had grown to all its former beauty ere the coffin lid
> was closed.
>
> The witch did not triumph, for the Trows took possession of her
> and punished her as she deserved.
>
> She was compelled to wander about their haunts and live in a strange
> manner. She was shadowed day and night (she said) by evil fancies.
> Whenever she tried to sleep the Trows would come and make queer
> noises so that she could not rest. Eventually she was spirited away
> altogether!

HUNT's story of 'The Mermaid's Vengeance' in *Popular Romances of
the West of England* is on similar lines, but we are not told explicitly that
Selina, a girl of MERMAID origins, had golden hair, only that she was
very beautiful.

Good manners. A polite tongue as well as an incurious eye is an important asset in any adventure among FAIRIES. There is one caution, however: certain fairies do not like to be thanked. It is against etiquette. No fault can be found with a bow or a curtsy, and all questions should be politely answered. See FAULTS CONDEMNED BY THE FAIRIES; VIRTUES ESTEEMED BY THE FAIRIES.

[Motif: F348.5.2]

Good neighbours, the. Of the many EUPHEMISTIC NAMES FOR THE FAIRIES, 'the Good Neighbours' is one of the most common. It will be remembered in the rhyme on 'Naming the Fairies' given by Chambers in *Popular Rhymes of Scotland*:

> Gin guid neibour ye ca' me,
> Then guid neibour I will be.

Montgomerie in *The Flouting of Polwart* calls the unattractive crowd whom he calls to mind 'The Guid Neeburs'.

[Motif: C433]

Good People, the. Another example of EUPHEMISTIC NAMES FOR THE FAIRIES.

Gooseberry Wife, the. One of the most obvious of the country NURSERY BOGIES; no grown-up person could ever have believed in her. She is known in the Isle of Wight and takes the form of an enormous hairy caterpillar who guards the gooseberry bushes. 'If ye goos out in the gearden, the gooseberry-wife'll be sure to ketch ye.'

Grant, the. GERVASE OF TILBURY, the 13th-century author of *Otia Imperialia*, includes a good many pieces of fairy belief in Part III of that work, some of them English and some from other parts of Europe. The Grant seems to be a close relation of the HEDLEY KOW, the Picktree BRAG and those other spirits whose most natural shape was that of a horse. He seems, however, to be a warning spirit and to be in character more like a BANSHEE than like the dangerous and malicious KELPY or EACH UISGE. Gervase explicitly places the Grant in England (KEIGHTLEY, *The Fairy Mythology*, p. 286):

> There is in England a certain kind of demon whom in their language they call Grant, like a yearling foal, erect on its hind legs, with sparkling eyes. This kind of demon often appears in the streets in the heat of the day, or about sunset. If there is any danger impending on the following day or night, it runs about the streets provoking the dogs to bark, and, by feigning flight, draws the dogs after it, in the vain hope of catching it. This illusion warns the inhabitants to beware of fire,

and the friendly demon, while he terrifies those who see him, puts by his coming the ignorant on their guard.

[Motif: F234.1.8]

Grateful fairies. The FAIRIES showed constant kindness to some of their favourites, generally because of the GOOD MANNERS and discretion which they showed towards them. They also repaid acts of kindness, either by a single reciprocal act or by steady gifts of good luck and prosperity. The many variants of the story of the BROKEN PED combine both of these rewards, for not only was the benefactor rewarded with a small gift of FAIRY FOOD, but continual good fortune followed his acceptance of the gift. The loan of meal or drink was often rewarded by the return of inexhaustible meal, as will be seen in FAIRY BORROWING. MIDWIVES TO THE FAIRIES often forfeited the reward they might have received by the breach of the TABOO against touching their own eye with the FAIRY OINTMENT given them to bestow fairy sight on the child. Cromek, however, favourable as usual to the fairies, has a variant of the story in which the results to the foster-mother are less disastrous. It is to be found in his *Remains of Galloway and Nithsdale Song* (pp. 302–3):

A fine young woman of Nithsdale, when first made a mother, was sitting singing and rocking her child, when a pretty lady came into her cottage, covered with a fairy mantle.

She carried a beautiful child in her arms, swaddled in green silk: 'Gie my bonnie thing a suck,' said the Fairy. The young woman, conscious to whom the child belonged, took it kindly in her arms, and laid it to her breast. The lady instantly disappeared, saying, 'Nurse kin' an' ne'er want.' The young mother nurtured the two babes, and was astonished whenever she awoke at finding the richest suits of apparel for both children, with meat of most delicious flavour. This food tasted, says tradition, like loaf mixed with wine and honey. It possessed more miraculous properties than the wilderness manna, preserving its relish even over the seventh day. On the approach of summer, the fairy lady came to see her child. It bounded with joy when it beheld her. She was much delighted with its freshness and activity; taking it in her arms, she bade the nurse follow. Passing through some scroggy woods, skirting the side of a beautiful green hill, they walked midway up. On its sunward slope a door opened, disclosing a beauteous porch, which they entered, and the turf closed behind them. The fairy dropped three drops of a precious dew on the nurse's left eyelid, and they entered a land of most pleasant and abundant promise. It was watered with fine looping rivulets, and yellow with corn; the fairest trees enclosed its fields, laden with fruit, which dropped honey. The nurse was rewarded with finest webs of cloth, and food of ever-enduring substance. Boxes of salves, for restoring mortal health, and curing mortal wounds and infirmities, were bestowed on her, with a promise of never needing. The Fairy dropped a green dew over her right eye, and bade her look. She beheld many of her lost friends and acquaintances doing menial drudgery, reaping the corn and gathering the fruits. This, said she, is the punishment of evil deeds! The Fairy passed her hand over her eye, and restored its mortal faculties.

She was conducted to the porch, but had the address to secure the heavenly salve.

She lived, and enjoyed the gift of discerning the earth-visiting spirits, till she was the mother of many children; but happening to meet the fairy lady who gave her her child, she attempted to shake hands with her. 'What ee d'ye see me wi'?' whispered she. 'Wi' them baith,' said the dame. She breathed on her eyes, and even the power of the box failed to restore their gifts again!

In this tale the young woman had acted more criminally than the mid-wives often do, for she had stolen the fairy liquid, yet she was only deprived of fairy sight, not of the sight of her eye. A suck of human milk was such a coveted boon that the fairy did not forget her gratitude.

Any share in humanity is coveted by the fairies, except for a gift of human clothing to BROWNIES and other helpers. There was, however, at least one gift of fairy clothing which earned a lasting reward. The tale is told in W. W. Gibbings, *Folk-Lore and Legends, Scotland*.

A poor man of Jedburgh was on his way to the market at Hawick and was passing over the side of Rubislaw when a great clamour arose in that lonely place. He could see nothing, but there was suddenly a great clamour of mirth and jollity, in the midst of which a terrible wailing arose. He could make out the words: 'O there's a bairn born, but there's naething to pit on 't!' The cry was repeated again and again. The man was sure that it was the fairies rejoicing at the birth of a baby, but in consternation that they had nothing to clothe it in. He was terrified, but he had a kind heart. He at once stripped off his plaid and threw it on the ground. It was at once snatched away and the sounds of rejoicing were redoubled. He did not stay to hear more, but drove his single sheep on to the market. It sold for a most unusual price and ever afterwards luck was with him, and he grew to be a rich and prosperous man.

Sometimes a piece of courtesy and consideration obtains a substantial reward, as in SCOTT's anecdote, in *Minstrelsy of the Scottish Border* (vol. II, p. 359), of Sir Godfrey MacCulloch, who happened to live above a house owned by the SUBTERRANEANS. One day, as Sir Godfrey was riding over his estate, he was joined by a little old man on a white palfrey who complained to him that his 'room of dais' was entirely spoiled by Sir Godfrey's main sewer which ran straight into it. Sir Godfrey was rather startled, but guessed what kind of person was speaking to him, apologized with great courtesy and promised to have the direction of the drain changed immediately. He went home and did so at once. Some years later he was so unfortunate as to kill a neighbour in an affray, and was sentenced to have his head struck off on the Castle Hill in Edinburgh. No sooner had he ascended the scaffold than a little old man on a white palfrey pressed through the crowd. He beckoned Sir Godfrey to jump down behind him, and no sooner had he done so than the two vanished like lightning and were never seen again.

The Laird o' Co was rescued in the same way, but this was as a reward for the honourable performance of a promise, and hence for another of the VIRTUES ESTEEMED BY THE FAIRIES.

It will be seen that the fairies are not generally devoid of gratitude, though a few, like YALLERY BROWN, are of such an evil disposition that it is a misfortune ever to befriend them.

[Motifs: F330; F333; F338]

Great Giant of Henllys, the. Like the ROARING BULL OF BAGBURY, the Great Giant of Henllys, whose story appeared in the *Athenaeum* in 1847, is the ghost of the dead man who turns into a demon, as the ghost of Glam did in the Icelandic saga, *Grettir the Strong*. It incidentally gives a typical account of how a ghost or a devil was traditionally laid.

Some time in the 18th century there lived on the banks of the Wye a man so rich, wicked and tyrannous that he was called 'The Great Giant of Henllys'. All the countryside rejoiced when he died, but they did not rejoice long, for he came again in a form so terrible that no one dared to be out of doors after dark, and even the horses and cattle huddled round the farms. At length it was determined that he must be laid, and three clergymen went at dead of night to the church of Henllys to exorcize him. They drew a circle before the altar, and took their stand within it. Each man had a lighted candle in his hand, and together they began their prayers. Suddenly a terrible monster appeared in the church and came roaring up towards them, but when it came to the circle it stopped as if it had hit against a stone wall. They went on with their prayers, but so terrible were the roarings and so close did the monster come that one man's heart failed him, and the candle that he held went out. But they continued with their exorcism. Then the giant reappeared as a roaring lion, and then as a raging bull; then it seemed as if a wave of the sea was flooding the church, and then as if the west wall was falling down. The second man wavered in his faith, and the second candle went out. Still the third went on, though his candle was faint. At last the Great Giant appeared in his mortal form, and they questioned him, and asked him why he had come in such dreadful shapes. 'I was bad as a man,' he said, 'and I am worse now as a devil.' And he vanished in a flash of fire. Then their candles all burned up again and they prayed steadily, and the Great Giant appeared in smaller and smaller forms, until at last he was only a fly, and they conjured him into a tobacco box, and threw him into

Llynwyn Pool, to lie there for ninety-nine years. Some say that it was for nine hundred and ninety-nine; but at any rate they are very careful not to disturb the tobacco box when they are dredging Llynwyn Pool.

[Motif: D2176.3]

Green. As fairy colour. See DRESS AND APPEARANCE OF THE FAIRIES.

Green Children, the. Very curious fairy anecdotes are to be found in the MEDIEVAL CHRONICLES. One of the strangest of them is the account of the Green Children given by both Ralph of Coggeshall and William of Newbridge. Ralph of Coggeshall in the original Latin is to be found in the *Rolls Series*, No. 68. KEIGHTLEY gives an English translation of it in *The Fairy Mythology* (pp. 281–3):

Another wonderful thing happened in Suffolk, at St Mary's of the Wolf-pits. A boy and his sister were found by the inhabitants of that place near the mouth of a pit which is there, who had the form of all their limbs like to those of other men, but they differed in the colour of their skin from all the people of our habitable world; for the whole surface of their skin was tinged of a green colour. No one could understand their speech. When they were brought as curiosities to the house of a certain knight, Sir Richard de Calne, at Wikes, they wept bitterly. Bread and other victuals were set before them, but they would touch none of them, though they were tormented by great hunger, as the girl afterwards acknowledged. At length, when some beans just cut, with their stalks, were brought into the house, they made signs, with great avidity, that they should be given to them. When they were brought, they opened the stalks instead of the pods, thinking the beans were in the hollow of them; but not finding them there, they began to weep anew. When those who were present saw this, they opened the pods, and showed them the naked beans. They fed on these with great delight, and for a long time tasted no other food. The boy, however, was always languid and depressed, and he died within a short time. The girl enjoyed continual good health; and becoming accustomed to various kinds of food, lost completely that green colour, and gradually recovered the sanguine habit of her entire body. She was afterwards regenerated by the laver of holy baptism, and lived for many years in the service of that knight (as I have frequently heard from him and his family), and was rather loose and wanton in her conduct. Being frequently asked about the people of her country, she asserted that the inhabitants, and all they had in that country, were of a green colour; and that they saw no sun, but enjoyed a degree of light like what is after sunset. Being asked how she came into this country with the aforesaid boy, she replied, that as they were following their flocks, they came to a certain cavern, on entering which they heard a delightful sound of bells; ravished by whose sweetness, they went for a long time wandering on through the cavern, until they came to its mouth. When they came out of it, they were struck senseless by the excessive light of the sun, and the unusual temperature of the air; and they thus lay for a long time. Being terrified by the noise of those who came on them, they wished to fly, but they could not find the entrance of the cavern before they were caught.

William of Newbridge (a monastery in Yorkshire) adds several details to this account. He says that he had not at first believed it, but further investigation convinced him of its truth. The children appeared in King Stephen's reign. He says that the girl called the country St Martin's Land and said that its inhabitants were Christians. It might be noted that green is the Celtic colour of death and that beans are traditionally the food of the dead.

[Motif: F233.1]

Green Mist, the. Mrs Balfour, in her collection of unusual stories from Lincolnshire to be found in her 'Legends of the Lincolnshire Cars', gives us a striking variant of the SEPARABLE SOUL theme, in which a life is bound up in an external object. It was told her by an old man of Lindsey and is presented in full dialect, like her other stories. This summary is taken from K. M. Briggs, *A Dictionary of British Folk-Tales in the English Language* (Part A, vol. I). Examples of the dialect are given in the STRANGERS.

In the old days, the 'car-folk', as the people of the Fens were known, had many strange ways and words to keep danger from them, and to bring good luck. In the churches the priests would sing their services, but the old people set more store by the old ways that the priest knew nothing about.

In the winter the BOGLES and such had nothing but evil to do, but in the spring the earth had to be wakened and many strange words were spoken that the people did not understand themselves: they would turn a mould in each field, and every morning at first dawn they would stand in the doorway with SALT and BREAD in their hands waiting for the Green Mist to creep up which meant that spring had come. There was one family that had done all that had to be done year after year, and yet for all that, one winter heavy sorrow came on them, for the daughter, who had been the prettiest lass in the village, grew so pining and sickly, that at last she could not stand upon her feet. But she thought if she could greet the spring again she would live. Day after day they carried her out to watch, but the wintry weather held on, and at length she said to her mother: 'If the Green Mist doesna come tomorrow, I can stay no longer. The earth is calling me and the seeds are bursting that will cover me, but if I could only live as long as one of those cowslips that grow by the door each spring, I swear I'd be content.' The mother hushed her, for she did not know who might hear; the air was full of listeners in those days. But the next day the Green Mist came, and the girl sat in the sun, and crumbled the bread in her thin fingers, and laughed with joy; and as the spring went on she grew stronger and prettier every day that the sun shone, though a cold day could make her white and shivery as ever, and when the cowslips flowered she grew so strange and beautiful that they almost feared her. But she would never let her mother pluck a cowslip. But one day a lad came to her cottage, and he plucked a cowslip and played with it as they chatted. She did not see what he had done till he said goodbye, and she saw the cowslip lying on the earth.

'Did thee pull that cowslip?' she said, and her hand went to her head.

'Aye,' he said, and stooped and gave it to her, thinking what a pretty lass she was.

She took it from him and stood looking round the garden, and then she gave a cry and ran into the house. They found her lying on the bed with the cowslip in her hand, and all day long she faded, and next morning her mother found her lying dead and withered like the withered flower in her hand.

The bogles had heard her wish and granted her to live as long as the cowslips, and fade with the first that was plucked.

[Motif: E765.3.4]

Green Sleeves. The story of Green Sleeves, published in Peter Buchan's *Ancient Scottish Tales*, is an excellent example of the SUPERNATURAL WIZARD such as we find in the tales of NICHT NAUGHT NOTHING and the Battle of the Birds. These are all Celtic tales which have survived in full, but of which fragments are to be found in England. 'Green Sleeves' is a story of the 'supernatural bride' type and is rich in motifs which seem peculiar to the Celtic genius, though it also contains many universal motifs. To begin with, Green Sleeves procures the presence of the prince-hero by winning a game of skill against him. In most of the Celtic tales the game is CHESS, but in this it is skittles. Then we have the travels in search of the challenger, where the hero is helped successively by three very aged, almost immortal brothers. Then we come to the SWAN MAIDEN theme with the three daughters of the WIZARD. The help of one of them is secured by taking her swan garment and returning it to her. We next move on to the miraculous tasks demanded by the wizard and performed for the hero by his daughter, the selection of the bride among a number of maidens who appear identical with her, the marriage and escape by means of an object which magically answers for the lovers. The flight and the pursuer delayed by magical objects, the SEPARABLE SOUL and the death of the wizard are all a common sequence of motifs in this type of story. It is almost inevitably followed by the separation of the lovers because of the violation of a TABOO, the theme of the bartered bed, the awakening of the husband's memory, and the final reunion of the lovers. The theme of the would-be lovers magically delayed is treated as a complete story in 'The Three Feathers', included by Jacobs in his *English Fairy Tales*. The Aarne-Thompson Types 400, 'The Search for the Lost Bride' and 425, 'The Search for the Lost Husband' are combined in this tale. Its subject is plainly a journey into a supernatural world and the winning of a supernatural bride. The wizard enjoys a conditional and magical immortality which is paralleled by many of the TUATHA DE DANANN. Age and disease cannot kill them, but they can be killed by violence, as AED the son of DAGDA was killed by a blow from a jealous husband. Green Sleeves is typical of many supernatural wizards whose life is buttressed by magic. The summary which follows is taken from *A Dictionary of British Folk-Tales* (Part A, vol. 1):

A King of Scotland had a son who was devoted to gambling and excelled at the game of skittles, so that no one dared compete with him in that game. A strange old man suddenly appeared and challenged him to play, on condition that the winner might ask of the loser whatever he wished, and the loser must comply on pain of death. The old man won, and charged the prince to tell him his name and place of abode before that day twelve months.

The prince took to his bed in despair, but was at last persuaded by his father, first to tell him the cause of his distress, and then to go and seek the answers to the old man's questions. After a long day's travel an old man, sitting outside his cottage, told him the rogue was named Green Sleeves. He was 200 years old, and sent the Prince 200 miles on to his brother, 400 years older, with the aid of magic slippers and a ball, to guide him. The slippers and ball would return of themselves on being kicked.

Eight hundred miles on, the third brother, 1,000 years older, sent him to the river Ugie to intercept the three daughters of Green Sleeves, who would come to bathe, disguised as swans. He stole the swan-skin of the youngest, which had one blue wing, and so induced her to tell him the way to Green Sleeves' castle. Being unwillingly admitted by Green Sleeves, the prince found endless difficulties – a bed of broken glass fragments, fish-skins and mouldy bread to eat – and three impossible tasks were imposed on him by Green Sleeves, but Blue Wing secretly helped him through all, with the aid of a magic box containing thousands of fairies. The tasks were, first, to build a castle 1,000 miles in length, breadth and height, including a stone from every quarry in the world, and covered with feathers of every kind of bird. The next task was to sow, reap and replace in the cask from which it came, a quantity of lint seed, as before in the space of a single day. Third and last was to clear a stable where 200 horses had stood for 200 years, and recover from it a golden needle lost by Green Sleeves' grandmother 1,000 years before.

Green Sleeves now offered the prince one of his daughters in marriage. They would have murdered him, but Blue Wing, by a trick, again saved him and they fled. Magic cakes hung on their bed delayed the pursuit, but finally Green Sleeves in seven-leagued boots followed them. Magic obstacles, a forest, a great rock, and a rushing river, enabled the prince, directed by Blue Wing, to procure an egg from a certain bird's nest on top of a high hill. With this egg, aimed at a special point of his breast, Green Sleeves was slain, and the prince rode home to procure a fitting escort for his bride before making her known to his parents. Blue Wing warned him against being kissed, but a lap-dog sprang up and licked him, and he forgot her.

Blue Wing hid in a tree above a pool, and two servants of a neighbouring goldsmith, mistaking her reflection for their own, refused, through pride in their supposed beauty, to serve him any more. Blue Wing took their place, and served the goldsmith, until two of his customers, a prince's groom first, and then the Duke of Marlborough himself, fell in love with her. She tricked them both, by magic, having promised to sleep with each of them for one night, and then kept them spell-bound to some menial task, and so made her way, as the duke's partner, to a ball at court. Here, when the dancing was over, and tales were told and songs sung, Blue Wing produced a golden cock and hen, which talked, and reminded the prince of all that had happened.

The new bride to whom he had been promised was dismissed, and Blue Wing and the prince were married, with all honour and joy, and lived to see their large family grow up to take their place in due time.

[Types: 313; 425. Motifs: D361.1; D672; D721; D1313.1; D1521.1; D2004.2.1; D2006.1.1; G465; H151.1; H335.0.1; H1010; H1102; H1219.1; N2.0.1]

Greencoaties. One of the names given to FAIRIES in the Lincolnshire Fen country. Here, as elsewhere, it was thought unlucky to mention the word 'fairies', and they are called 'the STRANGERS', 'the TIDDY ONES', or 'the Greencoaties', which are thus all EUPHEMISTIC NAMES FOR THE FAIRIES. The name 'Greencoaties' is mentioned by both Mrs Balfour in her 'Legends of the Lincolnshire Cars' and Mrs Wright in *Rustic Speech and Folk-Lore*.

Greenies. According to Bowker, the Greenies are the FAIRIES of Lancashire, dressed in green with red caps on their heads. Bowker tells a story of a fisherman's visit to a fairyland gained from Morecambe Bay, where he was given fairy food and gold and fell violently in love with the

Fairy Queen. He was punished because he tried to kiss her feet, and found himself back in his boat, with not a coin of gold on him. A year later he and his boat were lost. These fairies of Bowker's, with their mushroom tables and sophisticated talk, are very much in the style of the literary JACOBEAN FAIRIES and seem to rely for the details of the stories on Drayton's *Nimphidia* and the other poems in the same fashion.

[Motifs: F236.1.6; F236.3.2]

Grey Neighbours, the. One of the EUPHEMISTIC NAMES FOR THE FAIRIES given by the Shetlanders to the TROWS, the small grey-clad GOBLINS whom the Shetlanders used to propitiate and fear, using against them many of the means used all over the islands as PROTECTION AGAINST FAIRIES.

Grig. Rather a debatable fairy. The *Oxford Dictionary* gives the word as meaning a DWARF or something small, a baby eel, a cricket. There is, however, a fairly widespread idea that the proverbial expression 'As merry as a grig' relates to FAIRIES, and in Somerset 'griggling apples' are the small apples left on the trees for the fairies. Ruth Tongue heard a story, 'The Grig's Red Cap', from a groom at Stanmore, Harry White, in 1936, and an earlier version of it from the Welsh Marches in 1912. According to both of these, the grigs were small, merry fairies dressed in green, with red stocking caps, a costume which could indeed apply to fairies in a good many places, as, for example, the WEE FOLK in Ireland. It is possible that the idea of smallness and the expression 'merry as a grig' built up a kind of pseudo-fairy about the word 'grig'.

[Motifs: F236.1.6; F236.3.2]

Grim. A venerable name among the GOBLINS, known internationally in the *Fossegrim* of Norway and the Swedish *Kirkegrimm*, who is the same as our CHURCH GRIM. The Grim's Dykes straggling over the country are evidence of the antiquity of the spirit. It was at one time a by-name for ODIN and later for the Devil. Jabez ALLIES' LIST OF THE FAIRIES cites many place-names that begin with 'Grim'. The Church Grim usually took the form of a BLACK DOG, and the Fairy Grim in THE LIFE OF ROBIN GOODFELLOW sometimes assumed that form:

> I walke with the owle, and make many to cry as loud as she doth hollow. Sometimes I doe affright many simple people, for which some have termed me the Blacke Dog of Newgate. At the meetings of young men and maydes I many times am, and when they are in the midst of all their good cheare, I come in, in some fearefull shape and affright them, and then carry away their good cheare, and eat it with my fellow fayries. 'Tis I that do, like a skritch-owle, cry at sicke men's windowes, which make the hearers so fearefull, that they say that the

sick person cannot live. Many other wayes have I to fright the simple,
but the understanding man I cannot moove to feare, because he
knowes that I have no power to do hurt.

> My nightly businesse have I told,
> To play these trickes I use of old;
> When candles burn both blue and dim,
> Old folkes will say, Here's fairy Grim.

[Motif: DI812.5.1.12.2]

Grindylow. Like JENNY GREENTEETH, this is a Yorkshire water-demon
who lurks in deep stagnant pools to drag down children who come too
near to the water. It is mentioned by Mrs Wright in a list of cautionary
NURSERY BOGIES.
[Motif: F420.5.2]

Grogan, or Grogach. One of the BROWNIE-like spirits of the Highlands. GRUAGACH has many points in common with this brownie, and
in Ulster becomes the 'Grogan', according to Wood-Martin, or the
'Grogach', according to Lewis Spence. In *Traces of the Elder Faiths in
Ireland* (vol. II, p. 3), Wood-Martin describes the Grogan as 'low of
stature, hairy, with broad shoulders and very strong, "an unco wee body,
terrible strong"'. Spence in *The Fairy Tradition* (p. 101) gives a more
detailed account of him. There is an unusual feature in the story of the
Grogach of Ballycastle, where the poor Grogach kills himself from over-
work. It was the custom in the farm to lay out a number of sheaves in the
granary overnight for the Grogach to thresh by morning. One morning
the farmer left the flail on top of the cornstack and forgot to lay out the
usual number of sheaves. The Grogach took it that he was to thresh the
whole stack, but in the morning he was found dead on top of the grain.
The farmer gave him honourable burial, and he was long mourned. The
Highland Gruagachs were often richly dressed, with GOLDEN HAIR, and
watched over the cattle, but the Ulster Grogachs were naked and hairy
little men, about four feet in height. In another description, the Grogach
has a large head and soft body, and seems to have no bones as he comes
tumbling down the hillside. One Ulster grogach, like his Highland
counterpart, herded and watched over the cattle. The farmer's daughter,
pitying his nakedness, made him a shirt, but he thought that they were
trying to lay him, and went away, weeping bitterly.
[Motifs: F480; F488.1]

Gruagachs. Much has been written about the Gruagachs, and out of a
wealth of information from J. F. CAMPBELL and J. G. CAMPBELL, from
Alexander Carmichael, Donald Mackenzie and Lewis Spence, three
different types of Gruagach seem to emerge. In the Highlands there is

the fairy lady dressed in green with long GOLDEN HAIR, sometimes beautiful and sometimes wan and haggard, who is the guardian of cattle and is a kind of fairy chatelaine to a farm. Mackenzie is inclined to think that she is truly a GLAISTIG and that Gruagach, 'the hairy one', is an epithet attached to her. Like the Glaistig she travelled extensively and was connected with water. It was her habit to come dripping into houses and ask to dry herself by the fire. There were also male gruagachs in the Highlands, some handsome, slender youths wearing green and red, but for the most part naked and shaggy and performing BROWNIE labours about the farm which they patronized. Both kinds had offerings of milk made to them. In northern Ireland the GROGANS followed the brownie tradition, but in southern Ireland, the Gruagach was a SUPERNATURAL WIZARD, often a GIANT after the style of the Wizard in NICHT NAUGHT NOTHING. A clear account of all these three gruagachs is given by Lewis Spence in *The Fairy Tradition*.

[Motifs: F480; F488.1]

Guardian Black Dog, the. BLACK DOGS are as a rule considered sinister creatures, either ominous of death or a direct cause of it, like the MAUTHE DOOG of Man, but there are fairly widespread stories which were particularly current at the beginning of this century of a benevolent black dog which either guarded or guided travellers. A representative specimen is from Augustus Hare's repertoire. It is to be found in *In My Solitary Life* (p. 188):

> Mr Wharton dined. He said, 'When I was at the little inn at Ayscliffe, I met a Mr Bond, who told me a story about my friend Johnnie Greenwood of Swancliffe. Johnnie had to ride one night through a wood a mile long to the place he was going to. At the entrance of the wood a large black dog joined him, and pattered along by his side. He could not make out where it came from, but it never left him, and when the wood grew so dark that he could not see it, he still heard it pattering beside him. When he emerged from the wood, the dog had disappeared, and he could not tell where it had gone to. Well, Johnnie paid his visit, and set out to return the same way. At the entrance of the wood, the dog joined him, and pattered along beside him as before; but it never touched him, and he never spoke to it, and again, as he emerged from the wood, it ceased to be there.
>
> 'Years after, two condemned prisoners in York gaol told the chaplain that they had intended to rob and murder Johnnie that night in the wood, but that he had a large dog with him, and when they saw that, they felt that Johnnie and the dog together would be too much for them.
>
> 'Now that is what I call a useful ghostly apparition,' said Mr Wharton.

I myself heard in 1910 a very similar story told in London by a Mr Hosey, an old clergyman. One of the same type was told in Yorkshire about a well-known Nonconformist minister who was making a charitable collection in a lonely part of the country.

Birdlip Hill in Gloucestershire is said to be haunted by a good black dog which guides travellers who are walking on the hills or in darkness, but Somerset seems to have the liveliest tradition of the guardian black dogs. This may be connected with the CHURCH GRIM. It used to be the custom to bury a black dog, without a white hair in its coat, in a newly consecrated cemetery to perform the duties that would otherwise fall to the first corpse to be buried there. He would act as a guardian of the churchyard against the Devil. Ruth Tongue gives two anecdotes of good black dogs in Somerset in *County Folklore* (vol. VIII, pp. 108–9):

> An old lady of eighty-five told me in 1960 of a Black Dog experience of hers in Canada. She had apparently carried the belief out with her from Somerset and brought it back again.
> 'When I was a young girl I was living outside Toronto in Canada and I had to go to a farm some miles away one evening. There were woods on the way and I was greatly afraid, but a large black dog came with me and saw me safely to the door. When I had to return he again appeared, and walked with me till I was nearly home. *Then he vanished.*'
> A more indisputably Somerset story was told me by a very sweet and gentle cottager who had once had occasion to climb the Quantocks late one winter afternoon. When he had climbed up Weacombe to the top the sea mist came down, and he felt he might be frozen to death before he got home. But as he was groping along he suddenly touched shaggy fur and thought that old Shep, his sheep-dog, had come out to look for him. 'Good dog, Shep. Whoame, boy!' he said. The dog turned and led him right to his cottage door, where he heard his own dog barking inside. He turned to look at the dog who had guided him, which grew gradually larger and then faded away. 'It was the Black Dog, God bless it!' he would always say. It is unusual for anybody to touch the Black Dog without coming to harm.

[Motif: F401.3.3]

Gull. The name of one of the FAIRIES introduced into the LIFE OF ROBIN GOODFELLOW. He is one of the tricksy fairies, but his name is not to be found in any of the local traditions. His own account is true enough to the HOBGOBLIN's habits:

> When mortals keep their beds I walke abroad, and for my prankes am called by the name of Gull. I with a fayned voyse doe often deceive many men, to their great amazement. Many times I get on men and women, and soe lye on their stomackes, that I cause their great paine,

for which they call me by the name of HAGGE, or NIGHT-MARE. Tis I
that doe steale children, and in the place of them leave CHANGELINGS.
Sometimes I also steale milke and creame, and then with my brothers,
PATCH, PINCH and GRIM, and sisters, SIB, TIB, LICKE and LULL,
I feast with my stolne goods.

Gunna (*goona*). A kind of out-of-door BROWNIE whose chief concern is
herding the cattle. J. G. CAMPBELL says that he is known on the Isle
of Tiree, where he keeps the cattle from the growing crops. He is
miserably thin, and naked except for a ragged fox-skin wrapped round
him. He has long yellow hair like a GRUAGACH. A second-sighted man
saw him, and pitying his nakedness, tried to give him clothes, but, like a
true brownie, he was driven away by this attempted kindness. D. A.
Mackenzie quotes a poem written in sympathy for his plight:

> For he'll see him perched alone
> On a chilly old grey stone
> Nibbling, nibbling at a bone
>   That we'll maybe throw away.

> He's so hungry, he's so thin,
> If he'd come we'd let him in,
> For a rag of fox's skin
>   Is the only thing he'll wear.

> He'll be chittering in the cold
> As he hovers round the fold,
> With his locks of glimmering gold
>   Twined about his shoulders bare.

[Motif: F475]

Guytrash. Another of the sinister North Country spirits, a form of the
TRASH or SKRIKER. Like the Trash it is a death portent, but instead of
appearing like a shaggy dog with saucer eyes, it takes the shape of an evil
cow. Mrs Wright mentions it in *Rustic Speech and Folk-Lore* (p. 194),
but it is not mentioned by William Henderson, nor in the DENHAM
TRACTS. It is possible that she may have learnt of it orally from her
husband, Professor Wright of the great *Dialect Dictionary*.
[Motif: F401.3.1]

Gwartheg Y Llyn (*gwarrtheg er thlin*). These, the fairy cattle of Wales,
were among FAIRY ANIMALS very closely akin to the CRODH MARA of
the Highlands, except that they are generally said to be milk-white,
though in one story at least the cow is described as speckled or particoloured. These cattle in Wales were often given as part of the dowry of
a GWRAGEDD ANNWN, a Lake Maiden, but a water-bull would some-

times visit earthly herds with most fortunate results for the farmer. On one occasion at least a stray fairy cow attached herself to an earthly bull, and the farmer succeeded in catching her. From that moment his future was made. The number and quality of the calves born to the stray cow were unsurpassable. Never was such milk or butter or cheese. The farmer became the richest man in the countryside. But as years passed the rich farmer became prouder and more grasping. He began to think that the stray cow's heyday had passed and that it was time to fatten her for the market. She was as industrious at fattening as she had been at breeding or giving milk. Soon she was a prodigy of fatness. The butcher was called, the neighbours assembled to see the death of the far-famed cow. The butcher raised his sharp knife; but before the blow could be struck his arm was paralysed and the knife dropped from his hand. A piercing scream rang out, and the crowd saw a tall figure in green standing on the crag above Llyn Barfog. She chanted out in a great voice

'Come thou, Einion's Yellow One,
Stray-horns, the Particoloured Lake Cow,
And the hornless Dodin;
Arise, come home.'

As she sang the stray cow broke loose, and followed by all her progeny, raced up the mountain-side to the fairy lady. The farmer followed frantically after them, only to see them surrounding the green lady, who formed them into ranks and led them down into the dark waters of the lake. She waved her hand derisively to the farmer, and she and her herd disappeared into the dark waters, leaving only a cluster of yellow water-lilies to mark the place where they had sunk. The farmer became as poor as he had been rich.

The Highland version of this story is the ELF-BULL, though no lake maiden appears.

[Motif: F241.2]

Gwarwyn-a-Throt (*gwarrwin-a-throt*). The hidden name of a Monmouthshire BWCA. See also HABETROT; PEERIFOOL; SECRET NAMES OF THE FAIRIES; TOM TIT TOT.

Gwrach Y Rhibyn (*gwrarch er hreebin*). This rather obscure name is used in Cardiganshire for the Welsh BANSHEE, sometimes called y Cyhiraeth. She would go invisibly beside the person she wished to warn, and if she came to cross-roads or to a stream she would burst out into a ghastly shriek, beating the ground or the water and crying out, 'My husband! My husband!' if she was accompanying a woman, or, 'My wife!' if a woman's death was foretold. Or again, 'My little child! O my little child!' if it was a child who would die. Inarticulate screams meant the death of the hearer himself. She was described as very hideous, with tangled hair, long black teeth and long withered arms out of all proportion to the length of her body. Rhys, who gives this description of her in *Celtic Folk-Lore* (vol. II, pp. 452–5), considers that she is generally regarded as an ancestral figure, but thinks it possible that she may be one of the mother goddesses, like ANU or the CAILLEACH BHEUR.

[Motif: M301.6.1]

Gwragedd Annwn (*gwrageth anoon*). Of all the folk fairy tales of Wales, that of the Lake Maidens who married mortals has had the widest distribution and the longest life. There are many sinister fairies in Welsh tradition, but the Welsh water-fairies are not among them. They are beautiful and desirable, but they are not sirens or. nixies. John Rhys devotes a chapter in *Celtic Folk-Lore* (Chapter I) to 'Undine's Kymric Sisters'. The best-known and the earliest of the stories about the Gwragen Annwn is the story of the lady of Llyn y Fan Fach, a small and beautiful lake near the Black Mountains. It happened in the 12th century that a widow with a farm at Blaensawde, near Mydfai, used to send her only son two miles up the valley to graze their cattle on the shores of Llyn y Fan Fach. One day, as he was eating his midday snack, he saw the most beautiful lady he had ever seen, sitting on the surface of the lake combing the curls of her long GOLDEN HAIR with the smooth water as her mirror. He was at once fathoms deep in love, and held out his hands with the bread in them, beseeching her to come to shore. She looked kindly at him, but said, 'Your bread is baked too hard' and plunged into the lake. He went back and told his mother what had happened. She sympathized with him and gave him some unbaked dough to take next day. That was too soft, so the next day his mother gave him lightly baked bread. That passed the test, for three figures rose from the lake: an old man of noble and stately bearing with a beautiful daughter on each side of him. The old man spoke to the farmer saying that he was willing to part with his daughter if the young man could point out to him the one on whom his love was set. The fairy ladies were as like as two peas, and the farmer would have given it up in despair if one of them had not slightly moved her foot so that he recognized the distinctive lacing of her sandal and made the right choice. The fairy father gave her a dowry of as many cattle as she could count in a breath – and she counted quickly – but warned her future husband that he must treat her kindly, and if he gave her three causeless blows she and her dowry would be lost to him for ever. They married and were very happy, and had three beautiful boys, but she had strange, fairy-like ways; she fell some-times into a kind of trance, she was apt to weep when other people rejoiced, as at weddings, and to laugh and sing when other people were mourning, as at a child-funeral, and these peculiarities were the cause of his giving her three causeless blows, mere love-taps but a breach of the TABOO, so that she was forced to leave him, taking with her all her cattle and their descendants, even to the slaughtered calf hanging against the wall. She did not forget her three sons, however, for she visited them and taught them deep secrets of medicine so that they became the famous physicians of Mydfai, and the skill descended in their family until it died out in the 19th century. This tale Rhys reproduced from *The Physicians of Mydfai* by Rees of Tonn, but he also recorded variations of it from oral collections, adding fresh details in some versions, though some were rudimentary. Wirt Sikes in *British Goblins* tells the same story in considerable detail, but without giving his source, as Rhys is careful to do. In all the stories the taboo is, in the end, violated and the fairy disappears, just as the wedded SEAL MAIDENS regain their skins and return to their element.

[Motifs: F241.2; F300; F302.2]

Gwydion (*gwideeon*). The WIZARD and Bard of North Wales, who was the son of the Welsh goddess, DON, the equivalent of the Irish DANA. Don had three children: Gwydion the Wizard, Gofannon the Smith, and a daughter Arianrhod, the mother of Llew. In the *Mabinogi of Math ab Mathonwy*, Math and Gwydion make a bride for Llew – Blodeuwed, the flower-like – who fell in love with another man and betrayed Llew to his death. In the MABINOGION, Gwydion performed many works of magic against the men of southern Wales.

Gwyllion (*gwithleeon*). The evil mountain FAIRIES of Wales. They are hideous female spirits who waylay and mislead travellers by night on the mountain roads. Sikes devotes a chapter of *British Goblins* (Chapter 4) to the Gwyllion, contrasting them with the more friendly ELLYLLON. He regards the OLD WOMAN OF THE MOUNTAIN as one of the Gwyllion. They are defeated by drawing a knife against them; they seem to be sensitive to the power of cold IRON. They were in the habit of visiting the houses of people at Aberystwyth, especially in stormy weather, and the inhabitants felt it necessary to greet them hospitably for fear of the harm they might do. They were friends and patrons of the goats, and might indeed take goat form. It was the TYLWYTH TEG, however, who combed the goats' beards on Fridays.

[Motifs: F460; F460.4.4]

Gwyn ap Nudd (*gwin ap neethe*). The reputed king of the underworld since the earliest of the Arthurian Romances, *Kilwch and Olwen*, appeared in the MABINOGION. There he is listed in the Court of King Arthur, but was said also to be confined to the underworld, where it was his duty to control the imprisoned devils and prevent them from destroying mankind. He had clearly been a Celtic Pluto. As time went on he dwindled to a fairy and became king of the PLANT ANNWN, the subterranean fairies. Evans Wentz, in his *Fairy-Faith in Celtic Countries*, mentions him in his examination of King Arthur and his followers as early Celtic gods dwindled into FAIRIES, and a more sober assessment of him is given by John Rhys in *Celtic Folklore*.

Gyl Burnt-tayl. A jocular name for a female WILL O' THE WISP. She is to be found in Gayton's *Festivious Notes* (1654). She is mentioned by Gillian Edwards in *Hobgoblin and Sweet Puck*, who considers that 'Jill' was generally used as a slightly opprobrious term, in the sense of a flirt or a wanton. Perhaps it was more usually a rustic name, as in 'Jack shall have Jill'.
[Motif: F491]

Gyre-Carling. The name given to the Queen of the Fairies in Fife. She seems to be a spinning fairy like HABETROT, for J. E. Simpkins in *County Folk-Lore* (vol. VII) quotes *Jamieson's Dictionary*:

Superstitious females in Fife, are anxious to spin off all the flax that is on their rocks, on the last night of the year; being persuaded that if they left any unspun, the Gyre-Carling, or – as they pronounce the word – the Gy-carlin, would carry it off before morning.

It is still considered unlucky to leave a piece of knitting unfinished at the end of the year, but this is not now with any reference to the Gyre-Carling.

Habetrot. The name of the Border patron fairy of spinning. William Henderson in *Folk-Lore of the Northern Counties* (pp. 258–62) tells a story from the Wilkie manuscript about this fairy which has many points of interest. A Selkirkshire gudewife had a bonny, idle daughter who much preferred roaming over the countryside gathering flowers to blistering her fingers with spinning. The gudewife did all that she could to make the lassie a notable spinster, but all in vain, till one day she lost patience, gave her daughter a sound whipping, threw down seven heads of lint in front of her, and told her that they must all be spun up into yarn within three days, or it would be the worse for her. The lassie knew her mother meant what she said, so she set to work in earnest, and worked hard for a whole day, but she only blistered her soft little hands and produced a few feet of lumpy, uneven thread. When it grew dark she cried herself to sleep. She woke up on a glorious morning, looked at her wretched stint, and despaired. 'I can do no good here,' she thought, 'I'll away oot into the caller air.' She wandered here and there down the stream and at last sat down on a SELF-BORED STONE and burst into tears. She had heard no one come near, but when she looked up there was an old wife beside her, plying her spindle busily and pulling out her thread with a lip that seemed made for that very purpose. The lass was a friendly wee thing, and she wished the old wife a kind good morning. Then like the bairn she was she asked, 'Whit way are ye sae lang lipit, gudewife?' 'With drawing the thread, ma hinnie,' said the old wife, well pleased with her. 'That's what I sud be doing,' said the lassie, 'but it's a' nae gude.' And she told the old wife her story. 'Fetch me yir lint, and I'll hae it spun up in gude time,' said the kind old wife; and the lassie ran home and fetched it. 'What's yir name, gudewife?' she asked, 'and whaur will I get it?' But the old wife took the lint without answering – and was nowhere. The girl sat down, thoroughly bewildered, and waited. Presently the hot sun made her drowsy, and she fell asleep. The sun was setting when she woke, and she heard a whirring sound and voices singing coming from under her head. She put her eye to the self-bored stone and beneath her she saw a great cavern, with a number of queer old wives sitting spinning in it, each on a white marble stone, rounded in the river, called a 'colludie stone'. They all had long, long lips, and her friend of that morning was walking up and down among them, directing them all, and as the lassie peeped in she heard her say, 'Little kens the wee lassie on the brae-head that Habetrot is my name.' There was one spinner sitting a little apart from the rest who was uglier than all of them. Habetrot went up to her and said: 'Bundle up the yarn, SCANTLIE MAB, for it's time the wee lassie sud gie it to her Minnie.' At that the lassie knew that it was time for her to be at the cottage door, and she got up and hurried home. She met Habetrot just outside, who gave her seven beautiful hanks of yarn. 'Oh whit can I dae for ye in return?' she cried. 'Naething, naething,' said Habetrot, 'but dinna tell yer mither whae spun the yarn.'

The lassie went into the cottage treading on air but famished with hunger, for she had eaten nothing since the day before. Her mother was in the box-bed fast asleep, for she had been hard at work making black puddings, 'sausters' they called them round there, and had gone to bed early. The lassie spread out her yarn so that her mother could see it when she waked, then she blew up the fire, took down the frying-pan and fried the first sauster and ate it, then the second, then the third, and so on till she had eaten all seven. Then she went up the ladder to bed.

The mother was awake first in the morning. There she saw seven beautiful skeins of yarn spread out, but not a trace of her seven sausters except a black frying-pan. Half-distracted between joy and anger, she rushed out of the house singing:

'Ma daughter's spun se'en, se'en, se'en,
Ma daughter's eaten se'en, se'en, se'en
And all before daylight!'

And who should come riding along but the young laird himself. 'What's that you're crying, Goodwife?' he said, and she sang out again:

'Ma daughter's spun se'en, se'en, se'en,
Ma daughter's eaten se'en, se'en, se'en,

an' if ye don't believe me, come and see for yersel!'

The laird followed her into the house, and when he saw the smoothness and evenness of the skeins, he wanted to see the spinner of them, and when he saw the bonny lass, he asked her to be his wife.

The laird was handsome and braw, and the lass was glad to say yes, but there was one thing that troubled her, the laird kept talking of all the fine yarn she would be spinning for him after the wedding. So one evening the lassie went down to the self-bored stone and called on Habetrot. Habetrot knew what her trouble would be, but she said, 'Never heed, hinnie, bring your jo here and we'll sort it for ye.' So next night at sunset the pair of them stood at the self-bored stone and heard Habetrot singing, and at the end of the song she opened a hidden door and let them into the mound. The laird was astonished at all the shapes of deformity he saw before him and asked aloud why their lips were so distorted. One after another they muttered in hardly intelligible tones, 'With sp-sp-

spinning.' 'Aye, aye, they were once bonnie eneugh,' said Habetrot, 'but spinners aye gan of that gait. Yer own lassie 'ill be the same, bonnie though she is noo, for she's fair mad about the spinning.' 'She'll not!' said the laird. 'Not another spindle shall she touch from this day on!' 'Just as ye say, laird,' said the lassie; and from that day on she roamed the countryside with the laird or rode about behind him as blithe as a bird, and every head of lint that grew on their land went to old Habetrot to spin.

This pleasant version of Grimm's tale of 'The Three Spinners' is more than a mere folk-tale, for Habetrot was really believed to be the patroness of spinners, and it was seriously held that a shirt made by her was a sovereign remedy for all sorts of diseases. It is strange that so many of these spinning fairies had names ending in 'trot', 'throt' or 'tot'. There is TRYTEN-A-TROTEN, GWARYN-A-THROT and TOM TIT TOT. Habetrot, however, is not sinister like the others, though the over-hearing of her name suggests a similar motif which somehow got overlaid.

[Type: 501. Motifs: D2183; F271.4.3; F346; G201.1; H914; H1092; J51]

Hagge, the. One 16th-century name for a NIGHT-MARE, conceived of as a hideous succubus who sat on a man in his sleep, squeezing his stomach and causing horrible dreams.

[Motifs: F471.1; F471.2.1]

Hags. Ugly old women who had given themselves over to witchcraft were often called 'hags', but there were thought to be supernatural hags as well, such as those who haunted the Fen country in Mrs Balfour's story of the DEAD MOON; and giant-like hags which seem to have been the last shadows of a primitive nature goddess, the CAILLEACH BHEUR, BLACK ANNIS or GENTLE ANNIE.

[Motif: A125.1]

Hairy Jack. The name given to one of the Lincolnshire BLACK DOGS of the BARGUEST type. This particular barguest haunted an old barn near Willoughton Cliff, and others of the same breed were said to haunt lonely plantations and waste places. Mrs Gutch, after mentioning Hairy Jack in *County Folk-Lore* (vol. v), cites from *Notes and Queries* the legend of a lame old man who was reputed to turn himself into a black dog and bite cattle. One neighbour claimed to have seen the transformation from dog to man.

[Motifs: D141; F234.1.9]

Halliwell, James Orchard (1820–89), later Halliwell-Phillipps. One of the literary folklorists rather than one of the collectors. He was an antiquarian who did a great service to folklore by tracing current rhymes, beliefs and customs back to early broadsides and pamphlets and to the works of the 17th-century antiquarians. He made great use of AUBREY. His books that deal most with fairy-lore are *Illustrations of the Fairy Mythology of 'A Midsummer Night's Dream'* (1845), *Popular Rhymes and Nursery Tales* (1849), and *A Dictionary of Archaic and Provincial Words* (1847), which contains an interesting collection of traditional names for natural objects under the heading 'Fairy': 'fairy-butter', 'fairy-circles', 'fairy-darts', 'fairy-loaves', etc.

Halliwell occasionally pieced together rhymes to form a consecutive folk-tale in a rather tricksy way, but it is fair to say that he was a good guesser and that folk-tales subsequently and independently collected come pretty close to his versions. A more serious accusation made against him at the age of twenty-four was that of stealing manuscripts from Cambridge University Library to add to his considerable collection. His finances were precarious until 1867, when his wife inherited the fortune of her father, the antiquarian scholar Sir Thomas Phillipps, who could not endure his son-in-law. Even so, Halliwell hyphenated his name to Halliwell-Phillipps in 1872. J. O. Halliwell was a man of great charm and brilliance in spite of his erratic character.

Hard delivery, or barrenness. This was sometimes taken to be a fairy curse, probably called down by the unfortunate positioning of a house. Sometimes stock only were affected, and sometimes the wife as well as the stock would be cursed by barrenness. It was, however, more commonly attributed to witchcraft. The ballad 'Willie's Mother', in which the mother-in-law was a rank witch and help was given by a domestic fairy, BILLY BLIND, gives almost a recipe for inhibiting birth. See BLIGHTS AND ILLNESSES ATTRIBUTED TO THE FAIRIES.

[Motif: T591]

Hartland, Edwin Sidney (1848–1927). One of the great founder-members of the Folklore Society. Like many of 'The Great Team' described by Professor R. M. Dorson in *The British Folklorists*, he was no professor. He was a Gloucestershire solicitor, who combined an analytical mind with an extraordinary width of reading. As his work went on, he achieved a happy marriage between folklore and anthropology, but in his earlier researches he was particularly interested in the folk-tale. His *English Fairy and Folk-Tales* (1890) is a particularly good selection of sagas, *Märchen* and folk legends. Its collection of fairy anecdotes is of special interest. In the next year he brought out *The Science of Fairy Tales* in which many fairy beliefs, such as the miraculous passage of TIME IN FAIRYLAND and the FAIRY BRIDE stories, are incorporated. In *The Legend of Perseus*, Hartland covered an enormous range of legends in his investigation into the idea of supernatural birth. Here he left his original attachment to English folklore and first began excursions into anthropology. He was President of the Folklore Society in 1900 and

1901, and was always a diligent and valuable contributor to their journal. His many reviews were particularly notable.

Hedley Kow. A perfect but localized form of a BOGY OR BOGEY-BEAST. Jacobs, in *More English Fairy Tales* (pp. 50–53), gives a delightful story of the Hedley Kow which he heard from Mrs Balfour. It is a variant of Hans Andersen's 'The Goodman is Always Right'. The determined optimism of the old dame upon whom the Hedley Kow is playing his tricks triumphs over every change for the worse.

' Well!' she said at last, 'I *do* be the luckiest body hereabouts! Fancy me seeing the Hedley Kow all to myself, and making so free with it too! I can tell you, I *do* feel that GRAND.'

William Henderson in *Folk-Lore of the Northern Counties* (pp. 270–71) gives a description which covers all its activities and could hardly be bettered.

The Hedley Kow was a bogie, mischievous rather than malignant, which haunted the village of Hedley, near Ebchester. His appearance was never very alarming, and he used to end his frolics with a horse-laugh at the expense of his victims. He would present himself to some old dame gathering sticks, in the form of a truss of straw, which she would be sure to take up and carry away. Then it would become so heavy she would have to lay her burden down, on which the straw would become

'quick', rise upright, and shuffle away before her, till at last it vanished from her sight with a laugh and shout. Again, in the shape of a favourite cow, the sprite would lead the milkmaid a long chase round the field, and after kicking and routing during milking-time would upset the pail, slip clear of the tie, and vanish with a loud laugh. Indeed the 'Kow' must have been a great nuisance in a farmhouse, for it is said to have constantly imitated the voice of the servant-girl's lovers, over-turned the kail-pot, given the cream to the cats, unravelled the knitting, or put the spinning-wheel out of order. But the sprite made himself most obnoxious at the birth of a child. He would torment the man who rode for the howdie, frightening the horse, and often making him upset both messenger and howdie, and leave them in the road. Then he would mock the gudewife, and, when her angry husband rushed out with a stick to drive away the 'Kow' from the door or window, the stick would be snatched from him, and lustily applied to his own shoulders.

Two adventures with the Hedley Kow are thus related.

A farmer named Forster, who lived near Hedley, went out into the field one morning, and caught, as he believed, his own grey horse. After putting the harness on, and yoking him to the cart, Forster was about to drive off, when the creature slipped away from the limmers 'like a knotless thread', and set up a great nicker as he flung up his heels and scoured away, revealing himself clearly as the Hedley Kow. Again, two young men of Newlands, near Ebchester, went out one evening to meet their sweethearts; and arriving at the trysting-place, saw them, as it appeared, a short distance before them. The girls walked on for two or three miles; the lads followed, quite unable to overtake them, till at last they found themselves up to the knees in a bog, and their beguilers vanished, with a loud Ha! ha! The young men got clear of the mire and ran homewards, as fast as they could, the bogie at their heels hooting and mocking them. In crossing the Derwent they fell into the water, mistook each other for the sprite, and finally reached home separately, each telling a fearful tale of having been chased by the Hedley Kow, and nearly drowned in the Derwent.

[Type: 1415 (distant variant). Motifs: E423(b); F234.0.2; F234.3; F399.4; F402.1.1; J346]

Henkies. One name given to the TROWS of Orkney and Shetland. Like many of the Scandinavian and Celtic FAIRIES they had one of the DEFECTS OF THE FAIRIES by which they could be recognized, and these Shetland trows limped or 'henked' as they danced. John Spence, in *Shetland Folk-Lore* (p. 39), quotes a pathetic little song which illustrates the use of the word. It was sung by a little trow-wife who could find no partner in the dance.

'Hey!' co Cuttie; an 'ho!' co Cuttie;
'An' wha 'ill dance wi' me?' co Cuttie.
Sho luked aboot an' saw naebody;
'Sae I'll henk awa mesel',' co Cuttie.

[Motif: F254.1]

Herla's Rade. See KING HERLA.

Herne the Hunter. According to Shakespeare in *The Merry Wives of Windsor*, Herne the Hunter was the ghost of a forest hunter who had hanged himself on Herne's oak. Spirits, however, are often euhemerized into ghosts of human people, as the CAULD LAD OF HILTON was, and many people think that Herne the Hunter, with the stags' horns on his head, was a woodland spirit or a demon of the oak. In 1915 one of the teachers at my school in Edinburgh told me that her father, who was a retired colonel with apartments in Windsor Castle, used to see Herne the Hunter on moonlight nights standing under his oak. Ruth Tongue collected and recorded a story in 1964 told her at Cecil Sharp House by a Berkshire Morris member of the English Folk Dance and Song Society, and reproduced it in *Forgotten Folk-Tales of the English Counties* (No. 24):

Three silly young chaps were out for mischief. One of them was a teddy-boy come for the day and the other two were from Windsor – so they went in the forest and began breaking down the young trees.

Then the teddy-boy gave a shout: 'Coo! look what I found. Who's been filming Robin Hood now?' The Windsor chaps didn't answer and looked a bit queer at him – then he began to feel a bit off himself; no film could have been shot among those bushes.

'Leave it lay,' said one of the Windsor lads and run like hell! 'Don't touch it!' shouts the other and took off too.

Well, being a teddy-boy he had to show off and blow it. The horn gave such a groan and a blast he nearly fainted and as he stood shaking there was a terrible yell among the trees and great hounds baying. He took off too but he couldn't catch up with the Windsor lads who were going hell for leather to church – and run as he might he kept stumbling and shivering and listening to the feet behind him.

The Windsor lads safe inside the church-door saw him staggering on and heard the dogs baying. He was nearly to the door when the pursuer stopped; they heard the twang of an arrow and the teddy-boy threw up his arms and screamed and fell flat on his face in the porch, quite dead.

There was no arrow through him, and there were no hounds and no hunter.

Heroic Fairies. The fairy knights and ladies of the medieval romances, and those that occur in the Celtic legends, are of human or more than human size and of shining beauty. The Lady Tryamour who bestowed her favours on SIR LAUNFAL and the elfin woman who was captured by WILD EDRIC from her band of dancing sisters are examples of the fairy damsels; YOUNG TAMLANE, though a transformed human, is to all appearance a typical fairy knight, though he had an ulterior motive for his courtship. The truest type of all are the DAOINE SIDHE of Ireland, dwindled gods, and the Fingalian knights, who spend their time in the aristocratic pursuits of hunting, fighting, riding in procession, as well as the DANCING and music that are beloved by all FAIRIES. The SIZE OF THE FAIRIES is variable, and even in medieval times there are both tiny and rustic fairies as well as hideous and monstrous ones, just as in modern times some are still stately, but in terms of FASHIONS IN FAIRY-LORE one tends to think of the heroic fairies as characteristic of medieval times.

Herrick, Robert (1591-1674). One of the group of poets who called themselves the 'Sons of Ben Jonson', who wrote and exchanged among themselves poems, some of them considerable, and some short lyrics. The thing that interests us here is that they carried on the Elizabethan literary treatment of the small FAIRIES, originated, or at least made fashionable, by a MIDSUMMER NIGHT'S DREAM. Michael Drayton in his *Nimphidia* wrote of these DIMINUTIVE FAIRIES at greater length than Herrick, but among Herrick's *Hesperides* two different types of fairy lyric will be found. The first type, examples of which are 'The Chapel', 'Oberon's Feast', 'Oberon's Palace' and 'The Beggar's Petition to Queen Mab', is full of conceits of littleness, satires on the fairy court, and is on the whole far removed from the folk tradition, but they agree with it in the touches of erotic fancy, which remind one of the fairy connection with fertility, and in some references to folk magic and to some BLIGHTS such as canker, which were ascribed to fairy ill-will. Besides these, however, there are two or three short rhymes directly in the folk tradition, such as 'If you will with Mab find grace', 'If you fear to be affrighted', and 'Larr's Portion'. Herrick's poems had passed out of fashion when they were published in 1647, but they were doubtless handed round and well known before that.

Hillmen. See HOGMEN.

Hinky-Punk. One of the many names for WILL O' THE WISP. It occurs on the Somerset–Devon borders. In appearance it seems to be something like the Highland DIREACH, for it was described to Ruth Tongue by members of the Dulverton Women's Institute as having 'one leg and a light, and led you into bogs'.

[Motif: F491]

Hob, or Hobthrust. Hob is the general name for a tribe of kindly, beneficent and occasionally mischievous spirits to which the BROWNIE belongs. They are generally to be found in the North Country or northern Midlands. William Henderson in *Folk-Lore of the Northern Counties* (p. 264) mentions a localized hob who lived in a hobhole in a natural cave in Runswick Bay near Hartlepool. His speciality was the cure of whooping-cough. Parents would bring their sick children into the cave and whisper:

> 'Hobhole Hob! Hobhole Hob!
> Ma bairns gotten t' kink cough,
> Tak't off; tak't off',

and the cure was as good as effected.

A more sinister hob, also mentioned by Henderson, was Hob Headless who haunted the road between Hurworth and Neasham, but could not cross the little river Kent, which flowed into the Tees. He was exorcized and laid under a large stone by the roadside for ninety-nine years and a day. If anyone was so unwary as to sit on that stone, he would be unable to quit it for ever. The ninety-nine years is nearly up, so trouble may soon be heard of on the road between Hurworth and Neasham.

Another hob or hobthrust mentioned by Henderson was very much of the brownie type. He was attached to Sturfit Hall, near Reeth in York-shire. He churned milk, made up the fires, and performed other brownie labours, till his mistress, pitying his nakedness, gave him a cloak and a hood, on which he exclaimed,

> 'Ha! a cloak and a hood,
> Hob'll never do mair good'

and vanished for ever. Another brownie-like hob, who worked at a farm in Danby, seems to have been dissatisfied with the quality of the clothes provided for him, for his rhyme ran:

> 'Gin Hob mun hae nowght but Harding hamp,
> He'll come nae mair to berry nor stamp.'

Many tales of Hob and Hobthrust are reproduced by Mrs Gutch in *County Folk-Lore* (vol. II), among them the story of the hempen shirt told of Hart Hall in Glaisdale, and several versions of 'Aye, George, we're Flitting', generally told of a BOGGART. There is also a tale of a hobthrust who lived in a cave called Hobthrust Hall and used to leap from there to Carlow Hill, a distance of half a mile. He worked for an innkeeper named Weighall for a nightly wage of a large piece of bread and butter. One night his meal was not put out and he left for ever. Mrs Gutch derives 'Hobthrust' from 'Hob-i-t'-hurst', but Gillian Edwards in *Hobgoblin and Sweet Puck* maintains that it should more properly be derived from 'Hob

Thurse', an Old English word 'thyrs' or 'thurs' for a GIANT of heathen mythology and in Middle English used, as PUCK or 'Pouk' was, for the Devil. If this be so, the friendly prefix of 'hob' draws some of the sting. Mrs Gutch and Henderson use HOBMEN as the generic name for the whole race of Hobs. They were very nearly as various as, though less sinister than, the great tribe of the Highland FUATH.

[Motif: F381.3]

Hobgoblin. Used by the Puritans and in later times for wicked goblin spirits, as in Bunyan's 'Hobgoblin nor foul fiend', but its more correct use is for the friendly spirits of the BROWNIE type. In a MIDSUMMER NIGHT'S DREAM a fairy says to Shakespeare's PUCK:

> 'Those that Hobgoblin call you, and sweet Puck,
>   You do their work, and they shall have good luck:
>   Are you not he?'

and obviously Puck would not wish to be called a hobgoblin if that was an ill-omened word. 'Hob' and 'Lob' are words meaning the same kind of creature as the Hobgoblin, and more information will be found about these under HOB, OR HOBTHRUST and LOBS AND HOBS.

Hobgoblins and their kind do not strictly belong to the TROOPING FAIRIES, nor yet to demons and GOBLINS, though WILL O' THE WISPS and other tricksy spirits can be included in this category. They are, on the whole, good-humoured and ready to be helpful, but fond of practical joking, and like most of the FAIRIES rather nasty people to annoy. BOGGARTS hover on the verge of hobgoblindom. BOGLES are just over the edge.

[Motif: F470]

Hobmen. The generic name for all the various types of LOBS AND HOBS, to which ROBIN GOODFELLOW, ROBIN ROUNDCAP, PUCK, the LUBBARD FIEND, PIXIES, the Irish PHOOKA, the Highland GRUAGACH, the Manx FENODEREE, the North Country SILKIES, KILLMOULIS and many others belong. Even BOGGARTS and the various forms of WILL O' THE WISP may be described as hobmen.

Hobs. See HOB, OR HOBTHRUST; LOBS AND HOBS.

Hobyahs. These make a solitary appearance in folklore in a story in Jacobs's *More English Fairy Tales*, reproduced from the *Journal of American Folk-Lore* (vol. III), communicated by a Mr S. V. Proudfit who had it from a Perthshire family. There is no trace of Scottish dialect about it. The Hobyahs were horrifying GOBLINS who ate people and kidnapped children. They were, however, terrified of dogs, and with good reason, for they were finally all eaten up by a large black dog. This is an authentic

frightening NURSERY BOGIE tale, of the same type as 'The Old Man in the White House', but there is no sign that the hobyahs were objects of real belief.

Hogg, James (1770–1835), called 'the Ettrick Shepherd'. A self-taught man who had had less than a year's schooling in his life and had been set to work at the age of seven. He began to make verses and trained himself to write them. He submitted some poems to Sir Walter SCOTT, who became his steady friend and employed him to collect oral material. His mother contributed many ballads to Scott's collection, but Hogg preferred to invent his own. He wrote several prose collections of stories. He knew his background extremely well, but unfortunately preferred to decorate his narrative, not believing that a simple, straightforward style could be acceptable to an educated audience. Among his best-known prose works is *The Brownie of Bodsbeck*; his greatest poem, 'Kilmeny', is on the well-known theme of a VISIT TO FAIRYLAND and the return after a supernatural passage of time, seven years in this tale. Fairyland in this poem is the land of the dead, and – unusually – of the blessed dead. Kilmeny returns with a supernatural message to deliver, and dies when she has delivered it. The poem has the rhythm and flow of a ballad, and one verse is reminiscent of an early religious poem, 'The Faucon Hath Borne My Make Away':

> In yon green-wood there is a waik,
> And in that waik there is a wene,
> And in that wene there is a maike,
> That neither has flesh, blood, nor bane,
> And down in yon green-wood he walks his lane.

The poem is full of overtones and undertones, and so is the curiously touching poem, 'The Mermaid', which turns on the difference between human time and FAIRY TIME, the long-lived, soulless MERMAID and the short-lived mortal with an immortal soul. The mermaid mourns her human lover whose grave has been green a hundred years, and feels the Judgement Day drawing slowly nearer, when she will perish with the earth and never know a union with her resurrected true love. It is a subtle conception, simply and movingly expressed.

Hogmen, or Hillmen. These are among the more formidable of the Manx fairy people. They are described at some length in *A Mona Miscellany* by W. Harrison. They changed their quarters at Hollantide (11 November), and people kept indoors on that night to avoid meeting them. They were propitiated with gifts of fruit.

Holy water. One of the chief protections against FAIRY THEFTS, spells or ill-wishing. See also PROTECTION AGAINST FAIRIES.

Hookeys. In Lincolnshire, the expression 'By the hookeys' is supposed to refer to the FAIRIES, presumably because they were pilferers.

Hooper of Sennen Cove, the. BOTTRELL, in the *Traditions and Hearth-side Stories of West Cornwall* (vol. II), tells of a beneficent spirit in Sennen Cove called the Hooper who gave warning of coming storms, rather like the Manx DOOINNEY-OIE. It appeared like a curtain of cloud across the bay, with a dull light in the middle of it. Strange hooting sounds came from it. It always appeared before serious storms, and people who attempted to set out to sea felt an unaccountable resistance. Once a fisherman and his sons defied the warning and sailed out. The threatened storm arose, their boat was lost, and the Hooper never returned to warn the fishermen.
  [Motif: J1050]

'Horse and Hattock'. See AUBREY, JOHN; FAIRY LEVITATION.

Horseshoes. A horseshoe hung up above a stable or a house prevented the entrance of FAIRIES and witches, and hence constituted a PRO-TECTION AGAINST FAIRIES.

Host, the. See SLUAGH.

Hounds of the Hill, the. A name sometimes used in English for the hunting-dogs of the FAIRIES who live in the hollow hills. As FAIRY DOGS they are distinct from the GABRIEL HOUNDS, the DEVIL'S DANDY DOGS and other spectral packs whose duty it is to hunt souls rather than fairy deer. The Hounds of the Hill are generally described as white with red ears rather than dark green like the CU SITH described by J. G.

CAMPBELL. Ruth Tongue, in *Forgotten Folk-Tales of the English Counties*, reports an anecdote heard in Cheshire in 1917 and again in 1970 about a Hound of the Hill befriended by a young labourer. It was the size of a calf with a rough white coat and red ears. Its paws seemed sore, and the boy treated them with wet dock-leaves. Some time later, going through a haunted wood, he was attacked by a spectral goat and rescued by the hound. The episode has a Highland rather than a Welsh flavour.

Howlaa. This is given in Moore's *Vocabulary of the Manx Dialect* as the name of a spirit who howls before storms. Actually, this is the sound made by the DOOINNEY-OIE.

[Motif: F433]

Hunt, Robert (b.1790). Hunt wrote the Preface to the third edition of *Popular Romances of the West of England* in 1881. The book had first been published in 1865, but it was the fruit of long collection. He gives some account of this in the introduction to the first edition:

The beginning of this collection of Popular Romances may be truly said to date from my early childhood. I remember with what anticipations of pleasure, sixty-eight years since, I stitched together a few sheets of paper, and carefully pasted them into the back of an old book. This was preparatory to a visit I was about to make with my mother to Bodmin, about which town many strange stories were told, and my purpose was to record them. My memory retains dim shadows of a wild tale of Hender the Huntsman of Lanhydrock; of a narrative of streams having been poisoned by the monks; and of a legend of a devil who played many strange pranks with the tower which stands on a neighbouring hill. I have, within the last year, endeavoured to recover those stories, but in vain. The living people appear to have forgotten them; my juvenile note-book has long been lost: those traditions are, it is to be feared, gone for ever.

Fifteen years passed away – about six of them at school in Cornwall, and nine of them in close labour in London, – when failing health compelled my return to the West of England. Having spent about a month on the borders of Dartmoor, and wandered over that wild region of Granite Tors, gathering up its traditions, – ere yet Mrs Bray had thought of doing so, – I resolved on walking through Cornwall. Thirty-five years since, on a beautiful spring morning, I landed at Saltash, from the very ancient passage-boat which in those days conveyed men and women, carts and cattle, across the river Tamar, where now that triumph of engineering, the Albert Bridge, gracefully spans its waters. Sending my box forward to Liskeard by a van, my wanderings commenced; my purpose being to visit each relic of Old Cornwall, and to gather up every existing tale of its ancient people. Ten months were delightfully spent in this way; and in that period a large number of the romances and superstitions which are published in these volumes were collected, with many more, which have been weeded out of the collection as worthless.

He goes on to tell how, when staying for a few weeks on the borders of Dartmoor, he was placed in the very centre of people who believed that there were once GIANTS in their neighbourhood, that the OLD PEOPLE still existed, and that a man might save himself from being PIXY-LED by turning his coat-sleeve or stocking.

As a young boy he was first introduced to the fairy beliefs by a beautiful and romantic girl older than himself who used to take him to seek for the FAIRIES on Lelant Towans. They used to spend hours listening to the stories of an old woman who lived in a cottage on the edge of the sandhills there.

When his health compelled him to leave town, he became secretary to the Royal Cornwall Polytechnic Society and travelled constantly in the country places, meeting the miners and the peasantry and learning a great deal from them.

Always delighting in popular tales [he says], no opportunity of hearing them was ever lost. Seated on a three-legged stool, or in a 'timberen settle', near the blazing heath-fire on the hearth, have I elicited the old stories of which the people were beginning to be ashamed. Resting in a level, after the toil of climbing from the depths of a mine, in close companionship with the homely miner, his superstitions, and the tales which he had heard from his grandfather, have been confided to me.

Even before they were published, many of these tales had faded from popular tradition. In 1849, there were still wandering drolls, and Hunt owed some of his stories to them. By 1865 they had vanished. Hunt quotes a long account of a typical WANDERING DROLL-TELLER, Uncle Anthony James, given him by 'a gentleman to whom I am under many obligations'. This would no doubt be William BOTTRELL. Though the quoted account had been given to him individually, it is in substance the same as that given by Bottrell in his *Traditions and Hearthside Stories of West Cornwall*. These two men between them rescued many fairy anecdotes and beliefs that would otherwise have been lost to the world.

Huon of Bordeaux. A French prose romance of the 15th century, translated into English by Lord Berners in the 16th century. It became very popular in England, and though the earlier editions have disappeared, the third, of 1601, still remains. This is the first literary use of OBERON as the fairy king, though there are MAGICIANS' recipes for conjuring Oberion or Oberycom into a crystal stone. He was a dwarfish or

DIMINUTIVE FAIRY, of the size of a three-years child, though with a most beautiful face. This small size was attributed in the romance to the ill offices of an offended fairy at his birth – one of the earliest examples of a wicked fairy at a christening – but, since 'Auberon' is the French translation of the German 'Alberich', it seems likely that Oberon was dwarfish from the beginning.

This Oberon haunted a part of the forest through which Huon had to pass in his eastern travels. He was a master of GLAMOUR and was regarded as a tempting devil who must on no account be answered when he spoke. Huon was most earnestly warned about this by a good hermit, but when his courtesy was too strong for him and he answered Oberon's touchingly earnest entreaties, nothing but good came of it. Oberon was deeply grateful and became Huon's constant friend. In the end, Oberon's soul was admitted to Heaven and Huon of Bordeaux was crowned king of Fairyland in his place. It is not often in folk tradition that the pendulous, immortal state of the FAIRIES is resolved on the heavenly side.

It will be remembered that Rudyard KIPLING makes Huon of Bordeaux the king of the PEOPLE OF THE HILLS in *Puck of Pook's Hill*.

Hurling. An account of a hurling match, one of the most popular of the SPORTS OF THE FAIRIES among the Irish, is given in Douglas HYDE's tale of 'Paudyeen O'Kelly and the Weasel' in *Beside the Fire* (pp. 87–9). It is a good example of the DEPENDENCE OF FAIRIES ON MORTALS.

The green hill opened, and the pair went into a fine chamber.

Paudyeen never saw before a gathering like that which was in the Doon. The whole place was full up of little people, men and women, young and old. They all welcomed little Donal – that was the name of the piper – and Paudyeen O'Kelly. The king and queen of the fairies came up to them, and said:

'We are all going on a visit to-night to Cnoc Matha, to the high king and queen of our people.'

They all rose up then and went out. There were horses ready for each one of them and the *coash-t'ya bower* for the king and the queen. The king and queen got into the coach, each man leaped on his own horse, and be certain that Paudyeen was not behind. The piper went out before them and began playing them music, and then off and away with them. It was not long till they came to Cnoc Matha. The hill opened and the king of the fairy host passed in.

Finvara and Nuala were there, the arch-king and queen of the fairy host of Connacht, and thousands of little persons. Finvara came up and said:

'We are going to play a hurling match to-night against the fairy host of Munster, and unless we beat them our fame is gone for ever. The match is to be fought out on Moytura, under Slieve Belgadaun.'

The Connacht host cried out: 'We are all ready, and we have no doubt but we'll beat them.'

'Out with ye all,' cried the high king; 'the men of the hill of Nephin will be on the ground before us.'

They all went out, and little Donal and twelve pipers more before them, playing melodious music. When they came to Moytura, the fairy host of Munster and the fairy men of the hill of Nephin were there before them. Now, it is necessary for the fairy host to have two live men beside them when they are fighting or at a hurling-match, and that was the reason that little Donal took Paddy O'Kelly with him. There was a man they called the '*Yellow Stongirya*', with the fairy host of Munster, from Ennis, in the County Clare.

It was not long till the two hosts took sides; the ball was thrown up between them, and the fun began in earnest. They were hurling away, and the pipers playing music, until Paudyeen O'Kelly saw the host of Munster getting the strong hand, and he began helping the fairy host of Connacht. The *Stongirya* came up and he made at Paudyeen O'Kelly, but Paudyeen turned him head over heels. From hurling the two hosts began at fighting, but it was not long until the host of Connacht beat the other host. Then the host of Munster made flying beetles of themselves, and they began eating every green thing that they came up to. They were destroying the country before them until they came as far as Cong. Then there rose up thousands of doves out of the hole, and they swallowed down the beetles. That hole has no other name until this day but Pull-na-gullam, the dove's hole.

There was great zest about this game, but it seems it had something in common with modern cricket's test matches.

[Motif: F267]

Hyde, Douglas (1860–1949). The first of the Irish folklorists to pursue the fully scholarly methods of research initiated by J. F. CAMPBELL. In his collection of folk-tales, *Beside the Fire*, he puts the Irish and the English on alternate pages for the first time in an Irish folk-tale book. His introduction was a most scholarly piece of work, criticizing keenly but not unkindly the work of his predecessors, and noticing particularly the handicap under which Lady WILDE laboured in knowing no Irish, and strongly advising all collectors to take careful note of the source of their tales. Dr Hyde was the founder of the Irish League to promote the study of Irish Gaelic. He was a close collaborator with YEATS and Lady Gregory in their Irish renaissance, and was elected Ireland's first President in 1938. The tales he reproduces in *Beside the Fire* were more of ghosts and witchcraft than of FAIRIES, but 'Guleesh' is a notable story of FAIRY LEVITATION and of the rescue of a mortal CAPTIVE IN FAIRYLAND. It also illustrates the DEPENDENCE OF FAIRIES ON MORTALS for certain activities.

Hyter sprites. Lincolnshire and East Anglian fairies. They are small and sandy-coloured with green eyes, like the FERIERS of Suffolk. They assume the bird form of sand martins. They are grateful for human kindnesses, and stern critics of ill-behaviour. Ruth Tongue has permitted an otherwise unpublished story about the Hyter Sprites to appear in Part B of *A Dictionary of British Folk-Tales*. It is a tale traditional in her family. She also reports that the Hyter Sprites have been known to bring home lost children, like the GHILLIE DHU of the Highlands.

[Motif: F239.4.3]

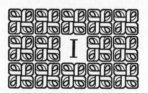

'I weat, you weat'. The FAIRIES appear to have lived on thefts of human food. The Celtic fairies were thought to take the FOYSON or goodness from it, but some lived off the land like mice, carrying away the grain early. Here is a condensed account of a Hampshire farmer's losses by FAIRY THEFTS, given by KEIGHTLEY in *The Fairy Mythology* (pp. 305–6):

> A farmer in Hampshire was sorely distressed by the unsettling of his barn. However straightly over-night he laid his sheaves on the threshing-floor for the application of the morning's flail, when morning came, all was topsy-turvy, higgledy-piggledy, though the door remained locked, and there was no sign whatever of irregular entry. Resolved to find out who played him these mischievous pranks, Hodge couched himself one night deeply among the sheaves, and watched for the enemy. At length midnight arrived, the barn was illuminated as if by moonbeams of wonderful brightness, and through the key-hole came thousands of elves, the most diminutive that could be imagined. They immediately began their gambols among the straw, which was soon in a most admired disorder. Hodge wondered, but interfered not; but at last the supernatural thieves began to busy themselves in a way still less to his taste, for each elf set about conveying the crop away, a straw at a time, with astonishing activity and perseverance. The key-hole was still their port of egress and regress, and it resembled the aperture of a bee-hive, on a sunny day in June. The farmer was rather annoyed at seeing his grain vanish in this fashion, when one of the fairies said to another in the tiniest voice that ever was heard – '*I weat, you weat.*' Hodge could contain himself no longer. He leaped out crying, 'The devil sweat ye. Let me get among ye!' when they all flew away so frightened that they never disturbed the barn any more.

In a Suffolk version, BROTHER MIKE, the little fairy's complaint is:

> 'Oh how I du twait,
> A carrying o' this air o' wate.'

This anecdote ends sadly, with the capture and death of the little fairy. It is one of the most tragic of the stories of CAPTURED FAIRIES.

[Motifs: F239.4.3; F365]

Ignis Fatuus. This, which literally means 'the foolish fire', is traditionally called WILL O' THE WISP, but has many other names and is given several origins. Mrs Wright in *Rustic Speech and Folk-Lore* gives a long, but not exhaustive, list: corp-candle or dead-candle (see CORPSE-CANDLE) when it is regarded as a death omen, and more generally: Billy-wi'-t'-wisp (West Yorkshire), Hobbledy's-lantern (Warwickshire, Worcestershire, Gloucestershire), Hobby-lantern (Worcestershire, Hertfordshire, East Anglia, Hampshire, Wiltshire, west Wales), Jack-a-lantern (see JACKY LANTERN), Jenny-burnt-tail (Northamptonshire, Oxfordshire), Jenny-wi'-t'-lantern (Northumberland, North Yorkshire), JOAN-IN-THE-WAD or Joan-the-wad (Somerset, Cornwall), Kit-in-the-Candlestick (Hampshire) (see KIT WITH THE CANSTICK), Kitty-candle-stick (Wiltshire), Kitty-wi'-the-wisp (Northumberland), the Lantern-man (East Anglia), Peg-a-lantern (Lancashire), PINKET (Worcestershire). To these may be added FRIAR RUSH, GYL BURNT-TAYLE, HINKY PUNK, SPUNKIES, PUCK or Pouk and ROBIN GOODFELLOW, who also amused themselves with Will-o'-the-Wisp pranks at times. Various legends account for the Ignis Fatuus. Sometimes it is thought to be a tricksy BOGGART, and where it is called 'Hobbledy's lantern', this is plainly so; sometimes it is ghostly in origin, a soul who for some sin could not rest. For instance, a man who had moved his neighbour's landmarks would be doomed to haunt the area with a flickering light. In Shropshire, Will the Smith, after being given a second spell of life by St Peter, spent it in such wickedness that he was debarred both from Heaven and Hell. The most the Devil would do for him was to give him a piece of burning pit coal to warm himself, with which he flickers over boggy ground to allure poor wanderers to their death. In other versions of the tale, the smith tricks the Devil into a steel purse, in which he so hammers him that the Devil dare not admit him into Hell, but in this version the smith tricks his way into Heaven. In the Lincolnshire fen country, the WILL O' THE WYKES are BOGLES, intent upon nothing but evil.

[Motifs: F369.7; F402.1.1; F491; F491.1]

Ill-temper. A notorious scold was supposed to draw down the ill-favour of the FAIRIES, and a nagging husband or a wife-beater was often misled by the fairies. A well-known case is the story of Old Farmer Mole given

by Ruth Tongue in *County Folklore* (vol. VIII, p. 115). See also FAULTS
CONDEMNED BY THE FAIRIES; VIRTUES ESTEEMED BY THE FAIRIES.

Impetigo. Impetigo and other skin diseases were sometimes attributed
to the FAIRIES and were the result of the infringement of some fairy
TABOO. The sensitive Irish, however, could be brought out in a rash by
a lampoon from a bard whom they had displeased. It was one of the
common sources of power in the Bardic community. See also BLIGHTS
AND ILLNESSES ATTRIBUTED TO THE FAIRIES.
[Motif: F362]

Imps, impets. An 'imp' is an off-shoot or cutting. Thus an 'ymp tree'
was a grafted tree, or one grown from a cutting, not from seed. 'Imp'
properly means a small devil, an off-shoot of Satan, but the distinction
between GOBLINS or BOGLES and imps from hell is hard to make, and
many in the Celtic countries as well as the English Puritans regarded all
FAIRIES as devils. TOM TIT TOT is called an impet. The fairies of
tradition often hover uneasily between the ghostly and the diabolic state.

Ina Pic Winna. In *County Folklore* (vol. VIII), Ruth Tongue records
some of the local fishermen's superstitions. The most interesting is that
about Ina Pic Winna.

> At Worle, when the fishermen go down to sea, they each put a white
> stone on the cairn or 'fairy mound' on the hillside and say,

> > 'Ina pic winna
> > Send me a good dinner.'

> And more times than not they come [back] with a load of fish.

> This was told her by a Weston-super-Mare fisherman.
> [Motif: F406]

Incubus. Technically, an 'Incubus' was a devil which assumed the
appearance of a man and lay with a woman, as a succubus or NIGHT-
MARE assumed the appearance of a woman or HAGGE to corrupt a man.
Merlin was supposed to be the child of an incubus, and almost every
16th-century book on witchcraft mentions the Incubus. He is, however,
rather vaguely coupled with the BROWNIE by Reginald SCOT as a spirit
who has offerings of milk left out for him.
[Motif: F471.2]

Infantile paralysis. A disease not so much attributed to the FAIRIES
as the cause of an attribution of child theft and of the substitution of a
fairy in the place of the real child. Any disease that suddenly altered the
appearance and powers of a child was liable to the suspicion of

CHANGELING substitution, and must have caused an immense amount of suffering where the fairy beliefs were prevalent. A description of a supposed changeling in Waldron's *Isle of Man* demonstrates this. See BLIGHTS AND ILLNESSES ATTRIBUTED TO THE FAIRIES.

Infringement of fairy privacy. From the earliest times the FAIRIES have been noted as secret people. They do not like to be watched, their land must not be trespassed on, their kindnesses must not be boasted of. Fairy lovers come and go in secret. Dame Tryamour, the lover of SIR LAUNFAL in the 12th-century metrical romance, comes and goes invisible to mortal eyes, and her love must not be boasted of. When Launfal is goaded into talking of her, all the costly presents he has been given melt away and he is left to poverty. In the end, however, his fairy relents and takes him back to favour, an unusually happy ending to what is almost invariably a tragedy. In one of the Highland legends in *Waifs and Strays of Celtic Tradition* (vol. v), 'The Two Sisters and the Curse', Mairearad (Margaret) has a fairy lover who forbids her to speak of him, but in a moment of confidence she tells her sister about him, who promises that it will 'as soon pass from her knee as from her lips'. She is false to her word, however, and spreads the tale, so that Margaret loses her lover. She wanders away from home and into the hills where she is heard singing laments until at length she fades away. Nothing more is seen of her until she or her child comes out of the cairn to avenge Dun Ailsa's treachery on Brown Torquil, her son.

One of the commonest tales from Elizabethan times to the present day is of mortals favoured by the fairies, who have been given fairy money till they tell the source of it, when the gifts cease for ever. This trait is often mentioned in Elizabethan accounts of the fairies, and exactly the same story is recorded in the archives of the School of Scottish Studies, and a similar anecdote, 'Fairy Money', is told also by Seán O' Súilleabháin in *Folktales of Ireland*. Fairy privacy must be respected even by passers-by. The girl who saw WILD EDRIC's Rade was told by her father to put an apron over her head so as not to watch them. In Bowker's *Goblin Tales of Lancashire*, the two villagers who see the FAIRY FUNERAL pass by withdraw beneath an oak to avoid being seen, and only when their curiosity is excited do they press forward to see the corpse on the bier and recognize it as the younger of the pair. In many Irish anecdotes, people sleeping innocently on a fairy hill have been blinded or pushed over a rock by the angry fairies who inhabit it. In Ulster, people avoid fairy roads, especially on quarter days, when the fairies are ordinarily on the move.

In short, though fairies are ready to reveal themselves to mortals whom they favour, or whose services they wish to secure, they are quick to resent and revenge any presumption upon that favour.

[Motif: F361.3]

Ingelow, Jean (1820–97). Famous in her lifetime as a poet, and perhaps still best remembered by her poem 'The High Tide on the Coast of Lincolnshire'. When Tennyson died, many people thought that Jean Ingelow should succeed him as Poet Laureate, but no one remembers many of her poems now, and she is most notable as the authoress of a children's fairy book, *Mopsa the Fairy*, written without a trace of condescension or moralizing. It is a fantasy of a boy's journey from the outskirts of Fairyland through several of its countries. In one of the outlying countries, he buys a little old slave with a piece of mortal money which has immense value in that land (an example of the DEPENDENCE OF FAIRIES UPON MORTALS). The little old slave turns into a fairy queen, and they come into her own land, the land of the one-foot-one fairies, where again we have an example of this dependence, as these fairies can neither laugh nor cry unless a mortal does so. Instances of this kind of thing are scattered through the book, not exact copyings of tradition, but true to fairy psychology. There is some resemblance in style and atmosphere to George MACDONALD's *Phantastes*, but it is less moral and less allegorical. A wild, fairy air blows through it.

Iron. Cold iron repels FAIRIES. A knife, or a CROSS of iron, are sovereign protections against witchcraft and evil magic of all kinds. A pair of open scissors hung above a child's cradle is said to protect it from being carried off by the fairies. It is a dual protection because it is in the form of a cross, and is also made of steel. See also PROTECTION AGAINST FAIRIES.

[Motif: F382.1]

Isle of Pabaidh, the. J. F. CAMPBELL in *Popular Tales of the West Highlands* (vol. II, p. 51) gives a terse, representative account of GRATEFUL FAIRIES:

> There came a woman of peace (a fairy) the way of the house of a man in the island of Pabaidh, and she had the hunger of motherhood on her. He gave her food, and that went well with her. She stayed that night. When she went away, she said to him, 'I am making a desire that none of the people of this island may go in childbed after this.' None of these people, and none others that would make their dwelling in the island ever departed in childbed from that time.

In this case, the reward matched the benefaction. Here we have an example of a fairy woman giving birth to a child, which, according to the FAIRY DWELLING ON SELENA MOOR, was thought to be a rare occurrence; but the FAIRIES in Cornwall were at a more advanced stage of being DIMINUTIVE FAIRIES than were the Highland fairies.

[Motif: F332]

'Isle of Sanntraigh, The'. This tale, which occurs in J. F. CAMPBELL's *Popular Tales of the West Highlands* (vol. II, pp. 52–4), gives an interesting example of FAIRY BORROWING which turns into theft if the operative words are not spoken. This may also be called a story of TRAFFIC WITH THE FAIRIES, for the transaction is profitable to the human as well as to the fairy wife:

There was a herd's wife in the island of Sanntraigh, and she had a kettle. A woman of peace (fairy) would come every day to seek the kettle. She would not say a word when she came, but she would catch hold of the kettle. When she would catch the kettle, the woman of the house would say –

> A smith is able to make
> Cold iron hot with coal.
> The due of a kettle is bones,
> And to bring it back again whole.

The woman of peace would come back every day with the kettle and flesh and bones in it. On a day that was there, the housewife was for going over the ferry to Baile a Chaisteil, and she said to her man, 'If thou wilt say to the woman of peace as I say, I will go to Baile Castle.' 'Oo! I will say it. Surely it's I that will say it.' He was spinning a heather rope to be set on the house. He saw a woman coming and a shadow from her feet, and he took fear of her. He shut the door. He stopped his work. When she came to the door she did not find the door open, and he did not open it for her. She went above a hole that was in the house. The kettle gave two jumps, and at the third leap it went out at the ridge of the house. The night came, and the kettle came not. The wife came back over the ferry, and she did not see a bit of the kettle within, and she asked, 'Where was the kettle?' 'Well then I don't care where it is,' said the man; 'I never took such a fright as I took at it. I shut the door, and she did not come any more with it.' 'Good-for-nothing wretch, what didst thou do? There are two that will be ill off – thyself and I.' 'She will come tomorrow with it.' 'She will not come.'

She hasted herself and she went away. She reached the knoll, and there was no man within. It was after dinner, and they were out in the mouth of the night. She went in. She saw the kettle, and she lifted it with her. It was heavy for her with the remnants that they left in it. When the old carle that was within saw her going out, he said,

> Silent wife, silent wife,
> That came on us from the land of chase,
> Thou man on the surface of the 'Bruth',
> Loose the black, and slip the Fierce.

The two dogs were let loose; and she was not long away when she heard the clatter of the dogs coming. She kept the remnant that was in the kettle, so that if she could get it with her, well, and if the dogs should come that she might throw it at them. She perceived the dogs coming. She put her hand in the kettle. She took the board out of it, and she threw at them a quarter of what was in it. They noticed it there for a while. She perceived them again, and she threw another piece at them when they closed upon her. She went away walking as well as she might; when she came near the farm, she threw the mouth of the pot downwards, and there she left them all that was in it. The dogs of the town struck (up) a barking when they saw the dogs of peace stopping. The woman of peace never came more to seek the kettle.

This tale could be cited by any supporters of David MAC RITCHIE's contention that the fairy beliefs were founded on a memory of the aboriginal inhabitants of the land. It will be noticed that the FAIRY DOGS in this tale were no more potent than the human ones.

This is the reverse story to that of the FAIRY LOAN as shown in AUBREY's story of the fairy caldron of Frensham.

It. This amorphous creature, described by Jessie Saxby in *Shetland Traditional Lore* (Chapter 9), might be thought of as the Shetland version of BONELESS or of the HEDLEY KOW. It seems to be such a master of GLAMOUR that no two people looking at it see the same thing. One noteworthy point made in her account is that Christmas is the season when TROWS have the greatest power of mischief, probably because it is the time when the nights are longest. Several of her tales illustrate the same point:

There was a creature known as 'it' which no person could describe properly. One said, It looked like a large lump of 'Slub' (jellyfish). Next It would seem like a bag of white wool. Another time It appeared like a beast wanting legs. Again, like a human form without the head. Never twice did It appear in the same guise. Without legs or wings It could run faster than a dog, and fly faster than an eagle. It made no sound of any sort, yet folk could understand what It meant to say, and repeated what It told one without a word being uttered.

Every year at Yule a certain house was troubled by It. Once a man sat in a room of that house with a lighted candle and a Bible. Suddenly he heard as if dead meat were flung down – 'just as a body micht fling da carkeesh o' a grice.' With the Bible in one hand and an axe in the other he rushed out. It took the road to the cliffs; he followed hard after. Just as It was going to slide over a cliff into the sea he said a holy word and slung his axe which stuck fast in It.

Hasting home he persuaded some friends to accompany him to the spot. There It was with the axe sticking in it. Then men flung earth over It. They could not tell whether It was alive or not; nor could they describe It's appearance. It looked different in the eyes of each. When they had covered It with earth they dug a wide deep trench around It, so that neither beast nor body could get near It. But indeed no one had the courage to approach the spot. The case was left to a fremmd person to investigate. When he went to raise the earth to discover what lay beneath, a strange lurid light and thereafter a 'lockit mist' surrounded him, and something rose out of the hole and rolled into the sea.

Could It have been an otter or a seal, the sceptic asked, and was gravely answered with a shake of the head: 'We all ken there's mony kinds of life that lives in the air, in the earth and water – forby the clouds abune. And we, poor mortals, have no vision to hear or see, or understand the like. We must just leave all that to the Powers abune.'

[Motif: F402.1.12]

Jack-in-Irons. This is a gigantic figure in clanking chains which may at any minute leap out on a benighted wayfarer going by a lonely road. It operates in Yorkshire, where they are ingenious in inventing BOGIES and other night horrors.

[Motif: F470]

Jacky Lantern. Another of the numerous names for WILL O' THE WISP, generally found in the West Country.

[Motifs: F491; F491.1]

Jacobean fairies. The Jacobean FAIRIES continue to extend the FASHIONS IN FAIRY LORE set in Elizabethan literature with an added emphasis on the minuteness of the small fairies, so that at one time people found it difficult to think of fairies at all without thinking of small-ness. The HOBGOBLIN type is exactly the same in both periods, except that the extreme Puritans regarded all fairies as devils. The most compre-hensive poem on ROBIN GOODFELLOW has been plausibly attributed to Ben Jonson. It seems to have been written to introduce a masque and has all Ben Jonson's vigour. A few verses will show its quality and its truth to tradition. The whole is to be found at the end of Carew Hazlitt's *Illustrations of the Fairy Mythology of Shakespeare.*

From Oberon, in fairyland,
   The king of ghosts and shadows there,
Mad Robin, I at his command,
   Am sent to view the night-sports here;
     What revel-rout
     Is kept about
   In every corner where I go,
     I will o'ersee,
     And merry be,
   And make good sport, with ho, ho, ho!

More swift than lightning can I fly
   About this airy welkin soon,
And, in a minute's space, descry
   Each thing that's done below the moon:
     There's not a hag,
     Nor ghost shall wag,
   Nor cry, ware Goblin! where I go;
     But Robin I
     Their feats will spy,
   And fear them home, with ho, ho, ho!

If any wanderers I meet,
   That from their night-sport do trudge home,
With counterfeiting voice I greet,
   And cause them on with me to roam;
     Through woods, through lakes,
     Through bogs, through brakes,
   O'er brush and brier, with them I go,
     I call upon
     Them to come on,
   And wend me laughing, ho, ho, ho!

In the course of the thirteen verses, all the Puckish activities are covered.

As for the DIMINUTIVE FAIRIES, the descent to triviality is well seen in Drayton's *Nimphidia*. The fairies in a MIDSUMMER NIGHT'S DREAM are small, but they are still formidable. Their dissensions affect the seasons, they have power over the unborn offspring of mortals; they can bless and ban. Though they are small, they can assume human size and they have the power of rapid motion. We have only to compare this with Drayton's flustered, frustrated OBERON and the little ladies of MAB's court, bustling about tearing their tiny ruffs and dropping their little gloves. The whole pleasure in them is in their littleness. It is a court intrigue through a minifying-glass. HERRICK's fairies are in the same vein, with a hint of scurrility about them which reminds us that the fairies were fertility spirits.

Towards the end of the 17th century, we reach the nadir of the fairies' powers with the Duchess of Newcastle's fairies, who are no bigger than microbes. After that, we have to wait for the Romantic revival and the rebirth of folklore.

Jeannie of Biggersdale. An evil spirit of the North Riding of Yorkshire who lived at the head of the Mulgrave Woods in Biggersdale. She was much dreaded, but one night a bold young farmer, rather flown with wine, betted that he would rouse her from her haunt. He rode up to Mulgrave Wood and called to her to come out. She answered angrily: 'I'm coming.' He made for the stream with her hard on his heels. Just as he got to the water she smote at his horse and cut it clean in two. He shot over the horse's head and landed safe on the far side, but the hind-quarters of the poor beast fell on Jeannie's side of the stream.

Jefferies, Anne. The affair of Anne Jefferies of St Teath in Cornwall and the FAIRIES caused almost as great a stir, even in the troubled times of the English Civil War, as the notorious case of the Demon Drummer of Tedworth. It is better documented than many other cases, which appeared only in pamphlets. There was even a letter about her in the Clarendon Manuscripts as early as March 1647, and in 1696, while Anne was still alive, Moses Pitt, the son of Anne's old master and mistress, wrote a printed letter to the Bishop of Gloucester in which he gives an account of Anne Jefferies's later life and of his early memories. Moses Pitt was only a boy when Anne, at the age of nineteen, came into service to his parents. In 1645 she fell into a fit, and was ill after it for some time, but when she recovered she declared that she had been carried away by the fairies, and in proof of this she showed strange powers of clairvoyance and could heal by touch. The first she healed was her mistress. After a time, Anne told some of her fairy experiences, and these are retold by HUNT in *Popular Romances of the West of England* (pp. 127-9), who also summarizes and gives extracts from Moses Pitt's letter in an appendix (pp. 470-71).

Anne was a clever girl, full of enterprise and curiosity, though she never learned to read. Her curiosity was chiefly excited by the stories she had heard of the fairies, and she was always searching for them. It was the tiny fairies of the West Country that she was looking for, and she was often out after sunset turning up the fern leaves and looking into the foxglove bells, singing,

> 'Fairy fair and fairy bright;
> Come and be my chosen sprite.'

And on fine moonlight nights she would roam down the valley, singing,

> 'Moon shines bright, waters run clear,
> I am here, but where's my fairy dear?'

The fairies afterwards told her they heard her well enough, and would run from frond to frond of the fern as she was searching. In the end they decided to show themselves.

Anne was knitting one day in a little arbour just outside the garden gate when she heard a rustling among the branches as if someone was peeping at her. She thought it was her sweetheart and took no notice. There was silence for a while, except for the click of her needles; then the branches rustled again and there was a suppressed laugh. Anne said rather crossly, 'You may stay there till the cuney grows on the gate ere I'll come to 'ee.' Immediately there was a tinkling sound and a ringing, musical laugh. Anne was frightened, for she knew it was not her sweetheart's, but she stayed where she was, and presently she heard the garden gate open and shut gently, and six little men appeared in the arbour. They were very beautiful, all dressed in green and with the brightest of eyes. The grandest of them had a red feather in his cap and spoke to her lovingly. She put her hand down to him. He jumped on to her palm and she lifted him up on to her lap and he clambered up to her bosom and began kissing her neck. She was perfectly charmed with the little gentleman's love-making and sat there in ecstasy until he called his five companions and they swarmed up her skirts and dress and began to kiss her chin and cheeks and lips, and one put his hands over her eyes. She felt a sharp pricking and everything was dark. Then she was lifted into the air and carried she knew not where, until she felt herself set down, and someone said, 'Tear! tear!' Her eyes were opened again and she found herself in a gorgeous fairyland.

She was surrounded by temples and palaces of gold and silver; there were trees covered with fruit and flowers, lakes full of golden and silver fish and bright-coloured birds singing all around. Hundreds of splendidly dressed people were walking in the gardens or dancing and sporting or reposing themselves in flowery arbours. Anne herself was dressed as finely as any of them. To her surprise they seemed no longer small, but of human size. Anne could have stayed forever in that happy place. She was surrounded and courted by her six friends, but the finest of them still made her his prime favourite, and presently they managed to steal away together and were in the height of happiness when there was a clamour, and her five followers broke in on them, followed by an angry crowd. Her lover drew his sword to protect her, but he was wounded and fell at her feet. The fairy who had first blinded her put his hands over her eyes again. She was whirled up into the air with a great humming, and at length regained her sight to find herself lying on the floor of the arbour surrounded by anxious friends.

Anne never revisited Fairyland, but the fairies did not withdraw their favours. They were with her constantly (though no one else could see them), and nourished her with FAIRY FOOD. Moses Pitt says in his letter:

She forsook eating our victuals, and was fed by these fairies from that harvest time to the next Christmas-day; upon which day she came to our table and said, because it was that day, she would eat some roast beef with us, the which she did – I myself being then at the table.

He adds later that Anne 'gave me a piece of her bread, which I did eat, and I think it was the most delicious bread that ever I did eat, either before or since'.

After her illness, Anne became very fervent in her devotions, though it was the church Prayer Book that she wished to hear, for she was a fervent Episcopalian and all her prophecies were of ultimate victory to the king. People resorted to her for cures from Lands End to London, and her prophecies had great vogue. It was these even more than her dealings with the fairies which caused her to be prosecuted. She was arrested in 1646 at the suit of John Tregeagle, who was to attain a post-humous supernatural reputation as the Demon Tregeagle, some stories of whom Hunt also tells. He committed her to prison and gave orders that she was not to be fed, but she made no complaints and continued in good health. In 1647, the Clarendon Correspondence notes, she is detained in the house of the Mayor of Bodmin and is still not fed. In the end she was released, went into service with a widowed aunt of Moses Pitt and married a labourer named William Warren.

Moses Pitt was a printer in London when he published the letter to the Bishop of Gloucester, and since he could not himself visit Anne Jefferies, he sent an old friend, Mr Humphrey Martin, to whose little daughter Anne had once given a silver cup from the fairies, to confirm her account of her fairy experience. She would tell him nothing. He wrote:

As for Anne Jefferies, I have been with her the greater part of one day, and did read to her all that you wrote to me; but she would not own anything of it, as concerning the fairies, neither of any of the cures that she did. She answered, that if her own father were now alive, she would not discover to him those things which did happen then to her. I asked her the reason why she would not do it; she replied, that if she should discover it to you, that you would make books or ballads of it; and she said she would not have her name spread about the country in books or ballads of such things, if she might have five hundred pounds for it.

Poor Anne had no desire to suffer again the things she had suffered at Justice Tregeagle's hands.

The subject-matter of Anne's delusion, the type of fairies that occurred to her, are of great interest. In this remote part of Cornwall, not fifty years after the first performance of a MIDSUMMER NIGHT'S DREAM, we have an illiterate country girl building up a courtly Fairyland of

DIMINUTIVE FAIRIES with all the minuteness and amorousness of the fairies in Shakespeare, Drayton and HERRICK. It is clear that the poets built on a real country tradition.

[Motifs: F235.3; F236.1.6; F239.4.3; F282; F301; F320; F329.2; F343.19; F370]

Jenny Greenteeth. There are many NURSERY BOGIES, invented by mothers and nurses to inculcate good behaviour or to keep children from danger. A good many of these last are designed to keep children from rivers and ponds. The Lancashire version of these is Jenny Greenteeth, who is supposed to seize children in her long, green fangs and drag them down into stagnant pools at the river's edge. Her counterpart in the river Tees is PEG POWLER.

[Motifs: F420.1.4.8; F420.5.2]

Jenny Permuen. The heroine of HUNT's story, 'The FAIRY WIDOWER', a rather less detailed and interesting version of 'CHERRY OF ZENNOR'.

Jimmy Squarefoot. This curious apparition is described at some length by Walter Gill in *A Manx Scrapbook* (pp. 356–7). He haunted all round the Grenaby district of Man, and in later times he appeared as a man with a pig's head and two great tusks like a wild boar's. Formidable though he looked, he does not seem to have done great damage. In earlier times he was a giant pig, and was ridden over land and sea by a FOAWR who lived on Cronk yn Irree Lhaa. Like most Foawr, he was himself a stone-thrower, and he seems usually to have thrown his stones at his wife, with whom he was on very bad terms. Gill suggests that she may have been the CAILLAGH NY GROAMAGH, who lived in exactly that locality: one of the rocks was Greg yn Arran, and another, which was a wide miss, fell at Cloughur in the south. The wife left him, and he himself presumably followed her, but they left their steed behind. After that he assumed a semi-human form and roamed about the countryside, possibly as far as Glen Rushen, where a BUGGANE appeared which changed its shape between that of a black pig and a man.

[Motifs: A963.5; F511.0.9; F531.4.11]

Joan the Wad. One of the local and obscure types of IGNIS FATUUS, and, though she has lately been publicized as one of the Cornish PISKIES, we owe our knowledge of her to Jonathan Couch's *History of Polperro*. She has, however, the distinction of being invoked in a rhyme: 'Jacky Lantern, Joan the Wad . . .'. From her tickling habits it seems likely, as Couch claimed, that she was a pisky, and the probability is that, if properly invoked, she and JACKY LANTERN would lead travellers aright instead of misleading them.

[Motif: F491]

Joint-eater. The name given by KIRK to what the Irish call 'Alp-Luachra'; but, according to Kirk, this Joint-eater is a kind of fairy who sits invisibly beside his victim and shares his food with him. In *The Secret Commonwealth* (p. 71) he says:

> They avouch that a Heluo, or Great-eater, hath a voracious Elve to be his attender, called a Joint-eater or Just-halver, feeding on the Pith or Quintessence of what the Man eats; and that therefoir he continues Lean like a Hawke or Heron, notwithstanding his devouring Appetite.

In Ireland this phenomenon is accounted for by the man having swallowed a newt when sleeping outside by a running stream. In Douglas HYDE's *Beside the Fire*, there is a detailed account of a man infested by a pregnant Alp-Luachra, and the method by which he was cleared of the thirteen Alp-Luachra by Mac Dermott the Prince of Coolavin. In all the stories the method is the same: the patient is forced to eat a great quantity of salt beef without drinking anything, and is made to lie down with his mouth open above a stream, and after a long wait the Alp-Luachra will come out and jump into the stream to quench their thirst. But this is folk-medicine, not fairy-lore; it is Kirk who attributes the unnatural hunger to an Elf (see ELVES).

'Kate Crackernuts'. An unusual Orcadian tale, collected by D. J. Robertson and published in *Folk-Lore* (September 1890). It is a tale of enchantment and disenchantment, and the fairy power to draw humans into their hills and to wear out their lives with DANCING.

Once upon a time there was a king and a queen, and they each had a daughter called Kate. But the king's Kate was far bonnier than the queen's Kate, and the queen was jealous of her stepdaughter's beauty and determined to spoil it, but the two Kates loved each other dearly. So the queen went to the hen-wife, her wicked crony, and took council with her.

'Send the bonny burd to me one morning, first thing,' said the hen-wife, 'and I'll spoil her beauty for her.'

So next day the queen sent the king's Kate down to the hen-wife to fetch a basket of eggs for their breakfast. It happened that Kate was hungry, and as she passed the kitchen she snatched up a bannock and munched it on her way. She came to the hen-wife's, and asked for the eggs. 'Go in hen and lift the lid of the pot while I get them,' said the hen-wife. The king's Kate lifted the lid, and a great steam rose up, but she was none the worse for that.

'Go home to your minnie,' said the hen-wife, 'and tell her to keep her larder door better snibbit.'

Next day the queen saw Kate as far as the palace door; but on the way to the hen-wife's she spoke to some reapers in the field, and they gave her some ears of corn, which she ate as she went. Again she went home scatheless, and the hen-wife said: 'Tell your minnie that the pot winna boil if the fire's away.'

The third day the queen went with her to the hen-wife's, and when Kate lifted the lid of the pot, a sheep's head rose out of it and fastened on her shoulders, covering her own pretty head.

The queen was delighted, but the queen's Kate was very angry. She wrapped her sister's head in a linen cloth, and took her by the hand, and they went out together to seek their fortunes. They walked until they got to the next kingdom, and the queen's Kate went to the palace, and got work as a kitchen-maid, and leave to keep her sick sister in the attic. The eldest son of the king was very ill. No one knew what ailed him, and all who watched by his bed at night disappeared. When the queen's Kate heard this she offered to watch by his bed for a peck of silver. All was quiet till midnight; then the prince rose and dressed like one in a daze, and went out and mounted on his horse. Kate followed him, and jumped up behind him. They rode through a close wood of hazels, and Kate picked the nuts as she passed. Soon they came to a fairy mound, and the prince said: 'Let the prince in with his horse and hound,' and Kate said:

'And his fair lady him behind.' And a door opened in the hillside and let them in. Kate slipped off and hid behind the open door, but the prince went in and danced till he fainted with weakness. When dawn came he mounted his horse, and Kate climbed up behind him. Next night she offered to watch again for a peck of gold, and followed the prince as before. That night a little fairy boy was playing about among the dancers, astride of a silver wand. One of the dancers said to him: 'Tak' tent o' that wand, for one stroke of it would give back the king's Kate her ain heid again.'

When the queen's Kate heard that she began to roll the nuts she had gathered out, one by one, from behind the door, till the fairy child laid down the wand and went after them. Then she snatched it, and carried it with her when she rode back behind the prince. When the day came, and she could leave the prince, she ran up to her attic and touched the king's Kate with the wand, and her own looks came back to her, bonnier than ever. The third night Kate watched; but this night she must marry the prince for her reward. She followed the prince again, and this time the fairy child was playing with a little dead bird.

'Now mind,' said one of the dancers, 'not to lose that birdie; for three tastes of it, and the prince would be as well as ever he was.'

When Kate heard that, she rolled out the nuts faster than before, and the fairy boy laid down the bird and went after them. As soon as they got home Kate plucked the bird and set it down to the fire to roast. At the first smell of it the prince sat up in bed and said: 'I could eat that birdie.'

At the third mouthful he was as well as ever he had been; and he married Kate Crackernuts, and his brother married the king's Kate, and

> They lived happy, and they died happy,
> And they never drank from a dry cappie.

[Motifs: D683.2; D764; D771.4; D1766.8; F211; F302.3.4; F302.3.4.2; F370; P284; S31]

Keightley, Thomas (1789–1872). The author of *The Fairy Mythology*, a remarkable collection of international fairy episodes. We owe this book to the inspiration of Crofton CROKER, who drew on the memories of Irish folk traditions stored in Keightley's receptive and retentive brain. Keightley had started life as an Irish barrister, but a breakdown in health forced him to go to London to earn his living by writing educational textbooks. There he made friends with both Croker and Douce, another well-known antiquarian. *The Fairy Mythology* was first published in 1828, and followed in 1834 by *Tales and Popular Fictions*. Two further and enlarged editions of *The Fairy Mythology* were brought out in 1860 and 1878. Keightley wrote many other books, but these are his great contributions to folklore.

Kelpies. The best-known of the Scottish WATER-HORSES. The Kelpie haunted rivers rather than lochs or the sea. He could assume human form, in which he appeared like a rough, shaggy man. In this shape he used sometimes to leap up behind a solitary rider, gripping and crushing him, and frightening him almost to death. Before storms, he would be heard howling and wailing. His most usual shape was that of a young horse. He played the ordinary BOGY OR BOGEY-BEAST trick of alluring travellers on to his back and rushing with them into a deep pool, where he struck the water with his tail with a sound like thunder and disappeared in a flash of light. He was suspected of sometimes tearing people to pieces and devouring them. A picturesque version of the story of 'The Time is Come but not the Man' is told of the river Conan in Sutherland, in which the Kelpie seems to figure as the hungry spirit of the river. In his horse form, the Kelpie sometimes had a magic bridle. Grant Stewart in his *Popular Superstitions* tells how a bold MacGregor, nicknamed Wellox, took his bridle off the Kelpie. The Kelpie begged him to restore it, but he kept it and used it to work magic. On the other hand, the man who put a human bridle on the Kelpie could subdue him to his will. Chambers tells us that Graham of Morphie once bridled a kelpie and used him to drag stones to build his new castle. When the castle was built he took off the bridle, and the poor, galled kelpie dashed into the river, but paused in the middle to say:

> 'Sair back and sair banes
> Drivin' the Laird o' Morphie's stanes.
> The Laird o' Morphie'll never thrive
> Sae lang as the Kelpie is alive!'

From then misfortune dogged the Grahams of Morphie until their lives ended.

[Motifs: B184.1.3; D1311.11.1; F234.1.8; F401.3.1; F420.1.3.3; G302.3.2; G303.3.3.1.3]

Killmoulis. A grotesque kind of HOB or BROWNIE who haunts mills. It is described at some length by William Henderson in *Folk-Lore of the Northern Counties* (pp. 252–3). Every mill used to be supposed to have its killmoulis, or mill-servant. He was not very pleasant to look at, for he had no mouth but an enormous nose, up which he must have snuffed his food, for a rhyme quoted by Henderson runs:

> Auld Killmoulis wanting the mow,
> Come to me now, come to me now!
> Where war ye yestreen when I killed the sow?
> Had ye come ye'd hae gotten yer belly fou.

Perhaps he fed on the FOYSON of food.

Killmoulis was deeply devoted to the welfare of the miller and his family, and wailed like a BANSHEE before illness or misfortune, but he was more than half a BOGGART, and delighted in practical jokes, such as blowing ashes over the shelled oats spread out to dry. Only the miller could keep him in order by calling out his invocation: 'Auld Killmoulis, etc.,' when the hob would appear, puffing and blowing, and be given his orders. In an emergency he would thrash the corn, or ride for the howdie (or midwife) if the miller's wife needed her, and he was also used at Hallowe'en in divination. He generally lived in the killogee, the space before the fireplace in the kiln. He seems to have been a Lowland spirit, for the Highland mills were haunted by BROWNIES, URISKS and BROLLACHANS, most of them more sinister than Killmoulis. In Holland, however, the mill spirit Kaboutermannekin is more helpful and industrious.

[Motifs: F480; F482.5.3; F482.5.4.1]

King Herla. Walter Map, the 12th-century author of *De Nugis Curialium*, gives one of the earliest stories of the variation of TIME IN FAIRYLAND to account for Herla's Rade. He places it locally on the Welsh Border, but the Ride of Harlequin was also reported at Bonneval in France in 1091, where it was supposed to be the Ride of the Dead. Map's pleasing but rather diffuse account was slightly shortened by E. M. Leather in *The Folk-Lore of Herefordshire*:

Herla was king of the Ancient Britons, and was challenged by another king, a pigmy no bigger than an ape, and of less than half human stature. He rode on a large goat; indeed, he himself might have been compared to Pan. He had a large head, glowing face, and a long red beard, while his breast was conspicuous for a spotted fawnskin which he wore on it. The lower part of his body was rough and hairy, and his legs ended in goats' hooves. He had a private interview with Herla, in which he spoke as follows: 'I am lord over many kings and princes, over a vast and innumerable people. I am their willing messenger to you, although to you I am unknown. Yet I rejoice in the fame which has raised you above other kings, for you are of all men the best, and also closely connected with me both by position and blood. You are worthy of the honour of adorning your marriage with my presence as guest, for the King of France has given you his daughter, and indeed the embassy is arriving here to-day, although all the arrangements have been made without your knowledge. Let there be an everlasting treaty between us, because, first of all, I was present at your marriage, and because you will be at mine on the same day a year hence.' After this speech he turned away, and moving faster even than a tiger, disappeared from his sight. The king, therefore, returned from that spot full of surprise, received the embassy, and assented to their proposals. When the marriage was celebrated, and the king was seated at the customary feast, suddenly, before the first course was served, the pigmy arrived, accompanied by so large a company of dwarfs like himself, that after they had filled all the seats at table, there were more dwarfs outside in tents which they had in a moment put up, than at the feast inside. Instantly there darted out from these tents servants with vessels made out of precious stones, all new and wondrously wrought. They filled the palace and the tents with furniture either made of gold or precious stones. Neither wine nor meat was served in any wooden or silver vessel. The servants were found wherever they were wanted, and served nothing out of the king's or anyone else's stores, but only from their own, which were of quality beyond anyone's thoughts. None of Herla's provisions were used, and his servants sat idle.

The pigmies won universal praise. Their raiment was gorgeous; for lamps they provided blazing gems; they were never far off when they were wanted, and never too close when not desired. Their king then thus addressed Herla: 'Most excellent King, God be my witness that I am here in accordance with our agreement, at your marriage. If there is anything more that you desire, I will supply it gladly, on the condition that when I demand a return, you will not deny it.' Hereupon, without waiting for an answer he returned to his tent and departed at about cockcrow with his attendants. After a year he suddenly came to Herla and demanded the observance of the treaty. Herla consented, and followed at the dwarf's bidding. They entered a cave in a very high cliff, and after some journeying through the dark, which appeared to be lighted, not by the sun or moon, but by numerous torches, they arrived at the dwarf's palace, a splendid mansion.

There the marriage was celebrated, and the obligations to the dwarf fittingly paid, after which Herla returned home loaded with gifts and offerings, horses, dogs, hawks, and all things pertaining to hunting and falconry. The pigmy guided them down the dark passage, and there gave them a (small) bloodhound (*canem sanguinarium*) small enough to be carried (*portabilem*), then, strictly forbidding any of the king's retinue to dismount until the dog leapt from his carrier, he bade them farewell, and returned home. Soon after, Herla reached the light of day, and having got back to his kingdom again, called an old shepherd and asked for news of his queen, using her name. The shepherd looked at him astonished, and said, 'Lord, I scarcely understand your language, for I am a Saxon, and you a Briton. I have never heard the name of that queen, except in the case of one who they say was Herla's wife, queen of the earliest Britons. He is fabled to have disappeared with a dwarf at this cliff, and never to have been seen on earth again. The Saxons have now held this realm for two hundred years, having driven out the original inhabitants.' The king was astonished, for he imagined that he had been away for three days only. Some of his companions descended from horseback before the dog was released, forget-

ful of the dwarf's commands, and instantly crumbled to dust. The king
then forbade any more of his companions to descend until the dog
leapt down. The dog has not leapt down yet. One legend states that
Herla for ever wanders on mad journeys with his train, without home
or rest. Many people, as they tell us, often see his company. However,
they say that at last, in the first year of our (present) King Henry (the
second) it ceased to visit our country in pomp as before. On that
occasion, many of the Welsh (*Wallenses*) saw it whelmed in the Wye,
the Herefordshire river (*Waiam Herefordiae flumen*). From that hour,
that weird roaming ceased, as though Herla had transferred his wandering (*Errores*, a pun containing the idea of error) to us, and had gained
rest for himself. (A hit at contemporary politics.)

[Type: 766 (variant). Motifs: C521; C927.2; C984; E501.1.7.1:
F241.1.0.1; F377; F378.1; F379.1

King Orfeo. The legend of Orpheus and Eurydice is reshaped in a
Middle English verse romance of which three manuscripts survive.
HALLIWELL chose MS. Ashmole 61 to reproduce in his *Illustrations of
the Fairy Mythology of Shakespeare*, which was reprinted by W. C.
Hazlitt in *Fairy Tales, Legends and Romances Illustrating Shakespeare*
(1875).
It is a delightful poem, in which Pluto is turned into the fairy king, as
Chaucer, a little later, called the fairy queen Persephone in the WIFE OF
BATH'S TALE. According to this romance, Orfeo was king of Tracyens
and his queen was Dame Meroudys. One May Day, Queen Meroudys
went with three of her ladies to sport herself in an orchard and she fell
asleep under an ymp tree; that is, a grafted apple-tree, which was always
supposed to be magical. Her ladies did not like to wake her, so they let
her sleep on until twilight. Suddenly she started up out of her sleep,
crying and wailing, and began to tear her cheeks and rend her clothes.
Her ladies were frightened, and ran to fetch all the knights and ladies out
to help them. They carried her up to her room, and King Orfeo begged
her to tell him what was the matter. At first she cried and wailed and
struggled, all unlike herself, who had been gentle and still and happy, but
at last she spoke and told him what had happened to her. She had been
lying asleep under the ymp tree, when a nobly caparisoned knight rode
up to her and told her to go with him to his lord, the King of Fairy. She
answered that she dared not and would not go. With that the king himself rode up, lifted her up on to his horse and carried her away to a noble
palace in a fair country. He showed her everything and then took her
back to the apple-tree; but before he left her he told her that she must be
there next day at twilight ready to go with him, and if she resisted he
would tear her in pieces, but he would take her. Orfeo said he would go
with her and protect her: so at twilight next evening he was with her,

with all his army ringing the tree around in a deep band. The host of the fairy king appeared, and they began to fight, but suddenly Meroudys was drawn away invisible from the very middle of the ring, and no one could find her. Then Orfeo was like a man distracted, and when no trace of Meroudys could be found he called his nobles together, and appointed his steward regent in his absence and his successor if he died. He laid aside his robes and his crown, and barefoot and in rags he went out into the wilderness. The only possession he took with him was his harp, for he was the best harper in the world. For ten years he lived in the wilderness, his only shelter a hollow tree, his clothing moss and leaves and his own long beard and hair, his food wild fruits in the summer and leaves and roots in the winter. But when the warm days came he sat in the sun and harped, so that all wild beasts came round him, tamed by his music, and the birds filled every tree. Then one day he heard the sound of horns, and a troop of fairy knights rode past him hunting, and a little after them came a bevy of ladies hawking, and among them he saw Dame Meroudys, and she saw him and knew him and said nothing, but her tears fell to see him so lean and shaggy and ragged, burnt black with sun and frost. And when the ladies saw that the two knew each other they turned about and bore Meroudys away, but Orfeo followed them, running as fast as their horses could gallop, and he saw them go into a cleft in the rock and followed them through a long winding cave, until he came out into full light and saw before him a fair country with a great palace standing up in the distance, all built of shining crystal and precious stones, and he went towards it. He knocked at the gate of the shining palace, and when the porter opened it he claimed a minstrel's right of entry. Inside the walls he saw the standing forms of dead men, some headless, some armless, some who had been strangled treacherously, all it seemed who had died before their time. Beyond them he saw men and women sleeping in the twilight, and among them his wife Meroudys under her ymp tree. Beyond them was the royal throne-room, and on the dais sat the king and queen in shining splendour surrounded by a great and rich company. Orfeo went up to the foot of the throne and fell on his knees. 'Lord,' he said, 'is it thy will to hear my minstrelsy?'

> Then seyd the kyng, 'what arte thou
> That hether arte i-come now?
> I, no' none that is with me
> Never zit sent after the;
> Never seth that my reyne be-gan,
> Fond I never none so herdy man
> That hyder durst to us wend,
> Bott iff I wold after hym send.'

So it runs in the 15th-century manuscript. Orfeo returned without fear that he was a harper, and that it was the duty of all such to offer their music to kings and nobles if they desired to hear it. The king gave him permission to play, he tuned his harp and began. From every room in the palace the FAIRIES poured in to listen, and cast themselves down at his feet. At the end the king promised him any boon he asked, and he asked for the lady asleep under the ymp tree.

'That would be a bad coupling,' said the king, 'for you are wild and rough and lean and she is fair and gentle. It would be a foul thing to give her to you.'

'Yet it would be a fouler thing,' said Orfeo, 'for a great king to break his plighted promise made before all his knights.'

'You are a brave man,' said the king in admiration. 'Take her with you.' So the two left the underworld in great joy. There was no looking back or loss; they went home in great happiness. When they got back to Tracyens the steward had been true to his trust; they were welcomed back with joy and lived out their lives in great happiness. It is a true fairy-story ending.

This early tale has so many correspondences with later folk-tales of Celtic Britain that is seems likely that it was of Celtic origin. Stories like ETHNA THE BRIDE and MIDHIR and ETAIN spring to mind at once. The dangerous time of twilight, the magic apple-tree, the connection between the fairies and the dead, are all part of Celtic tradition. It is possible that it may have been translated from a French source, but the roots are in Britain.

[Motifs: D950.10; F81.1; F241.1.0.1]

Kipling, Rudyard (1865–1936). Kipling wrote a number of short stories on supernatural themes, ghosts, witchcraft and curses, but his great contribution to literature for fairy-lore was made in the two volumes, *Puck of Pook's Hill* (1906) and *Rewards and Fairies* (1910). About certain of his books he said that his demon had been at work, so that he could not go wrong, and he rated these among them, and rightly. About the beginning of this century fairy-tales for children had fallen into a morass of prettification and sentimentality. From the 17th century onwards, the English FAIRIES had been assailed by various hazards, owing to the vagaries of FASHIONS IN FAIRY LORE. There was first a tendency to prettification and the diminution of the fairies. The DIMINUTIVE FAIRIES of Shakespeare (see MIDSUMMER NIGHT'S DREAM) had retained their powers and quality, Drayton's were reduced to a courtly parody, HERRICK's retained some of the phallic qualities which belonged to the fairies as the guardians of fertility, but much emphasis was laid on their tiny size, and the Duchess of Newcastle's dwindled into miracles of littleness. At the end of the century came the fascinating but sophisticated stories of PERRAULT and Madame D'AULNOY which proliferated into the *Cabinet des Fées*, some seventy volumes of it, growing ever further from traditional sources. In the 18th century, with the increasing production of books specially designed for children, fairies became instruments of edification; but there was little excuse for the gauzy fairies of the early 1900s, for at the beginning of the 19th century authentic fairy tradition became available, at first from Germany and Scandinavia, but very soon from all over Britain: Crofton CROKER and HYDE from Ireland, J. F. CAMPBELL, J. G. CAMPBELL and others from the Highlands, SCOTT, Chambers, William Henderson from the Border Country, HUNT and BOTTRELL from Cornwall, John Rhys and Wirt Sikes from Wales, to mention only a few. In literary fairy tales, too, there were sturdier creations: Jean INGELOW's and Mrs EWING's.

In spite of all this good material, a sentimental attitude towards children in literature communicated itself to the fairy writing. Kipling struck a ringing blow against this. His PUCK is of the real, homely ROBIN GOODFELLOW type, squat and strong and brown, broad-shouldered and pointy-eared, with a hearty contempt for the modern butterfly-winged, gauzy impostors. The PEOPLE OF THE HILLS have all gone, he says, and he is the last 'Old Thing' left in England. He brings the past back to the children who have unconsciously summoned him, but there are no fairy encounters. He tells them tales of the old gods who had sunk to fairies, of Wayland Smith in particular, and of a human foundling adopted by the Lady Esclairmonde, King HUON's Queen, and of the Dymchurch Flit, one chapter in the DEPARTURE OF THE FAIRIES. Otherwise it is the human past into which he admits them, and old Sussex that he brings to life.

Kirk, Robert (1644–92). The author of the fullest and most authoritative treatise on the fairy-lore of his period; it is, indeed, one of the most important works ever written on the subject. He is unusual, too, in being a folklorist who is the subject of a fairy-tale. Kirk was a Gaelic scholar and in 1682 he published the first metrical translation of the Psalms into the Gaelic tongue. This received a great welcome and made his reputation in his time, but some time in 1691 he produced a manuscript which was to give his name a much wider currency. It was *The Secret Commonwealth of Elves, Fauns and Fairies*. The book was not printed till 1815, reprinted in 1893, edited, with an introduction, by Andrew Lang. By this time the manuscript, which had been lodged in the Advocates' Library, had disappeared. Lang's emendations were necessarily conjectural. The book was published again in 1933 with a further introduction by Cunninghame Graham and a reproduction of D. Y. Cameron's painting of 'The Fairy Knowe at Aberfoyle'. Now, most fortunately, a fuller transcript has come to light in the Laing Collection in the University of Edinburgh Library. This has been examined and edited by Stewart Sanderson and there are plans for its publication. In the meantime, we must content ourselves with the present editions, supplemented by a delightful paper, 'A Prospect of Fairyland', delivered by Stewart Sanderson to the Folk-

lore Society and published in *Folklore* (vol. 75, Spring 1964). Robert
Kirk had been born at Aberfoyle, where his father was minister, and
after twenty-one years of serving as minister at Balquidder, he was called
to Aberfoyle on his father's death. In both places he had an admirable
opportunity of studying the fairy beliefs of the Highlanders, and he
examines them with calm detachment and impartiality, but apparently
with an ultimate conviction of their truth. All aspects of the Highland
fairy-lore are presented in this short treatise, which would be an encyclopedia in little if it were alphabetically arranged. Various theories of the
ORIGIN OF FAIRIES are presented: fairies as the dead, or alternatively
as 'Of a midle Nature betwixt Man and Angel, as were Daemons thought
to be of Old'; of DEPENDENCE OF FAIRIES UPON MORTALS, shown by
the CO-WALKER and JOINT-EATER; of FAIRY THEFTS, FAIRY FOOD,
FAIRY CRAFTS, FAIRY LEVITATION, the DRESS AND APPEARANCE OF
THE FAIRIES, ELF-SHOT, FAIRY OINTMENT, CAPTIVES IN FAIRYLAND
and many other aspects of fairy-lore. The whole is written in the
admirable prose of the 17th century:

> They are not subject to sore Sicknesses, but dwindle and decay at a
> certain Period, all about ane Age. Some say their continual Sadness is
> because of their pendulous State, as uncertain what at the last Revolu-
> tion will become of them, when they are lock't up into ane unchange-
> able Condition; and if they have any frolic Fitts of Mirth, 'tis as the
> constrained grinning of a Mort-head, or rather as acted on a Stage,
> and moved by another, then cordially comeing of themselves.

Kirk's parishioners evidently felt that he had infringed the TABOO
against spying upon the FAIRIES, for when his body was found beside
the Fairy Knowe at Aberfoyle, it was soon whispered around that what
was buried was only a STOCK and that the minister himself was with the
SUBTERRANEANS under the Fairy Knowe. In Walter SCOTT's time the
legend was still current and was recorded by the Reverend P. Grahame,
Minister of Aberfoyle, in his *Sketches of Picturesque Scenery in the
Southern Confines of Perthshire* (1806). Scott reproduces his tale in his
Letters on Demonology and Witchcraft. It seems that after his funeral
Robert Kirk appeared to one of his relations in the night-time and told
him to go to Grahame of Duchray with a message from him. He was a
prisoner in Fairyland, but he had one chance of escape. His posthumous
child had just been born, and would be christened at the Manse. At the
christening feast Kirk would appear, and if Duchray kept his dirk in his
hand and threw it over Kirk's spectral form, he would be disenchanted
and free to enter the mortal world again. Kirk duly appeared, but
Duchray was too startled to fling the dirk and the chance was lost. Never
again could Kirk be father to a 'chrisom' child. However, a tradition
still lingered which gave him a second chance. In the Second World War
an officer's young wife was a tenant of Aberfoyle Manse and was expecting

a child. She had been told that if a christening was held at the Manse, Kirk could still be disenchanted. The chair that was traditionally his still stood in the dining-room, and if anyone stuck a dirk into the seat of it, Kirk would be freed. The young wife hoped that they would not be posted before her baby was born. Presumably Kirk would appear only to crumble into dust, but his soul would have been saved and freed from the sad merriment of Fairyland. As it is, Kirk's story must be numbered among those tragic tales of the unrescued CAPTIVES IN FAIRYLAND.

[Motifs: F320; F375]

Kit with the Canstick, or candlestick. In SCOT's 'List of Hobgoblins and Night Fears', reproduced in the DENHAM TRACTS, Kit with the Canstick is included, and he is also mentioned by Samuel Harsnet in his *Egregious Papist Impostures*. Mrs Wright also includes him with WILL O' THE WISP and other forms of IGNIS FATUUS.

[Motif: F491]

Klippe. The Forfarshire name for a fairy. E. B. Simpson gives a short reference to them in *Folk Lore in Lowland Scotland* (p. 93):

A well-known minister of the Church of Scotland related, this century, at a dinner in Edinburgh, how his father had met a klippe in a bare moorland in Forfarshire, a little brown-faced elf who started up on the path before him, walked before him awhile and then vanished.

Knockers. The Cornish mine spirits, not evil and malicious like the German *Kobolds*, but friendly to the tin-miners, for they knock to indicate where a rich ore is to be found. They used to be supposed to be the ghosts of the Jews who worked the mines, and primitive smelting-houses sometimes found in the mines were called 'Jews' houses'. The story was that the Jews who took part in the Crucifixion were sent to work in the Cornish mines as a punishment. Jews did indeed join the mines in the 11th and 12th centuries, but tradition puts their working much earlier. HUNT reports that the miners often say they see little demons or IMPS in the mines, sitting on pieces of timber or tumbling about in curious attitudes. They welcome them, for they only come where a good lode is to be found. These presumably are knockers, though they are usually only heard, mimicking the sounds made by the miners, but continuing their work by night, long after the humans have left. The little, impish creatures may possibly be SPRIGGANS, who are also supposed to visit the mines. Two northern mine spirits are CUTTY SOAMS and BLUECAP.

The knockers are sometimes called BUCCAS, which is a Cornish name for a GOBLIN. Mrs Wright, in *Rustic Speech and Folk-Lore*, gives a list of the Cornish mine spirits. She says:

Buccas, Gathorns, Knockers, Nickers, Nuggies and Spriggans are individual and collective appellations for the sprites that haunt the tin-mines of Cornwall – They are for the most part a harmless folk, occupied in mining on their own account, out of sight of the human miners. These latter, however, take pains not to annoy the goblin workers; whistling and swearing, for instance, are held to be obnoxious to mine-spirits, and must therefore be avoided.

She does not mention another TABOO recorded by Hunt which has a more sinister flavour. It seems the mine spirits cannot endure the sign of the CROSS, and therefore the miners avoid marking anything with a cross for fear of annoying them. The generally friendly disposition of the knockers, however, is confirmed by a story from Hunt in *Popular Romances of the West of England* (pp. 90–91):

At Ransom Mine the 'Knockers' were always very active in their subterranean operations. In every part of the mine their 'knockings' were heard, but most especially were they busy in one particular 'end'. There was a general impression that great wealth must exist at this part of the 'lode'. Yet, notwithstanding the inducements of very high tribute were held out to the miners, no pair of men could be found brave enough to venture on the ground of the 'Bockles'. An old man and his son, called Trenwith, who lived near Bosprenis, went out one midsummer eve, about midnight, and watched until they saw the 'Smae People' bringing up the shining ore. It is said they were possessed of some secret by which they could communicate with the fairy people. Be this as it may, they told the little miners that they would save them all the trouble of breaking down the ore, that they would bring 'to grass' for them, one-tenth of the 'richest stuff', and leave it properly dressed, if they would quietly give them up this end. An agreement of some kind was come to. The old man and his son took the 'pitch', and in a short time realized much wealth. The old man never failed to keep to his bargain, and leave the tenth of the ore for his friends. He died. The son was avaricious and selfish. He sought to cheat the Knockers, but he ruined himself by so doing. The 'lode' failed; nothing answered with him; disappointed, he took to drink, squandered all the money his father had made, and died a beggar.

We see here the ordinary fairy-lore of just dealings, and the story of 'Barker's Knee', also told by Hunt (p. 88), shows that they share the fairy dislike of spies among the INFRINGEMENTS OF FAIRY PRIVACY. According to this tale, the knockers inhabited not only the mines, but rocks, caves and wells in Cornwall, and carried on their mining works wherever they lived. In the parish of Towednack there was once an idle, hulking fellow, who was always playing truant from the mines. He conceived a great curiosity about the knockers, and found out that they haunted a well in the parish, where, crouched among the ferns, he had a good opportunity of watching them. Day after day and night after night he lay, looking and listening. He learned their hours and their methods, heard them singing and playing, found out their holidays – the Jews' Sabbath, Christmas Day, Easter Day and All Saints – and at length even began to understand their speech. All this time he flattered himself that they knew nothing about the watch he kept, until one day when they were knocking off for work he heard them telling each other where they were going to hide their bags of tools. 'I'll put mine in this cleft here,' said one. 'I'll hide mine under these ferns,' said another. 'I'll put mine on Barker's knee,' said a third, and at once a great heavy but invisible bag of tools landed smack on Barker's knee-cap. He was lame all the rest of his life, and ever after if one of the miners suffered from rheumatism he would say, 'I be as stiff as Barker's knee.'

BOTTRELL, in his *Traditions and Hearthside Stories of West Cornwall* (vol. I, p. 77), gives an account of an old man, Captain Mathy, who was one of the few who claimed to have seen the 'knackers' when, following their knocking, he broke into a rich vug (an aperture in a lode, frequently lined with crystals):

When I rubbed my eyes and looked sharper into the inner end there I spied three of the knackers. They were no bigger, either one of them, than a good sixpenny doll; yet in their faces, dress, and movements, they had the look of hearty old tinners. I took the most notice of the one in the middle. He was settan down on a stone, his jacket off and his shirt-sleeves rolled up. Between his knees he held a little anvil, no more than an inch square, yet as complete as any you ever seed in a smith's shop. In his left hand he held a boryer, about the size of a darning-needle, which he was sharpan for one of the knackers, and the other was waitan his turn to have the pick he held in his hand new cossened, or steeled.

These knackers did not punish the intruder as Barker was punished, but seized the opportunity when Mathy turned aside to get them one of his candles, to disappear, and he heard them tittering and squeaking but never saw them again.

[Motifs: F456; F456.1.1; F456.1.1.1; F456.1.2.1.1; F456.1.2.2.1; M242]

Knocky-Boh. Mentioned by Mrs Wright in *Rustic Speech and Folk-Lore* as a North Yorkshire BOGIE who knocks behind wainscots. He seems to have been a kind of BOGGART, or poltergeist.

Knowe. The Scottish version of the word 'knoll', equivalent to the Irish 'knock'. It sometimes relates to a tumulus and sometimes to the buried ruins of a castle. See also BRUCH and SITHEIN.

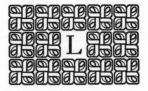

Lady of the Lake, the. She is one of the most mysterious and un-explained of the fairy ladies who appear and disappear in the Arthurian legends. By the time Malory collected the MATTER OF BRITAIN the FAIRIES had been euhemerized into enchantresses, but in the earlier romances their fairy nature is apparent. The German *Lanzelet* by Ulrich von Zatzikhoven, a translation of a French romance left in Austria by the de Morville who was one of the hostages for Richard Coeur de Lion, probably represents a very early version of the Lancelot legend. In this version the Lady of the Lake is a true lake maiden, like the GWRAGEDD ANNWN, the queen of an isle of maidens in the middle of an enchanted lake, where winter never comes and no one knows sorrow. She breeds up the young Lancelot to be the champion who shall protect her cowardly son, Mabuz the Enchanter, from the incursions of his neighbour Iweret. In the 15th-century prose *Lancelot* she is a sorceress, as MORGAN LE FAY is in Malory, and the lake is an illusion. Jessie Weston in *The Legend of Sir Lancelot du Lac* points out that the original germ of the Lancelot legend is the story of the capture of a royal child by a water-fairy, for, in *Lanzelet*, Lancelot has not become the lover of Guinevere, and Sir Gawaine is still Arthur's chief knight. The Lady of the Lake makes appearances in other parts of the Arthurian legends. It will be remembered that she gives Excalibur to Arthur at the beginning of his reign, and receives it again as a token of his mortal wounding and a summons to fetch him with the three other queens of faerie to be tended in the Isle of Avalon. She is generally identified with NIMUE.

[Motifs: D813.1.1; D878.1; F371; F420.5.1.9; F421.1]

'Laird of Balmachie's Wife, The'. The most serious of all the FAIRY THEFTS was the theft of human beings: human babies taken to reinforce the fairy stock and CHANGELINGS left in their place, children enticed away, young maidens to be brides, newly delivered mothers to act as nurses to fairy babies and others. Once these humans had been made CAPTIVES IN FAIRYLAND it was very difficult, though not impossible, to rescue them, but there are quite a number of anecdotes of the pre-vention of theft or of rescues before the captive had reached fairyland. 'The Laird of Balmachie's Wife', from Gibbings's *Folk-Lore and Legends, Scotland*, is a representative example. It is reproduced in *A Dictionary of British Folk-Tales in the English Language* (Part B, vol. 1):

In the olden times, when it was the fashion for gentlemen to wear swords, the Laird of Balmachie went one day to Dundee, leaving his wife at home ill in bed. Riding home in the twilight, he had occasion to leave the high road, and when crossing between some little romantic knolls, called the Cur-hills, in the neighbourhood of Carlungy, he encountered a troop of fairies supporting a kind of litter, upon which some person seemed to be borne. Being a man of dauntless courage, and, as he said, impelled by some internal impulse, he pushed his horse close to the litter, drew his sword, laid it across the vehicle, and in a firm tone exclaimed:

'In the name of God, release your captive.'

The tiny troop immediately disappeared, dropping the litter on the ground. The Laird dismounted, and found that it contained his own wife, dressed in her bedclothes. Wrapping his coat around her, he placed her on the horse before him, and, having only a short distance to ride, arrived safely at home.

Placing her in another room, under the care of an attentive friend, he immediately went to the chamber where he had left his wife in the morning, and there to all appearance she still lay, very sick of a fever. She was fretful, discontented, and complained much of having been neglected in his absence, at all of which the laird affected great concern, and, pretending much sympathy, insisted upon her rising to have her bed made. She said that she was unable to rise, but her husband was peremptory and having ordered a large wood fire to warm the room, he lifted the impostor from the bed, and bearing her across the floor as if to a chair, which had been previously prepared, he threw her on the fire, from which she bounced like a sky-rocket, and went through the ceiling, and out at the roof of the house, leaving a hole among the slates. He then brought in his own wife, a little recovered from her alarm, who said that some time after sunset, the nurse having left her for the purpose of preparing a little caudle, a multitude of ELVES came in at the window, thronging like bees from a hive. They filled the room, and having lifted her from the bed, carried her through the window, after which she recollected nothing further, till she saw her husband standing over her on the Cur-hills, at the back of Carlungy. The hole in the roof, by which the female fairy made her escape, was mended, but could never be kept in repair, as a tempest of wind happened always once a year, which uncovered that particular spot, without injuring any other part of the roof.

[Motif: F322]

'Laird o' Co, The'. See VIRTUES ESTEEMED BY THE FAIRIES.

Lake Maidens. See GWRAGEDD ANNWN.

Lambton Worm. One of the North Country DRAGONS, for the Norse and Saxon name for dragon was '*worm*'. Even in Somerset some of the dragons were called WORMS, as 'The Gurt Vurm of Shervage Wood'. Occasionally one hears of a winged worm, and sometimes of a legless one, but as a rule they are wingless and lizard-like in form. The tale of the Lambton Worm is of particular interest, for we hear of its life from the beginning to the end. William Henderson put together the particulars in *Folk-Lore of the Northern Counties* (pp. 287–92) from Sharpe's *Bishoprick Garland*.

The Heir of Lambton in the 14th century was a wild youth, and delighted to outrage public opinion. One fine Sunday morning he was sitting fishing in full view of all the tenants going to Brugeford Chapel on the bridge over the Wear close to Lambton Castle. He had had no luck, and just as the last of the church-goers were hurrying in, he burst out into a stream of oaths. As the church-bell stopped he had a bite, and after a fierce struggle he landed his catch. It was not a fish, but a creature so horrible that he took it off the hook and threw it into the well close at hand, still called 'Worm's Well'. A stranger passing asked what sport he had had. 'I think I've caught the Devil,' said the heir. 'Look and see what you make of him.' 'He looks like an eft,' said the stranger, 'except that he's got nine holes round his mouth. I think he bodes no good.' And he went on.

Time passed. The heir seemed a sobered man, and after a while he went to the Holy Land. The eft grew and grew, till it was too big for the well and curled itself round Worm's Hill, whence it ravaged the country-side. They put a great trough outside the castle gates, and filled it every day with the milk of nine cows, but that did not content it. Brave knights came to destroy the worm, but when it was cut in two it joined together again as worms do, and it crushed the knights to death.

At length the heir returned, a Knight of Rhodes now, and was horrified to learn what his folly had done. He was determined to destroy the worm, but when he heard how all earlier attempts had failed he went to a wise woman to learn what he should do. She scolded him fiercely for the sufferings he had caused, but in the end she told him exactly what he must do. First he must go to the chapel and vow to kill the first living creature that met him on his return from the battle with the worm. If he failed to carry this out, no Lord of Lambton for nine generations would die in his bed. Then he must go to a smith and have his armour covered with spikes, and thirdly he must take his stand on the great rock in the middle of the river Wear, and there he must fight the worm as he came down to drink at sunset. All this he did. He told the servants to loose his favourite dog as soon as he blew his trumpet after the battle; then he went down to the fight. At his first stroke the worm turned to strangle him in its folds; but the more fiercely it squeezed the more it wounded itself, till the Wear ran red with its blood. At last he cut it in pieces, and the swiftly flowing river carried them away before they could reunite. The heir staggered home with hardly strength to blow his horn. But his old father, who had been waiting in terrible suspense, ran out to greet him. The heir, in horror, blew his horn again, and the servants loosed the dog. The heir killed it with one thrust, but the condition was broken, the father had reached him first, and for nine generations no Lord of Lambton died in his bed.

[Type: 300. Motifs: BII.2.I.3; BII.2.12; BII.II; BII.12.4.I; C631; C984; C987; MI0I]

Lamia. A fairy creature which never got out of book-lore into living tradition, though it must have been a familiar figure to a great number of literate children in the 17th century, for it appeared in Topsell's *The Historie of Foure-Footed Beastes* (1607). All the early copies of this book

are in poor condition because they were so much handled by children. The Lamia is an invention of the classical imagination, but it is clear that this was working upon a foundation of traditional folklore. Topsell's article is illustrated by a woodcut of a creature as unlike one's ordinary idea of a fairy as possible: a scaly, four-legged creature, with hoofs behind and paws in front, with a woman's face, a hermaphrodite with a man's organ and woman's breasts.

The first paragraph tells of SHAPE-SHIFTING spirits, which were conjured away by railing as a WAFF can be dismissed.

This word *Lamia* hath many significations, being taken sometimes for a beast of *Lybia*, sometimes for a fish, and sometimes for a Spectre or apparition of women called Phairies. And from hence some have ignorantly affirmed, that either there were no such beasts at all, or else that it was a compounded monster of a beast and a fish, whose opinions I will briefly set downe. *Aristophanes* affirmeth, that he heard one say, that he saw a great wilde beast having severall parts resembling outwardly an Oxe, and inwardly a Mule, and a beautifull woman, which he called afterwards *Empusa*.

When *Appollonius* and his companions travailed in a bright Moone shine night, they saw a certaine apparition of Phairies, in latine called *Lamia*, and in Greeke *Empusa*, changing themselves from one shape into another, being also sometimes visible, and presently vanishing out of sight againe: as soone as he perceaved it, he knew what it was and did rate it with very contumelious and despightfull words, exhorting his fellowes to do the like, for that is the best remedie against the invasion of Phairies. And when his companions did likewise raile at them, presently the vision departed away.

Some kind of use as a NURSERY BOGIE is suggested in the next paragraph:

Of these, *Angelus Policianus* relateth this old wives story, in his preface uppon *Aristotles* first booke of *Analitickes*, that his grandmother tolde him when he was a childe, there were certaine Lamiae in the wildernes, which like Bug-beares would eat up crying boies, and that there was a little Well neare to *Fesulanum*, being very bright, yet in continuall shaddow, never seeing Sun, where these Phairy women have their habitation, which are to be seene of them which come thither for water.

Topsell goes on to tell at some length the story of Apollonius and Menippus, which was afterwards more concisely told by BURTON in *The Anatomie of Melancholy*. It is worth giving in that form as being the passage upon which Keats founded his poem 'Lamia'. It is quoted by Buxton Forman in his edition of Keats:

Philostratus, in his fourth book *de Vita Apollonii*, hath a memorable instance in this kind, which I may not omit, of one Menippus Lycius, a young man twenty-five years of age, that going betwixt Cenchreas and Corinth, met such a phantasm in the habit of a fair gentlewoman, which, taking him by the hand, carried him home to her house, in the suburbs of Corinth, and told him she was a Phoenician by birth, and if he would tarry with her, he should hear her sing and play, and drink such wine as never any drank, and no man should molest him; but she, being fair and lovely, would live and die with him, that was fair and lovely to behold. The young man, a philosopher, otherwise staid and discreet, able to moderate his passions, though not this of love, tarried with her a while to his great content, and at last married her, to whose wedding, amongst other guests, came Apollonius; who, by some probable conjectures, found her out to be a serpent, a lamia; and that all her furniture was, like Tantalus' gold, described by Homer, no substance but mere illusions. When she saw herself descried, she wept, and desired Apollonius to be silent, but he would not be moved, and thereupon she, plate, house, and all that was in it, vanished in an instant: many thousands took notice of this fact, for it was done in the midst of Greece.

Topsell interprets the lamiae as allegories of harlots:

So the Lamiae are but poeticall alligories of beautifull Harlottes, who after they have had their lust by men, doe many times devour and make them away, as we read of *Diomedes* daughters, and for this cause also Harlots are called *Lupae*, shee-Wolves, and *Lepores*, Hares.

[Type: 507C. Motif: B29.1]

Land of the Young, the. See TIR NAN OG.

Last Word, the. In dealing with evil spirits and BOGLES as well as the Devil, it was important to have the last word. The BLUE MEN OF THE MINCH are an example of this. They were evil sea-spirits who used to swim out by the Minch (the strip of water between Lewis and the mainland of Scotland), and the captain of the boat had to hold parley with them and get the last word, preferably in rhyme, or they would sink his ship.

Lazy Laurence. According to Ruth Tongue, Lazy Laurence was a guardian spirit of the orchard, both in Hampshire and in Somerset. Probably the name was once more widely spread, if the title of Maria Edgeworth's story *Lazy Laurence* (set in the village of Aston, near Bristol) is more than a coincidence. In Hampshire, he sometimes took the form of a colt and chased orchard thieves, like the COLT-PIXY. In Somerset, Lazy Laurence seems rather to afflict the thieves with what is described in one of the night spells (to be found in British Museum MS. 36674), as 'Crampe and crookeing and fault in their footing'. The Somerset proverbial saying runs,

> Lazy Laurence, let me goo,
> Don't hold me Summer and Winter too.

From this we may deduce that Lazy Laurence is one of the cautionary fairies, like MELSH DICK and AWD GOGGIE.
[Motifs: F234.1.8; F403]

Leanan-Sidhe (*lan-awn shee*), the 'Fairy Mistress'. Virtually the same as the LHIANNAN-SHEE of Man, though a different and more favourable interpretation is put on her by Lady WILDE in *Ancient Legends of Ireland* (vol. I, p. 257). She says, 'The *Leanan-Sidhe*, or the spirit of life, was supposed to be the inspirer of the poet and singer, as the *Ban-Sidhe* was the spirit of death, the foreteller of doom.' YEATS, however, explains the Leanan-Sidhe as the spirit that inspires poets and singers, burning them up, so that their earthly life is brief.

[Motifs: A465.1.1; F471.2.1]

'Legend of Mullaghmast, The'. Earl Fitzgerald (Gearoidh Iarla) is the Irish hero of the widespread legend of the SLEEPING WARRIORS. He was the son of the fairy AINE and Gerald, Earl of Desmond. Through the breach of a TABOO he had disappeared into an underground resting-place, but there are different versions of the story. This, which is the best-known, is given by Patrick Kennedy in his *Legendary Fictions of the Irish Celts* (pp. 153–6). Earl Fitzgerald was a champion of the Irish against the Normans, and as well as a great warrior he was a great master of magic. His lady had often heard of his power of SHAPE-SHIFTING, but she had never seen any evidence of it and she kept begging him to show her what he could do. He often put her off, and at last he warned her that if she cried out or gave any sign of fear while he was under enchantment he would disappear out of this world and would have no power to return to it till many generations of men had passed away. But she said proudly that she was the wife of a great warrior and knew better than to show fear. So he turned himself in a twinkling into a beautiful goldfinch and flew up on to her hand. They played merrily together, and he flitted out of the window for a moment, but sped in again to take refuge in her breast with a great hawk behind him. His lady screamed out and beat at the hawk and it swerved and dashed against the wall and fell dead. But when his lady looked down for her goldfinch he was nowhere to be seen, and she never saw Earl Fitzgerald again. He and his warriors are sleeping in a long cave under the Rath of Mullaghmast, as Arthur sleeps under Cadbury. Once in seven years they ride round the rath on white horses shod with silver. Their shoes were once half an inch thick and when they are worn as thin as a cat's ears, Earl Fitzgerald will return again and reign as king over Ireland. Once in seven years the door of the cave is open, and one night, over a hundred years ago, a drunken horse dealer went in. He was terrified at the sight of the slumbering host, and when one of them raised his hand and said, 'Is it time yet?' he answered hastily, 'Not yet, but it will be soon,' and fled from the cave. Arthur and Fitzgerald both had fairy blood in them; but the same may not be true of Charlemagne or Frederick Barbarossa, two other famous sleeping warriors.

[Type: 766. Motifs: A560; A571; D150]

Lepracaun (*lep-ra-chawn*). Now generally described as a fairy shoemaker, while the CLURICAUNE haunts cellars and spends his time in
drinking and smoking and the FIR DARRIG is the practical joker of this
trio of SOLITARY FAIRIES. Crofton CROKER, however, merges the
lepracaun and cluricaune together, and regards the differences of names
as merely regional. He says (vol. I, p. 140):

> The Cluricaune of the county Cork, the Luricaune of Kerry, and
> the Lurigadaune of Tipperary, appear to be the same as the Leprechan
> of Leinster, and the Loghery man of Ulster; and these words are
> probably provincialisms of Luacharma'n, the Irish for a pigmy.

On the other hand, Douglas HYDE derived the word 'lepracaun' from
leith bhrogan, the 'one-shoemaker', because he was generally seen working
at a single shoe. YEATS seems to think that the three names may represent
three aspects of one kind of fairy. For some reason the Lepracaun is now
used to represent all kinds of Irish fairies, but it is undoubted that the
Lepracaun and the Cluricaune are both solitary fairies, though it will be
seen that there are two aspects of the Fir Darrig. The various stories of
the Lepracaun are well and pleasantly represented by William Allingham's
poem, 'The Lepracaun':

I

Little Cowboy, what have you heard,
  Up on the lonely rath's green mound?
Only the plaintive yellow bird
  Sighing in sultry fields around,
Chary, chary, chary, chee-ee! –
Only the grasshopper and the bee? –
  'Tip-tap, rip-rap,
  Tick-a-tack-too!
  Scarlet leather, sewn together,
  This will make a shoe.
  Left, right, pull it tight;
  Summer days are warm;
  Underground in winter,
  Laughing at the storm!'
Lay your ear close to the hill.
Do you not catch the tiny clamour,
Busy click of an elfin hammer,
Voice of the Lepracaun singing shrill
  As he merrily plies his trade?
  He's a span
  And a quarter in height.
Get him in sight, hold him tight,
  And you're a made
  Man!

II

You watch your cattle the summer day,
Sup on potatoes, sleep in the hay;
   How would you like to roll in your carriage,
   Look for a duchess's daughter in marriage?
Seize the Shoemaker – then you may!
     'Big boots a-hunting,
      Sandals in the hall,
    White for a wedding-feast,
      Pink for a ball.
    This way, that way,
      So we make a shoe;
    Getting rich every stitch,
      Tick-tack-too!'
Nine-and-ninety treasure-crocks
This keen miser-fairy hath,
Hid in mountains, woods, and rocks,
Ruin and round-tow'r, cave and rath,
   And where the cormorants build;
     From times of old
     Guarded by him;
     Each of them fill'd
     Full to the brim
      With gold!

III

I caught him at work one day, myself,
   In the castle-ditch, where foxglove grows, –
A wrinkled, wizen'd, and bearded Elf,
   Spectacles stuck on his pointed nose,
   Silver buckles to his hose,
   Leather apron – shoe in his lap –
     'Rip-rap, tip-tap,
     Tack-tack-too!
   (A grasshopper on my cap!
     Away the moth flew!)
   Buskins for a fairy prince,
     Brogues for his son, –
   Pay me well, pay me well,
     When the job is done!'
The rogue was mine, beyond a doubt,
I stared at him; he stared at me;
   'Servant, Sir!' 'Humph!' says he,
   And pull'd a snuff-box out.

> He took a long pinch, look'd better pleased,
> The queer little Lepracaun;
> Offer'd the box with a whimsical grace, –
> Pouf! he flung the dust in my face,
> And, while I sneezed,
> Was gone!

This follows the general plot of the lepracaun stories, in which the human captor of a lepracaun is always thwarted, but Lady WILDE has a rather different account of them in her *Ancient Legends of Ireland* in 'The Leprehaun' (vol. I, p. 103). In this the Leprehaun is described as a merry little fellow dressed all in green, instead of wearing a red cap, a leather apron, drab clothes and buckled shoes, and the boy, who has fairy blood in him, succeeds in winning a wealth of treasure from an underground cave, keeps his gain secret and is the founder of a prosperous family. The last thing to expect from folk tradition is consistency.

[Motifs: F369.4; F451.0.1]

Lhiannan-Shee (*lannan-shee*), **the**. The Lhiannan-Shee of Man is generally treated as a vampirish spirit who attaches herself to one man, to whom she appears irresistibly beautiful, but is invisible to everyone else. If he yields to her seduction, he is ruined body and soul. The Irish LEANAN-SIDHE is more favourably regarded, as a life-giving spirit, the inspiration of poets and minstrels. Both names mean 'the fairy sweetheart'. The Lhiannan-Shee of Ballafletcher was, however, the tutelary spirit of the Fletchers, and gave them the FAIRY CUP, which was drained every Christmas in her honour. Like MELUSINE, the Lhiannan-Shee haunted wells and springs.

[Motif: F471.2.1]

Liban. The sanctified MERMAID, who may possibly account for the presence of some of the mermaids who so often occur in church carvings.

Liban is briefly mentioned in *The Annals of the Kingdom of Ireland* by the Four Masters, a history compiled in the 17th century and covering the time from the creation of the world down to the year 1616. The year 558 is given as the one in which Liban was caught in a net on the strand of Ollarbha, but her personal history goes back some 300 years earlier. Her whole story is given by P. W. Joyce in *Old Celtic Romances* (1894).

Liban was one of the daughters of EOCHAID and presumably of ETAIN. In the year 90 a sacred spring which had been sacrilegiously neglected overflowed its bounds and formed the great water of Lough Neagh. Eochaid and all his family were overwhelmed and drowned, except his two sons, Conang and Curman, and his daughter Liban. Liban was indeed swept away by the waters, but she and her pet dog were supernaturally preserved and carried into a subaqueous cave where she spent a year in her bower with no company except her little dog. She grew weary of this after a time, and prayed to God that she might be turned into a salmon and swim around with the shoals of fish that passed her bower. God so far granted her prayer as to give her the tail of a salmon, but from the navel upwards she retained the shape of a beautiful woman. Her dog was turned into an otter, and the two swam round together for 300 years or more. In this time Ireland had become Christian and St Comgall had become Bishop of Bangor. One day Comgall dispatched one of his clergy, Beoc, to Rome to consult Pope Gregory about some matters of order and rule. As they sailed they were accompanied by a very sweet voice singing from under the water. It was so sweet that Beoc thought that it must be an angel's voice. At that Liban spoke from under the water and said: 'It is I who am singing. I am no angel, but Liban the daughter of Eochaid, and for 300 years I have been swimming the seas, and I implore you to meet me, with the holy men of Bangor, at Inver Ollarba. I pray you tell St Comgall what I have said, and let them all come with nets and boats to draw me out of the sea.'

Beoc promised to do as she asked, pressed on on his errand, and before the year was over had returned from Rome, in time to tell St Comgall of Liban's prayer. On the appointed day a fleet of boats was there, and Liban was drawn out of the water by Beoan, son of Inli. They half-filled the boat in which she was caught with water, and crowds of people came to see her swimming around. A dispute arose as to who had the right to her. St Comgall thought she was his as she was caught in his diocese; Beoc claimed her because she had made her appeal to him; and even the man who had drawn her out of the sea staked his claim. To avoid dissension all the saints of Bangor embarked on a night of fasting and prayer. An angel spoke to them and said that on the next morning a yoke of two oxen would come to them. They were to put Liban into a chariot and harness the oxen to it; wherever they stopped, that was the territory. It was a method employed in many saints' legends to settle the place where a church should be erected, and the expedient did not fail this time. The oxen drew their chariot undoubtingly to Beoc's church, Teo-da-Beoc. There she was given her choice whether to die immediately and ascend at once to heaven or to stay on the earth as long as she had lived in the sea, and to ascend to heaven after 300 years. She chose immediate death. St Comgall baptized her by the name of Murgen, or 'sea-born', and she made her entry into heaven. She was accounted one of the Holy Virgins, and signs and wonders were done through her means in Teo-da-Beoc.

[Motifs: F420.5.1.1; V229.2.12]

Licke. The name given to one of the small female fairies in the LIFE OF ROBIN GOODFELLOW. She is mentioned in ALLIES'S LIST OF THE FAIRIES, but Allies does not seem to have found any place-names which begin with 'Licke'. *The Life of Robin Goodfellow* makes her, by virtue of her name, the fairy cook:

> Licke is cook and dresseth meate,
> And fetcheth all things that we eat.

Life of Robin Goodfellow, The. A 17th-century pamphlet republished by HALLIWELL(-Phillipps) in *Illustrations of the Fairy Mythology of Shakespeare* and giving a very fair account of the traditions current at that time about ROBIN GOODFELLOW, or, as he is indifferently called, PUCK. The title 'The Life of Robin Goodfellow' was given to it by Halliwell, the black letter tract of 1628 which he reproduced being called *Robin Goodfellow; his mad prankes, and merry jests, full of honest mirth, and is a fit medicine for melancholy.* Carew Hazlitt combined Halliwell's book with Ritson's *Fairy Tales,* giving them together the title of *Fairy Tales, Legends and Romances illustrating Shakespeare and other Early English Writers.*

Li'l Fellas, the. This, like the GOOD NEIGHBOURS, the Mob, THEM-SELVES, is one of the Manx EUPHEMISTIC NAMES FOR THE FAIRIES, or FERRISHYN.

Linton Worm. A WORM or DRAGON supposed in the 12th century to have infested the small parish of Linton in Roxburghshire. It was probably a legless WORM and had a poisonous breath, which destroyed the cattle and men which it devoured. It was destroyed by Somerville of Lariston, who thrust a peat dipped in burning pitch down the throat of the monster. This not only neutralized its poisonous breath but burned out its entrails. The spiral ridges on Wormington Hill still bear witness to the worm's dying agonies. In the same way, ASSIPATTLE killed the MEISTER STOORWORM. Further details of the Linton Worm are given by William Henderson in *Folk-Lore of the Northern Counties* (pp. 295–7).
[Motifs: A2468.3; B11.2.1.1; B11.2.11.2]

Little Folk, the. See SLEIGH BEGGEY.

Little Old Man of the Barn, the. See BODACHAN SABHAILL.

Little People of the Passamaquoddy Indians, the. There are two kinds of Little People among the Passamaquoddy Indians, the Nagumwa-suck and Mekumwasuck. Both kinds are two and a half to three feet in height, and both are grotesquely ugly. For the following particulars we are indebted to Susan Stevens, an anthropologist married to the Chief of the Passamaquoddies.
   The Passamaquoddy Indians, of whom there are about 1,200 living

close to the Canadian border, used to migrate to the ocean in the summer and move inland in the winter. When they moved, their FAIRIES moved with them. Now they live permanently in two reservations, each of which has Nagumwasuck attached to it. These fairies are closely involved in all that happens to their humans, and can be heard singing laments when there is a death in the tribe and rejoicing and DANCING when there is a wedding. When a new church was built in the 1930s, they made a tiny stone church on the lake shore. People heard them hammering and singing at night, and in the morning discovered the church. They are very conscious of their ugliness, and do not like to be seen. It is almost fatal to laugh at them. Some little clay cylinders found on the shore at the ocean reservation are said to be the pipes of the Nagumwasuck, just as small clay pipes dug up in Ireland are said to belong to the fairies. One old lady told Susan Stevens that she and some other women had seen the Nagumwasuck leaving the reservation early one morning, going over the lake in a stone canoe. They said they might return one day when more people believed in them.

These Little People are seen only by the Indians. It is the same with the Mekumwasuck, who are also about two and a half to three feet in height. They live in the woods and are fantastically and individually dressed. Their faces are covered with hair, which strikes an alien note to the Indians. According to the oral report, they were made of stone, but this is omitted in Susan Stevens's written account. They are the guardians of the Catholic Church. The Passamaquoddy people were converted by the Jesuits at the very beginning of the 17th century. The Mekumwasuck are much dreaded, for if they look directly at any Indian he dies or is attacked by a contagious disease; an interesting example of BLIGHTS AND ILLNESSES ATTRIBUTED TO THE FAIRIES. One woman seeing a Mekumwasuck managed to avoid his gaze, but her companions were overlooked, and all fell ill; some died.

Some time about 1970 the priest was on vacation and some drunk men broke into the church to steal the holy wine, but the Mekumwasuck were on guard and drove them out of the church. One man stuck in the window, and they belaboured him until he broke loose. In 1971 or so a dance was held in Lent, at which Susan Stevens acted as chaperone. The priest had given permission, but the old people were uneasy about it. Suddenly a boy of sixteen who was taking part saw one of the Mekumwasuck. He was terrified and went to fetch his cousin to see if he could see it too. The cousin was very unwilling to look for fear he should draw a dangerous glance on him, but at length he looked and saw the spirit. The report went round, and the entire company of seventy-five people were out of the room in two minutes. It was much feared that a death would follow this visitation. Nothing happened, but there have been no dances in Lent since then. It seems possible that these Indian spirits are not native but are imported gargoyles. The function of gargoyles is to guard the church from the Devil by staring out in all directions. None of the glories of a Gothic church would be known to the converts, but homesick missionaries describing their native land might well give the impression to the Indians that the gargoyles were hideous spirits guarding the church. It is not the only time when carved figures have been taken for fairies. The CHESSMEN OF LEWIS are by now a well-known example.

[Motifs: F234.2.2; F239.4.3; F242.2; F246; F271.2; F388]

Little-Washer-by-the-Ford. A EUPHEMISTIC NAME for the BANSHEE and the BEAN-NIGHE.

Llamhigyn Y Dwr (*thlamheegin er doorr*), **or The Water-Leaper.** The Water-Leaper was the villain of Welsh fishermen's tales, a kind of water-demon which broke the fishermen's lines, devoured sheep which fell into the rivers, and was in the habit of giving a fearful shriek which startled and unnerved the fisherman so that he could be dragged down into the water to share the fate of the sheep. Rhys, from a second-hand account of it given him by William Jones of Llangollen, learned that this monster was like a gigantic toad with wings and a tail instead of legs.

[Motif: F420.5.2]

Llyr (*thleer*). The Welsh equivalent of the Irish god Lir, and possibly an underworld god. He was the father of Manawyddan and of BRAN THE BLESSED, whose tragedy is the subject of one branch of the MABINOGION. It has been suggested that King Lear was an euhemerized version of Llyr, but there seems to be no correspondence in their stories.

Lob-Lie-by-the-Fire. One of the old family of BROWNIES, larger than most, if Beaumont is to be believed, who says in *The Knight of the Burning Pestle* 'There is a pretty tale of a witch . . . that had a giant to her son that was called Lob-Lie-by-the-Fire.' He is generally equated with MILTON's 'Lubbar Fend' in *L'Allegro*. It will be remembered that in Blake's illustration of that passage the LUBBARD FIEND is of gigantic size.

Juliana Horatia EWING, in one of her excellent short stories founded on folk tradition, makes use of the legend of Lob-Lie-by-the-Fire. She sets it on the Scottish Border country and it is possible that she may have come across the tradition there, though it is not to be found in the list of spirits in the DENHAM TRACTS nor in William Henderson, and the literary references come from further south. Mrs Ewing's folklore is, however, generally reliable, so we may give her the benefit of the doubt.

Lobs and Hobs. Though the word 'HOBGOBLIN' is sometimes used to mean a devil, as in Bunyan's phrase 'Hobgoblin nor foul fiend shall daunt my spirit', and LOB-LIE-BY-THE-FIRE is called 'the Giant who had a witch to his Mother' by the Citizen's Wife in *The Knight of the*

Burning Pestle, the general use of the words 'hob' and 'lob' is a friendly one with rustic associations. The words belong to FAIRIES of the BROWNIE type, and only Puritans who thought all fairies were devils regarded them, as MILTON did, as fiends. See also HOB OR HOBTHRUST; HOBMEN.

[Motif: F475]

Loireag (*lorryack*). In the Hebrides the Loireag is a water-fairy, but like the Lowland HABETROT she is a patroness of spinning. Grant Stewart in his *Popular Superstitions* said, 'She presided over the warping, weaving and washing of the web, and if the women omitted any of the traditional usages and ceremonies of these occasions, she resented their neglect in various ways.' Like all FAIRIES she was a connoisseur of music and was angry if one of the women had a harsh voice or sang out of tune. In Carmichael's *Carmina Gadelica*, the Loireag is described by a man from Benbecula as 'a small mite of womanhood that does not belong to this world but to the world thither', and as a 'plaintive little thing, stubborn and cunning'.

[Motifs: F271.4.3; F420.5.1]

Lone Sod, the. See STRAY SOD.

Love-Talker, the. See GANCONER.

Lubbard Fiend, the. John MILTON's country roots were at Forest Hill, and his fairy traditions were true to those of Oxfordshire and the surrounding counties. It is worth giving the whole fairy passage in *L'Allegro* in spite of its general familiarity:

> With stories told of many a feat,
> How Faery Mab the junkets eat,
> She was pincht, and pull'd she sed,
> And he by Friars Lanthorn led
> Tells how the drudging Goblin swet,
> To ern his Cream-bowle duly set,
> When in one night, ere glimps of morn,
> His shadowy Flale hath thresh'd the Corn
> That ten day-labourers could not end,
> Then lies him down the Lubbar Fend,
> And stretch'd out all the Chimney's length,
> Basks at the fire his hairy strength;
> And crop-full out of dores he flings,
> Ere the first Cock his Mattin rings.

'Lubbar Fend' is Milton's name for LOB-LIE-BY-THE-FIRE, a HOB-GOBLIN who performs the usual BROWNIE feats of threshing and cleaning, and like the brownie and many other hobgoblins is a spirit of the hearth. Though it is a youthful poem, Milton's Puritan bias is shown in his calling Lob a fiend as well as a GOBLIN. Some though not all Puritans identified all FAIRIES with the lesser devils, though Baxter and Cotton Mather considered the possibility that they might be 'spiritual animals'. William Warner, in his poem *Albion's England* (Chapter 21), made the ingenious suggestion that the brownie actually did no work himself, but got the housewife out of bed to do it in her sleep. All kinds of theories were brought forward in the long debate about the ORIGIN OF FAIRIES. The bleaker view is not original to the Puritans, but is to be found in such tales as ST COLLEN AND THE FAIRY KING.

The rest of the passage is also interesting with its reference to fairy MAB and the incident of the stolen junket; at least one may presume that this is a version of the tale of 'The Brownie of Cranshaws'. 'Friar's Lanthorn' as a name of WILL O' THE WISP has led to the presumption that it is attached to FRIAR RUSH. This connection is not mentioned in the chapbook version of the tale, and has been disputed, but it may be considered as a possibility.

Lubberkin. An Elizabethan diminutive of 'lubber', probably from the same stem as LOB. Used of foolish and clownish people, as in 'land-lubber'. The ABBEY LUBBER is the most familiar use in fairy-lore.

'Lucky Piggy'. See ARKAN SONNEY.

Lug, or Lugh (*lugh*). Lug, called *Lamfhada* ('of the long arm') or *Samildanach* ('many-skilled'), was one of the sons of the DAGDA to whom a BRUGH was allotted when ANGUS OG was forgotten. A story was told about him in *The Book of Conquests* of how he came to Tara in the time of Nuada of the Silver Hand and asked to join the Tuatha. He was told that only one claiming a special skill could be admitted. He claimed skill as a carpenter, a smith, a warrior, a poet, a harper, a historian, a hero and a sorcerer. He was told that all these posts were already filled. He asked if there was any man there who possessed all the skills at once; on those grounds he was admitted into the Tuatha. Lug was handsome and polished, unlike his father, the Dagda, who was a more primitive deity. It was Lug who killed Balor of the one eye, the leader of the FOMORIANS, and put an end to the long war between them and the TUATHA DE DANANN.

[Motifs: A141; A151.1.1]

Luideag (*lootchak*). This name, which means 'The Rag', belonged to a murderous female demon who haunted a lochan (the Lochan of the Black Trout) in Skye. She was as squalid in appearance as she was evil in disposition and an account of her can be found in Mackenzie, *Scottish Folk Lore and Folk Life* (p. 251).

[Motifs: G11.3; G346.2]

Lull. The name of one of the female FAIRIES in the the LIFE OF ROBIN GOODFELLOW. Following as usual the guidance of the name, the anonymous author makes her the nurse of the fairy babies:

> Lull is nurse and tends the cradle,
> And the babes doth dresse and swadle.

In ALLIES'S LIST OF THE FAIRIES he finds quite a number of place-names beginning with 'Lul'.

Lunantishee. Evans Wentz was told by an informant, Patrick Waters, who was enumerating the different types of FAIRIES, that the Lunantishee are the tribe that guards the blackthorn bushes, and will allow not a stick to be cut on 11 November (originally All Hallows Day) or on 11 May (originally May Day). If you cut blackthorn on those days, some misfortune will befall you. Blackthorn is one of the FAIRY TREES.

[Motif: F441.2]

Luridan. The unknown author of the 'Discourse upon Divils and Spirits' which was inserted into the 1665 edition of Reginald SCOT's *Discoverie of Witchcraft* included an account of an astral spirit or familiar which worked like a BROWNIE but seems to have talked rather like the spirits raised by DEE whose conversation was reported by Meric Casaubon. The whole chapter is as unlike as possible to the sturdy scepticism shown by Scot, and well illustrates the uprise of credulity towards the end of the 17th century, when the belief in FAIRIES and magic flickered high like a dying flame.

> Luridan, a familiar [the author says], did for many years inhabit the Island Pomonia, the largest of the Orcades in Scotland, supplying the place of Man-servant and maid-servant with wonderful diligence to these Families whom he did haunt, sweeping their rooms, and washing their dishes and making their fires before any were up in the morning. This Luridan affirmed, That he was the Genius Astral, of that Island, that his place or residence in the dayes of Solomon and David was at Jerusalem; That then he was called by the Jewes Belelah, and after that he remained Long in the Dominion of Wales, instructing their Bards in Brittish Poesy and Prophesies, being called Urthin, Wadd, Elgin: And now said he, I have removed hither, and alas my continuance is but short, for in 70 years I must resigne my place to Balkin, Lord of the Northern Mountains.

[Motifs: F480; F482.5.4]

Lutey and the Mermaid. Long ago Lutey of Cury, near Lizard Point, a Cornish fisherman and wrecker, was combing the beach for jetsam when he found a beautiful MERMAID stranded in a pool by the receding tide. She persuaded him to carry her down to the sea. As they went she offered him three wishes, and he chose those he thought would do good: the power to break the spells of witchcraft and to compel familiar spirits for the good of others, and that these powers should descend in his family. She granted these, and because he had wished unselfishly said that none of his family should come to want, and gave him her comb by which he could summon her. Then, as they grew near the sea, the more sinister side of her nature showed itself. She began to allure him to go with her, and tightened her grasp on his neck. So great were her allurements that he would have gone with her, but his dog howled to him from the shore, and he saw his own cottage where his wife and children lived,

13. Sir John Everett Millais: Ferdinand Lured by Ariel

14. Sir Joseph Noel Paton: The Reconciliation of Oberon and Titania

15. Sir Joseph Noel Paton: Thomas the Rhymer

16. Edward William Hopley: A Fairy and a Moth

17. R. Huskisson: Titania Asleep

18. Vernon Hill: Allison Gross

19. Thomas Stothard: illustration to *The Rape of the Lock*

Gorse

20. Cicely Mary Barker: Gorse

21. Kay Nielsen: illustration from *In Powder and Crinoline*

and told her to let him go. Even so she clung to him, and would have pulled him down, but he flashed his knife in her face, and, presumably repelled by the IRON, she plunged into the sea, calling, 'Farewell my sweet, for nine long years, then I'll come for thee my love.'

The mermaid was as good as her word, and for generations the Luteys of Cury were famous healers, and prospered by their art. The first Lutey, however, only enjoyed his powers for nine years, for at the end of that time, when he was out in his boat with one of his sons, a beautiful woman rose out of the sea and called him. 'My hour is come,' he said, and he plunged into the water, never to be seen again. And they say that ever after, every nine years, one of his descendants was lost in the sea. This is the grimmer version given by BOTTRELL from the narrative of a WANDERING DROLL-TELLER in *The Traditions and Hearthside Stories of West Cornwall* (vol. I). The mermaid in HUNT's 'OLD MAN OF CURY' is a less sinister character.

[Type: ML4080. Motifs: B81.13.2; B81.13.13*; F420.3.1; F420.5.2.1; F420.5.2.1.6]

Mab. In the 16th and 17th centuries most of the poets made Queen Mab the queen of the Fairies, and particularly of the DIMINUTIVE FAIRIES of Drayton's *Nimphidia*. Shakespeare's Queen Mab as mentioned in *Romeo and Juliet*, the fairies' midwife, who gives birth to dreams, is of the same sort, with a coach drawn by insects – a very much less dignified person than his TITANIA in a MIDSUMMER NIGHT'S DREAM. This minute Queen Mab, however, probably comes from a Celtic strain and was once much more formidable, the Mabb of Wales, with possibly some connection with the warlike Queen MAEVE of Ireland. In Ben Jonson's *Entertainment at Althorpe* she is a PIXY type of fairy, described as an 'Elfe' with no royalty about her:

> This is MAB, the mistris-Faerie,
> That doth nightly rob the dayrie;
> And can hurt, or helpe the cherning,
> (As shee please) without discerning...
> Shall we strip the skipping jester?
> This is shee, that empties cradles,
> Takes out children, puts in ladles:
> Traynes forth mid-wives in their slumber,
> With a sive the holes to number.

> And then leads them, from her borroughs,
> Home through ponds, and water furrowes.

In one of the British Museum magical manuscripts (Sloane MS. 1727), she is mentioned as 'Lady to the Queen'. Jabez ALLIES in his chapter on the IGNIS FATUUS in *The Antiquities of Worcestershire* says that 'Mab-led' was used for PIXY-LED. Evidently Jonson followed the same tradition.
   [Motif: F369.7]

Mabinogion (*mabinogeeon*), **The.** Originally a selection of eleven stories from the two most famous of the ancient books of Wales, the *White Book of Rhydderch* (written down about 1300–25) and the *Red Book of Hergest* (1375–1425), and from the 16th-century manuscript, the *Hanes Taliesin*. They were chosen and translated by Lady Charlotte Guest in 1840, and it was she who first named the book *The Mabinogion*, which she believed to be the plural of 'Mabinogi', a title that applies properly only to the first Four Branches of Pwyll, Branwen, Manawydan and Math, but which became so well-known that it has been used also for later translations. The book contains the Four Branches of the Mabinogi, 'The Dream of Macsen Wledig' and 'Lludd and Llefelys', then the early Arthurian tale, 'Culhwch and Olwen', 'The Dream of Rhonabwy' and three later Arthurian romances 'The Lady of the Fountain', 'Peredur' and 'Gereint Son of Erbin'. These last show how the Norman-French has entered into the Welsh Arthurian legend of the MATTER OF BRITAIN, but in *Culhwch and Olwen* we are half-way back to the mythological Arthur and in the land of fairy-tales where the hero is accompanied by a picked band of strong men with magical, specialized powers to aid him in the perform-ance of his quest. These manuscripts appear to represent the material used by the Welsh bards or *cyfarwydd's*. This was transmitted by word of mouth, and it would be centuries before it was written down, and there-fore these tales were probably very ancient indeed, as can be judged by the customs and linguistic turns which are built into them.

Macdonald, George (1824–1905). He was not a collector of folk-tales, though he was well versed in the folk traditions of his native county of Aberdeenshire. He was of Highland stock on both sides. His father was descended from one of the 120 fugitives who escaped from the Massacre of Glencoe. His great-great-grandfather – a piper – was blinded at Cul-loden. His grandfather – born on the day of the same battle – was a staunch Jacobite, but a more Puritan strain seems to have come into the family with his grandmother, and his parents were Congregationalists. His father was a farmer in the country near Huntly. George Macdonald obtained a small bursary at Aberdeen University, and later became a Congregationalist minister. His doctrine, however, was too broad for his flock, and he was asked to resign. As a layman, his sermons were in great

demand, and he supported himself by his writings. His fame chiefly rests
now on his fairy books and allegories, *The Princess and the Goblin*, *The
Princess and Curdie*, *Phantastes*, *The Lost Princess*, and *At the Back of the
North Wind*. He also wrote a number of short fairy-stories. Many of these
are founded on the French fairy tradition, but interesting touches of folk
tradition are to be found in the GOBLIN stories, such as the toeless feet of
the goblins, an example of the DEFECTS OF THE FAIRIES, as in the
tradition recorded in *Sir Gibbie* of the undivided fingers of the BROWNIE.
There are fascinating glimpses of fairy traditions running through
Phantastes, and C. S. Lewis has well described George Macdonald as a
'myth-maker', a quality he shares with TOLKIEN.

Macha (*ma-cha*). One of the triple forms taken by the ancient Irish war
goddess BADB. All are in the shape of Royston or hoodie crows. Macha
is a fairy that 'riots and revels among the slain', as Evans Wentz puts it in
his analysis of Badb's triple form.
  [Motifs: A132.6.2; A485.1]

Mac Ritchie, David (b. 1800). Though his private life seems to have
been largely forgotten, Mac Ritchie was chief author of one of the

THEORIES OF FAIRY ORIGINS which received wide support when it was first brought forward in his two books, *The Testimony of Tradition* (1890) and *Fians, Fairies and Picts* (1893). In the introduction to the second of these books, Mac Ritchie describes how the idea of an ethnological origin of the fairy traditions first came into his head. He says:

It is now a dozen years or thereabouts since I first read the 'Popular Tales of the West Highlands', by Mr J. F. Campbell, otherwise known by his courtesy-title of 'Campbell of Islay'. Mr Campbell was, as many people know, a Highland gentleman of good family, who devoted much of his time to collecting and studying the oral traditions of his own district and of many lands. His equipment as a student of West Highland folklore was unique. He had the necessary knowledge of Gaelic, the hereditary connection with the district which made him at home with the poorest peasant, and the sympathetic nature which proved a master-key in opening the storehouse of inherited belief. It is not likely that another Campbell of Islay will arise, and, indeed, in these days of decaying tradition, he would be born too late.

In reading his book, then, for the first time, what impressed me more than anything else in his pages were statements such as the following:–

'The ancient Gauls wore helmets which represented beasts. The enchanted king's sons, when they come home to their dwellings, put off *cochal* (a Gaelic word signifying, the husk), and become men; and when they go out they resume the *cochal*, and become animals of various kinds. May this not mean that they put on their armour? They marry a plurality of wives in many stories. In short, the enchanted warriors are, as I verily believe, nothing but real men, and their manners real manners, seen through a haze of centuries.'

And much more to the same effect, with which it is unnecessary to trouble the reader. Now, all this was quite new to me. If I had ever given a second thought to the so-called 'supernatural' beings of tradition, it was only to dismiss them, in the conventional manner, as creatures of the imagination. But these ideas of Mr Campbell's were decidedly interesting, and deserving of consideration. It was obvious that tradition, especially where there had been an intermixture of races, could not preserve one clear, unblemished record of the past; and this he fully recognized. But it seemed equally obvious that the 'matter-of-fact' element to which he refers could not have owed its origin to myth or fancy. The question being fascinating, there was therefore no alternative but to make further inquiry. And the more it was considered, the more did his theory proclaim its reasonableness. He suggests, for example, that certain 'fairy herds' in Sutherlandshire were probably reindeer, that the 'fairies' who milked those reindeer were probably of the same race as Lapps, and that not unlikely they were the people historically known as Picts. The fact that Picts once occupied northern

Scotland formed no obstacle to his theory. And when I learned that the reindeer was hunted in that part of Scotland as recently as the twelfth century, that remains of reindeer horns are still to be found in the counties of Sutherland, Ross, and Caithness, sometimes in the very structures ascribed to the Picts, then I perceived this to be a theory which, to quote his words, 'hung well together'.

At the Congress of the Folk-Lore Society held in 1891, the theory which Mac Ritchie brought forward was the subject of lively debate which is reproduced in R. M. Dorson's *Peasant Customs and Savage Myths* (vol. II, pp. 550–60). The views were given strong support on one side and opposed on the other. One may say that this is still to a certain extent true, though the idea has been a seminal one to some theorists.

Maeve (*mayv*), **or Medb**. Maeve Queen of Connacht was the famous warrior queen of the Ulster Cycle. She was a mortal queen, but in continual strife with Ethal Anbual, king of the SIDH of Ulster, and with the mortal king of Ulster and his champion CUCHULAIN. It was she who led the Cattle Raid of Cuailagne in which the Brown Bull and the White Bull were captured, whose passionate enmity had all but destroyed Ireland. She was famous for her great display and her war chariots. The story of her raid and of the combats between her and the Sidh of Ulster is retold by James Stephens in his book, *In the Land of Youth*; and also in Eleanor Hull's book, *The Cuchullin Saga*.
[Motif: F364.3]

Magicians. Those learned men who, like Dr DEE, stretched the area of their learning to include magic and intercourse with spirits. Some of them restricted their studies to theurgic magic, in which they approached God by intensive prayer, and sought intercourse with angels; others called up the spirits of the dead in a kind of refinement of necromancy called 'sciomancy'. A step lower was to reanimate a corpse – true necromancy – as Edward Kelly was said to have done. Others engaged in more dangerous experiments still and tried to call up devils and confine them into a stone or magic circle. This was an exceedingly tedious, and was felt to be a highly dangerous, proceeding, for if the spirit raised succeeded in frightening the magician to the edge of his ring, so that a step backward would cause a fold of his robe or the heel of his foot to protrude, he would be liable to be seized and carried down to Hell. It was the tediousness and danger of these efforts to control the Devil that induced some magicians to take the last step down the slippery slope and sign the Diabolic Contract, thus becoming WIZARDS. There was an alternative to raising devils, and that was TRAFFIC WITH THE FAIRIES, of which we have mentions in the Scottish witch trials and in the North of England. To the Puritans as a whole, all FAIRIES were devils, but the country people generally took a more lenient view of the GOOD NEIGHBOURS.

'Maides Metamorphosis, The' (anon). See DIMINUTIVE FAIRIES.

Malekin. The 13th-century chronicler, Ralph of Coggeshall, produced three of the best of the EARLY FAIRY ANECDOTES: (a) the one of the GREEN CHILDREN; (b) a tale of the capture and escape of a MERMAN; and (c) a fascinating anecdote of a little fairy who haunted Dagworthy Castle in Suffolk. This fairy spoke in the voice of a one-year-old child and called herself Malekin. She was generally invisible, but she claimed to be a human child, stolen by the FAIRIES when her mother had carried her out into the cornfield and left her there while she worked. The knight's wife and the family were at first frightened of her, but soon got used to her and found her conversation and her pranks amusing. She talked broad Suffolk with the servants but Latin to the chaplain, with whom she discussed the Scriptures. Food was left out for her in an open armoire, and it always disappeared. She was on particularly friendly terms with one of the chamber-maids, and once this girl persuaded her to appear, after solemnly promising that she would neither touch nor try to detain her. She said that she looked like a tiny child, wearing a white tunic. Malekin said that seven years of her captivity was gone, and that after another seven she would be able to return to her home. Presumably the human food was of importance to her, as to eat FAIRY FOOD would mean that she was a perpetual CAPTIVE IN FAIRYLAND.

It is most interesting that in this, the earliest account of the CHANGE-LING from a fairy point of view, it is a little girl child who is taken, for in nearly all the later tales it is a boy, though of course young maidens are often carried off into Fairyland.

[Motifs: F321; F375]

Manannan (*manan-awn*) **son of Lir.** The chief Irish god of the sea, the equivalent of the Welsh LLYR, though their functions seem to have been rather different. Manannan had the Isle of Man under his protection, but he travelled the sea in his self-propelling boat, which went wherever he willed without oars or sail. His swine were the chief food of the TUATHA DE DANANN, for they were killed and eaten every day and came alive again the next morning. There seems a suggestion here of the feasting in the Scandinavian Valhalla on the carcase of a mighty wild boar which was hunted each day and feasted on every night. Manannan travelled the sea beyond which lay TIR NAN OG, the Land of the Young in which the Tuatha de Danann had taken refuge. Manannan was a war god with invulnerable armour, an invincible sword and a helmet which glinted like the sun on water. His father, Lir, a vaguer character, was yet more definitely a water-god.

[Motifs: A132.7; A421]

Mara, or Mera. An Old English name for a demon, which survives in NIGHT-MARE and 'mare's nest'. Gillian Edwards, in *Hobgoblin and*

Sweet Puck, discussing the origin of 'Mirryland', mentioned in ballads and sometimes in the witch trials, accepts D. A. Mackenzie's explanation of it as deriving from 'Mera'.

Marool, the. Perhaps the most malevolent of the Shetland MONSTERS. It is briefly but vividly described by Jessie Saxby in *Shetland Traditional Lore* (Chapter 9):

> The Marool was a sea-devil who took the form of a fish, and was a very malignant creature. He had a crest of flickering flame, and eyes all over his head. He often appeared in the centre of mareel – that is sea-foam when it is phosphorescent. He delighted in storm, and was heard to shout his wild exultant song when some luckless bark went under.

[Motif: G308]

Matter of Britain, the. The Arthurian legends were first called 'The Matter of Britain' by a 12th-century French poet, Jean Bodel, who spoke of 'those idle and pleasant tales of Britain' (*Chanson des Saisnes*, edited by Michel, Paris, 1939, vols. 6 ff.). He treated them frankly as legendary, but they had been thought of as genuine history as early as the year 679 by Nennius of South Wales in his *Historia Britonum*. He speaks of 'the warrior Arthur', and gives a list of the twelve battles in which he was victorious, ending with Mount Badon, where Arthur slew 960 men in one onslaught; 'no one laid them low save he'. Professor Collingwood in his book *Roman Britain* came to the conclusion that Arthur was an actual warrior who led a picked band, armed and deployed in the almost forgotten manner, to aid whatever king was in need of his services against invading Saxons. By Nennius's time, however, it is plain that legend had been at work, and indeed Nennius, among his 'wonders', gives us a real piece of Celtic tradition in the mark left by Arthur's foot in his legendary hunting of the boar Troynt with his dog Cabal.

As early as 1090 the Celtic traditions of Arthur had spread even down into Italy, and many children were baptized by the name of Artus. By the year 1113, the 6th-century warrior Arthur had become a King of Fairy, one of the SLEEPING WARRIORS whose return was confidently expected. At that date a riot broke out in Bodmin church. Some monks of Laon, visiting Cornwall on a collecting expedition, were shown King Arthur's chair and oven and their servants openly mocked the Cornishmen's belief that Arthur was still alive and would return to help his countrymen. The sacredness of the place in which they spoke did not prevent a furious retaliation.

It is of these beliefs that William of Malmesbury, a serious and scholarly historian, wrote a few years later in his *Gesta Regum Anglorum* (*Exploits of the English Kings*, 1125), 'He is the Arthur about whom the Britons rave in empty words, but who in truth is worthy to be the subject not of deceitful tales and dreams, but of true history.' The mythological treatment of the Matter of Britain is clearly shown in the tale of 'Culhwch and Olwen' from the Red Book of Hergest, a part of the MABINOGION. Here we have a god-like king surrounded by a lesser pantheon of knights with special and magical skills, very much like in atmosphere to many of the early Irish folk-tales. Something of this was known, as we have seen, outside the Celtic folk-tales, but it received comparatively little attention until in 1135 GEOFFREY OF MONMOUTH launched it as serious history in *Libellus Merlini*, afterwards incorporated into his *Historia Regum Britanniae*. This hit the popular taste between wind and water, in spite of the horrified protests of such serious historians as William of New-bridge and GIRALDUS CAMBRENSIS. R. F. Treharne in *The Glastonbury Legends* has pointed out how well suited Geoffrey's treatment was to catch the taste of the tough fighting men of his period, and how it became modified in the gentler and more civilized society of the later 12th and 13th centuries, so that the idea of a *gentleman* was evolved in the writings of Marie de France in England and Chrétien de Troyes in France, and in the works of many anonymous poets and prose writers. Geoffrey of Monmouth brought nationalistic fervour, delight in combat and a simple pleasure in magic into his historical background, but the later authors introduced their countrymen to chivalry and the idea of gentleness; and it was in a fairy world that they both moved.

Mauthe Doog. The local name for the MODDEY DHOO which haunted Peel Castle on the Isle of Man in the 17th century. It owes its fame to the lines in SCOTT's *Lay of the Last Minstrel* (Canto VI, v. 26):

> For he was speechless, ghastly, wan,
> Like him of whom the story ran,
> Who spoke the spectre-hound in Man.

[Motifs: F401.3.3; F402.1.11; G302.3.2]

Meanness. The country TROOPING FAIRIES were fertility spirits who admired lavish behaviour and were particularly annoyed by all grudging and covetous persons. They did labour without specific reward, but many BROWNIES left the service of a farm if a new inmate gave them inferior rations of milk and bread. Many fairy stories are based on the ill-luck of refusing a gift of BREAD to anyone who asks it. See also FAULTS CONDEMNED BY THE FAIRIES; VIRTUES ESTEEMED BY THE FAIRIES.

Medb (*mayv*). See MAEVE.

Medieval chronicles. It must not be supposed that the monastic chroniclers led entirely cloistered lives. It must be remembered that the monasteries acted as hospices in medieval times and that first-hand accounts of battles, crusades and courtly politics could be gathered by the

monks who were in charge of the chronicles. There was lively intercourse between the monasteries, and often personal friendships. It seems
likely, for instance, that Ralph of Coggeshall and William of Newbridge
were friends and exchanged material. Strange happenings and supernatural occurrences were eagerly recorded, and it is from these that we
gain some of the EARLY FAIRY ANECDOTES. Some chroniclers, however,
though they were churchmen were not monastics. Among these were
GEOFFREY OF MONMOUTH and his friend Walter Map – or Mapes,
GIRALDUS CAMBRENSIS and GERVASE OF TILBURY.

All these chroniclers record fairy beliefs of great interest. Ralph of
Coggeshall tells the story of MALEKIN and the GREEN CHILDREN, and
he gives a long account of a MERMAN:

> In the time of King Henry II, when Bartholomew de Glanville kept
> Orford Castle, it happened that the sailors there, fishing in the sea,
> caught a wild man in their nets, whom they brought to the Castellan
> as a curiosity. He was completely naked, and had the appearance of a
> man in all his parts. He had hair too; and though the hair of his head
> seemed torn and rubbed, his beard was profuse and pointed, and he
> was exceedingly shaggy and hairy about the breasts. The Castellan had
> him guarded for a long time, by day and night, lest he should escape
> into the sea. What food was put before him he ate eagerly. He preferred
> raw fish to cooked; but when they were raw he squeezed them tightly
> in his hands until all the moisture was pressed out, and so he ate them.
> He would not utter any speech, or rather he could not, even when hung
> up by his feet and cruelly tortured. When he was taken into the church
> he showed no sign of reverence or even of belief, either by kneeling or
> bowing his head at the sight of anything sacred. He always hastened to
> bed as soon as the sun sank, and stayed there until it rose again. Once
> they took him to the sea-gate and let him go into the water, after placing
> a triple row of very strong nets in front of him. He soon made for the
> deep sea, and, breaking through all their nets, raised himself again and
> again from the depths, and showed himself to those watching on the
> shore, often plunging into the sea, and a little after coming up, as if
> he were jeering at the spectators because he had escaped their nets.
> When he had played there in the sea for a long time, and they had lost
> all hope of his return, he came back to them of his own accord, swim-
> ming to them through the waves, and remained with them for another
> two months. But when after a time he was more negligently kept, and
> held in some distaste, he escaped secretly to the sea, and never after-
> wards returned. But whether he was a mortal man, or a kind of fish
> bearing a resemblance to humanity, or an evil spirit lurking in the body
> of a drowned man, such as we read of in the life of the blessed Audon, it
> is difficult to decide, all the more so because one hears of so many
> remarkable things, and there is such a number of happenings like this.

Walter Map gives an account of Nicholas Pipe, a Merman, but he was in Mediterranean waters.

William of Newbridge confirms the account of the Green Children, and tells of a fairy mound and the theft of a drinking horn – one of the earliest examples of THEFTS FROM THE FAIRIES.

Walter Map in *Nugis Curialium* has many stories, not all of them confined to England, for he was a travelled man. He tells the story of KING HERLA, and later in the book gives a reference to Herla's Rout. His story of WILD EDRIC is one of the earliest of the FAIRY BRIDE legends, with its characteristic TABOO. His 'Fairy Wife of Brecknock Mere' is even closer to modern Welsh tradition, and he gives a MELUSINE story, 'Henno cum Dentibus', and a story of a wife rescued from a troop of the dead which is very like a CAPTIVES IN FAIRYLAND tale.

Map's friend Geoffrey of Monmouth has earned great fame from giving the first literary presentation of the Arthurian legends, or the MATTER OF BRITAIN, and we are indebted to Giraldus Cambrensis for ELIDOR AND THE GOLDEN BALL. From Gervase of Tilbury we have the PORTUNES and the GRANT and the first MIDWIFE TO THE FAIRIES story, told about the Dracae of Brittany. Indeed, we reap a rich harvest from these early chronicles.

[Motif: B82.6]

Meg Mullach, Maug Moulach, or Maggie Moloch. Meg Mullach (Hairy Meg) is first mentioned in AUBREY's *Miscellanies* as one of a couple of BROWNIES who had long haunted the castle of Tullochgorm belonging to the Grants of Strathspey. In the letter which Aubrey quotes from a Scottish correspondent, they are mentioned incidentally: 'Whether this man saw more than Brownie and Meig Mallach, I am not very sure. . . Others affirm he saw these two continually, and sometimes many more.' Aubrey glosses this:

> *Meg Mullack*, and *Brownie* mentioned in the end of it, are two Ghosts, which (as is constantly reputed) of old haunted a Family in Strathspey of the Name of Grant. They appeared in the likeness of a young Lass: The Second of a young Lad.

In 1823, Grant Stewart amplified this account in his *Popular Superstitions of the Highlanders of Scotland*. He gives the male Brownie's name as BROWNIE-CLOD and describes 'Maug Vuluchd' as a most excellent housekeeper, overseeing the maid-servants and serving meals as by magic. 'Whatever was called for came as if it floated on the air, and lighted on the table with the utmost ease and celerity; and for cleanliness and attention, she had not her equal in the land.'

Elsewhere her powers of prophecy are celebrated, and it is said that she used to stand invisibly behind the laird's chair and direct his play at CHESS. At some time she and her companion – whether husband or son is left rather in doubt – went from Tullochgorm, and more sinister aspects of her character began to develop. According to Grant Stewart, she was called 'Hairy Meg' because of her wealth of brown hair, but it was later suggested that it meant 'the one with the hairy hand', and it was even reported to the synod of the local church that it was her hairy paw that came down the chimney and carried off babies. This was probably a confusion with that hairy claw which carried off children in several of the Irish fairy tales. For in this case Maug Moulach is called 'he'. George Henderson, in *Survivals in Beliefs Among the Celts*, goes so far as to call her the Devil. Nevertheless she has remained a brownie right into the present century. In a story preserved in the tape-recordings of the School of Scottish Studies and reproduced in *A Dictionary of British Folk-Tales in the English Language* (Part B), Maggie Moloch and her companion were haunting the mill of Fincastle in Perthshire in a dangerous way. The Nemo story, 'Me Myself', which we find in AINSEL, was reproduced here. The male brownie was scalded to death by a girl who was protecting herself from him. Maggie Moloch was temporarily deceived, but when she accidentally learned what had happened, she killed the girl who had destroyed her man. She still, however, continued to work as a brownie, and when a miserly farmer began to pay off his servants because she could do the work of all of them, she appeared among them and claimed her dismissal wages too, so that he had to change his plan to keep her.

It is unusual to have a female brownie, though the SILKIES do brownie work, and perhaps Maggie Moloch is distinguished also by the length of time her tradition has lasted, from at least the 17th century until well into the 20th.

[Type: 1137. Motifs: F346(a); F482.5.5; K602.1]

Melsh Dick. The wood-demon who protects the unripe nuts from children in the West Riding of Yorkshire. Through most of the North Country it is a female spirit, CHURNMILK PEG, who performs this office. The importance of nut thickets in earlier rural economy may be judged by the number of supernatural beliefs surrounding them, such as the appearance of the Devil to Sunday nut-gatherers, and the fertility value ascribed to nuts. 'So many cratches [baskets], so many cradles' is a Somerset proverb.

Melusine. The story of Melusine may be called the French romance version of the classical LAMIA. She was in folk tradition before the 14th century, when the legends about her were collected by Jean D'Arras in the *Chronique de Mélusine*. This was afterwards amplified by Stephen, a Dominican friar of the House of Lusignan. The story of Melusine was summarized by KEIGHTLEY in *The Fairy Mythology*. It is interesting as being the French version of the FAIRY BRIDE theme, repeated in two generations with the characteristic TABOO, violated as usual. The hero of the first part is a king of Albany, that is of Scotland, and one wonders if the first germ of the tale came from there.

King Elinas of Albania had lately lost his wife, and to divert his sorrow gave a great deal of his time to solitary hunting. One day he went to quench his thirst in a fountain, and as he approached it heard the sound of singing and found sitting beside it a most beautiful woman, the FAY Pressina. He fell at once in love with her, and she consented to marry him on the condition that he should never visit her at the time of her lying-in. In due time she had three daughters at a birth, Melusina, Melior and Palatina. The king's son by his first marriage ran to tell his father of the birth, and the king, overjoyed, hastened to her room, forgetting his promise. He found his wife bathing the babies. She cried out that he had broken his word and, snatching up the children, she vanished. She took refuge in Cephalonia, the Hidden Island, mentioned in the romance of HUON OF BORDEAUX. It was like that island off the coast of Wales which could only be found by chance. From the heights of the island she could see Albany, and she showed it to her children every day, telling them that if it was not for their father's perfidy they would all be living there in happiness. The children naturally became embittered against their father and resolved to revenge themselves on him. Melusina took her two sisters and together they enclosed their father and all his wealth in Mount Brandelois. Then they returned in triumph to their mother, who was much displeased, and punished Melusina by turning her into a serpent from the waist downwards. This infliction would come on her periodically until she met a man who would marry her on the condition of never seeing her on a Saturday, and who would keep that promise for ever. Melusine wandered through France in search of such a man until she came to the forest of Colombiers in Poitou, where the fays of the region greeted her and made her their queen. There Raymond of Poitou met her at the Fountain of Thirst, and married her under the stipulated condition. They were deeply in love with each other, and out of her fairy wealth she built for him many noble castles, the chief of them the Castle of Lusignan, near the Fountain of Thirst, or the Fountain of the Fays, as it was also called. They would have been blissfully happy but for the fact that every child born to them was deformed in some way. Raymond still loved his wife passionately, but one of his cousins poisoned his mind with suggestions that these children had another parent, and that Saturday was kept sacred for his visits. At length Raymond could bear the suspicion no longer, he hid behind the arras one Saturday night and saw his wife emerging from her bath one half a serpent. He still loved her so much that he resolved to keep her secret and say nothing even to her of what he had seen. The secret could not be kept. Some of their children were not only monstrous in appearance but in character. One of them, Geoffroi with the Tusk, was particularly evil. He was quarrelling with his brother Freimond, and when Freimond took refuge in the Abbey of Melliers, he set fire to it and burned his brother and a hundred monks. When the dreadful news came to Melusine she hurried to comfort her desolate husband; but in his grief he burst into reproaches: 'Get out of my sight, you pernicious snake! You have contaminated my children!' Melusine fainted at his words. When she revived she said: 'The curse is come on me. I must go. I am condemned now to fly through the air in pain till the Day of Judgement. Until this castle falls I shall appear before the death of each Lord of Lusignan, wailing and lamenting for the sorrows of the House.' She leapt on the window-sill, where the print of her foot remained as long as the castle stood, and vanished from the sight of Count Raymond and the court.

Melusine became the BANSHEE of Lusignan; and after the family had been destroyed and the castle had fallen to the Crown, she appeared before the death of any king of France, until at last the castle was destroyed by fire.

[Motifs: C31.1.2; F471.2.1; F582.1]

Mermaids. The general characteristics of a mermaid are clear and well defined. They date from times of great antiquity and have been retained unaltered almost to the present day. According to this set of beliefs, the mermaids are like beautiful maidens from the waist upwards, but they have the tail of a fish. They carry a comb and a mirror and are often seen combing their long and beautiful hair and singing with irresistible sweetness on some rock beside the sea. They allure men to their death and their appearance is ominous of storms and disasters. According to this set of beliefs, mermaids are not only ominous of misfortunes but actually provoke them, and are avid for human lives, either drowning men or devouring them. In some of the early Celtic descriptions they are monstrous in size, like that recorded with some detail in *The Annals of the Four Masters*. She was 160 feet in length, her hair eighteen feet (comparatively short), her fingers were seven feet in length, and so was her

nose. These exact measurements were possible because she was cast up by the sea. This was said to have happened in about A.D. 887.

Some sea monsters, such as NUCKELAVEE, were allergic to fresh water, but mermaids penetrated up running streams and were to be found in fresh-water lakes. They were still called mermaids. A typical example of a ravening mermaid is to be found in the story of 'The Laird of Lorntie' told by Robert Chambers in *Popular Rhymes of Scotland*:

> The young Laird of Lorntie, in Forfarshire, was one evening return-ing from a hunting excursion, attended by a single servant and two greyhounds, when, in passing a solitary lake, which lies about three miles south from Lorntie, and was in those times closely surrounded with natural wood, his ears were suddenly assailed by the shrieks of a female apparently drowning. Being of a fearless character, he instantly spurred his horse forward to the side of the lake, and there saw a beautiful female struggling with the water, and, as it seemed to him, just in the act of sinking. 'Help, help, Lorntie!' she exclaimed. 'Help, Lorntie – help, Lor –,' and the waters seemed to choke the last sounds of her voice as they gurgled in her throat. The laird, unable to resist the impulse of humanity, rushed into the lake, and was about to grasp the long yellow locks of the lady, which lay like hanks of gold upon the water, when he was suddenly seized behind, and forced out of the lake by his servant, who, farther-sighted than his master, perceived the whole affair to be the feint of a water-spirit. 'Bide, Lorntie – bide a blink!' cried the faithful creature, as the laird was about to dash him to the earth; 'that wauling madam was nae other, God sauf us! than the mermaid.' Lorntie instantly acknowledged the truth of this asse-veration, which, as he was preparing to mount his horse, was confirmed by the mermaid raising herself half out of the water, and exclaiming, in a voice of fiendish disappointment and ferocity:

> 'Lorntie, Lorntie,
>   Were it na your man,
> I had gart your heart's bluid
>   Skirl in my pan.'

This may be called the general picture, but no folk traditions are absolutely consistent, and there are a number of stories, like HUNT's 'The OLD MAN OF CURY', which show gentler traits. Possibly these may be influenced by the Scandinavian strain in Scotland, for the Danes, Swedes and Norwegians take a much more lenient view of the sea people than the Scots. A pleasant story of a mermaid giving medical advice is again quoted by Chambers from Cromek's *Nithsdale and Galloway Song*:

> A charming young girl, whom consumption had brought to the brink of the grave, was lamented by her lover. In a vein of renovating

sweetness, the good mermaid sung to him:

> 'Wad ye let the bonnie May die i' your hand,
> And the mugwort flowering i' the land?'

He cropped and pressed the flower-tops, and administered the juice to his fair mistress, who arose and blessed the bestower for the return of health.

Cromek always gives a favourable view of the FAIRIES, but this story is confirmed by a Renfrewshire anecdote of a mermaid who rose from the water as the funeral of a young girl passed, and said mournfully:

> 'If they wad drink nettles in March
> And eat muggons in May,
> Sae mony braw maidens
> Wadna gang to the clay.'

Muggons is mugwort, or southernwood, and was much used for consumptive disorders. Mermaids had a great knowledge of herbs as well as prophetic powers. The most noble of all the mermaids, however, is that in the Orcadian story who gave her life for one of the SELKIES. This story, by the way, raises an interesting point, for this mermaid, like the ASRAI, died from too long exposure to the air of this world, while others, like the selkies or ROANE, seem native to the air and need a cap or a magical property with which to make their passage through the sea. Some of them, like the selkies, were courted by human lovers and became unwilling wives, bequeathing webbed hands and feet to their children, but often also great skill in medicine, like that bequeathed in the story of LUTEY AND THE MERMAID.

Mermaids were often caught and held to ransom for the sake of the wishes they could grant or the knowledge they could impart. They always held exactly to their bargains, as even the Devil must do by the condition of his being, though the wishes are twisted if it can be contrived.

In Scotland and in Ireland the question of the possibility of final salvation for the mermaids, as for other fairies, is raised; it is always denied in Scotland, but in Ireland there is one mermaid, LIBAN, who died in the odour of sanctity, though it is only right to say that she was not born a mermaid, any more than Fintan, who was converted by St Patrick and afterwards canonized, was born a merman.

Anyone who wishes to study this long and complicated subject might well start by reading *Sea Enchantress* by Benwell and Waugh, which, starting with fish-tailed gods and working through classical myths and early zoology, comes down to the most recent beliefs in mermaids and other water creatures and embraces the beliefs of almost all nations. See also MERMEN.

[Types: ML4071*; ML4080. Motifs: B81.2.2; B81.3.1; F420.5.1; F420.5.1.8; F420.5.2; F420.5.2.1; F420.5.2.7.3]

Mermen. Though generally wilder and uglier than MERMAIDS, mermen have less interest in mankind. They do not, like the SELKIES, come ashore to court mortal women and father their children, nor are they jovial and friendly to men like the Irish MERROWS, and they do not crave for salvation like the Scandinavian *Neck*. If the gentle little mermaid who was put into the sea by the OLD MAN OF CURY was to be believed, they were rough husbands and were even capable of eating their own children if they were left hungry. They seem to personify the stormy sea, and it is they who raise storms and wreck ships if a mermaid is wounded. Benwell, however, describes the Scandinavian Merman or *Havmand* as a handsome creature with a green or black beard, living on cliffs and shore hills as well as in the sea, and says that he was regarded as a beneficent creature.

[Motifs: B82.6; F420.5.2]

Merrows, or the Murdhuacha (*muroo-cha*). The Irish equivalent of MERMAIDS. Like them they are beautiful, though with fishes' tails and little webs between their fingers. They are dreaded because they appear before storms, but they are gentler than most mermaids and often fall in love with mortal fishermen. The offspring of these marriages are some-times said to be covered with scales, just as the descendants of the ROANE, or SEAL PEOPLE, are said to have webs between their fingers. Sometimes they come ashore in the form of little hornless cattle, but in their proper shape they wear red feather caps, by means of which they go through the water. If these are stolen they cannot return to the sea again.

If the female merrows are beautiful, the male are very ugly indeed, with green faces and bodies, a red, sharp nose and eyes like a pig. They seem, however, to be generally amiable and jovial characters. A lively story by Crofton CROKER gives a pleasant picture of a merrow. It is called 'Soul Cages' and comes in *Fairy Legends of the South of Ireland* (vol. II, p. 30). This is a shortened version:

The female merrows are a lovely sight, with their flowing hair and their white, gleaming arms and their dark eyes; but the male merrows are nothing worth looking at, for they have green hair and green teeth and little pig's eyes and long red noses, and short arms more like flippers than any respectable arm that could do a day's work. For all that there was once one man that was very anxious to see a merrow, and that was Jack Dogherty, that lived with his wife Biddy in a snug little cabin hard by the seashore not far from Ennis. It was the more provoking that Jack could never catch a glimpse of one because his own grandfather had been so chief with a merrow that, if it hadn't been for offending the priest, he'd have asked him to stand godfather to his children; and here was Jack living in the very place and looking out day and night without so much as the glimpse of a fin. At last one day, on a rock about half a mile along the coast, Jack made out a shape of a creature, standing as still as a stone with

a thing like a red cocked hat on its head. It stood so still that he almost
thought it was a piece of the rock with the sunset on it; when suddenly he
gave a sneeze, and the thing plunged into the water, so Jack knew that he
had seen a merrow at last. But he was not content with that. He wanted a
word with it; and he hung round the merrow's rock day in, day out, and
sometimes he got a glimpse of it; but it was not until the powerful storms
set up at the back end of the year that he saw the creature at all close.
Then it would play about the rock as fearless as a pike after salmon, and
it happened at last one blowy day that Jack got right up to it. And an ugly
old fellow it was, with its scaly legs, ending in a bit of a tail, and its finny
arms and its long, strong, green teeth. But it rolled a friendly eye at him,
and said, just like a Christian: 'Good day to you, Jack Dogherty, and how
have you been keeping this while back?'

'Your Honour's very pat with my name,' said Jack, surprised.

'And why wouldn't I know your name?' said the merrow, 'and I like
a brother almost with your own grandfather. That was a great man, Jack.
There was never a one could put him under the table. I wonder now, do
you take after him.'

'I may not take after him all ways,' said Jack. 'But if it's liking liquor
and good liquor you mean I'm the very double to him. But I wonder
where Your Honour'd get the liquor out of the sea; unless it might be salt
water, which isn't to every man's taste.'

'Faith, and where do you get it yourself, Jack?' said the merrow,
winking at him.

Now Jack got the most of what he drank and what he sold too out of
the sea, for there was many a cask of good wine drifted up out of the
Atlantic to his cabin door; and though he'd never have been the one to
hurt poor sailors, he thought it no harm to take what they were past
wanting and could never use. So Jack winked back at the merrow, and
said:

'Oh, I take Your Honour now. But it's a big cellar ye'll be needing and
a dry cellar to keep all the sea gives you.'

'So it is then,' said the merrow. 'And if you come to this rock at this
time on Monday, we'll go further into the subject.' And with that it
turned and dived into the sea.

Next Monday Jack was there for certain; for he didn't mean to lose
his chance of making friends with a merrow after all the trouble he'd been
at. The merrow was there before him, and he had two cocked hats under
his arm instead of one.

'Here's a chance for you now, Jack,' he said. 'I've got a loan of a
second hat for you. Put it on, and you shall come and see my cellar, and
get a taste of it into the bargain.'

'Thank you, Your Honour,' said Jack. 'But a plain man like me would
be drowned plunging down into the sea like a fish.'

'Tush,' said the merrow. 'You're not a quarter what the grandfather

was before you. He never stood a minute when he first got the chance to
come down and see me.'

'Well, I won't be a worse man than my grandfather,' said Jack, 'so
lead on.'

'Well said!' said the merrow. 'Follow me, and hold on to my tail when
I go down.'

They swam out straight enough to a rock a little way out, and Jack
began to wonder what would happen next, when the merrow said: 'Hold
on now!' and down they went; down, down, down, with the water
rushing past Jack's head, so that he could neither see nor breathe, and it
was all that he could do to hold on. At last they landed bump on to some
soft sand, and Jack found he was in air again, as good to breathe as ever
he smelt. He looked up, and there was the sea above them, as it might be
the sky, and the fishes swimming about over their heads, like the birds
flying. In front of them was the merrow's house, with a strong spurt of
smoke going up from the chimney. They went inside, and a good dinner
was cooking of all kinds of fish, and a good meal they made of it, and a
grand drinking at the end of all kinds of strong spirits. Jack had never
felt his head cooler, it must have been the cold water above him; but the
old merrow got quite boisterous, and roared out all manner of songs,
though Jack couldn't call any of them to mind afterwards. He told Jack
his name too – Coomara it was, and Coo to his friends, for by this time
they were pretty snug together.

After they'd drunken as much as was comfortable, Coomara took Jack
to see his curiosities, and a grand museum of things he'd got, all of them
dropped out of the sea. The thing that puzzled Jack most was a great row
of wicker baskets, something like lobster pots.

'And what might you keep in those, Coomara?' he said.

'Oh, those are soul cages,' said Coomara.

'But the fish haven't souls, surely,' said Jack.

'No, not they,' said Coomara. 'Those are the souls of fishermen. I like
to have them about the place. So whenever there is a big storm up above,
I sprinkle those about the sand; and when the souls come down, they are
cold and frightened, having just lost their men, and they creep in here for
warmth; and then it fails them to get out again. And aren't they lucky,
now, to have a warm, dry place like this to stay?'

Jack said never a word, but he bent down by the soul cages, and
though he could see nothing, he fancied he heard a breath like a sob
when old Coo talked of their good luck. So he said goodbye; and old Coo
gave him a back up, and shoved him up into the sea; and he shot up faster
than he had come down, and threw his cocked hat back as Coomara had
told him, and went home very sad to think of the poor souls imprisoned
in their lobster cages.

Jack Dogherty turned over and over in his mind how he could free the
poor souls, but for a while nothing came to him. He didn't like to ask the

Priest, for he didn't want to get Coomara into trouble, and he didn't care to tell his wife or friends, for perhaps a man mightn't be well thought of who had dealings with the merrows; so at last he decided he must ask Coomara to his own house and make him very drunk, and then nip off his cap and go down and free the poor souls so that Coomara would never be the wiser. The first thing was to get his wife out of the way. So Jack turned very pious all of a sudden, and he told his wife it would be a grand thing if she would make a pilgrimage to pray for his soul and the souls of all poor fishermen drowned at sea. His wife was ready enough to go, for whoever heard of a woman would refuse a pilgrimage; and no sooner had he seen her back than Jack nipped over to the merrow's rock and invited old Coomara to come and dine with him at one o'clock next day and to see what he had about the place in the way of drink. Coomara came readily enough; and they kept it up together, drinking and singing; but Jack forgot this time that he had not the sea above him to keep his head cool; and the first thing he knew he wakened up with a black head-ache, and there was not a sign of old Coomara, who had drunk him under the table and walked off as cool as you please.

Poor Jack was quite downcast to think that the caged souls were as far from their freedom as ever; but luckily Biddy was to be a week away, and before that time was past he had a thought that gave him a glimmer of hope. Coomara was well seasoned to whiskey and brandy and rum; but it was likely he had never tasted a drop of the real Irish potcheen, for that is a spirit that is seldom put upon the sea. Now as it happened, Jack had a keg of it, brewed by his own wife's brother, so he thought he would see what it would do for Coomara. So back he went to the merrow's rock, where he found Coomara very cock-a-hoop at having put him under the table.

'I'll not deny that you're a sturdy drinker, Coomara,' said Jack. 'But I have something put aside that you've never tasted, and that's a keg of the real potcheen that I'd kept till last; only you slipped out whilst I was considering to myself for a few moments. Come back tomorrow and you shall have a taste of it; and that's a thing I wouldn't offer to everyone, for it's hard to come by.'

Coomara was very ready to come, for he had a curiosity to taste the stuff; and next day they set to it again. I wouldn't say Jack drank entirely fair, for he put water to what he took and Coomara took it neat, but fair or unfair he drank Coomara under the table; and he was no sooner there than Jack nipped the hat off his head and set off to the rock as fast as he could run. There was nobody to be seen at the bottom of the sea, and that was a lucky thing for Jack, for he'd have been hard put to it to explain what he was doing in Coomara's house. He took a great armful of the soul cages and took them out of the house and turned them up. He saw nothing at all, except it might be a little flicker of light coming out of each of them, and he heard a sound like a faint whistle going past him.

He emptied all the soul cages and put them back just as they had been, and then he was hard put to it to make his way up to the sea above him without Coomara to give him a back. But as he looked round he saw one bit of the sea that hung down lower than the rest, and as he walked under it a cod happened to put his tail down into the air, and quick as lightning Jack jumped up and caught the tail, and the cod pulled him into the sea and the red cap carried him up in a flash; and so he got to land. Coomara was still asleep, and when he waked he was so ashamed to be out-drunken that he sneaked off without a word. But he and Jack stayed very good friends, for he never noticed that the soul cages were empty; and often after a storm Jack would make some excuse to go down, and would free all the new souls that had been caught. So they went on in great friendship for many years; until one day Jack threw his stone into the water without success. Coomara never came. Jack did not know what to make of it. Coomara was a young slip of a fellow as merrows went, not more than a couple of hundred years at the most. He couldn't have died on him. So all Jack could think was that Coomara must have flitted and be living in another part of the sea. But Coomara had the second cocked hat, so Jack could never go down to find out.

[Motif: F725.3.3]

Merry Dancers. See FIR CHLIS.

Mester Stoorworm, the. The Orcadian Mester Stoorworm is a prime example of the Scandinavian DRAGON in Britain. There are two main types of dragon in these islands: the heraldic dragon, winged and usually fire-breathing, and the WORM, for which one generally supposes a Scandinavian origin, which is generally huge, often wingless and most commonly a sea monster. These worms are not fire-breathing, but have a poisonous breath. The Mester Stoorworm fulfilled all these qualifications. Traill Dennison, whose manuscript is reproduced in *Scottish Fairy and Folk Tales*, gives several descriptions of the creature.

> Now you must know [he says] that this was the largest, the first, and the father of all the Stoorworms. Therefore was he well named the Mester Stoorworm. With his venomous breath he could kill every living creature on which it fell, and could wither up everything that grew.

A little later, as ASSIPATTLE sails out towards the Stoorworm, the description becomes even more gargantuan:

> The monster lay before him like an exceedingly big and high mountain, while the eyes of the monster – some say he had but one eye – glowed and flamed like a ward fire. It was a sight that might well have terrified the bravest heart. The monster's length stretched half across the world. His awful tongue was hundreds on hundreds of miles long.

And, when in anger, with his tongue he would sweep whole towns, trees, and hills into the sea. His terrible tongue was forked. And the prongs of the fork he used as a pair of tongs, with which to seize his prey. With that fork he would crush the largest ship like an egg-shell. With that fork he would crack the walls of the biggest castle like a nut, and suck every living thing out of the castle into his maw.

Later, in his dying agony, he spews out his teeth and they become the Orkneys, the Faroes and the Shetland Islands. His forked tongue entangles itself on one horn of the moon and his curled-up body hardens into Iceland. The whole thing is an extravaganza, a fairy-tale, not a legend.

[Motifs: BI1.2.1.3; BI1.11]

Micol. A queen of the DIMINUTIVE FAIRIES, according to the 17th-century MAGICIANS. The spell for raising her is to be found in full in SPELLS TO OBTAIN POWER OVER FAIRIES. Lilly mentions it as used by Sarah Skelhorn. It begins, '*Micol, O tu Micol, Regina Pigmeorum*'.

[Motif: F239.4.3]

Midhir, or Midar. The fairy lover of ETAIN, the queen. According to Lady WILDE in her *Ancient Legends of Ireland* (vol. 1, pp. 179–82), Etain was a human, the wife of EOCHAID of Munster, and her beauty was so great that it reached the ears of Midar, one of the kings of the TUATHA DE DANANN, and he desired her, and won her from her husband in a game of CHESS. The more usual story is more complicated. According to this, Etain was the wife of Midhir in the land of TIR NAN OG, but his jealous first wife, Fuamnach, cast a spell upon her, turning her into a midge, and blew her on a bitter wind out of Tir Nan Og and into Ireland. Midhir searched for her and at last found her as the queen of Munster. When he had won her he appeared in the palace, ringed as it was with an armed guard, and he and Etain flew away through the lifted roof of the palace as two white swans linked with a golden chain. But that was not the end of it, for Eochaid brought bitter war against Midhir, and in the end, it is said, Etain went back to her mortal husband, and the great power of the Tuatha de Danann declined and dwindled for ever.

[Motifs: F322; F322.2]

Midsummer Night's Dream, A. The DIMINUTIVE FAIRIES of which we have some mentions in the MEDIEVAL CHRONICLES were first introduced into literature in the poetry and drama of Elizabethan times. We find them first in Lyly's *Endimion*, but here they are incidental. In *A Midsummer Night's Dream* they are among the principal characters with a sub-plot of their own, but are important agents in the main plot as well. There is no doubt that the FAIRIES are small – the ELVES creep into acorn cups to hide, find a bee's honey bag a heavy burden and a bat a formidable adversary. But they still have their powers. All of them can travel immense distances as swiftly as the moon. The chief ones among them can change their size and shape. When they quarrel, all nature is affected and the seasons are out of gear. Like all fairies they have great herbal knowledge; they have power over human offspring and can bless marriage beds. Like most fairies they are amorous of mortals. They have their FAIRY RADES like the HEROIC FAIRIES. These are good fairies, the SEELIE COURT, benevolent to mortals except for an occasional jest, ready to help those who are in need.

In other plays of Shakespeare there are mentions of fairies, the best-known, perhaps, being Mercutio's description in *Romeo and Juliet* of Queen MAB, the midwife of dreams, an intentionally comic description. There is the invocation to the fairies in *Cymbeline*, where, in pagan Britain, the fairies take the place of God. When we come to *The Tempest* we have full treatment of a fairy again, if we may call Ariel a fairy; he is perhaps rather an elemental – a sylph; but he can summon fairies to help him in his revels and he sings their songs.

Midwife to the fairies. From the earliest times there have been stories of mortal women summoned to act as midwives to fairy mothers among the themes of the DEPENDENCE OF FAIRIES ON MORTALS. One of the latest of these was of a district nurse summoned by a queer old man who boarded a bus near Greenhow Hill in Yorkshire. He conducted the nurse to a cave in the side of Greenhow Hill, and the occupants turned out to be a family of PIXIES. The interesting point here, since the pixies are not native to Yorkshire, is that Greenhow Hill was said to have been mined by Cornishmen. The anecdote had currency in the 1920s and after. The FAIRY OINTMENT motif does not occur in this version. The earliest version of the midwife tale is to be found in GERVASE OF TILBURY'S 13th-century *Otia Imperialis*. The fullest of all, perhaps the only com-

plete fairy midwife story, is given by John Rhys in *Celtic Folklore* (vol. i, pp. 211–13). He gives the Welsh version, written down by William Thomas Solomon, who had it from his mother, who in her turn had learned it from an old woman at Garth Dorwen some eighty years earlier, and the English translation, as follows:

An old man and his wife lived at the Garth Dorwen in some period a long while ago. They went to Carnarvon to hire a maid servant at the Allhallows' Fair; and it was the custom then for young men and women who stood out for places to station themselves at the top of the present *Maes*, by a little green eminence where the present Post Office stands. The old man and his wife went to that spot, and saw there a lass with yellow hair, standing a little apart from all the others; the old woman went to her and asked if she wanted a place. She replied that she did, and so she hired herself at once and came to her place at the time fixed. In those times it was customary during the long winter nights that spinning should be done after supper. Now the maid servant would go to the meadow to spin by the light of the moon, and the *Tylwyth Teg* would come to her to sing and dance. But some time in the spring, when the days had grown longer, Eilian escaped with the Tylwyth Teg, so that she was seen no more. The field where she was last seen is known to this day as Eilian's Field, and the meadow is called the Maid's Meadow. The old woman of Garth Dorwen was in the habit of putting women to bed, and she was in great request far and wide. Some time after Eilian's escape there came a gentleman to the door one night when the moon was full, while there was a slight rain and just a little mist, to fetch the old woman to his wife. So she rode off behind the stranger on his horse, and came to Rhos y Cwrt. Now there was at that time at the centre of the *rhos*, somewhat of rising ground that looked like an old fortification with many big stones on the top, and a large cairn of stones on the northern side: it is to be seen to this day, and it goes by the name of Bryn i Pibion, but I have never visited the spot. When they reached the spot, they entered a large cave, and they went into a room where the wife lay in her bed; it was the finest place the old woman had seen in her life. When she had successfully brought the wife to bed she went to the fire to dress the baby; and when she had done the husband came to the old woman with a bottle of ointment that she might anoint the baby's eyes; but he entreated her not to touch her own eyes with it. Somehow, after putting the bottle by, one of the old woman's eyes happened to itch, and she rubbed it with the same finger that she used to rub the baby's eyes. Then she saw with that eye how the wife lay on a bundle of rushes and withered ferns in a large cave, with big stones all round her, and with a little fire in one corner; and she saw also that the lady was only Eilian, her former servant girl, whilst, with the other eye, she beheld the finest place she had ever seen. Not long afterwards the old midwife went to Carnarvon to market, when she saw the husband, and said to him, 'How is Eilian?'

'She is pretty well,' said he to the old woman. 'But with what eye do you see me?'

'With this one,' was the reply; and he took a bulrush and put her eye out at once.

In conversation old Solomon mentioned the enormous quantities of flax spun by Eilian when she sat in the meadow with the fairies. Here we have the story of the girl with GOLDEN HAIR beloved by the FAIRIES or the TYLWYTH TEG, the half-human baby who needs fairy ointment to clear its sight, the GLAMOUR cast over human eyes and the blinding of the seeing eye. These midwife stories are common, and according to the FAIRY DWELLING ON SELENA MOOR the pure fairies are shy breeders, but it seems a not unreasonable assumption from this story and CHERRY OF ZENNOR that the fairy children who need the ointment are hybrids.

[Motifs: F235.4.1(a); F372.1]

Milesians. See THEORIES OF FAIRY ORIGINS.

Milton, John (1608–74). Though brought up in London, Milton's family roots were in Oxfordshire, at Forest Hill, where his grandfather had once lived and from which he drew his first, Royalist, bride. In 1632 his father retired to Horton in Buckinghamshire, and Milton joined him there for some time. He had therefore an opportunity of knowing something of the Midland fairy traditions, and his few mentions of the FAIRIES ring true to the country lore. The best-known is the fairy passage in *L'Allegro* (quoted under the LUBBARD FIEND). Here we have Faery MAB, with a suggestion of a similar tale to that of the BROWNIE of Cranshaws later told by Chambers, far away on the Scottish Border, of the regular pinching and pulling of the fairies, a WILL O' THE WISP story generally connected with FRIAR RUSH, and one of the HOB-GOBLIN tales of LOB-LIE-BY-THE-FIRE.

In one of his *Vacation Exercises*, we hear of the fairies appearing like the Norns or Parcae at a birth – not like PERRAULT's fairies at a christening:

> Good luck befriend thee Son; for at thy birth
> The Faery Ladies daunc't upon the hearth;
> Thy drowsie Nurse hath sworn she did them spie
> Come tripping to the Room where thou didst lie;
> And sweetly singing round about thy Bed
> Strew all their blessings on thy sleeping Head.

In *Comus* we have a mention of 'the pert fairies and the dapper elves'. Years later a sudden rural freshness steals through the austere air of

Paradise Lost when the willing compression and diminution of the fallen angels in Hell is compared to a gathering of fairies in the English country-side:

> they but now who seemd
> In bigness to surpass Earths Giant Sons
> Now less then smallest Dwarfs, in narrow room
> Throng numberless, like that Pigmean Race
> Beyond the *Indian* Mount, or Faerie Elves,
> Whose midnight Revels, by a Forrest side
> Or Fountain some belated Peasant sees,
> Or dreams he sees, while over head the Moon
> Sits Arbitress, and neerer to the Earth
> Wheels her pale course, they on thir mirth & dance
> Intent, with jocond Music charm his ear;
> At once with joy and fear his heart rebounds.

These few fairy cameos are scattered through the vast scope of Milton's poetry; few, but worth the finding.

Mine goblins. The mine GOBLINS of England have names of their own, COBLYNAU, CUTTY SOAMS, DUNTERS, KNOCKERS and the like, but there was one kind that was imported into English literature in the 17th century, and was so often mentioned as to be almost proverbial – 'the goblins who laboured in the mines'. These references were founded on Georgius Agricola's work, *De animantis subterranibus* (Basle, 1651). They were mine-spirits who made a great show of working, were seen and heard blasting, wielding picks and shovels and wheeling away ore, but without leaving any palpable traces of their labours. There is a pleasant illustration of them on the title page of *Golden Remains of the Ever-memorable Mr John Hales* (1653), and we shall find references in such writers as BURTON, Dr Thomas Browne and Heywood. They were indeed a gift to the moralist.

Miser on the Fairy Gump, the. The Gump near St Just in Cornwall had been famous as the meeting-place of the SMALL PEOPLE. Robert HUNT, in *Popular Romances of the West of England* (pp. 98–101), gives a vivid description of a fairy gathering as tiny, bejewelled and courtly as any to be found in the poetry of HERRICK or Drayton.

The old people of St Just had long told their children and grand-children of the great spectacle there, of the music, DANCING and feasting. Modest spectators were not punished, and some had even been given tiny but most precious gifts.

There was one old miser, however, who could never hear of riches without desiring them, and on a night of the full harvest moon he set out to see what he could steal. As he began to climb the Gump he heard music all round him, but he could see nothing. As he climbed higher it became louder, and he suddenly realized that it was under his feet, and in a moment the hill burst open and a hideous crowd of SPRIGGANS poured out, followed by a great band of musicians and a troop of soldiers. At the same time the whole hillside was lit up; every blade of grass and every furze bush sparkled with jewels. He stared at them greedily, but was disturbed to see that a number of the spriggans were gathering round him like a kind of guard. None of them was higher than his shoestring, however, so he consoled himself by the thought that he could trample them underfoot, and stood his ground. Then out came a great crowd of servants, carrying the riches that he was waiting for, hundreds of tables set out in the finest order with gold and silver plates, and goblets carved out of rubies and diamonds and all varieties of rich food. He was greedily wondering where to pounce when the fairy court came out in their thousands followed by troops of fairy children scattering scented flowers which rooted themselves as they touched the ground, and last of all came the prince and princess, and moved to the high table upon the dais. This was the richest focus of the miser's greed, and, crouching down, he began to creep up behind it to catch the whole brilliant minuscule of jewels and gold and silk under his broad-brimmed hat. He crept up as the FAIRIES moved in ordered companies to do homage to their rulers and to take their proper places at the tables, apparently unconscious of what was overhanging them. He was so absorbed with his stealth that he never noticed that the spriggans were moving with him and that each one had cast a shining rope around him. At last he was behind the dais and raised himself to his knees with his hat above his head. Then he suddenly saw that every eye in that great assembly was fixed on him. As he paused, a whistle sounded, every light went out and he was jerked sideways by hundreds of thin cords; he heard the whirr of wings and was pierced all over and pinched from head to foot. He lay stretched on his back, pinned to the ground, while the biggest of the spriggans danced on his nose with shouts of laughter. At length the spriggan shouted, 'Away, away! I smell the day!' and disappeared. The miser found himself lying stretched at the foot of the mound covered with dewy cobwebs. He broke through them and managed to stagger to his feet and totter home. It was a long time before he confessed to anyone what happened to him that night.

It seemed that Hunt's 19th-century love of ornament ran away with him in this tale; but unless it is a complete invention – of which he has never been accused – we have here a tradition of the DIMINUTIVE FAIRIES and the royal court such as Herrick may well have found 200 years earlier. It also differs from the FAIRY DWELLING ON SELENA MOOR in being an entirely sympathetic approach to the fairies, treating them presumably as flower spirits, with the spriggans as their body-guard rather than as spirits of the dead.

[Type: 503 III. Motifs: F211; F239.4.3; F262.3.6; F340; F350; F361.2; F361.2.3]

Moddey Dhoo (*moor tha do*). The most famous of the BLACK DOGS of the Isle of Man was the Moddey Dhoo or MAUTHE DOOG of Peel Castle, made famous by Walter SCOTT. In the 17th century when the castle was garrisoned, a great, shaggy black dog used to come silently into the guard-room and stretch himself there. No one knew whom he belonged to nor how he came, and he looked so strange that no one dared to speak to him, and the soldiers always went in pairs to carry the keys to the governor's room after the castle was locked up. At length one man, the worse for drink, taunted his companions and mocked the dog. He snatched up the keys, dared the dog to follow him, and rushed out of the room alone. The dog got up and padded after him, and presently a terrible scream was heard and the man staggered back, pale, silent, shuddering. The dog was never seen again, but after three days of silent horror the man died. That was the last thing seen of the Mauthe Doog, but the Moddey Dhoo persists to modern times. Walter Gill gives two accounts of his appearances, of which one was in 1927 near Ramsey at the Milntown corner when a friend of Walter Gill met him, black, with long, shaggy hair and eyes like coals of fire. He was afraid to pass it, and they looked at each other till the dog drew aside and allowed him to pass. The man took it for a death token, for shortly after his father died. The other account was of a doctor in 1931 and at the same corner. He passed it on his way to a confinement, and it was there still when he came back two hours later. He described it as being nearly the size of a calf, with bright, staring eyes. We are not told if his patient died.

One story is told by Gill of a black dog in Peel who acted as a GUAR-DIAN BLACK DOG and prevented the deaths of several men. A fishing-boat was waiting in Peel Harbour for its skipper to command the crew on a night's fishing. They waited all night, and the skipper never came. In the early morning a sudden gale sprang up in which the boat might well have been lost. When the skipper rejoined his crew he told them that his way had been blocked by a great black dog, and whichever way he turned it always stood before him till at length he turned back. The story was told to Walter Gill by one of the crew. This story of the guardian black dog appears in other parts of Britain. It was said that the Mauthe Doog was no dog, but the ghost of a prisoner – some said of the Duchess of Gloucester, but this holds good of many black dogs. The Black Dog of Newgate, for instance, was said to be the ghost of Luke Hutton, a notorious highwayman who had been hanged there. Other black dogs were thought to be the Devil himself.

[Motif: F401.3.3]

Monsters. GIANTS and DRAGONS generally absorb the greater part of the monsters of British fairy-lore. Heraldic monsters, properly speaking, are those that display a mixture of parts of the body belonging to other creatures, as, for example, a griffin, which has the head and wings and

forefeet of an eagle, the body, hindquarters and tail of a lion and ears which appear to be its own invention. Griffins are occasionally mentioned in some of the fairy-stories. In 'Young Conall of Howth', for instance, which is included in Ó'Súilleabhaín's *Folktales of Ireland*, a volume of the *Folktales of the World* series, there is a casual mention of an old man having been carried to Ireland by a griffin, but these heraldic monsters are given little importance. Less formal creatures occupy the imagination of both the Celts and the Saxons, HAGGES of extraordinary

hideousness, with their eyes misplaced and hair growing inside their mouths, the DIREACH, with one leg, one hand and one eye, the skinless NUCKELAVEE, the shapeless BROLLACHAN and BONELESS and water-monsters like the AFANC and the BOOBRIE; these are felt to be more satisfactory than the mathematical conceptions of the heralds.

Mooinjer Veggey (*moo-in-jer vegar*). An alternative name in the Isle of Man for SLEIGH BEGGEY.

Morgan (*morrgan*). There is a mysterious story about the Morgan who was supposed to haunt the Lake Glasfryn Uchaf in the parish of Llangybi. It is one of quite a number of lakes which were said to have burst forth from a covered well when the cover had been removed and the well exposed. Rhys, in *Celtic Folklore* (vol. I, pp. 365–76), carefully explores all the various forms in which he received the legend. The one that he finds of special interest is that of the Morgan, which is said to come from the lake and carry away naughty or over-adventurous children. He believes that the Morgan was originally a MERMAID of the same breed as the Breton MORGENS and connected with MORGAN LE FAY. 'Morgan' in Welsh, however, was always a man's name, and Rhys suggests that the water spirit became male in this tradition because of the Welsh usage.
   [Motifs: F420.1.1; F420.1.2*]

Morgan le Fay. By the time that Malory was handling the MATTER OF BRITAIN, the godlike and fairy elements of many of the characters, so evident in such early Celtic legends as 'Culhwch and Olwen' from the *Red Book of Hergest*, reproduced in the MABINOGION, had been ob-scured and euhemerized almost beyond recognition; yet Morgan le Fay remains an obstinately fairy-tale character. The modernists of the 14th century did their best for her by making her an enchantress instead of a fairy. 'And the third sister, Morgan le Fay,' says Malory, 'was put to school in a nunnery, and there she learned so much that she was a great clerk of necromancy.' Outside the Arthurian stories, *Fata Morgana* still preserved her memory as a sea fairy, and the lesser MORGANS of Wales and Brittany still remind us of her earlier nature. In Arthurian legend, Morgan le Fay played the part of Arthur's evil fairy as the LADY OF THE LAKE was his good fairy. She was constantly bent on his death or the defamation of his court.
   The Fourth Book of Malory is largely occupied by a plot of Queen Morgan to compass Arthur's death by the means of his own sword and the unwitting help of her lover Sir Accolon. In *Sir Gawayne and the Green Knight*, the whole incident is designed by Morgan to bring the Round Table into disrepute, and she herself plays a part in it as the ancient duenna of the lady. In the ballad of 'The Boy and the Mantle' in the Child collection (No. 29), the magic cup and mantle are sent to Arthur's

court for the same purpose. She is a consistently evil and malicious character until the time of Arthur's death, when she is one of the four queens who bear him away to the Isle of Avalon. This amoral character might well belong to a fairy, but it possibly points to an earlier function as a goddess, for the Celtic pantheon seem to have been as fluctuating in their morals as the gods of Ancient Greece.

[Motif: F360]

Morgens. The Breton MERMAIDS. They are conjectured by Rhys in *Celtic Folklore* to be the same as the Welsh MORGANS.

Morrigan (*moreeghan*), **or Morrigu.** One of the forms taken by the ancient Irish war goddess BADB. In the CUCHULAIN epic, *Tain Bo Cuailnge*, in which the great war between the FOMORIANS and the TUATHA DE DANANN is celebrated, the three war goddesses in the form of crows are NEMAN, MACHA and Morrigu, of whom Morrigu is the greatest. As Evans Wentz analyses the legend, they are the tripartite form of 'Badb'. Neman confounds the armies of the enemy, so that allies wage mistaken war against each other, Macha revels in indiscriminate slaughter, but it was Morrigu who infused supernatural strength and courage into Cuchulain, so that he won the war for the Tuatha de Danann, the forces of goodness and light, and conquered the dark Fomorians, just as the Olympic gods conquered the Titans.

[Motif: A485.1]

Moruadh. See MERROWS.

Muilearteach (*moolyarstuch*), **the.** The watery form taken by the CAILLEACH BHEUR, according to D. A. Mackenzie in *Scottish Folk Lore and Folk Life*. As a water-spirit, he would list her among the FUATHS. As a sea spirit, she had a reptilian as well as a human form. But, on land, she appeared as an old HAGGE, and the story of her begging to be allowed to warm herself at a fire and gradually swelling in size and ferocity, which was later told of human witches, is early told as an encounter with FIONN in a Gaelic folk-poem. Like the Cailleach Bheur, she had a blue-black face and only one eye. She raised winds and sea-storms. It is difficult to distinguish her from the Cailleach except by her connection with the sea.

[Motif: F430]

Mumpoker. One of the frightening figures, or NURSERY BOGIES, listed by Mrs Wright in *Rustic Speech and Folk-Lore*. He comes from the Isle of Wight.

Murdhuacha (*muroo-cha*). See MERROWS.

Muryans. *Muryan* is the Cornish word for 'ant'. The Cornish belief about the FAIRIES was that they were the souls of ancient heathen people, too good for Hell and too bad for Heaven, who had gradually declined from their natural size, and were dwindling down until they became of the size of ants, after which they vanished from this state and no one knew what became of them. For this reason, the Cornish people thought it was unlucky to kill ants. In the FAIRY DWELLING ON SELENA MOOR the reason given for the dwindling size of the SMALL PEOPLE OF CORNWALL was that they had the power of changing into birds or other forms, but after every such change, when they resumed their former shape, they were rather smaller, and therefore as time went on they dwindled.

[Motif: F239.4.3]

Nanny Button-cap. A little West Yorkshire spirit. Not much is known about her, but she is a good fairy. Mrs Wright gives a nursery rhyme about her:

> The moon shines bright,
> The stars give light,
> And little Nanny Button-cap
> Will come to-morrow night.

[Motif: F403]

Neamhan. See NEMAN.

Neatness. The country TROOPING FAIRIES no less than the BROWNIES and HOBGOBLINS are great exponents of order and are annoyed if a house is left dirty or untidy. See also FAULTS CONDEMNED BY THE FAIRIES; VIRTUES ESTEEMED BY THE FAIRIES.

Nelly Long-arms. See NURSERY BOGIES; PEG POWLER.

Nelson, Mary. There are only a few stories of a successful attempt to rescue one of the CAPTIVES IN FAIRYLAND. Occasionally CHANGELINGS are detected and driven out, so that the true child is returned; sometimes, too, a fairy attempt at abduction is thwarted, as, for instance, in the story of SANDY HARG'S WIFE, but there are many pathetic stories of failures at rescue and only a few when the attempt succeeds. One such is told by Walter SCOTT in *Minstrelsy of the Scottish Border*. He got it, he says, 'from a broadside still popular in Ireland'.

The story is told at some length, and is here condensed.

Mary Campbell of Aberdeenshire was married to John Nelson, a young goldsmith, who set up a shop in Aberdeen to work at his trade. They lived in great happiness together until the time of her laying-in for her first child. On the night when her delivery was expected she was well provided with gossips and nurses, but at midnight there was a loud and horrible noise and all the candles went out. All the women fell into a panic, and it was some time before they got the lights rekindled, and when they did they saw a corpse lying on the bed. There was terrible consternation, and John Nelson was distracted with grief. People of all sects came to her wake, and among them was the Reverend Mr Dodd, who at the first sight of the corpse said: 'That's not the body of any Christian, Mrs Nelson must have been carried away by the fairies, and some substance left in her place.' No one believed him, and he refused to attend the funeral.

One evening some time later John Nelson was riding in his own field, where there was a KNOWE, or 'moat', and he heard a pleasant consort of music coming out of it. A veiled figure in white came towards him. Though he could not see her face he rode up to her and asked her kindly why she chose to walk alone so late in the evening. She threw back her veil and burst into tears, and he at once knew her for his wife. 'In the name of God,' he said, 'what has disturbed you? And what has caused you to appear at this hour?' 'I can come at any hour,' she replied, 'for though you believe me dead and buried, I am not. I was carried away at the time of my delivery, and you buried a piece of wood in my place. You can still free me if you use the proper means, but I fear we shall not reach our child; it has three nurses to attend on it, but I fear I cannot bring it away. The greatest hope I have is in my brother Robert, and his ship will be home in ten days.'

John Nelson asked her what they should do to win her back, and she said that he would find a letter addressed to her brother on his desk the next Sunday. He was to give it to Robert Campbell as soon as he got home. She told him to look over her right shoulder and he would see her companions. He did so, and saw kings and queens sitting crowned and guarded in front of the Knowe. 'We shall never win you away from such company,' he said. 'Robert can do it,' she said, 'but do not you attempt it, or I shall be lost for ever. Even now I am threatened with dreadful punishments for speaking to you, but ride up to the moat and threaten to burn all the thorns and brambles that grow on it if they do not promise that I shall get no punishment.' At that she vanished, and he rode up to the moat, and though he saw no one he called out as she had told him with great resolution. A voice came out of the air telling him to throw away the book in his pocket, and they would agree. He said that nothing would make him part from the book, but that if they did not obey him they would feel the effects of his wrath. On that the voice said that Mary

Nelson would be forgiven if he promised to do no harm to the moat. He agreed to that and a sound of pleasant music was heard. He rode away, and told everything to Mr Dodd, who came home with him, and stayed with him till the next Sunday, when the promised letter appeared. In a few days Captain Robert Campbell came home, and they gave him the letter at once. It ran as follows:

Dear Brother,
My husband can relate to you my present circumstances. I request that you will (the first night after you see this) come to the moat where I parted from my husband: let nothing daunt you, but stand in the centre of the moat at the hour of twelve at night, and call me, when I, with several others, will surround you; I shall have on the whitest dress of any in the company; then take hold of me, and do not forsake me; all the frightful methods they shall use, let it not surprise you, but keep your hold, suppose they continue till cockcrow, when they shall vanish all of a sudden, and I shall be safe, when I will return home and live with my husband. If you succeed in your attempt, you will gain applause from all your friends, and have the blessing of your ever loving and affectionate sister,
Mary Nelson.

When Robert Campbell read this letter he vowed to rescue his sister and her child that very night. He went back to his ship and told his men the work he was going on. They all offered to go with him, but he answered that it was better for him to go alone. He set out at ten o'clock, and as he left the ship an enormous lion came roaring towards him. He cut at it with his sword and it vanished into air, so he went forward with better heart than ever, for he knew that the things that would attack him were illusions. He came to the moat, and on the top of it he saw a white handkerchief spread out, so he stood on it and called for his sister. He was at once surrounded by a crowd of ladies in white clothes, but one shone the whitest of all and he knew it for his sister. He took her by the right hand, and cried out, 'By the help of God I will preserve you from all these infernal imps.' A terrible wailing broke out all round him and a great circle of fire surrounded them, out of which came the shapes of terrible birds. But he stood firm through it all, for an hour and three quarters, till the distant cocks began to crow in the country round. Then the fire faded, the ugly shapes all around them disappeared and his sister stood shivering near him in the cold wind of dawn. He wrapped his coat round her and thanked God for her safety. She embraced him and cried out that she was safe now that he had put one of his garments on her, and they went home to Aberdeen in great joy.

Robert Campbell was still determined to win the baby back too. And he and John Nelson were talking of burning all the thorns and brambles on the moat when a voice spoke out of the air: 'You shall have your child back on condition that you do not till the ground within three perches of the moat, and leave the thorns and brambles untouched.' They agreed to that and in a few moments the child was laid on his mother's knee, and they all knelt down and gave thanks to God. It is said that the FAIRIES were able to steal the baby because some of the women watching the mother were drunk.

There are great resemblances here to Burd Janet's rescue of YOUNG TAMLANE. The illusions, the necessity of holding the captive firmly, the saining power of a human garment are all the same.

[Motifs: F322; F372; F379.1; R112.3; R156]

Neman, or Neamhan. The ancient Irish war goddess BADB took a triple form, Neman, MORRIGU and MACHA, all in the shape of royston or hoodie crows, a form taken in modern Irish fairy-lore by the BEAN-SIDHE. Each manifestation has a different function and Neman is 'the confounder of armies'. It is she who causes bands of the same army to fight together, mistaking each other for the enemy. Evans Wentz, in *The Fairy-Faith in Celtic Countries* (pp. 302–7), gives a useful account of these war spirits, founded mainly on *Silva Gadelica* and *The Book of Conquests*, but with other comparisons and references.

[Motifs: A132.6.2; A485.1]

'Nicht Nought Nothing', or 'Nicht Nocht Naethin'. An example of a widespread story of which the earliest example is that of Jason and Medea. Andrew Lang published it in *Folk-Lore* (vol. I). In this version we have the SUPERNATURAL WIZARD as the hero's father-in-law. The tale is still alive, and was recorded and published by Dr Hamish Henderson in *The Green Man of Knowledge*, where the heroine is a SWAN MAIDEN:

> There once lived a king and a queen. They were long married, and had no bairns; but at last the queen had a bairn, when the king was away in far countries. The queen would not christen the bairn till the king came back, and she said: 'We will just call him *Nicht Nought Nothing* until his father comes home.'
>
> But it was long before he came home, and the boy had grown a nice little laddie. At length the king was on his way back; but he had a big river to cross, and there was a spate, and he could not get over the water. But a giant came up to him and said, 'If you will give me Nicht Nought Nothing, I will carry you over the water on my back.' The king had never heard that his son was called Nicht Nought Nothing, and so he promised him. When the king got home again, he was very pleased to see his queen again, and his young son. She told him she had not given the child any name but Nicht Nought Nothing until he should come home himself. The poor king was in a terrible case. He

said: 'What have I done? I promised to give the giant who carried me over the river on his back Nicht Nought Nothing.'

The king and the queen were sad and sorry, but they said: 'When the giant comes, we will give him the hen-wife's bairn; he will never know the difference.' The next day the giant came to claim the king's promise, and he sent for the hen-wife's bairn; and the giant went away with the bairn on his back.

He travelled till he came to a big stone, and there he sat down to rest. He said: 'Hidge, Hodge, on my back, what time of day is it?' The poor little bairn said, 'It is the time that my mother, the hen-wife, takes up the eggs for the queen's breakfast.' The giant was very angry, and dashed the bairn on the stone and killed it. They tried the same with the gardener's son, but it did no better. Then the giant went back to the king's house, and said he would destroy them all if they did not give him Nicht Nought Nothing this time. They had to do it; and when they came to the big stone, the giant said, 'What time o' day is it?' and Nicht Nought Nothing said: 'It is the time that my father, the King, will be sitting down to supper.' The giant said: 'I've got the right one now'; and took Nicht Nought Nothing to his own house, and brought him up till he was a man.

The giant had a bonny dochter, and she and the lad grew very fond of each other. The giant said one day to Nicht Nought Nothing, 'I've work for you to-morrow. There is a stable seven miles long, and seven miles broad, and it has not been cleaned for seven years, and you must clean it to-morrow, or I'll have you for my supper.' The giant's dochter went out next morning with the lad's breakfast, and found him in a terrible state, for aye as he cleaned out a bit, it aye fell in again. The giant's dochter said she would help him, and she cried a' the beasts o' the field, and a' the fowls o' the air, and in a minute they carried awa' everything that was in the stable, and made it a' clean before the giant came home. He said, 'Shame for the wit that helped you; but I have a worse job for you to-morrow.' Then he told Nicht Nought Nothing that there was a loch seven miles long, and seven miles deep, and seven miles broad, and he must drain it the next day, or else he would have him for his supper.

Nicht Nought Nothing began early next morning, and tried to lave the water with his pail, but the loch was never getting any less; and he did not ken what to do; but the giant's dochter called on all the fish in the sea to come and drink the water, and they soon drank it dry. When the giant saw the work done, he was in a rage, and said: 'I've a worse job for you to-morrow; there's a tree, seven miles high, and no branch on it, till you get to the top, and there is a nest, and you must bring down the eggs without breaking one, or else I will have you for my supper.' At first the giant's dochter did not know how to help Nicht Nought Nothing, but she cut off first her fingers, and then her toes and made steps of them, and he clomb the tree, and got all the eggs safe, till he came to the bottom, and then one was broken. The giant's dochter advised him to run away, and she would follow him. So he travelled until he came to a king's palace, and the king and queen took him in, and were very kind to him. The giant's dochter left her father's house, and he pursued her, and was drowned. Then she came to the king's palace where Nicht Nought Nothing was. And she went up a tree to watch for him. The gardener's dochter, going down to draw water in the well, saw the shadow of the lady in the water, and thought it was herself, and said: 'If I'm so bonny, if I'm so brave, do you send me to draw water?' The gardener's wife went, and said the same thing. Then the gardener went himself, and brought the lady from the tree, and had her in. And he told her that a stranger was to marry the king's dochter, and showed her the man, and it was Nicht Nought Nothing, asleep in a chair. And she saw him, and cried to him: 'Waken, waken, and speak to me!' But he would not waken, and syne she cried:

'I cleared the stable, I laved the loch, and I clomb the tree,
And all for the love of thee,
And thou wilt not waken and speak to me.'

The king and queen heard this, and came to the bonny young lady, and she said: 'I canna get Nicht Nought Nothing to speak to me, for all that I can do.'

Then were they greatly astonished, when she spoke of Nicht Nought Nothing, and asked where he was, and she said, 'He sits there in the chair.'

Then they ran to him and kissed him, and called him their own dear son, and he wakened, and told them all that the giant's dochter had done for him, and of all her kindness. Then they took her in their arms, and kissed her, and said she should be their dochter, for their son should marry her. And they lived happy all their days.

[Type: 313. Motifs: B451; D672; D2004.2.1; G465; H151; H335.0.1; H1010; H1102; H1235]

Nicnevin. Alexander Montgomerie in his poem 'Flyting with Polwart' calls the GYRE-CARLING, the Scottish Lowland Queen of Elfame, Nicnevin, a name which suggests something diabolic, 'Nicnivin with hir nymphis in nomber anew'. The whole poem is devoted to the darker aspect of the fairies, so that the FAIRY RADE appears almost like a rade of witches:

Some saidland a sho aipe all graithid into greine,
Some hobland one ane hempstalk, hovand to the heicht.
The King of pharie, and his Court, with the elph queine,
With mony elrich Incubus was rydand that nycht.

[Motif: F252.2]

Night-Mare. One form in which the name of MARA, a demon, survives. The other is 'mare's nest'. Other names for Night-Mare are Succubus and the HAGGE.

[Motifs: F471.1; F471.2.1]

Nimble Men, the. See FIR CHLIS.

Nimphidia (Drayton). See DIMINUTIVE FAIRIES.

Nimue. The name generally given to the LADY OF THE LAKE.

Noggle, or Nuggle, or Nygel. This creature, whose name is variously spelt, is the Shetland KELPIE. It appears like a beautiful little grey horse, about the size of a Shetland pony, bridled and saddled. It is less malicious than the Kelpie and much less dangerous than the EACH UISGE, but it has two mischievous tricks. Its peculiarity is that it is much attracted by water-mills, and if the mill was running at night it would seize the wheel and stop it. It could be driven off by thrusting a burning brand or a long steel knife through the vent-hole of the mill. Its other trick was to loiter along the mill-stream and allure pedestrians to mount it. It would then dash away into the sea and give its rider a severe and even dangerous ducking; but it did not, like Each Uisge, tear its victim to pieces, it merely rose through the water and vanished in a blue flame. Before mounting a stray horse it was wise to look well at its tail. The Noggle looked like an ordinary horse, but it had a tail like a half-wheel, curled up over its back. Some people called the Noggle a SHOOPILTIE, but it seems to have shared this name with the merpeople (see MERMAIDS; MERMEN). Anecdotes and descriptions of the Noggle have been brought together from various sources by A. C. Black in *County Folk-Lore* (vol. III, pp. 189–93).

[Motifs: F234.1.8; F420.1.3.3]

'Noman' story. See AINSEL; BROLLACHAN; BROWNIES; MEG MULLACH.

Nuala. Mentioned incidentally by Evans Wentz as the wife of FIN BHEARA, the king of the fairies of Connaught and king of the dead whose wife, according to Lady WILDE, is OONAGH.

[Motif: F252.2]

Nuckelavee. One of the most repulsive creatures which the Scottish imagination has conceived; and the Scots are expert in horrors. He was an Orcadian sea-monster, a kind of hideous centaur, for like a centaur he rose out of a horse's back and had no human legs. He came out of the sea and spread evil wherever he went, blighting crops, destroying livestock and killing every man whom he could encounter. Though he was a sea spirit he could not endure fresh water, and the only escape from him was to cross a running stream. In Douglas's *Scottish Fairy and Folk Tales* an article contributed by Traill Dennison to the *Scottish Antiquary* is reproduced. Mr Dennison met an old man, Tammas, who claimed to have met Nuckelavee, and after much persuasion, he described the encounter.

He was walking late one clear, starlight night along a narrow strip of land between a fresh-water loch and the sea, when he saw something moving along towards him. It seemed to him some monster, but he could go neither to the right nor the left and he had always been told that the worst thing to do was to run from supernatural creatures, so he took his courage in both hands, and went steadily, if slowly, forward. As the thing came nearer he recognized it as Nuckelavee. Traill Dennison gives the gist of his description:

The lower part of this terrible monster, as seen by Tammie, was like a great horse with flappers like fins about his legs, with a mouth as wide as a whale's, from whence came breath like steam from a brewing-kettle. He had but one eye, and that as red as fire. On him sat, or rather seemed to grow from his back, a huge man with no legs, and arms that reached nearly to the ground. His head was as big as a clue of simmons (a clue of straw ropes, generally about three feet in diameter), and this huge head kept rolling from one shoulder to the other as if it meant to tumble off. But what to Tammie appeared most horrible of all, was that the monster was skinless; this utter want of skin adding much to the terrific appearance of the creature's naked body, – the whole surface of it showing only red raw flesh, in which Tammie saw blood, black as tar, running through yellow veins, and great white sinews, thick as horse tethers, twisting, stretching, and contracting as the monster moved. Tammie went slowly on in mortal terror, his hair on end, a cold sensation like a film of ice between his scalp and his skull, and a cold sweat bursting from every pore. But he knew it was useless to flee, and he said, if he had to die, he would rather see who killed him than die with his back to the foe. In all his terror Tammie remembered what he had heard of Nuckelavee's dislike of fresh water, and, therefore, took that side of the road nearest to the loch. The awful moment came when the lower part of the head of the monster got abreast of Tammie. The mouth of the monster yawned like a bottomless pit. Tammie found its hot breath like fire on his face: the long arms were stretched out to seize the unhappy man. To avoid, if possible, the monster's clutch, Tammie swerved as near as he could to the loch; in doing so one of his feet went into the loch, splashing up some water on the foreleg of the monster, whereat the horse gave a snort like thunder and shied over to the other side of the road, and

Tammie felt the wind of Nuckelavee's clutches as he narrowly escaped the monster's grip. Tammie saw his opportunity, and ran with all his might; and sore need had he to run, for Nuckelavee had turned and was galloping after him, and bellowing with a sound like the roaring of the sea. In front of Tammie lay a rivulet, through which the surplus water of the loch found its way to the sea, and Tammie knew, if he could only cross the running water, he was safe; so he strained every nerve. As he reached the near bank another clutch was made at him by the long arms. Tammie made a desperate spring and reached the other side, leaving his bonnet in the monster's clutches. Nuckelavee gave a wild unearthly yell of disappointed rage as Tammie fell senseless on the safe side of the water.

[Motifs: F401.5; F420.1.4; F420.5.2; G303.16.19.13; G308]

Nursery bogies. There is a group of spirits that seem as if they had never been feared by grown-up people but had been invented expressly to warn children off dangerous ground or from undesirable activities. They are what are listed by Professor William Jansen as 'Frightening Figures'. Mrs Wright in *Rustic Speech and Folk-Lore* gives quite a list of them. Some of them are used in threats: 'If yo' dunna tak' car' I'll shewn yo' Jack up the orchut,' or 'I'll send MUMPOKER after ye,' or 'By goy! but auld Scratty'll git thi if thoo doesn't come in!' – with a whole host more, RAWHEAD-AND-BLOODY-BONES, TANKERABOGUS, TOM DOCKIN, TOM-POKER; and others with special functions, as to protect fruit and nut trees: LAZY LAURENCE, CHURNMILK PEG and MELSH DICK, AWD GOGGIE and the GOOSEBERRY WIFE; or to frighten children from dangerous water: GRINDYLOW, JENNY GREENTEETH and Nelly Long-arms. All these, however revolting they might be, no doubt played a useful part in inducing children to be cautious, but no one over the age of ten would be likely to believe in them. They were a class in themselves.

[Motif: F420.5.2.1.2]

Oakmen. There are scattered references to oakmen in the North of England, though very few folktales about them: there is no doubt that the oak was regarded as a sacred and potent tree. Most people know the rhyming proverb 'Fairy folks are in old oaks'; 'The Gospel Oak' or 'The

King's Oak' in every considerable forest had probably a traditional sacredness from unremembered times, and an oak coppice in which the young saplings had sprung from the stumps of felled trees was thought to be an uncanny place after sunset; but the references to 'oakmen' are scanty. Beatrix Potter in *The Fairy Caravan* gives some description of the Oakmen, squat, dwarfish people with red toadstool caps and red noses who tempt intruders into their copse with disguised food made of fungi. The fairy wood in which they lurk is thrice-cut copse and is full of blue-bells. *The Fairy Caravan* is her only long book, and is scattered with folktales and folk beliefs. It is probable that her Oakmen are founded on genuine traditions. In Ruth Tongue's *Forgotten Folk-Tales of the English Counties* there is a story from Cumberland, 'The Vixen and the Oakmen', in which the Oakmen figure as guardians of animals. This rests on a single tradition, a story brought back by a soldier from the Lake District in 1948, and may well have been subject to some sophistication, but these two together make it worth while to be alert for other examples.

[Motif: F441.2]

Oberon. Much more generally used as a name for the fairy king than TITANIA for the fairy queen, even if we regard the Scottish 'Diana' as the same as Titania. Oberon was the fairy king in the 15th-century French prose romance, HUON OF BORDEAUX, translated into English in 1548 by Lord Berners. This king was an example of a DIMINUTIVE FAIRY, the size of a three-years child, but this small size was the result of a curse laid on him by a malicious fairy at his christening. Shakespeare's Oberon is a typical fairy king, even in his amorous interest in mortals, and it will be noticed that Drayton makes his fairy king 'Oberon', even though he changes 'Titania' to Queen MAB. In early Renaissance times, familiar spirits were called 'Auberon' and 'Oberycom'. Some people derive 'Auberon' from the same source as the German dwarf 'Alberich'.

[Motif: F252.1]

Odin, or Woden. It seems likely that Odin was the original leader of the WILD HUNT in England, as he was until recent times in Scandinavia, where, however, he chased the harmless little wood-wives instead of the souls of damned men. It was common for Satan to take over the role of any influential god, and Odin, as the leader and chooser of the dead, had a special right to play the Devil's part. Brian Branston, in *The Lost Gods of England*, devotes a chapter to Woden and maintains his right to serve as the first leader of the Wild Hunt, the DEVIL'S DANDY DOGS and other sinister routs of the same kind.

[Motif: E501.1]

Ogme, the champion. One of the sons of the High King DAGDA to whom Dagda gave one of his BRUGHS when he was forced to take refuge underground before the advance of the invading Milesians. The whole incident is to be found in the *Lebor Gebar* (*Book of Battles*), which is one of the ancient books of Ireland.

Ogres. The word 'ogres' is used sometimes to describe man-eating GIANTS, monstrous both in shape and habits, but it may also be taken to mean a race of creatures of mortal size who are anthropophagous. George MACDONALD in *Phantastes* uses the word in this sense to describe the sinister woman with the pointed teeth who sits quietly reading and looks up from her book to advise the hero not to look in a certain cupboard, advice that has more the effect of a temptation than a warning. It is possible that the giant in 'Mallie Whuppie', the Scottish version of 'Hop O' My Thumb', was an ogre rather than a giant, for his children were certainly of ordinary mortal size, though they would have grown up with a hereditary taste for human flesh.
  [Motif: G312]

Oisin. The poet and recorder of the FIANNA and the last survivor of the band. He was the son of FINN Mac Cumhal and of Sadbh, a woman of the SIDH, who had been turned into a fawn by the Dark Druid, Fear Doirche, who was pressing his love on her. She took refuge with the Fianna where she could regain her woman's shape, and Finn loved her and married her, but when Finn was called away to war Fear Doirche took the appearance of Finn and lured her away, and Finn searched everywhere, but he could never find her again. But one day when he was hunting there was a great outcry among the hounds, and when the huntsmen rode up they found BRAN AND SCEOLAN protecting a beautiful little boy against all the rest of the pack. Finn leapt from his horse and picked up the child: 'O Oisin – my little fawn!' he said. For he knew Sadbh's child and his own son. Later, when Oisin could speak, he told how he had been watched and nursed by a deer, and how a dark man had taken her away.
  When he grew up Oisin became the sweetest singer and one of the most valiant fighters of the Fianna, and he lived to see the beginning of the dark days of the Fianna, for he lived through the Battle of Gabhra where Osgar, his son, who was next to him in valour, was killed. But one day the fairy princess, Niamh of the GOLDEN HAIR, fetched him away to TIR NAN OG, the Land of the Young, and none of the Fianna ever saw him again; but hundreds of years after he had gone he came back, riding the white horse on which he had departed, but he set down his foot for an instant to lift a great stone trough, and he fell down an old, old man, and the horse shied and galloped away so that Oisin could never return to Tir Nan Og. And by that time Christianity had come to the land, and St Patrick was the great man there, and he listened eagerly to all that Oisin told him of the days of the Fianna. But though Patrick tried to win him to

Christianity, Oisin continued to lament the days of the Fianna until he died.

[Type 766 (variant). Motifs: c521; c984; f302.1; f378.1]

Old Bloody Bones. This Cornish version of RAWHEAD-AND-BLOODY-BONES is mentioned by F. W. Jones in *Old Cornwall* as inhabiting KNOCKERS Hole near Baldhu. There was said to have been a massacre near, and Goon Gumpus once ran with blood. Old Bloody Bones may have been a ghost, or an evil spirit attracted by the carnage.

Old Lady of the Elder Tree, the. Of all the sacred and FAIRY TREES of England, the surviving traditions of the elder tree seem to be the most lively. Sometimes they are closely associated with witches, sometimes with FAIRIES, and sometimes they have an independent life as a dryad or goddess. These traditions are not now generally believed, but they are still known to some of the country people. Formerly the belief was more lively. Mrs Gutch in *County Folk-Lore* (vol. v) quotes from a paper given by R. M. Heanley to the Viking Club in 1901:

> Hearing one day that a baby in a cottage close to my own was ill, I went across to see what was the matter. Baby appeared right enough, and I said so; but its mother promptly explained. 'It were all along of my maister's thick 'ed; it were in this how: T' rocker cummed off t' cradle, an' he hedn't no more gumption than to mak' a new 'un out on illerwood without axing the Old Lady's leave, an' in coorse she didn't like that, an' she came and pinched t' wean that outrageous he were a' most black i' t' face; but I bashed 'un off, an' putten an' esh 'un on, an' t'wean is as gallus as owt agin.'
>
> This was something quite new to me, and the clue seemed worth following up. So going home I went straight down to my backyard, where old Johnny Holmes was cutting up firewood – 'chopping kindling,' as he would have said. Watching the opportunity, I put a knot of elder-wood in the way and said, 'You are not feared of chopping that, are you?' 'Nay,' he replied at once, 'I bain't feared of choppin' him, he bain't wick (alive); but if he were wick I dussn't, not without axin' the Old Gal's leave, not if it were ever so.' . . . (The words to be used are): 'Oh, them's slape enuff.' You just says, '*Owd Gal, give me of thy wood, an Oi will give some of moine, when I graws inter a tree.*'

[Motif: f441.2.3.2]

'Old Man of Cury, The'. HUNT's gentler version of BOTTRELL's story of LUTEY AND THE MERMAID. The MERMAID here is a much gentler character than Bottrell's mermaid, and there is no hint of the tragic ending. The following shortened version gives the general flavour of the tale.

An old fisherman of Cury was walking near Kynance Cove at low tide, when he saw a girl sitting on a rock near a deep pool, deserted by the retreating sea. As he came up she slipped into the pool; and when he ran up to rescue her he found that it was not a girl but a mermaid, who had been cut off from her home by a long stretch of sand. She entreated him with tears to carry her to the water, for she had left her husband asleep, and he was both jealous and ferocious. The old man took her on his back, and as he trudged over the sand she promised him any reward he chose. 'I've no need of money,' he said, 'but I should like the power to help others. Teach me how to break spells and to discover thefts and to cure illness.'

'That I will,' she said, 'but you must come to that rock at high tide and moonshine, and I will teach you.'

She took the comb from her hair, and told him to comb the sea with it when he wanted to speak to her. Then she slipped from his back, kissed her hand to him, and dived out of sight. But whenever he stroked the sea she came to him, and taught him many things. Sometimes he carried her on his back to see the strange land people, but he never accepted her invitation to visit her under the waves. The mermaid's comb and some part of the old man's skill stayed in his family for several generations.

[Motifs: D1410.4; F420.3.1; F420.4.4; F420.5.1.7.3]

Old People, the. One of the Cornish EUPHEMISTIC NAMES FOR THE FAIRIES. It was founded on the belief that the SMALL PEOPLE OF CORNWALL were the souls of the heathen people of the old times, who had died before the days of Christianity and were too good for Hell and too bad for Heaven. They were therefore pendulous till the Day of Judgement between Hell and Heaven. This belief was found by Evans Wentz in the early 1900s to be held by a proportion of the population in most of the Celtic countries which he explored.

[Motif: C433]

Old Shock. A Lincolnshire variant of SHOCK, mentioned by Mrs Wright in *Rustic Speech and Folk-Lore* (p. 194).

[Motif: G302.3.2]

Old Woman of Gloominess. See CAILLAGH NY GROAMAGH.

Old Woman of the Mountains, the. An individual member of the GWYLLION of Wales. Her special function seems to be to lead travellers astray. Both Wirt Sikes and Rhys mention the Gwyllion in some detail.

[Motifs: F491; F491.1]

Oonagh (*oona*). According to Lady WILDE in her *Ancient Legends of Ireland*, Oonagh is the wife of FINVARRA, the king of the western fairies and of the dead. She says:

Finvarra the King is still believed to rule over all the fairies of the west, and *Oonagh* is the fairy queen. Her golden hair sweeps the ground, and she is robed in silver gossamer all glittering as if with diamonds, but they are dew-drops that sparkle over it.

The queen is more beautiful than any woman of earth, yet Finvarra loves the mortal women best, and wiles them down to his fairy palace by the subtle charm of his fairy music.

NUALA is also said to be Finvarra's wife, but perhaps it is not surprising that so amorous a fairy should have several wives.
[Motif: F252.2]

Orfeo, King. See KING ORFEO.

Origin of fairies. Those inhabitants of Britain who used to believe in the FAIRIES, and that small number who still believe in them, have various notions about their origin, and this variety is not purely regional but is partly founded on theological differences. Folklorists and students of fairy-lore who have not committed themselves to personal beliefs also put forth a selection of THEORIES OF FAIRY ORIGINS, which for the sake of clarity can be examined separately.

A valuable work of research on the beliefs held about fairy origins among the Celts was published by Evans Wentz under the title *The Fairy-Faith in Celtic Countries* (1911). In the course of his work he travelled in Ireland, the Highlands of Scotland, Wales, the Isle of Man, Cornwall and Brittany, interviewing first eminent scholars, such as Douglas HYDE in Ireland and Alexander Carmichael in the Highlands, and also people of all classes and types who were believed to have information about the fairies. He found that, among the older people, many of the opinions of the 17th and 18th centuries still prevailed.

There seemed to be some trace of the prehistoric beliefs left, though these were not so explicit as the beliefs in the fairies as the dead, or as fallen angels, or occasionally as astral or elemental spirits.

Sometimes the particular class of the dead is specified. The SLUAGH or fairy Hosts are the evil dead, according to Highland belief. FINVARRA's following in Ireland seem to comprise the dead who have recently died as well as the ancient dead; but they are almost as sinister as the Sluagh. In Cornwall the SMALL PEOPLE are the souls of the heathen dead, who died before Christianity and were not good enough for Heaven nor bad enough for Hell, and therefore lingered on, gradually shrinking until they became as small as ants, and disappeared altogether out of the world. The FAIRY DWELLING ON SELENA MOOR gives a good account of this theory. In Cornwall and Devon too the souls of unchristened babies were called PISKIES, and appeared at twilight in the form of little white moths. The KNOCKERS in the tin mines were souls of the dead too, but of the Jews who had been transported there for their part in the Crucifixion. In Wales the belief in the fairies as the dead does not seem to have been so common. They were often described as a race of 'beings half-way between something material and spiritual, who were rarely seen', or 'a real race of invisible or spiritual beings living in an invisible world of their own' (Wentz, p. 145). In the Isle of Man a passage on the 'Nature of Fairies' is something the same:

> 'The fairies are spirits. I think they are in this country yet: A man below here forgot his cow, and at a late hour went to look for her, and saw that crowds of fairies like little boys were with him. (St) Paul said that spirits are thick in the air, if only we could see them; and we call spirits fairies. I think the old people here in the island thought of fairies in the same way.' [Wentz, p. 125]

The belief in the fairies as the dead may well come from pre-Christian times, but with the fairies as fallen angels we come into the post-Christian period. In Ireland, in spite of the lively belief in Finvarra and his host, there is also an explicit belief in the fairies as fallen angels. Lady WILDE contradicts the usual trend of her testimony in one chapter of her *Ancient Legends of Ireland* (vol. I), 'The Fairies as Fallen Angels' (p. 169):

> The islanders, like all the Irish, believe that the fairies are the fallen angels who were cast down by the Lord God out of heaven for their sinful pride. And some fell into the sea, and some on the dry land, and some fell deep down into hell, and the devil gives to these knowledge and power, and sends them on earth where they work much evil. But the fairies of the earth and the sea are mostly gentle and beautiful creatures, who will do no harm if they are let alone, and allowed to dance on the fairy raths in the moonlight to their own sweet music, undisturbed by the presence of mortals.

From the Scottish Highlands, Evans Wentz (p. 85) quotes a lively account of the story behind this, given to him by Alexander Carmichael, who heard it in Barra in company with J. F. CAMPBELL:

> 'The Proud Angel fomented a rebellion among the angels of heaven, where he had been a leading light. He declared that he would go and found a kingdom for himself. When going out at the door of heaven the Proud Angel brought prickly lightning and biting lightning out of the doorstep with his heels. Many angels followed him – so many that at last the Son called out, "Father! Father! the city is being emptied!" whereupon the Father ordered that the gates of heaven and the gates of hell should be closed. This was instantly done. And those who were in were in, and those who were out were out; while the hosts who had left heaven and had not reached hell flew into the holes of the earth, like the stormy petrels.'

The greater part of these angels were thought of, like the Cornish MURYANS, as 'too good for Hell and too bad for Heaven', but with the growth of Puritanism the view of the fairies became darker and the fallen angels began to be regarded as downright devils, with no mitigating feature. We find this in 17th-century England. William Warner in *Albion's England* goes so far as to deny all performance of household tasks to ROBIN GOODFELLOW, saying ingeniously that he got the housewives up in their sleep to clean their houses. Robin got the credit of the work, and the poor housewife got up in the morning more tired than she had gone to bed. This is to deprive the fairy character of all benevolence. On the other hand, two of the Puritan divines of the same period allow the fairies to be a kind of spiritual animal, of a middle nature between man and spirit. It is clear that there was no lack of diversity between those who believed in the real existence of fairies.

[Motifs: F251; F251.1; F251.2; F251.3; F251.6; F251.7; F251.11; F251.12]

Ossian (*isheen*). 'Ossian' has been the usual Highland spelling of the Irish OISIN since the time of James Macpherson's poem *Ossian*, loosely founded on the Highland Ossianic legends. J. F. CAMPBELL, in his discussion of the Scottish Ossianic legends in his *Popular Tales of the West Highlands* (vol. IV), well establishes the widespread knowledge of the Ossianic poems and ballads in 18th-century Scotland and of the Fingalian legends. All over the Highlands, Ossian was known as the great poet and singer of the Feinn, who survived them all and kept the memory of them alive by his songs. Many of the Fenian legends survived in these songs, and in such early manuscripts as *The Book of Leinster*. 'The Death of Diarmid' and other tragic stories of the last days of the Feinn were deeply remembered and the tragic plight of Ossian, old, blind and mighty, is the most vivid of all. What is not recorded in the Highlands is his visit to TIR NAN OG and the happy centuries he passed with Niam of the GOLDEN HAIR.

Ouph. An Elizabethan variant of ELF. It does not appear to be in common use now, but is to be found in literature.

Padfoot. A BOGY OR BOGEY-BEAST creature common about Leeds, of which several rather various descriptions are given by Henderson in *Folk-Lore of the Northern Counties* (pp. 273–4). Old Sally Dransfield, the carrier from Leeds to Swillington, claimed to have often seen it in the form of a wool-pack, rolling along the road in front of her or bursting through a hedge; J. C. Atkinson of Danby spoke of it as a death-warning, sometimes visible, sometimes invisible, padding lightly along behind a traveller or coming up to his side, roaring with a sound unlike any other animal, and occasionally rattling a chain. It was about the size of a sheep, with long, smooth hair. It must never be touched. A man in Horbury saw it like a white dog. He struck at it with his stick; the stick went through it, and it looked at him with great saucer eyes and he ran for home. He had been so frightened that he took to his bed and died. Padfoot is only one of many 'frittenings'. See also, for instance, BARGUEST, TRASH and SKRIKER, all road-haunters and products of the North Country imagination.

[Motifs: F234.0.2; G302.3.2]

Patch, or Pach. A common name for a court fool; Henry VII and Henry VIII both had fools called 'Pach'. In the LIFE OF ROBIN GOOD-FELLOW, Pach seems to perform the function of a censor of housewifery and care of the stock rather than Court Jester:

> About mid-night do I walke, and for the trickes I play they call me Pach. When I find a slut asleepe, I smuch her face if it be cleane; but if it be durty, I wash it in the next pissepot that I can finde: the balls I use to wash such sluts withal is a sows pancake, or a pilgrimes salve. Those that I find with their heads nitty and scabby, for want of combing, I am their barbers, and cut their hayre as close as an apes tayle; or else clap so much pitch on it, that they must cut it off themselves to their great shame. Slovens also that neglect their master's businesse, they doe not escape. Some I find that spoyle their master's horses for want of currying: those I doe daube with grease and soote, and they are faine to curry themselves ere they can get cleane. Others that for laysinesse will give the poor beasts no meate, I oftentimes so punish them with blowes, that they cannot feed themselves they are so sore.

He adds sanctimoniously in his final verse:

> Thus many trickes, I, Pach, can doe,
> But to the good I ne'ere was foe:

> The bad I hate and will doe ever,
> Till they from ill themselves doe sever.
> To help the good Ile run and goe,
> The bad no good from me shall know.

Jabez Allies (see ALLIES'S LIST OF THE FAIRIES) finds numerous place-names beginning with 'Patch' in his essay 'On Ignis Fatuus, or Will o' the Wisp, and the Fairies'.

[Motif: F360]

Peallaidh (*pyaw-le*), **the 'Shaggy One'**. A Perthshire URISK from which the place-name Aberfeldy is said to be taken. The whole tribe of evil spirits of this type are called FUATH. Most of them haunt rivers, lochs or the sea-shore. Donald Mackenzie in *Scottish Folk-Lore and Folk Life* has a chapter on these Fuath. A Lowland form of Peallaidh is SHELLYCOAT. In the Gaelic dialect of Lewis, 'Pwllardh' is used for the Devil, as PUCK or 'Pouk' was in Middle English.

[Motif: F360]

Pechs, or Pehts, or Picts. Pechs and Pehts are Scottish Lowland names for FAIRIES and are confused in tradition with the Picts, the mysterious people of Scotland who built the Pictish BRUGHS and possibly also the Fingalian BROCHS, the round stone towers, of which the most perfect examples are the Round Towers of Brechin and Abernethy. At the end of the 19th century, David MAC RITCHIE made out a good case for his THEORY OF FAIRY ORIGINS that the FEENS or Fians of the Highlands and Ireland were substantially identical with the PECHS of the Lowlands and the TROWS of Shetland. R. Chambers in his *Popular Rhymes of Scotland* says:

> Long ago there were people in this country called the Pechs; short wee men they were, wi' red hair, and long arms, and feet sae braid, that when it rained they could turn them up owre their heads, and then they served for umbrellas. The Pechs were great builders; they built a' the auld castles in the kintry; . . .

Mac Ritchie quotes the evidence of a young Shetlander in Kettlester:

> It may be mentioned that when I asked my young guide at Kettlester the exact height of the small Pechts he had just been speaking of, he said, 'About that height,' indicating at the same time a stature three feet or so. Whatever their height really was, this young Shetlander's ideas were in agreement with those held 'throughout Scotland'.

Mac Ritchie also cites an account given by James Knox in 1831 in *The Topography of the Banks of the Tay* (p. 108) in which he says 'the Pechs were unco wee bodies, but terrible strang' and adds, 'They are said to have been about three or four feet in height.' The Pechs were tremendous castle builders and were credited with the construction of many of the ancient castles and churches. Their method was to shape the stones in the quarry, and, forming a long chain from the quarry to the site, pass the stones from hand to hand and erect the whole tower in the course of a night. They could not bear the light of day and always took refuge in their brughs or SITHEANS at sunrise. This is a convincing picture of the hill fairies in Scotland and the Border Country. Whether it is a work of euhemerization to identify them with a former race or no is an open question. It seems likely that some historic memory of an aboriginal race contributed one strand to the twisted cord of fairy tradition.

[Motif: F239.4.2]

Peerifool. The name of the Orcadian TOM TIT TOT, which also contains some elements of HABETROT. The youngest of three princesses captured by a GIANT shares her porridge with some yellow-headed peerie folk who enter the house, and afterwards a peerie boy comes in to do spinning for her. A beggar woman looks through a hole into a fairy dwelling as the lassie did in 'Habetrot' and sees the Peerie Boy going round the spinners saying: 'Tease, teasers, tease; card, carders, card; spin, spinners, spin, for peerie fool, peerie fool is my name.' She told this to gain a night's lodging, and so the princess learned the needed name, which is hence one of the SECRET NAMES OF THE FAIRIES.

[Types 311; 500. Motifs: C432.1; D2183; F271.2; F381.1; N475]

Peg o' Nell. An evil spirit which haunts the river Ribble near Clitheroe, and Waddow Hall in particular. One year in seven she claims a victim for the river, and if a cat or dog has not been drowned by Peg o' Nell's Night, the Ribble will claim a human victim. A well in the grounds of Waddow Hall is named after her, and a headless stone figure standing near it is supposed to represent her. It seems likely that she was originally the nymph of the Ribble; if so, tradition has replaced her by a human ghost. Long ago, it is said, there was a maidservant named Peg o' Nell at Waddow Hall. She and her mistress quarrelled, and as she picked up her pail to fetch water from the well her mistress wished she might fall and break her neck. The ground was covered with ice and the wish was fulfilled. Peg did not turn into a mild, complaining ghost. A curse was on the place. Misfortunes to the stock and the illness of children were all blamed on her. But the worst of all was her seven-year toll of a life. We hear the details, with the confirmatory story of a drowning on Peg's Night, from William Henderson in *Folk-Lore of the Northern Counties* (p. 265).

[Motif: F420.5.2.1.6]

Peg Powler. If PEG O' NELL is a wronged ghost, Peg Powler is a relative of JENNY GREENTEETH, true-bred water-demon, though, according to the DENHAM TRACTS (vol. II, p. 42), she must be rated as a NURSERY BOGIE.

Peg Powler is the evil goddess of the Tees; and many are the tales still told at Piersebridge, of her dragging naughty children into its deep waters when playing, despite the orders and threats of their parents, on its banks – especially on the Sabbath-day. And the writer still perfectly recollects being dreadfully alarmed in the days of his childhood lest, more particularly when he chanced to be alone on the margin of those waters, she should issue from the stream and snatch him into her watery chambers.

Henderson gives a more explicit description of the spirit in *Folk-Lore of the Northern Counties* (p. 265):

The river Tees has its spirit, called Peg Powler, a sort of Lorelei, with green tresses, and an insatiable desire for human life, as has the Jenny Greenteeth of Lancashire streams. Both are said to lure people to their subaqueous haunts, and then drown or devour them. The foam or froth, which is often seen floating on the higher portion of the Tees in large masses, is called 'Peg Powler's suds'; the finer, less sponge-like froth is called 'Peg Powler's cream'.

GRINDYLOW and NELLY LONG-ARMS are both mentioned by E. M. Wright in *Rustic Speech and Folk-Lore* (p. 198) as similar GOBLINS who drag children down into water. She gives the last a wider range than the others (Yorkshire, Lancashire, Cheshire, Derbyshire, Shropshire), but gives no special description of her.

[Motifs: F420.1.4.8; F420.5.2.1.2]

Pellings, the. A prosperous and respected family living at the foot of Snowdon who were supposed to have fairy blood in them. They had fair complexions and GOLDEN HAIR like the TYLWYTH TEG, and were said to be the children of a fairy wife, Penelope, one of the GWRAGEDD ANNWN whose story was much like that of the Lady of Fan y Fach. The imputation of fairy blood seems to have been resented by most Welshmen, but it was respected in the Pellings, as in the Physicians of Mydfai.

[Motif: F305]

People of Peace, the, or Daoine Sidhe. These, of the Highlands, are very much the same as the DAOINE SIDH of Ireland, except that they have – with the exception of the FEENS, who exactly reproduce the stories of FINN of the FIANNA – no monarchical government. They are TROOPING FAIRIES who live under the green hills and ride on the Middle Earth, hunting and dancing like other FAIRIES. As individuals, they visit mortals as lovers. The earliest study of them was made by

KIRK in *The Secret Commonwealth*. There are ample accounts of them in the writings of J. G. CAMPBELL and J. F. CAMPBELL, of J. G. Mackay, Mrs Watson, Mrs Grant, Donald Mackenzie and others. In the Lowlands, the ELVES or GOOD NEIGHBOURS have a king and a queen – NICNEVIN or the GYRE-CARLING – and in later days were suspected of having a good deal of intercourse with witches and of paying a tribute to the Devil.

People of the Hills, the. A widespread euphemism for the FAIRIES who live under the green mounds, or tumuli, all over England. It is the name chosen by Rudyard KIPLING to be used in *Puck of Pook's Hill* and *Rewards and Fairies*.

[Motif: C433]

Perrault, Charles (1628–1703). Perrault may, almost with certainty, be presumed to be the author of *Histoires et Contes du Temps Passé avec des Moralités* (1697) which contains 'Cinderella', the world's most popular fairy story. The reason that there is any doubt about the matter is that the dedication of the book was signed Pierre Darmancour, which was the name used by Perrault's third son, a boy of eighteen when the book was first published. Iona and Peter Opie, in their scholarly work *The Classic Fairy Tales*, have examined the matter with characteristic thoroughness and have decided with much probability on the father. It was said that Charles Perrault heard these stories being told to his little son by the child's governess, and it is conceivable that he got the child to repeat them to him and therefore might have given him credit as the author. The tales are incomparable in their period for their simple, direct narrative style, with a certain spice of elegance and humour which is still characteristic of oral French tradition. The tales immediately conquered the taste of the court and initiated a fashion for fairy tales which was followed in a more luxuriant style by Madame D'AULNOY. In 1729, Robert Samber's translation of Perrault appeared in England, and the French invasion of English nurseries began. It is not astonishing that children's imaginations were captured, for the English fairy traditions were then represented only by scattered and inartistic chapbooks. Nothing that could be described as a collection appeared before Ritson. Perrault's stories have been altered and prettified, but they still capture the imagination.

Perry Dancers. The Suffolk name for the Aurora Borealis. See also FIR CHLIS.

Pharisees. See FARISEES.

Phenodyree (*fin-ord-er-ree*). See FENODEREE.

Phouka (*pooka*), **the.** The Irish word 'Phouka' is sometimes used, as 'Pouk', or PUCK, was in Middle English, for the Devil. More usually he is a kind of BOGY OR BOGEY-BEAST, something like the Picktree BRAG of the North of England, who takes various forms, most usually a horse, but also an eagle or a bat, and is responsible for people falling as well. Many a wild ride has been suffered on the Phouka's back. It is he who spoils the blackberries after Michaelmas. This is Crofton CROKER's view of him. According to Lady WILDE, however, he was nearer to the BROWNIE or HOBGOBLIN. There is a charming story, 'Fairy Help', in her *Ancient Legends of Ireland* in which a young boy, a miller's son, makes friends with Phouka and throws his coat over it as it rushes like a mad bull towards him. Afterwards he sees the Phouka directing six younger ones to thrash his father's corn while the miller's men are

asleep. In this form the Phouka is like an old withered man dressed in rags. The boy tells his father and together they watch the phoukas at work through the crack of the door. After this the miller dismisses his men, and all the work of the mill is done by the phoukas. The mill became very prosperous. The boy Phadrig became very fond of the Phouka and night after night he watched him through the keyhole of an empty chest. He became more and more sorry for the Phouka, so old and frail and ragged, and working so hard to keep the idle little phoukas up to their work. At length, out of pure love and gratitude, he bought stuff and had a beautiful coat and breeches made for the Phouka, and laid them out for him to find. The Phouka was delighted with them, but decided that he was too fine to work any more. When he left all the little phoukas ran away, but the mill kept its prosperity, and when Phadrig married a beautiful bride he found a gold cup full of wine on the bridal table. He was sure it came from the Phouka and drank it without fear, and made his bride drink too.

A better-known story is that of 'The Phooka of Kildare', in which the brownie-like spirit keeps its animal form of an ass, but describes itself as the ghost of an idle kitchen boy. It too is laid by a gift of clothing, but in this case because it has at length earned a reward by its labours. These stories show the Phooka very near to ROBIN GOODFELLOW, or Puck, tricksy, mischievous, practical-joking, but helpful and well-disposed to the human race.

[Motifs: E423; F234.0.2; F343.14; F381.3; F399.4; F401.3.1; F482.5.4]

Phynnodderee (*fin-ord-er-ree*). See FENODOREE.

Picktree Brag. See BRAG.
   Motifs: E423; E423.1.3.5(b); F234.0.2; F399.4]

Picts. See PECHS.

Pigsies. See PIXIES.

Pinch. One of the FAIRIES mentioned in the 17th-century pamphlet on ROBIN GOODFELLOW which is reproduced in Carew Hazlitt's *Fairy Tales, Legends and Romances Illustrating Shakespeare*. He, PATCH, GULL and GRIM are mentioned as adepts in SHAPE-SHIFTING:

> 'Pinch and Patch, Gull and Grim,
>   Goe you together,
> For you can change your shapes
>   Like to the weather.'

Pinket. A Worcestershire name for IGNIS FATUUS, particularly located by ALLIES in the parish of Badsey, although he finds 'Pink's Field', 'Pink's Green' and 'Pink's Meadow' more widely scattered through the country. He also points out that 'Pinck' is the name of one of Drayton's DIMINUTIVE FAIRIES. HINKY-PUNK, a name given to the Ignis Fatuus on the borders of Devon and Somerset, seems to suggest a slightly different version of the same name.
   [Motif: F491]

Pishogue (*pish-ogue*). An Irish fairy spell, by which a man's senses are bemused, so that he sees things entirely different from what they are in actuality. The FIR DARRIG is a master at pishogues, and the tale of the Fir Darrig in Donegal is a good example, but pishogues are thickly scattered through the Fenian legends. In English it is called GLAMOUR, and examples of it are to be found in Malory and in many English folktales.
   [Motif: D2031]

Piskies. The name for the Cornish Piskies is metathesized in Somerset and Devon to PIXIES or Pigsies, though they are, on the whole, very like in character and habits. The Cornish Piskie, however, is older, more wizened and meagre than the sturdy, earthy pixies of Somerset and the white, slight, naked pixies of Devon. BOTTRELL describes the Piskie as a weird, wizened-looking old man, who threshes corn, piskie-rides horses and leads folks astray. HUNT has a story of piskie-threshing, very like that given by Mrs Bray except that Hunt's piskie is a little old man in a ragged green suit, and Mrs Bray's pixy is 'fair and slim, with not a rag to cover him'. Both are delighted with the gift of a fine new suit, put it on and run away to show it off at the fairy court.

[Motif: F200.1]

Pixies, or Pigsies, or Piskies. These are West Country FAIRIES, belonging to Somerset, Devon and Cornwall. There is indeed a tradition of pixies at Greenhow Hill in Yorkshire, but this was once worked by Cornish miners, and they seem to have left their pixies behind them. They were first introduced to the literary world by Mrs Bray in her series of letters addressed to Robert Southey published under the title of *The Borders of the Tavy and the Tamar*. Mrs Bray was not native to the West Country, and occasionally gives some fairy traits to the Pixies and draws on literature as well as tradition. For all that, she opened a rich vein of folklore and her findings are confirmed by true West Countrymen such as HUNT and BOTTRELL in their accounts of Cornish PISKIES.

There are varying traditions about the size, appearance and origin of the Pixies, but all accounts agree about their being dressed in green, and about their habit of misleading travellers. They also will help their favourites like BROWNIES, and like brownies are laid by a gift of clothes. They are generally thought to be homelier in appearance than are fairies. The most recent and some of the most vivid descriptions of the Pixies are those given by Ruth Tongue in *County Folklore* (vol. VIII). According to her, the Pixies defeated the Fairies in a pitched battle and drove them across the river Parrett, so that everywhere to the west of the Parrett is now Pixyland. Pixies, even when they assume a mortal size, are easy to recognize. They are red-headed, with pointed ears, turned-up noses and short faces. They often squint. Green is their colour. It is their habit to steal horses at night and ride them round in circles, called 'gallitraps', a term for fairy rings. Anyone who puts both feet into one of these is a prisoner; if only one foot goes in he can see the pixies, but can still escape. A criminal putting even one foot into a gallitrap will be hanged.

Pixies play all the pranks that are elsewhere ascribed to ROBIN GOOD-FELLOW or PUCK, but they are particularly fond of misleading travellers. Anyone who comes unadvisedly and without precaution across pixy ground is liable to be PIXY-LED, and can only save himself by turning his coat, if he has not had the foresight to carry a wicken-CROSS or a piece of

BREAD with him, but a man who by ill-conduct or churlish ways has made himself disliked by the pixies is not likely to be let off so lightly. Ruth Tongue (pp. 115–16), after several stories of bad characters left in bogs or streams, tells one with a well-deserved fatal ending, the tale of 'Old Farmer Mole':

> They'll tell 'ee three things 'bout an Exmoor Pony 'can climb a cleeve, carry a drunky, and zee a pixy'. And that's what old Varmer Mole's pony do.
>
> Old Varmer Mole were a drunken old toad as lived out over to Hangley Cleave way and he gived his poor dear wife and liddle children a shocking life of it. He never come back from market till his pockets were empty and he was zo vull of zider he'd zit on pony 'hind-zide afore' a zingin' and zwearin' till her rolled into ditch and slept the night there – but if his poor missus didn't zit up all night vor 'n he'd baste her and the children wicked.
>
> Now the pixies they did mind'n and they went to mend his ways.
>
> 'Twad'n no manner of use to try to frighten pony – he were that foot-sure and way-wise he'd brought Varmer safe whoame drunk or asleep vor years, wheresoever the vule tried to ride'n tew.
>
> This foggy night the old veller were wicked drunk and a-waving his gad and reckoning how he'd drub his Missus when he gets to whoame when her zee a light in the mist. 'Whoa, tha vule!' says he, 'Us be to whoame. Dang'n vor lighting a girt candle like thic. I'll warm her zides for it!'
>
> But pony he wouldn' stop. He could a-zee the pixy holdin' thic light and 'twere over the blackest, deepest bog this zide of the Chains – zuck a pony down in a minute 'twould, rider and all.
>
> But the old man keeps on shouting, 'Whoa, fule, us be tew whoame!' And rode straight for the bog – but pony digged in his vour liddle veet 'n her stood!
>
> Varmer gets off'n and catches'n a crack on the head and walks on to light. He hadn' goed two steps when the bog took and swallowed 'n!
>
> Zo old pony trots whoame. And when they zee'd 'n come alone with peat-muck on his legs they knowed what did come to Varmer – and they did light every candle in house and *dancey*!
>
> After that Missus left a pail of clean water out at night vor pixy babies to wash in, pretty dears, and swept hearth vor pixies to dancey on and varm prospered wondervul, and old pony grew zo fat as a pig.

Similar stories are told of the Piskies of Cornwall, who are occasionally called, as they are sometimes in Somerset, the 'Pigsies'. Hunt gives one about the night-riding of a fine young horse. These pigsies were presumably the same as the Piskies, who were of the usual small size and rode twenty or so to each horse.

The tale of the FAIRY PED is also told about the Somerset Pixies.

One of the various origins ascribed to the Pixies and Piskies all over the West Country is that they are the souls of unchristened children; another is that they are the souls of the Druids or of heathen people who died before the coming of Christ and were not fit for Heaven but not bad enough for Hell. This they have in common with many ideas about the ORIGIN OF FAIRIES, and it will be seen that though some distinctions can be drawn between pixies and fairies, they yet have so much in common that they belong to the same genus.

Type: ML6035. Motifs: F361.16; F369.7; F381.3; F402.1.1; F405.11]

Pixy-led. One of the most common traits of the FAIRIES was their habit of leading humans astray. POUK-LEDDEN was the Midlands term for it, the stories of the STRAY SOD give us the Irish version, and ROBIN GOODFELLOW, or PUCK, was often credited with it by the early poets.

As Drayton says in his account of the DIMINUTIVE FAIRIES in *Nimphidia*:

> This *Puck* seemes but a dreaming dolt,
> Still walking like a ragged Colt,
> And oft out of a Bush doth bolt,
>   Of purpose to deceive us.
> And leading us makes us to stray,
> Long Winters nights out of the way,
> And when we stick in mire and clay,
>   *Hob* doth with laughter leave us.

Many of the fairies are credited with this kind of trickery, among them the GWYLLION of Wales, but in modern times the West Country PIXIES or the Cornish PISKIES are the most usual practitioners of the art. Two accounts collected by Ruth Tongue from the Nettlecombe Women's Institute in 1961 are given in K. Briggs, *The Fairies in Tradition and Literature* (pp. 138-9). One is in the regular country tradition:

> I were pixy-led once in a wood near Budleigh Salterton. I couldn't find my way out, though 'twas there, plain to see. I went all around about it three times, and then somebody coom along to find me, and I thought how could I miss the path. They said others was pixy-led there too.

The second, given by the President, was more sophisticated, but perhaps even more interesting:

> I went a journey to a house in Cornwall to do some secretarial work. When the farm came in sight I walked in and asked if I were on the right track to the Manor. They all looked a little queer, – I thought it was because they never saw any strangers, – but the farmer's wife was very kind and gave me careful directions. I was to cross certain fields, and then go down a certain track to where there were *two* gates, and I

must take the white one. She was so insistent on this that I had visions of a bull in the other field, or fierce watch-dogs; and the farm men who sat by (they were having a meal) all agreed in silence. Well, I came to the bridle track; it was a misty, snowy, depressing day and I didn't want to be late, – I had to walk home after. Then I came to a gate at the end, set in a thick hawthorn hedge, *one* gate, and it wasn't white, and I had a most creepy feeling. I was determined not to lose that job. I was just starting work and I needed the pay. Well, I went all along that hedge, and I pricked my fingers too, but there was only one gate. Then somebody came up the bridle track whistling, and the thick mist cleared, and there was no hedge. It was one of the farm lads sent after me who knew what to do. 'Here's your white gate, Miss,' he said, and, sure enough, there it was, beside the other one. He didn't stop for thanks, but turned back to the farm, still whistling loudly. The old Manor House was there, right in front of me, and I went in at a run. My job didn't take me more than an hour, and I simply ran past the farm. The woman looked out, and I waved and hurried on. I wish now I'd had the courage to ask if her boy wore hob-nailed boots, or carried salt in his pocket, or if he had been told to sing or whistle.

To avoid being pixy-led it is necessary to know the correct methods of PROTECTION AGAINST FAIRIES.

[Motifs: F369.7; F385.1; F402.1.1]

Plant Annwn (*plant anoon*), the. The Welsh FAIRIES of the underworld, whose entrance to the human world is by the lakes. Their king is GWYN AP NUD, and they are chiefly known to men through their maidens, the GWRAGEN ANNWN, by their white or speckled cattle, the GWARTHEG Y LLYN, and by their swift white hounds, the CWN ANNWN, who were sometimes seen with their fairy mistresses, but more often heard on summer nights in full cry after the souls of men who had died unassoiled and impenitent. The Lake Maidens made loving and docile wives until the TABOO attached to them was violated; the Lake Cattle brought wealth and prosperity to any farmer who was lucky enough to keep one; but the hounds of the underworld betray the nature of these underwater people: they were the company of the dead, like the subjects of FIN BHEARA in Ireland. In a story told by Pugh of Aberdovey and preserved by John Rhys, Gwyn ap Nud is called king of Annwn, but elsewhere Rhys calls ARAWN, the friend of Pwyll of Dyfed, the undoubted king of the underworld. He is called so in the MABINOGION.

[Motif: F212]

Plant Rhys Dwfen (*plant hrees thoovn*). This, meaning the family of Rhys the Deep, is the name given to a tribe of fairy people who inhabited a small land which was invisible because of a certain herb that grew on it.

They were handsome people, rather below the average in height, and it was their custom to attend the market in Cardigan and pay such high prices for the goods there that the ordinary buyer could not compete with them. They were honest and resolute in their dealings, and grateful to people who treated them fairly. One man called Gruffid always treated them so well that they took a great liking to him and invited him to their country, which was enriched with treasures from all over the world. They loaded him with gifts and conducted him back to their boundary. Just before he took leave of them he asked how they guarded all their wealth. Might not even one of their own people betray them into the hands of strangers? 'Oh no,' said his guide. 'No snakes can live in Ireland and no treachery can live here. Rhys, the father of our race, bade us, even to the most distant descendant, honour our parents and ancestors; love our own wives without looking at those of our neighbours; and do our best for our children and grandchildren. And he said that if we did so, no one of us would ever prove unfaithful to another, or become what you call a traitor.' He said that a traitor was an imaginary character with them, shown in a symbolic drawing with the feet of an ass, the head of the devil and a bosom full of snakes, holding a knife in his hand, with which he had killed his family. With that he said goodbye, and Gruffid found himself near his own home, and could no longer see the Country of Plant Rhys. After this time he prospered in everything and his friendship with the Plant Rhys continued. After his death, however, the farmers became so covetous that the Plant Rhys no longer frequented Cardigan Market, and were said to have gone to Fishguard. This land of virtuous, honest fairy people is like that visited by Elidor in the story of ELIDOR AND THE GOLDEN BALL in medieval times. John Rhys in *Celtic Folk-Lore* quotes this account from the *Brython* (vol. 1).

Plentyn-newid (*plentin newid*). Wirt Sikes in *British Goblins* gives a full account of a plentyn-newid, or Welsh CHANGELING, left by the TYL-WYTH TEG in exchange for the beautiful human child which they coveted. The Welsh changelings differed very little from those elsewhere, and received the same harsh treatment. Sikes says:

> The plentyn-newid has the exact appearance of the stolen infant at first; but its aspect speedily alters. It grows ugly of face, shrivelled of form, ill-tempered, wailing, and generally frightful. It bites and strikes, and becomes a terror to the poor mother. Sometimes it is idiotic; but again it has a supernatural cunning, not only impossible in a mortal babe, but not even appertaining to the oldest heads, on other than fairy shoulders.

Among the cruelties practised to drive away the fairy was the placing of the child on a heated shovel, as in Ireland, where a baby was actually killed by the neighbours in the 19th century. A Welsh method is to bathe

the child in a solution of fox-gloves. This is said to have killed a Caer-narvonshire baby in 1858. The brewery of eggshells is used in Wales as in Scotland to discover a changeling, or sometimes porridge is made in an eggshell, or a blackbird roasted to make a dinner for fifteen reapers, and the changeling's exclamation, 'I have seen the acorn before the oak,' is as common in Wales as in Scotland. These close resemblances in Celtic areas which have been long separated seem to mark the changeling beliefs as very early ones.

[Motif: F321.1]

Pokey-Hokey. Mrs Wright in *Rustic Speech and Folk-Lore* mentions Pokey-Hokey of East Anglia among her frightening figures, together with KNOCKY-BOH and MUMPOKER. It is possible that the colloquial phrase, 'There's been some hokey-pokey about this,' may derive from this GOBLIN, though it could be the other way round.

Portunes. Small agricultural FAIRIES described by GERVASE OF TIL-BURY in *Otia Imperialia*, written in the 13th century. It was their habit to labour on farms, and at night when the doors were shut they would blow up the fire, and, taking frogs from their bosoms, they would roast them on the coals and eat them. Gervase describes them as very tiny, only half an inch in height, but KEIGHTLEY suggests that by a copyist's error *pollicis* was substituted for *pedis*. It would certainly take a fairy of at least a foot high to carry even the smallest newly-hatched frog in his bosom. They were like very old men with wrinkled faces and wore patched coats. If anything had to be carried into the house or any arduous labour had to be undertaken, they would perform it, however hard it was. In fact they were all for good and never for ill, except for one mischievous trick. If any man was riding alone on a dark night, a portune would sometimes take his horse's bridle, lead it into a pond and make off with a loud laugh. In fact, the Portune was very like ROBIN GOODFELLOW, except that he seems a gregarious rather than a SOLITARY FAIRY. The PIXIES and other small fairies, however, have been known to work for humans just as these portunes did, and in their shabby clothes they resemble the BROWNIE. It is interesting to find this type so persistent in our fairy-lore.

Pouk. See PUCK.

Pouk-ledden. The Midland equivalent of PIXY-LED. It will be remem-bered that among the mischievous tricks of Shakespeare's PUCK is 'to mislead night-wanderers, laughing at their harm'. In medieval times, 'Pouk' was a name for the Devil. Langland speaks of *Pouk's Pinfold*, meaning Hell. By the 16th century, however, Pouk had become a harm-less trickster, and only the Puritans bore him a grudge.

[Motif: F402.1.1]

Power over fairies. Country people and learned MAGICIANS both desired power over FAIRIES and chose it rather than the double-edged weapon of submission to Satan. They generally pursued their end by rather different methods. The most brutal and straightforward was by direct capture. Fairy wives were caught in this way, as in the story of WILD EDRIC and many tales of the ROANE or SEAL MAIDENS. But other CAPTURED FAIRIES were caught from covetousness, like SKILLY-WIDDEN, the fairy boy. The fairies which were most eagerly seized were the LEPRACAUNS, or fairy shoemakers, of the same type as the CLURI-CAUNE, but there is no example of their being retained by their captors. A typical tale about them is that told by Thomas KEIGHTLEY in *Fairy Mythology* (pp. 373–5). Thomas Fitzpatrick, a young farmer of Kildare, was sauntering along one holiday when it came into his head to shake out the hay and bind up the oats, as the weather looked like changing. As he was doing so he heard a stump-tapping sound like a stonechat, only it was late in the season for a stonechat to be calling. So he stole along to see what it might be, and, peering through the bushes, he saw a little wee man with a wee leather apron tied round his waist hammering away fitting a heelpiece to a little bit of a brogue. Tom knew it was no other than the Lepracaun. He knew the Lepracaun was the richest creature in all Fairyland and he knew if he could keep his eye fixed on him he could force him to give up one at least of the crocks of gold he had hidden about in the fields. So he made a sharp pounce on him and held him tight and threatened him with all the worst things he could think of unless he showed him where his gold was hidden. He was so fierce that the little man was quite frightened, and he said, 'Come along with me and I'll show ye where it's hidden.' Tom fairly glued his eyes to the little fellow, who directed him through sticks and stones, and up and down and to-fro till they got to a field just covered with bolyawn buies (ragwort). He pointed to a tall one and said: 'Dig under that bolyawn and ye'll get a crock chuck full of golden guineas.' It was a holiday, so Tom hadn't his spade by him, so he tied his red garter round the bolyawn. 'You'll not be wanting me again,' said the Lepracaun. 'No, no,' says Tom. 'Now you've showed it me I'll off away for a spade.' So the Lepracaun melted away like a drop of water in sand. Tom ran for his spade as fast as the wind. He was gone no time at all, but when he got back there was a red garter round every bolyawn in that field. That, or something like it, was what happened to everyone who tried to enrich himself at the expense of a lepracaun.

An occasionally successful way of acquiring power over a fairy is to learn his name. An attempt to do so is always resented, and sometimes the bestowal of even a nickname will banish a haunting fairy. The stories of TOM TIT TOT and WHUPPITY STOURIE illustrate this power. Edward CLODD wrote an important book, *Tom Tit Tot*, on the power of the spoken name. The acquiring of fairy possessions, the red caps of Scandinavian ELVES, a MERMAID's comb, and so on, can give equal power; but all these methods can be dangerous when used by the unskilled, and the conjurations of the magicians were generally thought to be more effective. Some fairy rhymes and calls were used by unsophisticated people like Anne JEFFERIES, but the more elaborate SPELLS FOR OBTAINING POWER OVER FAIRIES, and particularly the enclosing of them in a crystal or a ring, are to be found in the magical manuscripts of the 16th and 17th centuries.

[Motif: C432.1]

Powries. See DUNTERS.

Prayers. Naturally, prayers are a chief form of protection in any super-natural peril, and particularly the Lord's Prayer. Against the Devil it used to be supposed that this was much more efficacious if said aloud, because the Devil could not read man's thoughts, and could only judge the state of his soul by his words and actions, and therefore he was fatally discouraged by hearing people praying aloud. The same no doubt would apply to evil FAIRIES when seeking adequate PROTECTION AGAINST FAIRIES.

[Motifs: F382.6; G303.16.2]

Protection against fairies. People walking alone by night, especially through fairy-haunted places, had many ways of protecting themselves. The first might be by sacred symbols, by making the sign of a cross or by carrying a CROSS, particularly one made of IRON; by PRAYERS or the chanting of hymns, by HOLY WATER, sprinkled or carried, and by carrying and strewing CHURCHYARD MOULD in their path. BREAD and SALT were also effective, and both were regarded as sacred symbols, one of life and the other of eternity. As HERRICK says:

> For that holy piece of bread
> Charmes the danger and the dread.

BELLS were protective; church bells, the bells worn by morris dancers and the bells round the necks of sheep and oxen. So was whistling and the snapping of clappers. A man who was PIXY-LED, wandering around and unable to find his way out of the field, would generally turn his coat. This act of TURNING CLOTHES may have been thought to act as a change of identity, for gamblers often turned their coat to break a run of bad luck.

Certain plants and herbs were also protective counter-charms. The strongest was a FOUR-LEAFED CLOVER, which broke fairy GLAMOUR, as well as the FAIRY OINTMENT, which was indeed said by HUNT to be made of four-leafed clovers. ST JOHN'S WORT, the herb of Midsummer, was potent against spells and the power of FAIRIES, evil spirits and the Devil. Red verbena was almost equally potent, partly perhaps because of its pure and brilliant colour. DAISIES, particularly the little field daisies, were protective plants, and a child wearing daisy chains was supposed to be safe from fairy kidnapping. Red-berried trees were also protective, above them all ROWAN or mountain ash. A staff made of rowan wood or a rowan cross or a bunch of ripe berries were all sure protections, and where rowan did not grow ASH was a good substitute.

If chased by evil fairies, one could generally leap to safety across RUNNING WATER, particularly a southward-flowing stream, though there were evil water-spirits such as the KELPIE who haunted fresh-water streams.

A newly-christened child was safe against being carried off by the fairies, but before christening 'the little pagan' was kept safe by his father's trousers laid over the cradle, or an open pair of scissors hung above it. This last had a double potency as being made of steel and as hanging in the form of a cross, on the same principle that the child's garments were secured by pins stuck in cross-wise. The house and stock were protected by iron HORSESHOES above the house and stable doors, and horses were protected from being elf-ridden by SELF-BORED STONES hung above the manger.

With so many methods of protection, it was surprising that such a number of babies were stolen and replaced by CHANGELINGS and so many travellers were pixy-led.

[Motifs: D788; D950.6; D1385.2.5; F321.2; F366.2; F382; F382.1; F382.2; F383.2; F384.1]

Puck. Shakespeare in his MIDSUMMER NIGHT'S DREAM has given Puck an individual character, and it no longer seems natural to talk, as Robert BURTON does in *The Anatomie of Melancholy*, of *a* puck instead of 'Puck', nor, like Langland, equate Puck with the Devil and call Hell 'Pouk's Pinfold'. Shakespeare's Puck is the epitome of the HOBGOBLIN, with the by-name of ROBIN GOODFELLOW. In folk tradition emphasis is perhaps most laid on Puck as a misleader, and 'POUK-LEDDEN' is a commoner phrase than 'Hobberdy's Lantern'. Shakespeare's Puck plays all the pranks described in the LIFE OF ROBIN GOODFELLOW. His self-descriptive speech to TITANIA's fairy could not be bettered as the description of a hobgoblin:

> I am that merry wanderer of the night.
> I jest to Oberon, and make him smile,
> When I a fat and bean-fed horse beguile,
> Neighing in likeness of a filly foal:
> And sometime lurk I in a gossip's bowl,
> In very likeness of a roasted crab;
> And, when she drinks, against her lips I bob,
> And on her wither'd dew-lap pour the ale.
> The wisest aunt, telling the saddest tale,

Sometime for three-foot stool mistaketh me;
Then slip I from her bum, down topples she,
And *tailor* cries, and falls into a cough;
And then the whole quire hold their hips, and loffe;
And waxen in their mirth, and neeze, and swear
A merrier hour was never wasted there.

Human follies are his perpetual entertainment, but, like all hobgoblins, he has his softer moments, his indignation is always raised against scornful lovers and he feels real compassion for Hermia, scorned and deserted by the man with whom she had fled. Puck in Drayton's account of DIMINUTIVE FAIRIES in *Nimphidia* shows many of the same characteristics. For the rest, we shall find that Puck's traits correspond with those to be found in the Celtic parts of these islands, in the PWCA, PHOUKA and PIXIES. Like all hobgoblins, he is a SHAPE-SHIFTER, but he also performs BROWNIE labours for humans, and like a Brownie he is laid by a gift of clothing. Shakespeare's Puck differs in one thing from ordinary pucks of tradition: he belongs to the fairy court and cannot be called a SOLITARY FAIRY.

[Motifs: F234.0.2; F381.3; F399.4; F402.1.1; F482.5.4]

Puddlefoot. A Perthshire BROWNIE who lived in a small burn on the road between Pitlochry and Dunkeld. He used to splash and paddle about in the burn, and then would go up with very wet feet to a farm nearby and do a certain amount of household work, but rather more mischief. What was tidy he untidied, and what was untidy he tidied. People were afraid of passing the burn at night because they heard Puddlefoot, but one night a man coming back market-merry from Dunkeld heard him splashing about in the burn and called to him, 'Hoo is't with thee noo, Puddlefoot?' Puddlefoot hated the name. 'Oh, oh, I have gotten a name. It's Puddlefoot they call me!' With that he vanished, and was never seen or heard of again. For a parallel story, the SHORT HOGGERS OF WHITTINGHAME provides an example.

[Motifs: C432.1; F346; F381.1; F399.4]

Pwca (*pooka*). The Welsh version of the English PUCK. His actions and character are so like those of Shakespeare's Puck that some Welsh people have claimed that Shakespeare borrowed him from stories told him by his friend Richard Price of Brecon who lived near Cwm Pwca, one of the Pwca's favourite haunts. Sikes in *British Goblins* reproduces a rather pleasing drawing of the Pwca, done with a piece of coal by a Welsh peasant. The Pwca in this picture has a head rather like a fledgeling bird's and a figure not unlike a tadpole's. No arms are shown, but the figure is in silhouette. One story about the Pwca shows that a tribute of milk was left for him. This may possibly have been in payment for his services as a cowherd, though that is not expressly mentioned. A milkmaid at Trwyn Farm near Abergwyddon used to leave a bowl of milk and a piece of white bread for Pwca in a lonely place on the pastures every day. One day, out of mischief, she drank the milk herself and ate most of the bread, so that Pwca only got cold water and a crust that day. Next day, as she went near the place, she was suddenly seized by very sharp but invisible hands and given a sound whipping, while the Pwca warned her that if she did that again she would get worse treatment.

Pwca is best known, however, as a WILL O' THE WISP. He will lead a benighted wanderer up a narrow path to the edge of a ravine, then leap over it, laughing loudly, blow out his candle, and leave the poor traveller to grope his way back as best he can. In this behaviour he is like the Scottish SHELLYCOAT as well as the English Puck.

[Motif: F402.1.1]

Rade. See FAIRY RADE; KING HERLA; WILD EDRIC.

Ralph of Coggeshall (12th–13th cent.). See GREEN CHILDREN.

Ratchets. See GABRIEL HOUNDS; GABRIEL RATCHETS.

Rawhead-and-Bloody-Bones. This was the full name, but it is sometimes shortened to 'Bloody Bones' or 'OLD BLOODY BONES', and sometimes to 'Tommy Rawhead'. Samuel Johnson in his dictionary defines it as 'The name of a spectre, mentioned to fright children', and quotes instances from Dryden and Locke. In Lancashire and Yorkshire, 'Tommy Rawhead' or 'Rawhead-and-Bloody-Bones' is a water-demon haunting old marl-pits or deep ponds to drag children down into their depths, like the other NURSERY BOGIES, PEG POWLER and Nelly Longarms. Mrs Wright, in *Rustic Speech and Folk-Lore*, quotes a typical warning: 'Keep away from the marl-pit or rawhead and bloody bones will have you.' In *County Folklore* (vol. VIII, p. 123), Ruth Tongue quotes two informants for Bloody-Bones who lived in dark cupboards, generally under the stairs.

> If you were heroic enough to peep through a crack you would get a glimpse of the dreadful crouching creature, with blood running down his face, seated waiting on a pile of raw bones that had belonged to children who told lies or said bad words. If you peeped through the keyhole at him he got you anyway.

Redcap. One of the most malignant of old Border GOBLINS, Redcap lived in old ruined peel towers and castles where wicked deeds had been done, and delighted to re-dye his red cap in human blood. William Henderson gives a full account of him in *Folk-Lore of the Northern Counties* (pp. 253–5). He describes him as 'a short thickset old man, with long prominent teeth, skinny fingers armed with talons like eagles, large eyes of a fiery-red colour, grisly hair streaming down his shoulders, iron boots, a pikestaff in his left hand, and a red cap on his head'. Human strength can avail little against him, but he can be routed by scripture or the sight of a CROSS. If this is held up to him, he gives a dismal yell and vanishes, leaving one of his long teeth behind him. The wicked Lord Soulis of Hermitage Castle had Redcap as his familiar, who made him weapon-proof so that he was only finally destroyed by boiling him in oil in a brazen pot on Nine-stane Rig.

In Perthshire, however, there is a milder Redcap, a little man who lives in a room high up in Grantully Castle and whom it is fortunate to see or hear. The Dutch redcaps, or *Kaboutermannekin*, are of the true BROWNIE nature and typical brownie tales are told about them.

[Motif: F363.2]

Redshanks. See DANES.

Rheumatism. The twisting and deformities which follow on rheumatism used to be suspect as a sign that the sufferer was a witch, especially if it came on suddenly. Severe lumbago was a dangerous affliction to have in the 16th and 17th centuries, for a witch was often supposed to be bent like a hoop; but it was also, in more minor forms, as a result of having displeased the FAIRIES in some way, and particularly when it took the form of lameness, as of the lazy dairymaid who refused to get up and put out water for the fairies and was afflicted with a seven-years' lameness. An account of this is to be found in Mrs Bray's *The Borders of the Tamar and the Tavy*. See also BLIGHTS AND ILLNESSES ATTRIBUTED TO THE FAIRIES.

Roane, the. 'Roane' is the Gaelic name for a seal, but the old people believed, as the Shetlanders believed of their SELKIES, that these were a kind of fairy creature, who wore their skins to travel through the sea, but could cast them off and appear in human shape. The Roane were the gentlest of all the fairy people. The Selkies avenged the death of their kin by raising storms and sinking the boats of the seal-catchers, but the Roane seem to have borne little resentment against their persecutors. Grant Stewart, in his *Highland Superstitions and Amusements* (pp. 65–71), tells of a seal-catcher who lived near John O'Groats, who had one day lost his clasp-knife in the attempt to kill a large dog-seal. That night there came a knock at his door and a stranger leading a fine horse asked his name and told him that he had been sent to order a large number of seal-skins from him. The customer was at hand, and would make the bargain with him himself. The two got on, and the horse plunged away at such a pace that the following wind seemed to blow in their faces. They rode along the wild coast until they reached a great crag above the sea. 'Where are you taking me?' said the fisherman. 'Get down, and you'll soon see,' said the stranger, and as their feet touched the land he seized the fisherman and leapt with him right over the crag. Down and down they went into the depths of the sea until they came to a cave which was full of the seal people, and the fisherman perceived that he himself had become a seal. His companion was a seal too, but he and all the rest spoke and behaved like human mortals. They were all very sad. The fisherman was in great terror, for he knew that he must have killed many of their friends. His guide showed him a clasp-knife. 'Do you know this knife?' he said, and the fisherman had no choice but to confess that it was his, though he feared that in a moment it would be plunged into him. 'It was with this knife that you wounded my father,' said the stranger, 'and only you can heal him.' He led the fisherman into an inner cave where the big dog-seal that had escaped that day lay in great pain. The seal people told him what to do, and with the knife he made a circle round the wound and smoothed it with his hand, wishing with all his heart that it might be healed. And so it was, and the old seal got up from his couch as well as he had ever been. The fisherman still feared that he would be punished, but they told him not to be afraid; if he would swear a solemn oath never to kill a seal again he should be taken back to his wife and children. He took the oath with full solemnity; the stranger took him back to the cliff where their horse was waiting, and left him at his own door, with a gift of money that was worth the price of many seal-skins.

It is the SEAL MAIDENS, too, who sometimes cast off their seal-skins and dance together on the shore. There are many tales in the Scottish Highlands, as well as in the Orkneys and Shetlands, of how mortal fishermen have sometimes seized a skin and taken captive one of the Roane as a wife. But the wife always recovers her skin and escapes back to the sea, just as the GWRAGEDD ANNWN of Wales always leave their mortal husbands in the end. There is no lasting union between FAIRIES and mortals.

[Type: ML4080. Motif: E731.6]

Roaring Bull of Bagbury, the. An example of a ghost who has taken over the character and functions of a BOGIE, or even of a devil. His story is told in Burne and Jackson's *Shropshire Folk-Lore* (pp. 108–11). He had been a very wicked man who lived at Bagbury Farm. He had only done two good deeds in his life, given a waistcoat to an old man and a piece of bread and cheese to a poor boy, but those deeds were not enough to save his soul, and after he died he came back in the shape of a monstrous bull which haunted the farm and the outbuildings, roaring and bellowing so loud that tiles and shutters would fly off. At last the people could stand it no longer, so they called together twelve parsons to lay him. They got him under, but they could not lay him, so they drove him before them to Hyssington Church. All the twelve of them had lighted candles, and eleven held them in their hands, but one old blind parson knew the bull's tricks, and when they got him into church he tucked his candle into his top-boot. Sure enough, the bull made a great rush, and he blew out all the eleven candles. But the old parson said, 'Light all your candles from mine.' They did so, and the bull raged round till he cracked one wall of the church. But they conjured him down, smaller and smaller, till they got him into a snuff-box, and he asked to be laid under Bagbury Bridge, so that every mare that passed over should lose her foal, and every woman her child. They would not consent to that, but sent him off to the Red Sea for 1,000 years. For all that, the people of Hyssington crossed Bagbury Bridge very cautiously for a good few years to come.

Here the procedure of laying is the same as that used in laying a demon or devil. The method is even more clearly shown in the story of the GREAT GIANT OF HENLLYS. These are undoubtedly ghost stories, but here we see the balance trembling towards those fairy stories in which the FAIRIES are regarded as the dead.

[Motifs: E423; E443.0.1; E443.2.4.1]

Robin Goodfellow. The best-known and most often referred to of all the HOBGOBLINS of England in the 16th and 17th centuries. Indeed, in a sense he seemed to swallow all others and their names were made nicknames of his. Even in Shakespeare, Robin Goodfellow and PUCK are identified. In the very informative conversation between Puck and the wandering fairy in a MIDSUMMER NIGHT'S DREAM, she begins by calling him 'Robin Goodfellow', but seems to consider that he prefers the name of 'Puck':

> Those that Hob-goblin call you and sweet Puck,
> You do their work, and they shall have good luck.

And yet one would imagine 'Robin Goodfellow' to be a more flattering name than 'Puck', which in earlier times was used without equivocation for the Devil. The black-letter pamphlet of 1628, *Robin Goodfellow, his mad Pranks and Merry Jests*, first reprinted by Collier as the LIFE OF ROBIN GOODFELLOW, makes him a half-fairy, the son of OBERON by a country wench. His mother was kept well supplied by his fairy friends with rich clothes and food and wines, but though he had the fairy precocity and prankishness he had no special powers until, at about six years old, he ran away from home. As he was wandering he had a vision of fairies, and when he woke found a golden scroll beside him from his father granting him the power of obtaining whatever he wished and of SHAPE-SHIFTING. These powers were to be used against the ill-disposed and in aid of honest folks. In the end he was promised the sight of Fairyland. He immediately tried these fairy powers and found that he truly possessed them. Accordingly he entered on his career as a hobgoblin, and each short chapter describes one of his pranks, generally ending with Robin Goodfellow's characteristic 'ho! ho! ho!' and a snatch of song of very varying merits. There are such episodes as the tricking of a lecherous old man who was making love to his own niece, the misleading of way-farers, practical jokes at a wedding, some love passages with a miller's wife in the course of which the miller, trying to throw Robin into the water, finds himself in the mill-pond instead, BROWNIE services to a maid, terminated in the usual way by a gift of clothing, and various other exploits. Finally Robin is led into Fairyland by OBERON and the various hobgoblins and fairies describe themselves and their activities in short verses. TOM THUMB is their piper.

This is a piece of popular journalism, but there is a good deal of true folk tradition included in it. The idea that half-fairies have to be given fairy powers by charms and potions seems to be borne out in the many stories of the FAIRY OINTMENT. Alfred Nutt, in his *Fairy Mythology of Shakespeare*, took this idle pamphlet seriously, pointing out its resemblance to the Celtic mythological legend of MANANNAN SON OF LIR. Like Robin Goodfellow, Manannan was the son of a supernatural being and a human mother, and was watched over and admitted into the pantheon by his father. In fact, Nutt sees Robin Goodfellow as the humble and distant descendant of the mythological hero.

There are many mentions of Robin Goodfellow in 17th-century literature, as, for instance, in Rowland's *More Knaves Yet*:

> Amongst the rest, was a good fellow devill,
> So called in kindness, cause he did no evill,

Knowne by the name of Robin (as we heare)
And that his eyes as bigge as sawcers were,
Who came a nights, and would make Kitchins cleane
And in the bed bepinch a lazie queane.
Was much in Milles about the grinding Meale,
(And sure I take it, taught the Miller steale,)
Amongst the creame bowles, and milke pans would be,
And with the country wenches, who but hee.
To wash their Dishes for some fresh-cheese hier:
Or set their Pots and Kettles bout the fier.

A more musical poem than many of the others was that which used to
be attributed to Ben Jonson and which reads as if it were part of a masque.
In its thirteen verses it touches on nearly all the hobgoblin activities, and
seems to epitomize the Robin Goodfellow pamphlet. It is particularly
vivid on his misleading and BOGY OR BOGEY-BEAST pranks:

If any wanderers I meet,
    That from their night-sport do trudge home,
With counterfeiting voice I greet,
    And cause them on with me to roam;
        Through woods, through lakes,
        Through bogs, through brakes,
    O'er bush and brier, with them I go,
        I call upon
        Them to come on,
    And wend me laughing, ho, ho, ho!

Sometimes I meet them like a man,
    Sometimes, an ox, sometimes, a hound;
And to a horse I turn me can,
    To trip and trot about them round;
        But if, to ride,
        My back they stride,
    More swift than wind away I go;
        O'er hedge and lands,
        Through pools and ponds,
    I whinny laughing, ho, ho, ho!

This poem, with nearly all the literary references to Robin Goodfellow,
may be found in Carew Hazlitt's *Fairy Tales, Legends and Romances
Illustrating Shakespeare*.
    [Motif: F399.4]

Robin Hood. The school of witchcraft theory initiated by Dr Margaret
Murray puts forward the proposition that the medieval witches and their
successors were a Stone Age fertility cult with a dying god who was bled

to death on May Day to give new life to the land and who from the Middle Ages onward was called Robin Hood. Later Dr Murray explored the theory of a rather more long-lived god, the actual king of the realm or his substitute, and suggested William Rufus, Thomas à Becket, Joan of Arc and Gilles de Rais as victims. Presumably, if that was so, Robin Hood would merely become part of the May Day celebrations. It has also been suggested that the outlaw Robin Hood took the name of a woodland spirit. Recent investigations, however, seem to point to a solid historical foundation for the legends, and to an aristocratic rather than a popular cult.

Robin Round-cap. Robin Round-cap of Spaldington Hall was a domestic spirit of the true HOBGOBLIN type. He used to help thresh the corn or do chores about the house, but when he was in a mischievous mood he would mix the chaff with wheat again, kick the milk-pail over or put out the fire. Nicholson, in *The Folk Speech of East Yorkshire*, says that the BOGGART story, 'Aye, George, We're Flitting', was told of him, but in the account of him quoted by Mrs Gutch in *County Folk-Lore* (vol. VI) he was, by the PRAYERS of three clergymen, laid for a certain number of years in a well which is still called 'Robin Round-cap's Well'.

[Motifs: F346; F382; F482.5.5]

Rossetti, Christina (1830–94). See GOBLIN MARKET.

Rowan, or mountain ash. The tree which above all others offered the best protection against fairy enchantments and witchcraft. As the Scottish rhyme goes:

> Rowan, lamer [amber] and red threid,
> Pits witches to their speed.

It will be noticed that all these are reddish, and the red berries of the rowan-tree make it specially effective. A staff of rowan, a CROSS made of rowan, a bunch of rowan berries, all these were effective, and it was customary in the Highlands to plant a rowan-tree outside every house. Where rowans were scarce, ASH-trees took their place. An ashen gad was supposed to be protective of cattle. See also PROTECTION AGAINST FAIRIES.

[Motifs: D950–6; D1385.2.5]

Running water. This, particularly southward-running water, is holy, and cannot be passed by evil spirits. See also PROTECTION AGAINST FAIRIES.

[Motif: F383.2]

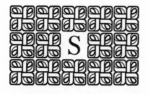

St Collen (*kothlen*) **and the Fairy King.** St Collen was a Welsh saint
of the 7th century. Like many of the Celtic saints, he was of a pugnacious
and restless disposition, and during his career he spent some time in
Somerset. It was here that he encountered the fairy king. S. Baring-
Gould, in his *Lives of the Saints*, summarizes his story from a Welsh
Life of St Collen, not translated into English at the time when Baring-
Gould was writing. This accounts for the confusing statement that the
king of the FAIRIES on Glastonbury Tor was called GWYN AP NUDD,
and his dominion was over Annwn.

St Collen, after three years at Glastonbury, had been elected abbot,
but he soon renounced his abbacy for the heavier and harder life of a
hermit, and found a cell at the foot of Glastonbury Tor. As he was
meditating in it one day he heard two men saying that Gwyn ap Nudd,
king of Annwn, had his castle on the top of the Tor. St Collen stuck his
head out of the window and rebuked them for talking in such good terms
of devils from Hell. The men warned him not to talk in that way of
Gwyn ap Nudd, or it would be the worse for him. But Collen persisted.
A few days later a messenger came to the cell inviting Collen to visit the
fairy king. Collen refused, but day after day the invitation was repeated,
and at last the messenger lost patience and said that it would be the worse
for him if he did not come. Collen went with him, but he picked up a
stoup of HOLY WATER and hid it under his cassock.

At the top of the Tor he found the most beautiful castle that the mind
of man could conceive, troops of bodyguards and a number of musicians
with all kinds of instruments, bevies of maidens, and gallant young men
riding around on beautiful horses. He was conducted into the banqueting
hall where the king pressed him courteously to sit down and eat. A great
banquet was carried in by fair pages in uniforms of scarlet and blue. 'Eat
and drink,' said the king, 'and if this does not please you, there is plenty
more of all sorts.' But Collen, whose eyes were not blinded by GLAMOUR,
replied, 'I do not eat the leaves of a tree.' A shudder ran through the
shining assembly, but the king still spoke courteously: 'Tell me, have
you ever seen attendants better dressed than my pages in their fair
liveries of scarlet and blue?' 'They are suitably dressed,' said Collen,
'for what they are.' 'And what is that?' said the king. 'Scarlet is for the
ever-living flames,' Collen replied, 'and blue for the eternal ice of Hell.'
With that he dashed the holy water over them all. The gorgeous show

vanished in a minute, and Collen found himself standing in the pale light of dawn among the grassy tumps at the summit of the Tor.

It is clear that Collen made nothing of the need of GOOD MANNERS in dealing with the fairies, but he was fully alive to the danger of eating FAIRY FOOD.

[Motifs: D2031; F160.0.2; F167.12; F382.2]

St John's wort. This (*Hypericum*) is one of the most beneficent of the magic herbs, protecting equally against FAIRIES and the Devil. Sir Walter SCOTT gives a rhyme spoken by a demon lover who could not approach a girl because she was carrying St John's wort and verbena:

> 'If you would be true love mine,
>   Throw away John's Wort and Verbein.'

See also PROTECTION AGAINST FAIRIES.
 [Motif: D1385.2]

Salt. A universal symbol of preservation, eternity, and of goodwill. See also PROTECTION AGAINST FAIRIES.
 [Motif: F384.1]

Sandy Harg's wife. Alexander Cromek, in his *Remains of Galloway and Nithsdale Song* (p. 305), gives an excellent example of a STOCK – that is, the replacement of the stolen human being by a piece of wood, given by GLAMOUR the appearance of the stolen human. In this story the attempt failed.

> Alexander Harg, a cottar, in the parish of New-Abbey, had courted and married a pretty girl, whom the fairies had long attempted to seduce from this world of love and wedlock. A few nights after his marriage, he was standing with a *halve* net, awaiting the approach of the tide. Two old vessels, stranded on the rocks, were visible at mid-water mark, and were reckoned occasional haunts of the fairies, when crossing the mouth of the Nith. In one of these wrecks a loud noise was heard, as of carpenters at work; a hollow voice cried from the other: 'Ho, what're ye doing?' 'I'm making a wife to Sandy Harg!' replied a voice in no mortal accent. The husband, astonished and terrified, throws down his net, hastens home, shuts up every avenue of entrance, and folds his young spouse in his arms. At midnight a gentle rap comes to the door, with a most courteous three-times touch. The young dame starts to get up; the husband holds her in forbidding silence and kindly clasps. A foot is heard to depart, and instantly the cattle low and bellow, ramping as if pulling up their stakes. He clasps his wife more close to his bosom, regardless of her entreaties. The horses, with most frightful neighs, prance, snort, and bound, as if in the midst of flame. She speaks, cries, entreats, and struggles: he will not move, speak, nor

quit her. The noise and tumult increases, but with the morning's coming it dies away. The husband leaps up with the dawn, and hurries out to view his premises. A piece of moss-oak, fashioned to the shape and size of his wife, meets his eye, reared against his garden-dyke, and he burns this devilish effigy.

The importance of maintaining silence and a firm grasp in combatting fairy enchantments is shown in this story.
[Motifs: F322; F380]

Scantlie Mab. The name of HABETROT's principal assistant. She was the plainest member of the assembly, for besides her deformed lip she had starting eyes and a long, hooked nose among her DEFECTS OF THE FAIRIES.

Sceolan (*shkeolawn*). As FINN's second hound, Sceolan was bound to him by a hidden blood-tie, for he was born while his mother, Finn's aunt, was in the form of a hound. See BRAN AND SCEOLAN.

Scot, Michael (1175?–1234?). See WIZARDS.

Scot, Reginald (1535?–1599). The author of two books, both original in conception and treatment, of which the second, *The Discoverie of Witchcraft* (1584), concerns us, though not so closely as if we had been treating primarily of witchcraft. Scot, after going down from Hart Hall, Oxford, spent a quiet, studious life in his native Kent. He was not, however, entirely abstracted from public business and concerned himself in local affairs to good purpose. In the course of his public services he became much concerned at the cruelty and injustice with which old women suspected of the practice of witchcraft were treated, and he set himself to expose the superstitions and fallacies on which the witchcraft beliefs were founded. This he did with great learning, and in a racy and engaging style which captured popular attention. In the course of the book he once or twice mentioned the FAIRIES and gave the famous list of fairies believed in in his boyhood which was reproduced in the DENHAM TRACTS. In Book IV, Chapter 10, he refers to the BROWNIE:

> In deede your grandams maides were woont to set a boll of milke before him and his cousine Robin good-fellow, for grinding of malt or mustard, and sweeping the house at midnight: and you haue also heard that he would chafe exceedingly, if the maid or good-wife of the house, having compassion of his nakednes, laid anie clothes for him, beesides his messe of white bread and milke, which was his standing fee. For in that case he saith; What haue we here? Hemton, hamten, here will I neuer more tread nor stampen.

And in his address 'To the Reader' Scot mentions these beliefs as long past:

> For I should no more prevaile herein, than if a hundred yeares since I should have intreated your predecessors to beleeve that Robin goodfellowe, that great and ancient bulbeggar, had beene but a cousening merchant, and no divell indeed . . . But Robin goodfellowe ceaseth now to be much feared, and poperie is sufficiently discovered.

Scot's book attracted considerable attention and was translated into Dutch. King James of Scotland took strong exception to it, and wrote his *Daemonologie* to refute it. He also mentions the fairies with a description of the FAIRY RADE and a mention of the brownie as a present, not a past belief, in a devil who haunts the house, doing no evil, 'but doing as it were necessarie turnes up and down the house: and this spirit they called *Brownie* in our language, who appeared like a rough-man: yea, some were so blinded, as to beleeve that their house was all the sonsier, as they called it, that such spirites resorted there'.

Not content with writing to refute the book, James, on his accession to the English throne, ordered that it should be burnt by the public hangman. It was perhaps as well that Scot had died some years before. The book was not, however, finally suppressed, and in 1665 the third edition was brought out with nine chapters added at the beginning of the Fifteenth Book and a *Discourse upon Devils and Spirits* in a very different style from the sturdy scepticism of Reginald Scot, for that curious fashion of credulity had set in which coincided with the foundation of the Royal Society. It includes some pretty fairy passages:

> And more particularly the *Faeries* – do principally inhabit the Mountains, and Caverns of the Earth, whose nature is to make strange Apparitions on the Earth in Meddows, or on Mountains being like Men and Women, Souldiers, Kings, and Ladyes Children, and Horsemen cloathed in green, to which purpose they do in the night steal hempen stalks from the fields where they grow, to Convert them into Horses as the Story goes . . . Such jocund and facetious Spirits are sayd to sport themselves in the night by tumbling and fooling with Servants and Shepherds in Country houses, pinching them black and blew, and leaving Bread, Butter and Cheese sometimes with them, which if they refuse to eat, some mischief shall undoubtedly befall them by means of these Faeries. And many such have been taken away by the sayd Spirits, for a fortnight, or month together, being carryed with them in Chariots through the Air, over Hills, and Dales, Rocks and Precipices, till at last they have been found lying in some Meddow or Mountain bereaved of their sences, and commonly of one of their Members to boot.

Scott, Sir Walter (1771–1832). The author who was the great originator
of the Romantic Revival in 19th-century English literature. He received
the impulse as a boy from Percy's *Reliques* and was ever after entranced
by myths and legends and historical traditions, more particularly in his
own native Border Country. The first book he published, *The Minstrelsy
of the Scottish Border*, contained traditional ballads that he had collected
and slightly refurbished, as well as some literary poems on traditional
subjects. Vol. II is notable for his essay on 'Fairies of Popular Superstition', an important contribution to the fairy-lore of Scotland, which
shows how much he had profited from his collecting expeditions in the
Border Country and farther afield in the Scottish Highlands. *The
Minstrelsy* contained versions of YOUNG TAM LIN and TRUE THOMAS,
but the long introductory essays were the most valuable part of the book.
The essay on the FAIRIES was later supplemented by Chapters 4–6 in
Demonology and Witchcraft (1830), which is full of interesting references
to the fairies in the witch trials and to fairy references in early literature.
In 1805, a poem which established Scott's fame, *The Lay of the Last
Minstrel*, appeared. It is founded on the tricks played by Gilpin Horner,
a BOGGART-like HOBGOBLIN who haunted one of the Border farms. His
cry of 'Lost! Lost!' is borrowed from the SHELLYCOAT who haunted
Eskdale, but in the poem he is supposed to be a devil who had been
called up by Michael SCOT and had escaped. This was the only one of the
poems which used a folk theme for its subject, but in *The Lady of the
Lake*, which was perhaps the most popular of all, a complete fairy ballad
was introduced as the ballad sung by Allan Bain, Douglas's harper. This
poem, 'Alice Brand', introduces many interesting pieces of fairy tradition, the perilous state of unconsciousness in which mortals can be
snatched away into Fairyland, the shifting appearance of the fairies, the
unluckiness of wearing green near fairy territory, the possibility of
rescuing CAPTIVES IN FAIRYLAND by the use of objects sacred to
Christianity, the CROSS, a Bible, BREAD, with its sacramental connection.
Throughout his poems and novels snatches of folk-belief and tradition
are to be found. The generous interest he took in fellow authors, in
James HOGG, Chambers, Crofton CROKER, the Grimm brothers and
many more, gave prestige to folklore studies everywhere.

Seal Maidens. The seal people have long been regarded as the gentlest
of the sea spirits, and the seal maidens are among the more recent of the
traditions of the FAIRY BRIDES. Occasional families have a hereditary
horny growth between their fingers which is supposed to be an inheritance
from a seal ancestress. 'The MacCoddrums of the Seals' are the most
famous example. The pattern of the story is almost invariable and is to
be found in Orkney and Shetland, where the seal people are known as
SELKIES, as well as in the Highlands and Islands, where they are called
the ROANE. A fisherman sees some beautiful maidens dancing by the sea.

He creeps up to them unobserved and carries away and hides one of the skins he finds lying on the rocks by the water. The seal maidens take alarm, pull on their seal-skins and plunge into the sea. Only one is left behind, searching desperately for her skin. She begs for it unavailingly, but at length she is persuaded to marry the fisherman, though she always has a wistful eye on the sea. She makes a good and domesticated wife until at length she discovers her hidden seal-skin, when she at once hurries down to the sea and returns to her first husband. Sometimes she returns to bestow medical knowledge upon her children, as, in Wales, did Penelope of the GWRAGEDD ANNWN. But here, as in other fairy bride stories, the rule is that unions between mortals and immortals are destined for breach and bereavement.

[Motifs: B651.8; D721; D1025.9; F420.1.2*]

Secret names of the fairies. Certain classes of FAIRIES or IMPS seem to regard the secrecy of their own names as a necessary protection to be guarded as carefully as primitive man guarded his ritual name. At the same time, an irresistible urge for the proclamation of the name drove them to shout it aloud as soon as they believed themselves to be unobserved. The same pattern is to be found in the well-known Grimm story of 'Rumpelstiltskin'. The best and the best-known English version is the Suffolk TOM TIT TOT, examined in a monograph, *Tom Tit Tot*, by Edward CLODD in 1898. He discusses the anthropological aspects of the tale. There are many variants scattered over the country. The demon TERRYTOP, the subject of one of the Cornish drolls, is the longest version. WHUPPITY STOORIE, with a female fairy, and the cure of a pig as its central theme, is a lively version from Scotland. HABETROT, the story of the patron fairy of spinners, only touches on the subject of her name, which is of no importance to the plot. FOUL WEATHER's name is given away by his wife singing it to his baby. Other secret names are the Welsh SILI FFRIT and TRWTYN-TRATYN, and the story of GWARYON-THROT provides another variation.

[Type: 500. Motifs: C432.1; C433; F381.1]

Seeing fairies. It is generally supposed that FAIRIES can present themselves to human sight if they wish to do so, but there seem to be also certain means and certain times when they can be caught unawares. One of the most general means is by a FOUR-LEAFED CLOVER, or by the use of the well-known FAIRY OINTMENT, compounded of four-leafed clovers, which disperses the GLAMOUR that fairies can cast over human senses. Once a human eye has been touched by the ointment it can penetrate fairy disguises, and this power is only removed by a blast of fairy breath or the more vindictive blinding of the seeing eye, as occurs in one of the MIDWIFE TO THE FAIRIES stories.

There are, however, certain people who have permanent or sporadic power of seeing fairies without fairy permission. These are the 'second-sighted' Highlanders, or those called 'gifted' in Somerset or the south-west, and 'sighted' in Ireland. John AUBREY made some researches into the beliefs about second-sighted men in Scotland, and gives the result of them in his *Miscellanies*. He issued a questionnaire, like those later used by folklorists, posing such questions as whether second sight consists in 'the discovery of present or past events only, or if it extend to such as are to come', and, 'If the objects of this knowledge be sad and dismal events only; such as deaths and murders? or, joyful and prosperous also?' The answers vary, as one comes to expect in folklore research. In KIRK's *Secret Commonwealth* there is frequent mention of second-sighted men, who either have the gift by nature or acquired it by magical art. Often they find the gift very onerous. Kirk says:

The TABHAISVER, or Seer, that corresponds with this kind of Familiars, can bring them with a Spel to appear to himselfe or others when he pleases, as readily as Endor Witch to those of her Kind. He tells, they are ever readiest to go on hurtfull Errands, but seldome will be the Messengers of great Good to Men. He is not terrified with their Sight when he calls them, but seeing them in a surprize (as often he does) frights him extreamly. And glaid would he be quite of such, for the hideous Spectacles seen among them; as the torturing of some Wight, earnest ghostly stairing Looks, Skirmishes, and the like.

However, there are some who wish to acquire the power, and Kirk gives the details of the rather hazardous ceremony by which they acquire it:

He must run a Tedder of Hair (which bound a Corps to the Bier) in a Helix (?) about his Midle, from End to End; then bow His Head downwards, as did Elijah, I Kings, 18. 42., and look back thorough his Legs untill he sie a Funerall advance till the People cross two Marches; or look thus back thorough a Hole where was a Knot of Fir. But if the Wind change Points while the Hair Tedder is ty'd about him, he is in Peril of his Lyfe. The usewall Method for a curious Person to get a transient Sight of this otherwise invisible Crew of Subterraneans, (if impotently and over rashly sought) is to put his (left Foot under the Wizard's right) Foot, and the Seer's Hand is put on the Inquirer's Head, who is to look over the Wizard's right Shoulder, (which hes ane ill Appearance, as if by this Ceremony ane implicit Surrender were made of all betwixt the Wizard's Foot and his Hand, ere the Person can be admitted a privado to the Airt;) then will he see a Multitude of Wight's, like furious hardie Men, flocking to him haistily from all Quarters, as thick as Atoms in the Air; which are no Nonentities or Phantasms, Creatures proceiding from ane affrighted Apprehensione, confused or crazed Sense, but Realities, appearing to a stable Man in his awaking Sense, and enduring a rationall Tryall of their Being.

Contact with the seer is recognized as a common way of seeing fairies
for a short time. Some years ago an account was sent me by a Mrs
Stewart, the wife of a minister in Edinburgh, of how her father, as a small
boy on the Isle of Skye, was once given the opportunity of seeing the
fairies dancing. He and his sister had been left with their grandmother
for the day while their mother went to nurse a sick neighbour. Another
little boy was keeping them company. Time went on and the children
grew tired, and had begun perhaps to be a little troublesome to the old
lady, when a friend came in whom they all liked and who had the reputation of having 'the gift'. She saw how things were and said: 'Come with
me and I'll show you something you'll like to see.' She made them hold
hands to form a chain, and led them out into the gloaming. There was a
little burn running past the cottage and a hillside beyond it. On the
hillside a fire was burning and a circle of little people was dancing round
it. The children gazed entranced until their friend led them back, and
when their mother came to fetch them they had a great tale to tell her.
In the morning they looked for the place where the fire had been, but
there was no trace of it, nor any charring. When Mrs Stewart was a child
she and the rest of the family liked no tale so much as that of 'How Papa
had Seen the Fairies'. Years later, her aunt came back from Canada and
confirmed the tale, and later still she met the old man who had been the
third child there, and he remembered the happening as if it had been
yesterday.

There are certain times which are specially suitable for seeing the
fairies. Twilight is one of them, midnight and the hour before sunrise,
and noon, when the sun is at its meridian. It will be remembered that the
DEPARTURE OF THE FAIRIES in Hugh Miller's story was witnessed at
midday. It is said, too, that you can only see the fairies as long as you can
look at them steadily; that is why captured LEPRACAUNS try to make
people look aside. If you hold a fairy in your eye it cannot escape, but if
you so much as blink it vanishes.

These are the rules in folk tradition. Lewis Carroll, in that curious
holdall of a book, *Sylvie and Bruno*, makes an attempt to lay down the
conditions of fairy vision. It seems he was thinking of the midday hour,
while Mrs EWING, in *Amelia and the Dwarfs*, is describing late twilight.

The next question [Lewis Carroll says] is, what is the best time for
seeing Fairies? I believe I can tell you all about that.

The first rule is, that it must be a *very* hot day – that we may consider
as settled: and you must be just a *little* sleepy – but not too sleepy to
keep your eyes open, mind. Well, and you ought to feel a little – what
one may call 'fairyish' – the Scotch call it 'eerie', and perhaps that's a
prettier word; if you don't know what it means, I'm afraid I can hardly
explain it; you must wait till you meet a Fairy, and then you'll
know.

And the last rule is, that the crickets should not be chirping. I can't stop to explain that: you must take it on trust for the present.

So, if all these things happen together, you have a good chance of seeing a Fairy – or at least a much better chance than if they didn't.

[Motifs: F235.1; F235.4.6; F235.5.1; F235.5.2]

Seelie Court. The name given to the kindly fairy HOST. 'Seelie' is 'blessed'. The malignant FAIRIES were sometimes called the UNSEELIE COURT. Macpherson, in *Primitive Beliefs in the North-East of Scotland* (pp. 98–100), gives a good account of the Seelie Court, with instances from Gregor, Grant Stewart and the *Aberdeen Journal* of 1910. He mentions first their purely benevolent activities, such as gifts of BREAD and seed corn to the poor and the help they give to their favourites. An example drawn from Gregor in *Folk-Lore Record* (vol. I) is of an Aberdeenshire farmer who suspected his thresher of using uncanny help. He hid himself in the barn to watch the threshing. His man came in, picked up the flail and approached the sheaves. Then he looked around and said, 'Come awa', ma reed cappies.' After that he made the motions of threshing, but invisible hands performed the labour. The farmer stayed hidden and said nothing, but he got rid of his uncanny helper on the first opportunity. The fair folk were benefactors also to anyone who did them a kindness. A story from Grant Stewart illustrates this. A poor woman, who could ill afford it, gave a fairy who begged from her a measure of meal. It was returned to her, and during a wintry shortage her meal bin never ran dry. Even the Seelie Court, however, readily revenged any injury or insult. People emptying slops into their underground dwellings were fairly warned, but if they paid no attention to the warning, they were punished by loss of stock or by the destruction of their house. Other offences met with appropriate punishment, but human beings were not wantonly injured, as by the Unseelie Court.

[Motifs: C433; F340; F346; F403]

Self-bored stones. These stones, meaning stones with a hole bored through them by the action of water, not only formed an aperture through which one could look at FAIRIES, but hung up over the stalls of stables very close to the horse's back, were effective in brushing off the fairies, who were fond of riding the horses round the field at night and exhausting them. AUBREY gives this recipe. See also PROTECTION AGAINST FAIRIES.

Selkies. The selkies of Orkney and Shetland are very like the ROANE of the West Highlands, but there are some differences in the beliefs about them. In Orkney the small, common seal, called by the Orcadians 'tang fish', was supposed to belong entirely to the animal world, but all the larger seals, the great seal, the grey seal, the crested seal and others, are called 'the selkie folk' because it is believed that their natural form is human, that they live in an underwater world or on lonely skerries and put on seal-skins and the appearance of seals to enable them to pass through the waters from one region of air to another. The Irish MERROWS exist under the same conditions, but wear red caps instead of seal-skins to enable them to pass through the waters. Like other Scottish fairy creatures, they were supposed to have been angels driven out of Heaven for some lesser fault, but not bad enough for Hell. Another explanation was that they were a human race, banished to the sea for their sins, but yet allowed to wear human shape upon land. Some men thought that they might yet be capable of salvation. In their human form, the male and female selkies were more beautiful than ordinary mortals, though they were uncouth and shapeless as seals, their beauty only showing in their large, liquid eyes. The male selkies were amorous, and used to make expeditions ashore to court mortal women, but they would never stay with them long. The human offspring of these unions, like those of the SEAL MAIDENS, had webbed hands and feet, and the webs when cut grew into horny excrescences which made it impossible to do some kinds of work. G. F. Black in *County Folk-Lore* (vol. III) gives a comprehensive account of the selkie beliefs, and among other tales quotes a story by Traill Dennison about a proud and passionate girl – Ursilla, Dennison calls her – who, dissatisfied with the husband she had chosen, summoned a selkie to be a lover. This was done by sitting on a rock at high tide and dropping seven tears into the sea. The selkie came to her bed time and again, and she had many children by him, but each one had webbed hands and feet, and their descendants after them. Traill Dennison himself tells of hiring a man to work in the harvest who could not bind a sheaf because of the horny growth on his hands. He was a descendant of Ursilla. The selkie maidens do not seem to seek for human lovers, but are captured unwillingly by the theft of their skins. This is the most widespread of the tales, a variant of the SWAN MAIDEN type. It is told in Shetland and Orkney as well as in the Highlands. The best-known of the Orkney stories is 'The Goodman of Wastness', and in Shetland there is a similar story told of an inhabitant of Unst. The Shetland story of the selkie lover is told in the ballad of 'The Great Silkie of Sule Skerry'.

Hibbert describes the selkies of Shetland as MERMEN and merwomen, but this is a confusion of his own, for the distinction is clear, though there was great kindness between selkies and MERMAIDS, as a story quoted by Black from Edmonston shows. There is some compunction felt by the Shetlanders when they kill and skin the selkies. Because of this a young fisherman who came on one after stunning and skinning it threw its body into the sea and pretended to his companions when he joined them in the boat that he found a dead seal and skinned it. But the seal was still alive. It regained consciousness, cold and in misery, and somehow made its way down beneath the sea into a cave inhabited by a mermaid. The only way in which the mermaid could help it was to try to regain its skin, and she bravely allowed herself to be caught in the nets of the boat where her friend's skin lay. The young fisherman was already remorseful about the death of the seal, and he was horrified when a mermaid was drawn on board. He begged earnestly that she might be set free, but his mates were anxious to sell her on shore and they made towards the land. The poor mermaid, tangled in the net, was laid on the seal-skin. Like the ASRAI she could not long endure in the upper air, and she felt her life beginning to fade. She knew that her death would release a storm and sink the boat and hoped that at least the skin would be swept down to her cave to save the selkie. And so indeed it happened; the boat was sunk, too late to save the mermaid, but with her body the skin was swept down to her cave and the selkie could put on his skin again. For this reason the selkie people do all that they can to warn and help the mermaids, and often risk themselves to save them. It is difficult to understand how this tale came to mortal knowledge, unless a mermaid told it to a man.

It was believed in both Orkney and Shetland that when the blood of a selkie is shed in the sea a storm arises that is often fatal to shipping. In this story the death of a mermaid had the same effect.

[Types: ML4080; ML4081*; ML4083*. Motifs: B81.13.11; F420.1.2*; F420.5.1]

Separable soul, or external soul. The separable or external soul is a magical stratagem generally employed by SUPERNATURAL WIZARDS or GIANTS. We do not find it so commonly used by FAIRIES. Somewhat allied to this power is a general invulnerability qualified by one vulnerable spot, like the heel of Achilles and the shoulder of Siegfried. Both these were acquired by immersion. Another kind of invulnerability is like that enjoyed by Llav Llew Giffes in the MABINOGION, who could only be killed in circumstances so peculiar that the opportunity had to be elaborately engineered. However, the separable soul was the more usual expedient. For this, the giant or wizard removed his life, or soul, from his body and placed it in an egg, which was concealed in the body of a duck, in the belly of a sheep, hidden in a STOCK or under a flagstone or in some comparable series of hiding-places. Most of the British stories in which this motif occurs come from the Highlands and bear a general resemblance to each other. Examples are 'The Bare-Stripping Hangman', recorded in *Waifs and Strays of Celtic Tradition* (vol. III), 'Cathal O'Cruachan and the Herd of the Stud' in Macdougall and Calder's *Folk Tales and Fairy Lore*, and 'How the Great Tuairisgeal was put to death' in McKay's *More West Highland Tales* (vol. I). GREEN SLEEVES comes from Peter Buchan's *Ancient Scottish Tales*, just outside the Celtic area. It is on the usual plot of NICHT NOUGHT NOTHING with the SWAN MAIDEN motif added, and the unusual addition of the separable soul, contained in this tale in an egg hidden in a bird's nest. J. F. CAMPBELL's tale, 'The Young King of Easaidh Ruadh', contains all the elements of the story in a comparatively concise form, beginning with the gambling challenge as in the MIDHIR and ETAIN story, except that in this case the first challenge was the hero's.

The young king of Easaidh Ruadh, after he had come to his kingdom, resolved to go and play a bout of CHESS games against a GRUAGACH called Gruagach carsalach donn – that is, the brown curly-haired Gruagach – who lived in the neighbourhood. He went to his soothsayer about it, who advised him to have nothing to do with the Gruagach, but when he insisted on going told him to take nothing as his stakes but the cropped rough-skinned maid behind the door. He went and had a good reception, and that day he won the game, and named as his stakes the cropped rough-skinned maid behind the door. The Gruagach tried to make him change his mind and brought out twenty pretty maids, one after the other, but the young king refused them all till the cropped rough-skinned maid came out, when he said, 'That is mine.' So they went away, and they had not gone far when the maid's appearance changed, and she became the most beautiful woman in the world. They went home in great joy and contentment and spent a happy night together; but the next morning the young king got up early to spend another day with the Gruagach. His wife advised against it. She said that the Gruagach was her father and meant him no good, but he said he must go. She advised him, if he won, to take nothing for his prize but the dun shaggy filly with the stick saddle. That day he won again, and when he put his leg over the filly he found she was the best mount he had ever ridden. That night they spent together in great enjoyment, but the young queen said that she would rather that he did not go to the Gruagach that day. 'For,' she said, 'if he wins he will put trouble on thy head.' He answered that he must go, so they kissed each other and parted. It seemed to him that the Gruagach was glad to see him that day, and they settled to gaming again, but this time the Gruagach won. 'Lift the stake of thy game,' said the young king, 'and be not heavy on me, for I cannot stand to it.' 'The stake of my play is,' said the Gruagach, 'that I lay it as crosses and as spells on thee that the cropped rough-skinned creature, mᴏᴇ uncouth and unworthy than thou thyself, should take thy head, and thy neck if thou dost not get for me the Glaive of Light of the King of the Oak Windows.'

The young king went home heavily and gloomily that night, and, though he got some pleasure from the young queen's greeting and her beauty, his heart was so heavy when he drew her to him that it cracked the chair beneath them. 'What is it ails you that you cannot tell it to me?' said the young queen; so he told her all that happened and of the crosses laid on them. 'You have no cause to mind that,' she said. 'You have the best wife in all Erin and the next to the best horse, and if you take heed to me you will come well out of this yet.'

In the morning the young queen got up early to prepare everything for the king's journey and brought out the dun shaggy filly to him. He mounted her, and the queen kissed him and wished him victory of battlefields. 'I need not tell you anything,' she said, 'for the filly will be your friend and your companion, and she will tell you all that you must do.'

So the young king set off and the filly galloped so fast that she left the March wind behind her and outstripped the wind in front of her. It was far they went, but it did not seem far until they got to the court and castle of the King of the Oak Windows. They stopped then, and the dun filly said, 'We are come to the end of our journey, and if you listen to my advice you can carry the Sword of Light away. The King of the Oak Windows is at dinner now, and the Sword of Light is in his chamber. I will take you to it; there is a knob on its end; lean in at the window and draw out the sword very gently.' They went to the window. The young king leaned in and drew out the sword. It came softly, but when the point passed the window-frame it gave a kind of a 'sgread'. 'It is no stopping time for us here,' said the dun filly. 'I know the king has felt us taking out the sword.' And they sped away. After a time the filly paused and said to him, 'Look and see what is behind us.' 'I see a crowd of brown horses coming madly,' said the young king. 'We are swifter than those ones,' said the dun filly, and sped on. When they had gone some long way she paused, and said, 'Look and see what is behind us.' 'I see a crowd of black horses coming madly,' said the young king, 'and in front of them is a black horse with a white face, and I think there is a rider on him.' 'That horse is my brother and he is the swiftest horse in Erin. He will come past us like a flash of light. As they pass his rider will look round, and try then if you can cut his head off. He is the King of the Oaken Windows, and the sword in your hand is the only sword that could take the head off him.' The young king did just that and the dun filly caught the head in her teeth. 'Leave the carcass,' she said. 'Mount the black horse and ride home with the Sword of Light, and I will follow as best I can.'

He leapt on the black horse and it carried him as if it were flying, and he got home before the night was over, with the dun filly behind him.

The queen had had no rest while he was away, and be sure they got a hero's welcome, and they raised music in the music place and feasting in the feasting place; but in the morning the young king said, 'I must go now to the Gruagach, and see if I can lift the spells he has laid on me.'

'He will not meet you as before,' said the young queen. 'The King of the Oaken Windows is his brother, and he will know that he would never part with the Glaive of Light unless he was dead. He will ask you how you got it, but only answer that if it were not for the knob at its end you would not have got it, and if he asks again give the same answer. Then he will lift himself to look at the knob and you will see a wart on his neck. Stab it quickly with the Glaive of Light, for that is the only way in which he can be killed, and if it is not done we are both destroyed.'

She kissed him and called on victory of battlefields to be with him and he went on his way.

The Gruagach met him in the same place as before.

'Did you get the sword?'

'I got the sword.'

'How did you get the sword?'

'If it had not been for the knob on its end I had not got it.'

'Let me see the sword.'

'It was not laid on me to let you see it.'

'How did you get the sword?'

'If it were not for the knob that was at its end I got it not.'

The Gruagach lifted his head to look at the sword; the young king saw the mole; he was sharp and quick, he plunged the sword into it and the Gruagach fell down dead.

The young king went back rejoicing, but he found small cause of rejoicing at home. His guards and servants were tied end to back, and his queen and the two horses were nowhere to be seen. When the king loosed his servants, they told him that a huge giant had come and carried away the queen and the two horses. The young king set off at once to find them. He followed the giant's track all day long, and in the evening he found the ashes of a fire. He was blowing it up to spend the night there when the slim dog of the green forest came up to him. 'Alas,' he said, 'thy wife and the two horses were in a bad plight here last night.' 'Alas indeed,' said the young king. 'It is for them I am seeking, and I fear that I shall never find them.' The dog spoke cheerily to him and caught him food. He watched over him through the night, and in the morning he promised that the young king had only to think of him if he was in need, and he would be there. They wished blessings on each other, and parted. The young king travelled on all day, and at night found the ashes of another fire, and was cheered, fed and guarded by the hoary hawk of the grey rock. They parted with the same promise of help. The third night he spent with the brown otter of the river, who fed and guarded him as the others had done and was able to tell him that he would see his queen that night. Sure enough he came that night to a deep chasm in which was the giant's cave, where he saw his wife and the two horses. His wife began to weep when she saw him, for she was afraid for his safety, but the two horses said he could hide in the front of their stable and they would make sure that the giant would not find them. They were as good as their word, for when the giant came to feed them they plunged and kicked, till the giant was almost destroyed. 'Take care,' said the queen.

'They will kill you!' 'Oh, they'd have killed me long ago,' said the giant, 'if I'd had my soul in my body, but it is in a place of safety.' 'Where do you keep it, my love?' said the queen. 'I'll guard it for you.' 'It's in that great stone,' said the giant. So next day when the giant had gone out, the queen decked the stone with flowers and cleaned all around it. When the giant came back at night he asked why she had dressed up the stone. 'Because your soul is in it, my dear love,' she replied. 'Oh, I see you really respect it,' said the giant. 'But it's not there.' 'Where is it then?' 'It is in the threshold.' So next day she cleaned and dressed up the threshold. This time the giant was really convinced that she cared for him, and he told her where it was hidden – beneath a great stone under the threshold there was a living wether, and in the wether's belly was a duck, and in the duck's belly was an egg, and in the egg was the giant's soul. When the giant was fairly away next morning they set to work. They lifted the great stone, and the wether leapt out and escaped, but she was fetched back by the slim dog of the green forest and the duck was caught by the hoary falcon and the egg found and brought back from the sea by the brown otter. By this time the giant was returning; the queen crumbled the egg in her fingers and he fell dead to the ground. They parted lovingly from their helpers and returned to the young king's castle where they had a hero's banquet, and lived lucky and happy after that.

This type was used by George MACDONALD in one of his fairy-tales, 'The Giant's Heart'. The motif of the vulnerable spot was used by TOLKIEN in *The Hobbit*.

[Motifs: B571.1; E710; E711.1]

Seven Whistlers, the. These are allied in people's minds with the GABRIEL HOUNDS, the WISH HOUNDS, and others, but are not thought of as hounds with a spiritual huntsman but as seven spirits, death portents like the BANSHEE. William Henderson in *Folklore of the Northern Counties* (p. 131) quotes a Folkestone fisherman who well knew what caused the sound, but still thought it ominous.

'I heard 'em one dark night last winter,' said an old Folkestone fisherman. 'They come over our heads all of a sudden, singing "ewe, ewe," and the men in the boat wanted to go back. It came on to rain and blow soon afterwards, and was an awful night, Sir; and sure enough before morning a boat was upset, and seven poor fellows drowned. I know what makes the noise, Sir; it's them long-billed curlews, but I never likes to hear them.'

Wordsworth in one of his sonnets mentions the Seven Whistlers, and connects them with the Gabriel Hounds:

He the seven birds hath seen that never part,
Seen the seven whistlers on their nightly rounds,

> And counted them! And oftentimes will start,
> For overhead are sweeping Gabriel's hounds,
> Doomed with their impious lord the flying hart
> To chase for ever on aërial grounds.

[Motif: E500]

Shag-foal, or tatter-foal. These are practically the same. They are the Lincolnshire members of that tribe of BOGY OR BOGEY-BEASTS that are adept at SHAPE-SHIFTING, can take many forms but seem to prefer to go about as shaggy, fiery-eyed horses, foals or donkeys. The Picktree BRAG and the HEDLEY KOW are famous examples. Examples are given in *County Folk-Lore* (vol. v) by Gutch and Peacock:

> *Shag-foal.* – An old lady used to talk of a mysterious phantom like an animal of deep black colour, which appeared before belated travellers. On hearing that we had been attacked at midnight by a large dog, she eagerly inquired: 'Had it any white about it?' and when we assured her that it had a white chest, she exclaimed in thankfulness: 'Ah! then it was not the shag-foal!'

Here the old lady makes no distinction between the shag and the shag-foal. Eli Twigg in the next extract sticks closer to the usual type:

> *Tatter-foal.* – 'Why, he is a shagg'd-looking hoss, and given to all manner of goings-on, fra cluzzening hold of a body what is riding home half-screwed with bargain-drink, and pulling him out of the saddle, to scaring a old woman three parts out of her skin, and making her drop her shop-things in the blatter and blash, and run for it.'

[Motifs: E423.1.3.5(a); F234.1.8]

Shape-shifting. A magical accomplishment, common in a greater or lesser degree to FAIRIES, WIZARDS and witches. Not all fairies are shape-shifters. The small, powerless fairies like SKILLYWIDDEN have no power to take any other shape or even to alter their size, as SPRIGGANS can do, and CHERRY OF ZENNOR's master. Some, like the EACH UISGE, have two forms at their disposal, a young man or a horse. The Cornish fairies whose habits are treated in such detail in 'The FAIRY DWELLING ON SELENA MOOR' seem to be able to assume only the form of a bird, and they pay for each change by a diminution in size. The fairies into whose house the human MIDWIFE TO THE FAIRIES is brought can change their appearance and the appearance of their dwellings, but this is probably not a real shape-shift, only the effect of GLAMOUR, a kind of hypnotism which affects the senses of the beholder, and a hypnotism against which ST COLLEN was armed by his sanctity.

The BOGY OR BOGEY-BEASTS and all their kind are true shape-shifters, and so are such HOBGOBLINS as PUCK. They exercise their powers for mischief rather than for malevolence. A typical story is that of the HEDLEY KOW.

Wizards, and particularly SUPERNATURAL WIZARDS, are the true shape-shifters, able to change the form of other people as well as to shift from one shape to another. The ordinary fairy people seem as helpless as humans against this kind of magic, as ETAIN was when the wizard turned her into a midge. Some fairies, however, presumably those who had studied magic, had the power. Uchtdealb turned Tuiren into a dog and herself into the appearance of FINN's messenger. The second seems to have been an illusion, the first a real change of form, for Tuiren's offspring were irrecoverably puppies.

Human wizards as well as supernatural creatures are capable of becoming masters of shape-shifting according to the fairy-tales, and to some legends. A Celtic tale of which there are a good many variants is that of which McKay's story, 'The Wizard's Gillie', to be found in *More Highland Tales*, is a good example. A man apprentices his son to a MAGICIAN for a stated period of years, which is afterwards extended and then extended more indefinitely, until the son does not return at all and his father goes out to look for him. He finds him a captive of the magician's and manages to get him away by recognizing him in his transformed shape. The father and son go off together, and in order to gain money the son transforms himself into various creatures whom the father sells, but he must always retain the strap by which the creature is led, for the son's soul is in that, and as long as his father has it he can always resume his own shape and return. The wizard is the purchaser each time, and each time the gillie escapes until the father is so much elated by the magnificent price paid that he forgets to remove the strap and his son is thrown into harsh captivity. By his ingenuity he manages to escape, the wizard pursues him and the two engage in a transformation combat, at the end of which the wizard is destroyed. The theme is roughly the same as that of the folk-song 'The Coal Black Smith'. Other tales on the same plot are 'The King of the Black Art', a particularly good version collected by Hamish Henderson from John Stewart, and 'The Black King of Morocco', from Buchan's *Ancient Scottish Tales*.

Tales of people changed into another shape by a wicked enchantment are very common. Many of them are variants of the Cupid and Psyche story. 'The Black Bull of Norroway' is the best-known of these, but there are others, such as 'The Hoodie'. Escapes by temporary transformations are another use of shape-shifting. MORGAN LE FAY used this expedient once in Malory's *Morte d'Arthur*. Ordinary witches were commonly accused of shape-shifting, generally into stereotyped forms such as hares or hedgehogs, but here we are off the road of fairy-lore.

[Motifs: A1459.3; D610; F234.0.2]

Shefro, or Siofra (*Sheaf-ra*). In Crofton CROKER's *Fairy Legends of the South of Ireland*, Shefro is the name given to the small TROOPING FAIRIES of Ireland. They are supposed to wear caps like foxglove bells on their heads. Stories of CHANGELINGS, of the carrying off of young girls and of the usual fairy activities are told of them. In the 'Legend of Knocksheogowna', the queen of the clan inhabiting that hill plays as many SHAPE-SHIFTING pranks as a BRAG or HEDLEY KOW could do. Like the Highland fairies, the Shefro show anxiety about their possible salvation.

[Motifs: F234.0.2; F241.1.0.1]

Shellycoat. A Lowland water-BOGLE described by SCOTT in *Minstrelsy of the Scottish Border*. He frequented fresh-water streams, and was festooned about with shells which clattered when he moved. Scott has a tale of two men being led all one dark night up the banks of the river Ettrick by a voice calling dolefully from the stream, 'Lost! Lost!' By daybreak they had reached the source, when Shellycoat leapt out from the spring and bounded down the other side of the hill with loud bursts of laughter. Like the Picktree BRAG and the HEDLEY KOW, Shellycoat delights in teasing, tricking and bewildering human beings, without doing them actual harm; and like ROBIN GOODFELLOW, he applauds his success with loud laughter.

[Motif: F402.1.1]

Shock, the. The Suffolk shock is a BOGY OR BOGEY-BEAST, generally appearing like a horse or donkey. *County Folk-Lore* (vol. 1) includes some personally collected material, among it some letters written to a Mr Redstone. One records an example of a very palpable shock:

In Melton stands the 'Horse and Groom' – in the days of toll-gates (thirty years ago) occupied by one Master Fisher. It was a dark night when Goodman Kemp of Woodbridge entered the inn in a hurried frightened manner, and asked for the loan of a gun to shoot a 'Shock' which hung upon the toll-gate here. It was a 'thing' with a donkey's head and a smooth velvet hide. Kemp, somewhat emboldened by the support of companions, sought to grab the creature and take it to the inn to examine it. As he seized it, it turned suddenly round, snapped at Kemp's hand and vanished. Kemp bore the mark of the Shock's bite upon his thumb to his dying day.

Some of the Suffolk shocks take the form of dogs or calves with shaggy manes and saucer eyes. They are supposed to be ghosts. The Shock is not unlike the Lincolnshire Shag, or SHAG-FOAL.

[Motif: E423]

Shony (*shaw nee*). An ancient sea spirit of the Isle of Lewis, to whom an oblation was made even as late as the 18th century. Martin, in *A Descrip-*

tion of the Western Isles of Scotland (1716), gives an account of the celebration by which Shony was propitiated at Hallowtide, not for a yield of fish, but of seaweed to manure the land:

> They gathered to the Church of St Mulvey, Lewis: each family furnished a peck of malt, and this was brew'd into ale: one of their number was picked out to wade into the sea up to the middle, and carrying a cup of ale in his hand, standing still in that posture, cry'd out with a loud voice saying: '*Shony, I give you this cup of ale, hoping that you'll be so kind as to send us plenty of sea ware, for enriching our ground the ensuing year*,' and so threw the cup of ale into the sea. This was performed in the night time. At his return to land they all went to church; there was a candle burning on the altar: and then, standing silent for a little time, one of them gave a signal at which the candle was put out, and immediately all of them went to the fields, where they fell a-drinking their ale, and spent the remainder of the night in dancing and singing.

Ruth Tongue records tributes paid to a similar sea spirit in Somerset, INA PIC WINNA.

[Motif: A421; V12.9]

Shoopiltee. The Shetland water horse, or CABYLL-USHTEY. He is described by KEIGHTLEY in the Shetland section of *Fairy Mythology* (p. 171):

> The water-spirit is in Shetland called Shoopiltee; he appears in the form of a pretty little horse, and endeavours to entice persons to ride on him, and then gallops with them into the sea.

[Motif: F420.5.2.1]

Short Hoggers of Whittinghame. A solitary example of the little ghosts who cannot rest because they have died unchristened. When these ghosts congregate together, they are called SPUNKIES in Lowland Scotland and in Somerset, and 'Pisgies' in the West Country, where they take the form of small white moths. In this story we are shown that it is the name not the baptism that is important to the little spirit.

The village of Whittinghame was haunted for a long time by the unhappy spirit of an unwanted baby who had been murdered by his mother and buried at the foot of a tree near the village. On dark nights it used to run up and down between the tree and the churchyard wailing, 'Nameless me!' and no one dared to speak to it, for it was believed that whoever addressed it would die. Late one night, however, a drunk man, too merry for fear, heard it wailing, and called out: 'How's a wi' you this morning, Short Hoggers?'

The little ghost was delighted.

'O weel's me noo, I've gotten a name;
They ca' me Short-Hoggers o' Whittinghame!'

he cried, and ran joyfully off to Heaven.

Chambers learned the story and the rhyme from an old woman of Whittinghame, who claimed to have seen the ghost. 'Short-hoggers' is a name for babies' bootees.

PUDDLEFOOT, the BROWNIE, was laid in the same way by a drunk man, but he was displeased and driven off by the naming.

[Motif: F251.3]

Si. See SIDH.

Sib. The principal female fairy, who acts as spokeswoman of the rest in the LIFE OF ROBIN GOODFELLOW. She speaks for herself and her sister FAIRIES:

> To walke nightly, as do the men fayries, we use not; but now and then we goe together, and at good huswives fires we warme and dresse our fayry children. If wee find cleane water and cleane towels, wee leave them money, either in their basons or in their shooes; but if wee find no cleane water in their houses, we wash our children in their pottage, milke or beere, or what-ere we finde; for the sluts that leave not such things fitting, wee wash their faces and hands with a gilded child's clout, or els carry them to some river, and ducke them over head and eares. We often use to dwell in some great hill, and from thence we doe lend money to any poore man or woman that hath need; but if they bring it not againe at the day appointed, we doe not only punish them with pinching, but also in their goods, so that they never thrive till they have payd us.

[Motif: F361.17.5]

Sidh, Sith, or Si (*shee*). The Gaelic name for FAIRIES, both in Ireland and the Highlands of Scotland, as in the BEAN SI or the DAOINE SIDH.

Sili Ffrit and Sili-Go-Dwt. The names of two female fairies to whom the same rather fragmentary story as TRWTYN-TRATYN is attached by Rhys. It is a version of the TOM TIT TOT or WHUPPITY STOORIE tale and hinges on the power given by knowledge of the name of a supernatural creature, or a SECRET NAME OF THE FAIRIES.

[Type: 500. Motif: C432.1]

Silky. BROWNIES are generally male spirits, though there are occasional female brownies, such as MEG MULLACH, mentioned by AUBREY as attached to the Grants, and GRUAGACHS, who were as much female as male. The Northumbrian and Border silky, however, is always female, like the BANSHEE. She is a spirit dressed in rustling silk, who does domestic chores about the house and is a terror to idle servants. Like the CAULD LAD OF HILTON, she is a ghostly spirit. The Silky of Black Heddon, mentioned by William Henderson in *Folk-Lore of the Northern Counties* (p. 269), was the most famous of them all, and more mischievous than helpful, for though she tidied what was left in disorder, she would often throw about anything that had been neatly arranged. She would spend a great part of the night sitting in an old tree near an artificial lake. The tree was long called 'Silky's Chair'. From this position she used often to stop carts and halt horses, and could only be countered by somebody wearing a CROSS made of ROWAN wood. One day a ceiling in Heddon Hall suddenly gave way and a large, rough skin filled with gold fell into the room below. The silky never haunted Heddon Hall after that, and it was thought that she was the ghost of someone who had hidden treasure and died without disclosing it. There was one at Hurdwood in Berwickshire, and another mentioned by Henderson at Denton Hall near Newcastle. There is later news of this silky; for a friend, one of the Sowerbys of Northumberland, used to visit two old ladies, the Hoyles of Denton, long ago, when she was a girl. The hall was too big for them, and they used sometimes to say to their intimate friends that they did not know how they could manage if it had not been for Silky, who laid and lighted fires for them and did all manner of chores about the house. My friend married and moved away, and did not return to Newcastle till the Second World War. The Misses Hoyle had died long before and the house had been let to another old acquaintance of Margery Sowerby. He was not at all the kind of person to commend himself to a spirit, and he had become the victim of all sorts of practical jokes. He was so angry that he could not bear to talk about it, and at last he had to move out of Denton Hall. The brownie had become a BOGGART.

A story with an ultimate gipsy origin, 'Gilsland's Gry', is told by Ruth Tongue in *Forgotten Folk-Tales of the English Counties* (pp. 201-4). Here the silky is a more formidable character than in any of the other tales. She is devoted to the interests of Gilsland, and does full brownie labours about the house, but at night she guards the gate from her tree, and lets any friend through, though with a scared horse, but she remorselessly kills any ill-wisher to the house. In this tale she slowly strangles a murderous robber who falls into her clutches. A silky who did little domestic work but haunted an avenue near North Shields, seems to have been more truly a ghost, the spectre of a mistress of the Duke of Argyll in the reign of William III, supposed to have been murdered by her lover.

[Motifs: E451.5; F480; F482.5.4; F482.5.5]

Siofra (*sheaf-ra*). See SHEFRO.

Sir Gawain and the Green Knight. This superb medieval poem was written somewhere about 1350 in north-west Midland dialect, that of Cheshire or South Lancashire, treated with great richness and mastery. The poem exists only in one manuscript (MS. Nero A.x. in the Cotton Collection at the British Museum). *The Pearl, Cleanliness* and *Patience* are in the same volume and written in the same hand. They are judged to be the work of the same author by the evidence of dialect and style. The name of the author is unknown, but Ormerod Greenwood, working on *The Pearl*, has suggested on the evidence of numerology – a cryptic method very fashionable in the 14th century – that he was a member of the Masci family, called Hugo de Masci. A short comment on the poem itself will be found under FAIRIES OF MEDIEVAL ROMANCES.

Sir Launfal. One of the early romances about Arthur or the MATTER OF BRITAIN, written by the 13th-century Marie de France, was translated with some alterations by a man calling himself Thomas of Chester. It is a true FAIRY BRIDE story, something after the style of the Irish tale 'Oisin and Niam of the Golden Hair'. Lancelot has not yet appeared on the scene, though Guinevere is there in the role of a villainous character. Sir Launfal was a famous and liberal knight of King Arthur's court, who disapproved of his marriage with Guinevere, and was accordingly hated by her. She put a public slight upon him at her marriage feast, and he withdrew from the court at Carlisle to go to Caerleon. King Arthur parted from him regretfully and gave him two knights to attend him. Launfal's liberality, however, outran his means, and after a while he could no longer afford maintenance for his knights. Things had come to a bad pass with him, when he was one day approached by two dazzlingly beautiful maidens who invited him to visit their mistress, the fairy princess Tryamour, the daughter of the fairy king Olyroun. He found her in a gorgeous pavilion lying on a bed with all her charms alluringly displayed. They came immediately to an understanding. She would bestow on him all earthly riches with a fairy squire and a milk-white fairy horse, and if he went into any secret place and wished for her company, she would immediately appear to him. She only made one stipulation: their love must be kept secret. If he boasted of her love he would lose her and all her gifts for ever.

The pact was concluded with great joy. Tryamour gave Launfal a Fortunatus, or inexhaustible, purse – out of which he could draw limitless stores of gold – a great white charger, and Gyfre, Tryamour's own attendant, as squire. A procession of young knights brought him rich clothes and equipment, and he gave out his charity more lavishly than he had ever done. A great tournament was given in his honour in which he distinguished himself signally. After some time of great happiness, Launfal was summoned to a tournament in Lombardy by an orgulous knight, Sir Valentyne. He went and, with much help from Gyfre, killed

Sir Valentyne and overcame the crowd of local knights who assailed him all together. The news of this great feat spread, and reached Carlisle. King Arthur invited Sir Launfal to return. Seven years had now passed since he left the court. He obeyed, and he was still able to enjoy Tryamour as before. Queen Guinevere, however, who had once hated him, now fell in love with him, and one day when King Arthur was out hunting made amorous advances towards him, which he refused. The queen was furiously angry and began to abuse him as an old bachelor whom no woman would look at and who had never had a love. Sir Launfal lost his temper and replied that the least of his lady's maidens was more beautiful than Queen Guinevere. They parted; Sir Launfal went to his chamber and called on Tryamour to appear. She did not come and he began to realize what he had done. He went to his coffers and found them empty. Gyfre had gone, as had Blanchard, his fairy horse. He flung himself on the ground and began to lament his folly and falsehood to his word. In the meantime King Arthur had returned from the hunt, and found his queen in her chamber, with her clothes and hair torn. She begged him to put Sir Launfal to death, who had tried to rape her, and when she repelled him had said that the least of his true love's maidens was more beautiful than she was. The king was unsuspicious of this double accusation, and at once sent a posse of knights to find Launfal and bring him to judgement. The king was for his immediate execution, but the court, knowing Queen Guinevere, ruled otherwise. They gave him a year and a fortnight to produce his true love, and if she was judged fairer than Guinevere, then Launfal must go free. The time passed, and Launfal appeared to clear the sureties who had stood for him, but he said he could not produce his lady. At this a great clamour broke out in the court; some wished to acquit him and some to banish him, and as they were disputing a beautiful damsel rode up to them, and all thought her more beautiful than Guinevere; but Launfal said: 'That is not my love.' Then one bevy after another of maidens rode up, and at last Tryamour appeared and rode up to Guinevere. She publicly declared that Guinevere had made a false accusation against an innocent man, then touched her eye so that she could no more see. Then she and Launfal rode off on Blanchard to the fairy island of Olyroun, from which he never returned, except that once a year his horse is heard to neigh from Fairyland, and any knight may challenge Sir Launfal to ride a course with him.

Here we have a good example of a fairy bride complete with the TABOO, though in this tale it is not pressed to a tragic conclusion, and the mortal and the fairy are reunited.

Oisin, or OSSIAN, and Niam were parted for ever, but Marie of France was more lenient to her characters than popular tradition usually allowed.

[Motifs: C31; C31.5; F300; F302.3.2; F302.6.2]

Sith. See SIDH.

Sithein (*sheean*). The Gaelic name for the fairy hill, or KNOWE seen from outside. If it opens on pillars, the interior is called the BRUGH.

Size of the fairies. The fairy people are good and bad, beautiful and hideous, stately and comical, but one of the greatest of their many variations is that of size. This variation is sometimes within the control of the FAIRIES; by SHAPE-SHIFTING they can monstrously enlarge themselves or shrink into midgets of their own volition, but this is not always so. Some of them seem to be controlled by the very essence of their being and to be small, powerless creatures of the class of DIMINUTIVE FAIRIES. The *Oxford Dictionary*, by defining a fairy as 'one of a class of beings of diminutive size', seems to cast its vote for the small ELVES so much beloved in Jacobean England, and this indeed is one true element in folk tradition. Among the tiny medieval fairies are the PORTUNES described by GERVASE OF TILBURY, which, as far as one can make out,

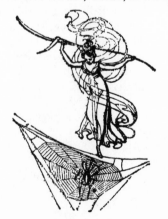

were about a finger's length in size, or such as the Danish troll which occurs in the Ballad of 'Eline of Villenokor' quoted by KEIGHTLEY in *The Fairy Mythology* (p. 95):

> Out then spake the tinyest Troll,
> No bigger than an emmet was he;

or the tiny fairies visited by ELIDURUS in GEOFFREY OF MONMOUTH, and little MALEKIN, described by Ralph of Coggeshall as the size of the tiniest child. All these are medieval fairies, although the FASHION IN FAIRYLORE in earlier times laid more stress on supernatural creatures of human or more than human size, WHITE LADIES, FAYS, HAGS, MAGICIANS, GIANTS and fairy knights like the one in the story of SIR GAWAIN AND THE GREEN KNIGHT. These never disappeared from tradition, and were reinforced by the FAIRY GODMOTHER who invaded England from the courtly French tales, like those of PERRAULT. The commonest fairies of country tradition, however, are generally described as of the size of a three-years' child, the smaller size of human kind; or the smaller ones, 'a span and a quarter in height'. The insect-sized fairies are rarer in tradition, though very common in literature. In Hampshire, in the tale of 'I WEAT, YOU WEAT', we have fairies so small that a grain of wheat is a burden; the MURYANS of Cornwall reach the size of an ant only at the last stage of their appearance on earth. In that very interesting description of the conditions of fairy life, 'The FAIRY DWELLING ON SELENA MOOR', the CAPTIVE IN FAIRYLAND explains that every time one of the SMALL PEOPLE OF CORNWALL changes its shape – turns itself into a bird, for instance – it is rather smaller when it returns to its natural form, so that it gradually dwindles, until when it reaches the size of a muryan, or ant, it passes out of that state altogether. The fairies of variable size are all those with powers of shape-shifting, the HEROIC FAIRIES, the White Ladies, many of the hags and nearly all BOGLES and HOBGOBLINS, such as the BRAG, the GRANT and many of the GIANTS and WIZARDS. The SPRIGGANS of Cornwall are generally tiny, but are capable of shooting up into monstrous size, as in HUNT's story of 'The MISER ON THE FAIRY GUMP'.

[Motifs: F239.4; F239.4.1; F239.4.2; F239.4.3]

Skillywidden. This, as we learn at the end of the story of the same title, was the name of a little fairy caught by a farmer at Treridge in Cornwall, one of the CAPTURED FAIRIES. It is to be found in HUNT's *Popular Romances of the West of England* (pp. 450–51):

> I heard last week of three fairies having been seen in Zennor very recently. A man who lived at the foot of Trendreen hill, in the valley of Treridge, I think, was cutting furze on the hill. Near the middle of the day he saw one of the small people, not more than a foot long, stretched at full length and fast asleep, on a bank of griglans (heath),

surrounded by high brakes of furze. The man took off his furze cuff, and slipped the little man into it, without his waking up; went down to the house; took the little fellow out of the cuff on the hearthstone, when he awakened, and seemed quite pleased and at home, beginning to play with the children, who were well pleased with the small body, and called him Bobby Griglans.

The old people were very careful not to let Bob out of the house, or be seen by the neighbours, as he promised to show the man where the crocks of gold were buried on the hill. A few days after he was brought from the hill, all the neighbours came with their horses (according to custom) to bring home the winter's reek of furze, which had to be brought down the hill in trusses on the backs of the horses. That Bob might be safe and out of sight, he and the children were shut up in the barn. Whilst the furze-carriers were in to dinner, the prisoners contrived to get out, to have a 'courant' round the furze-reek, when they saw a little man and woman, not much larger than Bob, searching into every hole and corner among the trusses that were dropped round the unfinished reek. The little woman was wringing her hands and crying, 'O my dear and tender Skillywidden, wherever canst ah (thou) be gone to? shall I ever cast eyes on thee again?' 'Go 'e back,' says Bob to the children; 'my father and mother are come here too.' He then cried out, 'Here I am, mammy!' By the time the words were out of his mouth, the little man and woman, with their precious Skilly-widden, were nowhere to be seen, and there has been no sight nor sign of them since. The children got a sound thrashing for letting Skilly-widden escape.

[Type: ML6010. Motifs: F239.4.3; F329.4.3; F387]

Skriker. A GOBLIN from Yorkshire and Lancashire, sometimes called TRASH from the padding of his feet. He was thought to be a death portent. Sometimes he wanders invisibly in the woods, giving fearful screams; sometimes he takes a form like PADFOOT, a huge dog with large feet and saucer eyes. James Bowker, in *Goblin Tales of Lancashire*, tells of a skriker which retreated before its victim, drawing him irresistibly after it.

[Motifs: D1812.5.1.17; F234.0.2; F234.1.9; F235.1; G302.3.2]

Sleeping warriors. The theme of a sleeping champion in a cave under a hill is common through Europe. Sometimes the hero is Charlemagne, sometimes Barbarossa, sometimes King Marko, sometimes Holger the Dane. In Britain it was most commonly King Arthur in the MATTER OF BRITAIN legends, or in Ireland it was FINN Mac Cumhal, though some-times it was a mysterious, unspecified champion. At Sewing Shields in Northumberland, between the Roman Wall and the ancient military road, there is a persistent and ancient legend that King Arthur, with Queen

Guinevere and all his knights, lies in an entranced sleep awaiting a champion who shall awake them. An account of the time when they were nearly awakened is to be found in the DENHAM TRACTS. The tradition was that the warriors would be aroused if a champion could find his way into the vault where they lay, blow a horn that was lying near the king, and cut a garter lying beside him with a stone sword, but no one knew where among heaps of briar-covered rubble the entrance could be found. One day chance disclosed it to a shepherd, who was sitting knitting on one of the mounds. His ball slipped off his knee and rolled down a deep and narrow hole. The shepherd was convinced that he had found the entrance, and, cutting the thorns and brambles that covered the hole, he found a way down wide enough for him to enter, and soon found himself in a vaulted passage. The floor was covered with toads and lizards, bats brushed against his ears, but he followed his clew of wool downwards in the darkness, and at last saw a distant light. Encouraged by this, he made his way towards it and found himself in a huge vaulted room lit by a fire that burned without fuel. On a hundred rich couches round the room lay the sleeping bodies of King Arthur, Queen Guinevere and the king's knights; in the dim light behind the fire, sixty couple of noble hounds lay sleeping, and on a table in front of it were a horn, a stone sword and a garter. The shepherd went up to the table, drew the sword softly from its sheath and cut the garter. When he touched the sword all the company stirred, and as he cut the garter they rose up sitting on their couches, but as he pushed the sword gently back into its sheath sleep came over them again, and they sank on to their beds. Only the king lifted his hands and said in a strong voice:

> 'O woe betide that evil day
> On which the witless wight was born
> Who drew the sword – the garter cut,
> But never blew the bugle-horn.'

In Richmond in Yorkshire any decisive movement would have served. There, a smooth hill called Round Howe is the place where Arthur is said to be sleeping. A potter called Thompson was walking round the howe one night when a stranger met him and conducted him into the vault beneath it. He began to draw the sword, but put it hastily back when the company stirred. A great voice cried out,

> 'Potter, Potter Thompson,
> If thou hadst either drawn
> The sword or blown the horn,
> Thou'd been the luckiest man
> That ever was born.'

The Somerset legend of Arthur and his knights at Cadbury Castle is different. No one visits them, and anyone who tries to dig up the Round

Table will fail, because it only sinks deeper into the earth. But every Midsummer Eve, King Arthur and his knights come out of the mound and ride round it on horses shod with silver, as Earl Fitzgerald does at Mullaghmast. According to a Welsh legend recorded by John Rhys, King Arthur's knights sleep without him in a cave on Snowdon. Once a shepherd looking for a sheep found the entrance to it and made his way in timidly, but as he went through the door he brushed against a bell which rang out and waked the sleepers, who started up with such a monstrous din that the shepherd fled from the cave and never recovered from his terror.

There are two legends of a WIZARD seeking for horses for the sleeping host, one told of Alderley Edge in Cheshire, where an anonymous wizard, probably Merlin, is seeking to make up the full number of white horses sleeping in the stables until the time should come for them to ride out and save England. It was Thomas of Ercildoune, better known as THOMAS THE RHYMER, who was buying horses, black ones this time, for the sleeping place under the Eildon Hills. This time poor Canobie Dick, a horse-coper from whom Thomas had bought several horses, made a fatal error by blowing the horn before he had drawn the sword. All the sleeping knights started up, drew their swords and made for him. A great voice cried out:

'Woe to the coward, that ever he was born,
That did not draw the sword before he blew the horn!'

A whirlwind sprang up and swept him out of the cave and down a precipice, where he had only time to tell his story to the shepherds that found him before he died.

We cannot be sure who TRUE THOMAS's warriors were. There is one legend of Finn Mac Cumhal, 'The Smith's Rock in the Isle of Skye'. It is told by J. Macdougall in *Waifs and Strays of Celtic Tradition* (vol. III). The Fenians in this tale are GIANTS:

There was a report that the Fians (Fingalians) were asleep in this Rock, and that if anyone would enter it and blow the Wooden-Crier (Whistle), which lay beside Finn, three times, they would rise up alive and well as they formerly were.

A Smith who lived in the island heard the report, and resolved that he would attempt to enter the Rock. He reached the place where it was; and, having formed a good idea of the key-hole, he returned to the smithy, and made a key which fitted the hole. He then went back to the Rock, and, as soon as he turned the key in the hole, the door opened, and he saw a very great and wide place before him, and exceedingly big men lying on the floor. One man, bigger than the rest, was lying in their midst, having a large hollow baton of wood lying beside him.

He thought that this was the Wooden-Crier (Whistle). But it was so large that he was afraid that he could not lift it, much less blow it. He stood for a time looking at it, but he at last said to himself that, as he came so far, he would try at any rate. He laid hold of the Wooden-Crier, and with difficulty raised its end up to his mouth. He blew it with all his might, and so loud was the sound it produced that he thought the Rock and all that was over it came down on the top of him. The huge unwieldy men who lay on the floor shook from the tops of their heads to the soles of their feet. He gave another blast on the Wooden-Crier, and with one spring they turned on their elbows. Their fingers were like the prongs of wooden grapes, and their arms like beams of bog-oak. Their size and the terrible appearance they had put him in such fear that he threw the Wooden-Crier from him, and sprang out. They were then crying after him, 'Worse have you left us than as you found us, worse have you left us than as you found us.' But he looked not behind him until he got outside and shut the door. He then drew the key out of the hole, and threw it out into the lake which is near the Rock, and which is called to this day the Lake of the Smith's Rock.

[Motifs: c984; d1960.2; e502]

Sleigh Beggey (*sleigh beargar*), **or the 'Little Folk'.** A name given to the FAIRIES in the Manx tongue, though they are more usually spoken of as 'the LI'L FALLAS', 'THEMSELVES', or 'THEM THAT'S IN', which covers BUGGANES and other sinister characters as well as the fairies. Another Manx name for them is the FERRISHYN.

Sluagh (*slooa*), **the, or the Host.** This is the Host of the Unforgiven Dead. They are the most formidable of the Highland fairy people. There are several accounts of the host collected by Evans Wentz in *The Fairy-Faith in Celtic Countries* from named informants. A few of them regard 'The Host' as fallen angels, not the dead, but on the whole their accounts correspond closely to that given by Alexander Carmichael in *Carmina Gadelica* (vol. II, p. 357):

> *Sluagh*, 'the host', the spirit-world. The 'hosts' are the spirits of mortals who have died. The people have many curious stories on this subject. According to one informant, the spirits fly about in great clouds, up and down the face of the world like the starlings, and come back to the scenes of their earthly transgressions. No soul of them is without the clouds of earth, dimming the brightness of the works of God, nor can any win heaven till satisfaction is made for the sins of earth. In bad nights, the hosts shelter themselves behind little russet docken stems and little yellow ragwort stalks. They fight battles in

the air as men do on the earth. They may be heard and seen on clear frosty nights, advancing and retreating, retreating and advancing, against one another. After a battle, as I was told in Barra, their crimson blood may be seen staining rocks and stones. ('Fuil nan sluagh,' the blood of the hosts, is the beautiful red 'crotal' of the rocks melted by the frost.) These spirits used to kill cats and dogs, sheep and cattle, with their unerring venomous darts. They commanded men to follow them, and men obeyed, having no alternative.

It was these men of earth who slew and maimed at the bidding of their spirit-masters, who in return ill-treated them in a most pitiless manner. They would be rolling and dragging and trouncing them in mud and mire and pools.

In a report by Evans Wentz (p. 108), Marian MacLean of Barra distinguishes between the FAIRIES and the Host.

> Generally, the fairies are to be seen after or about sunset, and walk on the ground as we do, whereas the hosts travel in the air above places inhabited by people. The hosts used to go after the fall of night, and more particularly about midnight.

[Motif: F360]

Sluttishness. Fairies were lavish, but they were orderly and liked NEATNESS. It sometimes happened that a BROWNIE would put right whatever humans had left untidy and disarrange whatever had been tidied, but the TROOPING FAIRIES who visited houses expected to find them in apple-pie order. If clean water was not set out, they washed their children's feet in milk or in wine or beer set to ferment. Gifts of silver were often left to an industrious maidservant who cleaned the hearth well. See also FAULTS CONDEMNED BY THE FAIRIES; VIRTUES ESTEEMED BY THE FAIRIES.

Small People of Cornwall, the. The FAIRIES are sometimes spoken of as such in Cornwall, but they are more often called 'The Small People'. These are the type of DIMINUTIVE FAIRIES about which the Elizabethans and Jacobeans loved to write. In Cornwall, they were not only small but dwindling. They had once been life-sized, but in consequence of some forgotten sin they have dwindled down, at rather varying rates, until they turn into ants, or MURYANS. It is therefore considered wrong in Cornwall to kill muryans, for one is destroying a fairy. 'The FAIRY DWELLING ON SELENA MOOR' goes in some detail into this aspect of the fairy tradition. The Small People seem to have their houses underground, but come up to hills and flowery places to hold their festivities on moonlit nights. We see them in a private and family capacity in such stories as 'The FAIRY WIDOWER' and 'CHERRY OF ZENNOR'.

They were fond of visiting human houses, and some old and bedridden people found them good company and much enjoyed their gambols.

BOTTRELL in *Traditions and Hearthside Stories of West Cornwall* (vol. II, pp. 245–6) gives a general description which agrees closely with HUNT:

> The Innocent Small-people, on the contrary, are always described as being extremely beautiful by all who have the luck to see them, holding their merry fairs and sprightly dances on the velvety turf of the green, sheltered glades between the cairns, or in other sheltered, secluded places, dressed in bright green nether garments, sky-blue jackets, three-cornered hats on the men and pointed ones on the ladies, all decked with lace and silver bells . . . These good small folks often showed great kindnesses to those people to whom they took a fancy, and have frequently been known to come into poor cottages, divert good old bed-ridden folks with their merry pranks, and fill the air with the delicious odour of flowers and sweet melody.

This account seems almost a summary of some of Hunt's stories in *Popular Romances of the West of England*. The last phrase may be founded on Hunt's story 'The Small People's Gardens' (pp. 118–19), about 'little sheltered places between the cairns, close down to the water's edge, beautifully green spots, with here and there some ferns and cliff pinks'. So they are by day, but at night fishermen coming close to land have heard the sweetest of music, seen hundreds of little lights, and smelt sweet perfumes, even a mile out to sea. Those coming still closer on moonlight nights claim to have seen hundreds of flowers of brilliant colours, far brighter than those that grow in mortal gardens.

[Motif: F239.4.3]

Solitary fairies. As a rule the solitary fairies are chiefly malignant or ominous creatures, though there may be a few nature spirits or dwindled gods among them. An exception is the BROWNIE and his variants, though there are a few family groups among the brownies – MEG MOULACH with her son BROWNIE-CLOD, and the rather sinister brownie in the AINSEL story who was scalded to death in Fincastle Mill and who had a group ready to avenge him. The FENODEREE of Man is a solitary of the brownie type, but he is not solitary by nature or by choice – he was banished from the fairy court for making love to a mortal. The solitary fairies seem in general to have worn red coats while the TROOP-ING FAIRIES wore green coats. Some think that brownies were un-acceptable in Fairyland because of their ragged, unkempt appearance, and that they went off to the SEELIE COURT when they were properly dressed. However, that is only one school of thought on the subject.

YEATS's list of the solitary fairies contains the LEPRACAUN, another example of a spirit detached from humanity, neither ominous nor malignant, the POOKA, the BANSHEE and the FIR DARRIG. Macdougall in *Folk Tales and Fairy Lore* includes stories about the CAOINTEACH, a glasrig (which seems to be the same creature as a GLAISTIG), several glaistig stories, including one in which four appear at once, a HAG and several SHAPE-SHIFTING witches. In England we could list a number of BOGY OR BOGEY-BEAST creatures: BRAG and TRASH and HEDLEY KOW, DUERGAR and the BROWN MAN OF THE MUIRS, are true solitaries, more interested in protecting their territories from human intruders than in the mortal race. Others, like SHELLYCOAT, take a sneaking interest in men, and like to waylay and mislead them. Some are actively horrible, like NUCKELAVEE who comes out of the sea to do all the mischief he can. On the whole the solitary fairies are not an attractive set of supernaturals.

Spells to obtain power over fairies. Several 17th-century magical manuscripts contain spells to obtain POWER OVER FAIRIES. Some were to call them up, some to dismiss them from places where treasure was to be found, and some to gain their help and advice. The first two that follow are from the Bodleian Library (MS. Ashmole 1406), the next two from the British Museum (MS. Sloane 1727):

An excellent way to gett a Fayrie, but for my selfe I call margarett Barrance but this will obtaine any one that is not allready bound.

First gett a broad square christall or Venus glasse in length and breadth 3 inches, then lay that glasse or christall in the bloud of a white henne 3 wednesdayes or 3 fridayes: then take it out and wash it with holy aqua and fumigate it: then take 3 hazle stickes or wands of an yeare groth, pill them fayre and white, and make soe longe as you write the spiritts name, or fayries name, which you call 3 times, on every sticke being made flatt one side, then bury them under some hill whereas you suppose fayries haunt, the wednesday before you call her, and the friday followinge take them uppe and call hir at 8 or 3 or 10 of the clocke which be good plannetts and howres for that turne: but when you call, be in cleane Life and turne thy face towards the east, and when you have her bind her to that stone or Glasse.

An Ungt. to annoynt under the Eyelids and upon the Eylidds evninge and morninge, but especially when you call, or finde your sight not perfect. (That is, an ointment to give sight of the fairies) pt. (precipitate?) sallet oyle and put it into a Viall glasse but first wash it with rose water, and marygold flower water, the flowers be gathered towards the east, wash it til the oyle come white, then put it into the glasse, ut supra. and thou put thereto the budds of holyhocke, the flowers of mary gold; the flowers or toppes of wild time the budds of younge hazle, and the time must be gatherred neare the side of a hill where fayries use to go oft, and the grasse of a fayrie throne, there, all these putt into the oyle, into the glasse, and sett it to dissolve 3 dayes in the sonne, and thou keep it for thy use; ut supra.

To Call a Fairy

I. E. A. call the. Elaby: Gathen: in the name of the. father. of. the. sonne. and of the holy. ghost. And. I Adiure. the. Elaby. Gathen: Conjure. and. Straightly: charge. and Command. thee. by. Tetra-grammaton: Emanuell. messias. sether. panton. cratons. Alpha et Omega. and by. all. other. high. and. reverent. names. of all-mighty. god. both Effable. and. in. Effuable. and by. all. the. vertues. of the holy.ghost. by the dyetic grace. and. foreknowledge. of the.powers. and. grace. and. vertues. of. thee. Elaby. by.all.the.powers. and. grace. and. vertues. of. all. the. holy. meritorious. Virginnes. and. patriarches. And. I. Conjure. thee. Elaby Gathen. by. these. holy. names. of God. Saday. Eloy. Iskyros. Adonay. Sabaoth. that thou appeare presently. meekely. and myldly. in. this. glasse. without. doeinge. hurt. or. daunger. unto. me. or any other. livinge. creature. and to this I binde. thee. by. the. whole. power. and. vertue. of. our. Lord. Jesus. Christ. I. Commande. thee. by. the. vertue. of. his. uprisinge. and. by. the vertue. of. his flesh. and. body. that he. tooke. of the. blessed. Virginne. Mary. Empresse. of. heaven. and. hell. and. by. the. hole. power. of. god. and. his. holy. names. namely. Adonay. Adonatos. Eloy. Elohim. Suda. Ege. zeth. and. heban: that. is. to. say. Lord. of. vertue. and. King. of. Israell. dwellinge. uppon. the. whole. face. of. the. earth. whose. seate. is. in. heaven and. his. power. in. earth. and. by. him, &. by those glorious. and. powerfull. names. I. binde. thee. to. give. and. doe. thy. true. humble. and. obedient. servise. unto. me. E.A. and never. to depart. without. my. consent. and Lawfull. Authoritie. in.the.name.of. the. Father. and.the.holy.trinitie. And. I Command. thee. Elaby. Gathen. by. all. Angells. and. Arkangells. and. all. the. holy.company.of.heaven. worshippinge. the omnipotent. god. that. thou. doest. come. and. appeare. presently. to. me. E.A. in. this. christall. or. glasse. meekely. and myldely. to.my.true and. perfect. sight. and. truly. without. fraud. Dissymulation. or. deceite. resolve. and. satisfye me. in. and. of. all. manner. of. such. questions. and. commands. and. Demandes. as. I. shall. either. Aske. Require. desire. or. demande. of. thee. and. that. thou. Ellaby. Gathen. be. true. and. obedient. unto me. both. now. and, ever.heare-after. at. all. time. and. times. howers. dayes. nightes. mynittes. and. in. and. at. all. places. wheresoever. either. in field. howse. or. in. any. other. place. what-soever. &. wheresoever. I. shall. call. upon. thee. and. that. thou. Elaby: Gathen: doe. not. start. depart. or. desire. to. goe. or. departe. from. me. neyther. by. arte. or. call. of. any. other. Artist. of. any. degree. or. Learninge. whatsoever. but. that. thou. in. the. humblyest. manner. that. thou. mayest. be. commanded. to. attend. and. give. thy. true. obedience. unto. me. E.A.: and that. even. as. thou. wilt. Answer. it. unto. and. before. the. Lord. of. hoste. at. the. dreadfull. day. of. Judgment. before. whose. glorious. presence. both. thou. and. I. and all. other. Christian. Creatures. must. and shall. appeare. to. receive. our. Joyes. in. heaven. or. by. his doome. to. be. Judged. into. everlastinge. Damnation. even. into. the. deepe. pitt. of. hell. there. to. receive. our. portion. amongst the divell. and. his. Angells. to. be. ever. burninge. in. pitch. fier. and. brimstone. and. never. consumed. and, to. this. I. E.A. Sweare. thee. Elaby. Gathen. and. binde. thee. by. the. whole. power. of. god. the. Father. god. the. Sonne. & god. the. holy. ghost. 3. persons. and. one. god. in. trinitye. to. be. trew. and. faithfull. unto. me. in. all. Reverente. humillity. Let. it. be. done. in. Jesus. Jesus. Jesus. his name. quickly. quickly. quickly. come. come. come. fiat. fiat. fiat. Amen. Amen. Amen. etc.

This call ut supra is to call Elabigathan A. Fayrie.

A discharge of the fayres and other sps. or Elphes from any place or grounde, where treasure is layd or hidd. First shall the mgn: say in the name of the fa. the so. & the ho. Go. amen. and they say as followeth. – I conjure you sps. or elphes which be 7 sisters and have these names. Lilia. Restilia, foca, fola, Afryca, Julia, venulia, I conjure youe & charge you by the fa.: the so.: and the ho: Go.: and holy mary the mother of our blessed lord and Saviour Jesus Christ: and by the annunciation nativity and circumcision, and by the baptisme; and by his holy fasting; and by the passion, death and reserection of our blessed lord Jesus Christ and by the Comeing of the holy gost our sacred Comforter: and by all the Apostles Martyres confessors: and also virgins and all the elect of God and of our lord Jesus Christ; that from hensforth neither you nor any other for you have power or rule upon this ground; neither within nor without nor uppon this servant of the liveing god.: N: neither by day nor night; but the holy trinity be always upon itt & him or her. Amen. Amen:

A call to the Queen of the Fairies.
Micol o tu micoll regina pigmeorum deus Abraham: deus Isaac: deus Jacob; tibi benedicat et omnia fausta danet et concedat Modo venias et mihi moremgem veni. Igitur o tu micol in nomine Jesus veni cito ters quatur beati in qui nomini Jesu veniunt veni Igitur O tu micol in nomine Jesu veni cito qui sit omnis honor laus et gloria in omne aeternum. Amen Amen

[Motifs: C432.1; D1766.7]

Spenser, Edmund (1552–99). See FAERIE QUEENE.

Sports of the fairies. The TROOPING FAIRIES, whether large or small, commonly engaged in most of the sports which were enjoyed or admired by humans. The HEROIC FAIRIES, that is the FAYS of medieval England, the SEELIE COURT of Scotland and DAOINE SIDH of Ireland, were aristocrats and enjoyed aristocratic pastimes, DANCING, music, hunting and processional rides in the FAIRY RADES. In Ireland a favourite pursuit of the Daoine Sidh was inter-clan warfare, for which they sometimes borrowed human helpers, for the red blood of humanity had special potency. Evans Wentz reproduced the report of old Thady Steed about the warfare of the fairies in *The Fairy-Faith in Celtic Countries* (p. 44):

> When the fairy tribes under the various kings and queens have a battle, one side manages to have a living man among them, and he by knocking the fairies about turns the battle in case the side he is on is losing. It is always usual for the Munster king to challenge Finvara, the Connaught fairy king.

They also conducted fierce wars against human kings and queens, such as that waged by Ethal Anbual, the SIDH king of Connaught, against the warrior Queen Maeve and King Ailill of Cruachan. In the Highlands of Scotland, the Seelie Court waged constant war against the UNSEELIE COURT, for the evil fairies are strong and wicked in the Highlands, and the tradition of this unceasing war was still alive in the Islands within living memory. The SLUAGH, the 'Host of the Dead', are also at enmity with the Seelie Court. Wars, processions and hunting occupy them all.

Music is dear to them all, and human musicians are often lured into Fairyland for the sake of their skill. Many fairy tunes also have been learned by mortal pipers. The reel tune, 'The Fairy Dance', is one, and perhaps the best known is 'The Londonderry Air'. It is a beautiful tune, but no human words seem to fit it. The most famous piper of the famous Mac Crimmon family is said to have learnt his skill from a little fairy man when he was a boy. Dancing, particularly circular dancing, is universal among the fairies. If they have no companions they leap and dance alone. Even the wicked fairies, BOGLES and bogies and the blood-sucking BAOBHAN SITH leap and twirl out of the black joy of their hearts. The Lowland fairy, WHUPPITY STOORIE, gave herself away by dancing and singing to herself. Alexander Carmichael translated a description of the fairies dancing given by Angus Macleod of Harris in 1877.

> I have never seen a man fairy or a woman fairy, but my mother saw a troop of them. She herself and the other maidens of the townland were once out upon the summer sheiling (grazing land). They were milking the cows in the evening gloaming, when they observed a flock of fairies reeling and setting upon the green plain in front of the knoll. And, oh King! but it was they the fairies themselves that had the right to be dancing, and not the children of men! Bell-helmets of blue silk covered their heads, and garments of green satin covered their bodies, and sandals of yellow membranes covered their feet. Their heavy brown hair was streaming down their waist, and its lustre was of the fair golden sun of summer. Their skin was as white as the swan of the

wave, and their voice was as melodious as the mavis of the wood, and they themselves were as beauteous of feature and as lithe of form as a picture, while their step was as light and stately and their minds as sportive as the little red hind of the hill.

Hunting is common to the heroic fairies, whether good or evil. The good fairies chase fairy deer, though it is doubtful if they kill them, and their hounds are white with red ears; the Sluagh hunt human souls, as the Devil does, and sometimes in company with the Devil. They fly in the air with a noise like wild birds calling, and their horses have fiery eyes. In the North of England they are called GABRIEL RATCHETS. Evans Wentz in his collections in Ireland reported a description of fairy hunting given under the shadow of Ben Bulbin in *The Fairy-Faith in Celtic Countries* (p. 56). It was given him by Michael Oates, who acted as his interpreter.

I knew a man who saw the Gentry hunting on the other side of the mountain. He saw hounds and horsemen cross the road and jump the hedge in front of him, and it was one o'clock at night. The next day he passed the place again, and looked for the tracks of the huntsmen, but saw not a trace of tracks at all.

These were 'The GENTRY' and of human size. In another account at Aranmore a crowd of 'small fellows' were chasing a single deer, and on another occasion they chased a horse. In his MIDSUMMER NIGHT'S DREAM, Shakespeare makes the small fairies hunt bats and humble-bees, but one does not find traces of this in folk tradition.

Ball games were played by the fairies. The earliest mention is in GIRALDUS CAMBRENSIS, where a golden ball is stolen by ELIDOR to prove to his mother that he was speaking the truth about the fairies. In Ireland, football and HURLING are popular among the fairies, but these are mostly the GOOD PEOPLE, sportive and dwindled in size. The chief indoor game in which the heroic fairies engaged was CHESS or 'tables'. Contests in chess were often used to defeat humans, as MIDIR won ETAIN from Eochaid when she had been sent by enchantment into the human world.

Fairyland is again and again described as a place of endless delight and sparkling beauty, but there are dark whispers that suggest that this is the delusion of GLAMOUR and that under the gaiety there is a restless, unsatisfied yearning. As KIRK says, 'If they have any frolic Fitts of Mirth, 'tis as the constrained grinning of a Mort-head, or rather as acted on a Stage, and moved by another than cordially comeing of themselves.'

[Motifs: F241.1.0.1; F261; F262; F267]

Spriggans. BOTTRELL and HUNT give much the same picture of the Spriggans. Both agree that they are grotesquely ugly and that they seem to act as the fairy bodyguard. In Hunt's story of 'The MISER ON THE

FAIRY GUMP' in *Popular Romances of the West of England* it is the Spriggans who catch and bind the Miser, and in a story of Bottrell's, 'The FAIRIES ON THE EASTERN GREEN', in *Traditions and Hearthside Stories of West Cornwall*, one of the free-traders who had dared to mock the fairies is attacked by the Spriggans. Bottrell says about them in his descriptions of the various types of Fairy (vol. II, p. 246):

> The Spriggans, quite a different class of being, are the dourest and most ugly set of sprights belonging to the elfin tribe; they are only to be seen about old ruins, barrows, giants' quoits and castles, and other places where treasure is buried, of which they have the charge. They also steal children, leaving their own ugly brats in their place, bring bad weather to blight the crops, whirlwinds over the fields of cut corn, and do much other mischief to those that meddle with their favourite haunts.

According to Hunt, the Spriggans are the ghosts of the old GIANTS, and though they are usually very small, they can swell to enormous size. On the whole, despite their interest in promoting BLIGHTS AND ILL-NESSES, they seem less dangerous than the Highland BOGIES, being intent rather on frightening than damaging their victims. They are, how-ever, busy thieves. One of Hunt's stories (op. cit., pp. 113–14), 'The Old Woman Who Turned Her Shift', is of a band of spriggans who used to meet nightly in an old woman's cottage to divide their spoils. They always left a coin for her, but she was greedy for more, and one night contrived slyly to turn her shift inside out and so, by the act of TURNING CLOTHES, to possess herself of all they had taken. She was punished for her greed, for she always suffered agonies whenever she put on that shift.

[Type: ML6045. Motifs: F385.1; F456; F456.1; F456.1.1]

Sprites. A general name for FAIRIES and other spirits such as sylphs and nereids. It is not generally used for earthier fairy creatures.

Spunkies. In the Lowlands of Scotland, 'Spunkies' is the name given to the WILL O' THE WISP. In *County Folk-lore* (vol. VII), Simpson gives a quotation from Graham's *History of Buckhaven* in which Spunkie is blamed for wrecks at sea as well as misleadings on land.

> Willy and the Wisp, he is a fiery devil, and leads people off their road to drown them, for he sparks sometimes at our feet, and then turns before us, with his candle, as if he were two or three miles before us, many a good boat has Spunkie drowned; the boats coming to land in night-time, they observe a light off the land and set in upon it and drown.

Here there is no suggestion that the spunkie is the soul of a child, but in Somerset there is an explicit belief that Will o' the Wisp is a spunky, the soul of an unchristened child. Ruth Tongue in *County Folklore* (vol. VIII) says:

> Will o' the Wisps in Somerset are called *Spunkies* and are believed to be the souls of unbaptized children, doomed to wander until Judgement Day. These are sometimes supposed to perform the same warning office as the corpse candles.
>
> Stoke Pero Church is one of the places where 'they spunkies do come from all around' to guide this year's ghosts to their funeral service on Hallowe'en. One St John's Eve, an old carter called me to watch from Ley Hill. The marsh lights were moving over by Stoke Pero and Dunkery. 'They'm away to church gate, zo they are. They'm gwaine to watch 'tis certain, they dead cannles be.'
>
> Midsummer Eve is the night on which the spunkies go to church to meet the newly dead . . .

The Lowland legend, SHORT HOGGERS OF WHITTINGHAME, given in Chambers's *Popular Rhymes*, is founded on the same belief in the misery of namelessness, but here the bestowal of even a nickname is enough to rescue a child from the limbo inhabited by the nameless. In a similar legend of the Isle of Man told by Sophia Morrison, the little waif is saved by a token Christian baptism, an old fisherman who blesses some water, makes the sign of the CROSS in the air and says, 'I christen you as John if you be a boy and Jean if you be a girl.' Here the heathen name-giving has been christianized.

[Motifs: F251.3; F402.1.1; F491; F491.1]

Stock. The fairy CHANGELING which was supposed to be substituted for the mortal baby stolen by the FAIRIES was generally a fairy, either a fairy boy who did not thrive, an old fellow of whom they felt themselves well rid, or even at times a family man who wanted a rest from the responsibilities of his position. Occasionally, however, a piece of wood, roughly shaped, was transformed and left in the child's place, and this was often done when a nursing mother or human wife was stolen, as, for instance, almost happened in the case of SANDY HARG'S WIFE. This simulated image was called 'a stock'. This means was used also when the fairies stole cattle, as the fairies stole the TACKSMAN OF AUCHRIACHAN's ox. Occasionally, by association, a fairy changeling was described as 'a stock', but this was an extension of the idea. Generally, where a human was involved, she would appear to be unconscious like Grace Hutchens in 'The FAIRY DWELLING ON SELENA MOOR' or Robert KIRK, but changeling cattle moved about and appeared to be alive for a short time, although they soon withered and died.

[Motifs: F451.5.2.3.1]

Strangers, the. A Lincolnshire name for the FAIRIES. In those tales she collected from the area of drained fens in north Lincolnshire known as 'The Cars', Mrs Balfour recorded many savage and primitive beliefs and practices. She preserved the notes that she took down as she listened to the stories, and several times claimed to have reproduced the very words in which they were told. The uniqueness of her collection, published in her article on 'Legends of the Cars', has tempted some folklorists to disbelieve her report, but this is a heavy charge to bring, and the macabre temper of many of the stories in W. H. Barrett's *Tales from the Fens*, though different in subject matter, shows a suggestive similarity of mood and background. In 'The GREEN MIST' and 'The DEAD MOON' we are introduced to the sinister BOGLES and horrors and dead hands that haunted the Fens, but the TIDDY MUN and this tale of 'The Strangers' Share' deal with the nearest the fenmen could come to the SEELIE COURT, fertility spirits who gave life to grain and flowers and who controlled the flow of the waters. They were the best the fenmen knew, but they were grotesque and sinister enough in their way. This is the description given of them by the Lindsey man from whom Mrs Balfour collected the story:

But 'bout th' Stra'angers. Thou knows what they be – ay – thou's geyan ready wi' th' wo'd, but it be'nt chancy to ca'all 'em sich! Noa; an' ef thou'd seed 's much on 'em as a done, thou'd twist thy tongue into 'nother sha'ape, thou 'ould. Fo'ak i' these pa'arts, tha ca'alled um mostly tha 'Stra'angers' or th' 'tiddy people'; 'ca'se tha wor none so big's a new-born babby; or th' 'Greencoaties', fro' ther green jackets; or mebbe th' 'Yarthkin'; sence tha doolt i' th' mools. But mostly th' 'Stra'angers', as a said afore: fur stra'ange tha be – i' looks 'n wa'ays – an' quare i' ther loikins, an' stra'angers i' th' mid o' th' fo'ak. – Hev a seed un? – Ay, that a hev; often 'n often, an' no later 'n last spring. Tha be main tiddy critters, no more'n a span-hoigh, wi' a'arms 'n legs's thin's thread, but gre'at big feet 'n han'ds, 'n he'ads rowllin' 'bout on ther shouthers. Tha weers gra'ass-green jackets 'n breeches, 'n yaller bonnets, fur ahl th' wo'ld loike towdie-stools o' ther he'ads; 'n quare bit fa'aces, wi' long nosen, an' wide gobs, 'n great red tongues hangin' oot 'n flap-flappin' aboot. A niver heerd un sp'akin 's a can moind on; but whan tha be fratched wi' owt, tha girns 'n ye'ps loike 'n angry hound, an' whan tha feels ga'ay 'n croodlesome, tha twitters an' cheeps 's soft an' fond's th' tiddy bi'ds . . .

O' summer noights tha da'anced i' tha moonshine o' th' great flat sto'ans's thou sees aba'out; a do'ant know'a wheer tha come from, but ma gran'ther said's how 's gran'ther's gran'ther'd tou'd 'em at long agone th' fo'ak set fire on tha sto'ans, 'n smeared 'un wi' blood, an' thowt a deal more on 'un than o' th' pa'asson bodies an' th' cho'ch.

An' o' winter evens tha Stra'angers'd da'ance o' nights o' th' fire-

pla'ace, whan tha fo'ak wor to bed; an' tha crickets pla'ayed fur'n wi'
roight good will. An' tha wor allus theer, whativer wor goin' on. I' th'
har'st field, tha pu'd aboot th' yearn o' co'n 'n tum'led mid th' stooble,
'n wrastled wi' th' poppie he'ads; an' i' th' spring o' th' year tha want
to sha'akin' 'n pinchin' th' tree-buds to mak' 'em come o'pen; an'
tweakin' tha flower-buds, 'n cha'asin' th' butterflees, 'n toogin' th'
wo'ms oot o' th' yarth; allus pla'ayin' loike tom-fools, but happy
mischeevious bit creeturs, so long's tha wor'nt crossed. Thou'd on'y to
ho'd qui't 'n kep still's de'ath an' thou'd see th' busy tiddy things
rinnin' 'n pla'aying ahl roond tha.

Fo'ak thowt as tha Stra'angers he'ped th' co'n to ripen, an' ahl th'
green things to grow'a; an' as tha p'inted th' purty colours o' th'
flowers, an' th' reds 'n bra'owns o' th' fruit i' Yatum' an' th' yallerin'
leaves. An' tha thowt's how, ef tha wor fratched, th' things 'd dwine an'
widder, an' th' har'st'd fail, an' th' fo'ak go hungered. So tha did ahl's
tha cud think on to ple'ase th' tiddy people, an' kep' friends wi' un.
I' th' gy'ardens th' first flowers, 'n th' first fruit, 'n th' first cabbage, or
what not, 'd be took to th' nighest flat sto'an, 'n laid theer fur tha
Stra'angers; i' th' fields th' fust yearn o' co'n, or th' fust taters, wor
guv to th' tiddy people; an' to ho'am, afore tha 'gun to y'eat their
vittles, a bit o' bre'ad 'n drop o' milk or beer, wor spilled o' th' fire
place, to kep' th' greencoaties fro' hunger 'n thu'st.

According to the story, all went well with the people and the land as
long as they kept up these habits. But as time went on the people became
careless. No libations were poured out, the great flat stones were left
empty, and even sometimes broken up and carried away. There was more
church-going, and in time a generation sprang up that had almost forgotten about the Strangers. Only the wise women remembered. At first
nothing happened; the Strangers were reluctant to believe that their old
worshippers had deserted them. At last they became angry, and struck.
Harvest after harvest failed, there was no growth of corn or hay, the
beasts sickened on the farms, the children pined away and there was no
food to give them. Then the men spent the little they could get on drink,
and the women on opium. They were bewildered, and could think of
nothing to do; all except the wise women. They got together and made a
solemn ceremony of divination, with fire and blood. And when they
learnt what was working the mischief, they went all among the people,
and summoned them to gather at the cross-roads in the deep twilight,
and there they told them the cause of the trouble, and explained the
usages of the older people. And the women, remembering all the little
graves in the churchyard and the pining babies in their arms, said that the
old ways must be taken up again, and the men agreed with them. So they
went home, and spilled their libations, and laid out the firstlings of the
little that they had, and taught their children to respect the Strangers.

Then, little by little, things began to mend; the children lifted their heads, the crops grew and the cattle throve. Still, there were never such merry times as there had once been, and the fever still hovered over the land. It is a bad thing to forsake the old ways, and what is once lost can never be quite recovered.

[Motifs: C433; V12.9]

Stray Sod, the, or Foidin Seachrain, sometimes called 'The Lone Sod'. The Irish version of the state of being PIXY-LED or POOK-LEDDEN. It is not effected by lights or voices; the general explanation is that a fairy spell is laid on a piece of turf so that the human stepping on it is unable to find his way out of a well-known spot, and wanders helplessly, often for several hours, until the spell is suddenly lifted. References to this phenomenon are to be found in many of the learned writings of the 17th century, but the fullest modern account is given in *The Middle Kingdom* by D. A. Mac Manus, who devotes a short chapter to 'The Stray Sod'. Several anecdotes illustrate the belief, among them one of a rector who was called out one Midsummer Night to visit a sick parishioner who lived about seven miles off by road. A pleasant footpath more than halved the distance, so the rector determined to walk there. The footpath led through a strong gate to a field with a fairy oak in the middle of it and a stile at the other end of the path. The rector walked straight through the field, but when he got to the other side of it, the stile was not to be found, and what was more the path had gone. The rector walked along the hedge, feeling for any possible gap, but there was none. When he got back the gate had gone as well as the stile. He walked round and round the field, following the hedge for several hours, until suddenly the spell lifted and he found the gate. He went through it and home, where he took out his bicycle and went by the road. The usual spell in Ireland as in England against fairy misleading is to turn one's coat. The rector did not try the spell of TURNING CLOTHES, but D. A. Mac Manus says that it has been tried with the stray sod and has failed.

Ruth Tongue records a very similar experience told in a Somerset Women's Institute, and already quoted in PIXY-LED. This incident happened in Cornwall, and in this account a white gate vanished and was later found again. The narrator was rescued by a local boy who came to look for her. Here again there was no evidence of the presence of fairies except the disappearance of the path and gate. See also HINKY; JACKY LANTERN; JOAN THE WAD; PINKET; PUNK; WILL O' THE WISP.

[Motif: D394.1]

Stroke. The traditional name for a paralytic seizure. It was a shortened version of 'fairy-stroke' or 'elf-stroke'. It was generally believed that the victim had been carried away by the FAIRIES and what KIRK calls 'a lingering substituted image' left in his place. This was sometimes supposed to be a fairy baby or an aged fairy or, alternatively, a STOCK, a roughly-carved wooden image which was given by GLAMOUR the appearance of the victim. It was sometimes supposed to happen to cattle and other stock. An example occurs in 'The TACKSMAN OF AUCHRIACHAN', told in Stewart's *Popular Superstitions of the Highlands*. An example of a human image of wood occurs in the story of SANDY HARG'S WIFE. Honey-dew, the excreta of aphides, was also called 'stroke', and was associated with the smaller TROOPING FAIRIES who were supposed to feed on it. See also BLIGHTS AND ILLNESSES ATTRIBUTED TO THE FAIRIES; ELF-SHOT.

Subterraneans, the. Robert KIRK calls those Highland FAIRIES that live under the fairy hills, or BROCHS, Subterraneans. They do not always inhabit the same hill, but travel from place to place, moving their lodgings always at quarter day. In this they seem to differ from those fairies that live constantly under some human habitation and seem to resemble the Roman *lemures* in being the spirits of ancestral inhabitants. Kirk says, however, that the Highlanders believe these mounds to be the homes of their dead ancestors and therefore sacred. In their 'flitting' times, therefore, they may be equated with the SLUAGH.

[Motifs: F211.3; F282]

Supernatural wizards. It is sometimes difficult to distinguish the true supernatural wizard from the WIZARD who has acquired his skill, however unusual, from practical experience and training and some inborn aptitude. The wizards of the SIDH, such, for instance, as Bresil, the druid who laid the spell of diminishment on ETAIN, may be counted as minor supernatural wizards, and so may the GIANT wizards who have their lives hidden away in a SEPARABLE SOUL, such as the wizard giant in 'The Battle of the Birds'; but the true supernatural wizard is he who started as a god. GWYDION is an example of this; so is BRAN THE BLESSED.

[Motifs: D1711.5; D1810]

Swan maidens. The swan maiden story has currency all over the world, but in Britain it occurs most often in Celtic fairy-tales. In the general run of the stories, the enchanted maidens are the daughters of a royal MAGICIAN. The hero sees them bathing or dancing, falls in love with one of them and steals her feather cloak. A swan is one of the most usual forms for the maidens to assume, but they are often doves or partridges. In the main type of the swan maiden tale, the hero is set tasks by the WIZARD father and helped by his future wife. The story often follows the same pattern as NICHT NOUGHT NOTHING, with the obstacle flight, the destruction of the wizard and the breach of TABOO which causes magical forgetfulness resolved by the motif of the bartered bed. HARTLAND in

The Science of Fairy Tales analyses the swan maiden tale in detail and treats the SEAL MAIDEN legend as a variant of the same tale. This, however, is a much simpler tale, the seal-skin is a more necessary part of the seal maiden's life, the finding of the skin and escape into the sea is intrinsic to the seal maiden story, although it occasionally occurs in the pure swan maiden type.

A representative example of the Scottish swan maiden story is to be found in *Waifs and Strays of Celtic Tradition* (vol. III), the tale of 'The Son of the King of Ireland and the Daughter of the King of the Red Cap'.

[Motifs: B652.1; D361.1; D361.1.1; F302.4.2; H335.0.1]

Swarth. The appearance of a person as a death omen in Cumberland. Mentioned by William Henderson in *Folk-Lore of the Northern Counties* (p. 46). The Yorkshire equivalent is WAFF.

[Motif: E723.2]

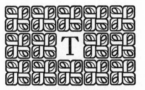

Taboo, or tabu. A recent term in English, first introduced into the language by Captain Cook in his *Voyage to the Pacific* (1777). It is to be found in various forms and spellings through the South Sea Islands, but always as an adjective, with the meaning of 'sacred' or forbidden. The verbal use of 'under a taboo' was introduced by Tylor in his *Early History of Man*. In that sense it is virtually the same as the Irish GEASA, a mysterious prohibition which was magically laid upon an individual, and once laid was irremovable. Some unfortunate people had conflicting geasas laid upon them, like CUCHULAIN, who might refuse no invitation to meat and might not eat the flesh of a dog. Other taboos that are not called geasas are like those laid on the men wedding FAIRY BRIDES who might not reproach them with their inhuman origin or might not give them three causeless blows. Some FAIRIES impose a taboo that they may not be thanked, and a taboo of secrecy is imposed by many, the 'Utter not we you implore' of the fairies in Ben Jonson's *Entertainment at Althorpe*.

[Motifs: C 0-980; F348.7; F348.8]

Tacksman of Auchriachan, the. Thomas KEIGHTLEY in *Fairy Mythology* (pp. 390–91) gives a condensed account of Grant Stewart's story of FAIRY THEFTS, which is typical of their technique. It raises other interesting points as well – the continued presence of THOMAS THE

RHYMER in Fairyland, the fairy nature of goats and the captivity of humans in Fairyland:

The tacksman (*i.e.* tenant) of the farm of Auchriachan in Strathavon, while searching one day for his goats on a hill in Glenlivat, found himself suddenly enveloped in a dense fog. It continued till night came on when he began to give himself up to despair. Suddenly he beheld a light at no great distance. He hastened toward it, and found that it proceeded from a strange-looking edifice. The door was open, and he entered, but great was his surprise to meet there a woman whose funeral he had lately attended. From her he learned that this was an abode of the fairies for whom she kept house, and his only chance of safety, she said, was in being concealed from them; for which purpose she hid him in a corner of the apartment. Presently in came a troop of fairies, and began calling out for food. An old dry-looking fellow then reminded them of the miserly, as he styled him, tacksman of Auchriachan, and how he cheated them out of their lawful share of his property, by using some charms taught him by his old grandmother. 'He is now from home,' said he, 'in search of our allies, his goats, and his family have neglected to use the charm, so come let us have his favourite ox for supper.' The speaker was Thomas Rimer, and the plan was adopted with acclamation. 'But what are we to do for bread?' cried one. 'We'll have Auchriachan's new baked bread,' replied Thomas; 'his wife forgot to cross the first bannock.' So said, so done. The ox was brought in and slaughtered before the eyes of his master, whom, while the fairies were employed about their cooking, his friend gave an opportunity of making his escape.

The mist had now cleared away and the moon was shining. Auchriachan therefore soon reached his home. His wife instantly produced a basket of new-baked bannocks with milk and urged him to eat. But his mind was running on his ox, and his first question was, who had served the cattle that night. He then asked the son who had done it if he had used the charm, and he owned he had forgotten it. 'Alas! alas!' cried he, 'my favourite ox is no more.' 'How can that be?' said one of the sons, 'I saw him alive and well not two hours ago.' 'It was nothing but a fairy stock,' cried the father. 'Bring him out here.' The poor ox was led forth, and the farmer, after abusing it and those that sent it, felled it to the ground. The carcase was flung down the brae at the back of the house, and the bread was sent after it, and there they both lay untouched, for it was observed that neither cat nor dog would put a tooth in either of them.

[Type: ML5081*. Motifs: F365; F370; F376; F380; F382.1; F382.1.1*]

Taghairm (*togherim*). Perhaps the most horrible of all recorded magical spells. It consisted of roasting a series of cats on spits until, in the end, a gigantic cat appeared and granted the wishes of the operants. The last known performance of this rite was at the beginning of the 17th century, and it was recorded in the *London Literary Gazette* (March 1824). It was quoted by Donald A. Mackenzie in *Scottish Folk-Lore and Folk Life*. The operants were Allan MacLean and Lauchlan MacLean, each of whom wished to secure a boon. They continued the operation for four days without tasting food. The barn became full of demon black cats yelling, and at length the master cat, BIG EARS, appeared and granted them their wishes, though it was said they would never look on the face of God, and indeed it seems unlikely that they would.

Tamlane. See YOUNG TAMLANE.

Tangie. So named because of the seaweed which covers it. It is one form of the NOGGLE of Orkney and Shetland; but in its horse form it is not sleek, but covered with rough hair and seaweed. In its human form it is an old man.
[Motif: B184.1.3]

Tankerabogus, or Tanterabobus. Names for one of the NURSERY BOGIES used to scare children into good behaviour, but they seem to be nicknames for the Devil, if we may judge from the example given by Mrs Wright in *Rustic Speech and Folk-Lore* (p. 198):

> 'Now, Polly, yu've abin a bad, naughty maid, and ef yu be sich a wicked cheel again, I'll zend var tankerabogus tu come and car yu away tu 'is pittee-awl [pit-hole].'

Tankerabogus is a Somerset BOGIE.
[Motif: E752.2]

Tarans. In the north-east of Scotland the spirits of babies who have died without baptism are called 'Tarans'. McPherson, in *Primitive Beliefs in the North-East of Scotland* (pp. 113–14), quotes from Pennant's *Tour of Scotland*, the Banff section:

> The little spectres, called Tarans, or the souls of unbaptized infants, were often seen flitting among the woods and secret places, bewailing in soft voices their hard fate.

In the Lowlands and in Somerset these would be called SPUNKIES. Little SHORT HOGGERS OF WHITTINGHAME was one of the spunkies.
[Motif: F251.3]

Tarroo-Ushtey (*tar-oo ushtar*). The water-bull of the Isle of Man. It is less malign than the CABYLL-USHTEY, just as the water-bull of the Highlands is less dangerous than the EACH UISGE, but it is as well to keep on the soft side of both of them. Dora Broome, in *Fairy Tales from the Isle of Man*, has a story of a cross-grained farmer at Sulby who found the Tarroo-Ushtey grazing with his herd. He recognized it by its round ears, but instead of treating it with civil avoidance he gave it a sharp hit with his stick and sent it plunging into the sea. His wife was much distressed and prophesied a blight on the crops. Sure enough, the corn came up blighted and the farmer was more furious against the Tarroo-Ushtey than before. The next time he saw the beast grazing with his herd he crept up behind it with a long loop of rope and lassooed it, but the bull twitched the rope out of his hand and plunged down into the sea again. This time the potatoes were blighted. Then the farmer did consent to go to the fairy doctor, as his wife had advised, but he paid no attention to the doctor's advice about treating fairy beasts with deference. He learned one thing, however, which was that a peeled ROWAN stick had power to subdue the Tarroo-Ushtey, and one day he crept up behind the creature and drove it with a rowan rod into a shed. In due course he drove it up to market. It was a beautiful beast, and there was nothing to tell that it was no earthly bull but its round ears and the wild glitter in its eyes, but no wise farmer would bid for it, and evening was falling when a simple fellow began to take an interest in it, and at last promised to buy it if the farmer would ride it, as he claimed to be able to do. The farmer climbed on its back and gave it a smart tap with his rowan gad and the bull set off at a gentle trot. Suddenly the slippery rowan wand slid out of his hand and he tried to get off and pick it up, but the bull put down his horns and up his heels and shot off at a wild gallop through the market place and out of the town, heading for the sea with the farmer clinging for dear life to his back. He had plenty of time to repent his uncivil ways as he went. They passed the farm and got to the shore; the bull plunged into the sea, but with his last strength the farmer leapt from his back into the deep water. More dead than alive he struggled to shore, and was a changed man ever afterwards.

[Type: ML6060. Motif: B184.2.2.2]

Tatterfoal. A Lincolnshire BOGY OR BOGEY-BEAST. See also SHAG-FOAL.

[Motif: E423.1.3.5(a); F234.1.8]

Teind. The old Lowland term for tithe. It was the tribute due to be paid by the FAIRIES to the Devil every seven years. The mention of it is to be found in the ballad of 'TRUE THOMAS and the Queen of Elfland'.

[Motif: F257]

Terrytop. The Cornish version of the Suffolk TOM TIT TOT had the demon Terrytop for its villain. HUNT, in *Popular Romances of the West of England* (pp. 239–47), summarizes the story as told by the old drolls, professional story-tellers who went from farm to farm entertaining the inhabitants through the long winter evenings. The story, 'Duffy and the Devil', as it was called, was also made the subject of one of the Christmas plays. Duffy was an idle, slovenly girl, but evidently a pretty one, for Squire Lovel of Trewoof, finding her in the middle of a quarrel with her stepmother about her idleness, believed her claim to be a champion spinner and knitter and carried her away to help his old housekeeper. Her helper was a devil, who helped her for three years on the usual terms. The name was discovered in the same way as in 'Tom Tit Tot', but when the devil was driven off, all his handiwork went up in smoke, and the squire had to walk home half-naked. The story meandered on in a long wrangle from which a compromise was at length arrived at with the help of Duffy's lover and the old housekeeper. The interest of the tale chiefly lies in the appearance of the 'Rumpelstiltskin' story type at the opposite side of England to 'Tom Tit Tot', and even more in this specimen of the work of the Cornish droll-tellers.

[Type: 500. Motifs: C432.1; D2183; F451.5.2; H521; M242; N475]

Thefts from the fairies. It would perhaps not be quite fair to say that men stole as much from the FAIRIES as the fairies stole from men by way of FAIRY THEFTS, but, considering the awe in which the fairies were held, it is surprising how many attempts, some of them successful, were made to take gold or silver plate out of the fairy mounds. The first accounts are in the MEDIEVAL CHRONICLES. There is the story of ELIDOR and his attempted theft of the golden ball which belonged to the little fairy prince, in order to satisfy his mother's curiosity. William of Newbridge tells of a barrow near his birthplace in Yorkshire which was occasionally open, with lights streaming from it and feasting going on inside. One night a peasant passed it and was invited in and offered a cup of wine. He poured out the contents and carried off the cup, which was afterwards given to Henry I. GERVASE OF TILBURY tells what seems like a variant of this FAIRY CUP story, though told of a different place. It is of a fairy cup-bearer who appeared from a mound near Gloucester and offered drink to any huntsman who asked for it. One was so ungrateful as to carry off the cup and present it to the Earl of Gloucester, who, however, executed him as a robber and gave the cup to Henry I. The Luck of Edenhall was stolen by the butler of Edenhall from a fairy gathering in something the same way, and carried with it a curse. Later attempts, like that of the MISER ON THE FAIRY GUMP, have often ended in ignominious failure. Ruth Tongue in *County Folklore* (vol. VIII) tells the story of a farmer who saw the FAIRY MARKET on Blackdown and tried to snatch a gold mug off one of the stalls. He galloped off with it, got safe home and took the mug to bed with him. Next morning there was nothing there but a large toadstool, and when he went down to look at his pony it was 'scamble-footed' and remained so for the rest of its life. J. G. CAMPBELL in his *Superstitions of the Highlands and Islands of Scotland* (pp. 52–7) gives several variants of the story of Luran, in some of which the hero is a dog, and in some a human – a crofter or a boy butler. In one version the fairies steal from Luran and he tries to make up his losses by stealing from the fairies. He is not finally successful. A feature of the story is the friendly adviser among the fairies. He is generally called 'The Red-headed Man' and is supposed to be a captured human who retains his sympathy with his fellow men:

The Charmed Hill (*Beinn Shianta*), from its height, greenness, or pointed summit, forms a conspicuous object on the Ardnamurchan coast, at the north entrance of the Sound of Mull. On 'the shoulder' of this hill, were two hamlets, Sginid and Corryvulin, the lands attached to which, now forming part of a large sheep farm, were at one time occupied in common by three tenants, one of whom was named Luran Black (*Luran Mac-ille-dhui*). One particular season a cow of Luran's was found unaccountably dead each morning. Suspicion fell on the tenants of the Culver (*an cuilibheir*), a green knoll in Corryvulin, having the reputation of being tenanted by the Fairies. Luran resolved to watch his cattle for a night, and ascertain the cause of his mysterious losses. Before long he saw the Culver opening, and a host of little people pouring out. They surrounded a grey cow (*mart glas*) belonging to him and drove it into the knoll. Not one busied himself in doing this more than Luran himself; he was, according to the Gaelic expression, 'as one and as two' (*mar a h-aon's mar a dhà*) in his exertions. The cow was killed and skinned. An old Elf, a tailor sitting in the upper part of the brugh, with a needle in the right lappel of his coat, was forcibly caught hold of, stuffed into the cow's hide, and sewn up. He was then taken to the door and rolled down the slope. Festivities commenced, and whoever might be on the floor dancing, Luran was sure to be. He was 'as one and as two' at the dance, as he had been at driving the cow. A number of gorgeous cups and dishes were put on the table, and Luran, resolving to make up for the loss of the grey cow, watched his opportunity and made off with one of the cups (*còrn*). The Fairies observed him and started in pursuit. He heard one of them remark:

'Not swift would be Luran
If it were not the hardness of his bread.'

His pursuers were likely to overtake him, when a friendly voice called out:
'Luran, Luran Black,
Betake thee to the black stones of the shore.'

Below high water mark, no Fairy, ghost, or demon can come, and, acting on the friendly advice, Luran reached the shore, and keeping below tide mark made his way home in safety. He heard the outcries

of the person who had called out to him (probably a former acquaintance who had been taken by 'the people') being belaboured by the
Fairies for his ill-timed officiousness. Next morning, the grey cow was
found lying dead with its feet in the air, at the foot of the Culver, and
Luran said that a needle would be found in its right shoulder. On this
proving to be the case, he allowed none of the flesh to be eaten, and
threw it out of the house.

One of the fields, tilled in common by Luran and two neighbours,
was every year, when ripe, reaped by the Fairies in one night, and the
benefit of the crop disappeared. An old man was consulted, and he
undertook to watch the crop. He saw the shïan of Corryvulin open, and
a troop of people coming out. There was an old man at their head,
who put the company in order, some to shear, some to bind the
sheaves, and some to make stooks. On the word of command being
given, the field was reaped in a wonderfully short time. The watcher,
calling aloud, counted the reapers. The Fairies never troubled the
field again.

Their persecution of Luran did not, however, cease. While on his
way to Inveraray Castle, with his Fairy cup, he was lifted mysteriously
with his treasure out of the boat, in which he was taking his passage,
and was never seen or heard of after.

[Type: ML6045. Motifs: F348.2; F350; F352; F352.1]

Themselves, or They, or Them that's in it. Manx EUPHEMISTIC
NAMES FOR THE FAIRIES, 'fairy' being generally considered an unlucky
word to use. It is sometimes said that 'Themselves' are the souls of those
drowned in Noah's Flood.

[Motif: C433]

Theories of fairy origins. The people who believed in their existence
had differing notions about the ORIGIN OF FAIRIES. Folklorists are more
concerned in the origin of fairy beliefs; what is important to them is not
so much whether the fairies really exist as whether their existence is
actually believed in by the people who tell about them. When that has
been discovered, the folklorist's next object is to find out the grounds on
which the belief was founded. Various suggestions have been put forward, either as full or partial solutions of the problem.

One of the most well-supported is that which equates the fairies with
the dead. Lewis Spence in *British Fairy Origins* makes a very plausible
case for this theory. He can bring forward plenty of evidence from tradition, as, for instance, Lady WILDE's accounts of FINVARRA's court, and
BOTTRELL's story 'The FAIRY DWELLING ON SELENA MOOR'. According to KIRK, the fairy KNOWES by the churchyard were supposed to be
places where the souls of the dead lodged, waiting to rejoin their bodies

on the Day of Judgement. The small size of the fairies might be plausibly accounted for by the primitive idea of the soul as a miniature replica of the man himself, which emerged from the owner's mouth in sleep or unconsciousness. If its return was prevented, the man died.

David MAC RITCHIE in *The Testimony of Tradition* and other writings was the chief exponent of the theory that the fairy beliefs were founded on the memory of a more primitive race driven into hiding by the invaders, lurking in caves or fens, some of them half-domesticated and doing chores about the houses like the shaggy and unkempt BROWNIE. Such tales as 'The ISLE OF SANNTRAIGH' give verisimilitude to the theory, but it does not cover all forms of fairy belief.

A third suggestion which attempts to cover only part of the ground is that the fairies are dwindled gods or nature spirits. This was undoubtedly true of the DAOINE SIDH and possibly of the TYLWYTH TEG, and of a few of the more primitive spirits such as the CAILLEACH BHEUR, the Hag of Winter, BLACK ANNIS and so on. Tree and water spirits might also be traced to this source. The psychological foundation of folk-tales, explored at some depth by C. G. Jung, may afford some valuable hints to folklorists probing into the foundation of fairy beliefs, and their curious plausibility as if the mind leapt to receive them. On the whole we may say that it is unwise to commit oneself blindfold to any solitary theory of the origins of fairy belief, but that it is most probable that these are all strands in a tightly twisted cord.

They. See THEMSELVES.

Thomas the Rhymer, or Thomas of Ercildoune. Famous for six centuries as a poet and prophet, Thomas the Rhymer was a real man living in the 13th century, as deeds signed by him and by his son show. In these documents he was called Thomas Rymour de Erceldoune. He is sometimes spoken of as Thomas Learmont of Erceldoune, but there is no documentary evidence of this name. He was supposed to have gained his prophetic knowledge from the Queen of Elfland. The romance of Thomas of Erceldoune gives an early account of this part of his life, together with a specimen of some of his prophecies. Several 15th-century manuscripts of this poem survive, and the poem itself may well be of the 14th century. The same story is told in the 'Ballad of TRUE THOMAS', but without the prophecies which were printed in chapbook form from the 16th to the 19th centuries, adapted from time to time to topical history. According to this part of the story, the Queen of Elfland became enamoured of True Thomas, carried him into Elfland and kept him there for seven years. At the end of that time the TEIND that the FAIRIES owed to Satan fell due, and the queen feared that Thomas would be chosen. To save him from this she returned him to the mortal world, bestowing upon him a tongue that could not lie. In some versions of the ballad,

Thomas protested against this embarrassing gift, but the queen bestowed it on him all the same. Here the romance ends, but tradition continues the story further, as SCOTT tells us in *Minstrelsy of the Scottish Border*. Thomas the Rhymer lived many years in Erceldoune after his return from Elfame, and became famous throughout Scotland for his gifts of prophecy. But Elfame did not loose its hold on him. One night, as he was feasting in his castle, a man came running in in great fear to say that a hind and a doe had left the forest and were pacing through the village towards the castle. Even now they were at his heels. At once Thomas the Rhymer got up from his seat and went to greet them. They turned round and led him into the forest and he never returned to live among men again. Yet he has been seen from time to time by those who have made VISITS TO FAIRYLAND. He always acts as councillor to the fairies, as he did in the fairy house visited by the TACKSMAN OF AUCHRIACHAN; sometimes he buys horses for SLEEPING WARRIORS under some of the Scottish hills.

[Motif: F234.1.4.1]

Thrummy-Cap. A North Country spirit who haunted the cellars of old houses and wore a cap made of weavers' thrums, the clippings of wool left at the ends of a web. It occurs in the list of FAIRIES and spirits in the DENHAM TRACTS with a footnote mentioning the Thrummy Hills near Catterick and adding, 'The name of this spirit is met with in the Fairy tales of Northumberland.'

Thrumpin. William Henderson in *Folk-Lore of the Northern Counties* (p. 262) cites the authority of the Wilkie manuscript for an instrument of fate called 'the thrumpin' who attended on every man like a dark guardian angel with the power to take away his life. This belief is found on the Scottish Border.

Tib. Lieutenant to SIB in the LIFE OF ROBIN GOODFELLOW. She seems to have no special attributes beyond her position as second-in-command, nor is it a name that belongs particularly to the FAIRIES, though like the other names it is short and thin in sound, to suggest the tiny size of the DIMINUTIVE FAIRIES and their whispering, sibilant voice.

Tiddy Mun, the. The Tiddy Mun was presumably an outstanding member of the TIDDY ONES, or STRANGERS, in Lincolnshire, but he seemed more concerned with the level of the waters than with fertility. Mrs Balfour collected this tale from an old woman who had lived all her life in the region of 'The Cars', and who had herself performed the ceremonies which she described. It is published in the local dialect, of which a specimen may be found in 'The Strangers' Share', and as much as possible in the exact words used. The old woman thought herself the only

person who still knew about Tiddy Mun. The tale is too long to be reproduced here, but anyone who wants to read it in its entirety – and it is
worth reading – must look up the article 'Legends of the Cars' in *Folk-
Lore* (vol. II, 1891, pp. 149–56).

The tale belongs to the time when the fens were drained by Dutch
workmen in the 17th century, though it relates to the later, final draining.
This was bitterly resented by the fenmen, who lived by fowling and fishing, and they believed that the spirits that haunted the fens resented it too.
For the bogs were haunted with spirits:

> Boggarts and Will-o'-tha-Wykes, an' sich loike; voices o' deed folks,
> an' hands wi'outen airms, that came i' tha darklins, moanin' an' cryin'
> an' beckonin' all night thruff; todlowries dancin' on tha tussocks, an'
> witches ridin' on tha great black snags, that turned to snakes, an' raced
> about wi' 'em i' tha watter.

The fenmen were terrified of all these, and would not venture out after
dark without a charm or a bible-ball (a leaf stolen from a bible and
crumpled into a small ball) in their pockets, but there was one whom they
loved as well as feared, Tiddy Mun, and they were afraid that when the
bogs were drained Tiddy Mun would go:

> For thee know'st, Tiddy Mun dwelt in tha watter-holes doun deep
> i' tha green still watter, an' a comed out nobbut of evens, whan tha
> mists rose. Than a comed crappelin out i' tha darklins, limpelty lobelty,
> like a dearie wee au'd gran'ther, wi' lang white hair, an' a lang white
> beardie, all cotted an' tangled together; limpelty-lobelty, an' a gowned
> i' gray, while tha could scarce see un thruff tha mist, an' a come wi' a
> sound o' rinnin' watter, an' a sough o' wind, an' laughin' like tha
> pyewipe screech. Tha wor none so skeered on Tiddy Mun like tha
> boggarts an' such hawiver. A worn't wicked an' tantrummy like tha
> watter-wives; an' a worn't white an' creepy like tha Dead Hands. But
> natheless, 'twor sort o' shivery-like when tha set round tha fire, to hear
> the screechin' laugh out by the door, passin' in a skirl o' wind an'
> watter.

For all his awesomeness they managed to come to terms with him, for
when the season was very wet, and when the water rose till it came to the
very doorstep, they waited till the next new moon, and then the whole
family would stand at the open door and call quaveringly into the
darkness:

> 'Tiddy Mun, wi'-out a name,
> tha watters thruff!'

Then they would listen, clinging to each other until they heard the call
of a pewit across the waters, and when they heard it they turned back

and shut the door, satisfied that the waters would go down. There was an old rhyme about the Tiddy Mun:

> 'Tiddy Mun, wi'-out a name
> White heed, walkin' lame;
> While tha watter teems tha fen
> Tiddy Mun'll harm nane.'

But that was the rub, the water was teeming no longer, the pools were draining, the bog-holes were turning into earth: there would soon be no place for the Tiddy Mun to live, and they feared his anger.

It fell on the Dutchmen first. One after another the Dutchmen disappeared and could never be found, lying deep in some bog-hole. The fenmen knew who had taken them. But more Dutchmen came and the work went on, and the waters fell lower. Then Tiddy Mun's anger fell on his own people. Cows died, and pigs starved and children fell ill and dwindled away, thatches fell in and walls fell out and all went arsy-varsy.

At first the Car people could not believe that their own Tiddy Mun had turned against them. They thought it might be the TOD-LOWERIES or the witches, but they used charms against one and ducked the others with no effect. At last it came to them that they must try if they could placate Tiddy Mun, for the graveyard was full and the cradles were empty; so they remembered what they used to do in the better times and they agreed all to meet together at the next new moon down by the cross-dyke near the new river. And they all came together creeping through the twilight, each one with a stoup of fresh water in his hands. It was dark when they came to the dyke edge, and they all emptied their stoups of water and cried out as loud as they could

> 'Tiddy Mun, wi-out a name,
> Here's watter for thee, tak' tha spell undone!'

They waited, and there was a daunting silence. Then, all of a sudden, a great wailing and crying and sobbing broke out all round them, and the mothers cried out that they heard their own dead babies weeping for them, and some said they felt cold lips kissing them and soft wings brushing their cheeks, and they thought the dead children were praying the Tiddy Mun to lift the curse and leave the other babies to thrive. Then the noise died down, and out of the river itself they heard the pewits call, low and sweet, and they knew Tiddy Mun had forgiven them. And the men shouted and leapt, and ran home with light hearts, but the women followed, crying for the babies they had left flitting about in the dark.

After that a time of great prosperity came to the Cars, children and stock throve and men found good work and prospered, and every new moon they went out to the dyke-side, and threw in their water and said their charm. If any man failed to do so sickness fell on him and they knew that Tiddy Mun was angry with him.

But now new ways and new times have driven him away.
[Motifs: F406; F422; Q552.10]

Tiddy Ones, Tiddy Men, Tiddy People. The Tiddy Ones, the
YARTHKINS and the STRANGERS, these were the Lincolnshire fenmen's
nature spirits, graphically described by Mrs Balfour in her article,
'Legends of the Cars'. Most of them were undifferentiated, a drifting
mass of influences and powers rather than individuals. The one among
them personally known and almost beloved was the TIDDY MUN, who
was invoked in times of flood to withdraw the waters. Even he did not
hesitate to call down pestilence on stock and children if he believed himself to be injured.

Time in Fairyland. The early fairy specialists had a vivid sense of the
relativity of time, founded, perhaps, on experiences of dream or trance,
when a dream that covers several years may be experienced between
rolling out of bed and landing on the floor. Occasionally the dimension
is in this direction. HARTLAND, in his exhaustive study of 'The Supernatural Lapse of Time in Fairyland', contained in *The Science of Fairy
Tales*, gives a Pembrokeshire example of a visit to Fairyland (p. 199). A
young shepherd joined a fairy dance and found himself in a glittering
palace surrounded by most beautiful gardens, where he passed many
years in happiness among the fairy people. There was only one prohibition: in the middle of the garden there was a fountain, filled with
gold and silver fish, and he was told he must on no account drink out of
it. He desired increasingly to do so, and at last he plunged his hands into
the pool. At once the whole place vanished, and he found himself on the
cold hillside among his sheep. Only minutes had passed since he joined
the fairy dance. More often this trance-like experience is told in a more
theological setting, the journey of Mahomet to Paradise, for instance, or
the experience of Brahmins or hermits. As a rule, however, time moves in
the other direction, both in VISITS TO FAIRYLAND and to other supernatural worlds. A dance of a few minutes takes a year and a day of
common time, as, in the tale of 'Rhys and Llewellyn', a few days of feasting and merriment have consumed 200 years in the mortal world (see
KING HERLA). This is not always so, for nothing in folk tradition can be
contained in an exact and logical system. ELIDURUS could go backwards
and forwards between Fairyland and his home with no alteration of time,
human MIDWIVES TO THE FAIRIES can visit fairy homes and return the
same night, the man who borrowed FAIRY OINTMENT from the fairy
hill was taken into it with impunity, and Isobel Gowdie visited the fairy
hills in the same way to obtain ELF-SHOT. Yet, on the whole, it may be
said that the man who visits Fairyland does so at a grave risk of not
returning until long after his span of mortal life has been consumed.

Sometimes, as in the Rip Van Winkle tale, a broken TABOO, the partaking of FAIRY FOOD or drink in Fairyland, is followed by an enchanted sleep during which time passes at a supernatural rate, but it is not always so. Certainly King Herla and his companions feasted in Fairyland, but there seems no suggestion that the passage of time was caused by this communion. The effect of the visit was disastrous, but the intention does not seem to have been unfriendly.

The OSSIAN story, in which the hero goes to live with a FAIRY BRIDE and returns after some hundreds of years, is widespread and is even to be found among the best-known of the Japanese fairy-tales, 'Urashima Taro'. Here, as in many other versions, his bride is a sea-maiden. Fairy-land is often under or across the sea, and MERMAIDS are amorous of mortals. When Urashima tries to return home, his bride gives him a casket in which his years are locked, and old age and death come on him when he opens it. Hartland in *The Science of Fairy Tales* (p. 141) noted an interesting Italian variant of the Ossian tale. In this, which begins as a SWAN MAIDEN tale, the hero's bride is Fortune, and after once losing her, he follows her to the Isle of Happiness, where he stays, as he thinks, for two months, but it is really 200 years. When he insists on returning to visit his mother, Fortune gives him a magnificent black horse to carry him over the sea, and warns him not to dismount from it, but she is more prudent than Niam of the Golden Locks, for she goes with him. They ride over the sea together, and find a changed country. As they go to-wards his mother's house they meet an old hag with a carriage-load of old shoes behind her, which she has worn out looking for him. She slips and falls to the ground, and he is bending down to lift her when Fortune calls out: 'Beware! That is Death!' So they ride on. Next they meet a great lord on a leg-weary horse, which founders at their side, but before the hero can come to his aid, Fortune cries out again: 'Be careful! That is the Devil!' And they ride on. But when the hero finds that his mother is dead and long since forgotten, he turns back with his bride to the Isle of Happiness, and has lived there with her ever since. This is one of the few stories of fairy brides and visits to Fairyland which ends happily.

One of the same motifs occurs in a Tyrolean story, also told by Hart-land (p. 185). A peasant followed his herd under a stone and into a cave, where a lady met him, gave him food and offered him a post as a gardener. He worked in the country for some weeks, and then began to be home-sick. They let him go home, but when he got back everything was strange, and no one recognized him except one old crone, who came up to him and said, 'Where have you been? I have been looking for you for 200 years.' She took him by the hand, and he fell dead, for she was Death.

When people return in this way after long absence they often fall to dust as soon as they eat human food. This is especially so in the Welsh stories. In a Highland version two men who had returned from Fairyland on a Sunday went to church, and as soon as the scriptures were read they crumbled into dust.

The suggestion behind all these stories is that Fairyland is a world of the dead, and that those who entered it had long been dead, and carried back with them an illusory body which crumbled into dust when they met reality.

In Ruth Tongue's moving story 'The Noontide Ghost' in *Forgotten Folk-Tales of the English Counties* (p. 53), this transformation has already occurred. The old man who long ago met the 'queer sort of chap' who delayed him with wagering-games and old merriment, returned as a ghost to look for his long-dead wife, and was called by her up to Heaven after he had told his story to a mortal listener. As in this tale, the fairy condition, or indeed the entry into eternity, often needs no entry into a geographical fairyland, underground or underwater. A fairy ring, the encounter with a FAIRY RADE, the singing of a supernatural bird, is enough to surround the mortal with the supernatural condition, so that he stands invisible and rapt away from the mortal world which continues all around him until the mysterious time-pattern ceases to have potency. For it is to be noticed that, whatever the differences in pace, human time and fairy time somehow interlock. The dancer in the fairy circle is nearly always to be rescued after a year and a day, sometimes after an exact year; two months equal 200 years; an hour may be a day and a night; there is some relationship. And if times are somehow interconnected, seasons are even more important. May Day, Midsummer Eve, Hallowe'en are all times when the doors open between the worlds. James Stephens's *In the Land of Youth*, a translation of one of the early Irish fairy legends, is a good example of this. Certain times of day are important too. The four hinges of the day, noontide, dusk, midnight and early dawn, are cardinal to the fairies. Certain days of the week are also important, days of danger and days of escape. In fact, however free and wild the course of fairy time appears to be, we find here as elsewhere traces of the DEPENDENCE OF FAIRIES UPON MORTALS.

[Motif: F377]

Tir Nan Og, or Tir Na N-og (*teer na nogue*), **meaning the Land of the Young.** This, which lay west across the sea, was one of the lands into which the TUATHA DE DANANN retreated when they had been conquered by the Milesians. They had other habitations, under the SIDH, the green mounds or tumuli of prehistoric Ireland, or the Land under the Waves, Tirfo Thuinn, but Tir Nan Og was the earthly paradise where time, like TIME IN FAIRYLAND, was no longer reckoned by mortal measures, a land of beauty, where the grass was always green and fruit and flowers could be picked together, where feasting, music, love, hunting and joyous fighting went on all day and death made no entry, for if in the fights men were wounded and killed one day they came to life again none the worse the next. Occasionally mortal men were invited to Tir Nan Og, as OSSIAN was, and if they wanted to revisit earth they were put under a

TABOO. When this was violated the weight of their mortal years came upon them and they were unable to return. In Wales a comparable story is that of KING HERLA.

If Tir Nan Og was the Celtic heaven, there are glimpses of a Celtic hell. In Ireland it was Scathach, visited by CUCHULAIN, the hero of the Ulster cycle, and in Wales Ysbaddaden, the land of the GIANTS visited by Culhwch in the MABINOGION.

[Motifs: F172.1; F377; F378.1]

Titania. As an epithet attached to Diana, Titania is Shakespeare's name for the fairy queen in his MIDSUMMER NIGHT'S DREAM, and he gives her a dignity which removes her from the more frivolous Queen MAB who ruled over the other DIMINUTIVE FAIRIES. It was a name not commonly used for the Fairy Queen, though in one of the magical manuscripts in the British Museum (Sloane 1727) 'Tyton, Florella and Mabb' are mentioned as 'the treasures of the earth'.

[Motif: F252.2]

Tod-lowery. The nickname of a fox in Lowland Scotland, but in Lincolnshire it is the name for a GOBLIN. A note on it can be found in *County Folk-Lore* (vol. v). Tod-loweries are mentioned among the bog spirits in Mrs Balfour's story, 'The DEAD MOON'. Sometimes the name is given as 'Tom-loudy'; it is one of the frightening figures – a NURSERY BOGIE.

Tolkien, J. R. R. (1892–1973). A new dimension in fairy fiction arose in our literature when the trilogy of *The Lord of the Rings* followed Tolkien's *The Hobbit*. These books were felt at once by a surprising number of people to have something significant to say about our modern problems and to hold an implicit message for young people all over the English-speaking world. Every detail was felt to be of interest. People used the elven script and learnt the elven tongue. One got the feeling that the whole of life was embraced in this archaic-seeming tale. It was about danger and endurance against heavy odds, about companionship and simple pleasures of food and song, about landscape, about the dreadful weight of a corrupting responsibility, the dangers of science and the terrible pressure of an evil will. There was no explicit preaching, but the will was braced by reading. The whole was not decorated but deepened by the use of traditional folklore which gave it that sense of being rooted in the earth which is the gift of folklore to literature.

The folklore used was in the main Scandinavian in tone. The DRAGONS, the GNOMES, the GOBLINS, the ELVES fit into the world of Scandinavian mythology. It was not of supreme importance what type of folklore was used so long as it was authentic and came like native air to the mind of the writer.

Tom Cockle. One of the travelling domestic FAIRIES who follow their families across the sea, like the Highland BAUCHAN and the other AMERICAN IMMIGRANT FAIRIES who crossed the Atlantic to America. Tom Cockle had served an Irish family for some hundreds of years, and was called their 'luck'. At last ill-fortune forced the family to leave Ireland, and move to the big, deserted Westmorland house which had been the mother's home in her girlhood. They had never seen Tom Cockle in their Irish home, but, however poor they were, he had always had a fire lit and a mouthful of food for them in their need. It was therefore with sad hearts that they called out to him to tell him that they had to leave him and go to England. It was a dismal journey, but at last it was over, and they were driving their little pony cart through the rain, down the steep Westmorland hills towards the empty, dreary house. When they got near it they saw lights in the windows, and inside there was a fire burning and food and drink on the table. Tom Cockle had got there before them. Ruth Tongue found three versions of this tale, one from Ireland, one from Westmorland and one in Warwickshire. She recorded it in *Forgotten Folk-Tales of the English Counties.*

[Type: ML6035. Motif: F346(a); F482.3.1]

Tom Dockin. Mrs Wright in her list of NURSERY BOGIES mentions a terrifying character called Tom Dockin, with iron teeth, who devours bad children. He belongs to Yorkshire.

[Motifs: F234.2.2; F402]

Tom-Poker. One of the NURSERY BOGIES who lives in dark cupboards, holes under stairs, empty cock lofts and other places appropriate to BOGIES. He is East Anglian and is mentioned by Mrs Wright in her list of cautionary nursery goblins in *Rustic Speech and Folk-Lore.*

Tom Thumb. The earliest surviving version of 'Tom Thumb' was written by a pamphleteer, Richard Johnson, and printed in 1621. Richard Johnson claims in the foreword that it is an ancient tale, and there is little reason to doubt his word, for the name was already proverbial. This pamphlet is reproduced in its entirety in Iona and Peter Opie's *The Classic Fairy Tales* without the modifications which the gentility of subsequent ages imposed on it. The story is left incomplete, with Tom happily returned to the court of King Arthur after his adventures with the pigmy king Twaddle. A metrical version which appeared in 1630 carried the story on to the death of Tom Thumb, though in later variants he was killed in a fight with a spider. In the first version, the setting is already the court of King Arthur. An honest farmer is one of the king's councillors, for in those democratic days rich and poor met in the court. The farmer and his wife had all that they needed to make them happy except that they yearned for a son, and at length the farmer sent his wife to beg the wizard

Merlin to find some way of obtaining one for them, even if he was no bigger than the farmer's thumb. Merlin was complaisant, and in an unusually short time a minute baby was born to the farmer's wife, who in four minutes grew to the length of the farmer's thumb and then stopped growing. This tiny size very much attracted the FAIRIES, for the Queen of the Fairies attended his mother as a midwife and his FAIRY GODMOTHER, and had a suit of fairy clothes made, in which he ran out at once to play with the other children, for he never grew older nor taller, but was at once at the full development of his powers. He played at pins and points with them, and when he lost all his pins or counters he crept into his playmates' pockets and purloined some of theirs. A playmate caught him at it and shut him up in a pin box without meat, drink, air or light. But by a gift of his fairy godmother he needed none of these, a faculty which was afterwards very useful to him, for he was destined to be swallowed a great many times. He had another miraculous art, which curiously enough he shared with some of the saints, St Kentigern among them; he could hang up pots and pans on a sunbeam. It was by this art that he revenged himself on his playmates, for he hung up his mother's pots on a sunbeam, and when they imitated him they got into trouble. After that he became less popular with the children and stayed about the house with his mother. Even there he was not free from adventure, for one day he fell into a bag pudding she was mixing, and when it was put in to boil he found the heat so disagreeable that he leapt and banged about so that his mother thought the pudding was enchanted, and gave it to a passing tinker. When Tom began to bang about again, the tinker thought the same and threw the pudding away, so Tom struggled out and made his way home. Another time, when his mother was out milking with him, one of the cows ate the thistle to which he was tethered and they had to give the cow a draught to rescue him. After that he was carried away by a raven, which landed with him on a GIANT's chimney. He fell down it, and after evading the giant for some time he was swallowed by him and kicked up such a rumpus in his belly that the

giant voided him into the sea, where he was again swallowed by a salmon
and carried to King Arthur's court, discovered by the cook when he was
gutting the fish, and presented to the king. He became a prime favourite
at court, but his career was chequered by various accidents. However,
some magical gifts bestowed on him by his fairy godmother made life
somewhat safer for him. The story becomes a series of incidents and stops
rather than ending. Some of the same incidents are found in German,
Indian and Japanese versions of the tale, and it is interesting that in
Hans Andersen's 'Thumbelina' her tiny size makes it natural for her to
be associated with the fairies.

[Type: 700. Motifs: F535.1; F535.1.1; F535.1.1.7; F535.1.1.14; T553]

Tom Tit Tot. The Tom Tit Tot story is the liveliest English version of
the type that is best known in Grimm's 'Rumpelstiltskin'. Edward
CLODD published a monograph, *Tom Tit Tot*, founded on the Suffolk
version of the tale, which he reproduced in full. It is one of the best of
the English folk-tales, lively in style and dialect, and deserves to be
included here in its complete form:

Well, once upon a time there were a woman and she baked five pies.
And when they come out of the oven, they was that overbaked, the
crust were too hard to eat. So she says to her darter –

'Maw'r,' says she, 'put you them there pies on the shelf an' leave
'em there a little, an' they'll come agin' – she meant, you know, the
crust 'ud get soft.

But the gal, she says to herself, 'Well, if they'll come agin, I'll ate
'em now.' And she set to work and ate 'em all, first and last.

Well, come supper time the woman she said, 'Goo you and git one
o' them there pies. I dare say they've came agin now.'

The gal she went an' she looked, and there warn't nothin' but the dishes. So back she come and says she, 'Noo, they ain't come agin.'

'Not none on 'em?' says the mother.

'Not none on 'em,' says she.

'Well, come agin, or not come agin,' says the woman, 'I'll ha' one for supper.'

'But you can't, if they ain't come,' says the gal.

'But I can,' says she. 'Goo you and bring the best of 'em.'

'Best or worst,' says the gal, 'I've ate 'em all, and you can't ha' one till that's come agin.'

Well, the woman she were wholly bate, and she took her spinnin' to the door to spin, and as she span she sang –

> 'My darter ha' ate five, five pies to-day –
> My darter ha' ate five, five pies to-day.'

The king he were a comin' down the street an he hard her sing, but what she sang he couldn't hare, so he stopped and said –

'What were that you was a singun of, maw'r?'

The woman, she were ashamed to let him hare what her darter had been a doin', so she sang, 'stids o' that –

> 'My darter ha' spun five, five skeins to-day –
> My darter ha' spun five, five skeins to-day.'

'S'ars o' mine!' said the king, 'I never heerd tell of any on as could do that.'

Then he said: 'Look you here, I want a wife, and I'll marry your darter. But look you here,' says he, ''leven months out o' the year she shall have all the vittles she likes to eat, and all the gownds she likes to git, and all the cumpny she likes to hev; but the last month o' the year she'll ha' to spin five skeins iv'ry day, an' if she doon't, I shall kill her.'

'All right,' says the woman: for she thowt what a grand marriage that was. And as for them five skeins, when te come tew, there'd be plenty o' ways of gettin' out of it, and likeliest, he'd ha' forgot about it.

Well, so they was married. An' for 'leven months the gal had all the vittles she liked to ate, and all the gownds she liked to git, an' all the cumpny she liked to hev.

But when the time was gettin' oover, she began to think about them there skeins an' to wonder if he had 'em in mind. But not one word did he say about 'em, an' she whoolly thowt he'd forgot 'em.

Howsivir, the last day o' the last month, he takes her to a room she'd niver set eyes on afore. There worn't nothin' in it but a spinnin' wheel and a stool. An' says he, 'Now, me dear, hare yow'll be shut in to-morrow with some vittles and some flax, and if you hain't spun five skeins by the night, yar hid'll goo off.'

An' awa' he went about his business.

Well, she were that frightened. She'd allus been such a gatless mawther, that she didn't se much as know how to spin, an' what were she to dew to-morrer, with no one to come nigh her to help her. She sat down on a stool in the kitchen, and lork! how she did cry!

Howsivir, all on a sudden she hard a sort of a knockin' low down on the door. She upped and oped it, an' what should she see but a small little black thing with a long tail. That looked up at her right kewrious, an' that said –

'What are yew a cryin' for?'

'Wha's that to yew?' says she.

'Niver yew mind,' that said, 'but tell me what you're a cryin' for.'

'That oon't dew me noo good if I dew,' says she.

'Yew doon't know that,' that said, an' twirled that's tail round.

'Well,' says she, 'that oon't dew no harm, if that doon't dew no good,' and she upped and told about the pies an' the skeins an' everything.

'This is what I'll dew,' says the little black thing: 'I'll come to yar winder iv'ry mornin' an' take the flax an' bring it spun at night.'

'What's your pay?' says she.

That looked out o' the corners o' that's eyes an' that said: 'I'll give you three guesses every night to guess my name, an' if you hain't guessed it afore the month's up, yew shall be mine.'

Well, she thowt she'd be sure to guess that's name afore the month was up. 'All right,' says she, 'I agree.'

'All right,' that says, an' lork! how that twirled that's tail.

Well, the next day, har husband he took her inter the room, an' there was the flax an' the day's vittles.

'Now, there's the flax,' says he, 'an' if that ain't spun up this night off goo yar hid.' An' then he went out an' locked the door.

He'd hardly goon, when there was a knockin' agin the winder.

She upped and she oped it, and there sure enough was the little oo'd thing a settin' on the ledge.

'Where's the flax?' says he.

'Here te be,' says she. And she gonned it to him.

Well, come the evenin', a knockin' come agin to the winder. She upped an' she oped it, and there were the little oo'd thing, with five skeins of flax on his arm.

'Here to be,' says he, an' he gonned it to her.

'Now, what's my name?' says he.

'What, is that Bill?' says she.

'Noo, that ain't,' says he. An' he twirled his tail.

'Is that Ned?' says she.

'Noo, that ain't,' says he. An' he twirled his tail.

'Well, is that Mark?' says she.

'Noo, that ain't,' says he. An' he twirled his tail harder, an' awa' he flew.

Well, when har husban' he come in: there was the five skeins riddy for him. 'I see I shorn't hev for to kill you to-night, me dare,' says he. 'Yew'll hev yar vittles and yar flax in the mornin',' says he, an' away he goes.

Well, ivery day the flax an' the vittles, they was browt, an' ivery day that there little black impet used for to come mornin's and evenin's. An' all the day the mawther she set a tryin' fur to think of names to say to it when te come at night. But she niver hot on the right one. An' as that got to-warts the ind o' the month, the impet that began for to look soo maliceful, an' that twirled that's tail faster an' faster each time she gave a guess.

At last te come to the last day but one. The impet that come at night along o' the five skeins, an' that said –

'What, hain't yew got my name yet?'

'Is that Nicodemus?' says she.

'Noo, t'ain't,' that says.

'Is that Sammle?' says she.

'Noo, t'ain't,' that says.

'A-well, is that Methusalem?' says she.

'Noo, t'ain't that norther,' he says.

Then that looks at her with that's eyes like a cool o' fire, an' that says, 'Woman, there's only to-morrer night, an' then yar'll be mine!' An' away te flew.

Well, she felt that horrud. Howsomediver, she hard the king a coming along the passage. In he came, an' when he see the five skeins, he says, says he –

'Well, me dare,' says he, 'I don't see but what yew'll ha' your skeins ready to-morrer night as well, an' as I reckon I shorn't ha' to kill you, I'll ha' supper in here to-night.' So they brought supper, an' another stool for him, and down the tew they sat.

Well, he hadn't eat but a mouthful or so, when he stops and begins to laugh.

'What is it?' says she.

'A-why,' says he, 'I was out a-huntin' to-day, an' I got away to a place in the wood I'd never seen afore. An' there was an old chalk pit. An' I heerd a sort of a hummin', kind o'. So I got off my hobby, an' I went right quiet to the pit, an' I looked down. Well, what should there be but the funniest little black thing yew iver set eyes on. An' what was that a dewin' on, but that had a little spinnin' wheel, an' that were a spinnin' wonnerful fast, an' a twirlin' that's tail. An' as that span, that sang –

"Nimmy nimmy not,
My name's Tom Tit Tot."'

NIMMY NIMMY NOT
YOUR NAME'S TOM
TIT
TOT

Well, when the mawther heerd this, she fared as if she could ha' jumped outer her skin for joy, but she di'n't say a word.

Next day, that there little thing looked soo maliceful when he come for the flax. An' when night came, she heerd that a knockin' agin the winder panes. She oped the winder, an' that come right in on the ledge. That were grinnin' from are to are, an' Oo! that's tail were twirlin' round so fast.

'What's my name?' that says, as that gonned her the skeins.

'Is that Solomon?' she says, pretendin' to be afeard.

'Noo, t'ain't,' that says, an' that come fudder inter the room.

'Well, is that Zebedee?' says she agin.

'Noo, t'ain't,' says the impet. An' then that laughed an' twirled that's tail till yew cou'n't hardly see it.

'Take time, woman,' that says; 'next guess, an' you're mine.' An' that stretched out that's black hands at her.

Well, she backed a step or two, an' she looked at it, and then she laughed out, an' says she, a pointin' of her finger at it –

'Nimmy nimmy not,
Yar name's Tom Tit Tot.'

Well, when that hard her, that shruck awful an' awa' that flew into the dark, an' she niver saw it noo more.

There is a gipsy sequel to this, recorded, as the first was, in the *Ipswich Journal*, in which the girl is rescued from the annual repetitions of the feat by the help of a gipsy woman and a noxious mixture of axle-grease and rotten eggs.

The Cornish version of Tom Tit Tot, 'Duffy and the Devil', has the devil TERRYTOP as its villain and is recorded by HUNT as one of the last of the Cornish drolls. In Scotland we have WHUPPITY STOORIE and one version of HABETROT. There is also the Orcadian PEERIFOOL and a fragmentary version in Wales of TRWTYN-TRATYN. It will be seen that the tale is well represented in these islands. There are many variants also in Europe. In Austria there is 'Kruzimügeli', in France 'Robiquet', in Hungary 'Winterkolbe' and 'Panczumanczi', in Iceland 'Gilitrutt', in Italy 'Rosania', in Russia 'Kinkach Martinko', and various others, some of the 'Tom Tit Tot' type and some more like 'Habetrot'.

[Type 500. Motifs: C432.1; D2183; F271.4.3; F346; F381.1; F451.5.2; H521; H914; H1092; M242; N475]

Traffic with the fairies. Among the Puritans in Britain, by whom the FAIRIES were generally thought of as minor devils, intercourse with the fairies was looked on with the gravest suspicion, though the country people looked on it more leniently and the Irish regarded a certain amount of homage paid to the fairies as a very justifiable piece of protection payment, though some of them at least took a darker view of the transaction. It was widely said that the witches, the fairies and the dead danced together on Hallowe'en. In the North of England, people accused of witchcraft sometimes claimed to work through the fairies rather than the Devil. Durant Hotham and Webster described how a man brought into court as a witch offered to lead the judge to see the fairy hill from which he received the medicine he used. The judge treated his plea harshly, but the jury refused to convict him. Durant Hotham in the introduction to his *Life of Jacob Behmen* is the first to mention the case in 1654:

> There was (as I have heard the story credibly reputed in this Country) a man apprehended of suspition of Witchcraft, he was of that sort we call white-witches, which are such as do Cures beyond the Ordinary reasons and deducing of our usual Practitioners, and are supposed (and most part of them truly) to do the same by the ministrations of Spirits (from whence, under their noble favour, most Sciences first grew) and therefore are upon good reason provided against by our Civil Laws as being waies full of danger and deceit, and scarce ever otherwise obtain'd than by a devilish Compact of the Exchange of ones Soul to that assistant Spirit for the honour of its Mountebankery. What this man did was with a white powder, which he said, he receiv'd from the Fayries, and that going to a hill he knocked three times, and the hill opened, and he had access to, and converse with, a visible people; and offer'd, that if any Gentleman present would either go himself in person, or send his servant, he would conduct them thither, and show them the place and persons from whence he had his skill.

Twenty-three years later Webster published *Displaying of Supposed Witchcraft*, perhaps the most influential book of its time in removing the practice of witchcraft from the Criminal Statute Book. Webster comments on Hotham's mention of the case, and brings fuller knowledge to bear on it, for he was himself present at the examination of the man:

To this I shall only add thus much, that the man was accused for invoking and calling upon evil spirits, and was a very simple and illiterate person to any mans judgment, and had been formerly very poor, but had gotten some pretty little meanes to maintain himself, his Wife and diverse small children, by his cures done with this white powder, of which there were sufficient proofs, and the Judge asking him how he came by the powder, he told a story to this effect. 'That one night before the day was gone, as he was going home from his labour, being very sad and full of heavy thoughts, not knowing how to get meat and drink for his Wife and Children, he met a fair Woman in fine cloaths, who asked him why he was so sad, and he told her that it was by reason of his poverty, to which she said, that if he would follow her counsel she would help him to that which would serve to get him a good living; to which he said he would consent with all his heart, so it were not by unlawful ways: she told him that it should not be by any such ways, but by doing of good and curing of sick people; and so warning him strictly to meet her there the next night at the same time, she departed from him, and he went home. And the next night at the time appointed he duly waited, and she (according to promise) came and told him that it was well he came so duly, otherwise he had missed of that benefit, that she intended to do unto him, and so bade him follow her and not be afraid. Thereupon she led him to a little Hill and she knocked three times, and the Hill opened, and they went in, and came to a fair hall, wherein was a Queen sitting in great state, and many people about her, and the Gentlewoman that brought him, presented him to the Queen, and she said he was welcom, and bid the Gentlewoman give him some of the white powder, and teach him how to use it; which she did, and gave him a little wood box full of the white powder, and bad him give 2 or 3 grains of it to any that were sick, and it would heal them, and so she brought him forth of the Hill, and so they parted. And being asked by the Judge whether the place within the Hill, which he called a Hall, were light or dark, he said indifferent, as it is with us in the twilight; and being asked how he got more powder, he said when he wanted he went to that Hill, and knocked three times, and said every time I am coming, I am coming, whereupon it opened, and he going in was conducted by the aforesaid Woman to the Queen, and so had more powder given him.' This was the plain and simple story (however it may be judged of) that he told before the Judge, the whole Court and the Jury, and there being no proof, but what cures he had done to very many, the Jury did acquit him: and I remember the Judge said, when all the evidence was heard, that if he were to assign his punishment, he should be whipped thence to Fairy-hall, and did seem to judge it to be a delusion or Imposture.

This seems to have been a gentler fairyland than that believed in by the Scottish witches, who evidently regarded their fairies as the SLUAGH, who employed them to shoot passers-by, a feat which the fairies seem unable to perform for themselves; this at least is the belief of Isobel Gowdie, who, apparently suffering from some form of nervous break-down, made a voluntary confession of her witchcraft practices and her association with the fairies. It is to be found in Pitcairn's *Criminal Trials* (vol. III, Part Two). Of the ELF-SHOT she says:

> As for Elf-arrow heidis, THE DIVELL shapes them with his awin hand, (and syne deliveris thame) to Elf-boyes, who whyttis and dightis them with a sharp thing lyk a paking neidle; bot (quhan I wes in Elf-land?) I saw them whytting and dighting them . . . Thes that dightis thaim ar litle ones, hollow and boss-baked. They speak gowstie lyk. Quhnn THE DIVELL giwes them to ws, he sayes,
>
> > 'SHOOT thes in my name,
> > And they sall not goe heall hame.'

In an earlier examination she had explained how she experienced FAIRY LEVITATION after using the 'Horse and hattock!' invocation mentioned by AUBREY.

> I haid a little horse, and wold say, 'HORSE AND HATTOCK, IN THE DIVILLIS NAME!' And then ve vold flie away quhair ve vold, be ewin as strawes wold flie wpon an hieway. We will flie lyk strawes quhan we pleas; wild-strawes and corne-strawes wilbe horses to ws, and ve put thaim betwixt our foot, and say, 'HORSE AND HATTOCK, IN THE DIVELLIS nam!' An quhan any sies thes strawes in a whirlewind, and doe not then sanctifie them selves, we may shoot them dead at owr pleasour. Any that ar shot be vs, their sowell will goe to Hevin, bot their bodies remains with ws and will flie as horsis to ws, als small as strawes.

There are a number of confessions of visits to elf-hills scattered through the Scottish witch-trials, and fragments of the belief are found all over England. As for normal and neighbourly associations, we can mention the putting out of BREAD and CLEAR WATER, the making up of a good fire and leaving the kitchen clean and a state of NEATNESS for their visits, often receiving a piece of money in exchange; putting flowers on stones sacred to the fairies and pouring milk into the holes of the cupped stones, and other observances half-way between acts of neighbourliness and of worship. All these can be counted as part of the normal traffic with

the fairies, as well as occasional practices of borrowing and FAIRY LOANS.
[Motifs: D1500.1.20; F282.2; F344.3]

Trash. Another name for the SKRIKER of Lancashire. As a skriker he is
generally invisible, but as a trash he takes the form of a large dog with
saucer eyes, shaggy coat and enormous pelt. He is called 'Trash' by the
splashy, squelchy sound he makes as he pads along, like someone walking
in worn-out shoes, or 'trashes'. He might equally be identified with
PADFOOT.
[Motifs: E423.1.1(b); G302.3.2]

Trees. See FAIRY TREES.

Trooping fairies. W. B. YEATS, in his delightful *Irish Fairy and Folk
Tales*, divides the FAIRIES into two main classes: trooping fairies and
SOLITARY FAIRIES. Much the same distinction is made by James
Macdougall in *Folk Tales and Fairy Lore*. It is a distinction that holds
good throughout the British Isles, and is indeed valid wherever fairy
beliefs are held. One might, however, add a third division, the domesticated
fairies, who live in small family groups, but these presumably would join
other fairies for FAIRY MARKETS and merry-making.

The trooping fairies can be large or small, friendly or sinister. They
tend to wear green jackets, while the solitary fairies wear red jackets. They
can range from the HEROIC FAIRIES to the dangerous and malevolent
SLUAGH or those DIMINUTIVE FAIRIES who include the tiny nature
fairies that make the fairy rings with their DANCING and speed the
growth of flowers. Among the trooping fairies mentioned by Yeats are
some so small that a heather bell is the size of their caps. Some are small
people three to four feet in height, the fairies who dance and sing inside
the fairy hills, those who are responsible for CHANGELINGS and FAIRY
BRIDES. He also includes the MERROWS, hideous, genial MERMEN of
Ireland.

Macdougall's fairies range through very small to those of human size
suitable for intercourse with mankind. In England it is the same. The
tiny fairies, so small that the whole royal dais can be caught under a
miser's hat, and the little fellows to whom a single grain of wheat is a
heavy burden, are as clearly trooping fairies as WILD EDRIC's ominous
rade. In Wales, the fairies love hunting and are great herdsmen. On the
whole, the characteristics and habits of the trooping fairies are alike,
though there are regional differences. The Irish fairies are particularly
fond of faction fights and HURLING matches, the Scots use ELF-SHOTS
and carry human beings with them through the air to operate them,
which they are apparently incapable of doing themselves. Throughout
the land they resemble each other more closely than the solitary fairies do.
[Motif: F241.1.0.1]

Trows. The trows of Shetland seem to be connected in some way with the Scandinavian trolls. Some of the trolls are gigantic and monstrous, often many-headed, like some of the British GIANTS, and others of human size and in many ways like ordinary rustic FAIRIES clothed in grey, and similar in many ways to the fairies and ELVES of other parts of Britain. The gigantic trolls, it will be remembered, could not live in the light of the sun, but turned into stone. This trait has been made familiar to many readers by its introduction into J. R. R. TOLKIEN's *The Hobbit*. The Shetland trows also found the light of the sun dangerous, but not fatal. A trow who is above-ground at sunrise is earthbound and cannot return to its underground dwelling until sunset. KEIGHTLEY draws his information about the trows from Hibbert's *Description of the Shetland Islands* (1822) and from Edmonston's *View of Zetland Islands* (1799), but some of the most interesting details about them are to be found in Jessie M. E. Saxby's *Shetland Traditional Lore*. Jessie Saxby was herself a Shetlander, a ninth child of a ninth child, and thus having from childhood unusual access to Shetland lore. This was hard to get, for the TABOO against any INFRINGEMENT OF FAIRY PRIVACY was strongly enforced in the Islands. However, she was privileged by right of her birth, and tells us much, as, for instance , the knowledge handed on by an old boat-builder about the Kunal-Trow or King-Trow, who had never before been described:

> One sort of Trow this old man called Kunal-Trows, very human sort of creatures, but their nature was morbid and sullen. They wandered in lonely places after the sun had set, and were seen at times to weep and wave their arms about. We cease to wonder at that when we learn that there are no female King-Trows. They marry human wives, and as soon as the baby-Trow is born the mother dies. No Kunal-Trow marries twice, so their period of matrimonial bliss is brief. It seems a wise arrangement that there should never be more than one son to inherit the questionable character of a Kunal-Trow.
>
> A Kunal-Trow can't die till his son is grown up, but some philosophers of the race have tried to live a bachelor life under the pleasing impression that thus they might become immortal; but the laws of this people have a statute for even such an emergency as that. The Trow who postpones matrimony beyond reasonable limits is outlawed until he brings to Trow-land an earthly bride. One Trow-King braved all consequences, and took up his abode in a ruined Broch, and for centuries he was the terror of the Isles. His only food was earth formed into perfect models of fish, birds, babies, and it was said that those images had the 'goo' (smell and taste) of what they represented in form.
>
> He seems to have found his solitary life unendurable, and met the advances of some humans with a certain amount of pleasure, but his

love of mischief usually brought all friendly overtures to an abrupt conclusion.

A witch who craved to know the secrets of Trow-land was assiduous in courting the bachelor, and persuaded him to marry her on the assurance that *her* art would show him how to prevent the death he dreaded. His history broke off at his marriage; but it was said that from this union sprang the Ganfer and the Finis.

The Finis is the being who appears before a death, personating the dying person. The Ganfer is what we – in modern days – would call the Astral, who (so say some spiritualists) is ever waiting to enter into some human being and ally itself to the physical life.

The witch whose charms proved irresistible to the bachelor Trow was said to have paid a clandestine visit to her mother and told her many secret things. She had created (her mother said) a sensation among the Trows; but we may suppose she had not found the life agreeable, for she gave her mother many instructions how to provide against the enchantment of all Trows who try to decoy unsuspecting girls into their unhallowed domain. Her parting words were: 'Noo, Mam, mind he hae the puir tings o' lasses well keust-aboot when the grey wumman-stealers are oot upon der pranks.'

Other trows were as often female as male, and exhibit many of the traits of ordinary fairies, though they have peculiarities of their own. Jessie Saxby tells us many interesting things about them in a rather random and disorganized way:

> Our Shetland fairies are very unlike Shakespeare's dainty little creatures and Lover's Irish 'good people'. They are small grey-clad men. They always walk backwards when under observation, facing the person who is ill luckit enough to spy them. They are so fond of music they play the fiddle continually. Their melodies are peculiarly wild and sweet, and have a lilt of Gaelic as well as Icelandic tunes. Their homes are located under green knowes or sunny hillsides. They can visit the upper air only after sunset, and if, by any evil chance, one remains above ground a second after sunrise, *there* he must stay till the Glüder (the sun) disappears again!
>
> There was a Trow called the Booner who came after dark and threshed the corn required during the Yules.
>
> When once the eye is on a Trow, and kept there, he can't get away. It is lucky to hear a Trow *speak* to another, and very unlucky for the person who *sees* one.
>
> When a bairn was Trow-stricken the mother begged three kinds of meal from nine mothers of healthy children, and with that fare the child was fed. If the cure failed, the child died! 'Yea, my lamb, what can a body do when a bairn has had the grey man's web about it?'
>
> A steel blade, a holy Book, a bit of silver, a good word, could

protect one from the Trows, and 'to sain' was an important duty. To sain means very much the same as sprinkling and consecration, and other ceremonies connected with religion in modern days. I daresay the saining was as effectual as the others!

When a Trow took a fancy to a family or district, these prospered. Broonie was a Trow well known in one locality. He took the 'yards' into his care; and often yarfasted the screws of corn and desses of hay against a storm, but if anyone interfered he resented that by laying both screws and desses 'in Herda' (in utter confusion).

Broonie once took a whole neighbourhood into his protection, and he was often seen gliding from yard to yard casting his spell upon them. The women felt sorry for Broonie exposed to the chill winter winds in his thin grey suit, so they made a cloak and a hood for him, and laid it in a yard which he frequented. Broonie took the well-intentioned gift as an offence, and he was never seen again.

The Trows were permitted freedom on the earth at one time of the year. That was during the Yules, therefore extra care was taken against their mischief at that season.

The folk strove at all times to propitiate the Trows, and were said to live sometimes on good terms with them. But on the whole they were feared and disliked even more than they seem to have deserved.

In her chapter 'Tales of the Trows', Jessie Saxby illustrates most of these qualities, which will be mentioned in connection with various fairy traits such as FAIRY MORALITY.
[Motif: F455.8.1]

True love. As spirits interested in fertility, FAIRIES are deeply sympathetic with lovers, and punish maidens who are niggardly of their favours. Campion's poem 'The Fairy Lady Proserpine' gives a true picture of the Queen of the Fairies as the patroness of lovers, and the same trait is shown in Shakespeare's MIDSUMMER NIGHT'S DREAM. See also FAIRY MORALITY; VIRTUES ESTEEMED BY THE FAIRIES.

True Thomas. The 'Ballad of True Thomas', which Child included in his collections as No. 37A, tells part of the story of Thomas Rymour of Erceldoune, most commonly called THOMAS THE RHYMER (this entry outlines his whole story). Whether or not such a character as Merlin ever existed as a real man, it is certain that Thomas Rymour of Erceldoune was an historic personage living in the 13th century. But much more important than his existence is his reputation as a prophet, which endured until the 19th century. The ballad, which tells of his meeting with the Queen of Elfland and his visit to that country, is founded on a 14th-century romance which can be read in Carew Hazlitt's *Fairy Tales*,

Legends and Romances Illustrating Shakespeare. The ballad, which was
not collected until the 19th century, tells the story more tersely and
vividly, without the series of prophecies appended to the Romance.

True Thomas lay oer yond grassy bank,
    And he beheld a ladie gay,
A ladie that was brisk and bold,
    Come riding oer the fernie brae.

Her skirt was of the grass-green silk,
    Her mantel of the velvet fine,
At ilka tett of her horse's mane
    Hung fifty silver bells and nine.

True Thomas he took off his hat,
    And bowed him low down till his knee:
'All hail, thou mighty Queen of Heaven!
    For your peer on earth I never did see.'

'O no, O no, True Thomas,' she says,
    'That name does not belong to me;
I am but the queen of fair Elfland,
    And I'm come here for to visit thee.

'But ye maun go wi me now, Thomas,
    True Thomas, ye maun go wi me,
For ye maun serve me seven years,
    Thro weel or wae as may chance to be.'

She turned about her milk-white steed,
    And took True Thomas up behind,
And aye wheneer her bridle rang,
    The steed flew swifter than the wind.

For forty days and forty nights
    He wade thro red blude to the knee,
And he saw neither sun nor moon,
    But heard the roaring of the sea.

O they rade on, and further on,
    Until they came to a garden green:
'Light down, light down, ye ladie free,
    Some of that fruit let me pull to thee.'

'O no, O no, True Thomas,' she says,
    'That fruit maun not be touched by thee,
For a' the plagues that are in hell
    Light on the fruit of this countrie.

'But I have a loaf here in my lap,
　　Likewise a bottle of claret wine,
And now ere we go farther on,
　　We'll rest a while, and ye may dine.'

When he had eaten and drunk his fill,
　　'Lay down your head upon my knee,'
The lady sayd, 'ere we climb yon hill,
　　And I will show you fairlies three.

'O see not ye yon narrow road,
　　So thick beset wi thorns and briers?
That is the path of righteousness,
　　Tho after it but few enquires.

'And see not ye that braid braid road,
　　That lies across yon lillie leven?
That is the path of wickedness,
　　Tho some call it the road to heaven.

'And see not ye that bonny road,
　　Which winds about the fernie brae?
That is the road to fair Elfland,
　　Where you and I this night maun gae.

'But Thomas, ye maun hold your tongue,
　　Whatever you may hear or see,
For gin ae word you should chance to speak,
　　You will neer get back to your ain countrie.'

He has gotten a coat of the even cloth,
　　And a pair of shoes of velvet green,
And till seven years were past and gone
　　True Thomas on earth was never seen.

[Motifs: C211.1; C405; F236.6; F302.3.1; F304.2; F379.1; F379.3]

Truth. The tricksiest FAIRIES, like the Devil, were not above equivocation, but they expected strict truth in the dealings of mortals. ELIDOR'S
fairies in the story told by GIRALDUS CAMBRENSIS were accustomed to
reprehend the deceitfulness of mortals. Theirs appeared to be a real
moral scruple, but anyone dealing with the Devil would have to be careful to speak the exact truth, because otherwise it gives the Devil power
against the mortal. Fairies, however, seem to have a disinterested love of
it. See also FAIRY MORALITY; VIRTUES ESTEEMED BY THE FAIRIES.

Trwtyn-Tratyn. A fragmentary story discovered by John Rhys in

Cardiganshire. He believes it to be part of a TOM TIT TOT story, a notion borne out by the surviving rhyme,

> Little did she know
> That Trwtyn-Tratyn
> Is my name!

In another version, the name is 'SILI-FFRIT', and yet again 'Sili-go-Dwt'. The same ending and the same desire to keep the name secret is to be found in the story of GWARWYN-A-THROT. Rhys does not consider the suffix 'Trot' or 'Throt' to be Welsh, but rather thinks it an echo of the English Tom Tit Tot or the Scottish HABETROT. In one version of 'Habetrot' the kindly spinning fairy is like the rapacious WHUPPITY STOORIE, and even in the usual version of 'Habetrot' there is a trace of the same motif in the unconnected remark of the fairy overheard by the heroine: 'Little kens the wee lassie at the brae-head that Habetrot is my name.' The widespread fairy desire to keep his name secret is fully analysed in Edward CLODD's monograph, *Tom Tit Tot*.

[Motif: C432.1]

Tuatha de Danann (*tootha day danan*). The people of the goddess DANA. In the traditional History of Ireland, these are supposed to be the race who inhabited Ireland after conquering the FIRBOLGS, and were in their turn dispossessed by the Milesians, and forced to take refuge under the grassy hills or in lands beneath the waters. They were great masters of magic, and became a fairy people, who in course of time dwindled down into the DAOINE SIDH, though sometimes glimpses of them in their old form of HEROIC FAIRIES are to be seen. Lady WILDE in *Ancient Legends of Ireland* (pp. 178–84) gives an eloquent account of the Tuatha de Danann under the heading of 'Cave Fairies'. It includes a shortened version of the Legend of MIDHIR and ETAIN, one of the most fruitful for modern poetry and drama. We read too in this section of FAIRY HOUSES OF THE TUATHA DE DANANN, as distinct from the AUGHISKY and PHOUKA which are not domesticated, but exist in their own right. YEATS in his *Irish Fairy and Folk Tales* tells stories of the Tuatha de Danann in the section on TIR NAN OG.

[Motifs: A1611.5.4.3; F211.0.2.1]

Tulman. A Gaelic name for the house inside a fairy KNOWE. It seems to be a single dwelling. J. F. CAMPBELL in *Popular Tales of the West Highlands* (vol. II, p. 49) gives a brief anecdote of a tulman which illustrates the use of GOOD MANNERS in dealing with the FAIRIES, and shows them in a benevolent light. The fairy woman had been given nothing but politeness and respect:

> There was a woman in Baile Thangusdail, and she was out seeking a couple of calves; and the night and lateness caught her, and there

came rain and tempest, and she was seeking shelter. She went to a knoll with the couple of calves, and she was striking a tether-peg into it. The knoll opened. She heard a gleegashing as if a pot-hook were clashing beside a pot. She took wonder, and she stopped striking the tether-peg. A woman put out her head and all above her middle, and she said, 'What business hast thou to be troubling this tulman in which I make my dwelling?' 'I am taking care of this couple of calves, and I am but weak. Where shall I go with them?' 'Thou shalt go with them to that breast down yonder. Thou wilt see a tuft of grass. If thy couple of calves eat that tuft of grass, thou wilt not be a day without a milk cow as long as thou art alive, because thou hast taken my counsel.'

As she said, she never was without a milk cow after that, and she was alive fourscore and fifteen years after the night that was there.

[Motif: F330]

Turning clothes. A method of protecting oneself against fairy enchantment, not invariably successful. See also PROTECTION AGAINST FAIRIES.

[Motif: F385.1]

Tylwyth Teg (*terlooeth teig*), **or the Fair Family.** The most usual name for the Welsh FAIRIES, though they are sometimes called BENDITH Y MAMAU, the Mother's Blessing, in an attempt to avert their kidnapping activities by invoking a EUPHEMISTIC NAME FOR THE FAIRIES. There seems no distinction between the types of fairies named. They are fair-haired, love GOLDEN HAIR and hence covet fair-haired human children. They dance and make the fairy rings. Their habitation is under the ground or under the water. The fairy maidens are easily won as wives and will live with human husbands for a time. The danger of visiting them in their own country lies in the miraculous passage of TIME IN FAIRYLAND. They give riches to their favourites, but these gifts vanish if they are spoken of. In fact, they have all the characteristics of the ordinary fairy people.

[Motifs: C433; F233.5]

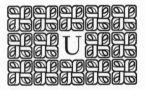

Unseelie Court, the. Members of the SEELIE COURT, which is the general Scottish name for the good FAIRIES, can be formidable enough when they are offended, but the Unseelie Court are never under any circumstances favourable to mankind. They comprise the SLUAGH, or

'The Host', that is, the band of the unsanctified dead who hover above the earth, snatching up with them undefended mortals whom they employ to loose ELF-SHOT against men and cattle, and those malevolent SOLITARY FAIRIES, the BROWN MAN OF THE MUIRS, SHELLYCOAT, NUCKELAVEE, REDCAPS, BAOBHAN SITH and many other ill-disposed natures whose chief pleasure is to hurt or distress mortal men . They can never be too much avoided.

[Motif: F360]

Urchins. 'Urchin' or 'Hurgeon' is a dialect name for a hedgehog, and small BOGIES or PIXIES often took hedgehog form and were therefore called 'urchins'. It will be remembered that Caliban was tormented by urchins at Prospero's command. 'Urchens' are mentioned by Reginald SCOT in his list of frightening spirits. The name came into use for small, impish boys and passed out of common use for FAIRIES.

Urisk, or Uruisg. The Urisk is a kind of rough BROWNIE, half-human, half-goat, very lucky to have about the house, who herded cattle and did farmwork. He haunted lonely pools, but would sometimes crave company and follow terrified travellers all night. Urisks lived as SOLITARY FAIRIES, but met together at stated times. Graham tells us in *Picturesque Sketches of Perthshire* that a corrie near Loch Katrine was their favourite meeting-place. D. A. Mackenzie in *Scottish Folk Lore and Folk Life* treats of the Urisks in some detail.

[Motif: F403.2]

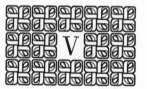

Verbena. See PROTECTION AGAINST FAIRIES.

Virtues esteemed by the fairies. The human virtues which commend themselves to FAIRIES are those which render human intercourse agreeable to them, for a point which is always striking us in fairy legend is the DEPENDENCE OF FAIRIES UPON MORTALS. Two different and almost contradictory traits are asked of humans: they should be close and private, well able to keep the fairy secrets and to guard against INFRINGEMENTS OF FAIRY PRIVACY, often fond of solitude and contemplation; and they should be open and capable of GENEROSITY, ready to share with anyone in need and to speak the TRUTH about their own plans and quests. The first is necessary if the traditional way of life of the 'Secret People' is to be preserved, and the second is congenial to the fairies as guardians of fertility and growth. In the interests of fertility, TRUE LOVE and the affairs of lovers are always under fairy patronage. Open, loving, free people are dear to them, but boasters and braggarts are unpopular. Gentleness and politeness are important to success. In a Russian fairy-tale, Father Frost's heart is won because the heroine politely refuses to complain of the cold although it is nearly killing her, and this is true to folk tradition everywhere, except in dealing with the most sinister of the supernaturals, where bragging and the LAST WORD is a recognized weapon.

Hospitality is one of the admired human virtues, and particularly hospitality towards the fairies, who must be made welcome in the houses which they visit by NEATNESS and good order, a freshly swept CLEAN HEARTH and clear fire, fresh, CLEAR WATER set out for drinking and to wash the fairy babies, and sometimes milk, BREAD and cheese. An unexpected stranger fed may well be a disguised fairy. Good fortune rests upon a miller who sets his mill ready for use on request, a woman who freely lends a measure of meal or gives a fairy baby a suck at her breast. Examples of all these are to be found in the Lowlands of Scotland, cited by J. G. CAMPBELL and William Henderson. FAIR DEALING and the keeping of promises always win respect and are often rewarded. A case in point is the story of 'The Laird o' Co', told by Chambers in his *Popular Rhymes of Scotland*. The Laird of Colzean Castle was accosted one day as he returned home by a small boy with an equally small can who begged for a drink of ale for his old, sick mother. The laird called the butler to fill the can to the brim. The butler took the can and emptied a whole cask into it without more than half-filling it. The butler in per-plexity sent to ask what he should do. The laird said: 'I promised to fill it, and filled it shall be if it takes all the ale in my cellar.' So the butler broached a new cask, and after one drop the can was full, and the little boy thanked him and took it away. Some years later the laird was fighting in the Low Countries and had been taken prisoner. He was languishing there when the door opened, the fairy boy appeared and transported him back to his own castle. A similar good fortune befell Sir Godfrey McCulloch on the eve of his execution because he had courteously moved his back door so that his cesspool should not leak into the living-room of a fairy man whose house was beneath his. These are two examples of GRATEFUL FAIRIES, who respected generosity, true dealing and courtesy when they met them. Merriment, CHEERFULNESS, music, DANCING and good fellowship are all endearing to those fairies who may be called the SEELIE COURT. The evil fairies of the UNSEELIE COURT are in-capable of affection. No man can endear himself to them.

[Type: ML5076*. Motifs: C51.4.3; C94.1; C311.1.2; F330; F332; F335; F348.5.2; F348.7]

Visits to Fairyland, or Visitors to Fairyland. It was most usual for people who had been drawn into Fairyland to find themselves unable to escape when they wished to do so, or to be unconscious of the passage of TIME IN FAIRYLAND, so that when they did return hundreds of years had passed. The classical versions of this theme are the return of OISIN, in which his age descended on him when he touched the earth, and KING HERLA, in which the dismounting knights crumbled into dust. This last is a common motif in some of the comparatively modern Welsh legends. A typical example, the tale of Taffy ap Sion, is given by Wirt Sikes in *British Goblins* (Chapter 6). Taffy ap Sion stepped one evening into a fairy circle and danced, as he thought, for a few minutes, but when he stepped out everything was changed. He made his way to his old cottage, but it was gone, and a handsome stone farm stood in its place. The farmer heard his story and treated him kindly. He offered him a meal, and promised to take him to see old Catti Shon, the oldest inhabitant, who might remember his name. The farmer led the way, but as he went he heard the footsteps behind him grow lighter and lighter and turned just in time to see Taffy crumble and fall to the ground as a little heap of ashes. This crumbling is a common motif in the legend. Sometimes it happens after a meal has been taken, sometimes after the revenant has gone to church and heard the first words of scripture, sometimes, as in this story, after he has told his tale. There are other pathetic stories of human CAPTIVES IN FAIRYLAND who have abstained from FAIRY FOOD in the hope of being rescued. Sometimes these efforts are successful, as in the tale of Mary NELSON; often they fail through human jealousy or cowardice.

There are cases, however, of humans who have gone in and out of Fairyland more or less unscathed. The medieval tale of ELIDOR AND THE GOLDEN BALL is a classic example of this. A later Welsh legend is that of Gitto Bach, a farmer's little son, who used to play with fairy children on the mountain nearby and bring back with him round pieces of white paper stamped to represent money. One evening he did not come back, and all hope of his return was given up. After two years, however, he knocked at the door with a bundle under his arm. It contained handsome-looking clothes, but they were made, like the money, of paper.

In the 17th century, several young people claimed to have visited Fairyland. J. F. CAMPBELL in *Popular Tales of the West Highlands* (vol. II, pp. 66–7) gives an account that he had lately heard of the Boy of Borgue, whose claim to acquaintanceship with the fairies is recorded in the Kirk Session books of the parish:

> Another story he [Johnny Nicholson] told me was about a boy of the name of Williamson, whose father, an Irish linen packman, was drowned on his way from Ireland, where he had gone to purchase linen; so the boy was brought up by his mother and grandfather, an

old man of the name of Sproat, who lived in Borgue. The boy disappeared often for two and three, and often ten days at a time, and no one knew where he went, as he never told when he returned, though it was understood the fairies took him away. Upon one occasion the Laird of Barmagachan was getting his peats cast, and all the neighbours round were assisting. At this time the boy had been away for ten days, and they were all wondering where he could be, when lo and behold, the boy is sitting in the midst of them. 'Johnny,' said one of the company, who were all seated in a ring, eating their dinner, 'where did ye come from?' 'I came with our folks,' said the boy (meaning the fairies). 'Your folks; who are they?' 'Do you see yon barrow of peats a couping into yon hole? there's where I came from.' An old man of the name of Brown, ancestor of the Browns of Langlands, who are still living in Borgue, advised the grandfather to send the boy to the Papist priest, and he would give him something that would frighten away the fairies; so they accordingly sent the boy, and when he returned home he wore a cross hung round his neck by a bit of black ribbon. When the minister and kirk-session heard of it they excommunicated the old grandfather and old Brown for advising such a thing. They believed in fairies, but not in anything a Papist priest could do. However, the boy was never after taken away; and some of the oldest men now alive remember that boy as an old man. The whole affair is recorded in the books of the kirk-session of Borgue, and can be seen any day.

This boy's contemporary, and a not too distant neighbour, was the Boy of Leith, another claimant whose story was reported to BOVET from a man who actually interviewed the boy. He reproduced the letter in *Pandaemonium, or the Devil's Cloyster Opened* (1684), published at a time when there was a recrudescence of witchcraft and folklore beliefs among the learned as well as the believers in witchcraft. George Burton's account is a good piece of reporting:

'About fifteen years since, having business that detained me some time at Leith, which is near Edinburgh, in the kingdom of Scotland, I often met some of my acquaintance at a certain house there, where we used to drink a glass of wine for our refection; the woman which kept the house was of honest reputation among the neighbours, which made me give the more attention to what she told me one day about a fairy boy (as they called him), who lived about that town. She had given me so strange an account of him that I desired I might see him the first opportunity, which she promised; and not long after, passing that way, she told me there was the fairy boy but a little before I came by; and, casting her eye into the street, said, Look you, sir, yonder he is at play with those other boys; and designing him to me, I went, and by smooth words, and a piece of money, got him to come into the house with me; where, in the presence of divers people, I demanded of him several astrological questions, which he answered with great subtilty; and, through all his discourse, carried it with a cunning much above his years, which seemed not to exceed ten or eleven.

'He seemed to make a motion like drumming upon the table with his fingers, upon which I asked him whether he could beat a drum? To which he replied, Yes, sir, as well as any man in Scotland; for every Thursday night I beat all points to a sort of people that used to meet under yonder hill (pointing to the great hill between Edenborough and Leith). How, boy? quoth I, what company have you there? There are, sir, said he, a great company both of men and women, and they are entertained with many sorts of musick, besides my drum; they have, besides, plenty of variety of meats and wine, and many times we are carried into France or Holland in a night, and return again, and whilst we are there we enjoy all the pleasures the country doth afford. I demanded of him how they got under that hill? To which he replied that there was a great pair of gates that opened to them, though they were invisible to others; and that within there were brave large rooms, as well accommodated as most in Scotland. I then asked him how I should know what he said to be true? Upon which he told me he would read my fortune, saying I should have two wives, and that he saw the forms of them sitting on my shoulders; that both would be very handsome women. As he was thus speaking, a woman of the neighbourhood, coming into the room, demanded of him what her fortune should be? He told her that she had two bastards before she was married, which put her in such a rage, that she desired not to hear the rest.

'The woman of the house told me that all the people in Scotland could not keep him from the rendezvous on Thursday night; upon which, by promising him some more money, I got a promise of him to meet me at the same place, in the afternoon, the Thursday following, and so dismist him at that time. The boy came again, at the place and time appointed, and I had prevailed with some friends to continue with me, if possible, to prevent his moving that night. He was placed between us, and answered many questions, until, about eleven of the clock, he was got away unperceived by the company; but I, suddenly missing him, hasted to the door, and took hold of him, and so returned him into the same room; we all watched him, and, of a sudden, he was again got out of doors; I followed him close, and he made a noise in the street, as if he had been set upon; but from that time I could never see him.

'GEORGE BURTON.'

At the same kind of date in the south of England, Anne JEFFERIES was claiming close intimacy with the fairies, but though they took her with them once to the place where they lived, she was not so much a visitor to Fairyland as visited by them.

The witches in Scotland claimed to visit the fairy hills, and the most vivid picture of the place was by Isobel Gowdie, whose account is mentioned in TRAFFIC WITH THE FAIRIES. Her boss-backed ELVES, who spoke ghostie-like, are real IMPS of the Devil, who shapes the elf-arrows for ELF-SHOT; and the ELF-BULLS, 'routing and scoiling', are minor devils too. These are the UNSEELIE COURT, if ever there was one.

[Type: ML4075. Motifs: F370; F375; F377; F378.1; F379.1]

Vough. See FUATH.

Waff. The Yorkshire name for a wraith or double; in other words, it is a kind of CO-WALKER. It is believed to be a death token and may be seen either by the doomed man or by a friend. William Henderson gives several instances in *Folk-Lore of the Northern Counties* (p. 46). If a man sees his own waff, he can avert his fate by speaking to it severely. Henderson gives an example of a native of Guisborough who, on going into a shop at Whitby, saw his own waff. He addressed it boldly: 'What's thou doin' here? What's thou doin' here? Thou's after no good, I'll go bail! Get thy ways yom with thee! Get thy ways yom!' The waff slunk off, quite ashamed of itself, and he had no further trouble with it.

[Motifs: D1812.5.1.17; F405.4]

Wag-at-the-Wa'. This was a Border household spirit of the BROWNIE kind, though rather more eccentric. He is described at length, with the assistance of some rather obscure verses, by William Henderson in *Folk-Lore of the Northern Counties* (pp. 256–7). He loved human CHEERFUL-NESS and the company of children, and his usual seat was on the swinging pot-hook. When this was empty, he used to sit on it and swing himself to and fro, laughing and chuckling at the merriment of the company. He disapproved of any drink stronger than home-brewed ale, and used to cough angrily if strong spirits were drunk. Otherwise he was a convivial spirit, though very particular about the cleanliness or NEAT-NESS of the house and a torment to slovenly kitchen-maids. His cheerful-ness was a great credit to him, since he suffered from perpetual toothache. Henderson describes him with great minuteness:

His general appearance was that of a grisly old man, with short, crooked legs, while a long tail assisted him in keeping his seat on the crook. Sometimes he appeared in a grey mantle, with the remains of an old '*pirnicap*' (night-cap) on his head, drawn down over that side of the face which was troubled with toothache, a constant grievance of his; but he commonly wore a red coat and blue breeches, both garments being made of 'familie woo'.

Wag-at-the-Wa', like most brownies, seeems to have had no fear of cold IRON, but he was frightened of the sign of the CROSS; for when that was marked on the pot-hook to protect the fire from witches, Wag-at-the-Wa' disappeared too. Nevertheless, it was felt even in Henderson's time that to swing an empty pot-hook was to invoke him. Henderson tells us, on the authority of Mr Wilkie, that an old woman visiting a house got up and went when one of the laddies idly swung the pot-hook. She said, 'she wouldna abide in the hoose where sic mookerie was practised'.

[Motif: F480]

Wandering Droll-teller, The. In BOTTRELL's *Traditions and Hearthside Stories of West Cornwall* (vol. I,) there is an account of one of the wandering droll-tellers whom he had known in his youth, which gives us a useful insight into the way in which folk-tales were presented and propagated in Cornwall. Uncle Anthony James of Cury was an entertainer rather than a bard, and there is no indication of the careful accuracy of transmission which was so important to the Irish and Highland bards, where every deviation from strict tradition was frowned upon. Here, on the contrary, a spontaneous and happy innovation was apparently welcomed. It yet remains for someone to make an exhaustive study of different methods in which tales were orally transmitted.

This story of Uncle Anthony James of Cury was an introduction to the story of LUTEY AND THE MERMAID:

> From a period more remote than is now remembered, to the present time, some members of the family called Lutey, who for the most part, resided in the parish of Cury, or its vicinity, have been noted conjurors or white witches. They have long been known, all over the west, as the 'Pellar Family'. The word Pellar is probably an abridgement of repeller, derived from their reputed power in counteracting the malign influences of sorcery and witchcraft.
>
> According to an oft-told story, the wonderful gifts of this family were acquired by a fortunate ancestor, who had the luck to find a mermaid (here by us pronounced meremaid), left high and dry on a rock by the ebbing tide. Some forty years ago, uncle Anthony James – an old blind man, belonging to the neighbourhood of the gifted family – with his dog, and a boy who led him, used to make their yearly tour of the country as regularly as the seasons came round. This venerable wanderer, in his youth, had been a soldier, and had then visited many

foreign lands, about which he had much to tell; but his descriptions of outlandish people and places were just as much fashioned after his own imagination, as were the embellishments of the legends he related, and the airs he composed for many old ballads which he and his boy sang to the melody of the old droll-teller's crowd (fiddle). However, in all the farm houses, where this old wanderer rested on his journey, he and his companions received a hearty welcome, for the sake of his music and above all for his stories, the substance of most of which every one knew by heart, yet they liked to hear these old legends again and again, because he, or some of his audience, had always something new to add, by way of fashioning out the droll, or to display their inventive powers.

Water-bull. See WATER-HORSE AND WATER-BULL.

Water-horse. See CABYLL-USHTEY; EACH UISGE; KELPIE; WATER-HORSE AND WATER-BULL.

'Water-Horse and the Water-Bull, The'. J. F. CAMPBELL in his *Popular Tales of the West Highlands* (vol. IV, pp. 304-6) gives a version of the tale of 'The Water-Horse and the Water-Bull' written down for him by Mr Pattison of Islay:

In one of the islands here (Islay), on the northern side, there lived before now a great farmer, and he had a large stock of cattle. It happened one day that a calf was born amongst them, and an old woman who lived in the place, as soon as ever she saw it, ordered that it should be put in a house by itself, and kept there for seven years, and fed on the milk of three cows. And as every thing which this old woman advised was always done in the 'baile,' this also was done. (It is to be remarked that the progeny of the water-bull can be recognized by an expert by the shape of the ears.)

A long time after these things a servant girl went with the farmer's herd of cattle to graze them at the side of a loch, and she sat herself down near the bank. There, in a little while, what should she see walking towards her but a man (no description of him given in this version), who asked her to 'fàsg' his hair. She said she was willing enough to do him that service, and so he laid his head on her knee, and she began to arrange his locks, as Neapolitan damsels also do by their swains. But soon she got a great fright, for, growing amongst the man's hair, she found a great quantity of 'Liobhagach an locha,' a certain slimy green weed that abounds in such lochs, fresh, salt, and brackish. (In another version it was sand.) The girl knew that if she screamed there was an end of her, so she kept her terror to herself, and worked away till the man fell asleep, as he was with his head on her knee. Then she untied her apron strings, and slid the apron quietly on to the ground with its burden upon it, and then she took her feet home as fast as it was in her heart. (This incident I have heard told in the Isle of Man and elsewhere, of a girl and a supernatural.) Now when she was getting near the houses she gave a glance behind her, and there she saw her 'caraid' (friend) coming after her in the likeness of a horse.

He had nearly reached her, when the old woman who saw what was going on called out to open the door of the wild bull's house, and in a moment out sprang the bull.

He gave an eye all round about him, and then rushed off to meet the horse, and when they met they fought, and they never stopped fighting till they drove each other out into the sea, and no one could tell which of them was best. Next day the body of the bull was found on the shore all torn and spoilt, but the horse was never more seen at all.

The narrator prefaced this story by remarking that it was 'perfectly true,' for he had it from a lobster fisher, who heard it from an old man who witnessed the whole scene. It was suggested to him that the 'old woman' was a witch, but he would have his story told in his own way, and said, 'Well, I suppose she was a witch, but I did not hear it.'

Campbell enlarges this tale by some interesting glosses and a variant of the story in which the water-bull is a more fairy-like character with the gift of speech and song:

Mr Pattison, who wrote down this version, regrets that he did not get a fuller description of the animals. I have a fuller description of them, and of the girl, with all the names of the people, and the places, fully set forth. The bull was large and black, he was found groaning in a peat hag, and was helped by the girl's lover, who brought him food, though he suspected him to be the water-bull. The girl was dark-haired and brown-eyed, and the farmer's daughter. Her lover was an active Highland lad, and a drover, who went by the name of 'Eachan còir nan òrd,' 'Gentle Hector of the hammers', and he was fair-haired.

There was a rejected rival suitor who takes the place of the water-horse, who threw his plaid over the girl's head when she is at a shieling, and carried her off, but the black water-bull rushed in just at the nick of time, crushed the wicked wooer to the earth, invited the lady to mount on his back, and carried her safely home, when he disappeared, singing –

> 'Aid came to me by a gentle youth,
> And to a maiden I brought aid;
> After three hundred years of my hard age,
> Give me my freedom without delay.'

[Type: ML6060. Motifs: F420.1.3.3; F420.1.3.4]

Water-Leaper. See LLAMHIGYN Y DWR.

Water-wraith. A Scottish female water spirit, dressed in green, withered, meagre and scowling. Hugh Miller, in *My Schools and Schoolmasters* (p. 202), speaks of one such who haunted the river Conan in Ross-shire:

> . . . who used to appear as a tall woman dressed in green, but distinguished chiefly by her withered meagre countenance, ever distorted by a malignant scowl. I knew all the various fords – always dangerous ones – where of old she used to start, it was said, out of the river, before the terrified traveller, to point at him, as in derision, with her skinny finger, or to beckon him invitingly on; and I was shown the very tree to which a poor Highlander had clung, when, in crossing the river by night, he was seized by the goblin, and from which, despite of his utmost exertions, though assisted by a young lad, his companion, he was dragged into the middle of the current, where he perished.

J. M. McPherson in *Primitive Beliefs in the North-East of Scotland* (p. 63) mentions a water-wraith at the Linn of Lynturk. Her last appearance was when she attacked the Laird of Kincraigie on his way home from dining with the Laird of Tulloch. McPherson hints that these water-demons generally appeared when people were on their way home from a drinking bout.

[Motifs: F420.1.6.6.3; F420.5.2; F420.5.2.1]

Wee Folk, the. One of the Scottish and Irish EUPHEMISTIC NAMES FOR THE FAIRIES. We find it in Allingham's poem 'The Fairies': – 'Wee folk, good folk, trooping all together'. The Manx equivalent is 'The LIL' FELLAS'.

[Motif: C433]

Wee Willie Winkie. The best-known of our British nursery sleep spirits, many of whom were originated by William Miller, who published the earliest known version of this nursery rhyme in 1841. The first verse, which captured the popular imagination, ran:

> Wee Willie Winkie runs through the toun,
> Up stairs and down stairs in his nicht-goun,
> Tirling at the window, crying at the lock,
> Are the weans in their bed, for it's now ten o'clock?

It was soon anglicized and reproduced without acknowledgement in *Nursery Rhymes, Tales and Jingles* as early as 1842. There are five verses in Miller's poem; the other four are rather charming, but have not the traditional ring of the first verse. It is possible that Miller, like several other Scottish poets of the 19th century, took a traditional verse as the theme of his poem and expanded it. It is at any rate likely, if BILLY WINKER was current in Lancashire, that Wee Willie Winkie was known in Scotland before Miller wrote his poem. Peter Opie, however, in the

Oxford Dictionary of Nursery Rhymes, gives 1841 as the date of the whole rhyme.

White ladies. The use of 'White Ladies' for both ghosts and FAIRIES is an indication of close connection between fairies and the dead. Evans Wentz in *The Fairy-Faith in Celtic Countries*, tracing the supernatural elements in the early Arthurian MATTER OF BRITAIN legends, points out that 'Gwenhwyvar' or Guinevere originally meant 'white phantom', which has the same meaning as the Irish 'Bean Fhionn', or White Lady of Lough Gur, who claims a human life every seven years. Douglas HYDE, in his introduction to the Irish section of the same book, speaks in passing of the White Ladies of raths and moats as direct descendants of the TUATHA DE DANANN.

'Whuppity Stoorie'. The liveliest of the Scottish versions of 'Rumpel-stiltskin', to be found in Chambers's *Popular Rhymes of Scotland*. Chambers suggests that the name comes from the Scots 'stoor', meaning dust, and is inspired by the swirl of dust in which the FAIRIES are supposed to travel. He also mentions that in another version the name for the fairy is 'Fittletot'. Rhys points out that the names of many of these TOM TIT TOT fairies end in 'Tot', 'Trot' or other similar suffixes.

> The Gudewife of Kittlerumpit had lost her man, – they thought he was pressed for the sea, – and she had nothing to care for but a wee lad bairn still sucking and a muckle big soo that was soon to farrow, and she hoped for a big litter. But one fine morning she went round the hoose to the stye and poured the swill out in the trough, and there was the soo grainin' and gruntin' like one at death's door. She called and she coaxed, but never a stir was in it, and at last she sat down at the knockin' stane at her door, and she burst oot greetin'. And as she grat and roared she saw an old, queer-like leddy in green coming up the brae to her housie, which was on a hill with a green wood behind it. She had a long staff in her hand and there was something aristo-cratical aboot her, and when she got near the gudewife rose up and gave her a curchie and she says – 'Oh yir leddyship, I'm the maist waefulest woman in the world, and there's nane to help me.' 'I'm no wanting lang tales,' says the leddy. 'I ken what ails ye; ye've lost yir man and ye're like to lose yir muckle big soo. I'll no can help ye with the first, but what'll ye give me if I save the second?' 'I'm shair I'll gie ye onything I have to give,' says the gudewife, foolish woman! 'Let's weet thumbs on that,' says the leddy. So they wetted thumbs on the bargain, and the strange leddy went into the stye. She took a wee bottle oot of her pocket, and she muttered some words that sounded like 'Pitter, patter, holy water' and anointed the soo's neb with it; and the soo jumped up as well as ever she was, and gobbled up the swill. The gudewife knelt down, and she wad ha kissed the strange leddy's

green skirts, but the strange leddy says, 'I'm no ane for fashions, let's get to bargains. Ye've no muckle to give, so I'll e'en tak' yir bit bairn.' The gudewife knew then what kind of a creature she was, and she fleeched an she prayed at her for mercy, and at last the strange leddy said: 'It's yir bairn I want and it's yir bairn I'll get; but I'll tell ye this, – by the law we leeve on I canna tak it till the third day from this, and no even then if ye can tell me my richt name.' And with that she was awa'.

Well all that day the gudewife mourned and grat and kissed the bairn, and all that night she lay thinking on every name she could call to mind, but nane seemed right. So the evening of the second day she thinks to herself she'll do no good in the hoose, and maybe the caller air will clear her wits. So she picks up the bit bairn and awa' oot. She went this way and that through the wood ahint her hoosie, tills she comes to an old quarry, all o'ergrown with gorse, and with a bonnie spring in it. And she tippytaes to the edge o' the quarry, and there is the green leddy spinning, and singing o'er and o'er again

> 'Little kens oor gude dame at hame
> That Whuppity Stoorie is my name!'

Then thought the gudewife to herself: 'I've gotten the mason's word at last,' and she carried a licht heart back with her, that went oot with a heavy ane.

In the morn she thinks she'll hae some sport with the fairy, so she sits doon on the knockin' stane, wi' her mutch and her apron agley, and she makes a show of greeting and girning waur nor ever, and the old fairy comes up the braeside as licht as a lassie, and as she comes she skirls oot

'Ye ken what I come for! Stand and deliver!'

'Oh yir leddyship,' says the gudewife. 'Dinna tak my bit bairn, tak' the auld soo!'

'It's the bairn I want and the bairn I'll hae,' says the fairy.

'Tak me yir leddyship,' says the gudewife, 'but spare the bit bairn.'

'Dae ye think I'm daft that I'd tak sic a muckle, ill-faured skelloch as yirsel, Gudewife?'

Well the gudewife kent she was nae beauty, but she wasna one to be misca'ed. So she raised herself up, and then she gied a laigh curchie and she says: 'Ah micht hae kent that a puir body like masell was na fit to tie the shoe strings of the heih and michty Princess Whuppity Stoorie.'

At that the fairy gave a great loup, and then she twirled roun and roun doan the brae and the gudewife never seed her again, and she picked up the bit bairn and gaed into her hoosie as prood as a doggie wi' twa tails.

[Type: 500. Motifs: C432.1; F381.1; H521; M242; N475]

Wicht. The Scottish version of WIGHT.

Wife of Bath's Tale, The. Chaucer's *The Wife of Bath's Tale* is worthy of comment for two reasons. First, it is an early and excellent example of a fairy-tale, and secondly it contains a medieval example of the complaint of the DEPARTURE OF THE FAIRIES after the manner of Corbet's 'Farewell, Rewards and Fairies'. It seems that from the earliest times the FAIRIES have always been leaving us, and yet sometimes they never quite go.

> In th'olde dayes of the King Arthour,
> Of which that Britons speken greet honour,
> Al was this land fulfild of faierie.
> The elf-queene, with hir joly compaignie,
> Daunced ful ofte in many a grene mede.
> This was the olde opinion, as I rede;
> I speke of manie hundred yeres ago.
> But now kan no man se none elves mo,
> For now the grete charitee and prayeres
> Of limitours and othere hooly freres,
> That serchen every lond and every streem,
> As thikke as motes in the sonne-beem,
> Blessinge halles, chambres, kichenes, boures,
> Citees, burghes, castels, hye toures,
> Thropes, bernes, shipnes, daieries –
> This maketh that ther ben no faieries.
> For ther as wont to walken was an elf,
> Ther walketh now the limitour himself,
> In undermeles and in morweninges,
> And seyth his matins and his hooly thinges
> As he gooth in his limitacioun.
> Wommen may go now saufly up and doun.
> In every bussh or under every tree
> Ther is noon oother incubus but he,
> And he ne wol doon hem but dishonour.

In this passage the Wife of Bath takes her sly fling at the churchmen who were of the company, going as far as 'There is none other incubus but he.' The wanton friar is a common figure in folk tradition. One notices here that she identifies the fairies with the devils, for an INCUBUS is a devil who lies with a woman, though the Loathly Lady in the story is really a good fairy.

The tale itself is one that is a good deal used at that time. Gower used it at the same time as Chaucer in *Confessio Amantis*, and a 15th-century poem, 'The Weddyinge of Sr Gawen and Dame Ragnell', is printed in Madden's *Syr Gawayne*. There is a mutilated ballad 'The Marriage of

Sir Gawain' reprinted by Child from the Percy Manuscript. There is also a ballad of 'King Henry' (No. 32 of the Child ballads) with the same theme of courtesy and compliance to a hideous woman-creature. The story is attached to the Finne Fein in J. F. CAMPBELL's Gaelic tale, 'The Daughter of King Under-Waves', with Diarmid as its hero. Child cites a parallel from an Icelandic saga.

Chaucer's version of the tale differs a little from most of the others, though the plot is the same. An unnamed knight of Arthur's court, 'a lusty bachelor', riding back from hawking one day, raped a maiden and was condemned to die at first, but Guinevere begged that she might dispose of him. She set him a question – what is it that women desire most? – and gave him a year and a day to find the answer. If he failed his life was forfeit. He rode high and low and received a variety of answers, but none seemed better than the others. At length the time came to ride back to the court, but as he passed through a forest he came on an open green on which four-and-twenty ladies were dancing, and went eagerly up to them in the hope of getting the answer to his riddle, but before he reached them they all vanished into air, and when he came to the green he saw only one old woman, hideous beyond description, who hailed him and asked him what he sought there. He told her his plight, and she said that she knew the answer to his riddle, and would tell him if in return he would promise to grant a request she would make to him, provided it was within his power. He promised, and she whispered the answer into his ear. Then they went along together to the tribunal. The judges were maidens, wives and widows, presided over by the queen. The whole of King Arthur's court attended. The question was posed and the knight stepped forward boldly:

> 'My lige lady, generally,' quod he,
> 'Wommen desiren to have sovereintee
> As wel over hir housbond as hir love,
> And for to been in maistrie him above.
> This is youre mooste desir, thogh ye me kille.
> Dooth as yow list; I am heer at youre wille.'

And no one, maid, wife or widow, could gainsay him, so that he was judged to have fairly won his life. Then the old, foul woman started up, and claimed that she had taught him that answer and that he had promised to return to grant her any request that was in his power. So now she demanded that he should marry her. The young man admitted the truth of what she said, but begged that she would take some other recompense, but no other would do for her, so he wedded her, in haste and shame, and at night they went to bed together. As they lay she began to remonstrate with him because he would do nothing but groan and toss about. What had offended him? she asked. What had she done wrong? He answered that she was old and foul and poor, and of low estate. She answered him gently point by point, and at last said that she could amend it. He could choose if he would have her old and ugly, but gentle and loving, serving him in every way like a true wife, or beautiful and young, but froward and false, with a great resort of lovers to her door. He thought deeply, and at length asked her to take her choice herself, for she knew best. 'Then you give me the mastery,' she said. 'Yes,' he said, 'I think it best.' 'Come, kiss me,' she said, 'for I will be both to you, fair and good. Come, lift the curtain and see.' Then, when he saw her as fair as any lady in the world, and ready to pleasure him in any way he would, he kissed her a hundred times, and all their days were spent in love and gentleness.

Chaucer's story is different from the ballads and folk-tales in making the knight suffer for his own fault. In the other tales, the heroes undertake the quest on behalf of their king or leader, and the lady is suffering from an enchantment laid on her by a wicked stepmother, comparable to that of 'The Laidly Worm of Spindlestone Heugh'. This lady is a fairy, in complete control of the situation, while the others are victims, seeking disenchantment. It is perhaps a gentler, prettier tale than one would expect from the Wife of Bath, but it enforces her moral that husbands should be obedient to their wives.

[Motifs: D621.3; D732; H541]

Wight. A general Germanic word meaning 'being' or 'creature', but increasingly applied to either good or bad spirits, until it came to have a supernatural connotation. In late Saxon, 'unsele wiht' is 'uncanny creature', and in *The Canterbury Tales* Chaucer uses the word for dangerous spirits in 'I crouche thee from elves and fro wightes' in 'The Miller's Tale'. KIRK talks of seeing the FAIRIES crowding in from all quarters 'like furious hardie wights'. It was not a word objected to by the fairies, for in the fairy rhyme given by Chambers we have:

> Gin ye ca' me seelie wicht
> I'll be your freend baith day and nicht.

Of course, they would not welcome the title of 'wicked wight' by which the evil fairies of the UNSEELIE COURT were designated.

Wild Edric. Our earliest tale of the FAIRY BRIDE is that of 'Wild Edric', for among the MEDIEVAL CHRONICLES it was told in some detail by Walter Map in the 12th century. It is re-told by Burne and Jackson in *Shropshire Folk-Lore* (pp. 59–61):

Shropshire men must have been well acquainted with the fairies five hundred years ago. It was reported then, that our famous champion Wild Edric had had an Elf-maiden for his wife. One day, we are told, when he was returning from hunting in the forest of Clun, he lost his way and wandered about till nightfall, alone, save for one young page. At last he saw the lights of a very large house in the distance, towards which he turned his steps, and when he had reached it, he beheld within a large company of noble ladies dancing. They were exceedingly beautiful, taller and larger than women of the human race, and dressed in gracefully-shaped linen garments. They circled round with smooth and easy motion, singing a soft low song of which the hunter could not understand the words. Among them was one maiden who excelled all the others in beauty, at the sight of whom our hero's heart was inflamed with love. Forgetting the fears of enchantment, which at the first moment had seized him, he hurried round the house, seeking an entrance, and having found it, he rushed in, and snatched the maiden who was the object of his passion from her place in the moving circle. The dancers assailed him with teeth and nails, but backed by his page, he escaped at length from their hands, and succeeded in carrying off his fair captive.

For three whole days, not his utmost caresses and persuasions could prevail on her to utter a single word, but on the fourth day she suddenly broke the silence. 'Good luck to you, my dear!' said she, 'and you will be lucky too, and enjoy health and peace and plenty, as long as you do not reproach me on account of my sisters, or the place from which you snatched me away, or anything connected with it. For on the day when you do so you will lose both your bride and your good fortune; and when I am taken away from you, you will pine away quickly to an early death.'

He pledged himself by all that was most sacred to be ever faithful and constant in his love for her: and they were solemnly wedded in the presence of all the nobles from far and near, whom Edric invited to their bridal feast. At that time William the Norman was newly made king of England, who, hearing of this wonder, desired both to see the lady, and to test the truth of the tale; and bade the newly-married pair to London, where he was then holding his court. Thither then they went, and many witnesses from their own country with them, who brought with them the testimony of others who could not present themselves to the king. But the marvellous beauty of the lady was the best of all proofs of her superhuman origin. And the king let them return in peace, wondering greatly.

Many years passed happily by, till one evening Edric returned late from hunting, and could not find his wife. He sought for her and called her for some time in vain. At last she appeared. 'I suppose,' began he, with angry looks, 'it is your sisters who have detained you such a long time, have they not?'

The rest of his upbraiding was addressed to thin air, for the moment her sisters were mentioned she vanished. Edric's grief was overwhelming. He sought the place where he had found her at first, but no tears, no laments of his could call her back. He cried out day and night against his own folly, and pined away and died of sorrow, as his wife had long before foretold.

It is very curious to find that Wild Edric was already the centre of myth and legend within scarcely more than a century of his own life-time.

Walter Map tells us about the piety of Wild Edric's son, but there is a sequel which he does not record, for Wild Edric, like KING HERLA, rode after his death. Tradition restored him to his wife, and they rode together over the Welsh Border country for many centuries after his death. *Shropshire Folk-Lore* (pp. 28–9) records an eye-witness account of the Rade in the 19th century:

For it is not many years since, in the West Shropshire hills, in the very neighbourhood where Edric's estates lay, and where also lay the greater number of the very few Shropshire manors retained after the Conquest by Englishmen (no doubt Edric's old friends and comrades, perhaps his kindred), there were people to be found, if there are not some now, who believed Wild Edric to be still alive, imprisoned in the mines of that wild west country. He cannot die, they say, till all the wrong has been made right, and England has returned to the same state as it was in before the troubles of his days. Meantime he is con-demned to inhabit the lead-mines as a punishment for having allowed himself to be deceived by the Conqueror's fair words into submitting to him. So there he dwells with his wife and his whole train. The miners call them the 'Old Men,' and sometimes hear them knocking, and wherever they knock, the best lodes are to be found. Now and then they are permitted to show themselves. Whenever war is going to break out, they ride over the hills in the direction of the enemy's country, and if they appear, it is a sign that the war will be serious.

Such, in substance, was the account given some years ago by a young woman from Rorrington to her mistress, who repeated it to me. The lady, wishing to draw out the girl's knowledge, professed not to under-stand whom she meant by the 'Cong-kerry,' as she called him. 'What! did you never hear of the Cong-kerry, ma'am?' exclaimed the maid, who, by the way, could neither read nor write. 'Why, he used to hang up men by the heels because they were English! Oh, he was a bad man!'

She declared that she had herself seen Wild Edric and his men. It was in 1853 or 1854, just before the Crimean war broke out. She was with her father, a miner, at Minsterley, and she heard the blast of a horn. Her father bade her cover her face, all but her eyes, and on no account speak, lest she should go mad. Then they all came by; Wild Edric himself on a white horse at the head of the band, and the Lady Godda his wife, riding at full speed over the hills. Edric had short dark curly hair and very bright black eyes. He wore a green cap and white feather, a short green coat and cloak, a horn and a short sword hanging from his golden belt, 'and something zig-zagged here' (touching her leg below the knee). The lady had wavy golden hair falling loosely to her waist, and round her forehead a band of white linen, with a golden ornament in it. The rest of her dress was green, and she had a short dagger at her waist. The girl watched them pass out of sight over the hills towards the north. It was the second time her father had seen them. The former time they were going southwards. 'And then Napoleon Bonaparte came.'

'Many people say,' added our authority, 'that the miners always do seem to know when a war is going to be desperate!'

[Type: 400 (variant). Motifs: C31.2; C932; E501.1.7.3; F241.1.0.1; F302.2]

Wild Hunt, the. One name given to the GABRIEL RATCHETS, to the DEVIL'S DANDY DOGS, the SLUAGH, or 'The Host', and other soul-ravening hunts. Some of these, like the Gabriel Ratchets and the Host, are supposed to fly through the air, others, like the Devil's Dandy Dogs and the Wild Hunt, course along the ground, or only just above it. It was presumably the Wild Hunt that was described in the *Anglo-Saxon Chronicle* of 1127, quoted by Brian Branston in *The Lost Gods of England*:

> Let no one be surprised at what we are about to relate, for it was common gossip up and down the countryside that after February 6th many people both saw and heard a whole pack of huntsmen in full cry. They straddled black horses and black bucks while their hounds were pitch black with staring hideous eyes. This was seen in the very deer park of Peterborough town, and in all the wood stretching from that same spot as far as Stamford. All through the night monks heard them sounding and winding their horns. Reliable witnesses who kept watch in the night declared that there might well have been twenty or even thirty of them in this wild tantivy as near as they could tell.

The Wild Hunt has been long lived. In the 1940s it was said to be heard going through West Coker near Taunton on Hallow's E'en at night.
[Motifs: E501.1; E501.1.7.3; E501.13.1.4; E501.13.4]

Wilde, Lady, Jane Frances (1826–96). The wife of Sir William Wilde – famous for his advancement of aural and ophthalmic science and for his antiquarian knowledge – and the mother of Oscar Wilde. She was an ardent Irish nationalist and contributed, under the pseudonym of 'Speranza', many articles to the nationalist magazine *The Nation*. As is not unusual, her patriotism led her to study the folklore of her nation, and she became a friend of W. B. YEATS. Her most notable contribution to fairy-lore is *Ancient Legends, Mystic Charms and Superstitions of*

Ireland (2 vols., 1857). It is notable for the many instances she gives of the confusion between the FAIRIES and the dead which is a common ingredient in the Celtic beliefs on the ORIGIN OF FAIRIES in many parts of the British Isles.

Wilkie. At Westray in Orkney there were two burial mounds which were called 'Wilkie's Knolls'. Offerings of milk were said to be made to Wilkie, though nobody seems very clear about him. It is at least obvious that, like quite a number of other fairy types, Wilkie was closely connected with the dead.

Will o' the Wisp. The commonest and most widespread traditional name for IGNIS FATUUS. Also Will-with-the-Wisp, Willy Wisp, WILL O' THE WYKES.
[Motifs: F369.7; F402.1.1; F491; F491.1]

Will o' the Wykes. The Norfolk name for IGNIS FATUUS. It is to be found in Mrs Balfour's 'The DEAD MOON'.
[Motif: F491]

William of Newbridge (1136–98?), sometimes incorrectly called Newburgh. See GREEN CHILDREN.

Wisdome of Doctor Dodypol, The. Published by Thomas Creede in 1600, this is a rather miscellaneous and wandering play out of which can be abstracted the plot of a pleasant fairy interlude containing many folklore elements. The fairy theme is opened in Act Three, when a benighted peasant hears music coming out of a fairy mound. It opens to him, and a small dapper fairy comes out and offers him a goblet of wine. He asks for meat to go with it, and while the fairy goes to fetch it, runs off with the cup. The whole incident is like that about the FAIRY CUP recorded by William of Newbridge in one of the MEDIEVAL CHRONICLES. These SUBTERRANEANS are governed not by a king but by a WIZARD, like the 'maister man' who controlled a troop of FAIRIES which Katherine Carey, tried for witchcraft in 1610, met at the going down of the sun. This enchanter, seeing a young wife flouted and despised by her husband, draws them both into the hill, throws the husband into an enchanted sleep, and, having clouded the wife's memory with a spell, tries to make her believe that he is her lover. Throughout the play the plot hangs on the substantial indestructibility of love through every enchantment. In the following scene the idea is developed with some subtlety.

The Enchanter says to Lassenburg, the husband:

> Lie there, and lose the memorie of her
> Who likewise hath forgot the thought of thee
> By my inchantments: Come, sit downe faire Nimphe
> And taste the sweetnesse of these heavenly cates,
> Whilst from the hollow craines [crannies] of this rocke,
> Musick shall sound to recreate my love.
> But tell me, had you ever lover yet?

LUCILLA: I had a lover I thinke, but who it was,
> Or where, or how long since, aye me, I know not:
> Yet beat my timerous thoughts on such a thing,
> I feele a passionate heate, but finde no flame:
> Thinke what I know not, nor know what I thinke.

ENCHANTER: Hast thou forgot me then? I am thy love,
> Whom sweetly thou wert wont to entertaine,
> With lookes, with vowes of love, with amorous kisses,
> Look'st thou so strange? doost thou not know me yet?

LUCILLA: Sure I should know you.

ENCHANTER: Why love, doubt you that?
> Twas I that led you through the painted meades,
> Where the light Fairies daunst upon the flowers,
> Hanging on every leafe an orient pearle,
> Which strooke together with the silken winde,
> Of their loose mantels made a silver chime.
> Twas I that winding my shrill bugle horne,
> Made a guilt pallace breake out of the hill,
> Filled suddenly with troopes of knights and dames,
> Who daunst and reveld whilst we sweetly slept,
> Upon a bed of Roses wrapt all in goulde,
> Dost thou not know me yet?

LUCILLA: Yes now I know you.

ENCHANTER: Come then confirme thy knowledge with a kis.

LUCILLA: Nay stay, you are not he, how strange is this.

ENCHANTER: Thou art growne passing strange my love,
> To him that made thee so long since his bride.

LUCILLA: O was it you? Come then, O stay a while,
I know not where I am, nor what I am,
Nor you, nor these I know, nor any thing.

At this point her father enters the hill, and breaks the enchantment with a magic jewel, as the two brothers in *Comus* broke the enchantment with a flower. It is tempting to think that MILTON knew the play of *The Wisdome of Dr Dodypol* as a child. It comes even closer to *Comus* than Peele's *Old Wife's Tale*, which is generally considered the source of the *Comus* plot.

Wish Hounds, sometimes called Yell-hounds or Yeth-hounds. The spectral, headless hounds of Dartmoor which sometimes meet also in the valley of Dewerstone. They also run into Cornwall, hunting the demon Tregeagle. Their huntsman is presumably the Devil, though the ghost of Sir Francis Drake was sometimes said to drive a hearse into Plymouth, followed by a pack of headless hounds. HUNT also suggests that CHENEY'S HOUNDS are Wish Hounds. Hunt, who gives a short account of the Wish Hounds in *Popular Romances of the West of England*, suggests that they are the same as the DEVIL'S DANDY DOGS, but the Dandy Dogs have horns and fiery saucer eyes, while the Wish Hounds are headless.

    [Motifs: E500; G303.7.1.3]

Wizards. All wizards were not necessarily bad, though they were exposed to the temptations of power and tended rather to make use of it. Merlin is an example of a good wizard, though he was admittedly unscrupulous in the affair of Uther and Igraine, when he disguised Uther as the Duke of Tintagel, so that he begot Arthur on Igraine in the very hour in which the real duke was killed in battle. Merlin might almost count as a SUPERNATURAL WIZARD, for he was the child of an INCUBUS, who lay with a princess, and was therefore described as 'a child without a father'. He studied magic, however, under the famous MAGICIAN Blaise of Brittany.

    Michael Scot, the famous Scottish wizard, owed his introduction to magic, much as FINN had done, to having the first taste of a magical fish of knowledge, in his case a 'White Snake' which he had been set to watch as it cooked. He had burnt his fingers on it, and had put them to his mouth, so having the first potent taste. Many widespread stories are attached to Michael Scot, such as the magical flight to Rome, of which there are many versions, including one in the Faust legend. One collected in the 19th century is to be found in *Waifs and Strays of Celtic Tradition* (vol. I, pp. 47–53):

    When the country of Scotland was ruled by the Pope, the inhabitants were very ignorant, and nothing could be done or said by them until they would obtain the consent of the Pope. The Feast of Shrove-tide regulated all the feasts that followed it, during the whole year. So, when the date of Shrove-tide would be known, the date of every feast during the year was known. On Shrove-tide, Lent began; six weeks after that was Easter; and so on unto the end of the year.

A man left each country every year for Rome for the purpose of ascertaining the knowledge of the date of Shrove-tide, and on his arrival home, and on his telling the date of Shrove-tide in that year, an intelligent, clever, fearless, prudent, and well-bred man was selected to proceed to Rome on the following year to ascertain it.

On a certain year, Michael Scot, a learned man and famous, was chosen to proceed to Rome to obtain the knowledge of Shrove-tide; but, because of the many other matters he had to attend to, he forgot his duty until all the feasts of the year were over at Candlemas. There was not a minute to lose. He betook himself to one of the fairy riding-fillies, and said to her, 'How swift are you?' 'I am as fleet as the wind,' replied she. 'You will not do,' says Michael. He reached the second one. 'How swift are you?' 'I am as swift as that I can outspeed the wind that comes behind me, and overtake the wind that goes before me.' 'You will not do,' answered Michael. The third one was as fleet as the 'black blast of March'. 'Scarcely will you do,' says Michael. He arrived at the fourth one, and put his question to her. 'I am as swift as the thought of a maiden between her two lovers.' 'You will be of service,' says Michael; 'make ready.' 'I am always ready if the man were in accord with me,' says she.

They started. Sea and land were alike to them. While they were above the sea, the witch said to him, 'What say the women of Scotland when they quench the fire?' 'You ride,' says Michael, 'in your master's name, and never mind that.' 'Blessing to thyself, but a curse on thy teacher,' replied she. 'What,' says she again, 'say the wives of Scotland when they put the first weanling to bed, and a suckling at their breast?' 'Ride you in your master's name, and let the wives of Scotland sleep,' responded Michael. 'Forward was the woman who put the first finger in your mouth,' says she.

Michael arrived at Rome. It was the morning. He sent swift message to the Pope that the messenger from Scotland was at the door seeking knowledge of Shrove-tide, lest Lent would go away. The Pope came at once to the audience-room. 'Whence art thou?' he said to Michael. 'I am from thy faithful children of Scotland, seeking the knowledge of Shrove-tide, lest Lent will go away,' says Michael. 'You were too late in coming.' 'Early that leases me,' replied Michael. 'You have ridden somewhat high.' 'Neither high nor low, but right ahead,' says Michael. 'I see,' says the Pope, 'snow on your bonnet.' 'Yes, by your leave, the snow of Scotland.' 'What proof,' says the Pope, 'can you give me of that? likewise, that you have come from Scotland to seek knowledge of Shrove-tide?' 'That,' says Michael, 'a shoe is on your foot that is not your own.' The Pope looked, and on his right foot was a woman's shoe.

'You will get what you want,' says he to Michael, 'and begone. The first Tuesday of the first moon of Spring is Shrove-tide.'

Thus Michael Scot obtained knowledge of the secret that the Pope kept to himself. Before that time the messenger obtained but the knowledge that this day or that day was the day of Shrove-tide in the coming year; but Michael obtained knowledge of how the Pope himself came to ascertain the day. How Michael returned, history does not tell.

SHAPE-SHIFTING, which was a native power to all the more distinguished FAIRIES, could be acquired by wizards, as several stories of boys trained by wizards to transformation show. One is to be found in McKay's *More West Highland Tales* (vol. I), 'The Wizard's Gillie', in which a boy is hired from his father by a wizard and finally acquired as a permanent slave by trickery. His father manages to find him. Every day he transforms himself into a saleable form and is bought by the wizard, but so long as his father retains the strap that led him he can return in his own shape. When the father, elated by the large price paid, forgets to remove it, he is a prisoner. But he manages to make his escape and is pursued. A transformation conflict ensues in which the gillie finally outwits the wizard and destroys him. Powers of indestructibility and of externalizing their souls, making them SEPARABLE SOULS, can also be acquired by mortal wizards.

THOMAS THE RHYMER is an example of the acquisition of supernatural knowledge by means of the fairies. He was more fortunate than Merlin, for when he left Middle Earth he went into Fairyland, while Merlin was spell-bound under a rock. Some wizards acquired power over fairies, like the 'Master-Man' reported by Katherine Carey at her trial in 1610. But whether this was a magician or a wizard may be left to conjecture, since it was probably an illusion in any case.

[Motifs: B217.1.1; D2122; G303.3.3.1.3]

Woden. See ODIN.

Woodwose, or Wild Men of the Woods. In the programme book for the 25th Aldeburgh Festival in 1972, an article by Felicity Dracopoli appeared which explored the subject of the Woodwose so often to be found among the carvings and decorations of East Anglian churches. Mentions of these 'Wild Men of the Woods' are scattered sparsely through the literature of the 16th and 17th centuries. Such authors as Heywood and BURTON refer to them occasionally, and they occurred in processions and pageants. They were covered in hair, as the GREEN MEN were covered in leaves, but it is rather doubtful if they were thought of as supernatural creatures or as primitive inhabitants of the forests.

Worms. The worms of Great Britain, and particularly the Celtic worms, seem to show some influence from the Scandinavian worms or DRAGONS, though these were sometimes winged and fire-breathing. Smaug, the dragon in TOLKIEN's book *The Hobbit*, though he is a literary creation, is a good exemplar of a Scandinavian or Teutonic dragon. He is wily and able to talk, a treasure-guarder and winged, with only one vulnerable spot on him. Sometimes a dragon is a transformed man, as Fafnir was, the dragon which Siegfried slew. C. S. Lewis made use of this motif in one of his Narnia books, *The Voyage of the Dawn-Treader*, when Eustace, having fallen asleep lying on treasure, with covetous thoughts in his

heart, wakes to find himself transformed into a dragon. The only trace of this motif in English dragon traditions is in the half-farcical gipsy tale 'The Long, Long Worm', reported by Ruth Tongue in *Forgotten Folk-Tales of the English Counties*, in which the mile-long worm lightly buried under leaves is lying covering a long lair of golden treasure. Two typical British worm-dragons are the LAMBTON WORM from Yorkshire which is in the form of an 'eft' or newt, which grows monstrously after being pulled from the river Wear by the prodigal heir of Lambton, who is sacrilegiously fishing on a Sunday, and thrown into a neighbouring well. When it emerges it is in the form of an enormous lizard which ravages the countryside, sometimes curling round a neighbouring hill and some-times round a great rock in the river. It possesses the quality, super-stitiously attributed to serpents, of re-joining if it is cut in two, and its breath is poisonous rather than fiery. The Orcadian Mester Stoorworm in the story of ASSIPATTLE is a sea-serpent of monstrous size, for its burning body was screwed up in its last agony into the island of Iceland.

It was destroyed by thrusting a burning peat down its throat which ignited its internal fat.

The Dragon of Loschy Hill, whose story is quoted in *County Folk-Lore* (vol. II), was self-joining like the Lambton Worm, and was conquered by the help of the hero's dog, who carried it away piecemeal to prevent the reunion of the parts. The poisonous fumes of the monster proved fatal to both the master and the dog. The LINTON WORM, which was comparatively dwarfish, rather less than twelve feet in length, was conquered by Somerville of Lariston, as the Mester Stoorworm had been, by thrusting a burning peat on a long lance down its throat.

The Highland worms were generally closely connected with the sea or rivers. In J. F. CAMPBELL's 'The Sea-Maiden', a three-headed sea monster comes up to claim the princess as its prey, as the Mester Stoorworm claimed Gemdelovely.

There are a few Highland water creatures which might qualify as worms. J. G. CAMPBELL mentions the Big Beast of Lochave (Beathach mòr Loch Odha), but not very explicitly, only saying that it had twelve legs and was to be heard in winter breaking the ice. He adds that some say it was like a horse, others like a large eel. The notorious Loch Ness Monster is usually described as having a serpent-like head and bumps which appear above the water as it moves. Among the monsters described by J. G. Campbell in *Superstitions of the Highlands and Islands of Scotland* (p. 220) is the Sea Serpent (Cirein Cròin). He says of it:

> This was the largest animal in the world, as may be inferred from a popular Caithness rhyme:

'Seven herring are a salmon's fill,
Seven salmon are a seal's fill,
Seven seals are a whale's fill,
And seven whales the fill of a Cirein Cròin.'

To this is sometimes added, 'seven Cirein Cròin are the fill of the big devil himself.' This immense sea-animal is also called *Mial mhòr a chuain*, the great beast of the ocean, *cuartag mhòr a chuain*, the great whirlpool of the ocean, and *uile-bhéisd a chuain*, the monster of the ocean. It was originally a whirlpool, or the sea-snake of the Edda, that encircled the whole world.

There is a curious shortage of dragons or worms in the Irish fairy-tales or heroic legends. The main adversaries are GIANTS, of which there are a great number, and supernatural HAGS. Patrick Kennedy, however, in *Legendary Fictions of the Irish Celts* (p. 11), says that there are a number of traditions of conflicts with worms or serpents:

We have more than one large pool deriving its name from having been infested by a worm or a serpent in the days of the heroes. Fion M'Cumhaill killed several of these. A Munster champion slew a terrible specimen in the Duffrey (Co. Wexford), and the pool in which it sweltered is yet called Loch-na-Piastha.

It sounds as if these creatures might be something like the Welsh AFANC.
[Motifs: B11.11; B91]

Wright, Thomas (1810–77). One of the antiquarian folklorists, a successor to AUBREY and Glanville. He edited Walter Map and Thomas of Newbury, the *Gesta Romanorum*, and a collection of chapbook stories, among which is that of FRIAR RUSH. In *Essays on Subjects connected with Literature, Popular Superstitions, and History of England in the Middle Ages* (1846) he writes on FAIRIES and demonology, on legends of heroes and outlaws and many popular traditions and superstitions. He was a contemporary and friend of Crofton CROKER and J. O. HALLIWELL. He was secretary of both the Percy and the Camden Society, but died the year before the Folk-Lore Society was founded.

Wryneck. A malignant spirit of Lancashire and Yorkshire who chiefly survives in proverbial usage. He was evidently thought to be even worse than the Devil, for, according to William Henderson in *Folk-Lore of the Northern Counties* (p. 254), of a very unpopular character it used to be said, 'He caps Wryneck, and Wryneck caps the Dule.'

Wulver, the. A formidable-looking but harmless and even benevolent creature described by Jessie Saxby in *Shetland Traditional Lore* (Chapter 9):

The Wulver was a creature like a man with a wolf's head. He had short brown hair all over him. His home was a cave dug out of the side of a steep knowe, half-way up a hill. He didn't molest folk if folk didn't molest him. He was fond of fishing, and had a small rock in the deep water which is known to this day as the 'Wulver's Stane.' There he would sit fishing sillaks and piltaks for hour after hour. He was reported to have frequently left a few fish on the window-sill of some poor body.

[Motif: F420.5.1.1]

Y Fuch Laethwen Le Frith (*er viwch lighthwen levrith*). See DUN COW OF KIRKHAM.

Yallery Brown. An example of one of the evil FAIRIES, whom it is dangerous even to befriend. He undoubtedly belongs to the UNSEELIE COURT. His story is told in Mrs Balfour's article on 'Legends of the Cars', and he must have been one of the YARTHKINS or STRANGERS of the Fen Country. One night a young man called Tom Tiver, as he was going home from work, heard a most distressful crying, like an abandoned child, and made out at last that it came from under a great flat stone, half-buried in the grass, called 'The Strangers' Stone'. He managed to lift it up, and he saw underneath a little thing, the size of a year-old child, all wrinkled, and tangled up in its own shining GOLDEN HAIR and beard. It thanked him kindly enough for freeing it, and asked him

what he would like for a gift, a fine wife or a pot of gold. Tom said he
didn't care much for either, but the work of the farm was too hard for
him and he'd thank the little man for help with his work. 'Now mind
you, never thank me,' said the little thing with an ugly look. 'I'll do the
work for you and welcome, but if you give me a word of thanks you'll
never get a hand's turn more from me. If you want me just call, "Yallery
Brown, from out of the mools come to help me", and I'll be there.' And
with that he picked a dandelion clock, blew it into Tom's eyes, and
was gone.

In the morning Tom found all his work done, and he had no need to
do a single stroke. At first he thought he was in Paradise, but after a
while things did not go so well, for if his work was done all the other men's
work was undone and destroyed, and his fellow workmen began to blame
him for it. He thought he would do the work himself, and not be beholden
to Yallery Brown, but not a hand's turn could he do, and at last, when
the men had complained of him and the master had given him the sack,
he called out, 'Yallery Brown, from out of the mools come to me!'
Yallery Brown was there on the instant and Tom said to him, 'It's an ill
you've done to me and no good. I'll thank you to go away and leave me
to work for myself.' At that Yallery Brown burst out laughing, and piped
out: 'You've thanked me you fool! You've thanked me and I warned you
not. You'll get no more help from me; but if I can't help I'll hinder.'
And he burst out singing:

> 'Work as thou will
> Thou'lt never do well;
> Work as thou may'st
> Thou'lt never gain grist;
> For harm and mischance and Yallery Brown
> Thou'st let out thyself from under the stone.'

And ever after that nothing went well with poor Tom Tiver, and however
he worked he could never do good, and there was ill-fortune on whatever
he touched, and till the day of his death Yallery Brown never stopped
troubling him.

[Type: 331 (variant). Motifs: c46; f346; f348.5.2; f402; f451.5.2;
r181; r188]

Yarthkins. According to Mrs Balfour in her article 'Legends of the
Cars', this was one name for the fertility spirits of the Lincolnshire Fen
Country, who came from the earth and gave its increase for which they
expected tribute. When neglected they became dangerous. They were
also called TIDDY PEOPLE, or GREENCOATIES, and most often the
STRANGERS. The TIDDY MUN seems to have been a benevolent member
of the Yarthkins, and YALLERY BROWN a particularly malevolent one.

[Motifs: f422; v12.9]

Yeats, William Butler (1865–1939). He is chiefly remembered as a great poet, but he is also central to the renaissance of Irish folklore at the end of the 19th century, the close associate of Douglas HYDE, Lady WILDE and Lady Gregory. His *Irish Fairy and Folk Tales* (1888) is a standard work, and *The Celtic Twilight* (1893) made Irish traditions fashionable in England. He was himself a firm believer in FAIRIES, and he dabbled in various forms of spiritualism, but he also took part in practical matters, was an ardent nationalist and a promoter of the arts. And in spite of his mysticism and of the wistful music of his fairy poems –

Come away! O human child!
To the woods and waters wild,
With a fairy hand in hand,
For the world's more full of weeping than you can understand.

– in spite of these, Yeats is fully aware of the earthy and matter-of-fact quality of fairy tradition in the country. In the introduction to *Irish Fairy and Folk Tales* he says:

'Have you ever seen a fairy or such like?' I asked an old man in County Sligo. 'Amn't I annoyed with them,' was the answer.

Yell-Hounds, or Yeth-hounds. See WISH HOUNDS.

Young Tam Lin, or Tamlane. The subject of the ballad 'Young Tam Lin', of which there are many versions, both in the Border country and in Aberdeenshire. It is perhaps the most important of all the supernatural ballads because of the many fairy beliefs incorporated in it. The fullest version is No. 39A in Child's *The English and Scottish Popular Ballads.* At the beginning the king warns the maidens in his court not to go to Carterhaugh Wood, which is haunted by Young Tam Lin who exacts a pledge from every maiden who visits it, most likely her maidenhood. In spite of his warning his own daughter Janet goes to the well of Carterhaugh, summons Young Tam Lin by plucking a rose, and loses her maidenhood to him. The rest of the ballad is so vivid and so full of important detail that it would be a pity only to summarize it.

> Janet has kilted her green kirtle
>   A little aboon her knee,
> And she has snooded her yellow hair
>   A little aboon her bree,
> And she is to her father's ha,
>   As fast as she can hie.
>
> Four and twenty ladies fair
>   Were playing at the ba,
> And out then cam the fair Janet,
>   Ance the flower amang them a'.
>
> Four and twenty ladies fair
>   Were playing at the chess,
> And out then cam the fair Janet,
>   As green as onie glass.
>
> Out then spak an auld grey knight,
>   Lay oer the castle wa,
> And says, Alas, fair Janet, for thee
>   But we'll be blamed a'.
>
> 'Haud your tongue, ye auld fac'd knight,
>   Some ill death may ye die!
> Father my bairn on whom I will,
>   I'll father nane on thee.'
>
> Out then spak her father dear,
>   And he spak meek and mild;
> 'And ever alas, sweet Janet,' he says,
>   'I think thou gaes wi child.'

'If that I gae wi child, father,
  Mysel maun bear the blame;
There's neer a laird about your ha
  Shall get the bairn's name.

'If my love were an earthly knight,
  As he's an elfin grey,
I wad na gie my ain true-love
  For nae lord that ye hae.

'The steed that my true-love rides on
  Is lighter than the wind;
Wi siller he is shod before,
  Wi burning gowd behind.'

Janet has kilted her green kirtle
  A little aboon her knee,
And she has snooded her yellow hair
  A little aboon her bree,
And she's awa to Carterhaugh
  As fast as she can hie.

When she cam to Carterhaugh,
  Tam Lin was at the well,
And there she fand his steed standing,
  But away was himsel.

She had na pu'd a double rose,
  A rose but only twa,
Till up then started young Tam Lin,
  Says Lady, thou pu's nae mae.

Why pu's thou the rose, Janet,
  Amang the groves sae green,
And a' to kill the bonnie babe
  That we gat us between?

'O tell me, tell me, Tam Lin,' she says,
  'For's sake that died on tree,
If eer ye was in holy chapel,
  Or christendom did see?'

'Roxbrugh he was my grandfather,
  Took me with him to bide,
And ance it fell upon a day
  That wae did me betide.

'And ance it fell upon a day,
   A cauld day and a snell,
When we were frae the hunting come
   That frae my horse I fell;
The Queen o Fairies she caught me,
   In yon green hill to dwell.

'And pleasant is the fairy land,
   But, an eerie tale to tell,
Ay at the end of seven years
   We pay a tiend to hell;
I am sae fair and fu o flesh,
   I'm feard it be myself.

'But the night is Halloween, lady,
   The morn is Hallowday;
Then win me, win me, an ye will,
   For weel I wat ye may.

'Just at the mirk and midnight hour
   The fairy folk will ride,
And they that wad their true-love win,
   At Miles Cross they maun bide.'

'But how shall I thee ken, Tam Lin,
   Or how my true-love know,
Amang sae mony unco knights
   The like I never saw?'

'O first let pass the black, lady,
   And syne let pass the brown,
But quickly run to the milk-white steed,
   Pu ye his rider down.

'For I'll ride on the milk-white steed,
   And ay nearest the town;
Because I was an earthly knight
   They gie me that renown.

'My right hand will be glovd, lady,
   My left hand will be bare,
Cockt up shall my bonnet be,
   And kaimd down shall my hair,
And thae's the takens I gie thee,
   Nae doubt I will be there.

'They'll turn me in your arms, lady,
   Into an esk and adder;
But hold me fast, and fear me not,
   I am your bairn's father.

'They'll turn me to a bear sae grim,
    And then a lion bold;
But hold me fast, and fear me not,
    As ye shall love your child.

'Again they'll turn me in your arms
    To a red het gaud of airn;
But hold me fast, and fear me not,
    I'll do to you nae harm.

'And last they'll turn me in your arms
    Into the burning gleed;
Then throw me into well water,
    O throw me in wi speed.

'And then I'll be your ain true-love,
    I'll turn a naked knight;
Then cover me wi your green mantle,
    And cover me out o sight.'

Gloomy, gloomy was the night,
    And eerie was the way,
As fair Jenny in her green mantle
    To Miles Cross she did gae.

About the middle o the night
    She heard the bridles ring;
This lady was as glad at that
    As any earthly thing.

First she let the black pass by,
    And syne she let the brown;
But quickly she ran to the milk-white steed,
    And pu'd the rider down.

Sae weel she minded whae he did say,
    And young Tam Lin did win;
Syne coverd him wi her green mantle,
    As blythe's a bird in spring.

Out then spak the Queen o Fairies,
    Out of a bush o broom:
'Them that has gotten young Tam Lin
    Has gotten a stately groom.'

Out then spak the Queen o Fairies,
    And an angry woman was she:
'Shame betide her ill-far'd face,
    And an ill death may she die,
For she's taen awa the bonniest knight
    In a' my companie.

'But had I kend, Tam Lin,' she says,
 'What now this night I see,
I wad hae taen out thy twa grey een,
 And put in twa een o tree.'

Here we have the summoning of a spirit by breaking the branch of a tree
sacred to him, the FAIRY RADE with its jingling bells at Hallowe'en, the
time most sacred to the fairies, the fairy KNOWE, the TEIND to Hell –
so characteristic of Scottish Fairyland – the rescue from Fairyland by
holding fast, the SHAPE-SHIFTING of the captive, and the essential ill-
will of the Fairy Queen.

Tamlin, Tamlane, Tam-a-Lin were names often given to a fairy,
sometimes a page, sometimes a knight and sometimes a grotesquely
comic character, as in the nursery rhyme:

Tam-a-Lin and his wife, and his wife's mother,
They went over a bridge all three together;
The bridge was broken, and they fell in;
'The devil go with all!' says Tam-a-Lin.

[Type: 425 (variant). Motifs: C515, D610; D757; F301.1.1.2; F320;
R112.3]

𝕭𝖔𝖔𝖐-𝖑𝖎𝖘𝖙

A Selected List of Books Quoted, Cited and Consulted

AARNE, ANTTI, *The Types of the Folktale*, translated and enlarged by Stith Thompson, second revision, Folklore Fellows Communications No. 184, Helsinki, 1961.

ALLIES, JABEZ, *On the Ancient British, Roman and Saxon Antiquities and Folk-Lore of Worcestershire*, Marshall, London, 1840.

ALLINGHAM, WILLIAM, *Rhymes for the Young Folk*, Cassell, London, [1887].

AUBREY, JOHN, *Hypomnemata Antiquaria*, Bodleian MS. Aubrey III.

—, *Miscellanies*, 5th edition, Reeves & Turner, London, 1890.

—, *Natural History and Antiquities of the County of Surrey*, 5 vols., Curll, London, 1718–19.

—, *Remaines of Gentilisme and Judaisme*, edited by James Britten, first full edition, Folk-Lore Society, London, 1881.

BALFOUR, Mrs, 'Legends of the Cars', *Folk-Lore*, II, 1891.

—: *see also* Folklore Society County Publications, vol. IV.

BARRETT, W. H., *Tales from the Fens*, Routledge & Kegan Paul, London, 1963.

BEAUMONT, JOHN, *An Historical, Physiological and Theological Treatise of Spirits*, D. Browne, London, 1705.

BENWELL, GWEN, and WAUGH, ARTHUR, *Sea Enchantress*, Hutchinson, London, 1961.

BETT, HENRY, *English Myths and Traditions*, Batsford, London, 1952.

BILLSON, C. J.: *see* Folklore Society County Publications, vol. I.

BLACK, G. F.: *see* Folklore Society County Publications, vol. III.

BOTTRELL, WILLIAM, *Traditions and Hearthside Stories of West Cornwall*, Three Series, Bottrell, Penzance, 1870–90. (The title of the third volume in the series was *Stories and Folk-Lore of West Cornwall*.)

BOVET, RICHARD, *Pandaemonium, or The Devil's Cloyster*, J. Walthoe, London, 1684.

BOWKER, JAMES, *Goblin Tales of Lancashire*, Swan Sonnenschein, London, 1883.

BRANSTON, BRIAN, *The Lost Gods of England*, Thames & Hudson, London, 1957.

BRAY, Mrs A. E., *The Borders of the Tamar and the Tavy. Their Natural History, Manners, Customs, Superstitions, etc.*, new edition, 2 vols., John Murray, London, 1879.

BRIGGS, K. M., *The Fairies in Tradition and Literature*, Routledge & Kegan Paul, London, 1967.

—, *The Personnel of Fairyland*, Alden Press, Oxford, 1969.

—: *A Dictionary of British Folk Tales in the Eugern Language*, 4 vols., Routledge & Kegan Paul, London, 1970–71.

—, and TONGUE, R. L., *Folktales of England* (Folktales of the World series), Routledge & Kegan Paul, London, 1965.

BROOME, DORA, *Fairy Tales from the Isle of Man*, Penguin Books, Harmondsworth, 1951.

BROWN, THEO, 'The Black Dog', *Folklore*, 69, September 1958.

BROWNE, WILLIAM, *The Poems of William Browne of Tavistock*, edited by Gordon Goodwin, 2 vols., Lawrence & Bullen (The Muses' Library), London, 1894.

BUCHAN, PETER, *Ancient Scottish Tales*, Norwood Editions, Darby, Pa., 1973.

BURNE, C. S., and JACKSON, G. F., *Shropshire Folk-Lore*, Trübner & Co., London, 1883.

BURTON, ROBERT, *The Anatomy of Melancholy*, 5th edition, corrected and augmented by the author, Henry Cripps, Oxford, 1638.

CAMPBELL, J. F., *Popular Tales of the West Highlands*, 4 vols., new edition, Alexander Gardner, Paisley and London, 1890–93.

CAMPBELL, J. G., *Superstitions of the Highlands and Islands of Scotland*, J. MacLehose, Glasgow, 1900.

—, *Witchcraft and Second Sight in the Highlands and Islands of Scotland*, MacLehose, Glasgow, 1902.

CARMICHAEL, ALEXANDER, *Carmina Gadelica*, 4 vols., Oliver & Boyd, Edinburgh, 1928–41.

CARROLL, LEWIS, *Silvie and Bruno*, Macmillan, London, 1889.

—, *Silvie and Bruno Concluded*, Macmillan, London, 1893.

CHAMBERS, ROBERT, *Popular Rhymes of Scotland*, W. & R. Chambers, Edinburgh, 1870.

CHILD, F. J. (ed.), *The English and Scottish Popular Ballads*, Little, Brown; Shepard Clark & Brown, Boston, 1857–8; definitive edition: 5 vols., The Folklore Press in association with the Pagent Book Co., New York, 1957.

CHRÉTIEN DE TROYES, *Arthurian Romances*, edited by W. W. Comfort, Dent, London, 1914.

CLODD, EDWARD, *Tom Tit Tot, an Essay on Savage Philosophy*, Duckworth, London, 1898.

CORBET, RICHARD, *The Poems of Richard Corbet*, edited by Octavius Gilchrist, Longman, Hurst, Rees & Orme, London, 1807.

COURTNEY, MARGARET, *Cornish Feasts and Folk-lore*, Beare & Son, Penzance, 1890.

COXHEAD, J. R. W., *Devon Traditions and Fairy Tales*, Raleigh Press, Exmouth, 1959.

CROKER, T. CROFTON, *Fairy Legends and Traditions of the South of Ireland*, 3 vols., John Murray, London, 1825–8.

CROMEK, R. H., *Remains of Nithsdale and Galloway Song*, Cadell & Davies, London, 1810.

CROSSING, WILLIAM, *Tales of the Dartmoor Pixies: Glimpses of Elfin Haunts and Antics*, W. H. Hood, London, 1890.

CUNNINGHAM, ALLAN, *The Lives of the Most Eminent British Painters*, 1876.

DE LA MARE, WALTER, *Broomsticks*, Constable, London, 1925.

Denham Tracts, The, edited by James Hardy, 2 vols., Folk-Lore Society, London, 1892.

DORSON, RICHARD M., *The British Folklorists*, Routledge & Kegan Paul, London, 1968.

DOUGLAS, SIR GEORGE, *Scottish Fairy and Folk-Tales*, Walter Scott, London, [1893].

DRAYTON, MICHAEL, *Works*, edited by J. W. Hebel, 5 vols., Shakespeare Head, London, 1931.

EDMONSTON, ARTHUR, *A View of the Ancient and Present State of the Zetland Islands*, 2 vols., Edinburgh, 1809.

EDMONSTON, BIOT, and SAXBY, JESSIE M. E., *The Home of a Naturalist*, Nesbit, London, 1888.

EDWARDS, GILLIAN, *Hobgoblin and Sweet Puck*, Bles, London, 1974.

FANSHAWE, LADY, *Memoirs of Lady Fanshawe*, John Lane, London, 1905.

Folk-Lore Record, The, 5 vols., printed for the Folk-Lore Society by Nichols & Sons, London, 1878–82.

FOLKLORE SOCIETY COUNTY PUBLICATIONS:

County Folk-Lore, vol. I: *Gloucestershire*, edited, with suggestions for the collection of the Folk-Lore of the County, by E. S. Hartland, 1892; *Suffolk*, collected and edited by Lady E. C. Gurdon, 1893; *Leicestershire and Rutland*, collected and edited by C. J. Billson, 1895.

County Folk-Lore, vol. II: *North Riding of Yorkshire, York and the Ainsty*, collected and edited by Mrs Gutch, 1899.

County Folk-Lore, vol. III: *Orkney and Shetland Islands*, collected by G. F. Black, and edited by Northcote W. Thomas, 1901.

County Folk-Lore, vol. IV: *Northumberland*, collected by M. C. Balfour, edited by Northcote W. Thomas, 1903.

County Folk-Lore, vol. V: *Lincolnshire*, collected by Mrs Gutch and Mabel Peacock, 1908.

County Folk-Lore, vol. VI: *Concerning the East Riding of Yorkshire*, collected and edited by Mrs Gutch, 1911.

County Folk-Lore, vol. VII: *Fife, with Some Notes on Clackmannan and Kinross-Shires*, collected by John Ewart Simpkins, 1912.

County Folklore, vol. VIII: *Somerset Folklore* by R. L. Tongue, edited by K. M. Briggs, 1965.

GEOFFREY OF MONMOUTH, *Histories of the Kings of Britain*, edited by W. W. Comfort, Dent, London, 1914.

GERVASE OF TILBURY, *Otia Imperialia*, III, Hanover, 1856.

GIBBINGS, W. W., *Folk-Lore and Legends, Scotland*, London, 1889.

GILL, WALTER, *A Manx Scrapbook*, Arrowsmith, London, 1929.

—, *A Second Manx Scrapbook*, Arrowsmith, London, 1932.

GIRALDUS CAMBRENSIS, *The Historical Works*, edited by Thomas Wright, Bohn Library, London, 1863.

GLANVILL, JOSEPH, *Saducismus Triumphatus*, London, 1681.

GOMME, ALICE, *A Dictionary of British Folk-Lore*, Part I: *Traditional Games*, 2 vols., Nutt, London, 1898.

GOULD, S. BARING, *Lives of the Saints*, 16 vols., Nimmo, London, 1897–8.

GRAHAM, PATRICK, *Sketches Descriptive of Picturesque Scenery on the Southern Confines of Perthshire*, Edinburgh, 1806.

GREGORY, LADY, *Gods and Fighting Men*, with a Preface by W. B. Yeats, John Murray, London, 1910.

GRICE, F., *Folk Tales of the North Country*, Nelson, London and Edinburgh, 1944.

GUEST, CHARLOTTE (trans. and ed.), *The Mabinogion*, London, 1838. (See also *Mabinogion*.)

GURDON, Lady E. C.: *see* Folklore Society County Publications, vol. I.

GUTCH, Mrs: *see* Folklore Society County Publications, vols. II, V and VI.

HALLIWELL-PHILLIPPS, J. O., *Illustrations of the Fairy Mythology of the Midsummer Night's Dream*, Shakespeare Society, London, 1845.

HARLAND, J. A., and WILKINSON, T. T., *Legends and Traditions of Lancashire*, Routledge, London, 1873.

HARRISON, W., *A Mona Miscellany*, Manx Society, Douglas, 1869.

HARTLAND, E. S., *English Fairy and Folk Tales*, Walter Scott, London, [1893].

—, *The Science of Fairy Tales, an Inquiry into Fairy Mythology*, Walter Scott, London, 1891.

—: *see also* Folklore Society County Publications, vol. I.

HAZLITT, W. CAREW, *Fairy Tales, Legends and Romances Illustrating Shakespeare*, F. & W. Kerslake, London, 1875.

HENDERSON, GEORGE, *Survivals in Belief Among the Celts*, MacLehose, Glasgow, 1911.

HENDERSON, WILLIAM, *Folk-Lore of the Northern Counties*, Folk-Lore Society, London, 1879.

HERRICK, ROBERT, *Poems*, edited by R. W. Moorman, Oxford University Press, 1925.

HESLOP, R. O., *Northumberland Words*, English Dialect Society, Nos. 66, 68, and 71, London, 1892–4.

HEYWOOD, THOMAS, *The Hierarchie of the Blessed Angels*, Adam Islip, London, 1635.

HOGG, JAMES, *Selected Poems*, Oliver & Boyd, Edinburgh, 1940.

HULL, ELEANOR, *The Cuchullin Saga in Irish Literature*, Nutt, London, 1898.

—, *Folklore of the British Isles*, Methuen, London, 1928.

HUNT, ROBERT, *Popular Romances of the West of England*, 2 vols., Hotten, London, 1865; reprint of the 3rd edition, Chatto & Windus, London, 1923.

HUON OF BORDEAUX, *The Boke of Duke Huon of Bordeuxe done into English by Sir John Bourchier, Lord Berners*, Early English Text Society, London, 1883–7.

HYDE, DOUGLAS, *Beside the Fire*, Nutt, London, 1890.

JACOBS, JOSEPH, *English Fairy Tales*, Nutt, London, 1890.

—, *More English Fairy Tales*, Nutt, London, 1894.

JONSON, BEN, *Ben Jonson*, edited by C. Herford and P. Simpson, 11 vols., Oxford University Press, 1925–52.

JOYCE, P. W., *Old Celtic Romances*, 2nd edition, Nutt, London, 1894.

KEIGHTLEY, THOMAS, *The Fairy Mythology, Illustrative of the Romance and Superstition of Various Countries*, new edition, Bohn Library, London, 1850.

KENNEDY, PATRICK, *Legendary Fictions of the Irish Celts*, Macmillan, London, 1866.

KIPLING, RUDYARD, *Puck of Pook's Hill*, Doubleday, Page & Co., New York, 1906.

—, *Rewards and Fairies*, Macmillan, London, 1914.

KIRK, ROBERT, *The Secret Commonwealth of Elves, Fauns, and Fairies*, Mackay, Stirling, 1933.

KITTREDGE, G. L., 'Friar's Lantern', publications of the Modern Language Association of America, vol. XV, pp. 415–41.

KNOX, JAMES, *The Topography of the Basin of the Tay*, Anderson & Hunter, Edinburgh, 1831.

LEATHER, E. M., *The Folk-Lore of Herefordshire*, Sidgwick & Jackson, London, 1912.

Mabinogion, The, translated from the *White Book of Rhydderch* and the *Red Book of Hergest* by Gwyn Jones and Thomas Jones, Dent, London, 1948. (See also Guest, Charlotte.)

MACDOUGALL, J., and CALDER, G., *Folk Tales and Fairy Lore*, Grant, London, 1910.

MCKAY, JOHN G., *More West Highland Tales*, 2 vols., Oliver & Boyd, Edinburgh, 1940 and 1960.

MACKENZIE, DONALD A., *Scottish Folk Lore and Folk Life*, Blackie, London, 1935.

MACKENZIE, OSGOOD, *A Hundred Years in the Highlands*, Bles, London, 1949.

MAC MANUS, D. A., *The Middle Kingdom*, Max Parrish, London, 1959.

MCPHERSON, J. M., *Primitive Beliefs in the North-East of Scotland*, Longmans, London, 1929.

MAC RITCHIE, DAVID, *The Testimony of Tradition*, Kegan Paul, London, 1890.

MALORY, SIR THOMAS, *Works*, edited by E. Vinaver, 3 vols., Oxford University Press, 1947.

MAP, WALTER, *De Nugis Curialium*, Englished by Frederick Tupper and Marbury Bladen Ogle, Chatto & Windus, London, 1924.

MARIE DE FRANCE, *Poésies de Marie de France*, edited by B. de Roquefort, Paris, 1820.

MEYER, KUNO, and NUTT, ALFRED, *The Voyage of Bran Son of Febal* (Grimm Library No. 4), 2 vols., Nutt, London, 1895–7.

MILLER, HUGH, *The Old Red Sandstone*, Edinburgh, 1841.

MILTON, J., *The Poetical Works of John Milton*, edited by John Beeching, Oxford University Press, 1913.

MORRISON, SOPHIA, *Manx Fairy Tales*, Nutt, London, 1911.

NASHE, THOMAS, *The Works of Thomas Nashe*, 5 vols., edited by R. B. McKerrow, Bullen, London, 1904–10.

NENNIUS (9th century), British Museum MS. Harleian 3859 (11th century).

NICHOLSON, JOHN, *The Folk Speech of East Yorkshire*, London, 1889.

O'CURRY, EUGENE, *Lectures on the Manuscript Materials of Ancient Irish History*, Hinch & Traynor, London, 1878.

O'GRADY, STANDISH H., *Silva Gadelica*, Williams & Norgate, London, 1892.

Old Cornwall, Vol. II, 1931–6.

OPIE, IONA and PETER, *The Oxford Dictionary of Nursery Rhymes*, Oxford University Press, 1951.

—, *The Classic Fairy Tales*, Oxford University Press, 1974.

Ó SÚILLEABHÁIN, SEÁN, *Folktales of Ireland* (Folktales of the World series), Routledge & Kegan Paul, London, 1966.

PATON, LUCY ALLEN, *Sir Lancelot of the Lake*, Routledge, London, 1929.

PEACOCK, MABEL: *see* Folklore Society County Publications, vol. v.

RALPH OF COGGESHALL, Rolls Series 66, 1857.

RHYS, JOHN, *Celtic Folk-Lore, Welsh and Manx*, 2 vols., Oxford University Press, 1901.

ROBERTSON, T. A., and GRAHAM, JOHN J. (eds.), *Shetland Folk Book*, vol. 3, Shetland Times Ltd, Lerwick, 1957.

Robin Goodfellow his Mad Prankes and Merry Jests, London, 1628.

SANDERSON, STEWART, 'A Prospect of Fairyland', *Folklore*, 79, 1964.

SAXBY, JESSIE, M. E., *Shetland Traditional Lore*, Norwood Editions reprint, 1974.

SCOT, REGINALD, *The Discoverie of Witchcraft*, Brome, London, 1584; 'Discourse on Devils and Spirits' (anon.) inserted in 1665 edition.

SCOTT, SIR WALTER, *Minstrelsy of the Scottish Border*, with notes and introduction by Sir Walter Scott, revised and edited by T. F. Henderson, 4 vols., Oliver & Boyd, Edinburgh, 1932.

—, *Letters on Demonology and Witchcraft*, John Murray (Murray's Family Library), London, 1830.

—, *The Globe Edition of the Poetical Works*, edited by F. T. Palgrave, Macmillan, London, 1866.

SHAKESPEARE, WILLIAM, *The Works of William Shakespeare*, 3 vols., Oxford University Press, 1915.

SIKES, WIRT, *British Goblins*, Sampson Low, London, 1880.

SIMPKINS, J. E.: *see* Folklore Society County Publications, vol. VII.

SIMPSON, E. B., *Folk Lore in Lowland Scotland*, Dent, London, 1908.

Sir Gawayne and the Green Knight, edited by I. Gollancz, Early English Text Society, London, 1920.

SKENE, W. F., *The Four Ancient Books of Wales*, Edmonston & Douglas, Edinburgh, 1868.

SPENCE, JOHN, *Shetland Folklore*, Johnson & Greig, Lerwick, 1899.

SPENCE, LEWIS, *British Fairy Origins*, Watts, London, 1946.

—, *The Fairy Traditions in Britain*, Rider, London, 1948.

SPOONER, BARBARA C., *John Tregagle of Trevorder: Man and Ghost*, A. W. Jordan, Truro, 1935.

STEPHENS, JAMES, *In the Land of Youth*, Macmillan, London, 1924.

—, *Irish Fairy Tales*, Macmillan, London, 1920.

STERNBERG, W., *The Dialect and Folk-Lore of Northamptonshire*, London, 1851.

STEWART, W. GRANT, *Popular Superstitions of the Highlanders of Scotland*, Archibald Constable, London, 1823; Ward Lock reprint, London, 1970.

THOMAS, NORTHCOTE W.: *see* Folklore Society County Publications, vols. III and IV.

THOMS, W. J., *Early English Prose Romances*, Routledge (Routledge's Library of Early Novelists), 1907.

TOLKIEN, J. R., *The Hobbit*, Allen & Unwin, London, 1937.

—, *The Lord of the Rings*, 1-vol. edition, Allen & Unwin, London, 1968.

TONGUE, R. L., *Forgotten Folk-Tales of the English Counties*, Routledge & Kegan Paul, London, 1970.

—: *see also* Folklore Society County Publications, vol. VIII.

TOPSELL, EDWARD, *The Historie of Foure-Footed Beastes*, William Taggard, London, 1607.

TREHARNE, R. F., *The Glastonbury Legends*, Sphere Books, London, 1971.

Waifs and Strays of Celtic Tradition, vols. I–V, Argyllshire Series, Nutt, London, 1889.

WAINWRIGHT, F. T. (ed.), *The Problem of the Picts*, Nelson, London, 1955.

WALDRON, GEORGE, *A Description of the Isle of Man*, London, 1731.

WENTZ, W. Y. EVANS, *The Fairy-Faith in Celtic Countries*, Oxford University Press, 1911.

WESTON, JESSIE L., *The Legend of Sir Lancelot du Lac*, Nutt, London, 1901.

WILDE, Lady, *Ancient Legends, Mystic Charms and Superstitions of Ireland*, 2 vols., Ward & Downey, London, 1887.

WILKIE MS.: a collection of Border customs, superstitions and etc. made by a medical student at the desire of Sir Walter Scott.

WILLIAM OF MALMESBURY, *Chronicle of the Kings of England*, Bohn Library, London, 1841.

WILLIAM OF NEWBRIDGE, *Guilielmi Neubrigensis Historia sive Chronica Rerum Anglicarum*, Oxon, 1719.

WOOD-MARTIN, W. G., *Traces of the Elder Faiths of Ireland*, 2 vols., Longmans, London, 1902.

WRIGHT, E. M., *Rustic Speech and Folk-Lore*, Oxford University Press, 1913.

WRIGHT, THOMAS, *Essays on Subjects Connected with the Literature, Popular Superstitions and History of England in the Middle Ages*, 2 vols., J. R. Smith, London, 1846.

YEATS, W. B., *The Celtic Twilight: Men and Women, Ghouls and Faeries*, Lawrence & Bullen, London, 1893.

—, *Irish Fairy and Folk-Tales*, Walter Scott, London, [1893].

Index of Types and Motifs

A. Index of Types

Type 300: The dragon-slayer. ASSIPATTLE; LAMBTON WORM.

Type 311: Rescue by the sister. PEERIFOOL.

Type 313: The girl as helper in the hero's flight. GREEN SLEEVES; NICHT NOUGHT NOTHING.

Type 331 (variant): The spirit in the bottle. YALLERY BROWN.

Type 400 (variant): The man in quest for his lost wife. WILD EDRIC.

Type 425 (variant): Search for lost husband. YOUNG TAM LIN; GREEN SLEEVES.

Type 500: The name of the helper. FOUL-WEATHER; PEERIFOOL; SECRET NAMES OF THE FAIRIES; SILI FFRIT AND SILI-GO-DWT; TERRYTOP; TOM TIT TOT; WHUPPITY STOORIE.

Type 501: The three old women helpers. HABETROT.

Type 503 III: The companion punished. MISER ON THE FAIRY GUMP.

Type 507C: The serpent maiden. LAMIA.

Type 673: The white serpent's flesh. WIZARDS.

Type 700: Tom Thumb. TOM THUMB.

Type 766: The sleeping warriors. SLEEPING WARRIORS; LEGEND OF MULLAGHMAST.

Type 766 (variant): The seven sleepers. BRAN SON OF FEBAL; KING HERLA; OISIN.

Type 1030: The crop division. BOGIES.

Type 1090: Mowing contest. BOGIES.

Type 1137: The ogre blinded. AINSEL; MEG MOLOCH.

Type 1187: Meleager. GREEN MIST.

Type 1415 (distant variant): Lucky Hans. HEDLEY KOW.

Type ML.4071* (KMB): Malevolent mermaid. MERMAIDS.

Type ML.4075: Visits to fairy dwellings. CHERRY OF ZENNOR; FAIRY DWELLING ON SELENA MOOR; FAIRY WIDOWER; VISITS TO FAIRYLAND.

Type ML.4077*: Caught in Fairyland. CAPTIVES IN FAIRYLAND.

Type ML.4080: The seal wife. LUTEY AND THE MERMAID; MERMAIDS; ROANE; SELKIES.

Type ML.4081*: The wounded seal. SELKIES.

Type ML.4083*: The mermaid and the selkie. SELKIES.

Type ML.5006*: The ride with the fairies. FAIRY LEVITATION.

Type ML.5020: Troll legends. GIANTS.

Type ML.5076*: Fairy grateful. VIRTUES ESTEEMED BY THE FAIRIES.

Type ML.5080: Food from the fairies. BROKEN PED.

Type ML.5081*: Fairies steal food. TACKSMAN OF AUCHRIACHAN.

Type ML.5085: The changeling. CHANGELINGS; FAIRY THEFTS.

Type ML.6010: The capture of a fairy. BROTHER MIKE; CAPTURED FAIRIES; COLEMAN GRAY; SKILLYWIDDEN.

Type ML.6035: Fairies assist a farmer in his work. BODACHAN SABHAILL; BROWNIE; PIXIES; TOM COCKLE.

Type ML.6045: Drinking-cup stolen from the fairies. FAIRY CUP; SPRIGGANS; THEFTS FROM THE FAIRIES.

Type ML.6060: The fairy bull. ELF-BULL; TARROO-USHTEY; WATER-HORSE AND THE WATER-BULL.

Type ML.7010: Revenge for being teased. BOGGART; BROWNIE; BWBACHOD; BWCA.

Type ML.7015: The new suit. BROONIE; BROWNIE.

Type ML.7020: Vain attempt to escape from the Nisse. BOGGART.

B. Index of Motifs

A106.2.1.1: Banished devil appears on earth only on day of dark moon. DEAD MOON.

A125.1: Goddess of war in shape of hag. BLACK ANNIS; HAGS.

A132.6.2: Goddess in form of bird. BADB; MACHA; NEMAN.

A132.7: Swine-god. MANANNAN SON OF LIR.

A141: God as craftsman. LUG.

A151.1.1: Home of gods inside hill. LUG.

A300: God of the underworld. ARAWN.

A421: Sea-god. MANANNAN SON OF LIR; SHONY.

A465.1.1: Goddess of poetry. LEANAN-SIDHE.

A485.1: Goddess of war. BADB; MACHA; MORRIGAN; NEMAN.

A511.1.3.1: Demigod son of king's unmarried sister by god. CUCHULLIN.

A511.2.3: Culture hero is hidden in order to escape enemies. FINN.

A511.3: Education of culture hero. FINN.

A523: Giant as culture hero. BRAN THE BLESSED; GIANTS.

A524.1.1: Culture hero has marvellous dogs. FINN.

A525: Good and bad culture heroes. BRAN THE BLESSED.

A526.1: Culture hero can be wounded. CUCHULLIN.

A526.5: Culture hero has seven pupils in each eye, seven toes on each foot, seven fingers on each hand. CUCHULLIN.

A526.6: Culture hero, when angry, subject to contortions. CUCHULLIN.

A526.8: Culture hero can turn knees and feet backwards. CUCHULLIN.

A527.2: Culture hero has knowledge-giving member. FINN.

A536.1: Culture hero defends Ireland against foreign foes. CUCHULLIN.

A560: Culture hero's departure. LEGEND OF MULLAGHMAST.

A571: Culture hero asleep in mountain. LEGEND OF MULLAGHMAST.

A753: Moon as a person. DEAD MOON.

A754.1.1: Moon falls into a pit, but is rescued by man. DEAD MOON.

A758: Theft of moon: stolen and brought to earth. DEAD MOON.

A963.5: Hills from stones cast by giants. GIANTS; JIMMY SQUARE-FOOT.

A977.1: Giant responsible for certain stones. GIANTS.

A1135: Origin of winter weather: CAILLAGH NY GROAMAGH; CAILLEACH BERA; CAILLEACH BHEUR.

A1459.3: Acquisition of sorcery. SHAPE-SHIFTING.

A1611.5.4.3: Origin of Tuatha De Danann regarded as an early tribe. TUATHA DE DANANN.

A1657.2: Origin of the Fir Bolg. FIRBOLGS.

A1659.1: Origin of Fomorians. FOMORIANS.

A1659.1.1: Fomorians descended from Ham or Cain. FOMORIANS.

A2468.3: Why dragon dies by means of fire. ASSIPATTLE; LINTON WORM.

A2766.1: Why elder bleeds when cut. FAIRY TREES.

B11.2.1.1: Dragon as modified serpent. LINTON WORM.

B11.2.1.3: Dragon as modified fish. LAMBTON WORM; MESTER STOORWORM.

B11.2.11.2: Breath of dragon kills men. LINTON WORM.

B11.2.12: Dragon of enormous size. ASSIPATTLE; LAMBTON WORM.

B11.10: Sacrifice of human being to dragon. ASSIPATTLE.

B11.11: Fight with dragon. ASSIPATTLE; LAMBTON WORM; MESTER STOORWORM; WORMS.

B11.12.4.1: Dragon fed with great quantities of milk to keep him pacified. LAMBTON WORM.

B17.2.1: Hostile sea-beasts. CABYLL-USHTEY.

B29.1: Lamia: Face of woman, body of serpent. LAMIA.

B53.0.1: Siren in mermaid form. BEN-VARREY.

B81: Mermaid. CEASG.

B81.2.2: Mermaids tear their mortal lovers to pieces. MERMAIDS.

B81.3.1: Mermaid entices people into water. MERMAIDS.

B81.7: Mermaid warns of bad weather. BEN-VARREY.

B81.13.2: Mermaid is washed up on beach. LUTEY AND THE MERMAID; OLD MAN OF CURY.

B81.13.4: Mermaid gives mortals gold from sea bottom. BEN-VARREY.

B81.13.11: Mermaid captured. SELKIES.

B81.13.13* (Baughman): Mermaid rewards man who puts her back under water. LUTEY AND THE MERMAID; OLD MAN OF CURY.

B82.6: Merman caught by fisherman (afterwards released). MEDIEVAL CHRONICLES; MERMEN.

B91: Mythical serpent. WORMS.

B184.1.1: Horse with magic speed. ASSIPATTLE.

B184.1.3: Magic horse from water world. AUGHISKY; EACH UISGE; GLASTYN; KELPIES; TANGIE.

B184.2.2.2: Magic cow (bull) from water world. CRODH MARA; DUN COW OF KIRKHAM; GLASGAVLEN; TARROO-USHTEY.

B217.1.1: Animal languages learned from eating serpent. WIZARDS.

B251.1.2: Animals speak together on Christmas Eve. APPLE-TREE MAN.

B451: Helpful birds. NICHT NOUGHT NOTHING.

B571.1: Animals help man overcome monster with external soul. SEPARABLE SOUL.

B651.8: Marriage to seal in human form. SEAL MAIDENS.

B652.1: Marriage to swan maiden. SWAN MAIDENS.

B871.1.6: Giant cat. BIG EARS.

B872: Giant birds. BOOBRIE.

C 0–980: Taboo. TABOO.

C30: Taboo: offending supernatural relative. AINE.

C31: Taboo: offending supernatural wife. AINE; FAIRY BRIDES; GWRAGED ANNWN; SIR LAUNFAL.

C31.1.2: Taboo: looking at supernatural wife on certain occasions. FAIRY BRIDES; MELUSINE.

C31.2: Taboo: mentioning origin of supernatural wife. FAIRY BRIDES; WILD EDRIC.

C31.5: Taboo: boasting of supernatural wife. FAIRY BRIDES; SIR LAUNFAL.

C31.8: Taboo: striking supernatural wife. FAIRY BRIDES.

C46: Taboo: offending fairy. YALLERY BROWN.

C51.4.3: Taboo: spying on secret help of fairies. VIRTUES ESTEEMED BY THE FAIRIES.

C94.1: Taboo: uncivil answer to supernatural being. VIRTUES ESTEEMED BY THE FAIRIES.

C211.1: Taboo: eating in Fairyland. FAIRY DWELLING ON SELENA MOOR; TRUE THOMAS.

C311.1.2: Looking at fairies. VIRTUES ESTEEMED BY THE FAIRIES.

C405: Silence preserved in Fairyland. TRUE THOMAS.

C432.1: Guessing name of supernatural creature gives power over it. FOUL-WEATHER; PEERIFOOL; POWER OVER FAIRIES; PUDDLE-FOOT; SECRET NAMES OF THE FAIRIES; SILI FFRIT AND SILI-GO-DWT; SPELLS TO OBTAIN POWER OVER FAIRIES; TERRYTOP; TOM TIT TOT; TRWTYN-TRATYN; WHUPPITY STOORIE.

C433: Taboo: uttering name of malevolent creature (Eumenides). EUPHEMISTIC NAMES FOR THE FAIRIES; GENTRY; GOOD NEIGHBOURS; GOOD PEOPLE; OLD PEOPLE; PEOPLE OF THE HILLS; SECRET NAMES OF THE FAIRIES; SEELIE COURT; STRANGERS; THEMSELVES; TYLWETH TEG; WEE FOLK.

C515: Taboo: plucking flowers. YOUNG TAM LIN.

C521: Taboo: dismounting from horse. KING HERLA; OISIN.

C614.1.0.2: Taboo: hunting in certain part of forest. BROWN MAN OF THE MUIRS.

D1385.2.5: Ash (quicken rowan) protects against spells and enchantments. FAIRY TREES; PROTECTION AGAINST FAIRIES; ROWAN.

D1410.4: Possession of mermaid's belt (comb) gives power over her. OLD MAN OF CURY.

D1500.1.20: Magic healing powder. TRAFFIC WITH THE FAIRIES.

D1521.1: Seven-league boots. GREEN SLEEVES.

D1711.5: Fairy as magician. SUPERNATURAL WIZARDS.

D1766.7: Magic results from uttering powerful name. SPELLS TO OBTAIN POWER OVER FAIRIES.

D1766.8: Magic results from fasting. KATE CRACKERNUTS.

D1810: Magic knowledge. SUPERNATURAL WIZARDS.

D1812.5.1.12.2: Bird-calls as evil omen. GRIM.

D1812.5.1.17: Spectre as evil omen. SKRIKER; WAFF.

D1825.7.1: Foresight of funeral procession. FAIRY FUNERALS; FEEORIN.

D1870: Magic hideousness. WIFE OF BATH'S TALE.

D1960.2: King asleep in mountain. SLEEPING WARRIORS.

D2004.2.1: Dog's licking produces forgetfulness. GREEN SLEEVES; NICHT NOUGHT NOTHING.

D2006.1.1: Forgotten fiancée reawakens husband's memory by detaining lovers by magic. GREEN SLEEVES.

D2031: Magic illusion. GLAMOUR; PISHOGUE; ST COLLEN AND THE FAIRY KING.

D2031.0.2: Fairies cause illusions. GLAMOUR.

D2066: Elf-shot. AMERICAN FAIRY IMMIGRANTS; DEPENDENCE OF FAIRIES UPON MORTALS; ELF-SHOT; FAIRY MORALITY.

D2122: Journey with magic speed. WIZARDS.

D2176.3: Evil spirit is exorcised. GREAT GIANT OF HENLLYS.

D2183: Magic spinning performed by supernatural helpers. FOULWEATHER; HABETROT; PEERIFOOL; TERRYTOP; TOM TIT TOT.

E251.3.3: Vampire sucks blood. BAOBHAN SITH.

E422.1.1: Headless revenant. COLUINN GUN CHEANN.

E423: Revenant in animal form. BRAG; PHOUKA; ROARING BULL OF BAGBURY; SHOCK.

E423(b) (Baughman): Spirit animal changes shape. BRAG; HEDLEY KOW.

E423.1.1: Revenant as dog. BLACK DOGS.

E423.1.1.1(b) (Baughman): Ghostly black dog. BLACK DOGS; TRASH.

E423.1.3.5(a) (Baughman): Spirit horse lets man ride, then shakes him off into mud. BRAG; SHAGFOAL; TATTERFOAL.

E443.0.1: Laying ghost causes great storm. ROARING BULL OF BAGBURY.

E443.2.4.1: Ghost laid by group of ministers. ROARING BULL OF BAGBURY.

E451.5: Ghost laid when treasure is unearthed. SILKY.

E461: Fight of revenant with living person. COLUINN GUN CHEANN.

E500: Phantom hosts. SEVEN WHISTLERS; WISH HOUNDS.

E501.1: Leader of the wild hunt. ODIN; WILD HUNT.

E501.1.7.1: King Herla as wild huntsman. KING HERLA.

E501.1.7.3: Wild Edric as leader of wild hunt. WILD EDRIC; WILD HUNT.

E501.13.1.4: Wild hunt heralded by ringing of bells. BELLS; WILD HUNT.

E501.13.4: Wild hunt heralded by baying of hounds. CWN ANNWN; WILD HUNT.

E502: The sleeping army. SLEEPING WARRIORS.

E710: External soul. SEPARABLE SOUL.

E711.1: Soul in egg. SEPARABLE SOUL.

E723.2: Death token (seeing own wraith). BODACH GLAS; FETCH; SWARTH.

E731.6: Soul in form of seal. ROANE.

E752.2: Soul carried off by devil. TANKERABOGUS.

E765.3.4: Girl lives until her cowslip is pulled. GREEN MIST.

F68: Ascent to upper world by magic. ETAIN.

F81.1: Orpheus. KING ORFEO.

F103.1 (Baughman): 'Green children' visit world of mortals; continue to live with them. GREEN CHILDREN.

F109: Visit to lower world. FIN BHEARA.

F111: Journey to earthly paradise. BRAN SON OF FEBAL.

F112: Journey to Island of Women. BRAN SON OF FEBAL.

F160.0.2: Fairy otherworld confused with land of the dead. FIN BHEARA; ST COLLEN AND THE FAIRY KING.

F167.12: King of otherworld. FIN BHEARA; GWYN AP NUDD; ST COLLEN AND THE FAIRY KING.

F172.1: No gloom, no envy, etc., in otherworld. FAIRY MORALITY; TIR NAN OG.

F184: Otherworld king. FIN BHEARA.

F200–399: Fairies (or elves). ELLYLLON; ELVES.

F200.1: Pixies. PISKIES.

F211: Fairyland under hollow knoll. KATE CRACKERNUTS; MISER ON THE FAIRY GUMP; SUBTERRANEANS.

F211.0.2.1: Tuatha De Danann, conquerors of Ireland, are overcome by invaders. TUATHA DE DANANN.

F211.3: Fairies live under the earth. FAIRY WIDOWER; FRAIRIES; SUBTERRANEANS.

F212: Fairyland under water. PLANT ANNWN.

F232.2: Fairies have breasts long enough to throw over shoulders. BEAN-NIGHE.

F233.1: Green fairy. GREEN CHILDREN.

F233.3: Red fairy. FIR DARRIG.

F233.5: Fairies have yellow (golden) hair. GOLDEN HAIR; TYLWETH TEG.

F234.0.2: Fairy as shape-shifter. BARGUEST; BRAG; HEDLEY KOW; PADFOOT; PHOUKA; PUCK; SHAPE-SHIFTING; SHEFRO; SKRIKER.

F234.1.4.1: Fairy in form of doe. THOMAS THE RHYMER.

F234.1.8: Fairy in form of horse. AUGHISKY; GRANT; KELPIES; LAZY LAURENCE; NOGGLE; SHAGFOAL; TATTERFOAL.

F234.1.9: Fairy in form of dog. BARGUEST; BLACK DOGS; HAIRY JACK; SKRIKER.

F234.1.16: Fairy in form of insect. AWD GOGGIE; GOOSEBERRY WIFE.

F234.2.2: Fairy in hideous form. LITTLE PEOPLE OF THE PASSAMA-QUODDY INDIANS; TOM DOCKIN.

F234.3: Fairy in form of object. HEDLEY KOW.

F235.1: Fairies invisible. SEEING FAIRIES; SKRIKER.

F235.3: Fairies visible to only one person. JEFFERIES, ANNE.

F235.4.1: Fairies made visible through use of ointment. CHANGELINGS; CHERRY OF ZENNOR; FAIRY OINTMENT; FAULTS CONDEMNED BY THE FAIRIES.

F235.4.1(a) (Baughman): Midwife to fairies uses ointment. FAIRY OINTMENT; FAULTS CONDEMNED BY THE FAIRIES; MIDWIFE TO THE FAIRIES.

F235.4.6: Fairies made visible when one carries four-leafed clover. FOUR-LEAFED CLOVER; SEEING FAIRIES.

F235.5.1: Fairies made visible by standing on another's foot. SEEING FAIRIES.

F235.5.2: Fairies made visible when person steps into fairy ring. SEEING FAIRIES.

F236.1.3: Fairies in white clothes. FAIRIES.

F236.1.6: Fairies in green clothes. FAIRIES ON THE EASTERN GREEN; GREENIES; GRIG; JEFFERIES, ANNE.

F236.3.2: Fairies with red caps. FAIRIES ON THE EASTERN GREEN; GREENIES; GRIG.

F236.6: Fairies wear gay clothes. TRUE THOMAS.

F239.4: Size of fairies. SIZE OF THE FAIRIES.

F239.4.1: Fairies are the same size as mortals. SIZE OF THE FAIRIES.

F239.4.2: Fairies are the size of small children. PECHS; SIZE OF THE FAIRIES.

F239.4.3: Fairy is tiny. BROTHER MIKE; DIMINUTIVE FAIRIES; ELIZABETHAN FAIRIES; HYTER SPRITES; I WEAT, YOU WEAT; JEFFERIES, ANNE; LITTLE PEOPLE OF THE PASSAMAQUODDY INDIANS; MICOL; MISER ON THE FAIRY GUMP; MURYANS; SIZE OF THE FAIRIES; SKILLYWIDDEN; SMALL PEOPLE OF CORNWALL.

F241: Fairies' animals. FAIRY DOGS.

F241.1: Fairies' horses. FAIRY HORSES OF THE TUATHA DE DANANN; GWRAGEDD ANNWN.

F241.1.0.1: Fairy cavalcade. FAIRY LEVITATION; FAIRY RADE; KING HERLA; KING ORFEO; SHEFRO; SPORTS OF THE FAIRIES; TROOPING FAIRIES; WILD EDRIC.

F241.1.1.1: Fairies ride white horses. FAIRY HORSES OF THE TUATHA DE DANANN.

F241.2: Fairies' cows. CRODH MARA; GWARTHEG Y LLYN; GWRAGEDD ANNWN.

F241.4: Goats follow fairies. TACKSMAN OF AUCHRIACHAN.

F241.6: Fairy dogs. BRAN AND SCEOLAN; CU SITH; FAIRY DOGS; FARVANN.

F242.2: Fairy boat. LITTLE PEOPLE OF THE PASSAMAQUODDY INDIANS.

F243: Fairies' food. FAIRY FOOD.

F243.1: Fairies' bread. FAIRY FOOD.

F246: Fairy tobacco pipes. LITTLE PEOPLE OF THE PASSAMAQUODDY INDIANS.

F251: Origin of fairies. ORIGIN OF FAIRIES.

F251.1: Fairies as descendants of early race of gods. ORIGIN OF FAIRIES; THEORIES OF FAIRY ORIGINS.

F251.2: Fairies as souls of the departed. ORIGIN OF FAIRIES.

F251.3: Unbaptized children as fairies. ORIGIN OF FAIRIES; SHORT HOGGERS OF WHITTINGHAME; SPUNKIES; TARANS.

F251.6: Fairies as fallen angels. ORIGIN OF FAIRIES.

F251.7: Fairies as demons. ORIGIN OF FAIRIES.

F251.11: Fairies are people not good enough for heaven but not bad enough for hell. ORIGIN OF FAIRIES.

F251.12: Fairies are druids. ORIGIN OF FAIRIES.

F252.1: Fairy king. FIN BHEARA; OBERON.

F252.2: Fairy queen. NICNEVIN; NUALA; OONAGH; TITANIA.

F252.4: Fairies banished from Fairyland. FENODOREE.

F254.1: Fairies have physical disabilities. BANSHEE; DEFECTS OF THE FAIRIES; HENKIES.

F257: Tribute taken from fairies by fiend at stated periods. TEIND.

F258.1: Fairies hold a fair. FAIRY MARKET.

F261: Fairies dance. SPORTS OF THE FAIRIES.

F261.1.1: Fairies dance in fairy rings. ELIZABETHAN FAIRIES.

F262: Fairies make music. FAIRY CRAFTS; SPORTS OF THE FAIRIES.

F262.2: Fairies teach bagpipe-playing. AMERICAN FAIRY IMMIGRANTS; FAIRY CRAFTS.

F262.3.4: Fairy music causes sleep. AILLEN MAC MIDHNA.

F262.3.6: Fairy music causes joy. MISER ON THE FAIRY GUMP.

F265.1: Fairies use bath house. BATHING FAIRIES.

F267: Fairies attend games. DEPENDENCE OF FAIRIES UPON MORTALS; HURLING; SPORTS OF THE FAIRIES.

F268.1: Burial service for Fairy Queen is held at night in Christian church. FAIRY FUNERALS.

F271.0.1: Fairies as craftsmen. FAIRY CRAFTS.

F271.2: Fairies as builders. LITTLE PEOPLE OF THE PASSAMAQUODDY INDIANS; PECHS.

'F271.4.2: Fairies skilful as weavers. FAIRY CRAFTS.

F271.4.3: Fairies spin. FAIRY CRAFTS; HABETROT; LOIREAG; TOM TIT TOT.

F271.7: Fairies churn. FAIRY CRAFTS.

F271.10: Fairies bake bread. BROKEN PED; FAIRY CRAFTS.

F282: Fairies travel through air. FAIRY LEVITATION; JEFFERIES, ANNE; SUBTERRANEANS.

F282.2: Formulas for fairies' travel through air. FAIRY LEVITATION; TRAFFIC WITH THE FAIRIES.

F282.4(a) (Baughman): Mortal travels with fairies: feasts with them in various spots. FAIRY LEVITATION.

F300: Marriage or liaison with fairy. CAPTIVES IN FAIRYLAND; EILIAN OF GARTH DORWEN; FAIRIES OF MEDIEVAL ROMANCES; FAIRY BRIDES; GWRAGEDD ANNWN; SIR LAUNFAL.

F301: Fairy lover. JEFFERIES, ANNE.

F301.1.1.2: Girl summons fairy lover by plucking flowers. YOUNG TAM LIN.

F301.2: Fairy lover entices mortal girl. GANCONER.

F301.3: Girl goes to Fairyland and marries fairy. CAPTIVES IN FAIRYLAND; EILIAN OF GARTH DORWEN.

F302.1: Man goes to Fairyland and marries fairy. OISIN.

F302.2: Man marries fairy and takes her to his home. AINE; GWRAGEDD ANNWN; FAIRY BRIDES; WILD EDRIC.

F302.3.1: Fairy entices man into Fairyland. BRAN SON OF FEBAL; TRUE THOMAS.

F302.3.2: Fairy offers gifts to man to be her paramour. SIR LAUNFAL.

F302.3.4: Fairies entice men and then harm them. KATE CRACKERNUTS.

F302.3.4.2: Fairies dance with youth till he goes insane. KATE CRACKERNUTS.

F302.4.2: Fairy comes into man's power when he steals her wings; she leaves when she finds them. SWAN MAIDENS.

F302.4.2.1: Fairy comes into man's power when he steals her clothes. FAIRY BRIDES.

F302.5.2: Fairy mistress transforms man's human wife. BRAN AND SCEOLAN.

F302.6.2: Recovery of fairy mistress. SIR LAUNFAL.

F304.2: Fairy queen's beauty temporarily destroyed by intercourse with mortal. TRUE THOMAS.

F343.19: Fairies give mortals fairy bread. BROKEN PED; JEFFERIES, ANNE.

F344.3: Fairies give man white powder to cure mortals. TRAFFIC WITH THE FAIRIES.

F346: Fairy helps mortal with labour. AMERICAN FAIRY IMMIGRANTS; BODACHAN SABHAIL; BROWNIE; CAULD LAD OF HILTON; HABE-TROT; PUDDLEFOOT; ROBIN ROUND-CAP; SEELIE COURT; TOM TIT TOT; YALLERY BROWN.

F346(a) (Baughman): Fairy or brownie helps mortal with housework of all kinds. MEG MULLACH; ROBIN ROUND-CAP; TOM COCKLE.

F348.2: Cup stolen from fairy must not be broken: bad luck will follow. THEFTS FROM THE FAIRIES.

F348.5.2: Mortal not to thank fairy for gifts. GOOD MANNERS; VIRTUES ESTEEMED BY THE FAIRIES; YALLERY BROWN.

F348.7: Taboo: telling of fairy gifts: gifts cease. TABOO; VIRTUES ESTEEMED BY THE FAIRIES.

F348.8: Taboo: mortal for whom fairies work must not watch them. TABOO.

F350: Theft from fairies. MISER ON THE FAIRY GUMP; THEFTS FROM THE FAIRIES.

F352: Theft of cup from fairies. FAIRY CUP; THEFTS FROM THE FAIRIES.

F352.1: Theft of cup from fairies when they offer mortal drink. FAIRY CUP; THEFTS FROM THE FAIRIES.

F360: Malevolent or destructive fairies. MORGAN LE FAY; PATCH; PEALLAIDH; SLUAGH; UNSEELIE COURT.

F361.2: Fairy takes revenge for theft. MISER ON THE FAIRY GUMP; SPRIGGANS.

F361.2.3: Fairies bind man fast to ground after he has attempted to capture fairy prince and princess. MISER ON THE FAIRY GUMP.

F361.3: Fairies take revenge on person who spies on them. FAIRIES ON THE EASTERN GREEN; FAIRY FUNERALS; FAIRY OINTMENT; FAULTS CONDEMNED BY THE FAIRIES; INFRINGEMENT OF FAIRY PRIVACY.

F361.14: Fairy punishes servant girl who fails to leave food for him. FAULTS CONDEMNED BY THE FAIRIES.

F361.16: Fairies punish person because of his treatment of other mortals. PIXIES.

F361.17.5: Fairies bathe children in churn when housewife forgets to leave a supply of clear water for the fairies. SIB.

F362: Fairies cause diseases. BLIGHTS AND ILLNESSES ATTRIBUTED TO THE FAIRIES; IMPETIGO.

F363.2: Redcap murders travellers, catches their blood in his cap. REDCAP.

F364.3: War between fairies and mortals. MAEVE.

F365: Fairies steal. FAIRY MORALITY; FAIRY THEFTS; I WEAT, YOU
WEAT; TACKSMAN OF AUCHRIACHAN.

F365(c) (Baughman): Fairies steal grain, an ear at a time. BROTHER
MIKE; I WEAT, YOU WEAT.

F366.2: Fairies ride mortal's horses at night. PROTECTION AGAINST
FAIRIES.

F369.1: Fairies set fire to buildings. AILLEN MAC MIDHNA.

F369.4: Fairy tricks mortal. FIR DARRIG; LEPRACAUN.

F369.7: Fairies lead travellers astray. IGNIS FATUUS; MAB; PIXIES;
PIXY-LED; WILL O' THE WISP.

F370: Visit to Fairyland. CHERRY OF ZENNOR; ELIDOR; FAIRY
DWELLING ON SELENA MOOR; FAIRY WIDOWER; JEFFERIES,
ANNE; KATE CRACKERNUTS; TACKSMAN OF AUCHRIACHAN;
VISITS TO FAIRYLAND.

F371: Human being reared in Fairyland. LADY OF THE LAKE.

F372: Fairies take human nurse to wait on fairy child. CAPTIVES IN
FAIRYLAND; CHERRY OF ZENNOR; FAIRY DWELLING ON SELENA
MOOR; FAIRY WIDOWER; NELSON, MARY.

F372.1: Fairies take human midwife to attend fairy woman. MIDWIFE
TO THE FAIRIES.

F373: Mortal abandons world to live in Fairyland. BRAN SON OF FEBAL.

F375: Mortals as captives in Fairyland. CAPTIVES IN FAIRYLAND;
ETHNA THE BRIDE; FAIRY DWELLING ON SELENA MOOR; FIR
DARRIG; KIRK, ROBERT; MALEKIN; VISITS TO FAIRYLAND.

F376: Mortal as servant in Fairyland. CHERRY OF ZENNOR; FAIRY
WIDOWER; TACKSMAN OF AUCHRIACHAN.

F377: Supernatural lapse of time in Fairyland. BRAN SON OF FEBAL;
KING HERLA; TIME IN FAIRYLAND; TIR NAN OG; VISITS TO
FAIRYLAND.

F378.1: Taboo: touching ground on return from Fairyland. KING
HERLA; OISIN; TIR NAN OG; VISITS TO FAIRYLAND.

F379.1: Return from Fairyland. AEDH; CAPTIVES IN FAIRYLAND;
KING HERLA; NELSON, MARY; TRUE THOMAS; VISITS TO FAIRY-
LAND.

F379.3: Man lives with fairies seven years. TRUE THOMAS.

F380: Defeating or ridding oneself of fairies. SANDY HARG'S WIFE;
TACKSMAN OF AUCHRIACHAN.

F381.1: Fairy leaves when he is named. FOUL-WEATHER; PEERIFOOL;
PUDDLEFOOT; SECRET NAMES OF THE FAIRIES; TOM TIT TOT;
WHUPPITY STOORIE.

F381.3: Brownie leaves when given new clothes. AIKEN DRUM;
BROWNIE; CAULD LAD OF HILTON; FENODOREE; HOB OR HOB-
THRUST; PHOUKA; PIXIES; PUCK.

F382: Exorcizing fairies. BLUE BURCHES; BROWNIE; PROTECTION
AGAINST FAIRIES; ROBIN ROUND-CAP.

F419.3.1* (KMB): Spirit as protector of wild creatures. BROWN MAN OF THE MUIRS.

F420.1.1: Water-spirit as man. MORGAN.

F420.1.2* (Baughman): Water-spirit as woman. ASRAI; MORGAN; SEAL MAIDENS; SELKIES.

F420.1.2.2: Water-maidens are mute. ASRAI.

F420.1.3.3: Water-spirit as horse. EACH UISGE; KELPIES; NOGGLE; WATER-HORSE AND THE WATER-BULL.

F420.1.3.4: Water-spirit as bull. ELF-BULL; WATER-HORSE AND THE WATER-BULL.

F420.1.4: Water-spirits in abnormal form. AFANC; ASSIPATTLE; NUCKELAVEE.

F420.1.4.8: Water-spirits with green teeth. JENNY GREENTEETH; PEG POWLER.

F420.1.6.6.3: Water-spirits are dressed in green. WATER WRAITH.

F420.3.1: Water-spirits have family life under water. BEN-VARREY; LUTEY AND THE MERMAID; OLD MAN OF CURY.

F420.4.4: Water-spirits are grateful. OLD MAN OF CURY.

F420.5.1: Kind water-spirits. LOIREAG; MERMAIDS; SELKIES.

F420.5.1.1: Water-spirits warn sailors against storms. LIBAN; WULVER.

F420.5.1.7.3: Water-spirits give magic gifts. OLD MAN OF CURY.

F420.5.1.8: Water-spirits give advice. MERMAIDS.

F420.5.1.9: Water-spirits adopt human foundling. LADY OF THE LAKE.

F420.5.2: Malevolent water-spirits. AFANC; FIDEAL; FUATH; GRINDY-LOW; JENNY GREENTEETH; LLAMHIGYN Y DWR; MERMAIDS; MERMEN; NUCKELAVEE; WATER WRAITH.

F420.5.2.1: Water-spirits lure mortal into water. LUTEY AND THE MERMAID; MERMAIDS; SHOOPILTIE; WATER WRAITH.

F420.5.2.1.2: Water-spirits lure children into water. NURSERY BOGIES; PEG POWLER.

F420.5.2.1.6: Water-spirit claims a life every seven (or nine) years. LUTEY AND THE MERMAID; PEG O' NELL.

F420.5.2.7.3: Water-spirit wrecks ship. BLUE MEN OF THE MINCH; MERMAIDS.

F421.1: Lady of the lake. A female lake spirit. LADY OF THE LAKE.

F422: Marsh spirit. TIDDY MUN; YARTHKINS.

F430: Weather-spirits. CAILLEACH BHEUR; GENTLE ANNIS; MUILEARTEACH.

F433: Storm-spirit. HOWLAA.

F436: Spirit of cold. CAILLEACH BHEUR.

F441.2: Tree-spirit. LUNANTISHEE; OAKMEN.

F441.2.3.2: Tree-spirit in elder. FAIRY TREES; OLD LADY OF THE ELDER-TREE.

F451: Dwarfs. DWARFS.

F451.0.1: Lepracauns. LEPRACAUN.

F451.5.2: Malevolent dwarf. BROWN MAN OF THE MUIRS; DUERGAR; TERRYTOP; TOM TIT TOT; YALLERY BROWN.

F451.5.2.3.1: Wooden image substituted for child stolen by dwarfs. STOCK.

F455.8.1: Trolls turn to stone at sunrise. TROWS.

F456: Gnomes as mine-spirits. BLUE-CAP; COBLYNAU; CUTTY SOAMS; DWARFS; GNOMES; KNOCKERS; SPRIGGANS.

F456.1: Spriggans. BLUE-CAP; CUTTY SOAMS; MISER ON THE FAIRY GUMP; SPRIGGANS.

F456.1.1: Origin of knockers or spriggans. KNOCKERS; SPRIGGANS.

F456.1.1.1: Knockers as ghosts of Jews who crucified Christ. KNOCKERS.

F456.1.2.1.1: Knockers bring ill luck if one whistles in the mine. KNOCKERS.

F456.1.2.2.1: Knockers lead men to the richest lodes in the mines by knocking in those areas. KNOCKERS.

F456.2: Mining spirit, Blue-cap. BLUE-CAP.

F456.2.1: Blue-cap moves coal tubs for miners. BLUE-CAP.

F456.3: Mining spirit. CUTTY SOAMS.

F456.3.1: 'Cutty' cuts cords by which miners pull tubs of coal. CUTTY SOAMS.

F460: Mountain spirits. BEITHIR; GWYLLION.

F460.4.4: Malevolent mountain-men. GWYLLION.

F470: Goblins. FUATH; GOBLINS; HOBGOBLIN. Night-spirits. JACK-IN-IRONS.

F470.0.1: Friar Rush as mischief-maker. FRIAR RUSH.

F471.1: Nightmare. HAGGE; NIGHT-MARE.

F471.2: Incubus. INCUBUS.

F471.2.1: Succubus. BAOBHAN SITH; HAGGE; LEANAN-SIDHE; LHIANNAN-SHEE; MELUSINE; NIGHT-MARE.

F473.2.4: House burns for no apparent reason. BLUE BURCHES.

F473.6.4: Spirit eats food. BUTTERY SPIRITS.

F475: Friendly night-spirits. BLUE BURCHES; BROWNIE; GUNNA; LOBS AND HOBS.

F480: House-spirits. GROGAN; GRUAGACHS; KILLMOULIS; LURIDAN; SILKY; SUPERNATURAL WIZARDS; WAG-AT-THE-WA'.

F482: Brownies. BROWNIE; ELIZABETHAN FAIRIES.

F482.3.1: Brownies live in house. Move when persons move. AMERICAN FAIRY IMMIGRANTS; TOM COCKLE.

F482.3.1.1: Brownie moves with farmer. BAUCHAN; BOGGART.

F482.5.3: Brownies tease. KILLMOULIS.

F482.5.4: Helpful deeds of brownie or other domestic spirit. BILLY BLIND; BODACHAN SABHAIL; BROWNIE; LURIDAN; PHOUKA; PUCK; SILKY.

F482.5.4.1: Brownie rides for midwife. BROWNIE; KILLMOULIS.

F482.5.5: Malicious or troublesome actions of brownies. BAUCHAN; BOGGART; BROWNIE; BWCA; MEG MULLACH; ROBIN ROUND-CAP; SILKY.

F482.5.5(i) (Baughman): Robin Round-Cap remixes chaff with wheat. ROBIN ROUND-CAP.

F482.5.5(o) (Baughman): The fairy in the sack of a thief or poacher. CAPTURED FAIRIES.

F488: The stupid house-spirit. BROWNIE-CLOD.

F488.1: Household spirit herds sheep: trouble with smallest lamb (hare). GROGAN; GRUAGACHS.

F491: Will-o'-the-Wisp. ELLYLLDAN; GYL BURNT-TAYL; HINKY-PUNK; IGNIS FATUUS; JACKY LANTERN; JOAN THE WAD; KIT WITH THE CANSTICK; OLD WOMAN OF THE MOUNTAINS; PINKET; SPUNKIES; WILL O' THE WISP; WILL O' THE WYKES.

F491.1: Will-o'-the-Wisp leads people astray. ELLYLLDAN; IGNIS FATUUS; JACKY LANTERN; OLD WOMAN OF THE MOUNTAINS; SPUNKIES; WILL O' THE WISP.

F511.0.9: Person with animal's head. JIMMY SQUAREFOOT.

F351: Person of enormous size. BRAN THE BLESSED; GIANTS.

F531.4.11: Giant's enormous animals. JIMMY SQUAREFOOT.

F535.1: Person the size of a thumb. TOM THUMB.

F535.1.1: Adventures of thumbling. TOM THUMB.

F535.1.1.7: Thumbling swallowed by animals. TOM THUMB.

F535.1.1.14: Thumbling carried on hat brim. TOM THUMB.

F555.1: Gold hair. GOLDEN HAIR.

F582.1: Serpent damsel. Woman has serpent inside which comes out and kills her bridegrooms. MELUSINE.

F628.2.3: Strong man kills giant. GIANTS.

F725.3.3: Undersea house. MERROWS.

F1041.16: Extraordinary physical reactions to anger. BRAN THE BLESSED.

G11.3: Cannibal witch. LUIDEAG.

G100.1: Giant ogre (fomorian). FOMORIANS.

G201.1: Hags deformed from much spinning. HABETROT.

G211.1.7: Witch in form of cat. BLACK ANNIS.

G214.1: Witch with long teeth. BLACK ANNIS.

G261: Witch steals children. BLACK ANNIS.

G262.0.1: Lamia. Witch who eats children. BLACK ANNIS.

G269.4: Curse by disappointed witch. ALLISON GROSS.

G275.8.2: Witch overcome by help of fairy. ALLISON GROSS.

G302.3.2: Demon in animal form. BARGUEST; BIG EARS; BLACK DOGS; EACH UISGE; KELPIES; MAUTHE DOOG; OLD SHOCK; PADFOOT; SKRIKER; TRASH.

G303.3.3.1.3: Devil as horse. AUGHISKY; EACH UISGE; FRIAR RUSH; KELPIES; WIZARDS.

G303.4.1.2.4: Devil has saucer eyes. BARGUEST.

G303.4.6: The Devil's tail. BARGUEST.

G303.7.1.3: Devil rides horse at night hunting lost souls. DEVIL'S DANDY DOGS; GABRIEL HOUNDS; GABRIEL RATCHETS; WILD HUNT; WISH HOUNDS.

G303.9.3.1: Devil hires out to a farmer. FRIAR RUSH.

G303.9.4: The Devil as a tempter. FRIAR RUSH.

G303.16.2: Devil's power over one avoided by prayer. DEVIL'S DANDY DOGS; PRAYERS.

G303.16.19.13: Devil cannot cross running water. NUCKELAVEE.

G303.17.2.4: Devil and sinful priest disappear amid blaze of fire in the river. DANDO AND HIS DOGS.

G308: Sea-monster. MAROOL; NUCKELAVEE.

G312: Cannibal ogre. OGRES.

G346.2: Devastating demon kills and eats people. LUIDEAG.

G465: Ogre sets impossible tasks. GREEN SLEEVES; NICHT NOUGHT NOTHING.

H151: Attention drawn: recognition follows. NICHT NOUGHT NOTHING.

H151.1: Attention drawn by magic objects: recognition follows. GREEN SLEEVES.

H335.0.1: Bride helps suitor perform tasks. GREEN SLEEVES; NICHT NOUGHT NOTHING; SWAN MAIDENS.

H335.3.1: Suitor task: killing dragon to whom princess is to be sacrificed. ASSIPATTLE.

H509.3: Game of chess as test. CHESS.

H512: Guessing, with life as wager. FOUL-WEATHER.

H521: Test: guessing unknown propounder's name. FOUL-WEATHER; TERRYTOP; TOM TIT TOT; WHUPPITY STOORIE.

H541: Riddle propounded with penalty for failure. WIFE OF BATH'S TALE.

H900: Tasks imposed: a person's prowess tested. FIANNA.

H914: Tasks assigned because of mother's foolish boasting. HABETROT; TOM TIT TOT.

H1010: Impossible tasks. GREEN SLEEVES; NICHT NOUGHT NOTHING.

H1092: Task: spinning impossible amount. HABETROT; TOM TIT TOT.

H1102: Cleaning Augean stables. GREEN SLEEVES; NICHT NOUGHT NOTHING.

H1219.1: Quest assigned as payment for gambling loss. GREEN SLEEVES.

H1235: Succession of helpers on quest. GREEN SLEEVES; NIGHT NOUGHT NOTHING.

J51: Sight of deformed witches causes man to release wife from spinning duty. HABETROT.

J346: Better be content with what you have. HEDLEY KOW.

J1050: Attention to warnings. HOOPER OF SENNEN COVE.

K42.2: Mowing contest won by trickery. BOGIES.

K171.1: Deceptive crop division. BOGIES.

K602.1: Fairy child is injured by man who says his name is 'Self'. The fairy mother is told by child that 'Self did it'. Takes no revenge. AINSEL; MEG MULLACH.

K1987: Devil disguised as man goes to church. FRIAR RUSH.

L101: Male Cinderella. ASSIPATTLE.

L131.1: Ashes as hero's abode. ASSIPATTLE.

M101: Punishment for broken oaths. LAMBTON WORM.

M219.2.4: Devil carries off hunt-loving priest. DANDO AND HIS DOGS.

M242: Bargaining between mortals and supernatural beings. KNOCKERS; TERRYTOP; TOM TIT TOT; WHUPPITY STOORIE.

M301.6.1: Banshees as portents of misfortune. BEAN-NIGHE; BEAN-SITH; CAOID-HEAG (Welsh); CAOINEAG (Highland); CAOINTEAGH (Argyllshire); CYHRAETH; GWRACH Y RHIBYN.

N2.0.1: Play for unnamed stakes. GREEN SLEEVES.

N101.2: Death from violating taboo. BROWN MAN OF THE MUIRS.

N471: Foolish attempt of second man to overhear secrets from animals. APPLE-TREE MAN.

N475: Secret name overheard by eavesdropper. FOUL-WEATHER; PEERIFOOL; TERRYTOP; TOM TIT TOT; WHUPPITY STOORIE.

N541.1: Treasure reveals itself only on Christmas Eve at midnight. APPLE-TREE MAN.

N812: Giant as helper. GIANTS.

P284: Step-sister. KATE CRACKERNUTS.

Q552.10: Plague as a punishment. TIDDY MUN.

R112.3: Rescue of prisoners from fairy stronghold. NELSON, MARY; YOUNG TAMLIN.

R131.12: Fairy rescues abandoned child. GHILLIE DHU.

R156: Brother rescues sister. NELSON, MARY.

R181: Demon enclosed in bottle (under stone) released. YALLERY BROWN.

R188: Rescued person horrifies rescuers. YALLERY BROWN.

R227: Wife flees husband. ASSIPATTLE.

S31: Cruel stepmother. KATE CRACKERNUTS.

S241: Jephthah's vow. LAMBTON WORM.

S262: Periodic sacrifices to a monster (giant fomorian). FOMORIANS.

T68.1: Princess offered as prize to rescuer. ASSIPATTLE.

T553: Thumbling born as a result of hasty wish of parents. TOM THUMB.

T591: Barrenness induced by magic. HARD DELIVERY OR BARRENNESS.

V12.9: Libations. AUSTRALIAN FAIRY IMMIGRANTS; BUCCA; FRID; SHONY; STRANGERS; YARTHKINS.

V229.2.12: Extraordinary longevity of saints. LIBAN.

KATHARINE BRIGGS is one of England's most prominent folklorists and the author of *The Personnel of Fairyland, The Anatomy of Puck, Folktales of England, The Fairies in Tradition and Literature,* and the much-loved children's story *Hobberdy Dick.* She has been president of the English Folklore Society and has taught and lectured in American universities.